The Concise Encyclopedia
of English Pottery
& Porcelain

The Concise Encyclopedia of

ENGLISH POTTERY
AND PORCELAIN

by

Wolf Mankowitz

&

Reginald G. Haggar

Publishers

HAWTHORN BOOKS, Inc.

New York

Published in the United States of America by Hawthorn Books Inc.,
70 Fifth Avenue, New York City 11. All rights reserved, including
the right to reproduce any portions thereof in any form except for
the inclusion of a brief quotation in a review. Designed and produced
by Rainbird, McLean Ltd, London. Printed in Holland by Drukkerij
Meijer of Amsterdam. Color plates made by Austin Miles, London,
and printed in England by Tillotsons (Bolton) Ltd. Endpapers printed
in Holland by Van Leer of Amsterdam. The monochrome plates
were made by Van Leer. The binding is by
Van Rijmenam N.V. of The Hague.

Library of Congress Catalogue Card No. 57-6366.

Contents

The Colour Plates

1. BOW *Frontispiece*

Top: figure of a gardener, emblematic of Autumn. About 1770. Ht 14 ins. *Bottom right*: figure of a *General Wolfe*, copied from an engraving by Richard Houston after a sketch by Captain Hervey Smyth. Mark impressed. About 1760. Ht 13⅞ ins. *Bottom left*: figure of the *Marquis of Granby*, copied from an engraving by Richard Houston after a painting by Sir Joshua Reynolds. Mark 'T' impressed. About 1760. Ht 14⅛ ins.

2. BRISTOL (probably) *facing p. 1*

Dish of delftware painted with a representation of *The Fall*. 2nd half of the 17th century. Diam. 13¼ ins.

3. CHELSEA *facing p. 33*

Figure of a *Nurse and Child*, after Bartelemy de Blenod. Mark, an anchor in red. About 1755. Ht 7 ins.

4. CHELSEA *facing p. 48*

Group, *The Music Lesson*, adapted from an engraving by J. E. Nilson after the painting 'L'Agréable Leçon' by François Boucher. Mark, an anchor in gold, and 'R' impressed. About 1765. Ht 14 ins.

5. CHELSEA AND
CHELSEA-DERBY *facing p. 49*

Top: vase and cover. Celadon and Amelia, perhaps painted by Richard Askew after Angelica Kauffmann; the landscape probably painted by Zachariah Boreman. Marks, an anchor in gold and '86' incised. About 1782. Ht 15¼ ins. *Left*: pot-pourri vase and cover. Mark, an anchor in gold. About 1765. Ht 14⅛ ins. *Right*: pot-pourri vase and cover. Mark, an anchor in gold. About 1765. Ht 14⅜ ins.

6. COALPORT *facing p. 64*

Top: dish filled with modelled flowers and fruit. Mark, 'Coalport', in gold. About 1830. Diam. 10⅜ ins. *Left*: dish. About 1840. Width 8½ ins. *Right*: vase and cover, made in imitation of Sèvres porcelain. Mark, 'CBD' in monogram, in blue enamel. About 1850. Ht 13¼ ins.

7. DERBY *facing p. 65*

Left: flower pot and stand. Mark, 'D' surmounted by a crown and crossed batons with six dots, also '2' in red enamel. About 1820. Ht 7½ ins. *Right*: flower-pot and stand, painted by Daniel Lucas, senior. Mark, 'D' under a crown, and '33' in puce enamel. About 1820. Ht 7½ ins.

8. DERBY *facing p. 80*

Figure of a *Bagpiper*, perhaps copied from a Meissen original, based on an engraving by J. Daulle, about 1755. Ht 8¾ ins.

9. LOWESTOFT *facing p. 113*

Jug painted with a representation of a cricket-match, copied from a print by H. Roberts after L. P. Boitard. About 1765.

10. SCOTTISH *facing p. 128*

Figure of a Scottish Highlander, lead-glazed earthenware. Probably Portobello; first half of 19th century. Ht 12¼ ins.

11. SPODE *facing p. 129*

Stoke-on-Trent. *Centre*: vase painted with a view of 'The Mount', Penkhull, Staffordshire, the residence of the second Josiah Spode. Mark, 'Spode' in red enamel; early 19th century. Ht 10 ins. *Right*: vase. Mark, $\frac{3}{797}$ in red enamel, perhaps Spode. *Left*: spill vase. Mark 'SPODE 711', in red enamel. About 1820. Ht 4¾ ins.

12. SPODE   *facing p.* 144

'Cincinnati' plate commissioned by the Massachusetts Society of Cincinnati as a perfect facsimile of the original service made in Canton for George Washington. Coffee-pot Ht 8 ins. Coffee-cup, Ht 2½ ins. Saucer, diam. 4¼ ins. 'Cincinnati' plate, diam. 9¾ ins. 'Regent' pattern.

13. STAFFORDSHIRE   *facing p.* 145

Top left and right: pair of figures of swans, salt-glazed stoneware painted in enamel colours. About 1750. Ht 5½ ins. *Bottom right:* figure of swan, salt-glazed stoneware painted in enamel colour. About 1750. Ht 7⅜ ins. *Bottom left:* figure of a bird, salt-glazed stoneware painted in enamel colours. About 1760. Ht 5⅜ ins.

14. STAFFORDSHIRE   *facing p.* 160

Left: copy of the 'Portland Vase', jasper-ware. Mark, 'Neale & Co.' impressed. (Hanley Factory of Neale & Co.); about 1778–88. *Right:* vase, jasper-ware. Mark 'TURNER & CO.' impressed (Lane End Factory of Turner & Co); late 18th century. Ht 8½ ins.

15. STAFFORDSHIRE   *facing p.* 177

Figure of *Old Age*, lead-glazed earthenware. Mark, 'R. WOOD' impressed (Burslem, Ralph Wood's factory); about 1770. Ht. 8¾ ins.

16. STAFFORDSHIRE   *facing p.* 192

Dish of lead-glazed earthenware decorated in slip with 'the Pelican in her Piety'. (Made by Ralph Simpson); late 17th century. Diam. 17 ins. Dish of lead-glazed earthenware decorated in slip. (Made by Thomas Toft); about 1675. Diam. 17¼ ins.

17. STAFFORDSHIRE   *facing p.* 193

Punch-pot and cover, salt-glazed stoneware painted in enamel colours. About 1755–60. Ht 7½ ins.

18. STAFFORDSHIRE
(probably)   *facing p.* 208

Top left: goblet, decorated in lustre. First half of 19th century. Ht. 4½ ins. *Top right:* jug covered with canary-yellow enamel and decorated in lustre. Early 19th century. Ht 5¾ ins. *Bottom left:* dish, decorated in lustre. Early 19th century.

Diam. 8 ins. *Bottom right:* jug, STAFFORDSHIRE OR SWANSEA, decorated in platinum ('silver') lustre. Early 19th century. Ht 5½ ins.

19. SWANSEA   *facing p.* 209

Pair of spill vases, painted by Thomas Baxter. About 1817. Ht 5 ins.

20. WHIELDON (probably)   *facing p.* 224

Dessert dish, lead-glazed earthenware, c. 1755–60. WEDGWOOD (probably) tea-caddy and cover, lead-glazed pineapple-style earthenware, c. 1755–60

21. WEDGWOOD (Modern)   *facing p.* 225

Top: Taurus the Bull, designed by Arnold Machin, A.R.A., Ht 6 ins, width 15 ins. Centre left: Queensware, Napoleon Ivy Tea-pot. Centre right: Queensware, 'Cream colour on lavender' dinner plate. Diam. 10½ ins. Bottom left: bone china 'Turquoise Ulander' teacup and saucer. Tea-cup, Ht 2 ins. Saucer, diam. 5¾ ins. Bottom right: bone china 'Arras green Florentine' sugar box. Ht 4 ins, width 3 ins.

22. CHAMBERLAIN'S WORCESTER

Top left: bottom left and right: suite of three vases with covers and stands, painted by Thomas Baxter with subjects representing '*The Triumph of Mercy*', '*Cornelia, Mother of the Gracchi*' and '*Orpheus and Eurydice*'. Marks, 'Chamberlain's Worcester' in gold. about 1820. Hts 12¾ ins. 8 ins and 8 ins. Top right: vase. Mark 'Chamberlain's Worcester' in red enamel. About 1810. Ht 10½ ins.

23. WORCESTER   *facing p.* 241

Top: jug. Mark, a square in underglaze blue. About 1770–75. Ht 11½ ins. *Bottom:* pair of vases. About 1770. Hts 11¼ ins. and 11⅜ ins respectively.

24. WORCESTER   *facing p.* 256

Top left: plate and tureen 'Ruby'. This pattern was given by the Brigade of Guards as a wedding present to H.M. the Queen and is now in use as dessert service in Buckingham Palace. *Top right:* 'Saquenay' plate and soup-cup; *lower right,* 'Bernina' plate and coffee cup.

The Monochrome Plates

Acknowledgements

The authors, publishers and producers are particularly indebted to Mrs Colin McFadyean for help in the basic research necessary in the compilation of this book. They are also indebted to the following for help with the pieces of pottery and porcelain photographed on the wrapper: The Antique Porcelain Co. Ltd, Boswell and Ward, Gered (Antiques) Ltd, Frank Partridge & Sons Ltd, Josiah Wedgwood & Sons Ltd.

The colour plates were all taken by Percy Henell (by arrangement with the Metal Box Company) from pieces in the Victoria and Albert Museum, London, except for pl. 12 for which we thank W. T. Copeland & Son Ltd; pl. 21 for which we thank Gered (Antiques) Ltd; and pl. 24 for which we thank the Royal Worcester Porcelain Co. Ltd, for the loan of suitable pieces.

The monochrome plates are all from pieces in the Victoria and Albert Museum, London, unless otherwise acknowledged at the foot of each plate, and we wish to thank the following for lending us photographs: Ernest Allman, Esq., George L. Ashworth and Bros, Miss Winifred Ashworth, Miss G. V. Barnard, M. B. E., formerly Curator, Norwich Castle Museum, Geoffrey Bemrose, Esq., Curator of Museum and Art Gallery, Stoke-on-Trent, the British Museum, R. J. Charleston, Esq., Susie Cooper Pottery Ltd, J. Cushion, Esq., Doulton Fine China Ltd, Desmond Eyles, Esq., Miss Moira Forsyth, Mrs M. Bruce George, C. Gibbs-Smith, Esq., John V. Goddard, Esq., R. G. Haggar, Esq., Hanley Museum, Heal and Sons Ltd, Mrs J. Hollingsworth, Bernard Leach, Esq., Tom Lyth, Esq., Curator, Wedgwood Museum, Barlaston, Mr and Mrs Arthur M. Moorby, Mr and Mrs Frank Nagington, New Chelsea China Co. Ltd, Frank Partridge and Sons Ltd, Royal Crown Derby Porcelain Co. Ltd, Service Advertising Co. Ltd.

The line drawings are by Reginald G. Haggar, Audrey Frew and Mary Woodward.

Foreword

As well as constituting a summary of the reliable information contained in the standard works of reference on English ceramics, this book also comprises considerable original research into more obscure sources such as contemporary newspapers, early topographical histories, diaries, parish registers, and other documents.

The attempt to provide within the compass of a single volume concise but complete information concerning factories, manufacturers, artists, types of pottery and porcelain, their styles and decorations, would be an over-ambitious project were it not for the immense amount of work in detail which has been published over the past years in specialist journals, and in the papers of learned societies. To a great extent the function of the authors of this encyclopedia has been to organize and summarize that material, co-ordinating it with standard authorities, and adding information or changing dates where original documents or newspaper sources indicated such correction.

Works of the past on this subject have shown a tendency towards anecdote and irrelevance which make quick and easy reference difficult for the reader. The present volume is designed specifically for the practical collector of, or dealer in, ceramic objects. The authors' intention is to supply all information which can lead to accurate identification. To this end larger entries are sub-divided under dates and owners, marks, artists, work, and distinguishing characteristics. Where there is no likelihood of ambiguity, marks are simply described, but all individual, cypher or symbol marks have been newly copied from actual rather than published sources.

We have thought it more practical to illustrate the present work as far as possible from public collections, particularly that of the Victoria and Albert Museum, rather than to draw extensively upon private sources where examples are not on view to the public.

The compilation of an extensive work of reference, taking as it does a considerable time, is certain to omit those many small discoveries and corrections being made by specialized students from time to time. There is still much that is unclear in the early history of ceramics, particularly in the immensely active period of the second half of the eighteenth century. The authors have tried to include all ascertainable factual information, and while it is not unlikely that they have omitted some details, it is certain that they have firmly excluded all the guesswork and supposition which is a not uncommon feature of many works of the past.

W. M.

R. G. H.

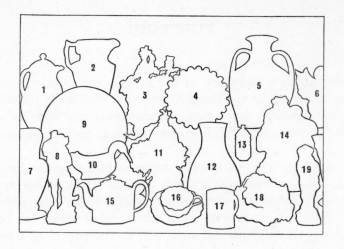

Key to the Endpapers

1. WEDGWOOD blue and white coffee-pot, c. 1785 (*Gered Ltd*)
2. STAFFORDSHIRE lustre jug, early nineteenth century (*Boswell & Ward Ltd*)
3. and 11. DERBY pair of porcelain candlesticks with figures,
    c. 1770 (*The Antique Porcelain Co. Ltd*)
4. COALPORT plate of flowers, c. 1830 (*Boswell & Ward Ltd*)
5. WEDGWOOD Black Portland vase; the Northwood copy of 1790 (*Josiah Wedgwood & Sons Ltd*)
6. WHIELDON figure of a squirrel, c. 1750 (*Frank Partridge & Sons Ltd*)
7. ASTBURY drinking cup and cover in the shape of an owl, late
    eighteenth century (*Frank Partridge & Sons Ltd*)
8. RALPH WOOD group 'lost sheep', c. 1770 (*Frank Partridge & Sons Ltd*)
9. DERBY plate with coat-of-arms, c. 1810 (*The Antique Porcelain Co. Ltd*)
10. WHIELDON sauce boat in the shape of a duck, c. 1750 (*Frank Partridge & Sons Ltd*)
11. See 3 above
12. WEDGWOOD jasper vase, c. 1785 (*Gered Ltd*)
13. WEDGWOOD scent bottle, c. 1785 (*Josiah Wedgwood & Sons Ltd*)
14. RALPH WOOD group, the 'flute player', c. 1770 (*Frank Partridge & Sons Ltd*)
15. WEDGWOOD Whieldon-type teapot, c. 1760 (*Gered Ltd*)
16. WORCESTER cup and saucer, c. 1765 (*The Antique Porcelain Co. Ltd*)
17. DERBY mug. c. 1775 (*The Antique Porcelain Co. Ltd*)
18. CHELSEA cauliflower dish and cover, c. 1760 (*The Antique Porcelain Co. Ltd*)
19. RALPH WOOD figure of 'bagpiper', c. 1770 (*Frank Partridge & Sons Ltd*)

A Selection of Impressed
and Incised Marks

A Selection of Impressed and Incised Marks

This small collection of intaglio marks has been selected to reveal the range and variety of such marks on English pottery and porcelain. It is by no means exhaustive. These marks have been reproduced against a coloured ground to make apparent as clearly as possible their texture and form. It will be evident to students that die-stamped impressions upon paper, however well-done, can only approximate to the quality of hand-impressed marks from a hard plaster or metal stamp on soft clay. Such marks vary considerably even from piece to piece. They may be partly illegible if the stamp is held at an angle to the piece when the pressure is applied. Moreover, the impress of such stamps sometimes results in a slight blur or roughness at the edges which cannot be reproduced.

Impressed or incised marks generally show most clearly on dry bodies like jasper, caneware basaltes, or parian. On pottery or porcelain which is glazed such impressions tend to fill up with glaze and may in consequence be difficult to decipher.

MINTON (Factory, date, workman's marks and mould numbers impressed all in one piece) 1871

CLOWES Impressed *c.* 1783

SWANSEA Impressed
1814-1817

NANTGARW Impressed
1813-1819

CAUGHLEY Impressed
Date uncertain

CHELSEA Incised
1745-1749
(Triangle mark)

DERBY Incised
1750

TURNER
Impressed with mould
number
1762-1787

BOW Incised
c. 1750

LEEDS (Impressed and incised workman's mark)
c. 1800

CHELSEA Incised
1745

P. & F. WARBURTON
Impressed
1800-1802

NEALE & CO. Impressed
c. 1780

RALPH WOOD Impressed
with mould number
c. 1770

GLASS Impressed
c. 1800

WOLFE Impressed
c. 1800

HAWLEY Impressed
c. 1810

ADAMS Impressed
1787-1805

TITTENSOR Impressed
1803-1823

FELL Impressed
c. 1820

WALTON Impressed
1805-1835

MARTIN BROS. Incised
1898

WEDGWOOD
1769-1780

WEDGWOOD Impressed
1769-1780

DAVENPORT Impressed
c. 1820

A

Abbey, Richard (born 1720 died 1801)

Apprenticed to John Sadler of the firm of Sadler & Green, Liverpool, as an engraver. He designed motifs for transfer-printing, including the 'Farmer's Arms'. He subsequently left Sadler and went first to Glasgow, then to France, and finally returned to Liverpool, where, with a man named Graham, he founded the Herculaneum Factory.

[L. Jewitt, *Ceramic Art of Great Britain*, 1878.]

Abbott (flourished c. 1781–1787)

Abbott is mentioned in Bailey's *Directory* 1781 and Tunnicliff's *Survey* of 1787 as being in partnership with John Turner, the firm being described as 'Turner & Abbott, Potters to the Prince of Wales, Lane End'. Possibly Abbott left the firm after Turner's death in 1787, joining Mist, a London dealer (formerly Turner's London agent) to form the partnership of 'Abbott & Mist', whose mark is found on black basaltes and other staple wares, largely in imitation of Turner's, but generally of much poorer quality and lacking originality.

[*Directories*, 1781–1787]

Abington, Leonard James (born 1785 died 1867)

Potter, designer, modeller and Baptist minister. Worked as carver and modeller for Benjamin Wyatt and Sir John Soane in London. Came to Hanley in 1819 and worked as modeller for Jacob Phillips and Joseph Mayer until 1831. Entered into partnership with William Ridgway in the firm of Ridgway and Abington in 1831, the partnership continuing until 1860. For this firm he modelled the 'Alhambra' Jug which was il-

lustrated in the *Art Union Journal* 1845. He was a friend of Joseph Mayer and a beneficiary under his will to the sum of nearly £10,000. In 1824 he edited the local Radical paper, *The Pottery Mercury*.

[Abington, *Personal Recollections of the late James Leonard Abington* (Hanley, 1868); *Art Union Journal*, 1845; *Rate Books, Stoke-on-Trent*].

Abraham, Robert Frederick (born 1827 died 1895)

Ceramic decorator. Studied art in Paris and Antwerp and said to have been a follower of Etty: worked for Mr Rose at Coalport and at the Hill Pottery, Burslem, as a decorator. In 1864 he was described as a china manufacturer, Northwood, Hanley. Later he became decorating manager and art director of Copelands, Stoke-on-Trent. Abraham painted portraits and historical subjects in oil, and exhibited at the Royal Academy and British Institution between 1846 and 1853. He died 24 September 1895. His son Robert John Abraham (born c. 1850 died c. 1925) modelled architectural faience for Copelands. Another member of the family, Francis Xavier Abraham (born 1861 died 1933) was a designer at S. Hancock & Sons.

[Information per Miss Abraham; L. Jewitt, *Ceramic Art of Great Britain*, 1878.]

Absolon, William (born 1751 died 1815)

Pottery decorator and china and glass dealer at Yarmouth. About 1790 he set up a pottery decorating business at a place on the Denes known as 'The Ovens' where he enamelled earthenware and porcelain bought 'in the white' from Staffordshire and Leeds. Absolon's mark, 'Absolon Yarme No 25' painted in red, occurs on wares bought from Turner, Wedgwood, Shorthose and Leeds and impressed with their marks.

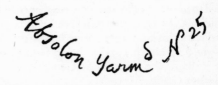

In 1808 Absolon purchased a shop at the corner of Market Row (Row No 63) Yarmouth, and

Colour plate 2, BRISTOL: *see page vii for caption*

he died in Yarmouth in 1815. A painted arrow is also said to be Absolon's mark. There are examples of Absolon's decorated pottery and glass in Norwich Castle Museum.
Plate 61 A.

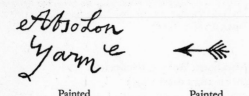

Painted   Painted

[Information per George Levine of Brundall, Norfolk, and Miss G.V.Barnard, M.B.E.]

Acid Gilding

A process of decorating china with patterns etched into the ware and covered with gold. The design, usually in the form of a narrow border is transfer-printed to the ware in an acid 'resist'. The rest of the plate is then stopped out, both back and front, and dipped in acid which corrodes away the exposed parts of the design to a certain depth. When the etching is completed, the ware is removed from the acid, the resist and 'stopping' dissolved and washed off and the etched border banded over in gold. After firing the ware is burnished, yielding a polished relief pattern against a duller matt gold background. First introduced by Mintons, 1863. A process which appears similar was invented by the Austrians and acquired, improved and worked by Powell & Bishop of Hanley.

[L. Jewitt, *Ceramic Art of Great Britain*, 1878.]

Acoustic Jars

The name is given to pottery vessels found embedded in the fabrics of many medieval churches, usually upon the top of the walls of the chancels. They are held to have been incorporated to improve or increase the resonance of the buildings. In 1954 two fifteenth century pots used for a similar purpose were reported (*Daily Telegraph* 27 March 1954) as being found under the joists of the choir of St George's Chapel, Windsor Castle.

They have been found in many counties – Berkshire, Devonshire, Dorsetshire, Kent, Nor-folk, Northamptonshire, Nottinghamshire, Rutland, Staffordshire, Suffolk, Sussex and Yorkshire.

[J.C.Cox, *English Church Fittings, Furniture and Accessories*, 1923.]

Adam and Eve

Arms of the Worshipful Company of Fruiterers of London, incorporated 1606 (A.C. Fox-Davies, *The Book of Public Arms*, 1915) and a subject occurring with some frequency on tin-glazed earthenware made at London (from 1635) and Bristol; on Staffordshire slipware with the name Thomas Toft and date, 1674 (Temple Newsam House, Leeds), or S.M., the initials of Samuel Malkin, c. 1725; and as a salt-glazed 'Pew' group, c. 1725-40, (Fitzwilliam Museum, Cambridge).

[F.H.Garner, *English Delftware*, 1948; B. Rackham, *Catalogue of the Glaisher Collection*, Fitzwilliam Museum, 1935; Ronald Cooper, *Pottery of Thomas Toft*, 1952.]

Adams Family, North Staffordshire

Family in Staffordshire of potters claiming descent from William Adams who held copyhold lands in Tunstall in 1299. The first member of the family referred to specifically as a potter is William Adams (born 1550 died 1617) of Burslem, from whom the present partners in the firm of William Adams & Son claim descent.

[P.W.L.Adams, *The Adams Family*, 1914; R. Nicholls, *Ten Generations of a Potting Family*, 1931.]

Adams, Benjamin (born 1787 died 1828), Greengates, Tunstall, Staffordshire

The only surviving son of William Adams of Greengates inherited the firm at too early an age to attend adequately to its business. Being of poor health and unfortunate in his attempt to develop trade with America, he was forced to sell the Greengates works in 1820 to Meir of Tunstall.

The firms's manufacture of jasper had ceased between 1805 and 1809, and without a master to supervise manufacture its wares degenerated both in quality and quantity. Even the blue-printed wares in which Benjamin Adams specialised varied a great deal in quality although finely engraved, many by William Brookes.

The Adams family bought back the Green-gates works about 1858.

MARK

B. ADAMS (impressed.)

[P.W.L. Adams, *The Adams Family*, 1914.]

Adams, Harvey (commenced 1862), Longton.

Messrs Harvey Adams and Scrivener commenced to manufacture in the Sutherland Road, Longton in 1862 under the title Adams & Scrivener. Scrivener retired about 1865 and, Adams having been joined by Titus Hammersley (died 1875), the firm became Harvey Adams & Co. At Hammersley's death his son, George Harris Hammersley took his place in the business which continued under the same name. The firm manufactured china, earthenware and stoneware, specialising in china with relief modelling of flowers, ferns and leaves.

ARTISTS

Mitchell, Henry Figure, landscape and animal
Swan Flowers
Longmore Birds
Clowes, W.M. Modeller

Harvey Adams & Co. introduced the moustache cup.

[*Directories*, 1864–75; L. Jewitt, *Ceramic Art of Great Britain*, 1878.]

Adams, John (born 1624 died 1687), Brick House, Burslem, Staffordshire

One of the earliest recorded potters of the Adams family who, about 1654, manufactured black, mottled and slipwares at Burslem where he built and occupied the town's first brick-made house called 'The Brick House', later an early factory of Josiah Wedgwood's.

John Adams's family also owned the Holden Lane, or Hulton Abbey Pottery, worked in John Adams's time by William Adams of Bagnall for the manufacture of salt-glazed stonewares.

After John Adams's death Holden Lane pottery was inherited and worked for a time by a younger brother, Edward. He subsequently let it to Beech.

[P.W.L. Adams, *The Adams Family*, 1914.]

Adams, J., and Co.

This firm flourished in the third quarter of the nineteenth century (not at the beginning of the century as frequently stated) and has been confused, because of its productions, with the older firm of Adams of Stoke and Tunstall. The firm was styled J.Adams & Co. until 1873 when it became known as Adams & Bromley. Their manufactures included jasper, majolica and parian (busts of Tennyson, Gladstone and Lord Derby).

MARKS (impressed) include:

ADAMS & BROMLEY
J. ADAMS & Co.

[*Directories*.]

Adams, John (born 1882 died 1953)

Pottery manufacturer and designer; pioneer in the revival of handcraft pottery; trained at Hanley and South Kensington; painted lustre and flambé pottery for Bernard Moore of Stoke-on-Trent; engaged on the decoration of the Palace of Peace at the Hague in Holland. Headmaster, School of Art, Durban, South Africa. Joint founder in 1921 and managing director 1921–49 of Carter, Stabler and Adams, Poole Pottery, Dorset.

 Personal mark of John Adams

[Obit. *Pottery Gazette*, September 1953; Reginald G. Haggar, *A Century of Art Education in the Potteries*, 1953.]

Adams, Richard (born 1739 died 1811)

Richard Adams of Cobridge Gate and Bank House, Bagnall was the son of William Adams (born 1702 died 1775) and Sarah Whieldon, his wife. He manufactured salt-glazed stoneware at Cobridge, and in 1770 signed an agreement with other potters concerning selling prices, (S. Shaw, *History of the Staffordshire Potteries*, 1829). He must have ceased business about 1780 for his name no longer occurs in Directories or Records of potters after that date.

[P.W.L. Adams, *The Adams Family*, 1914; R. Nicholls, *Ten Generations of a Potting Family*, 1931.]

Adams, William (born 1746 died 1805)

HISTORY

Son of Edward and Martha Adams: frequently but erroneously described as a pupil of Josiah Wedgwood, but now known to have served his time to John Brindley of Longport (*letter from Byerley to Josiah Wedgwood II*, dated 9 March 1800). William Adams was in business at a potworks at St John's Square, Burslem about 1769 and during the next decade built an extensive trade. The firm is listed in Bailey's *Western and Midland Directory* for 1783 as William Adams & Co., potters, Burslem.

It is said that in 1779 he started up another potworks at Greengates, Tunstall, and later at Newfield in the same area. The latter was abandoned in 1805, the year of his death, after which only the Greengates Pottery was continued by his executors. His son Benjamin Adams (born 1787 died 1828) appears to have taken control of the works from about 1809 but his interests were divided. The factory was sold in 1820.

MANUFACTURES

Tunnicliff's *Survey of* 1787 lists William Adams & Co. as manufacturers of 'Cream colour ware and china glazed ware painted'. Jasper was added to the firm's productions in the 1780's, including dark and light blue solid jasper, and pale green, dark green, lilac, pink and plum-coloured jasper dip. W.B.Honey states that Adams' jasper was 'quite equal' to that of Wedgwood but rather stronger and more violet in colour. Adams' jasper wares were sometimes sent to Thomas Law & Co. of Sheffield to be mounted. In 1791 Adams was competing severely with Josiah Wedgwood and undercutting his prices by 20%. Blue-printed earthenware was extensively made, and in the first decades of the nineteenth century so were brown-banded stoneware jugs, wine coolers, and teapots with sliding lids. All the general utility wares were manufactured including a fine cane ware with relief decorations sometimes in olive green or blue; and 'mocha' wares.

ARTISTS

William Adams is said by his descendants to have been an artist, but there is no clear indication in the wares of a developed personal style which can certainly be attributed to him.

W.Brookes Engraver.

Joseph Mongenot Designer and possibly modeller. (The name is given incorrectly as **Monglott** in all P. W. L. Adams' books on the Adams Family.)

MARKS

A D A M S & Co. (impressed) – on cream coloured earthenware 1770–1800.

A D A M S & Co. (impressed) – on solid jasper 1780–90.

A D A M S (impressed) – Stonewares, transfer-printed earthenware and jasper ware 1787–1805.

W. A D A M S & Co. (impressed) – Jasper.

[P. W. L. Adams, *The Adams Family*, 1914.]

Adams, William (born 1748 died 1831)

William Adams of Cobridge Hall and the Brick House, Burslem, was the son of John Adams and Dorothy Murhall, his wife.

HISTORY

He started to manufacture at Cobridge in 1769 at one of the factories formerly occupied by the Daniel family, and at the Brick House potworks, Burslem (so-called because it was the first brick-built house in Burslem) where he made painted and printed cream-coloured earthenware and red ware. He let the Brick House works in 1809 to William Bourne and concentrated his business at the larger Cobridge factories, one of which he let in 1813 to William Burdett Oliver and Timothy Bourne at a rental of £90 p.a., and another in 1817 to Ralph and James Clews at a rental of £216 p.a. A further factory he operated for a short time in partnership with Philip Eaton as a china manufactory but this came to an end in 1819.

William Davis, a workman from Worcester, is said by Simeon Shaw to have introduced transfer-printing at this factory by means of gelatine bats.

[P. W. L. Adams, *The Adams Family*, 1914; S. Shaw, *History of the Staffordshire Potteries*, 1829.]

4

Adams, William (born 1772 died 1829)

William Adams of Fenton Hall and Bagnall was the son of Richard Adams (born 1739 died 1811) of Cobridge.

HISTORY

He entered into partnership with Lewis Heath (born 1750 died 1801) potter of Burslem in 1773 and married his partner's eldest daughter. In 1804 he relinquished his share in the Burslem business and set up on his own at Cliff Bank, Stoke, where he made general earthenware (including blue-printed) and figures. The latter have never been identified. During the next 35 years Adams and his sons so extended the business that they acquired or worked no less than six factories in Stoke-on-Trent, and, in addition to the staple earthenware lines which included blue-printed wares for the American market, they made stoneware jugs, bone china services with elaborate painting and gilding, lustre and 'dipped' pottery, Egyptian black, earthenware decorated in 'flown blue', and later, parian statuary.

In 1819 William Adams took his eldest son, also named William Adams (born 1798 died 1865) into the business, and later his other sons, Edward Adams (born 1803 died 1872), Lewis Adams (born 1805 died 1850) and Thomas Adams (born 1807 died 1863), the business trading as William Adams & Sons. The elder William Adams died in 1829, the firm continuing under the same style until 1853 when William Adams, the eldest surviving brother, withdrew in order to work the factories at Greenfield, Tunstall, leaving the other brothers to continue at Stoke until 1863 when the Stoke factories were closed down.

MANUFACTURES

The more important of these were bone china which was manufactured from about 1810 and often lavishly painted and gilded in the contemporary romantic regency style (the chief artist was John Simpson), blue-printed earthenware for overseas markets and parian.

Blue transfer-printed designs included:

ENGLISH VIEWS with a border of bluebells and other flowers;

LONDON VIEWS with a foliage frame arranged from *Metropolitan Improvements of London*, 1829;

AMERICAN VIEWS with a border of flowers etc.;

COLUMBUS PICTURES with medallions of animals and flowers on the plate rim.

Other popular patterns in the mid-nineteenth century were 'Athens' and 'Bologna'. Examples of Adams' blue-printed ware in Princeton University Museum of Art and other American museums.

Parian statuary was made after models by Giovanni Meli and William Beattie.

MARKS

ADAMS (impressed) – on all kinds of ware (except blue-printed earthenware) 1804–1864.

An Eagle displayed surrounded by 'Adams warranted Staffordshire' – on blue transfer-printed earthenware 1810–1864.

A Crown surrounded by a double circle with the words 'Adams warranted Staffordshire' (impressed) – on various wares 1820–1850.

W. ADAMS & SONS STOKE-UPON-TRENT (Printed) – bone china, ironstone china and enamelled earthenware 1819–1864.

W. ADAMS & SONS
STOKE . UPON . TRENT

W. A. & S – various wares 1819–1864.

W A. & S.

[P. W. L. Adams, *The Adams Family*, 1914; R. Nicholls, *Ten Generations of a Potting Family*, 1931.]

Adams, William (born 1798 died 1865), Greenfield, Staffordshire

William Adams of Greenfield was the eldest son of William Adams of Stoke-on-Trent.

The Greenfield factory was founded in 1792 by Theophilus Smith, and worked for some time in conjunction with the Knowl and Longport factories. In 1797 it was bought by John Breeze, upon whose death in 1827 it was let until being taken over by William [Adams in 1834.

Greenfield principally produced useful wares, including enamel and gilt dessert services, black basalt tea services, and green glazed ware. During Adams' ownership no highly decorated work was produced, and the factory's output included sanitary and plain-printed wares. Sponged painted pottery was exported and, as at Stoke, blue-printed ware was made.

MARK

ADAMS (impressed)

[P.W.L.Adams, *The Adams Family*, 1914.]

Aerograph

An apparatus for applying evenly coloured grounds on pottery, invented in 1890 and used on cheap china and earthenware, instead of ground laying.

[J.C.Wedgwood, *Staffordshire Pottery and its History*, 1914.]

Aesop's Fables

Decorations occurring on Chelsea porcelain table wares, c. 1753, derived from Francis Barlow's folio edition of *Aesop's Fables*, 1687.

[H.B.Gardner, *The Connoisseur*, 1922.]

Agate

Salt-glazed stoneware or lead-glazed earthenware made in imitation of variegated natural stones, such as agate, by wedging together different coloured clays (early eighteenth century): more refined wares imitating semi-precious stones were made by Josiah Wedgwood. A surface agate, known as marbled ware, was produced by combing various coloured slips in the manner of marbled papers.

Albarello

A word of obscure derivation used to describe the nearly cylindrical form of the maiolica drug-pot which was introduced into Italy from Spain, and later copied by English makers of tin-glazed earthenware. Possibly derived from *el Barani*, a vase for drugs. Albarelli were used for ointments and dry medicines.

[H.Wallis, *The Albarello, a Study in early Renaissance Maiolica*, London, 1904.]

Alcock & Co., Samuel, The Hill Pottery, Burslem, Staffordshire

Commenced business in 1831 in premises formerly occupied by J. & R. Riley and John Robinson & Sons.

Alcock & Co. manufactured good quality porcelain, bisque figures modelled (some by Protât) from historical subjects, and parian vases and figures, until 1859 when the company failed.

The following marks are found both impressed and printed:

ALCOCK & CO.
HILL POTTERY
BURSLEM

Sam/ Alcock & Co.

S.A. & Co.

A beehive with the name above

[L.Jewitt, *Ceramic Art of Great Britain*, 1878.]

Alderholt, Hampshire

A manufactory producing coarse earthenware from local clay was worked here in the first half of the nineteenth century.

Alders, Thomas and John, Stoke-on-Trent

Manufacturers of buttons and knife-handles in agate and tortoiseshell earthenware and salt-glazed stoneware at Cliff Bank, Stoke, mid-eighteenth century. Thomas Alders in partnership with John Harrison the elder and Josiah Wedgwood 1752-54. Thomas Alders died 27 November 1781 (Gravestone, Stoke Churchyard). Jewitt gives the name as Aldersea.

Aldred, Obed

One of the original partners in the company set up to work the Lowestoft porcelain factory, 1757.

[Gillingwater, *An Historial Account of the Ancient Town of Lowestoft*, 1790; W.W.R.Spelman, *Lowestoft China*, 1905; A.E.Murton, *Lowestoft China*, 1932.]

Alfreton, Derbyshire

A red earthenware factory was operating here, early nineteenth century.

[S. Glover, *The History Gazetteer and Directory of the County of Derby*, Derby, 1829.]

'Alhambra' Jug

Jug decorated with pseudo-Moorish ornament derived from Murphy's *Alhambra*, made in 1845 by Ridgway and Abington.

[*Art Union Journal*, May, 1845, p. 135.]

Alken & Gerrard

Samuel Alken and Edward Gerrard manufactured earthenware at Longport from c. 1796 until 1798, when the partnership was dissolved.

[*Staffordshire Advertiser*, 10 March 1798.]

Allen, Robert (born 1744 died 1835)

China painter at Lowestoft, Suffolk, 1757 until about 1780 when he became manager. On the closure of the Lowestoft factory, about 1802, he set up an enamelling workshop in the town. The numeral '5' written in blue on the inner side of the foot-ring of Lowestoft porcelain is said to be the mark of Robert Allen, whose signature 'Allen Lowestoft' also occurs on a teapot painted by a Chinese hand with the Crucifixion, to which he probably added the flowers on the lid (Victoria & Albert Museum, London).

Allen Lowestoft

[W.B.Honey, *Old English Porcelain*, 1928, new edition 1948.]

Allen, Thomas (born 1831 died 1915)

Ceramic painter and designer; studied at Stoke School of Design and at South Kensington 1852-1854. *The Diary of Thomas Allen, Scholar* (1852-53) is now preserved in the Wedgwood Museum, Barlaston. From 1854 until 1875 he was employed as a porcelain painter of figure subjects at Mintons'; and from 1875 until 1906 at Wedgwoods' of Etruria, for whom he became art director and chief designer. His best known pattern is called 'Ivanhoe'.

[Obit. *Staffordshire Evening Sentinel*, 13 October 1915; Reginald G. Haggar, *A Century of Art Education in the Potteries*, 1953.]

Aller Vale, near Newton Abbot, Devon

Common brown-wares were made here from 1865 until 1868 when John Phillips & Co. took over and started to make architectural pottery.

Alsager

Made mechanical improvements in the potter's throwing wheel c. 1735.

[J.Aiken, *A Description of the Country... around Manchester*, 1795.]

American Views

Transfer-printed pottery decorated underglaze, with 'American Views', incidents from American history and portraits of famous American statesmen became popular in the first half of the nineteenth century. Often skilfully engraved and yielding considerable topographical and historical information, these prints are avidly sought after in America. The chief manufacturers to use them were: –

Enoch Wood & Sons, Burslem
James & Ralph Clews, Cobridge
Joseph Stubbs
Ralph Stevenson, Cobridge
J. & J. Jackson
J. Rogers & Son
Thomas Green
Joseph Heath & Co.
Andrew Stevenson, Cobridge
J. & W. Ridgway, Shelton
William Adams & Son
Thomas Godwin

Charles Meigh, Hanley
Mellor, Venables & Co.
Phillips & Co.
Examples in the Metropolitan Museum of Art,
New York; Princeton University Museum of
Historic Art; Gallery of Fine Arts, Yale Uni-
versity and the Boston Museum of Fine Art.

[N. Hudson Moore, *The Old China Book*, 1903, reprinted
1936; E.A.Barber, *Anglo-American Pottery*, 1899.]

'Apostle' Jug

A straight-sided jug modelled in relief with
figures of the Apostles under an elaborate gothic arcading, made by Charles Meigh in porcellanous stoneware, c. 1845.

'Apple-green'

A trade name for a ground colour used extensively at Worcester during the Wall period from
about 1770 when Sèvres influence was felt. The
colour was introduced at Sèvres in 1757. W.B.
Honey describes it as 'pea-green' (*Old English
Porcelain*, 1928, new ed. 1948).

[George Savage, *Eighteenth Century English Porcelain*,
1952; B.Rackham, *Catalogue of the Schreiber Collection*,
Vol. 1. Porcelain, 1928.]

Aquamanile

A ewer for handwashing in medieval times,
usually in the form of a mounted figure or
animal. Examples in museums at Scarborough,
Oxford and Lewes, Sussex.

[B.Rackham, *Mediaeval English Pottery*, 1948.]

Arbour Group

Lovers seated within an alcove or a leafy arbour,
made in Staffordshire white salt-glazed stoneware or 'Whieldon' ware. Examples in Hanley
Museum, Stoke-on-Trent, and the Victoria &
Albert Museum, London.

Arcanist

A person pretending to possess secret formulae.

Argil

Clay, especially potters' clay, hence the trade
name MASON'S CAMBRIAN ARGIL used for earthenware allegedly made from Welsh clay by the
firm of G. M. and C. J. Mason, c. 1820. 'Cambria
Clay' occurs in sale notices and means Welsh clay.

[Reginald G.Haggar, *The Masons of Lane Delph*, 1952.]

Argyll, Argyle

A double-walled vessel like a small coffee-pot,
for keeping hot, and serving, gravy.

Armitage, Staffordshire

Was 'famous for tobacco-pipes' in the time of
Dr Plot (writing 1686). Tobacco-pipes were
still made in the hamlet of Handsacre in this
village until 1841 when the pipe manufactory
was offered for sale (*Staffordshire Advertiser* 13
February 1841). A manufactory of cream-coloured earthenware was established in 1817; within
twenty years the population of the village
doubled, as trade developed and flourished.
John Tunnicliffe and John Hall, who were in
partnership in this concern dissolved partnership in 1833, (*Staffordshire Advertiser* 7 December
1833). In 1844 the factory was offered for sale or
to be let (*Staffordshire Advertiser* various dates
from 6 January until 18 May 1844). In 1854
Penman and Brown took over the works and
manufactured toilet wares, but after building
new premises ran into financial difficulties, were
compelled to dissolve the partnership, and closed
down in 1856 (*MSS Diary of John Hackett Goddard*, 24 July 1854 until 28 November 1856).

Armorial China

Services of porcelain with coats-of-arms and
crests were popular in the 18th century, but until 1755 all were made in China at Ching-te-Chen
and ordered through merchants at Canton or
through the East India Co. The decoration was
done from bookplates, engravings or sketches
specially sent to China. After 1755 some English Armorial services were made, notably at the
Worcester factory during the Dr Wall period
and also later. Champion produced armorial
porcelain at Bristol, and most of the factories
made pieces as replacements of broken Chinese
examples. Some armorial wares were made by
Josiah Wedgwood and the Leeds factory.

[James Tudor-Craig, *Concise Encyclopedia of Antiques*,
vol. 2, 1955; Sir A. Tudor-Craig, *Armorial Porcelain of
the 18th Century*, 1925.]

Arnoux, Joseph Léon François
(born 1816 died 1902)

Ceramist; son of Antoine Arnoux and his wife
Miette Fouque. Studied engineering in Paris at
the École des Arts et Manufactures where he

met Brongniart and obtained facilities to study pottery at the Paris depot of the Royal Manufactory of Sèvres in the rue de Rivoli. Before coming to England in 1848 he managed the Fouque factory at Valentine. In England he was taken up by Herbert Minton and from 1848 until his retirement in 1892 he held the position of art director of the Minton factory, Stoke-on-Trent. In 1878 he was awarded the Order of Francis Joseph and made Chevalier of the Legion of Honour. The Minton down-draught kiln was invented by him.

Ash, George

Manufacturer of parian statuary and majolica, Broad Street, Hanley, first of all in partnership with Wardle (as Wardle and Ash) c. 1860, and from 1865 until 1879 under his own name.

Ashby Wolds, Leicestershire and Derbyshire

An area remarkable for its fine clay deposits which gave rise at the beginning of the nineteenth century to the 'yellow ware' industry. It was perhaps the worst area in England for abuses of the work people and conditions of employment. Added to low prices, 'truck' and the 'allowance system' were rife. It was said, without dispute, that 'the whole of the earthenware manufacturers of Ashby Wolds are either publicans, Grocers, Drapers, Butchers, Hatters or Pedlars or a mixture of all put together'. In 1843 one master potter was described as 'a dealer in pigs, onions, Fir Tippets, ready-made Clothes, Hats, Bonnets and almost every article used by his *hands*'.

POTTERS

Cooper & Massey, Coppice-side 1845

John Hall, Wooden Box 1845

Thomas Hall, Wooden Box 1845

Brunt & Allerton, Hartshorne New Pottery before 1833

Thomas Brunt, Hartshorne New Pottery after 1833

T. Harrison, Wooden Box 1845

George Read, Wooden Box 1845

Richard Staley, Midway 1845

Joseph Thompson, Wooden Box, Hartshorne 1818–45 or later

Watts & Stanley, Wooden Box 1845

Tunnicliff & Croxall, Old Midway Pottery closed 1841

Thompson Brothers, Wooden Box, successors to J. Thompson

Thomas Sharpe (d. 1838) Swadlincote 1821-38

Sharpe Brothers & Co. Swadlincote 1838 onwards

[*Potters' Examiner & Workmans' Advocate*, 23 Dec. 1843, 24 May 1845; *Directories*.]
See also CHURCH GRESLEY, BRETBY ART POTTERY.

Ashworth, Geo. L. & Bros, Ltd

In 1857 Francis Morley of the Broad Street Manufactory, Hanley, manufacturer of ironstone china, who had acquired Mason's moulds and engravings and the right to use his backstamp, was joined by Taylor Ashworth (born 1839 died 1910) youngest son of George Ashworth of Rochdale. When Morley retired from business in 1862 George Ashworth purchased the business for his sons, and traded under the name of Geo. L. Ashworth & Bros. George Leach Ashworth (born 1823 died 1873; twice Mayor of Rochdale), the eldest brother, was head of the firm but like the other brothers his interests were in wool and cotton and public affairs in Lancashire, and he had little to do with the day-to-day running of the business which was in the hands of Taylor Ashworth, the resident partner, who built up a prosperous business in hotel, shipping and table wares as well as in insulators and sanitary pottery. The collapse of the woollen trade in Lancashire in 1883 (in which the brothers were deeply involved) caused them to sell the Hanley business to John Hackett Goddard for his son John Shaw Goddard (born 1857 died 1939) whose descendants have continued the business to date, manufacturing a durable earthenware to the designs and shapes of C. J. Mason. The latter's backstamp is the name MASON'S over a Crown and cartouche enclosing the words PATENT IRONSTONE CHINA, transfer-printed underglaze, and is the firm's trademark.

ASHWORTHS
REAL
IRONSTONE
CHINA

1870-1880
Transfer printed
and impressed

1870-1880
Transfer-printed and impressed

[Typescript history of the Ashworth family *Recollections of Family History* by G.H.Ashworth; Ashworth's business papers; Ashworth family correspondence.]

Askew, Richard

Well known as a painter of cupids which he executed *en camaieu* in rose colour, at Chelsea during the gold anchor period, and at Derby from 1772 until about 1795.

Asquith, John (c. 1756), Nottingham

Potter of salt-glazed stoneware, whose name occurs on a circular tea caddy incised 'John Asquith, maker, 1756' in Nottingham Castle Museum.

Astbury, John (born 1688 died 1743), Shelton

John Astbury is almost a legendary figure in Staffordshire pottery history, though little can be stated with certainty about him. Simeon Shaw's stories that he introduced the use of Devonshire white-firing clays and calcined flints into the earthenware body may be true but contemporary evidence in support is lacking. His gravestone in Stoke Parish churchyard (carefully preserved) gives the date of his death and age; 'John Astbury the elder, of Shelton, Potter, who departed this life March the 3rd, 1743, age 55'. The *Parish Registers* of Stoke record his christening, 14 May 1690. Percy Adams in *Notes on some North Staffordshire Families* (1930) printed his will in full, which proved that he had property in Shelton and that he bequeathed 'To son Joshua Astbury all my Tools, Implements etc in the trade of a Potter'. The will was proved at Lichfield, 16 June, 1744. On the strength of tradition John Astbury is credited with the manufacture of red earthenware teapots and other articles with applied white relief decorations, and image toys of musicians, soldiers etc. made in red and white clays under a lead glaze, sometimes crudely stained with colouring oxides. Both types were made by other Staffordshire potters.

Astbury's name does not occur in Wedgwood's list of early Staffordshire potters; nor are there any authentic examples marked with his name, although the impressed mark AST-BURY is recorded on productions by later members of the Astbury family potting at the Foley, Fenton.

Examples in the Art Institute of Chicago; Nelson Gallery of Art, Kansas City and the Metropolitan Museum of Art, New York.

Astbury Pedigree,
based on Gravestones, Registers etc.

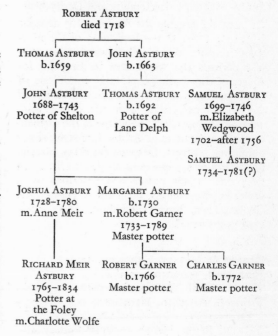

Astbury, Richard Meir (born 1765 died 1834)

Potter and merchant; son of Joshua Astbury (1728-1780) and Anne Meir his wife; succeeded his father at the Foley Pottery, Lane Delph, where he made useful wares, including Voyez's 'Fair Hebe' jug; mark recorded 'R.M.A.' or 'ASTBURY'; London warehouse at 151 Drury Lane; bankrupt 1797; removed to Manchester, where, with the help of his son John Meir Astbury, he made a fortune in cotton, became a landed proprietor and died at Strand Lodge, Radcliffe, Lancashire.

[P. W. L. Adams, *Notes on some North Staffordshire Families*, 1930; Reginald G. Haggar, *Staffordshire Chimney Ornaments*, 1955; Announcements in *Staffordshire Advertiser*, 1797.]

Astbury, Thomas, Lane Delph

Manufacturer of salt-glazed stoneware, first half of the eighteenth century; including probably Staffordshire image toys.

'Astbury' Type

A classification of Staffordshire pottery, produced about 1730-40, in which red and white clays are combined under a transparent lead glaze. Similar wares, in which the glaze is splashed or dabbed with metallic oxides, are generally called 'ASTBURY-WHIELDON'.
Plates 1–3.

Aston, Jabez

A painter of naturalistic flower and fruit panels of Coalport manufacture, mid-nineteenth century.

Ault Faience

'Art' pottery made by William Ault, at Swadlincote, near Burton-on-Trent, some from the special designs of Dr Christopher Dresser. Received the highest award at the Chicago World Fair, 1893.

Aylesford, c. 1850

Edward Betts established a terra cotta works at Aylesford about 1850, using a bed of plastic clay found in the neighbourhood. He exhibited a terra cotta vase with figure terminals, designed by John Thomas, at the Great Exhibition, 1851.

Ayliffe, John (c. 1635)

A brewer of Westminster, financially involved in the manufacture of stoneware and tiles. Took out a patent for stone jugs and pantiles, 1635.

Aynsley, Henry & Co. (c. 1870), Longton

Manufacturers of lustre, Egyptian black, drab wares, turquoise and painted earthenwares in Commerce Street, Longton, from about 1870.

Aynsley, John (born 1752 died 1829), Longton

Manufacturer of cream-coloured earthenware and porcelain in Longton. His earthenware is frequently decorated with black transfer-prints of popular subjects such as 'Keep within Compass', the fight between Humphries and Mendoza (1788), 'The Catch Club', etc., which are signed 'Aynsley, Lane End' or 'J. Aynsley, Lane End'. His obituary notice describes him as 'One of the first manufacturers of porcelain in Lane End, and the first lusterer'.

[Obit. *The Staffordshire Mercury*, 28 February 1829.]

Aynsley, John and Sons (c. 1860), Longton

Manufacturers of bone china, Longton. The founder of this firm was one of the most remarkable 'characters' in the Potteries, John Aynsley, four times Mayor of Longton, desscendant of John Aynsley (died 1829).

B

Bacchus, William (c. 1783-87),
Fenton, Staffordshire

Manufacturer of cream-coloured wares in all styles, recorded in *Directories* and *Surveys*, 1783-1787. The Thomas Bacchus recorded by Simeon Shaw (*History of the Staffordshire Potteries*, 1829) as marrying a widow named Astbury and as making cream-coloured and blue-painted earthenware may be an erroneous reference to William Bacchus.

Bacon, John, R.A. (born 1740 died 1799)

Sculptor and modeller. Apprenticed to Crispe of Bow Churchyard, 'an eminent maker of porcelain', in 1754. Tradition ascribes to him porcelain figures of Quin as Falstaff, Garrick as Richard III, figures of cooks, and John Wilkes. He is known to have worked for Wedgwood, for Duesbury who paid his account in 1769, possibly for Champion's Bristol Factory, and for Enoch Wood of Burslem. He certainly worked (after leaving Crispe) at Coade's Artifical Stone manufactory of which he eventually became manager. As a sculptor he produced a large amount of meritorious work including monuments to Pitt in Westminster Abbey, Dr Johnson in St. Paul's, and Blackstone in All Souls', Oxford.

Baddeley, John (born 1756 died 1841)

Son of William Baddeley of Eastwood, Hanley; lathe-maker to the pottery trade. In 1783 he charged £8 or £9 for the wood and ironwork of a lathe, and from 6/- to 10/- for the movements.

[Obit. *Staffordshire Advertiser*, 7 August 1841; *Letter* dated 8 September 1783, Birmingham Reference Library.]

Baddeley, Ralph, John and Edward, Shelton

For fifty years the Baddeley family potted at factories in Broad Street, Shelton. The original founder of the concern was John Baddeley of Shelton, son of a flint grinder owning and working a mill at Moddershall, near Stone (Shaw, *History of the Staffordshire Potteries*, 1829) who on 29 April 1754 married Anne Godwin at Wolstanton Church (*Parish Registers*). John Baddeley the elder manufactured salt-glazed stoneware and cream-coloured earthenware and established a successful European and overseas trade in rivalry to Josiah Wedgwood who acknowledged his pre-eminence among his competitors (*Letter, Wedgwood to Bentley*, 22 April 1771). There is evidence that Baddeley made salt-glazed pottery with basket mouldings in relief. A stoneware 'block' in the Victoria and Albert Museum with basket-work decoration is inscribed 'J. B. 1763'. Shaw says John Baddeley made the last improvements in cream colour prior to the production of Queen's ware by Josiah Wedgwood about 1751. John Baddeley appears to have played some part in the production of experimental porcelain pastes. His name was coupled with those of William Littler and John Yates as first attempting its manufacture in 1751 (*The Illustrated Exhibitor*, 15 November 1851). John Baddeley of Shelton and John Yates of Newcastle-under-Lyme were licensed to prospect for soaprock for ten years on the Erisey Estate in the Lizard Peninsula, Cornwall. Again Shaw tells us that about 1765 a good porcelain was made by John Baddeley in partnership with the father of Sir Thomas Fletcher of Newcastle. This partnership is confirmed by an entry in *Aris's Birmingham Gazette*, 14 August 1775. Their manager was stated to be William Littler of Brownhill and Longton Hall. John Baddeley died in 1772, leaving his sons John and Ralph to continue the business. John and Ralph Baddeley were progressive potters and modernised their plant, erecting four ovens behind their factory instead of two, and roofing the buildings with tiles instead of thatch. They effected improvements in transfer-printing from about 1777. Craftsmen named Harry Baker, William Smith (an engraver from Liverpool) and Thomas Davis (from Worcester) are cited in this connection. Two factories in Shelton were controlled and worked by the Baddeley family, the Broad Street Works (now Ashworths) by Ralph Baddeley; and the one adjoining by John Baddeley. In 1787 the second factory was under the control of John and Edward Baddeley who continued it until about 1802, when the two factories, the house in Broad Street, and the rest of the estate were offered for sale (*Staffordshire Advertiser*, 7 November 1801 and 27 February 1802). The business of J. & E. Baddeley was managed by Thomas Shelley, an unsuccessful china manufacturer (*Report on the Employment of Children in Factories*, 1842-43). Ralph Baddeley's premises were taken over by Boon & Hicks in 1802. John Baddeley of Shelton died 21 June 1813 aged 53 years.

IB1763

Incised

Baddeley, William, Eastwood, Hanley

Potter and lathe-maker at Eastwood, Hanley. William Baddeley commenced making brown ware at Eastwood about 1750, and about 1765 'having invented an engine-lathe he began to make turned articles in cane and brown ware'. His son, William, succeeded to the Eastwood pottery business and made improvements in the ware which Jewitt says he tried, by a badly impressed backstamp, to pass off as that of Wedgwood. Another son, John Baddeley, took over the craft of lathe-making.

On the death of the second William Baddeley the Eastwood Factory was sold, and his son, Henry William Baddeley (born 1807 died 1856) commenced to make terra cotta articles and pottery knobs for japanned tea- and coffee-pots. Jewitt says he was 'the first to make telegraph insulators at the Market Lane Works'. In 1846 the business was removed to Longton where he acquired or worked factories in Commerce Street and St Martin's Lane, and introduced pottery imitations of stag and buffalo horn and bone hafts for cutlery. After his death his widow carried on the business. She is described until 1875 as a manfacturer of rustic and terra cotta figures. The son of H. W. and Elizabeth Baddeley, also named William, opened a factory for similar products called Drury Works, Normacot Road, Longton.

The first two William Baddeleys produced excellent Egyptian black, and cane and red stoneware 'dry' bodies, which were impressed

EASTWOOD

[*Directories* from 1800–1875; *Parish Registers* of Stoke-on-Trent; L. Jewitt, *Ceramic Art of Great Britain*, 1878; S. Shaw, *History of the Staffordshire Potteries*, 1829.]

PEDIGREE

WILLIAM BADDELEY of Eastwood
Potter and lathe-maker
m. Sarah Edwards

JOHN BADDELEY 1756–1841 Lathe maker   WILLIAM BADDELEY Master potter of Eastwood   JAMES BADDELEY Silk throwster

HENRY WILLIAM BADDELEY 1807–1856 Master potter of Hanley & Longton

WILLIAM BADDELEY of Longton Master potter

Baggeley, Henry (c. 1860), Cobridge

A well-known potteries modeller who flourished in the 1860's. Described in 1864 as a designer and modeller. He modelled a 'Wedgwood' jug for Charles Meigh. The *Staffordshire Sentinel* (30 April 1864) contained an announcement of his 'Garibaldi' jug. At the *North Staffordshire Industrial Exhibition* in Hanley 1865 he exhibited a rustic garden seat and a 'Cobden Memorial Vase'.

Baggeley, Thomas

China and earthenware manufacturer in partnership with John Yates of Shelton as potters until 9 May 1803, and as china manufacturers until 25 May 1808. He then set up as a china manufacturer at Lane Delph, went bankrupt in 1814, started again (recorded in *Parson & Bradshaw's Directory* 1818) and ended up as a modeller and mould-maker in Tontine Street, Hanley, in 1834.

[*Directories*, 1818–1834; *Staffordshire Advertiser*, 1803, 1808, 1814, 1818; *Staffordshire Gazette*, 1814.]

Bagillt, Flintshire

A small potworks comprising one biscuit and one glost oven, was announced for sale in *The Pottery Mercury*, 13 December 1828.

Bagnall, Charles (born 1747 died 1814)

Potter and merchant, original partner in the New Hall joint stock company; partner in firm of Heath and Bagnall 1783-87 and Bagnall & Boon 1796. He signed the agreement of the Hendra Company, 1799 and is listed as lead merchant in 1800: W.B.Honey (*European Ceramic Art*, 1952) surmised that Charles Bagnall was the person mentioned by Chavagnac and Grollier as founding with M. de Saint-Cricq-Cazeaux a faience factory at Creil (Oise, France) in 1794. There is no evidence to support this. Bagnall as a private person enjoyed some status. He is listed on the Jurors' List for Penkhull Court 1784 (Salt Library, Stafford). He was 'Mayor' of the Mock Corporation of Hanley 1787 and subscribed to rebuilding of Hanley Church 1787. In 1802 he was member of committee, Pottery Subscription Library. He was also partner in the colliery concerns owned by Samuel Perry & Co which dissolved 29 September 1797.

[Bailey's *Directory*, 1783; Tunnicliff's *Survey*, 1787; Staffordshire Pottery Directory, c. 1796; Tregortha's *A View of the Staffordshire Potteries*, 1800; Holden's *Triennial Directory*, 1805-7; *Staffordshire Advertiser*, 29 April 1797; 17 April 1802; 29 December 1804, 1 and 15 July 1815; 9 December 1815; L.Jewitt, *Ceramic Art of Great Britain*, 1878; J.S.Crapper, *Revised History of the Ancient Corporation of Hanley*, 1882; G.E.Stringer, *New Hall Porcelain*, 1949; X. de Chavagnac and A. de Grollier, *Histoire de Manufactures Françaises de Porcelaine*, Paris, 1906; S.Shaw, *History of the Staffordshire Potteries*, 1829.]

Bagnall & Fletcher (c. 1786), Shelton

Sampson Bagnall the younger and Thomas Fletcher entered into partnership as earthenware manufacturers in Shelton, Stoke-on-Trent about 1786. The partnership was dissolved in 1796 (*Staffordshire Advertiser*, 30 April 1796), Fletcher taking over the printing business and Bagnall continuing as a pottery manufacturer at Booden Brook, Shelton.

[*Directories.*]

Bagnall, Sampson (born 1720 died 1803)

Master potter, Hanley, 1787, manufacturer of earthenware.

[Tunnicliff's *Survey*, 1787; *Parish Registers*, Stoke-on-Trent, 1803.]

Baguley, C, Hanley

The *Handbook to the Museum of Practical Geology* (1893) mentions a white figure group of children playing with a rabbit marked in relief:

PUBD. BY C. BAGULEY, Hanley
Staffordshire, 20 July 1818

Baguley, Isaac

Painter, first of all in Derby. In 1842 after the closure of the Rockingham Factory he took over a portion of the works as a china decorator, buying wares from Minton, Brown, Westhead, Moore & Co.; and Powell, Bishop and Stonier. His mark was 'Baguley Rockingham Works' with or without the griffin crest.

[L.Jewitt, *Ceramic Art of Great Britain*, 1878.]

Bailey & Batkin (c. 1815-29),

Lane End (now Longton), Staffordshire.
William Bailey and W.Batkin were possessors of a patent for the manufacture of lustred pottery. They were established c. 1815 and certainly continued until 1829. Their mark, 'Bailey & Batkin, SOLE PATENTEES' occurs on lustre-decorated wares in relief. Examples in the Art Institute of Chicago.

Balaam, W.

A slipware potter working in the Rope Walk, Ipswich, in the early part of the nineteenth century. A dish marked 'W.Balaam, Rope Lane Pottery, IPSWICH' is recorded by Rackham and Read.

[B.Rackham and H.Read, *English Pottery*, 1924.]

Ball clay

A very plastic clay from Devonshire and Dorsetshire used in the manufacture of earthenware so called from the manner of its excavation.

'The manner of procuring it after first clearing the soil and gravel from the top is to take a sharp knife or spade and cut or chop the surface into squares about nine or ten inches; then with an instrument like a carpenter's adze but much wider to dig them up and with a stick at the top of which is inserted a small pike to heave up the squares (or as they are called by the workmen balls) and throw them from the pit to be carried away.'

These balls varied according to locality from 30 to 35 pounds (or 70 balls to the ton) to 40 pounds (or 54½ balls to the ton). Eliza Meteyard said the weight of the balls was from 60 pounds to 70 pounds.

[R.Polwhele, *History of Devonshire*, 1797; E.Meteyard, *Life of Josiah Wedgwood*, 1865–66.]

Ball, Isaac

Izac Ball is listed in the *Tunstall Court Rolls* in 1671; and his son Isaac Ball is listed in the Wedgwood MS list of early eighteenth century potters as making wares to the value of £4 per ovenfull in the South West of Burslem. The *Parish Registers* of Burslem record the christening of Isaac, son of Isaac and Sarah Ball, 30 April 1669; those of Stoke his marriage to Sara Edge on 24 December 1696. The initials I.B. which occur with some frequency on early Staffordshire trailed slip posset-pots possibly refer to this potter. Dates on these posset-pots range from 1696 to 1700.
Plate 81 A.

[Reginald G. Haggar in *Apollo*, December 1953; *Parish Registers*, Burslem and Stoke.]

Ballot Box

A common name for a salt kit or barm pot.

'Bamboo' Ware

A dark shade of cane ware, made by Josiah Wedgwood in 1770, in imitation of bamboo.

[W.Mankowitz, *Wedgwood*, 1953.]

Bamford, John (c. 1850), Hanley

Manufacturer of toys and ornaments, china figures, stone jugs and teapots at Nelson Place, Hanley, from 1850 until after 1875.

[*Directories*, 1851, 1860, 1864, 1875.]

Banford, James and Bernice

James Banford commenced as a china painter at Bristol although the work that he did then cannot now be identified. He worked for the Derby factory from 1790 until 1795 having also done some work at Wedgwood's Chelsea decorating workshop. He was a man of improvident habits and addicted to the bottle, hence the necessity for his wife's support.

He excelled as a figure painter but did also flowers, landscapes and birds, turning his hand in fact to everything. Most of it was done to a small scale with miniature-like delicacy, often upon coffee-cans.

Bernice Banford was a pattern-painter.
Plate 40 C.

[George Savage, *Eighteenth Century English Porcelain*, 1952.]

Barberini Vase

See Portland Vase.

Barber's Dish

A wide-rimmed circular dish with a segment notch in the rim to fit the neck, part of the barber-surgeon's equipment.

Barker Family, Staffordshire

John Barker was hired by Thomas Whieldon in 1749 as an ovenman at 5/6 a week, with earnest of 2/6 paid in two instalments. He set up as a manufacturer of shining black wares at Row Houses, Foley, Fenton, about 1750 in partnership with his brothers. Later he made cream-coloured earthenware, china glazed and blue wares at Lane End. He married Mary Plant 21 May 1777 at Stoke church, and their eldest daughter married Josiah Spode. Tunnicliff in 1787 lists John, William and Richard Barker as manufacturers of cream-coloured earthenware at Lane End. In 1783 a Thomas Barker was potting at Lane Delph. In 1796 Richard alone of the brothers appears to have survived at Lane End; a Samuel Barker was at Lane Delph but was in financial difficulties in 1804. Richard alone is listed in Holden's *Triennial Directory*, 1805, as making earthenware.

Another generation entered upon the business between 1805 and 1818, when the firm is listed as R. J. and J. Barker, Flint Street. The partners were Richard, James and John, who became bankrupt in 1817, probably after the 1818 Directory was compiled. The Barker family was potting at a factory in the High Street in the 1830's. It was offered to be let (1831) and for sale (1833). In 1834 Thomas and Richard Barker are listed separately in Flint Street, Lane End, the one producing enamelled and gold burnished china, the other lustred earthenware. In 1851 William Barker alone is given as a manufacturer, Thomas Barker being described as a gilder, Stafford Street. In 1864 and 1875 the firm of Barker and Hill, china and earthenware manufacturers, was in King Street, Longton. In 1889 Barker Bros were in Barker Street.

Geoffrey Bemrose suggests that of the many Staffordshire figure makers 'the Barker family of Longton was the most prolific of all'. There is a teapot of 'Pratt' type, marked BARKER in the Victoria & Albert Museum, London.

[Whieldon's *Notebook*; *Directories*, 1783–1889; *Staffordshire Advertiser*, 1804, 1817, 1831, 1832, 1833; *Parish Registers*.]

Barker Family, Yorkshire

Peter Barker, son of Joseph Barker (the manager of Swinton Old Pottery) took over Mexborough Old Pottery in 1804 and worked it on his own account until 1822. From 1822 until 1833 the business was controlled by Peter Barker and his brother Jesse. Jesse's son, Samuel Barker, became proprietor in 1833 and continued the business until 1844 when it closed down. The chief output of the factory was printed earthenware.

Samuel Barker from 1834 also worked the Don Pottery. In 1852 the style of the firm was Samuel Barker & Son, and it traded under this name until the factory closed down in 1893. Edward Barker, the son, retired from the business in 1882. No marks have been recorded.

[A. Hurst, *The Boynton Collection of Yorkshire Pottery*, 1922.]

Barker, Sutton & Till

In 1833 William Barker of Snow Hill, Burslem, and James Sutton and Thomas Till of Liverpool Road, Burslem, took over the Sytch Pottery, trading as Barker, Sutton & Till. They made general earthenware, lustre wares and figures. In 1842 Sutton withdrew, and by 1850 Thomas Till was in sole possession of the business. Later he took his sons into partnership and changed the style to Thomas Till & Sons. Marks, 'B. S. & T. Burslem' and 'TILL' impressed.

[Reginald G. Haggar, *Staffordshire Chimney Ornaments*, 1955; L. Jewitt, *Ceramic Art of Great Britain*, 1878.]

Barleycorn

A subject of nineteenth and twentieth century Toby jugs, first recorded in old ballads and broadsides, such as *A Pleasant New Ballad of the Bloody Murther of Sir John Barleycorn* and *The Arraining and Indicting of Sir John Barleycorn, Knt*, printed for Timothy Tosspot. John Barleycorn was the personifiction of barley as providing malt liquors. The term was popularised by Robert Burns (1759–1796) in *Tam O'Shanter*.

Barlow, Thomas (c. 1870), Longton

Thomas Barlow manufactured china at Market Street, Longton in succession to the firms of Cyples and Cyples & Barker. In the 1870's he was producing distinctive neo-Greek cups and saucers with angular or fret handles, and straight sides. The feet were sometimes fretted and the decorations a curious combination of formal neo-Greek motifs with naturalistic flowers. Thomas Waterhouse Barlow manufactured earthenware in Commerce Street, Longton (recorded 1864 to 1889 or later.)

[L. Jewitt, *Ceramic Art of Great Britain*, 1878; *Directories*, 1864–1889.]

Barm Pot

A pot for storing barm or yeast.
See also SALT KIT.

Barnes, Zachariah (born 1743 died 1820), Liverpool.

Manufacturer principally of coarse delftware. Examples moulded in silver shapes and thickly

ASTBURY brown and white earthenware figure of a dancing actor under a lead glaze stained with metallic oxides. Staffordshire, c. 1740. Height 6½ inches. *(Courtesy Frank Partridge & Sons Ltd.)*

PLATE I

(A) ASTBURY-WHIELDON type teapot and cover, lead-glazed earthenware with relief decoration, c. 1740. Height 3½ inches.

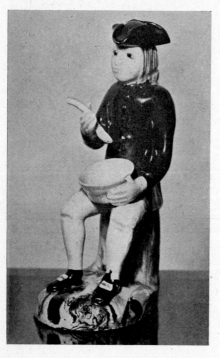

(B) *Left* ASTBURY figure of a seated man holding a bowl, c. 1740. Height 5 inches. (*Courtesy Frank Partridge & Sons Ltd.*)

(C) *Right* ASTBURY figure of a seated piper. Lead glaze stained with metallic oxides, c. 1740. Height 5½ inches. (*Courtesy Frank Partridge & Sons Ltd.*)

PLATE 2

ASTBURY-WHIELDON type. Staffordshire figure of a lady on horseback. Earthenware covered with a lead glaze stained with colouring oxides, c. 1740. Height 7⅝ inches.

PLATE 3

(A) BLUE-PRINTED EARTHENWARE. James and Ralph Clews. Earthenware plate transfer-printed in blue underglaze with 'The Landing of Lafayette' (engraved after a drawing by Samuel Maverick), 1824. Diameter 10⅛ inches. *(Courtesy of Mrs Frank Nagington.)*

(B) BLUE-PRINTED EARTHENWARE. G. M. and C. J. Mason. Ironstone china supper set transfer-printed in blue underglaze. Mark, MASON'S PATENT IRONSTONE CHINA within a cartouche beneath a crown, printed, c. 1825. *(Courtesy of Geo. L. Ashworth & Bros.)*

PLATE 4

BLUE-PRINTED EARTHENWARE. J. and R. Riley, Burslem. Earthenware dish transfer-printed underglaze in blue with an oriental scene, c. 1825. Diameter 20¾ inches. Mark, RILEY's Semi China, printed. (*Courtesy of Mrs Frank Nagington.*)

PLATE 5

BOW pair of figures, of a sportsman and sportswoman, porcelain, painted in colours, c. 1755. Mark, 'W' impressed. Height 7 inches; 6⅞ inches.

PLATE 6

(A) BOW pair of figures of owls, porcelain, painted in colours, c. 1760.
Height 7⅞ inches; 7¾ inches.

(B) BOW pair of figures from the Italian Comedy, porcelain painted in colours
and gilt, c. 1760–65. Height 7¼ inches.

PLATE 7

(A) BOW figure of a waterman wearing Dog-gett's Coat and Badge, porcelain, painted in colours and gilt, c. 1755. Height 8 inches.

(B) BOW figure of the Muse Erato, porcelain, painted in green, yellow, blue, crimson, brown and gilt, c. 1755. Height 6⅜ inches.

(C) BOW figure of a Nun reading, porcelain painted in enamel colours, c. 1760. Height 5⅝ inches.

(D) BOW group, lovers with a birdcage, porcelain, painted in colours and gilt, c. 1755. Height 7½ inches.

PLATE 8

(A) BOW figure, porcelain, c. 1750–55.
Height 8 inches.

(B) BOW figure, Quin as Falstaff, porcelain, c. 1750.
Height 9¼ inches.

(C) BOW group of a fortune teller and a girl, porcelain, c. 1750. Height 7⅛ inches.

(D) BOW figure of a lady with a negro page; porcelain, c. 1750–55. Height 6 inches.

PLATE 9

(A) BOW inkstand, porcelain, painted with enamel colours in Japanese (Kakiemon) style. Inscribed 'MADE AT NEW CANTON, 1751'. Height 1⅝ inches, diameter 4 inches.

(B) BOW sauce boat, moulded porcelain, painted with enamel colours. Mark, CT incised, c. 1750–55. Height 5¾ inches, length 8¾ inches.

PLATE 10

(A) BOW tureen, porcelain, painted in colours, c. 1765. Length 13½ inches.

(B) BOW mug, porcelain, painted in colours; height 5¾ inches; and porcelain dish, painted in colours. Mark, an anchor and dagger in red, c. 1770. Width 6¼ inches, length 8⅞ inches.

PLATE II

(A) BOW dish, porcelain, moulded in relief and painted in colours, c. 1770. Length 9⅝ inches, width 8⅛ inches.

(B) BOW plate, porcelain, painted with coloured panels on a powder-blue ground, c. 1765. Mark, six simulated Chinese characters within a double circle, in blue. Diameter 8⅝ inches.

(B)

(C) BOW plate, porcelain, painted in imitation of Imari ware, c. 1760–70. Diameter 7¼ inches.

(D) BOW plate, porcelain, painted in underglaze blue, c. 1760. Diameter 8¾ inches.

PLATE 12

BOW pair of vases, porcelain painted in colours and gilt, c. 1770. Mark, an anchor and a dagger in red. Height 8½ inches; 8⅛ inches.

PLATE 13

(B) CAUGHLEY jug, porcelain, with decoration moulded in relief and painted in colours and gilding. Mark, 'S' in underglaze blue, c. 1780. Height 8⅜ inches, diameter 5⅞ inches.

(A) CAUGHLEY chocolate cup, cover and saucer, porcelain, painted in blue and gold, c. 1790. Mark, 'S' in underglaze blue. Cup and cover, height 5¾ inches; saucer, diameter 6¼ inches.

PLATE 14

(A) CAUGHLEY teapot, cover and stand, porcelain, painted in colours and gilt, c. 1775. Height 4⅞ inches.

(B) CAUGHLEY plate, porcelain, painted in underglaze blue, c. 1780. Mark SALOPIAN impressed. Diameter 8⅛ inches.

(C) CAUGHLEY saucer, porcelain, painted in underglaze blue. Mark 'S' in underglaze blue, c. 1780. Diameter 5 inches.

PLATE 15

STAFFORDSHIRE SLIPWARE dish, red earthenware, decorated with white and buff slip, c. 1700. Diameter 13¾ inches.

PLATE 16

printed in underglaze dark blue are traditionally ascribed to Barnes and include a jug in the British Museum inscribed '*Frederick Heinzelman Liverpool 1779*' blue-printed with scroll work, flowers and liver-birds. Barnes also supplied Sadler & Green with blank white tiles for decoration.

Barnstaple, Devonshire

There were two potworks here of some importance from early times. (1) NORTHWALK POTTERY and (2) LITCHDON STREET POTTERY. The Northwalk Pottery was demolished within this century but had been in existence from the seventeenth century. In the nineteenth century it was occupied by Elias D. Rendell and later by Brannam. Many old embossed tiles found in West Country churches were made here. A wooden mould or former for such tiles was discovered at this factory as well as bats of clay impressed from similar moulds. The patterns included floral motifs, fleur-de-lis, Tudor Roses, lions, swans, human heads – all medieval in character. Some of the tiles were dated 1661.

A jug in the Fitzwilliam Museum with a sun-face decoration was made by Philip Burch of Barnstaple.

The Litchdon Street Pottery in the eighteenth century was worked by a potter named Lovering, subsequently by Rendell and finally by Brannam. The firm is now Charles H. Brannam Ltd.

C H Brannam
Barum

Barr, Martin

Partner in the firm of Flight & Barr 1792, Barr, Flight & Barr 1807, and Flight, Barr & Barr 1813, at Worcester. See under WORCESTER.

Barvas

Crude, grey, unglazed pottery, very thick and heavy, was made at Barvas in the Outer Hebrides in the nineteenth century or earlier. It was roughly built up without mechanical aids and looks more primitive and earlier than it is.

[J. A. Fleming, *Scottish Pottery*, 1923.]

Basaltes

'A black porcelain biscuit of nearly the same properties with the natural stone, striking fire from steel, receiving a high polish, serving as a touchstone for metals, resisting all acids and bearing without injury a strong fire – stronger indeed than the basaltes itself.' (Wedgwood *Catalogue*, 1787.)

Basaltes was a refinement of the 'dry' black stoneware originally made by Elers. Its black colour was due to the presence of iron and manganese in the 'body'. In addition to Wedgwood it was made by Adams, Neale & Co., Palmer, Turner, Birch, Mayer, Hollins, Walton and others.

Plates 111 B, 114 D, 115 C, 118 B, 120 A, 125 C.

[M. H. Grant, *The Makers of Black Basaltes*, 1910.]

Basket work

Shapes with embossed decoration resembling basketwork were common in salt-glazed stoneware c. 1760–1780 and are usually associated with the firm of Baddeley at Shelton. Openwork shapes formed upon a mould by interlacing strips of clay were popular in the 19th century and were made both in various china and other bodies.

Bas relief

Modelled decoration in low relief as on jasper ware.

Bates, Elliot & Company, Dale Hall, Burslem
Bates, Walker & Company

An extensive potworks at Dalehall, Longport, was worked successively by Joseph Stubbs (died 1836); Thomas, John and Joseph (or Joshua) Mayer; Mayer & Elliot; Liddle, Elliot & Co.; Bates, Elliot & Co., later Bates, Walker & Co.

Manufactures included a large variety of dinner, tea, toilet and other services in ironstone china, jet and stoneware. Blue-printed and 'flown' blue ware was produced. Jugs with relief decorations were a speciality.

Terra cotta statuary was made from red clay at Bradwell and was exceedingly well produced. In addition to classical models, special subjects were modelled by Grispie and William Beattie. Reproductions of Turner's jasper ware were made in the 1870's from original Turner moulds in their possession.

Other products included sanitary wares,

chemist's goods and garden pottery. Various patents were taken out by Bates, Walker & Co.

MARKS

BATES WALKER & CO. (impressed)
or B.W. & CO.

[*Directories*,1818–89; L. Jewitt,*Ceramic Art of Great Britain*, 1878.]

Bathwell, William, Thomas and Elijah, Burslem

William and Thomas Bathwell manufactured earthenware in the centre of Burslem from the beginning of the nineteenth century. William Bathwell died on Friday, 3 March 1815, 'in the prime of life'. (*Staffordshire Advertiser*, 11 March, 1815.) and the business was continued by Thomas and Elijah Bathwell. In 1818 the firm is listed as T. & E. Bathwell, Market Street, Burslem. Thomas Bathwell died in 1820 and his factory was offered for sale (*Staffordshire Advertiser*, 30 September, 14 October 1820.)

[*Directories*; *Staffordshire Advertiser*, 1815–1820.]

Bat-printing

Process of transfer-printing from engraved copper-plates in which a bat of gelatine takes the place of transfer tissue. Because of its sensitiveness to fine engraving the process was extensively used in the first decade of the nineteenth century at Minton's, Copeland's, etc., for transfer-printing vignettes of shells and flowers.

[W. Turner, *Transfer Printing on Enamels, Porcelain and Pottery*, 1907.]

Battam, Thomas (born 1810 died 1864)

Son of a porcelain painter: art director of Copeland at London and Stoke-on-Trent from 1835 until 1864. The introduction of parian is said to have been due 'to his taste and judgment' (*Art Journal*, Vol. 10, 1848). He died at Notting Hill, 28 October 1864.

[*Art Journal*, 1864.]

Battersea, London

A porcelain factory at Battersea was said to have existed in the early 1750's though no porcelain of such manufacture has been identified, and the description is probably an inaccurate one of the short-lived Battersea enamel factory (1753–56).

[Rouquet, *L'Etat des Arts en Angleterre*, 1755; Richard Pococke, *Travels through England*, 1750. Camden Soc., 1888.]

'Battle for the Breeches'

A theme of popular imagery concerning marriage, of great and almost universal antiquity; occurs on fourteenth and fifteenth century misericords at Ely and Bristol; on seventeenth century slipware dishes (example in the Fitzwilliam Museum, Cambridge); and as a subject for a figure group in the form of a spill vase, usually lettered 'WHO SHALL WARE THE BREECHES' and 'CONQUER OR DIE'; possibly made by Obadiah Sherratt, nineteenth century.

[Reginald G. Haggar, *Staffordshire Chimney Ornaments*, 1955.]

Baxter, Thomas (born 1782)

China painter. His father was the proprietor of an outside decorating business in London, and he worked for the Worcester factory. Baxter removed to Worcester in 1814, working as an instructor of apprentices and as an outside artist until 1816 when he went to Swansea. He returned, however, to Worcester, in 1818. He was a painter of landscapes, flowers and figures, subjects which he executed with careful regard to finish and detail. He was particularly successful with shells and feathers.

Plates 100 D, 134 B, 138 B, 141 A.

[W.B. Honey, *Old English Porcelain*, 1928, New Ed. 1948; George Savage, *Eighteenth Century English Porcelain*, 1952.]

Bear Jug

A jug modelled in the form of a bear hugging a dog, illustrating the sport of bear-baiting. The detachable head was used as a cup. It was made in white salt-glazed stoneware in Staffordshire and in brown stoneware at Nottingham and in Derbyshire, eighteenth century. Enamelled bear jugs were made in Staffordshire and Yorkshire in the late eighteenth and early nineteenth centuries.

Beech, James (born 1770 died 1854), Tunstall, Staffordshire

In 1821 James Beech and Abraham Lownds manufactured earthenware on a considerable scale at Newfield, Sandyford. The business was continued from 1834 by Beech alone until 1845. The output of the factory were staple Staffordshire products. Previous to setting up as a manufacturer Beech had been employed by William and Benjamin Adams. He died at Spotacre, Hilderstone, 25 May, 1854.

[P.W.L. Adams, *John Henry Clive*, 1947; L. Jewitt, *Ceramic Art of Great Britain*, 1878.]

Beech, William (died 1864), Burslem

William Beech, china figure manufacturer, later manufacturer of parian and ornamental china, started up in partnership with a man named Jones in 1836, at the Bell Works, Queen Street, Burslem. The partnership was dissolved in 1839, Beech continuing the business on his own account. In 1853 he took into partnership a Mr Brock who dropped out in 1855, Beech carrying on the business until his death in 1864. His widow, Jane Beech, worked the factory from 1864 in partnership with a man named Podmore (as Beech & Podmore) until 1876. She was described in Harrod's *Directory* 1870 as a manufacturer of water closets and china and earthenware toys, an odd combination. The factory was pulled down.

[*Directories.*]

'Beeley'

The name adopted by and sometimes used in connection with Billingsley after leaving Torksey.

Beevers & Ford, Mexborough, near Swinton, Yorkshire

Established towards the end of the eighteenth century by Beevers at the Rock Pottery, who in partnership with Ford & Simpson manufactured cane-coloured domestic wares.

The factory's products were improved by Reed & Taylor of Ferrybridge, James Reed continuing the works until 1849 when he was succeeded by his son John. Their products are impressed 'REED' in large capitals. The mark is also found printed in blue on stoneware. Sidney Woolfe & Co. of Ferrybridge took over the factory after the Reeds and worked it until its closure in 1883.

[Oxley Grabham, *Report, Yorkshire Philosophical Society*, 1916; A. Hurst, *Catalogue of the Boynton Collection of Yorkshire Pottery*, 1922.]

Belfast, County Down, Northern Ireland

Robert Leathes is said by Honey to have manufactured delftware here before 1686. Contempo-

rary with its manufacture in Staffordshire cream-coloured ware was also made, though certainly identified examples are not known.

Belfield, Charles, Prestonpans

Charles Belfield came from Derbyshire and made dinner and dessert services for the Duke of Buccleuch in a cream earthenware from clay quarried at Cousland near Dalkeith. He became manager to Fowler & Thomson and when they closed down started up in 1832 on his own account. His son James Belfield became a partner in 1836, (other sons later), the firm trading as Charles Belfield & Sons. Brown and yellow wares for domestic use were first made, with 'Rockingham' style teapots, hand-thrown drainpipes, and white sanitary pottery.

[J.A. Fleming, *Scottish Pottery*, 1923.]

Bell, John (died 1880) and Matthew Perston (died 1869), Glasgow

The Glasgow Pottery was founded early in the nineteenth century by John and Matthew Perston Bell for the production of fireclay, sanitary and garden pottery. From 1842 china and earthenware was made in a wide variety of styles and materials. Blue-printed earthenware was popular and included three well-known patterns, 'Willow', 'Damascus' and 'Triumphal Car'. Parian statuary, copies of Etruscan vases, and terra cotta goods were made. Artists included:

Copeland designer and modeller
Wagstaff painter

The firm became a public limited company in 1881, but after operating under the direction of a Mr Murdoch for ten years and Joseph Turner subsequently, it closed down.

MARKS

Transfer-printed

[J.A. Fleming, *Scottish Pottery*, 1923.]

Bell, Samuel (died 1754)

Potter, Lower Street, Newcastle-under-Lyme from c.1730–1754, where he made Astbury-type teapots of excellent shape and finish. In 1734 he had attained sufficient substance to be listed in the *Newcastle-under-Lyme Poll List* as a gentleman. Good examples of his pottery may be seen in Newcastle-under-Lyme Museum.

Bell, William, Belle Vue Pottery, Myton, Hull

A pottery was established here on the Humber bank in 1802. In 1825 it was acquired by William Bell who extended the manufacture, exporting good quality cream-coloured wares, painted and blue and brown transfer-printed pottery with various decorations through a depot in Hamburg managed by his brother, Edward Bell.

Earlier products of the factory are said to include green-glazed ware. Teapots made at this factory are sometimes distinguishable by a bell-shaped lid. The factory closed in 1840.

MARKS

Two bells overlapping each other, within a circular inscription, 'BELLEVUE POTTERY HULL.'

> Two bells overlapping (impressed).
>
> Two bells enclosed within a cursive inscription, 'Belle Vue Pottery, Hull' and scrollwork.

[A. Hurst, *Catalogue of the Boynton Collection of Yorkshire Pottery*, 1922; Oxley Grabham, 'Yorkshire Potteries, Pots and Potters' in *Yorkshire Philosophical Society Transactions*, 1916; L. Jewitt, *Ceramic Art of Great Britain*, 1878.]

Bellarmine

A stoneware ale-house bottle, big-bellied, narrow-necked, with a bearded mask opposite the handle. It was named after Cardinal Robert Bellarmine (born 1542 died 1621). First imported to this country from the Rhineland and Holland, it was later, in the seventeenth century, made in England by John Dwight (c.1633–1703) of Fulham and others.

The bellarmine is frequently mentioned or referred to in English seventeenth century literature, notably by Ben Jonson, Thomas Shad-

well and Thomas D'Urfey; and Hogarth figures a bellarmine in the sixth plate of *The Harlot's Progress* (published 1733–34).

It was also known as a Grey Beard or Long Beard.

For its use in witchcraft and magic see under WITCH BOTTLES.

Plate 48 A.

Belleek, Fermanagh, Ireland

A factory on an island in the river Erne was established by David McBirney and Robert Williams Armstrong in 1857, after preliminary trials with Cornish china clay and Irish felspar at Worcester. In 1878 some 200 workpeople were engaged at the factory. Armstrong was art director.

MARKS

Jewitt gives the following:

BELLEEK CO FERMANAGH

CHARACTERISTICS & WORK

China, parian, ironstone, and painted, printed and gilded earthenware were made. Its porcelain was notorious for a curious 'slimy nacreous lustre' which Charles Locke Eastlake in *Hints on Household Taste* (4th edition 1878) said 'glistens like wet barley sugar'. Important services were made, parian statuary, and imitations of shells marked by skilful workmanship.

[L. Jewitt, *Ceramic Art of Great Britain*, 1878.]

Bell Ringers' jugs

Jugs for serving ale to bell ringers, kept either in the church tower, as at Macclesfield, Cheshire; or in the home of one of the ringers. Newcastle-under-Lyme Museum possesses two capacious jugs, one evidently for civic occasions, the other in coloured slips dated 1845. In Derby Museum there is a large, brown stoneware jug, probably made at Belper, said to have been made for use at the Font of St. Werburgh's, Derby, in 1806, but possibly intended as a ringers' jug.

Belper, Derbyshire

A manufacture of coarse brown ware existed here from about 1750. The incised mark 'Belper' is recorded on a mug dated 1775. William Bourne took over the factory about 1800. It was closed down in 1834.

Bennet, John

Manufacturer of rustic and terra cotta figures at the Sneyd Pottery, Albert Street, Burslem, 1864.

Bennett, Robert

Potter at Brislington, Bristol, in 1669.

Benthall, Shropshire

The factory here, under John Thursfield, produced similar black-glazed wares to Jackfield. On his death in 1789 his son continued in partnership with W. Pierce until 1818.

Bentley, Thomas (born 1730 died 1780)

Partner with Josiah Wedgwood in the firm of Wedgwood & Bentley, potters. Born in 1730 and educated at a Presbyterian school at Findern, near Derby. Apprenticed in 1745 to a Manchester warehouseman, and subsequently went to the Continent, where he spent some time. Returning to Liverpool as a warehouseman he took into partnership Samuel Boardman.

His wife, Hannah Oates, whom Bentley married in 1754, died five years later. Bentley probably became acquainted with Josiah Wedgwood in 1762 becoming his partner in 1769.

He was a man of wide culture, possessing a knowledge of classical and renaissance art; he was also a gifted linguist. Through Bentley,

Wedgwood became known to Priestley and Matthew Boulton.

Bentley died in November 1780.

[Katherine Eufemia Farrer, *Letters of Josiah Wedgwood, 1762–80*, 1903; (Anonymous) *Thomas Bentley 1730–1780 Liverpool, Etruria and London*, 1927.]

Bentley, Wear & Bourne, Shelton

One of the most important nineteenth century engraving workshops was established in Vine Street, Shelton by William Bentley (1777–1833), William Wear and Samuel Bourne, about 1818.

The sequence of the firm was as follows:

Bentley, Wear & Bourne, 1818
Bentley & Wear, 1822–1833
Bentley, Wear & Wildig, 1833
Wildig & Allen, 1834–1837
Allen & Green, 1851

The firm engraved extensively for the trade, issued colour prints in lithography, and opened the first Art Gallery in North Staffordshire in 1825. The signature of the firm is sometimes found beneath engraved pottery pictures:

Bentley, Wear & Bourne, Engravers & Printers, Shelton, Staffordshire

Anglo-American subjects were taken from Abel Bowen's *Naval Monuments*, 1816. Examples in Gallery of Fine Arts, Yale University.

[*Directories: Staffordshire Advertiser; Pottery Mercury*, 1825; S. Shaw, *History of the Staffordshire Potteries*, 1829.]

Bentley, William (born 1777 died 1833)

Engraver in partnership in the firm of Bentley, Wear & Bourne, Vine Street, Shelton, c.1815–1823, later Bentley & Wear and finally Bentley, Wear & Wildig. Opened a picture gallery at his workshop, Shelton, in October 1825. His collection included works attributed to Wouverman, Teniers, Rembrandt, Berghem, Tintoretto Brueghel, Ostade, Guido, Bega and Brouwer (*Pottery Mercury*, 12th October 1825).

[S. Shaw, *History of the Staffordshire Potteries*, 1829; Obit. *Staffordshire Advertiser*, 1 June 1833.]

Bevington, Samuel and John, Shelton and Hanley

Samuel Bevington, who is variously described as 'artist', 'China figure maker', and 'toy and ornament' manufacturer, founded the firm which ultimately became known as Samuel Bevington & Son, at the Swan Works, Elm Street, Hanley, in 1835. He was also described as 'gilder, lusterer and enameller'. Samuel Bevington took his son into partnership and extended his business. Porcelain table services were exhibited at the 1862 Exhibition as well as parian statuary by Pradier, Morrey and Beattie.

John Bevington carried on the business after his father's death or retirement as a manufacturer of china, earthenware and parian until the end of the century.

Other sons of Samuel Bevington, James and Thomas, made useful and ornamental china in the second half of the nineteenth century.

The Bevingtons are said to have made imitation Sèvres in the 1870's.

[*Directories* 1846–1889; L. Jewitt, *Ceramic Art of Great Britain*, 1878; *Catalogue, 1862 Exhibition;* G. W. Rhead, *British Pottery Marks*, 1910.]

Bevington, Timothy and John, Swansea

The Bevingtons were in partnership with L. W. Dillwyn at Swansea from 1811 to 1817, and lessees until 1824. Quaker business men, they had nothing to do with the artistic production at Swansea. Their mark however, is found on a biscuit ornament of a reclining ram in the Victory and Albert Museum with the impressed initials of the modeller, Isaac Wood:

SWANSEA
Bevington & Co.

Bianco Sopra Bianco

Literally, white on white, but used as a form of white decoration upon a pale grey or blue ground at the Lambeth, Bristol, and Liverpool delftware factories from about 1750.

[F. H. Garner, *English Delftware*, 1948.]

Bideford, Devonshire

A number of factories operated in this town from an early date, making common country pottery. The more important were:

East-the-Water: Briant Ching is recorded here in 1850 (White's *Directory of Devonshire*, 1850)

to be followed by John Philips Royle whose name occurs on a pitcher dated 1857 in the Fitzwilliam Museum, Cambridge. Harry Phillips made handsomely decorated jugs and dishes here in the 1860's and 1870's. The factory survived into the twentieth century, making only common wares.

Crocker's Pottery: Established in 1668 and in continuous operation until early twentieth century, when it was demolished. Samuel Crocker was here in 1850. His factory was in the Strand. Bideford makers whose workshops are not known include Edward Reed, 1741 (jug in Hanley Museum, Stoke-on-Trent) and John Bird, 1818 (jug in Exeter Museum).

East-the-Water: 2nd factory which in 1850 was in the occupation of John Cole.

High Street: George Green was potting here in 1850.

Potter's Lane: John Tucker & Son, 1850.

Billing (Billin), Thomas (c. 1722)

His products are unidentified, but were probably salt-glazed stoneware and are described in his patent, October 17, 1722, as 'the most refined earthenware of a nature and composition not only transparent but so perfect in its kind as (contrary to the nature of all other earthenwares) to resist almost any degree of heat'.

[L. Jewitt, *Ceramic Art of Great Britain*, 1878.]

Billingsley, William (born 1760 died 1828)

A china painter and wandering arcanist who discovered the secret of a white and exceedingly translucent porcelain paste which could be produced only with incredible loss. His career was therefore dogged by disappointment and failure.

Born at Derby and apprenticed as a china painter at the Derby works in 1774; influenced by Boreman; became celebrated as a painter of flowers in a new naturalistic style marked by the illusion of depth, and the use of longish sprays of flowers spreading from a central bloom. He left Derby in 1796, entered into association with Coke at Pinxton as an arcanist, then went to Mansfield in 1799 and later to Torksey, Lincolnshire, where he decorated white china bought in Staffordshire. He found employment at Worcester in his trade in 1808 but left once more to become a china-maker at Nantgarw in 1813. His association with Dillwyn at Swansea in 1814 broke down in 1816, and he returned to Nantgarw. In 1819 Rose of Coalport bought his moulds and made use of his ideas.

He died in 1828 in greatly reduced circumstances. As a porcelain painter, his work seems always to have been in demand and to have reached a high quality.
Plates 41 B, 76 A.

[W. B. Honey, *Old English Porcelain*, 1928: new ed. 1948; George Savage, *Eighteenth Century English Pottery*, 1952.]

Billington, Dora May
Studio potter and teacher: studied at Hanley and South Kensington; author of *Art of the Potter*, 1937. Decorated industrial pottery made by Meakins. One of the first English studio potters to respond to modern continental tendencies, her work shows distinct originality of form and treatment.

 Incised

[J. Farleigh, *The Creative Craftsman*, 1950; G. W. Digby, *The Work of the Modern Potter in England*, 1952.]

'Billy Waters'
A celebrated early nineteenth century London black fiddler, with a wooden leg, who became the subject of popular pottery imagery. Edward Keys modelled a figure of him for Derby before 1826. A puppet of Billy Waters appeared in Chandler's Fantoccini in 1825.

[William Hone, *The Every Day Book*, 1825–27.]

Bilston, South Staffordshire
William Pitt, in his *Topographical History of Staffordshire* (1817), said, 'Potter's clay, for the most common wares, is found in Monway-field, and near Tipton, Wednesbury, and Bilston, where some small manufactures of this kind are now carried on'. The earliest reference to a Bilston potter occurs in a document dated 13 January 1801 (Birmingham Reference Library) which cites William Brereton of 'the liberty of Bilstone.'

The manufacture of earthenware in Bilston was continued throughout the nineteenth century.

The Bradley Pottery, Bilston is stated to have been built by John Wilkinson, the ironmaster. The factory changed hands many times during the next hundred years. In 1818 William Stinson worked the factory (*Parson & Bradshaw's Directory*, 1818) but shortly after it must have been taken over by Robert Jackson who continued it until June 1827 when he retired from the trade (*Pottery Mercury*, 6 June 1827). John Wild (or Wilde) who in 1818 was at the Pot House, New Town, Bilston, succeeded Jackson at Bradley, trading as John Wilde & Son and manufacturing coarse black wares. The Wildes continued until 1834 or later when they got into debt and eventually landed in prison as insolvent debtors. The appeal of John and Thomas Wilde under an act for the relief of insolvent debtors was heard at Stafford 18 August 1841 (*Staffordshire Advertiser*, 31 July 1841). In the announcement of this appeal they were described as formerly of Shropshire Row and later of Bradley.

Other potters are recorded in Bilston. Abraham Bruiton was at Shropshire Row in 1828 where he was followed by George Myatt some time before 1834.

The Myatts are the most important potters of Bilston. George Myatt made blue-and-white-earthenware. By 1834 Benjamin Myatt was manufacturing yellow wares at Bradley and probably the decorative wares which have survived were made by him. Before 1851 Robert Bew a pottery dealer took over the Bradley Potworks, employing Robert John Myatt as his manager (Melville's *Directory of Wolverhampton*, 1851.) Bew was succeeded by Alexander Turner & Son who made salt-glazed stonewares for chemical and domestic use.

The Bilston Museum possesses a small collection of Bilston pottery, consisting of vases, jugs and bowls, glazed olive green, tawny yellow and warm ochre. Incised decoration occurs on some pieces, the hollows of the incisions collecting glaze and emphasising pattern. Vases with goose-neck handles were peculiar to the factory. Slip decoration was successfully employed in the form of feathery leaf patterns. The impressed mark MYATT occurs on these types.

[Geo. T. Lawley, *History of Bilston*, 1893; Kelly's *Directory*, 1896.]

Bingham, Edward (born 1829)

Potter, Castle Hedingham, Essex, 1848, who made pseudo-Tudor and seventeenth century pottery, sometimes passed off as genuine early English pottery.

[W. B. Honey, *English Pottery and Porcelain*, 1933, later editions.]

Bingley, Thomas (fl. 1778-1806), Swinton

Thomas Bingley, in partnership with Sharpe and the two elder Bramelds, took over the Swinton works in 1778 for the manufacture of stoneware, and blue-and-white dinner and tea services, which were known as 'Rockingham ware'. He was associated with John and William Brameld and the Greens of the Leeds pottery from 1787 to 1806, trading successively as Thomas Bingley & Co. 1778–87; Greens, Bingley & Co. 1787–1800; and Greens, Hartley & Co. 1800–06. His impressed mark BINGLEY is found.

[A. Hurst, *Catalogue of the Boynton Collection of Yorkshire Pottery*, 1922.]

Birch, Edmund John, Shelton

The firm of Birch & Whitehead is recorded in the 1796 *Directory*, but later, in 1802, is under the name of Edmund John Birch, who made excellent black basaltes and jasper wares in the Wedgwood style which occur with his mark impressed:

BIRCH or Birch

Birch's factory was announced for sale in 1814 (*Staffordshire Advertiser*, 4 June 1814, *Staffordshire Gazette*, 7 June 1814).

[*Directories*, 1796/1805; M. H. Grant, *The Makers of Black Basaltes*, 1910.]

Bird call

A pottery whistle in the form of a small bird, made in slipware and stoneware in widely distributed districts. It is said to have been built in the chimneys of old houses as a charm against evil spirits. A whistle in the form of a cock made in salt-glazed stoneware decorated with manganese was discovered at Broughton Old Hall, Staffs., and is now in Hanley Museum and Art Gallery, Stoke-on-Trent.

Bird, Daniel, Cliff Bank, Stoke, Staffordshire

Mid-eighteenth century potter of agate and salt-glazed stoneware whose work cannot be definitely identified. He was called the 'Flint Potter' because, according to Simeon Shaw, he established the proper proportion of flint to clay to form a workable earthenware and stoneware body.

[S. Shaw, *History of the Staffordshire Potteries*, 1829.]

Bird, William (born 1717 died 1765)

Slipware potter, son of William and Anna Bird. A dish mould inscribed 'WILLIAM BIRD made me 1751' is in the British Museum.

Birks, Alboin (born 1861 died 1941)

Artist in pâte-sur-pâte and pupil of M. L. Solon from whom he learnt the technique; worked for Mintons Ltd, 1876–1937. His pieces were generally signed.

ABirks

Birks, Charles (born 1793 died 1834)

Manufacturer of china, High Street, Lane End, from 1819 to 1834.

[*Staffordshire Advertiser*, 2 August 1834, 18 October 1834.]

Biscuit porcelain

A porcelain paste, fired but left unglazed, used for making porcelain figures and groups in emulation of marble statuary at Bristol and Derby; and by Samuel Alcock at Burslem. It was superceded by parian.

[W.B.Honey, *Old English Porcelain*, 1928, new ed. 1948; G.V. J.Bemrose, *Nineteenth Century English Pottery and Porcelain*, 1952.]

Blackburton, Burton-in-Lonsdale, Yorkshire
Slipware was manufactured in the early eighteenth century by Thomas Bateson. In 1750 the Baggaley family established its manufacture. The ware is of dark red body, fired almost to stoneware hardness, the decoration being trailed white slip beneath a deep yellow glaze. The factory continued into the nineteenth century. Dated specimens made in this area range from 1774 to 1865.

[S.Lewis, *A Topographical Dictionary of England*, 7th ed. 1848; B.Rackham, *Catalogue of the Glaisher Collection*, 1935; Oxley Grabham, *Report, Yorkshire Philosophical Society*, 1916.]

Black Egyptian
See under BASALTES, and EGYPTIAN BLACK.

Black-glazed pottery
Red earthenware covered with a lustrous black or brownish-black glaze made in Staffordshire at Fenton Low by Whieldon and others; at Burslem by Thomas Holland (1748–1807) often erroneously stated as the 'first' maker of 'shining black' ware, and his widow Ann Holland (née Hill: 1773–1847); and in Shropshire at Jackfield, Benthall and Haybrook in Posenhall Parish. Jacobite emblems or inscriptions are not infrequent upon Jackfield ware, in glaze colours or leaf gold.
Plate 92 B.
[Sir Edward Benthall, 'Black Glazed Pottery of the Eighteenth Century', *Apollo*, 1955; Directories; Staffordshire Advertiser.]

Black-printing
Described by William Evans in *The Art and History of the Potting Business* in 1846 as 'a term for applying impressions to glazed vessels, whether the colour be black, red or gold', it was extensively used by outside decorators in Staffordshire and the potteries of Liverpool, York-

shire and the Tyne in the second half of the eighteenth century and first three decades of the nineteenth century. Black was more extensively used than other colours, hence the term. Many black-printers were probably included in the term decorator in old directories. The following were described specifically as black-printers, printers, or are known from signed works to have been such:

John Ansley, Lane End, fl. 1790–1829

Thomas Baddeley (Engraver and enameller) Chapel Fields, Shelton

Bentley, Wear & Bourne (Engravers and Printers) Vine Street, Shelton fl. 1818–1823. The engraving business was continued until late in the nineteenth century.

Bagnall & Fletcher, Booden Brook, Shelton, 1786–96

Cephas Shirley, Bowden Brook Shelton, 1818 onwards

Ellis & Shirley (Moses Ellis and Cephas Shirley) before 1818

Thomas Fletcher, Shelton, 1796–1810

Thomas Harley, Lane End, fl. 1800–32

John Robinson, Hill Top, Burslem, 1787–1818 or later

Francis Morris, Vale Pleasant, Shelton 1800–1802

Joseph Machin (and enameller) Old Croft, Nile Street, Burslem 180

John Johnson, Shelton, 1800

Charles Tittensor, Shelton, fl. 1800–1823

The most distinguished of the black-printers were SADLER & GREEN, Liverpool.

[Evans, *Art & History of the Potting Business*, 1846; Directories; Announcements in *Staffordshire Advertiser*, etc.]

Blackwell family, Cobridge, Staffordshire
The Blackwell family was potting at Cobridge from about 1780. In 1783 John Blackwell was listed as a potter (Bailey's *Directory*), and in Tunnicliff's *Survey* of 1787 Joseph and John Blackwell are listed separately as manufacturers of 'blue-and-white stoneware, cream and painted

wares, Cobridge'. They may have worked at the same factory.

In 1796 the firm was John and Andrew Blackwell. When Andrew died John Blackwell continued the business as a china and earthenware manufacturer (Holden's *Directory*, 1805–07). In 1818 the firm was John and Robert Blackwell. At some later date John Blackwell of the Grange entered into partnership with Francis and Nicholas Dillon which continued until 28 February 1832 (*Staffordshire Advertiser*, 24 Nov. 1832.) The Dillons continued to manufacture earthenware until 1843 or later.

[*Directories*, 1783–1830; *Staffordshire Advertiser*, 1832.]

Blake, William (born 1757 died 1827)

Artist and poet; engraved and drew items for the Wedgwood catalogue of cream-coloured earthenware, 1815–16. Blake's correspondence with Josiah Wedgwood II is printed in Geoffrey Keynes' *Blake Studies* (1949). See catalogue illustrations in Mankowitz's *Wedgwood*, 1953.

Blanc de Chine

Glazed but unpainted relief decorated Chinese porcelain table wares and figures, imitated at Bow, Bristol (soft-paste), Chelsea and early Derby.

Blanchard (M.H.), Son & Company, London

This firm was established by M.H.Blanchard at Blackfriars Road, London, in 1839. Blanchard served his apprenticeship to the firm of Coade & Sealey of Lambeth, and when that business ultimately closed down he purchased some of their moulds. He was awarded medals at the 1851 and 1862 Exhibitions.

Terra cotta statuary and architectural enrichments were executed for the South Kensington Museum, Charing Cross and Cannon Street Stations, and the Wedgwood Institute, Burslem.

[L.Jewitt, *Ceramic Art of Great Britain*, 1878.]

Blashfield, John Marriott, Stamford

J.M.Blashfield started as a manufacturer of scagliola and cement at Southwark Bridge Road and Mill Wall, London, until 1851, when, having acquired moulds from Coade's factory (many by reputable sculptors and modellers) he started to produce terra cotta. In 1858 he removed to Stamford, in Lincolnshire, and continued to produce architectural terra cotta and statuary. In 1874 the Stamford Terra Cotta Company was formed, but it failed in 1875 and was wound up.

MARKS

> J.M.BLASHFIELD (impressed)
> BLASHFIELD, STAMFORD

WORK

This firm exhibited a considerable array of busts, statues and animals at the 1862 International Exhibition after models by Henry Hale, Henry Gibson and John Bell. Weigall modelled a competent bust of Queen Victoria.

Bleu-de-Roi

A Sèvres colour imitated at Worcester and contemporaneously at Derby at the end of the Chelsea-Derby period, consisting of a bright lapis-lazuli opaque enamel.

Bleu persan

Semi-oriental type of decoration painted in opaque white over a dark blue ground colour which was used in France at the Nevers factory, and copied in England.

Bloor, Robert, Derby

Clerk to the Derby factory during Duesbury's ownership, and proprietor from 1811 until 1826 when he became insane.

Blore, Robert, Bridge Gate, Derby

Maker of biscuit figures similar to those of Cocker, nineteenth century.

[W.B.Honey, *Old English Porcelain*, 1928; new ed. 1948.]

Blue Clay

More commonly known as BALL CLAY. A plastic clay quarried in Devon and Dorset, forming the basis of most earthenware bodies, see BALL CLAY.

Blue-dash Chargers

Circular dishes painted with various figural or floral subjects with blue brush strokes or dashes at the edge, ranging in date from 1614 to 1740 or longer. The archaistic word 'charger' was applied to this purely decorative class of tin-glazed earthenware by E. A. Downman who collected them.

[E.A.Downman, *Blue Dash Chargers*, 1919; F.H.Garner, *English Delftware*, 1948.]

'Bocage'

Foliage or tree backgrounds to porcelain or earthenware figures or groups, eighteenth and nineteenth centuries.

Body

The prepared and blended materials from which pottery is made.

Bodley and Son, Burslem, Staffordshire

Edward F. Bodley became partner in the firm of Bodley and Diggory in 1870 working the Hill Pottery China Works. In 1871 he became sole owner and in 1874 traded as Bodley & Son. Edwin J.D. Bodley became proprietor in 1875 and continued until 1890 or later. Manufactures included earthenware, parian, and china, a speciality being elaborately ornamented vases for lamps and chandeliers. Geoffrey Bemrose accords them a mention in referring to the influence of the aesthetic movement of the 1880's. Mark: initials in monogram.

[*Directories*, 1873–89.]

Bolsover, Derbyshire

Slipware was manufactured through the second half of the eighteenth century. A dish dated 1784 is described by B.Rackham in the *Catalogue of the Glaisher Collection*, 1935.

Bone China

The standard English porcelain since 1800. It is basically hard-paste, modified by the addition of bone ash which may be as much as 40% of the ingredients of the bone china body. Josiah Spode is credited with stabilising the proportions, although bone as an ingredient of porcelain was used at Bow from 1749, Lowestoft, Chelsea and Derby in the eighteenth century and is stated by Church to have been common knowledge among potters in Staffordshire in Spode's time.

Boon, Joseph (c. 1760–1814)

Manufacturer of blue-printed earthenware in Shelton and Hanley from about 1760 until 1814. In 1802 he was in partnership with Ridgway in Hill Street, Hanley, and from 1805 until 1808 with Richard Hicks (Boon & Hicks) in Broad Street, Shelton. Afterwards he potted on his own account until 1814, when his factory equipment, copperplate engravings and stock of ware (comprising 28 crates of blue-printed earthenware) were offered for sale.

[*Indenture of Apprenticeship of Moses Colclough*, 1763; *Juror's List* Salt Library, Stafford; Bailey's *Directory*, 1783; Tunnicliff's *Survey*, 1787; *Rate Books*; information per Alfred Meigh; *Staffordshire Advertiser* various dates.]

Boot, Jonathan (born 1745 died 1806)

Toy maker and modeller, Cobridge, 1800, 1802.

[Gravestone, St John's Churchyard, Hanley; Reginald G. Haggar, *Staffordshire Chimney Ornaments*, 1955.]

Boote, T. & R.

Founded 1842 by Thomas Latham Boote and Richard Boote at the Central Pottery, Burslem; manufacturers of parian statuary and vases. Various factories were occupied, the Kilncroft Works, and finally the Waterloo Potteries. Tiles and 'Granite' earthenware were made from about 1850. When T.L.Boote retired in September 1879, the business was continued by Richard Boote (d.1891) with the help of his sons. In 1894 the firm became a limited liability company. Blackwall Tunnel was tiled throughout by T. & R. Boote. The Bootes disputed with Copelands and Mintons the invention of parian.

T. & R.B.

[W.J.Furnival, *Leadless Decorative Tiles, Faience and Mosaic Stone*, 1904.]

Booth, Bridgwood & Booth, Lane End

Joseph Booth, John Bridgwood and Thomas Booth were established as earthenware manufacturers under the style Booth, Bridgwood and Company at Lane End at the beginning of the nineteenth century. Their factory was offered for sale in December 1805 (*Staffordshire Advertiser*, 28 December 1805) and the partnership was dissolved 11 November 1806 (*Staffordshire Advertiser*, 6 December 1806). The business was carried on by Joseph and Thomas Booth who are listed as earthenware manufacturers in 1818 (Parson and Bradshaw's *Directory*). In 1834 the firm was trading as Booth & Son, Church Street, Lane End. Joseph Booth died 6 March 1848 aged 75 years (*Staffordshire Advertiser*, 1848) The firm was not listed in 1851.

Booth, Enoch (c. 1742), Tunstall, Staffordshire

A salt-glazed mug with 'scratch blue' decoration is inscribed with the name Enoch Booth and the date 1742. Booth improved the quality of the pottery body by mixing local clay with Devon and Dorset clays, together with flint and is credited by Shaw with the introduction of fluid glaze, (a mixture of lead and flint into which biscuit was dipped before second firing) about 1750. Enoch Booth married Ann, daughter of Thomas Child of Tunstall, and was succeeded by his son-in-law, Anthony Keeling, who continued the business until 1810.

[S. Shaw, *History of the Staffordshire Potteries*, 1829.]

Booth, Hugh, Stoke-on-Trent, Staffordshire

A well-known potter who in 1787 was manufacturing china-glazed earthenware and 'Queen's ware in all its branches at a factory on Cliff Bank, Stoke. Ephraim Booth, his brother, succeeded him on his death in 1789, and took his sons Hugh and Joseph into the business, trading as Booth & Sons. The factory was later taken over by Adams.

Booth, Richard (born 1804 died 1842)

'China toy manufacturer', Hanley; his small factory employed 19 persons.

[Obit. *Staffordshire Advertiser*, 28 May 1842; *Report on the Employment of Children in Factories* 1842–43; Reginald G. Haggar, *Staffordshire Chimney Ornaments*, 1955.]

Booth, Thomas, Burslem

Toy manufacturer at Portland Street, Burslem, 1865–1868.

Borax

Simeon Shaw said that considerable quantities of borax were used weekly in the potteries for glazes', but he does not say when or by whom borax was first used. It was, however, evidently in use in pottery manufacture from the closing years of the eighteenth century.

Ralph Wedgwood's patent for making a glaze on new principles specified borax (3 October 1796) and early glaze recipes purporting to be those in use at Nantgarw sometimes include borax. This was certainly one of the ingredients of John Rose's leadless Coalport glaze of 1820. Recipes in use by James Furnival from 1817 until 1840 also mention borax.

[S. Shaw, *Chemistry of Pottery*, 1837; L. Jewitt, *Ceramic Art of Great Britain*, 1878; Recipe books.]

Boreman, Zachariah (born 1738 died 1810)

Landscape painter on porcelain; worked originally at Chelsea but moved to Derby about 1783 when he renewed a contract with Duesbury for three years at two guineas a week wage; returned to London 1794 and worked as an outside decorator at one of the London establishments. His work, executed in quiet tones, possesses a certain sober dignity. It was painted in the eighteenth century water-colour technique of glazing local colours over a monochrome foundation, possibly learnt from Sandby.

[L. Jewitt, *Ceramic Art of Great Britain*, 1878.]

Botanical flowers

A type of floral decoration inspired originally by Meissen porcelain and occurring on Chelsea porcelain, 1750–56 (from engravings in Philip Miller's '*The Gardeners Dictionary*, 1724, issued in parts with numerous copperplate engravings from 1755); on Derby porcelain painted by William Pegg (1775–1851), early nineteenth century; on porcelain decorated at Yarmouth by William Absolon (1751–1815); and by Thomas Pardoe (1770–1823) on Swansea porcelain. Pardoe's careful imitations of plants and flowers from Curtis's *Botanical Magazine* were probably due to the influence of Lewis Weston Dillwyn who was a keen botanist. Decorations from the same source are recorded on earthenware, notably those made at the Cambrian Pottery, Swansea c.1800. Wedgwood's Lotus Service, made c.1781 for Erasmus Darwin, is an example of this kind. Philip Miller was the greatest gardener of his time and the author of the great *Gardeners' Dictionary* 1724, and *Figures of Plants* 1760 illustrated by Lancrake, Georg Dionysius Ehret, (1708–70), and others. The *Botanical Magazine* was founded in 1787 by William Curtis (1746–99). Most of the illustrations during its first 28 years were drawn by William Kilburn (1745–1818) James Sowerby (1757–1822) and Sydenham Edwards (1769?–1819) and engraved by F. Sansom.

[H. Bellamy Gardener, 'Sir Hans Sloan's Plants on Chelsea porcelain,' in *Transactions, English Porcelain Circle*, IV, 1932, p. 22; Arthur Lane, 'Flower Painting on Pottery and Porcelain' in *Geographical Magazine*, 18, pp. 522–30; *The Connoisseur*, September 1947; Wilfred Blunt, *The Art of Botanical Illustration*, 1950; W. B. Honey, *English Pottery and Porcelain*, 1933; later ed.; W.B.Honey, *Old English Porcelain*, 1928, later ed.]

Bott & Co., Lane End, Staffordshire

Early nineteenth century manufacturers, principally of earthenware busts and figures. A moulded flower stand printed in purple and painted in red and blue in the Victoria and Albert Museum is marked 'Bott & Co.' The mark also occurs on silver lustre wares and blue-printed earthenware.

Bott & Co Impressed

[Reginald G.Haggar, *Staffordshire Chimney Ornaments*, 1955; A.Hayden, *Chats on Old English Earthenware* 1909.]

Bott, Thomas John

Enamel painter at the Worcester factory in mid-nineteenth century who excelled in figure painting in translucent white enamel against a rich blue ground. Bott was trained at Worcester under R.W. Binns, and was extensively employed in the 1860's in reproducing on porcelain effects of Limoges enamels.

[L. Jewitt, *Ceramic Art of Great Britain*, 1878; G.Bemrose, *Nineteenth Century English Pottery and Porcelain*, 1952.]

Boullemier, Antonin (born 1840 died 1900)

Painter of figure subjects on porcelain; studied under a descendant of Fragonard, and excelled in the dexterous interpretation of eighteenth century French subjects after Boucher; worked at Sèvres until 1870 when he came to England where he was employed at Mintons.

a Boullemier

[Anon. *Antonin Boullemier*, New York, 1900.]

Boullemier, Lucien Emile (born 1876 died 1949)

Ceramic painter of figure and portrait subjects, son of A. Boullemier; worked at Minton's, and later as art director, Malings of Newcastle-on-Tyne.

Boulton, Matthew (born 1728 died 1809)

Partner with John Fothergill until 1781 and John Wall as manufacturer of metalwork, Soho, Birmingham. Mounted Wedgwood cameos, vases etc. in cut-steel and gilt-bronze.

Bourne, Charles

Manufacturer of porcelain, Foley pottery, Fenton. He retired from business about 1830 because of ill-health and his factory was offered for sale.

CB/No 1   CB/No 3

[*Pottery Mercury*, 1 November 1828; *Staffordshire Advertiser*, 13 November, 1830.]

Bourne & Baker, Fenton, Staffordshire

Ralph Bourne and William Baker manufactured staple products from about 1796, exporting them on a considerable scale. In 1829 they owned, according to Shaw, 'two extensive manufactories and a mill and two spacious mansions as residences'.

The firm at this time was known as Bourne, Baker & Bourne. John Bourne and William Baker died in 1833. The business was carried on for a few months by Ralph Bourne (1772/3–1835) jointly with their executors, but the partnership was dissolved 11 November 1833.

For a short time the firm traded as Bourne, Baker & Baker (with Ralph Bourne, William Baker junior and John Baker as partners) but in 1843 William Baker alone survived, the firm being carried on subsequently as William Baker & Co.

William Baker was born in 1800 and died on 1865.

[*Staffordshire Advertiser*, various dates; *Directories*, 1834–89; R. Simms, *Bibliotheca Staffordiensis*, 1894.]

Bourne, Ralph (born 1772/3 died 1835)

Principal partner in the firm of Bourne, Baker and Bourne; lived at Hilderstone Hall; contributed generously to the building of Fenton and Hilderstone Churches.

[Obit. *Staffordshire Advertiser*, 5 December 1835.]

Bourne & Son, Denby, Derbyshire

This firm of stoneware manufacturers which continues to this day was founded by Joseph Bourne in 1812. He was the son of William Bourne, master potter of Belper, and the Belper and Denby factories were carried on by the family simultaneously until 1834 when the Belper works was discontinued and its materials and plant were transferred to Denby. The Codnor Park works which passed into Bourne's control in 1833 was also finally closed down and its plant and workpeople brought to Denby in 1861. Similarly the Shipley Pottery acquired in 1845 was absorbed in 1856. Joseph Bourne died in 1860 and his son and successor, Joseph Harvey Bourne, in 1869.

MARKS

The name of the firm J. BOURNE & SON with PATENTEES DENBY POTTERY NEAR DERBY arranged variously, or BOURNE'S POTTERY BELPER & DENBY DERBYSHIRE.

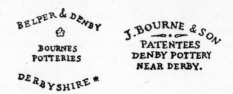

WORK

Excellent brown salt-glazed stonewares included hunting jugs with relief ornament and greyhound handles, Reform flasks and other ornamental wares.

Plate 159 B.

[L. Jewitt, *Ceramic Art of Great Britain*, 1878.]

Bourne, Samuel, Shelton

In partnership with John Bourne until 23 April 1803 (*Staffordshire Advertiser*, 29 October 1803). His name impressed S. BOURNE occurs on a figure of a reclining hind, coloured a deep ochreous yellow, with a green base, in Hanley Museum.

[Reginald G. Haggar, *Staffordshire Chimney Ornaments*, 1955.]

Bovey Tracey, Devonshire

Several potworks existed in this parish in the eighteenth century at INDEO and THE FOLLY. The Bovey Tracey Pottery Company was formed in 1841 for the manufacture of earthenware of the Staffordshire type and continued until December 1956 when the Directors decided to close (*Manchester Guardian*, 22 December 1956).

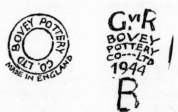

Bow, Straford-le-Bow, East London, Porcelain Manufactory

HISTORY AND OWNERS

The early history of the factory is obscure. In 1744 a copper and mineral merchant, Edward Heylin, and a mezzotint engraver and artist named Thomas Frye took out a patent for the manufacture of 'a certain material' equal in beauty and quality to imported porcelain, from a recipe including a material called unaker, 'the produce of the Chirokee nation in America'. Doubt has been cast upon the workableness of their specification, and no Bow porcelain of this early date has been identified with certainty.

Another patent was taken out by Frye alone in 1749 for a phosphatic porcelain including a percentage of bone-ash or 'Virgin Earth' which accounts for the high phosphorous content of identified early Bow porcelain.

By 1750 the manufactory had been taken over by Weatherby & Crowther, merchants, under the name 'New Canton', but Frye remained as manager until 1759. From that date the quality of the products deteriorated. Weatherby died in 1762, and in 1763 Crowther became bankrupt. The factory, however, was continued in operation until 1776 when it was taken over by William Duesbury who closed it down and removed the moulds to Derby.

MARKS

Numerous factory and workmen's or repairers' marks have been recorded on identified Bow porcelain, but before c.1760 wares can only be distinguished by qualities other than marks. The most generally recognized Bow marks after 1760 are an anchor and dagger in red or underglaze blue. Chaffers suggested that the dagger was adopted because Weatherby and Crowther were freemen of the City of London.

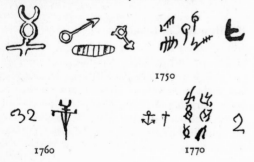

1750

1760   1770

ARTISTS

Thomas Frye, painter and engraver.

Sarah Wilcox, Frye's married daughter, who was a successful painter of figures and groups.

John Bacon, modeller, probably from 1762. A small 'B' has been found impressed on some Bow figures.

Thomas Craft, painter of a punch bowl c.1760 in the British Museum.

Simon François Ravenet, Robert Hancock. May have worked at Bow. Signed Hancock prints occur on some Bow porcelain.

Tebo (phonetic version of the French name Thibaut). Probably responsible for the 'T' or 'To' mark found on porcelain made at Bow 1750–65. He is thought to have been a repairer or assembler rather than a modeller.

Charles Weyman, c. 1772

Much Bow porcelain was decorated outside the factory.

DISTINGUISHING CHARACTERISTICS

The manufacture of Bow porcelain may be divided into four periods; (1) before 1749; (2) from 1749 until 1755; (3) from 1755 until 1760, when the most valued and typical Bow qualities appeared; and (4) after 1760, when there was a general lowering of quality apart from modelling, and the work became imitative in character.

(1) The wares made, if made at all, under the patent of 1744 were non-phosphatic. A number of figures, including the Kitty Clive as the 'Fine Lady' in the Schreiber Collection, Victoria and Albert Museum, on the evidence of style mannerisms, have been conjecturally attributed to this early period.

(2) From 1749 a creamy bone paste was produced, and wares were rather heavy in weight with an uneven glaze and of variable translucency. Plain white figures were made, and groups attributed on stylistic grounds to the 'Muses', modeller', often of women and children with round, doll-like heads and receding chins. These are generally treated with originality and painted sparingly with a limited palette of pigments. Useful wares followed Oriental porcelain shapes or contemporary silver, and were frequently decorated with versions of Chinese *famille rose* patterns; designs reminiscent of Japanese Ka-

kiemon; or with applied prunus sprays in relief on white wares.

(3) The distinctive qualities of Bow porcelain c.1755–60 are a rather waxy glaze, sometimes slightly iridiscent; the irregular spreading of the blue colour used for underglaze painting giving the surface a bluish tinge; and bright clear colouring with delicate flower painting. Figures display a liveliness of modelling and colour, in spite of strong Meissen influence. 'General Wolfe' and the 'Marquis of Granby' (c.1759) are examples of the best and most original Bow style. Figures tend to be a little heavy for their size and are sometimes provided with a square hole in which a support for candles could be placed. Mound bases gave place about 1758–60 to 4-footed rococo scroll pedestals tricked out in crimson and purple. Useful wares were decorated in Oriental styles, with Kakiemon patterns in red, blue and gold; with floral sprays dominated by two big peonies; or with 'botanical' flowers. Mixed decorative styles were sometimes used containing *motifs* from East and West. Transfer-printed decorations in black or brick red are beautiful but uncommon.

(4) Bow figures of the last period retained something of the charms of the earlier work, but the paste was greyer and the decoration tended to become over-elaborate. Useful wares in this phase follow Meissen, Chelsea and Worcester styles and marks. Examples: British Museum, Victoria & Albert Museum, Bedford Museum; Metropolitan Museum of Art, New York, the Art Institute of Chicago, and Rhode Island School of Design. See also FRYE, Thomas; BACON, John; MUSES MODELLER.
Colour plate 1 and Plates 6–13.

[*Bowcocke Papers*, British Museum; *Duesbury's Account Book*, British Museum; L.Jewitt, *Ceramic Art of Great Britain*, 1878; R.L.Hobson, *Catalogue of the Collection of Porcelain*, British Museum 1905; W.B.Honey, *Old English Porcelain*, 1928; new ed. 1948; J.L.Dixon, *English Porcelain of the 18th Century*, 1952; George Savage, *Eighteenth Century English Porcelain*, 1952; W.Chaffers, *Marks and Monograms on Pottery and Porcelain*, 14th ed. 1952; J. Haslem, *Old Derby China Factory*, 1876.]

Bowers, George Frederick,
Tunstall, Staffordshire

Manufacturer of porcelain tea wares with painted decorations at Brownhill, Tunstalls, from 1848 until 1860. At the 1851 Exhibition his wares were awarded a gold medal. Earthenware was subsequently made by him, and his son and successor, Frederick F. Bowers, until the business failed in 1871. The marks of the firm were the initials G.F.B. in a Staffordshire knot and G.F.BOWERS/TUNSTALL/POTTERIES.
[L.Jewitt, *Ceramic Art of Great Britain*, 1878.]

Boyle, John (died 1845)

Manufacturer of earthenware on own account at Keelings Lane, Hanley, from 1826. Partner to Herbert Minton in the firm of Minton & Boyle 1836–41, and with Wedgwood of Etruria from 1843 until his death. John Boyle contributed an important 'Account of Strikes in the Potteries in 1834–36' to the *Journal of the Statistical Society*, 1839.
[L.Jewitt, *Ceramic Art of Great Britain*, 1878.]

Boyle, Zachariah (or Zachary) (born 1783 died 1841)

Manufacturer of porcelain and pottery of quality. Boyle started as a china manufacturer trading as Zachariah Boyle & Son at a factory in upper Hanley about 1825. This potworks was announced 'to be let' in October 1828 (*Pottery Mercury*, 11 October 1828) when he took over Adams' factory in Stoke where the business was continued until 1850. Zachariah Boyle died in 1841 (Obit. *Staffordshire Advertiser*, 11 December 1841.)
[L.Jewitt, *Ceramic Art of Great Britain*, 1878.]

Brackley, Thomas

Potter at Buckland near Aylesbury whose name occurs with date 1759 inscribed on a jug at Chequers.
[B.Rackham and H.Read, *English Pottery*, 1924.]

Bradley & Co, London

John Bradley & Co. of 47 and 54 Pall Mall were dealers in and possibly decorators of basaltes, cream-coloured wares, Coalbrookdale, Coalport and perhaps Swansea and Nantgarw china. The mark 'Bradley & Co., Coalport,' is known. There is also a red script mark 'P.Bradley 1828' on a pastille burner probably of Coalport manufacture in the National Museum of Wales.

Bradwell Wood, near Burslem, Staffordshire

The traditional and generally accepted site in Staffordshire of Elers' factory. It was situated on a wooded ridge which separates Burslem from Newcastle-under-Lyme and this afforded some element of secrecy. Good red clay was abundant in the area, from which Elers made 'red china' teapots which gave him a national reputation. There are contemporary and eulogistic references by Dr Martin Lister and Dr Charles Leigh to his products. The premises, Bradwell Hall, are said to have been occupied by the Marsh family subsequently.

This site has been frequently investigated but little of any value has ever been discovered. Shaw says that Enoch Wood and John Riley measured the oven in 1808 and came to the conclusion that it was unsuitable for salt-glazed stoneware which Elers was alleged to have introduced into Staffordshire. In a memorandum written in 1814 into Cox's *Magna Britannia and Hibernia*, Enoch Wood recorded his opinion that it had been 'built to fire red china only'. The site has been frequently explored since Enoch Wood's time by the Rheads, by Thomas Pape, and recently in 1955 by A.R.Mountford who discovered fragments of 'red china.' The site awaits more thorough excavation.

[S. Shaw, *History of the Staffordshire Potteries*, 1829; G.W. Rhead, *The Earthenware Collector*, 1920; Thomas Pape, *Evening Sentinel*, 2 February 1944.]

Brain, E. and Company

The firm was founded by Edward Brain at the Foley, Longton, in 1850, and made china. Distinctive wares were produced for an exhibition held at Harrod's in 1934 for which the services of many distinguished painters were enlisted for new shapes and decorations, including:

Brangwyn, Sir Frank
Sutherland, Graham
Bell, Vanessa
Grant, Duncan
Forsyth, Gordon Mitchell
Rutherston, Albert
Proctor, Dod
Forsyth Moira
Gray, Milner

These have some collector's value, particularly as they were made only in small quantities.

FOLEY
ENGLISH BONE CHINA
PAINTED BY HAND.

Brameld, Thomas (died 1850), Swinton

One of three brothers, sons of William Brameld (died 1813) who worked the Rockingham Factory, Swinton, from the time of their father's death until 1842. They made porcelain from 1820 onwards. Jewitt described Thomas Brameld as 'a man of most exquisite taste'. His brothers, George Frederick Brameld (died 1853) and John Wager Brameld (died 1851) were engaged in the commercial and artistic aspects of the business respectively. J.W.Brameld was said to be a good porcelain painter of landscape, flower and figure subjects.

[L.Jewitt, *Ceramic Art of Great Britain*, 1878.]

Brammar, George (born 1800 died 1851)

China painter, Stafford Row, Shelton.

[Obit. *Staffordshire Advertiser*, 21 June, 1851.]

Brammer, Thomas and Elizabeth, Longton

Thomas Brammer manufactured earthenware toys at the Daisy Bank, Longton in 1830. In 1834 and 1835 the business was listed under the name of Elizabeth Brammer.

[*Directories;* Reginald G. Haggar, *Staffordshire Chimney Ornaments*, 1955.]

Brampton, Near Chesterfield, Derbyshire

Brown stonewares were made from early in the eighteenth century and throughout the nineteenth century. The principal potter in 1800 is said to have been William Bromley who was succeeded by Robert Bambrigge & Co.

Six factories existed in Brampton early in the nineteenth century:

Mrs Blake's factory which was formerly worked by her husband and later became part of Luke Knowles' works.

William Briddon founded the Walton factory in 1790. It was continued by his descendants.

Colour plate 3, CHELSEA: *see page vii for caption*

Brown stonewares in 'all their varieties' were made.

Luke Knowles' factory, which later became Matthew Knowles & Son. Stoneware bottles, kegs and barrels were manufactured.

Thomas Oldfield with others formed a company in 1810. The business passed to his nephew, John Oldfield, in 1838. Excellent salt-glazed stonewares were made in a great variety of shapes, and articles, including 'Welsh' trays, relief-ornamented jugs, figures, twisted pipes, puzzle jugs, bottles and Toby jugs.

John Wright's factory near St Thomas's Church, later discontinued.

Edward Wright & Son. This factory was still being worked in 1878 by the family.

MARKS

S. & H. BRIDDON
(Samuel & Henry Briddon) c.1848

OLDFIELD & CO. MAKERS
(Oldfield, Madin Wright, Hewitt & Company, or John Oldfield.)

J. OLDFIELD

OLDFIELD & CO.
CHESTERFIELD

DISTINGUISHING CHARACTERISTICS

The wares made at Brampton were in the nineteenth century classed with and are still when unmarked often mistaken for Nottingham wares They fall into two categories: one, of a fine chocolate colour similar to Belper wares, decorated with applied ornament; and two, wares varying in colour from buff to red of some brilliancy. This second group included Toby jugs as well as tea and coffee-pots, which were mostly made by Briddon or Oldfield c.1835. A characteristic feature of Brampton wares is an internal green glaze which occurs on dated specimens from 1820 to 1894.

[L. Jewitt, *Ceramic Art of Great Britain*, 1878; B. Rackham, *Catalogue of the Glaisher Collection*, 1935; John Drinkwater, *Transactions, English Ceramic Circle*, 1939.]

Briand, Thomas (died 1784)

Exhibited examples of a soft paste porcelain before the Royal Society in 1742–1743, and was part proprietor in the Chelsea porcelain factory.

Brede, Sussex

A potworks located in Brede Parish at Broadland Wood, fifteenth century; the Brede pottery said to have been established 1755; there is record of the marriage of a potter, John Eldridge of Brede, 22 May 1769; Henry Richardson (d. 1789) acquired the factory which was worked successively by Thomas Weller and his son, John Weller (1806–91); closed down 1892.

[J.M.Baines, *Sussex Pottery in East Sussex*, 1948.]

Breeze, John, Tunstall

John Breeze is first listed as an earthenware manufacturer at Burslem in 1796. In 1805 the firm is given as John Breeze and Son, Tunstall. John Breeze (born 1746 died 1821) of Greenfields, Tunstall and the Knowl, Burslem, married Mrs Elizabeth Mare (born 1736 died 1801) and by her had a son, Jesse Breeze (born 1776 died 1826) who eventually became sole owner of the business. The factory at\Greenfields was offered to be let in 1828 (*Pottery Mercury*, 28 September, 1828), and eventually passed to the Adams family, William Adams having married Jesse Breeze's daughter.

Breeze

[*Parish Registers*; *Directories*, 1796–1818.]

Breeze, William, Hanley

William Breeze of Hanley (born 1765 died 1828) was a much younger brother of John Breeze of Tunstall and Burslem. He potted in partnership with Joseph Leigh in the firm of Leigh and Breeze earthenware manufacturers, Hanley, from the opening years of the nineteenth century. This partnership was dissolved in 1808 (*Staffordshire Advertiser*, 21 December 1808). Afterwards Breeze potted on own account until he became bankrupt in 1817 (*Staffordshire Advertiser*). Later he became a partner in the firm of Wilson and Breeze. William Breeze died at the age of 64 at Stoke in 1828 (*Pottery Mercury*, 29 November 1828).

[*Directories*, 1805–1818; *Parish Registers*.]

Brentwood, Essex

A potter named Robert Longcroft worked at Brentwood mid-eighteenth century. He became bankrupt in 1754.

[London, *General Evening Post*, 24 September 1754, quoted in *Apollo*.]

Bretby Art Pottery

A modern art pottery was established at Woodville near Burton-on-Trent by Henry Tooth under the style of Bretby Art Pottery in 1883. Their manufactures are described by G.W. Rhead as 'extremely quaint and artistic'.

MARK

[G.W.Rhead, *The Earthenware Collector*, 1920.]

Brewer, John (born 1764 died 1815)

Said to have come from Madeley, Shropshire and worked in Derby as a landscape painter, drawing-master and china-painter. He painted at Derby landscapes and hunting scenes from 1795. In 1811 he held an exhibition of his drawings at his own home St. Mary's Bridge, Bridge Gate, Derby, charging one shilling for admission.

Brewer, Robert (died 1857)

Brother of John Brewer, and also china-painter at Derby, later at Coalport and Worcester. He is said to have been a pupil of Paul Sandby whose water-colour style influenced his work. He painted directly upon the ware without any preliminary underpainting.

Robert Brewer was also a drawing-master.

Brewster-shape

Oval, straight-sided teapots with lid set into an oval, vertical collar, made at the Wedgwood factory in the 1780's. This shape was popular at all potworks making wares in the neo-classic style.

[Illus. W.Mankowitz, *Wedgwood*, 1953.]

Bridgwood, Sampson, Longton

The business which eventually became Sampson Bridgwood & Son was established in Lane End in the early years of the nineteenth century at the Market Street works. In 1805 the firm is listed as Samuel Bridgwood, earthenware manufacturers. In 1818 Maria Bridgwood, and Kitty Bridgwood & Son are listed separately as manufacturers of earthenware in Market Street. Later control passed to Sampson Bridgwood by whom the business was continued first in Market Street, then in Stafford Street in a factory which was demolished to make way for Longton covered market, and finally at Anchor Road, where bone china was made. The firm subsequently reverted to earthenware which is still made.

MARKS

S. BRIDGWOOD & SON (impressed)

1860 Impressed

Impressed

WORK:

Wares made by Sampson Bridgwood were often painted and gilded. Fine white earthenware called 'Porcelaine Opaque' was impressed with the LIMOGES mark.

Brill, Buckinghamshire

A pottery-making centre from the thirteenth century. Not mentioned in later literature until the nineteenth century, although a splendid big-bellied jar in the Ashmolean Museum, Oxford, incised 'Thomas Hullocks, Brill 1791' suggests a firmly established tradition. Samuel Lewis (*A Topographical Dictionary of England* 7th ed. 1848) mentions 'A small manufactory for earthenware'. Lampstands, bottles, pitchers and money-boxes were made until as late as 1900.

Brindley, John (born 1718 died c. 1793), Longport, Staffordshire

Manufacturer of earthenware at a factory in Burslem from about 1750 where John Adams

(1746–1805) became in 1757/8 his apprentice. He used Tabernor's Mine Rock quarried at Lane End in his earthenware 'body'. About 1772 he built the potworks situated by the canal at Longport which he worked until 1793 when they were taken over by John Davenport. He was brother of the celebrated engineer, James Brindley the Schemer.

[L. Jewitt, *Ceramic Art of Great Britain*, 1878.]

Brislington

A delftware manufactory flourished here from c.1650 to 1750. See under Bristol.

Bristol, Gloucestershire. Earthenware

The most famous product of Bristol earthenware factories was tin-glazed pottery which was manufactured from c.1650 until late in the eighteenth century. The first factory was established at Brislington by potters from Southwark, London. Other factories sprang up in Bristol as offshoots, Temple Back in 1683, and Limekiln Lane and Redcliffe in 1706. Delftware was also manufactured at Wincanton in Somerset. Little tin-glazed pottery was made after 1770.

In the late eighteenth, and throughout the nineteenth century extensive manufactures of earthenware of Staffordshire type flourished.

OWNERS

Brislington 1652	**Robert Collins**
Temple Back 1683	**Edward Ward, senior**
Limekiln Lane 1706	**Woodes Rogers and Herby Hobbs**
Redcliffe 1706	**Thomas Frank**
Redcliffe 1739	**Thomas and Hugh Taylor, and Richard Riley**

MARKS

There are no undisputed factory marks. Identification of Bristol delftware is difficult, and depends upon local knowledge, style factors, and comparison with excavated specimens and surviving documentary pieces.

ARTISTS

John Niglett, apprenticed 1714 at Brislington.

Worked afterwards at Temple Back and Redcliffe.

John Bowen, apprenticed 1734 at Limekiln Lane. Said to have painted figure subjects and ships.

Michael Edkins, a blue-and-white plate in the Victoria and Albert Museum is attributed to him.

Joseph Flower, had a pottery shop in Bristol in 1767. His name or initials occur on delftware bowls, one of which is dated 1751.

Anthony Hassels, employed by Ring, 1786.

DISTINGUISHING CHARACTERISTICS AND WORK

The large output of delftware from Bristol factories included plain and scalloped–edged plates, punch bowls, 'brick' inkstands or flower holders, trays, puzzle-jugs, trinket-pots, teapots, bleeding-bowls, porringers, and the like. Identification is difficult because early wares were closely allied and similar to those of Lambeth, while later delft resembles the products of Liverpool. Some distinctive features have been noted by F. H. Garner.

Shapes: a footless plate with a straight rim forming a pronounced angle to the bottom; puzzle jugs with necks pierced with bands of intersecting circles; bleeding-bowls with indented handles and radiating grooves.

Glaze: pale purplish-blue in tint.

Pigment: a red which on early wares stands up in relief.

Decoration: *bianco-sopra-bianco* plates with borders of fir-cones, 5-petalled and many-petalled flowers alternating with foliage; election inscriptions; Chinese decorations with towers and pagodas; 'cracked ice' and trellis patterns. For earthenware of Staffordshire type see under POUNTNEY; see also BIANCO-SOPRA-BIANCO, 'CRACKED-ICE', WINCANTON.

[Hugh Owen, *Two Centuries of Ceramic Art in Bristol*, 1873; L. Jewitt, *Ceramic Art of Great Britain*, 1878; W. G. Pountney, *Old Bristol Potteries*, 1920; Sir Gilbert Mellor, 'Bristol Delftware' in *Transactions, English Ceramic Circle*; H. W. Maxwell, 'Recent Excavations in Bristol' in *Transactions, English Ceramic Circle*; F. H. Garner, *English Delftware*, 1948.]

Bristol, Gloucestershire. Porcelain.
c.1749–1752.

A type of soft-paste porcelain, making use of soapstone quarried in Cornwall, was made by William Miller and Benjamin Lund at a glasshouse at Redcliffe Backs, Bristol, known, because owned until 1745 by William Lowdin, as Lowdin's China House. A few pieces survive: Chinese-copy figures, and more rarely sauceboats decorated with flowers. They may be marked BRISTOLL, or BRISTOL 1750.

In 1752 the factory amalgamated with Worcester, from which its products are no longer distinguishable. In fact many pieces of disputed origin exist which may well have been made at Worcester shortly after the amalgamation.

There may have been a second Bristol factory producing porcelain until 1765, although when and by whom it was founded, and whether it was independent of the first factory or not, is not known.

[Richard Pococke, *Travels in England in 1750;* letter of Richard Champion dated 1766.]

1770–1781

Hard-paste porcelain was made at Bristol for only eleven years, first by William Cookworthy who moved his factory from Plymouth, later by Richard Champion his associate who acquired his patent and bought his business in 1773. Cookworthy's patent soon expired, and when its renewal was contested by Wedgwood, Turner and others in Staffordshire, he retained the sole use of Cornish china clay and china stone in translucent wares, but being unsuccessful he was compelled to sell his patent and abandon porcelain manufacture in 1781. The patent was acquired by a company of Staffordshire potters who traded from New Hall, Shelton.

ARTISTS

Banford, James, apprenticed to Champion.

Bone, Henry, enameller and miniaturist, with Champion until 1778.

Briand, Thomas, possibly the modeller of biscuit plaques.

Soqui, painter of bird subjects.

Stephens, William, apprentice with Bone.

MARKS

A cross, or a cross and a letter 'B' in blue enamel; or crossed swords with a cross in underglaze blue and blue enamel

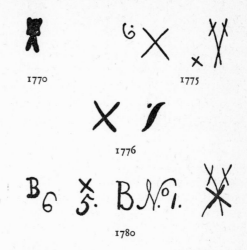

1770   1775

1776

1780

WORK AND DISTINGUISHING CHARACTERISTICS

Richard Champion claimed that his hard-paste porcelain rivalled that of Meissen for strength, and Sèvres for elegance. He manufactured with it a variety of useful wares ranging from ungilded cottage china decorated with sprigs of blossom to elaborate services with initials for his friends or to special order. Elegant Sèvres-style *cabarets* were also made.

Teapots in the form of an inverted pear with double curve handles are characteristic. Tightly bunched floral sprays, or sprays with angular spiky foliage recur. Typical colours are leaf green and clear deep red.

Sets of figures representing the *Seasons*, the *Elements* or *Venus and Adonis* decorated in the Sèvres style of Louis XVI period were made by Champion. Rockwork bases and a touch of sentiment are features of these wares.

Large hexagonal vases were decorated with masks and floral festoons in relief, and painted in colours.

Bristol porcelain is rare, much of it being made for presentation rather than sale, such as the Service, after a Dresden model, presented by Edmund Burke to Mrs Smith in 1774. The following Services are known:

Brice	Harford (Mark)
Burke	Harford (Joseph)

Butts   Leinster
Colston   Ludlow (Daniel)
Chough   Nelson
Cowles   Parliament
Edwards   Smith
Gainsborough   Smyth

Colour plate 2 and plates 17–20.

[H. Owen, *Two Centuries of Ceramic Art in Bristol*, 1873; F. Severne Mackenna, *Cookworthy's Plymouth and Bristol Porcelain*, 1946; F. Severne Mackenna, *Champion's Bristol Porcelain*, 1947; F. Hurlbutt, *Bristol Porcelain*, 1928; W. G. Pountney, *Old Bristol Potteries*, 1920.]

Brittan, John, Bristol

Foreman of Champion's Bristol China Manufactory. He was apprenticed to a Bristol potter named Cantle in 1749. He claimed in his evidence before the Committee of the House of Commons in 1775 to have had 'great experience of several China manufactures'. His initials occur on a plate described by Nightingale.

[J. E. Nightingale, *Contribution towards the History of Early English Porcelain from Contemporary Sources*, 1881; W. B. Honey, *Old English Porcelain*, 1928; new ed. 1948.]

Broom, A.

Figure maker: Mark A. BROOM recorded.

[G. J. V. Bemrose, *Nineteenth Century English Pottery and Porcelain*, 1952.]

Brown & Cartledge, Burslem

The short-lived earthenware concern which traded under this name in Burslem ended with the death of Brown on Saturday 13 May 1815.

[*Staffordshire Advertiser*, 11 and 25 November 1815.]

Brown, Henry and Company, Lane End

Manufacturers of earthenware toys at a potworks in the High Street, Lane End, 1828.

Brown, Westhead, Moore & Company, Cauldon Place, Shelton

Succeeded the Ridgways at Cauldon Place in 1859 and continued until 1920, and manufactured china, earthenware, parian of excellent workmanship and in the 'contemporary styles'. They contributed largely to exhibitions and endeav-oured to emulate the standards of Mintons, using coloured grounds, turquoise and pink particularly, painted decoration and lavish gilding. Polychrome colour printing was extensively used by them; charming porcelain figures in the earlier Staffordshire tradition were made; Toft's patent jug lid was taken up by them.

[G. J. V. Bemrose, *Nineteenth Century English Pottery and Porcelain*, 1952.]

Browne, Robert (1757-1771), Lowestoft, Suffolk

Formerly employed at Bow, Browne opened a small factory at Lowestoft in 1757, manufacturing a rough porcelain (described by Honey as 'peasant'), of similar bone-ash composition to that of the Bow factory. His production was probably restricted to table-wares, decorated in the Chinese styles of the Worcester factory. See also under LOWESTOFT.

[W. B. Honey, *English Pottery and Porcelain*, 1933; new ed. 1952; *Old English Porcelain*, 1928; new ed. 1948.]

Brownfield, William, Cobridge, Staffordshire.

William Brownfield succeeded to the business of Robinson, Wood and Brownfield in 1850 and manufactured good-class earthenware. W. Brownfield (d. 1873) took his son, William Etches Brownfield into partnership in 1871 when bone china was also manufactured, the firm trading as W. Brownfield & Son. W. E. Brownfield withdrew from the business about 1890 which was reconstituted by Arthur Brownfield on co-operative lines under the title Brownfield Guild Pottery. It failed soon after.

ARTIST
Louis Jahn
Frederick Alfred Rhead.

MARKS
Initials W. B. within a Staffordshire knot,

or   BROWNFIELD & SON
          COBRIDGE STAFFS

upon a scroll enclosing two globes.

W.B.

WORK

Coloured porcelain of excellent quality was used for statuettes and fine vases. Aventurine glaze effects were tried out. The Gladstone vase, decorated in pâte-sur-pâte by F. A. Rhead, was made by Brownfields for presentation to the Rt. Hon. W. E. Gladstone in 1888.

[L. Jewitt, *Ceramic Art of Great Britain*, 1878; G. W. and F. A. Rhead, *Staffordshire Pots and Potters*, 1906.]

Brunt, Thomas, Lane End

Toy and ornamental china manufacturer at Millfield Gate, Lane End 1835

Brunt, William, Lane End

Manufacturer of earthenware toys at the Daisy Bank, Longton in 1834. It is not known whether he was any connection of T. Brunt of Millfield Gate.

Buckland (c. 1701–93), Buckinghamshire

Slipware pottery was made at Buckland near Aylesbury. A red earthenware jug of dark brown manganese glaze incised after the application of the glaze but before firing 'John Revet, Esqr, 1759 THOMAS BRACKLEY POTTER AT BUCKLAND COMMON', is in the Chequers Collection (1923 catalogue). Colonel John Revet was owner of Chequers in 1759.

A similar jug in the same collection incised 'H. K. 1701' is unlikely to be the work of Brackley but is of the same locality.

[B. Rackham and H. Read, *English Pottery*, 1924.]

Buckley Mountain, Flintshire

A slipware factory existed here from eighteenth century, producing country pottery for local use.

Bull-baiting

Pottery groups showing a bull tossing or goring a dog, accompanied sometimes by a man brandishing a stick, or prostrate beneath the bull. Made in Staffordshire from the eighteenth century. A distinctive type, mounted upon a six-footed table-base is associated with the name of Obadiah Sherratt of Hot Lane c.1830–35. Bull-baiting was extremely popular at Wakes in North and South Staffordshire.

Plate 154 C.

[Reginald G. Haggar, 'Obadiah and Martha Sherratt of Hot Lane', *Apollo* Vol 50, 1949; ibid. *Staffordshire Chimney Ornaments*, 1955.]

Bullers Ltd, Milton, Staffordshire

For a short period this well-known firm of insulator and electrical porcelain manufacturers produced image toys in the Staffordshire tradition, and decorative pottery and kitchen wares of high quality, 1937–55. The department closed down in 1955.

ARTISTS

Anne Potts, figure maker

Agnete Hoy Bohrer, modeller and decorator

Incised   Painted

Harold Thomas, thrower
James Rushton, decorator

Good examples in Hanley Museum, Stoke-on-Trent.

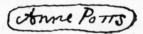

Incised

Burmantofts pottery, Leeds

A factory making fire-clay wares was started 1858. From 1882 until 1904 'Art' pottery including coloured wares, persian blue, sang de bœuf, etc. was made. The firm subsequently reverted to terra cotta faience. Mark; B U R M A N - T O F T S   F A I E N C E in two lines, impressed or BF in monogram. The business was run by WILCOCK & Co., Burmantofts Pottery Co., and later Leeds Fire-Clay Co.

[A. Hurst, *A Catalogue... of Yorkshire Pottery*, 1922.]

Burrow, Joseph, Lane End

Earthenware manufacturer at the Foley or Folly, Lane End in 1818. The factory and house, occupied by him were announced for sale in 1820.

[*Staffordshire Advertiser*, 2 September, 1820.]

Burslem, Staffordshire

The first of the Potteries towns of North Staffordshire to rise to commercial importance as a centre of pottery manufacture. In the seventeenth century its potters were largely concerned with meeting the requirements of neighbouring farms and dairies. Because of its extensive manufacture of butter-pots it became known as the butter pottery. Lead-glazed red wares were then the staple product. Presentation pieces were ornamented in slip with a contrasting colour. Salt-glazed stoneware was made from about 1690, and red unglazed stoneware ('red china') from the time of Elers, when the Staffordshire potter began to meet the demands of the new habit of tea drinking. About 1710–1715 there were at least 43 potworks in Burslem as against 7 listed for Hanley and 2 at Stoke. These figures (based upon the memory of an old person) are valuable only as indicating the relative size and importance of the pottery towns and villages at the beginning of the eighteenth century.

Wedgwood's list of Burslem potters in 1710–1715 contains many names which recur throughout the century: Wedgwood, Malkin, Adams, Shaw, Daniel, Warburton and Lockett; he himself, before moving to Etruria, potted successfully in Burslem. The important factories in Burslem at the end of the eighteenth century were those of the Woods, particularly Enoch Wood, William Adams & Co., and Timothy & John Lockett.

The construction of the canal led to the development of Burslem along the road to Wolstanton, hence arose Longport, Middleport and Newport which became important sub-centres of pottery activity. Davenport's factory which lasted nearly a century was at Longport.

The opening years of the nineteenth century saw other firms emerging to eminence; Riley, Alcock and Davenport to compete with Enoch Wood. Doultons and Maddocks emerge at the close of the century. John Maddock & Sons was founded in 1830.

Burton, G. and B, Hanley and Stoke

A firm of this name made 'earthenware and figures' at the Waterloo Works, Nelson Place, Hanley and in Registry Street, Stoke, 1889.

Burton-on-Trent, Staffordshire

A factory for the manufacture of china or 'artificial marble' and yellow-ware existed at the Hay, Burton-on-Trent in the 1830's under the direction of a Derby lawyer named William Edwards in financial partnership with one Tunnicliffe.

Edwards used the modeller Wornell, painters George and John Hancock and Joseph Bentley from the Derby works, and William Watson from Coalport. His manager was Isaac Bentley.

Statuary was attempted in 'artificial marble' but proved a failure. The factory closed soon after.

'Busha'

Phonetic rendering of the name Boucher, – 'enamelled in Cupids, after Busha' (*Sale catalogue*, Chelsea-Derby Factory, 1771).

Bussa

A large earthenware pot, commonly kept in old Cornish cottages, and used for salting down pilchards.

Also spelt BUZZARD.

Butter pot

Cylindrical vessel of coarse red earthenware, holding 14 lbs of butter, made at Burslem in the seventeenth century for use at Uttoxeter market. An act of 1661 regulated abuses in the manner of making or packing butter pots. The church-wardens' accounts of Uttoxeter for 1644 and 1645 contain references to 'potts of butter.'

[R. Plot, *The Natural History of the County of Stafford*, Oxford, 1686; F. Redfern, *History of Uttoxeter*, Derby, 1865, 2nd ed. Hanley, 1886.]

Byerley, Thomas (died 1810)

Nephew of Josiah Wedgwood and partner with him in the firms of Josiah Wedgwood, Son and Byerley (1790–1795), and of Wedgwood and Byerley (Josiah Wedgwood II, John Wedgwood and Thomas Byerley) (1795–1810).

[L. Jewitt, *Ceramic Art of Great Britain*, 1878.]

C

Cabbage-leaf jugs

There are two large jugs in Worcester Corporation Museum, moulded with overlapping leaves in relief, dated 1757, which were made at the Worcester porcelain factory. Worcester cabbage-leaf jugs have cylindrical necks, (later ones sometimes with masks), and ovoid relief-ornamented bodies upon which the decoration was superimposed. This type of jug was imitated later at Lowestoft and Caughley usually with the addition of a mask-lip spout.

Examples, Victoria and Albert Museum, British Museum, Worcester Museum, Norwich Castle Museum, and in the Irwin Untermyer collection.

Plates 14 B, 135 A and B.

[Illus. B. Rackham, *Catalogue of the Schreiber Collection, Victoria and Albert Museum*, 1928.]

Cadogan

A teapot or jug filled from a hole in the base, said to have been named after the Hon. Mrs Cadogan, who brought to this country an original Chinese teapot of this type. A Cadogan teapot is lidless and shaped like a Chinese peach-shaped wine pot. First made at Swinton, Yorkshire, about 1795, with a purple-brown 'Rockingham' glaze, Cadogan teapots became popular, and John Mortlock of Oxford Street, London, whose name, impressed, frequently occurs, bought and sold large quantities of them. In Staffordshire Cadogans were made by Davenports, Copelands and other firms.

[L. Jewitt, *Ceramic Art of Great Britain*, 1878.]

Calcine

To reduce to powder by heat.

Caldwell, James (born 1760 died 1838)

Partner in the firm of Wood & Caldwell, earthenware manufacturers, Burslem, 1790–1818. James Caldwell of Linley Wood was a prominent shareholder in the Trent and Mersey Canal, a Deputy Lieutenant for the County of Stafford, and later Recorder of Newcastle-under-Lyme.

Campana vase

A vase made in the neo-classic style, during the first decades of the nineteenth century. Possibly from 'campana', a church bell, hence bell-shaped.

**Campbell, Colin Minton
(born 1827 died 1885)**

Nephew of Herbert Minton and partner in the firm of Minton & Co. from 1849. High Sheriff

41

of Staffordshire 1869; Chairman of the North Stafford Railway; Conservative Member of Parliament for North Staffordshire 1874 until 1880. His statue by Sir Thomas Brock R.A. (born 1847 died 1922) stands outside the new Minton factory. It was reproduced to small scale in parian by Mintons in 1887.

[R.Simms, *Bibliotheca Staffordiensis*, 1894.]

Cane

A tan-coloured stoneware 'dry' body made by Josiah Wedgwood in 1770 by refining the red and buff clays used by local potters. Similar bodies were made by John Turner of Lane End, Elijah Mayer and others in Staffordshire and the Out-Potteries. It was sometimes enamelled in blue and other colours.

[W.Mankowitz, *Wedgwood*, 1953.]

Can Marl

'Clay found in the coal-pits.'

[W.Pitt, *Topographical History of Staffordshire*, 1817.]

'Capacity' mugs

Measures: cylindrical mugs of a certified content, stamped with an excise mark, used in alehouses, or by street hawkers and shopkeepers; and made in salt-glazed stoneware in London, Staffordshire and elsewhere from the end of the seventeenth century, and in dipped, mocha, and banded earthenware from the end of the eighteenth century.

Cardew, Michael

Studio potter; pupil of Bernard Leach 1923–1926; acquired the Winchcombe Pottery, Gloucestershire 1926, where he produced English slipware until 1939. Started to make stoneware at Wenford Bridge, Cornwall, 1939, but left for Achimota College, Gold Coast 1942; started his own pottery at Vumé, Gold Coast, 1945.

[E.March, *The Studio*, May 1943.]

Carey, Thomas and John, Lane End

Earthenware and china manufacturers at Lane End from the second decade of the nineteenth century. The firm was first listed as Carey and Son in 1818. Later the firm was listed as Thomas and John Carey working three factories at Lane End, the Anchor Works in Market Street and potworks in King Street. Geoffrey Bemrose says they made 'curious chimney ornaments in a glassy porcelain not unlike Longton Hall' (*19th Century English Pottery & Porcelain*, 1952.) The partnership between Thomas and John Carey, earthenware manufacturers, flint grinders and farmers was dissolved 22 January 1842 (*Staffordshire Advertiser*, 29 February 1842.) Thomas Carey died c.1847 and the copperplate engravings and block and working moulds were disposed of by auction (advertisement *Staffordshire Advertiser*, 12 February 1848).

[*Directories*, 1818, 1823, 1834.]

Carpet balls

Taws or large marbles were used in the Victorian indoor game of carpet bowls. They were made in brown stoneware, agate ware, or earthenware coloured with striped, ringed, flowery or starry designs. A set of bowls comprised one plain or self-coloured taw and six patterned balls. They were made in many places in Scotland and England. Edward, John, Thomas and W.Parr of Burslem specialised in the manufacture of marbles. Their factories were called 'rock taw banks'.

Plate 78 A.

[*Directories*, 1860, 1864, 1868; information per Mrs B. Marsh, a descendant.]

Carrara

Name given to the parian paste by Josiah Wedgwood & Sons, Etruria.

Carr's Hill Pottery, near Gateshead, Tyneside

Earthenware of various kinds including brown ware and painted pottery was made by John Warburton in the second half of the eighteenth century. Chaffers recorded a transfer-decorated yellow ware jug, made c.1760, signed 'J. Warburton N. on Tyne'.

Isaac Warburton from 1795 onwards until 1801, and Ellen Warburton from 1801 to 1811, worked this factory which, apart from a small portion occupied by other proprietors, was closed down about 1817.

[F. Buckley, *Archaeologia Aeliana*, 1927; L. Jewitt, *Ceramic Art of Great Britain*, 1878.]

Carter, Henry (flourished 1790-1830),

Earthenware Manufacturer, Bristol

Henry Carter was concerned in various partnerships including Carter, Ring and Pountney, of Bristol who made 'painted, printed, enamelled and cream-coloured earthenware'.

[W. J. Pountney, *Old Bristol Potteries*, 1920.]

Carter, John, Hanley

Enameller, lusterer, and toy and ornament manufacturer at Mill Street, Hanley, 1841–1851.

Carter, Stabler & Adams, Poole, Dorset.

Earthenware manufactory

Founded in 1921 by Cyril Carter, John Adams, and Harold Stabler to take over and develop the decorative pottery produced at Poole by Owen Carter. Excellent tablewares and 'fancies' are made with decorations tellingly executed in a delft palette of colours. Good functional shapes, hygienic in appearance as well as form, are typical of this factory's productions.

ARTISTS

Harold Stabler RDI
Phoebe Stabler
John Adams

Truda Carter
Dora Batty
Marjorie Drawbell

MARKS:

Incised on lustre wares produced by Carter before 1921. Also Carter & Co.

Impressed 1921–24. After 1924, with addition of the word 'Ltd'.

Impressed after 1921. Also in black under glaze.

POOLE
ENGLAND

Impressed after 1921.

After 1919 in black underglaze

Plate 156.

[John Adams, 'Potters' Parade', *Pottery & Glass*, October 1950.]

Cartledge, Hugh, Burslem

Manufacturer of earthenware toys and figures at Low Street, Burslem, 1822–1823.

Cartlege, Cartledge or Cartlich, family of Burslem and Tunstall

Samuel and Thomas Cartlege are listed in the *Jurors List* for Tunstall Court 1784 as potters, and in Tunnicliff's *Survey* 1787 the firm is given as S. & J. Cartledge, which style was repeated in *The Staffordshire Pottery Directory*, 1796. In 1805 (Holdens *Directory*) the firm was once again Samuel and Thomas Cartlich. The Cartlichs manufactured earthenware at Tunstall.

Another firm is listed as Richard & James Cartledge, at Goldenhill in 1818 (Parson & Bradshaw's *Directory*).

Cartlidge, George (born 1868)

Ceramic craftsman; student at Hanley Art School 1878; teacher of painting in the School 1897. Made a considerable reputation as a portrait modeller and painter for pottery, and did portraits of many famous personalities, including Thomas Hardy (reproduced as frontispiece to Macmillan's standard edition of his works). Partner in firm of Sherwin & Cotton. Worked also for Barratts, Stoke-on-Trent.

[Reginald G.Haggar, *A Century of Art Education in the Potteries*, 1953.]

Cartlidge, John

Pottery figures holding candle sockets recorded, impressed 'JOHN CARTLIDGE at the Lodge in the plantation COWBRIDGE 1800.'

[Reginald G.Haggar, *Staffordshire Chimney Ornaments*, 1955.]

Cartwright

An early nineteenth century London decorator of porcelain.

[J.Haslem, *Old Derby China Factory*, 1876.]

Carving

Decoration cut through the outer wall of double-walled vessels such as jugs and teapots.

[Illus. *James Morley's Advertisement Sheet*, Bodleian library, Oxford.]

Castle Espie, County Down, Ireland.

Samuel Minland set up a brick and tile works which subsequently manufactured brown-glazed teapots, flower vases and kitchen crockery, third quarter nineteenth century.

Castleford, Yorkshire

At Whitwood Mere, David Dunderdale, an apprentice of the Leeds Pottery, established a factory c.1790 for the manufacture of cream-coloured earthenware, Egyptian black and felspathic stoneware. From 1793 until 1820 when it closed down, it traded as David Dunderdale and Co. The most typical products were in unglazed stoneware with relief decorations in panels. Similar wares, with or without panels picked out in blue, were made elsewhere. The marks used were:

[L.Jewitt, *Ceramic Art of Great Britain*, 1878.]

D D & Co.   D D & Co.   D D & Co.
CASTLEFORD CASTLEFORD CASTLEFORD
POTTERY   D D & CO.   POTTERY

Dunderdale issued a catalogue of cream-colour in several languages. In 1825 the factory was partly re-opened by Asquith, Wood & Co. and from that time onwards was continued by Asquith, Wood & Nicholson 1835; Samuel Wood & Co. 1838–54; T.Nicholson & Co. 1854–67; Clokie & Masterman 1871–1881; and from 1887 by Clokie & Co., as manufacturers of earthenware. Hurst listed over 20 other nineteenth century factories in the Castleford and Whitwood Mere parishes, as follows:

Mere Pottery, Whitwood Mere. 1821 Asquith & Co.; 1835 George Taylor & Co.; 1841 Taylor Harrison & Co.; 1867 Taylor & Harrison.
Earthenware mfrs.

Victoria Pottery. 1887–1901. Ford Bros. (Earthenware mfrs.)

Castleford. 1822 George Bateson; 1835 Bateson & Co.; 1838 and 1841 Bateson & Bros; 1849 and 1854 Christopher Bateson. (black earthenware and stoneware.)

Eagle Pottery, started 1854, John Roberts & Co., later Pratt & Co.; 1861 H.McDowall & Co.; 1867 McDowall & Roberts; then J.Roberts & Co.

Eleven Acres Pottery, Nicholson St. 1893 Robinson Bros; later John Robinson or John Robinson & Sons. (Common and black earthenware.)

Providence Pottery, Leeds Rd. 1867 G. Gill; 1887 William Gill (Domestic earthenware.)

Methley Rd, Whitwood Mere. 1867 C. Phillips, later Charles Phillips & Son. (Black, red and white wares.)

Another Pottery, Methley Rd. 1849 Wilson & Harling; 1854 Wilson Harling & Co.; 1861 Harling & Phillips; 1867 J.Harling & Son.

Castleford. 1822 Isaac Fletcher until after 1849. (Black earthenware and stoneware.)

Whitwood Mere. 1822 T. S. Russell. (Stoneware.)

Castleford. Cleggs and Wilson 1854. (Earthenware.)

Castleford 1854 Taylor & Hartley. (Black earthenware and stoneware.)

Whitwood Mere. 1854 Asquith, Ford & Co. (Earthenware.)

Whitwood. 1861 T. Wilson. (Black earthenware).

Castleford. 1861 T. Wilson & Son. (Earthenware).

Whitwood. 1861 Hurdus & Asquith. (Earthenware).

Castleford. 1861 Lowther & Ford. (Earthenware).

Providence Pottery, Castleford. 1849 Asquith Gill & Co.; 1861 Gill and Farquhar 1881 William Gill (Blue-and-white earthenware).

Calder Pottery, Castleford. 1881 Thos Poulson & Edwin Llewellyn.

Albion Pottery, Whitwood Mere. 1887 & 1888 Nicholson & Masterman.

Allerton Bywater or Allerton Pottery. 1838 Thomas Dobson; 1841 and 1849 Dibb & Hurdus; 1854 Gill & Dibb; 1861 and 1867 William Gill; 1881–87 Thomas Robinson; 1888 onwards, Executors of Thomas Robinson.

[A. Hurst, *The Boynton Collection of Yorkshire Pottery* 1922; L. Jewitt, *Ceramic Art of Great Britain,* 1878; W. B. Honey, *English Pottery and Porcelain,* 1933; *Victoria Country History of Yorkshire.*]

Castle Hedingham, Essex. See BINGHAM, EDWARD.

'Castle' painter

An unidentified porcelain decorator who painted landscapes with castles and other buildings on Longton Hall porcelain.

[G. Savage, *18th Century English Porcelain*, 1952.]

Castor ware

Roman pottery was extensively manufactured in the neighbourhood of Castor, near Peterborough, Northamptonshire, from the second century until the end of the fourth century or the beginning of the fifth century. It reached its climax in the third century. Various decorative treatments were employed, including trailed slip, roulette and relief ornament.

Cats

Made as chimney ornaments in tin-glazed earthenware, brown and white agate earthenware, agate salt-glazed stoneware and Whieldon ware; and as flower-holders in tin-glazed earthenware. Dates on tin-glazed specimens from 1613 until 1713. A seated cat, Cecil Higgins Museum, Bedford, lettered 'Cat i am Ms Oliver 1713.'

[J.E. & Edith Hodgkin, *Examples of Early English Pottery*, 1891.]

Caughley, near Broseley, Shropshire. Porcelain Manufactory.

Thomas Turner (born 1749 died 1809) is the dominant figure. He is described as a pottery chemist and engraver, and is said to have served his apprenticeship to Robert Hancock at Worcester. He left Worcester and became proprietor of the Caughley works in 1772. These had been worked as an earthenware factory since 1754 by Ambrose Gallimore, whose daughter Turner married.

Turner manufactured at Caughley a soapstone porcelain similar to that of Worcester but slightly different in colour and less well potted. In 1799 John Rose of Coalport, one of Turner's former apprentices, purchased the factory and used it to produce biscuit porcelain which was glazed and decorated at Coalport. The factory was closed down in 1814.

MARKS

A number of marks were used, some clearly imitating those of other English and foreign factories. The most notable are the letters 'S' or 'C' in blue, or the word 'Salopian' in upper or lower case letters, impressed.

Imitation Worcester

C S Sx C C

SALOPIAN

ARTISTS

Robert Hancock. Engraver: Turner had been his apprentice at Worcester. Some of his prints were used on Caughley porcelain.

Thomas Turner. Engraver and designer: he is stated to have brought back a number of artists from France after a visit in 1780.

Thomas Baxter. Decorated white ware sent to him in London from Caughley and Coalport.

Thomas Minton. Apprenticed to Turner: engraver of Willow and Broseley Blue Dragon patterns: founder of the firm of Mintons.

Richard Hicks. Engraver: apprenticed to Turner: founder of the firm of Hicks and Meigh, Shelton.

Much Caughley-Coalport porcelain was decorated in the London enamelling studios of Baxter, Sims, Robins & Randall, and Muss.

DISTINGUISHING CHARACTERISTICS

Caughley porcelain resembles that of Worcester except for the colour of the paste (blueing does not seen to have been employed at Caughley), and its less skilful finish. The bulk of the factory's output of useful wares was decorated in blue-and-white, sometimes by transfer-printing, in the Worcester manner. Two patterns which were originated here, the 'Willow' and 'Broseley Dragon', attained great popularity, and are known in numerous variations produced by later Staffordshire and other earthenware factories. Gilding was combined with blue decorations at the end of the century. A greyish and a bright purplish-blue was used for decoration, lighter and brighter than that of Worcester. Shapes and patterns followed Worcester lines.

Ambitious coloured decorations were produced. Jugs with mask lips and cabbage-leaf embossment were ornamented with exotic birds in hot 'sticky' colours. Sprays of closely packed flowers are characteristic of Caughley painting.

Other typical features are foot-rings of nearly rectangular section, and a circle underneath the centre of the base.

Caughley porcelain is well represented in the Victoria and Albert Museum, London.

Plates 14–15.

[L. Jewitt, *Ceramic Art of Great Britain*, 1878; W.B. Honey, *Old English Porcelain*, 1928; new ed. 1948; G. Savage, *Eighteenth Century English Porcelain*, 1952; J. L. Dixon, *English Porcelain of Eighteenth Century*, 1952.]

'Cauliflower' ware

Green and yellow glazed earthenware made in the form of cauliflowers, pineapples and other vegetables, by Whieldon, Wedgwood and others from 1750 onwards: cauliflowers were also made in porcelain – 'Two fine large colliflowers and leaves' Chelsea Catalogue, 1756) at Chelsea, at Longton Hall (advert, *London Public Advertiser*, 12 April 1757) and elsewhere.

W. Mankowitz, *Wedgwood*, 1953; G. Savage, *Eighteenth Century English Porcelain*, 1952]

Cave, Edward

Founder of the *Gentleman's Magazine* and subscriber to the Worcester porcelain company originally known as Worcester Tonquin Manufacture. The *Gentleman's Magazine* contained a number of articles on Worcester porcelain of a eulogistic character. The article on porcelain in *The Annual Register* 1763 may have been 'inspired' by him.

Chaffers, Richard (died 1765),
Liverpool, Lancashire

Chaffers established his pottery in 1752 largely for the manufacture of blue-and-white earthenware, which he exported in considerable quantities to the American colonies. Wedgwood's improved cream-ware was emulated by Chaffers, assisted by Podmore, a former employee of Wedgwood.

The factory continued successfully until the sudden death of both Chaffers and Podmore in 1765 after which, though Chaffers' son took over, the factory declined.

Chailey, Sussex

Good inlaid red and white pottery was made here in the first half of the nineteenth century, particularly by the Norman family, whose name occurs on some pieces. Clock-faced spirit flasks, money boxes, bowls, tobacco jars, teapots, harvest jugs, were made. There are specimens in the Sussex Archaeological Museum at Lewes:

Money box, inscribed A. NORMAN, April 13 1835.

Bowl, inscribed RICHARD NORMAN, 1827. CHAILEY.

Clock Spirit Flask, RICHARD NORMAN.

Chamberlain, Robert, Worcester

In 1783 Robert Chamberlain, a painter at the Worcester factory, severed his connection and opened a factory of his own in Worcester in rivalry to the old company. It was at first a decorating business, but porcelain of a dense, hard kind was made from 1792, and later in a much improved paste. Robert Chamberlain had for partners his son Humphrey Chamberlain and Richard Nash. In 1840 Chamberlain's factory and the old company were amalgamated. In 1850 W.H.Kerr joined the firm which traded as Kerr & Binns in 1852. In 1862 the firm became the Royal Worcester Porcelain Co.

MARKS

Various marks were used,

H. Chamberlain
& Sons
Worcester
(incised)

Chamberlains
Wars No 276

Chamberlain
Worcester.

Chamberlains
Worcester
403

CHAMBERLAINS   Chamberlains

Chamberlain's
Regent China
Worcester
& 155
New Bond Street,
London

Printed in red

WORK

Elaborately painted wares in a naturalistic style with lavish gilding and striking ground colours. Japans were popular and generally hideous.

Champion, Richard (born 1743 died 1791), Bristol

Porcelain manufacturer, Bristol; married 1765; joined forces with Cookworthy c.1770 and received from him a licence to manufacture under his hard-paste patent when he retired in 1772. In 1774 Cookworthy assigned his patent rights to Champion for a consideration and in 1775 Champion petitioned Parliament for an extension of the patent rights for a further 14 years. In this he was successful (in spite of the opposition of Josiah Wedgwood) but the business crippled him financially. By 1778 Champion's Bristol manufactory was in financial difficulties. In 1781 Champion sold the patent for the manufacture of hard-paste porcelain to a company in North Staffordshire (which became known as New Hall) and moved to the Potteries to supervise its manufacture. Appointed Deputy Paymaster General to the Forces 1781–84; emigrated to South Carolina 1784; died there 1791.

[G.Savage, *Eighteenth Century English Porcelain*, 1952; G.E.Stringer, *New Hall Porcelain*, 1949; F.S.MacKenna, *Champion's Bristol Porcelain*.]

Chandler, John, London

A potter who is alleged to have been enticed by Elers from the employment of John Dwight of Fulham before 1693.

[Sir A.H.Church, *Burlington Magazine*, 1907–08; *Catalogue, Burlington Fine Arts Club*, 1914.]

Charter of incorporation

The minutes of the Worshipful Company of Glass Sellers of London, 21 June 1722, make it evident that the London manufacturers of 'white and painted earthen wares glazed with lead and tin' were seeking a charter of incorporation in 1722.

[S.Young, *The History of the Worshipful Company of Glass Sellers of London*, London, 1913.]

Châtelaine

An ornamental appendage worn by women for supporting watches, scissors, seals, keys and other étuis, from a belt. Wedgwood jasper cameos were mounted as ornaments to chatelaines.

[Illus., W.Mankowitz, *Wedgwood*, 1953.]

Chatterley, Charles and Ephraim, Hanley

Manufacturers of cream coloured earthenware in succession to Samuel Chatterley in Hanley. They are first listed as potters in 1783. In 1783 Ephraim Chatterley became the first Mayor of the 'mock' Corporation of Hanley. They gave up the business to their nephews about 1793 when the firm became James & Charles Whitehead. Ephraim Chatterley died 7 May 1811 aged 66 years. (*Mural Monument, Hanley Church*) A William Chatterley was potting in Hanley in 1796.

[*Directories*.]

Chatterley, Samuel

Salt-glazed stoneware manufacturer in Hanley for whom (before he started potting on his own account) Elijah Mayer acted as foreign agent (J.C. Wedgwood, *Staffordshire Pottery and its History*, n.d.). He also made Egyptian black wares.

Cheam, Surrey

Site of an important medieval pottery at which jugs, bowls, pipkins, etc., were made in enormous quantities. Many of these appear to have been sent to London where they have been discovered (examples in the British Museum, Guildhall Museum and London Museum). Jugs of sturdy biconical form are typical. Boldly painted 'gothic' scrolls in red or dark brown slip occur on buff wares and have an appearance of primitive simplicity and strength belied by the date of their manufacture in the fourteenth century. Green and yellow lead-glazed wares were made in the fourteenth and fifteenth centuries.

[G.C.Dunning, *London Museum, Mediaeval Catalogue*, 1940; B.Rackham, *Medieval English Pottery*, 1948; C, Marshall 'Mediaeval Pottery Kiln at Cheam' in *Surrey Archaeological Collections*, 1924; G.C.Dunning, *Transactions-English Ceramic Circle*, 1946.]

Chelsea, Porcelain manufactory

EARLIEST DATE

The Chelsea Works was probably founded about 1745 or shortly before, judging by the earliest pieces of porcelain to survive, the 'goat and bee' cream jugs, some of which carry this date. The earliest contemporary reference occurs in the *London Tradesman* in 1747 which mentions manufactures of porcelain at Greenwich and Chelsea.

OWNERS

Until 1750 it is believed that Charles Gouyn, silversmith, was proprietor and chief manager of the factory. He is believed to have had the assistance of working potters from other factories, who left him to produce their own wares. In this they were unsuccessful, and some of them, who came from Staffordshire, returned to Burslem.

The name of Nicholas Sprimont first appears in connection with Chelsea in 1749 when he managed the factory for Sir Edward Fawkener, and on his death in 1758 became its owner. The factory changed hands in 1769, and again in 1770 when it was bought by William Duesbury and John Heath of Derby. From this time until its closure in 1784 its products followed Derby

Colour plate 4, CHELSEA: *see page vii for caption*

(A) BRISTOL dish of tin-enamelled earthenware with portrait bust of King James II painted in colours, c. 1685. Diameter 13¼ inches.

(B) BRISTOL plaque of tin-enamelled earthenware with portrait bust of Queen Anne after Kneller painted in under-glaze blue, first half of 18th century. 9 inches × 7¼ inches.

PLATE 17

(A) *Left above:* BRISTOL dish, porc. painted in colours, c. 1775. Mark, an arrow-head in blue. Length 11⅞ in, width 8¾ in.

(B) *Left under:* BRISTOL chocolate cup with lid and saucer, porc. painted in colours and gilt, eighteenth century. Mark, a cross and '2' in blue enamel. Ht 4½ in.

(C) *Right:* BRISTOL vase, with ormolu mounts, c. 1775. Height, 15½ inches.

(D) BRISTOL food-warmer, tin-enam-elled earthenware painted in under-glaze blue, first half of eighteenth cen-tury. Height 10 inches.

(E) BRISTOL coffee-pot and cover, painted in ena mel colours and gilt, 1780. Mark, a cross in over glaze blue. Height 9¼ in.

PLATE 18

(A) BRISTOL figure of a girl, porcelain, painted in colours, c. 1775. Height 8 inches.

(B) BRISTOL (Water Lane Pottery) panel of biscuit porcelain, stained lavender blue on the surface, with group of flowers modelled in white biscuit porcelain and applied. Made by Edward Raby, c. 1850. Height 10¾ inches, width 8½ inches, approximately.

(C) BRISTOL punch-bowl, tin-enamelled earthenware, painted in underglaze blue, dated 1731. Diameter 10⅛ inches.

(D) BRISTOL plate, tin-enamelled earthenware, painted in colours, c. 1760. Diameter 9 inches.

PLATE 19

(A) BRISTOL tea-pots and lids, porcelain, painted in colours and gilt, c. 1775. Height 6½ inches.

(B) BRISTOL dishes, tin-enamelled earthenware, painted in colours, middle of seventeenth century. Diameters 13 ⅜ inches. 13 ¼ inches, and 10 ¼ inches.

(C) BRISTOL plate enamelled earthenware, painted in colours, middle of eighteenth century. Diameter 9 inches. Plate, earthenware with whitish-blue enamel painted in blue and opaque white, made by Joseph Flower, middle of eighteenth century. Diameter 8¾ inches.

(D) BRISTOL punch-bowl of tin-enamelled earthenware, painted in underglaze blue, dated 1731. Diameter 10⅛ inches.

PLATE 20

CHELSEA teapot, porcelain, painted in colours on a claret ground. Mark, an anchor in gold. c. 1765. Height 5³⁄₈ inches; cream-jug, height 3 inches; saucers, diameter, 5¹⁄₈ inches; coffee cup, height 2³⁄₄ inches.

PLATE 21

(A) CHELSEA tureen with cover and stand, porcelain painted in colours, c. 1755.
Mark, an anchor in red. Height 8¾ inches, width 13¾ inches.

(B) CHELSEA vase, porcelain painted in colours,
turquoise ground, c. 1765. Mark, an anchor in
gold. Height 6¾ inches.

(C) CHELSEA vase and cover, decorated
in imitation of Japanese Kakiemon ware,
c. 1755. Height 10⅜ inches, diameter
6⅜ inches.

PLATE 22

(A) CHELSEA cup and saucer, porcelain painted in colours, c. 1750–55. Mark, an anchor in red. Cup, height 1⅝ inches, saucer, diameter 4⅞ inches.

(B) CHELSEA plate, porcelain painted in colours, c. 1755. Mark, an anchor in red. Diameter 9⅜ inches.

(C) CHELSEA dish, porcelain painted in colours, c. 1760. Mark, an anchor in red. Length 10¼ inches, width 7¼ inches.

PLATE 23

(A) CHELSEA cup and saucer, porcelain, c. 1745–50. Mark, a triangle incised. Height of cup 1¾ inches, diameter of saucer, 4⅝ inches; dish, porcelain, c. 1745–50, length 4¾ inches; 'Goat and Bee' jug, porcelain, c. 1745–50. Mark, a triangle incised. Height 4⅜ inches.

(B) CHELSEA plate painted in imitation of Chinese porcelain of the *famille rose*, c. 1755. Diameter 7 inches.

(C) CHELSEA vase and cover made in imitation of Sèvres porcelain, c. 1770. Mark, an anchor in gold. Height 9⅜ inches.

PLATE 24

(A) CHELSEA crested bird, porcelain, painted in colours, c. 1755. Mark, an anchor in relief painted in red. Height 6½ inches.

(B) CHELSEA figure of a bird, white glazed porcelain, c. 1750. Height 5¼ inches.

(C) CHELSEA pair of figures, a cock and a hen, porcelain, painted in colours, c. 1755. Mark, an anchor in red. Height 6⅝ inches. 5⅞ inches.

PLATE 25

CHELSEA group, Leda and the swan, porcelain painted in colours, c. 1755. Mark, an anchor in red. Height 6⅞ inches, width 6¾ inches.

PLATE 26

(A) CHELSEA dish, porcelain painted in colours, c. 1755.
Length 16 inches, width 13 inches.

(B) CHELSEA teapot and cover, porcelain, c. 1745–
50. Mark, a triangle incised. Height 6¾ inches.

(C) CHELSEA figure of a peasant, porcelain.
Mark, an anchor in red. c. 1755. Height 5¼ inches.

PLATE 27

(A) CHELSEA (probably) figures of a boy and girl, white glazed porcelain,
c. 1750. Height 5¾ inches.

(B) CHELSEA flower-holder in the form of
two boys with a fish, porcelain, painted in
colours, c. 1755. Height 8⅝ inches.

(C) CHELSEA figure of a carpenter,
porcelain, painted in colours, c. 1755.
Mark, an anchor in red.
Height 7¾ inches.

PLATE 28

(A) CHELSEA-DERBY figure of An-
dromache weeping over the ashes of
Hector, porcelain, painted in colours
and gilded, c. 1775. Mark, '100' incised.

(B) CHELSEA-DERBY group, Rinaldo and
Armida, porcelain, painted in colours, c. 1775.
Height 8⅜ inches.

(C) CHELSEA-DERBY figures of General Conway and John Wilkes, porcelain,
painted in colours and gilded, c. 1771. Height 12⅜ inches, 11¾ inches.

PLATE 29

CHELSEA-DERBY set of three vases, porcelain painted in blue, gilt and grey. Marks, 'D' under a crown on the top of the plinth of each, in gold; also on the smaller vases 'No. 67' incised. Height 13⅛ inches and 10 inches respectively.

PLATE 30

(B) CHELSEA-DERBY trembleuse saucer, porcelain painted in colours on a blue and gilt ground, c. 1775. Mark, an anchor in gold and 'N' incised. Saucer, diameter 6½ inches.

(A) CHELSEA-DERBY mug, porcelain painted in colours and gilt, c. 1775. Mark, 'D' intersected by an anchor in gold. Height 3⅞ inches.

PLATE 31

(A) CHELSEA-DERBY, cups and saucers, porcelain painted in colours, c. 1775. Cup, height 1⅞ inches, saucer, diameter 3⅞ inches; cup, height 3¼ inches, saucer, diameter 3 inches; cup, height 2¾ inches, saucer, diameter 5¼ inches respectively.

(B) CHELSEA-DERBY tea-pot and cover, porcelain painted in natural colours, c. 1775. Height 6 inches.

PLATE 32

rather than established Chelsea styles, and so this is known as the Chelsea-Derby period. In 1784 the Chelsea workshops and ovens were demolished and many moulds destroyed. Some were removed to Derby.

ARTISTS

Artists sometimes bought white porcelain in order to decorate it themselves. A number of anonymous Chelsea decorators have been identified, as 'the Chelsea painter' or 'the Fable painter'.

William Duesbury, was a decorator of Bow, Chelsea, Derby and Staffordshire porcelain from 1751–1756, when he became proprietor of Derby. He later acquired control of Longton Hall and Bow as well as Chelsea.

Richard (?) Dyer, said to have been at Chelsea, and may have been the enameller of that name employed by the Bow factory in 1760. Painter at Worcester 1770.

John Astbury, painter, 1747.

John Donaldson, miniaturist and porcelain painter, believed responsible for some important pieces.

Louis François Roubiliac, sculptor and modeller who may have modelled busts of royal family and some important large figures.

Richard Askew, painter of figure subjects at Chelsea and Derby.

Zachariah Boreman, landscape painter at Chelsea and Derby, probably the celebrated painter of birds on Chelsea services.

Nicholas-Joseph Gauron, the chief modeller at Tournai, may (or Nicholas-Francois) have been the Gauron who was later employed at Chelsea in 1773.

Joseph Willems, sculptor and modeller.

MARKS

| Incised | Incised 1745-49 | in applied relief 1750-53 | in under-glaze blue 1749 |

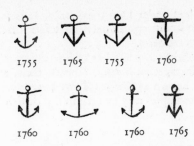

| 1755 | 1765 | 1755 | 1760 |
| 1760 | 1760 | 1760 | 1765 |

DISTINGUISHING CHARACTERISTICS

Four clearly defined periods of Chelsea manufacture are recognised: Triangle 1745–1749; Raised Anchor 1750–1753; Red Anchor 1753–1758; and Gold Anchor 1758–1770. The earliest Chelsea group, to which the 'goat and bee' jugs belong, bears the mark of an incised triangle.

Work of the 'raised' (i.e. embossed) and 'red anchor' periods enjoys the highest esteem, in spite of its imperfections, for the quality of its porcelain. This was made from a very fine soft paste which had the characteristic of forming transparent glass spots or 'moons' under firing. These can be seen when the ware is held up to the light. It has been claimed that this was necessary to strengthen the china body because of the softness of the paste. However, it was eliminated in the gold anchor period (and in occasional perfect red anchor pieces), but the ware also lost its celebrated creamy texture.

During Fawkener's ownership (c. 1749–1758), Meissen styles were most often copied, though the colouring and quality of the china give the ware an original beauty. Colour washes were employed to give simple effects in keeping with paste and form. Gilding was little used.

When Sprimont became owner, several changes occurred. Sprimont's is the gold anchor period, the red anchor being rarely used. Bone ash was introduced into the paste; Sèvres became the dominant influence; decoration became richer employing elaborate floral backgrounds; heavy gilding was used. Some fine ground colours were introduced, 'mazarine' (an uneven dark blue) and claret, as well as more flamboyant modelling. The resulting quality, though notable, was perhaps inferior to 'red anchor' Chelsea.

Under Duesbury the Chelsea and Derby styles gradually blended, the vigour of Chelsea being lost under Derby influence. It becomes difficult to distinguish between wares made at the two factories.

A considerable number of interesting miniature pieces, scent-bottles, flowers, seals, snuffboxes, known as Chelsea Toys, have survived. Good examples may be seen in the British Museum.

SUBJECTS

Triangle Period: Silver shapes predominate, with applied ornament, fluting and raised foliage and floral sprays. Painted subjects included Japanese patterns derived from Meissen examples. The apparently haphazard application of tiny flower sprigs or insects concealed imperfections of paste or glaze.

Not many Triangle figures are known. A notable class of uncoloured figures takes its name from the well-known 'Girl in a Swing' and is attributed on evidence of paste and style to the earliest Chelsea period.

Raised Anchor Period: Oriental influence via Meissen is strong in this phase of Chelsea. Decorations were applied with regard to the beauty of the paste and glaze. Aesop's Fables and the Lady and Pavilion are well-known patterns. Figures in this period are very uncommon; outstanding are Italian Comedy figures and the tender earthenware-derived 'Nurse'; portrait busts, and models of birds copied from George Edwards' *The Natural History of Uncommon Birds.*

Red Anchor Period: The finest of the Chelsea porcelains. Meissen, Chinese, and Japanese influences are strong. A version of botanical flowers, some adapted from Philip Miller's *Figures of Plants*, was an outstanding decoration. Fantastic animal and vegetable shapes were used for tureens and dishes, and gaily coloured. Crimson monochrome landscapes and Aesop's Fables again appear. Other subjects of this mature Chelsea phase are naked children at play, birds, moulded scroll borders, Watteau subjects, and bouquets of flowers.

Splendid figures were made, some derived from Meissen, others like Leda and the Swan from an engraving after Boucher. Notable specimens are the Ratcatcher, the Girl in a Nun's Costume, and the River Goddess.

Gold Anchor Period: Meissen influences yield to Sèvres, and the vigorous playfulness of the earlier phases gives way to a new elegance and sophistication. New colours were adopted including a rich sonorous blue. Elaborate gilding became fashionable, subjects for decoration included groups after Teniers, exotic or naturalistic birds, chinoiseries, flowers and fruits.

Figures with elaborate and fulsome bocages are typical, usually with rococo scroll bases. The large Roman Charity is an outstanding achievement.

Chelsea Porcelain is well represented in the Victoria and Albert Museum, the Bedford Museum, and the British Museum; and in the Irwin Untermyer Collection, Metropolitan Museum of Art, New York; Chicago Art Institute; Boston Museum of Fine Arts, and Rhode Island School of Design.

FAKES AND FORGERIES

Coalport nineteenth century imitations of marked gold anchor vases and 'goat and bee' jugs should be detected because of the clean whiteness of the ware. Tournai imitations of the same period (gold anchor) are in true soft paste and may be more easily mistaken although often decorated with impossible subjects. Some modern bone-china tablewares with distinctive Chelsea-Derby patterns have been provided with forged Chelsea-Derby marks.

Colour plates 3, 4 and 5; plates 21–32.

[W.King, *Chelsea Porcelain*, 1922; G.E.Bryant, *Chelsea Porcelain Toys*, 1925; Yvonne Hackenbroch, *Chelsea and other English Porcelain... in the Irwin Untermyer Collection*, 1957; F.Severne MacKenna, *Chelsea Porcelain; the Trinagle and Raised Anchor Wares*, 1948; *Chelsea Porcelain: Gold Anchor Wares*, 1952; Raphael Read, *Reprint of the Original Catalogue... Chelsea Porcelain Manufactory*, 1880; Articles by Dr Bellamy Gardner in *Apollo*, 1939 and the *Connoisseur*, 1923, 1926, 1942, and 1943; and by G.Savage in *Apollo*, 1941, 1952.]

'Chelsea' painter

An unidentified artist who worked for James Giles, whose touch is recognised in three of the plates presented to the Victoria and Albert Museum, London, by a descendant of Giles, Mrs Dora Grubbe. His work is to be found on Worcester, Chelsea and Chinese porcelain and is characterised by bright neat colouring with accentuated high lights and shadows, and a bold, fluent touch. He painted fruit, flowers, birds and more rarely figures.

[J.L.Dixon, *English Porcelain of the 18th Century*, 1952; W.B.Honey, *Old English Porcelain*, 1928 and later editions.]

Chemical, Alchemical and Astrological signs

Some of these occur as marks on Bow, Chelsea, Bristol, and early Worcester porcelain, and on Staffordshire earthenware such as Rogers' of Dale Hall. A sequence of signes is given below.

aer	Air
Terra	Earth
gnis	Fire : Water	Aqua
Dies	Day : Nox	Night
Fumus	Smoke : Cineres	Ashes
Sal	Salt
Sol	Gold
Luna	Silver
Jupiter	Tin
Saturn	Lead
Mars	Iron or Steel
Venus	Copper

Mercury	Quicksilver
Antimonium	Antimony
Orichalum	Brass
Faecis Vini	Lees of Wine
Albumen	White of Egg
Arena	Sand
Arsenicum	Arsenic
Atramentum	Ink
Creta	Chalk
Borax	

Chessmen

A set of chessmen was modelled by John Flaxman for Wedgwood in 1784–85. They were made in various coloured jasper, and in cream colour, and were exported to Germany and Russia.

Bone-china chessmen were made at Rockingham about 1825.

[E.Meteyard, *Life of Josiah Wedgwood*, 1865-66.]

Chesswas, Thomas Edensor (c. 1834), Lane End

Earthenware manufacturer, Lower Market Place, Lane End, in 1834. The factory which he occupied was announced for sale by auction in 1835 (*Staffordshire Advertiser*, 5 September 1835). Chesswas was living in Longton Road, Longton in 1851, but was apparently no longer potting on his own account.

Chester, Cheshire

From the *Port Books* of Bideford (1691) it is evident that a small export of North Devonshire clay was made to Chester at the end of the seventeenth century. It does not follow however that this was intended for dispatch overland to the Potteries. Dr Charles Leigh (1700) says fine clay pipes were made at Chester from clays imported from Poole, Bideford and the Isle of Wight.

[*Transactions, Devonshire Association*, 1955; C. Leigh, *Natural History of Lancashire, Cheshire and the Peak in Derbyshire*, 1700.]

Chesterfield

A centre noted for the manufacture of brown stonewares characterised by relief decorations of hunting scenes or drinking bouts: J. Aiken (*A Description of the Country round Manchester*, 1795) noted the existence of three potworks making coarse earthenware in 1795. In 1848 there were several potteries, chiefly for coarse brown and yellow stoneware 'which afford employment for upwards of 200 men' (Samuel Lewis, *A Topographical Dictionary of England*, 1848). Glover in his *Gazetteer* of the County of Derby (1829) said much the same thing. Llewellyn Jewitt cited evidence for the continuous production of pottery at Chesterfield from the early part of the sixteenth century.

See under BRAMPTON.

Chetham, family of Longton

The Chetham family occupied and worked a factory in Commerce Street, Longton for nearly three quarters of a century. Jewitt says the business was started by Richard Woolley, earthenware manufacturer (born 1765 died 1825) at the end of the eighteenth century. By 1796 it was styled Chetham & Woolley, the partners being James Chetham (died 1807) and Richard Woolley. The firm became famous for a fine grained white earthenware called 'pearl' ware, in which they made portrait busts and figures. 'Mr Chetham, a respectable manufacturer' died in 1807 (*Staffordshire Advertiser*, 22 August 1807) and for the next two years the business was carried on by his widow, Ann Chetham, in partnership with Richard Woolley under the same style. The partnership was dissolved by mutual consent in 1809 (*Staffordshire Advertiser*, 16 December 1809) when Ann Chetham continued at the Old Pottery and Richard Woolley set up on his own in Turner's Old Factory, where he became bankrupt in 1814 (*Staffordshire Gazette*, 23 August 1814). Richard Woolley 'formerly an earthenware manufacturer at Lane End' died 28 December 1826 at Stone (*Pottery Mercury*, 11 January 1826). His widow, Margaret, survived until 1850, dying at Oxted, Cheshire at the age of 85, on September 1st (*Staffordshire Advertiser*, 14 September 1850).

Ann Chetham continued the business which in 1818 was known as M. Chetham & Son, the son being Jonathan Lowe Chetham. John Robinson (born 1779 died 1840) became a partner in the concern in the 1820's or 1830's, and in 1834 the business traded as Chetham & Robinson. After Robinson's death in 1840 (*Staffordhires Advertiser*, 19 September 1840) the firm continued as Jonathan Lowe Chetham. Eventually his sons John, Robert and Frederick took over, working the factory until 1875 when it passed to the control of H. Aynsley and Company. J. R. & F. Chetham were manufacturers of 'lustre, drab, black, torquoise (sic) and printed wares' and 'stone mortars'.

*Chetham & Woolley
Lane End, 1798*

CHETHAM

[*Staffordshire Advertiser*, 22 August 1807, 16 December 1809, 22 March 1817, 19 September 1840, 14 September 1850; *Staffordshire Gazette*, 23 August 1814; *Pottery Mercury* 11 January 1826; *Directories*, 1796–1875; L. Jewitt, *Ceramic Art of Great Britain*, 1878; S. Shaw, *History of the Staffordshire Potteries*, 1829.]

Chetwynd, David

Pottery modeller at Burslem and Hanley from 1851 until 1865, and partner in firm of Cockson and Chetwynd, Cobridge, manufacturers of china from 1866 until 1876. Jewitt gives the mark as the Royal Arms and the name:

IMPERIAL IRONSTONE CHINA,
COCKSON & CHETWYND.

Chetwynd, Elijah

A well-known pottery modeller in Hanley who flourished from 1850–79. He was married to Mrs de Beauregard 18 March 1851 (*North Staffordshire Independent*, 23 March 1851), and in 1866 became partner in the firm of Cockson & Chetwynd (partners Charles Cockson, died 1873, Elijah Chetwynd and David Chetwynd). The business was continued after Cockson's death by his widow, under the same style until 1876 when the Chetwynds retired.

[*Directories*; *North Staffordshire Independent* 23 March 1851; L. Jewitt, *Ceramic Art of Great Britain*, 1878.]

Child, Smith (born 1730 died 1813),
Tunstall, Staffordshire

A manufactory of transfer-printed and other decorated cream-wares at Newfield, using the impressed mark CHILD, was established by Admiral Smith Child in 1763 and worked by him for twenty years.

In 1806 Child once more took over the factory and manufactured earthenware in partnership with John Henry Clive until 1813, under the style Child & Clive.

In 1829 the factory was taken over by Joseph Heath and Co.

The impressed mark C L I V E also occurs.

[P. W. L. Adams, *John Henry Clive*, 1947.]

Chimney ornament

A pottery or porcelain figure intended for display on the mantelpiece; often of a 'flat-back' type, modelled and decorated on one side only; 'six large and elegant China Chimney Ornaments of intrinsic value' (sale notice concerning Rupert Leigh of Cheadle, *Staffordshire Advertiser*, 2 January 1796).

China clay

A white burning refractory clay produced by the decomposition of felspathic rock, called by the Chinese *kaolin*, and quarried in Cornwall. It is an essential ingredient of hard-paste porcelain, and English bone china. The *unaker* specified in the patent of Heylin and Frye in 1744, was American china clay.

Chinaman

An importer of oriental porcelain; a pottery dealer; ('went to see a garden belonging to one Mr Bauldy, a china-man' – *Diary of Sylas Neville*, 20 September 1771.) Miles Mason was originally a chinaman.

Chinaman teapot

Grotesque teapots in the form of a squatting Chinaman, made at Chelsea in the triangle period, 1745–1749.

China-stone

A fusible felspathic rock, known to the Chinese as *petuntse*, used in the manufacture of porcelain, and generally known in England as china-stone, or, because quarried in Cornwall, Cornish stone.

Chinese Lowestoft

An incorrect name sometimes given to Chinese export porcelain.

'Chinese' marks

Marks imitating Chinese characters appear with some frequency on porcelain made at Bow, Worcester, Caughley, or by Spode and Mason in North Staffordshire, eighteenth and early nineteenth centuries.

They were also common on red wares of Elers type made in Staffordshire throughout the eighteenth century.

[W. Mankowitz, *Wedgwood*, 1953.]

Christening Goblet

Footed four-handled loving cup with whistle attached for calling for replenishment; used for christenings, harvest-homes and other convivial occasions, and specially associated with Wiltshire. A favourite inscription was HERE IS THE GEST OF THE BARLY KORNE GLAD HAM I THE CILD IS BORN. Dates recorded from 1603 until 1799.

[E. T. Stevens, *Catalogue of the Salisbury and South Wilts Museum*, Salisbury, 1870.]

Christian, Philip (c. 1765), Liverpool

Porcelain manufacturer at Shaw's Brow, and friend and associate of Richard Chaffers the principal Liverpool potter.

His products included large china vases in the Oriental style, tortoiseshell in round and octagonal forms, fine table wares and chimney vases.

His name occurs in Gore's *Liverpool Directory* 1766 and 1769 at Shaw's Brow.

Chrome Green

A colour discovered c.1795. Made from oxide of chromium, and rather more opaque and yellowish in appearance than copper-green.

Church Gresley, Leicestershire

A factory was established here in 1794 and was worked until 1808, but its work has not been identified. Sir Nigel Bowyer Gresley is said to have founded it, and William Coffee, the Derby modeller, to have been one of its workmen. Coffee stayed one year. In 1800 the business was purchased by W. Nadin who continued it until 1804. From 1804 until its closure it was run by a company.

A cream ware tureen painted with botanical specimens and impressed 'C. Gresley' may be a product of the factory which operated here.

W. B. Honey referred to Church Gresley bluntly as 'another myth'.

Church monuments

Josiah Wedgwood made a black basaltes vase for the mural monument to William Viscount Chetwynd (d.1770) in Ashley Church, Staffordshire in 1772; also jasper insets in the form of spandrels for the monument to Sir William Jackson Hooker in Kew Church, to designs by Reginald Palgrave. A number of important sculptural works in Doulton stoneware were designed and modelled by George Tinworth including the altarpiece in Shelton Church, Stoke-on-Trent; mural panels in Trentham Church, Staffs; Sandringham Church, Norfolk; and a reredos in York Minster.

Churchyard works, Burslem, Staffordshire

Occupied in 1710 by Josiah Wedgwood's grandfather Thomas and eventually by Thomas, the elder brother of Josiah, who inherited the family works in 1739.

Josiah served his apprenticeship at the Churchyard until 1749 and later took over the works himself, operating it together with the Bell Works and the Ivy House.

On the completion of the Etruria estate and factory, Josiah Wedgwood moved his activities there and the Churchyard works were taken over by his second cousin Joseph who worked for him as a sub-contractor until 1795 when Thomas Green took over the property. In 1811 the Churchyard was purchased by Joynson or Johnson, who later sold it to Moseley, whose upper-case impressed mark 'MOSELEY', is found on Wedgwood-style basaltes.

Cistercian ware

Red earthenware with a brownish-black or mirror-black glaze so named because often found on the sites of Cistercian Abbeys, notably Kirkstall and Fountains, although not exclusively. J. T. Micklethwaite first called attention to this pottery group which dates from the early sixteenth century (*Society of Antiquaries Proceedings* Series 2, Vol 15). There seems to have been continuity of the type, similar wares of seventeenth century date being known.

Claret

A ground colour introduced by Sprimont at Chelsea in 1760; a fine crimson. It was imitated at Derby and Worcester, although the claret ground of Derby tended to a brownish hue and was less attractive in appearance. The fine claret colour of Worcester, was produced, perhaps as suggested by W. B. Honey, with the help of migrant Chelsea craftsmen. Plymouth produced an unsuccessful claret-crimson.

Most of the nineteenth century Staffordshire bone china houses of repute produced a more-or-less successful crimson ground colour, notably Copelands, and Minton's.

[W. B. Honey, *Old English Porcelain*, 1928, new ed. 1948.]

Clementson, Joseph (born 1794 died 1871)

Master potter; b. Carrigill, Cumberland, 15 July; apprenticed at J. & W. Ridgway, 1820; started in partnership with Jonah Read in firm of Read & Clementson, earthenware manufacturers, at the Phoenix Works, Shelton, 1832–39, which he enlarged 1845. Purchased Bell Works 1856; Chief Bailiff of Hanley 1849, 50, 51; died at Prospect House 1871.

[Rupert Simms, *Bibliotheca Staffordiensis*, Lichfield, 1894; H. Smith & A.M. Beard, *Bethesda Chapel, Hanley*, 1899.]

Clewes, Ralph

This name, incised underneath the base of a silver-shaped New Hall teapot in the Victoria & Albert Museum, occurs with some frequency in Burslem and Wolstanton Parish Registers, but nothing further is known about him.

[Illustrated, G.E. Stringer, *New Hall Porcelain*, 1949.]

Clews (Clewes), Ralph and James, Cobridge

Ralph and James Clews rented a potworks at Cobridge from William Adams of Cobridge Hall in 1817 for £216 p.a., where they manufactured blue-printed earthenware, chiefly for the American market. According to their invoice headings they were Potters to Her Imperial Majesty the Empress of Russia. They also made ironstone china. The firm became bankrupt in 1835 and in the ensuing years numerous announcements appeared in the *Staffordshire Advertiser* (1834, 1835, 1836 various issues). James Clews at the time of the crash (1835) was about 44 years of age (*Staffordshire Advertiser*, 28 February 1835). R. & J. Clews produced a number of splendidly engraved views and decorations for the English and American markets including:

American views with border of scallops bearing the names of 15 States with stars between.

American views with scroll and floral border.

American views with a border of scrolls, flowers and birds.

Dr Syntax: 27 scenes after Rowlandson with a scroll and flower border.

Domestic Genre: pictures after Wilkie with a flower border.

Don Quixote: 21 Views with a scroll/floral border.

English views: border of bluebells and other flowers.

English views: scroll and foliage border.

Select views: bold floral border.

Zoological Pictures with twisted scroll border.

The Landing of Lafayette with floral border: centre after a drawing by S. Maverick.

Some of the Clews' engravings passed into the hands of Adams and were used at the Adams Factory. James Clews went to America in 1836, started a factory at Troy, Indiana, but failed again. He returned to England and died in 1856.

Examples in the Metropolitan Museum of Art, New York.

Plate 4 A.

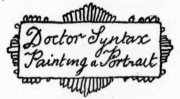

Transfer-printed

Transfer-printed

[R. Nicholls, *Ten Generations of a Potting Family*, 1932; L. Jewitt, *Ceramic Art of Great Britain*, 1878; Moore, *The Old China Book*, E.A. Barber, *Pottery and Porcelain of the United States*; *Staffordshire Advertiser*.]

Clevedon, Somerset

Hand-made 'Art' pottery was produced at the Sunflower Pottery, Clevedon by Sir Edmund H. Elton, Bart., from clay quarried on the Clevedon Estate, and decorated with coloured slips under a clear transparent glaze.

[*Official Catalogue of the Exhibition of Decorative and Artistic Pottery*, Imperial Institute, London, 1894.]

Clive, John Henry (born 1781 died 1853)

Master potter, engraver, colliery proprietor and inventor. Became partner in the firm of Child and Clive, cream-coloured earthenware manufacturers, Newfield Potteries, Tunstall. In 1805 they were producing good quality hand-painted ware. Clive wrote an important pioneer treatise on shorthand entitled *Mavor Abbreviated* which was published in Newcastle in 1810. He designed a double sextant in 1825, and in 1851 exhibited a model of a 'bar-trellis' suspension bridge at the Great Exhibition. His other interests encluded colliery undertakings, sewage and land-drainage schemes, and engraving.

[*Parson & Bradshaw's Directory*, 1818; P.W.L.Adams, *John Henry Clive*, Newcastle, 1947.]

Clobbering

Badly applied fake on glaze enamel colours which only partly obliterate underglaze printing or painting.

Close, Valentine

Hanley, Staffordshire

Manufacturer of earthenware at Keeling's Lane, Hanley from c.1795 until 1813 when he was bankrupt (*Staffordshire Advertiser*, 5 June 1813). He took out a patent, jointly with James Keeling of Hanley, 5 July 1796, for improvements in 'potter's ovens, or kilns for the firing of porcelain and earthenware'. (*Staffordshire Advertiser* 30 July 1796.) No wares identified.

Clowes, William & Company, Longport

William Clowes manufactured earthenware and excellent black basaltes at Longport, Burslem from about 1783. In 1796 the firm was styled Henshall, Williamson & Clowes, and by 1805 had become Henshall & Williamson. William Clowes was one of the original partners in the New Hall concern. His name occurs in documents from 1784 until 1813. He was one of the original members of the 'Mock' Corporation of Hanley, and he acted as arbitrator with Charles Daniel, china manufacturer of Shelton, in a dispute between William Adams and Oliver & Bourne. William Clowes died c.1815–16. The mark W. CLOWES impressed occurs on black basaltes candlesticks.

W Clowes

[*Directories* 1783, 1787, 1796, 1800, 1805-07, 1818; *Jurors List*, Salt Library, 1784; J.S.Crapper, *A Revised History of the Ancient Corporation of Hanley*, 1882; M.H.Grant, *The Makers of Black Basaltes*, 1910.]

Coade's Artificial Stone Works, Lambeth

A manufactory of moulded architectural stoneware to imitate carved stone was established by Batty Langley before 1738. About 1760 the Misses Coade set up a business under the name 'Coade's Lithodipyra, Terra Cotta, or Artificial Stone Manufactory'. A cousin of the Coades named Sealey joined the business in 1769, and the mark used was COADE & SEALEY, LAMBETH impressed.

Statuary, busts, church monuments and furnishings, and ornamental architectural details were made. Well known artists and sculptors were employed, including John Bacon, R.A. who eventually became manager, and John Charles Felix Rossi, R.A.

The relief upon the pediment over the west portico of Greenwich Hospital, the rood screen of St. George's Chapel, Windsor, and the statue of Britannia on the Nelson monument at Yarmouth were said to be the work of this firm.

When Sealey died the business passed through several hands, but continued until about 1840 when the moulds and plant were sold, many being acquired by H. M. Blanchard who had served his apprenticeship here, and Blashfield.

[L. Jewitt, *Ceramic Art of Great Britain*, 1878.]

Coalport or Coalbrookdale, Shropshire

John Rose left the Caughley factory after a difference with Thomas Turner and started on his own first at Jackfield and then at Coalport on the opposite bank of the river, c.1796. He took over an opposition works started by his brother and then, in an attempt to recover lost business, purchased Turner's Caughley factory after which biscuit china was made at Caughley and sent to Coalport for glazing and decoration. In 1814 the entire manufactory was removed to Coalport. John Rose bought the Cambrian Pottery at Swansea in 1820, and it was arranged that Billingsley and Walker should continue to make their high quality porcelain for Coalport.

There have been a number of different proprietors of Coalport since 1862 when the last representative of the Rose family, William Frederick Rose, retired from business. William Pugh, his partner, died in 1875. In 1885 the factory was bought by a member of the Bruff family and soon regained its position. In 1924 the firm was sold to Cauldon Potteries Ltd., and in 1926 moved to Staffordshire. Coalport china is now made at the Crescent Works, Stoke-on-Trent by Coalport China Ltd.

ARTISTS

Thomas Baxter (d.1821) is believed to have painted white porcelain sent to London for that purpose.

William Billingsley (d.1828) made porcelain and was also a flower painter.

W. J. Coffee (see Derby)

William Cook. Flower painter.

John James Spengler (see Derby)

Pierre Stephan. Modelled for Coalport as well as Derby.

Charles Walker. Painter.

MARKS

JOHN ROSE & Cº
COALBROOKDALE
SHROPSHIRE

DISTINGUISHING CHARACTERISTICS:

Early Coalport is indistinguishable from Caughley. From 1820 onwards the employment of Billingsley may have led to the use of the Nantgarw and Swansea formula and the product is extremely translucent. Bright flower painting particularly roses, with modelled and applied decoration, is characteristic of the Coalport style up to 1850. At the same time models of Sèvres, Dresden and Chelsea were not only imitated but skilfully faked at the Coalport factory. Less elaborate tea and table ware made from about

mid-century onwards is lightly decorated and makes use of pleasant green and rose coloured grounds.

Coalport China may be seen in London at the British Museum and Victoria and Albert Museum (Allen and Schreiber Collections) and Fitzwilliam Museum Cambridge.

Colour plate 6 and plates 33–36.

[W.B.Honey, *Old English Porcelain*, 1928, New Ed. 1948; Geoffrey Bemrose, *Nineteenth Century English Pottery and Porcelain*, 1952; L. Jewitt, *Ceramic Art in Great Britain*, 1878; C. Mackenzie, *The House of Coalport*; Otto Kurz, *Fakes*, 1948.]

Cobalt oxide

A powerful blue colouring material used for staining bodies and glazes from the beginning of the eighteenth century, known and used by John Dwight of Fulham.

Cocker, George (born 1794 died 1868)

Apprenticed in figure-making at the Derby China Works at the beginning of the nineteenth century but left within a few years of completing his apprenticeship in 1817. Worked for a time at Coalport and Worcester but returned to Derby in 1821 where he remained four years. Leaving Derby in 1825 he set up a small figure-making business with John Whitaker, Senior, as his partner. After twelve months Whitaker withdrew. Cocker carried on independently until 1840 when he went to London. In 1853 he came to the Potteries and for two years was employed by Herbert Minton and afterwards by John Mountford. Cocker died in the Potteries in 1868.

Cocker produced biscuit statuettes and portrait busts of popular contemporary celebrities, small animals and baskets of flowers. He was assisted by his family.

Cockpit Hill, Derby

Some slipwares were made at Cockpit Hill although the date of origin of this Derby potworks is unknown. Some white cream jugs marked DERBY and dated 1750 were probably made there although the factory may have been in production sometime before this date. From the early 1750's until 1779 the proprietors were W.Butts, Thomas Rivett, John and Christopher Heath. It is likely that the factory closure was due to the Heaths' bankruptcy and that the stock was acquired by William Duesbury (see also Bow, Chelsea, Derby). The ware was of a Staffordshire type and usually unmarked.

It is likely that Andrew Planché, who made the first porcelain in Derby, fired his figures at Cockpit Hill (c.1745) before Duesbury built his Derby Porcelain factory in 1756.

Thomas Radford, engraver, worked at the Cockpit Hill factory and an R surrounded by sun-rays is said erroneously to be his mark. Radford signed his work, T. Radford, Sc. Derby.

[F. Williamson, *The Derby Pot-Manufactory known as Cockpit Hill*, 1931.]

Codnor park, Derbyshire

A potworks was established here in 1821 by William Burton for the manufacture of stone-ware bottles from local clay, but closed in 1832 when Burton got into financial difficulties. Joseph Bourne of Denby re-opened the factory, which employed about 60 hands, in 1833, and continued to work it until 1861 when the workmen and plant were transferred to Denby.

Coffee, William

Modeller, started in his trade at Coade's factory in Lambeth, but later found employment at the porcelain factory, Derby, where he was working in 1794. In 1795 he is said to have gone to another and rather mysterious porcelain factory at Church Gresley, but returned to Derby. Subsequently he entered into partnership with a relative of Duesbury in a small china factory in Derby and when the partnership was dissolved commenced to make terra cotta. Finally he emigrated to America. His own productions in terra cotta are said to have been stamped.

W. COFFEE DERBY

Plate 43 A.

Cole, Sir Henry, C.B. (born 1808 died 1882)

Born at Bath and educated at Christ's Hospital; assistant keeper of the Records and helped to establish the Public Records Office. Head of the Science and Art Department, South Kensington and Director (from 1853 until 1873) of the Victoria and Albert Museum. As 'Felix Sum-merly' he designed (or caused to be designed) 'Art' pottery of a functional and ornamental kind, reproduced by Mintons, Wedgwood etc.

[Sir H.Cole, *Fifty Years of Public Work*, 1884; J.Steegman, *Consort of Taste 1830–1870*, 1950.]

Coleman, Helen Cordelia, A.R.W.S. (born 1847 died 1884)

Married Thomas William Angell; trained by her brother, W.S.Coleman. Produced some exquisite ceramic decorations under the direction of her brother for Mintons.

Coleman, William Stephen (born 1829 died 1904)

Illustrator of works of natural history and figure painter on pottery. Director of Mintons Art Studio in Kensington Gore.

[H.M.Cundall, *A History of British Water Colour Painting*, 2nd ed. 1929.]

Coles, William, Swansea

A potter who worked from c.1765 to 1800.

Collier Toby

Seated Toby jug, in form of a collier with blackened 'dirty' face and hands, late eighteenth and early nineteenth century date. Made in Staffordshire by James Neale and others.

Combed ware

Wares decorated by the application of two or more different coloured slips brushed or combed to produce an effect similar to marbled paper. The finer examples are called feathered wares.

Extensively used by Staffordshire slipware potters, late seventeenth and early eighteenth centuries.

[R.Plot, *Natural History of Staffordshire*, 1686.]

Comolera, Paul

A modeller of animals and birds at Mintons 1875 who came from Limoges.

Complin, George

A skilful fruit and bird painter who left the Derby factory in 1795.

Contour-framing

The isolation of an ornamental feature by means of a white or uncoloured border, more or less parallel, following its outline: a feature of near eastern Islamic pottery decoration from which it was derived via Italy and Holland. Recorded on a late sixteenth century tin-glazed earthenware vase.

Cook, William

A Coalport artist who specialised in finely executed trophies, flowers and birds in the Sèvres style.

[W.B.Honey, *Old English Porcelain*; 1928, new ed. 1948.]

Cookworthy, William (born 1705 died 1780)

Born at Kingsbridge in South Devon, of humble parentage. Apprenticed to a London apothecary named Bevans in 1719, he subsequently returned to Devon where he started a druggist's store under the name of Bevans & Cookworthy.

Cookworthy was a Quaker and married a Quakeress. His wife died ten years afterwards, in 1745, having borne her husband five daughters. After his wife's death Cookworthy took his brother into the druggist's business, leaving himself free to develop his researches into the secrets of porcelain-making. He journeyed into Cornwall many times, discovered the Cornish equivalents to *kaolin* and *petuntse*; and found a partner for his Plymouth hard-paste porcelain venture in Lord Camelford whom he visited with the object of securing the mineral rights of his land. The first fired experiments in hard-paste were made in 1765, and in 1768 he was sufficiently confident to take out a patent and form a company for its manufacture. The venture was transferred to Bristol in 1770, and in 1774 the patent was bought by Champion. Cookworthy died in 1780.

Coombes, Bristol

A repairer of china who re-marked and re-fired pieces from c.1780 until 1805. His address was Queen Street, Bristol. Also **Combes**.

Combes
Queen St
Bristol

Another Bristol repairer was a man named Daniel who flourished from 1789 until 1791, in David Street, near the Broad Main, Bristol.

[W.B.Honey, *Old English Porcelain*, 1928, subsequent editions.]

Cooper, Mrs A.

Manufacturer of china and parian figures at Etruria Road, Hanley in 1860.

Cooper, Susan Vera, R.D.I.

Studied at Burslem Art School from 1922; designer for A.E. Gray & Co., Stoke 1925; founder and managing director Susie Cooper Pottery, Burslem 1932, and Susie Cooper (China, Ltd., Longton. Manufacturer and designer of functional and visually satisfying shapes and patterns in the 'contemporary' style.
Plate 157 C.

A
SUSIE COOPER
PRODUCTION
CROWN WORKS
BURSLEM
ENGLAND

[Reginald G. Haggar, *Century of Art Education in the Potteries*, 1953].

Copeland, James, Hanley

James Copeland made china toys and figures at a small factory in New Street, Hanley, where he kept a beer-house, from 1834 until 1860 or longer. He married Mary Shirley at Norton-in-the-Moors January 27, 1812. She died aged 61, 17 June 1853 (*Staffordshire Advertiser*, 25 June 1853). His small works employed nine workpeople (*Government Report on Employment of*

Children, 1843). Copeland was a typical 'back street' potter.

[*Parish Registers*, Norton-in-the-Moors; *Poll List*, 1841.]

Copeland, William Taylor, M.P.
(born 1797 died 1868)

Son of William Copeland partner to Josiah Spode II; became sole owner of Spode's china manufactory, Stoke, 1833; Lord Mayor of London, 1835; Conservative M.P. Stoke-on-Trent 1837 to 1865; helped to form N. Staffs Railway 1846; dissolved partnership with Thomas Garrett 1847; took sons into business 1867.

[*Dictionary of National Biography;* J.C.Wedgwood, *Staffordshire Pottery and its History*, n.d.]

Copestick, Daniel, Lane Delph

Manufacturer of earthenware toys at Lane Delph from about 1817 until 1830.

Copper green

Copper was the source of most early green glaze stains such as those found upon Medieval, Tudor, and seventeenth and eighteenth century slipwares. Copper green pigment applied overglaze on earthenware and porcelain was a bright transparent green obtained from oxide of copper fritted with a flux and ground to powder. When applied over a black or brown transfer-print it shows the pattern or drawing beneath. Worcester apple-green was a copper green.

Cormie, John, Burslem

John Cormie, uncle of Thomas Pinder, succeeded J. & R.Riley at a factory in Nile Street, Burslem in 1814 which he continued to work as an earthenware manufacturer until he became bankrupt in 1840, when the factory was taken over by Mellor, Venables & Company. Cormie was probably in financial difficulties in 1831 when the fixtures of the Bell Works, Burslem, which for a time he also worked, were offered for sale (*Staffordshire Advertiser*, November 1831). Jewitt gives the name of this potter as James Cormie. John Cormie was Chief Constable of Burslem in 1827.

[*Staffordshire Advertiser* 1831, 1834, 1841.]

Corn, William and Edward, Burslem

Edward Corn, who came of farming stock, started to manufacture plain and fancy earthenware in Navigation Road, Burslem, in 1837. In 1875 the firm was listed as William and Edward Corn, who in addition to manufacturing earthenware, had flint-grinding and crate-making businesses in Burslem. In the 1890's tablewares were abandoned for tiles and a new company was started, using the second Christian names of the two brothers for its title, The Henry Richards Tile Co., shortened in 1934 to Richards Tiles.

MARK

W & EC

Cornwall

A principal source of pottery ingredients such as lead and tin used in glazings; high quality clays, particularly *kaolin* soaprock or soapstone (a natural mixture of steatite and China clay); and Moorstone or *petuntse* (china stone), a decomposed felspar used in porcelain manufacture.

The reason why no important ceramic manufactory flourished in the county is attributed to the resistance of Cornishmen engaged in the lead and tin industries. Country potteries existed, however, and that at Truro survives. Some attempts seem also to have been made to use local materials for 'porcelain' making in the eighteenth century. A small factory at Calstock had failed by 1755 while a Staffordshire man, named Horn, is alleged to have gone to Cornwall in 1755 for the purpose of 'setting up' a porcelain factory at Penryn.

[*Willaim Borlase MSS.*, letters March–December 1755, quoted by J.Rowe, *Cornwall in the Age of the Industrial Revolution*, 1953.]

Costrel

A pilgrim's bottle; a bottle with ears or handles for suspension from a cord or sling.

Cottage China

An inferior decorated Bristol hard-paste porcelain; sparsely decorated and without gilding, intended to compete with Staffordshire cream-

colour and usually known as 'cottage Bristol'. Similar wares were made at New Hall, Shelton, which is known from its final sale advertisement (1835) to have produced 'hawkers sets,' and other early Staffordshire porcelain houses.
[W.B.Honey, *Old English Porcelain*, 1928; new ed. 1948; R.G.Haggar, 'New Hall; the Last Phase' in *Apollo*, 1951.]

Cottages

Small porcelain models of cottages, churches, summer-houses and the like were extensively manufactured in the second quarter of the nineteenth century at Rockingham and in Staffordshire. Many were intended as pastille-burners. Earthenware cottages were commonly made in Staffordshire (particularly by Sampson Smith of Longton and Kent of Burslem), and in Yorkshire and Scotland over a more extended period of time. Simple cottages with a slot in the roof were used as money boxes and known as penny banks. See PASTILLE BURNERS.

'Cotton Stalk' painter

As unidentified ceramic artist, working at the Derby factory c.1760, who painted versions of Meissen flower sprays with fine stalks.
[W.B.Honey, *Old English Porcelain*, 1928 new ed. 1948; J.L.Dixon, *English Porcelain of the Eighteenth Century*, 1952.]

'Courtship and Marriage'

A popular contrast theme treated in various ways on cream-coloured earthenware as a black print. One version shows reversible masks of a grinning/grimacing man and women labelled COURTSHIP/MARRIAGE with the words below 'When two fond fools together meet / Each look gives joy each kiss so sweet; / But wed, how cold and cross they'll be / Turn upside down and then you'll see'. Another version based upon the painting of W. Williams, 1797, shows a girl being helped over a low stile by her lover and a woman climbing a five-barred gate while her husband walks on, with the verse: 'In courtship Strephon careful hands his lass / Over a stile a child with ease might pass. / But wedded Strephon now neglects his dame, / Tumble or not to him 'tis all the same'.

Cow milk jug

A model of a cow in which the mouth and tail form the spout and handle, filled from a hole in the back. Based upon a Dutch model introduced into England by John Schuppe about 1755, and made in South Wales, Yorkshire, Scotland and Staffordshire.

Cox, George

Pioneer studio potter and sculptor; established his kiln and workshop at Mortlake and sold his work at 9, South Kensington Arcade, London, c.1912; His venture turning out unsuccessful he went to America where he became a member of the staff of Columbia University, New York.
[John Adams, 'Potters' Parade', *Pottery and Glass*, January 1950.]

'Cracked Ice' pattern

Decoration resembling ice cracks, found on Bristol delftware, c.1770.
[F.H.Garner, *English Delftware*, 1948.]

Crackle

Intentional or controlled 'crazing', used extensively by the Chinese potters but not known in Europe until the nineteenth century. Used frequently by modern studio and artist potters.

Cradles

Presentation pieces commonly made in slipware for newly-married couples having the same fertility significance as the oval delftware *La Fécondité* dishes. Dated specimens are recorded from 1673 until 1839. Formerly they were stated to be commemoration pieces given to young couples on the occasion of the birth of their first children, but a comparison of the inscription upon a cradle in the Fitzwilliam Museum, Cambridge, 'ELISABATH CAPAR 1723' with the entry in the marriage registers of Stoke Parish Church, '31 December 1723 Nathaniel Kent & Elizabeth Capper' proves them to be wedding gifts. Cradles were used as hold-alls or pipetrays. Sometimes cradles were made in cream or white earthenware with representations of a child in them. These date from the end of the eighteenth century.
Plate 81 B.

Crane, Walter, R.W.S. (born 1846 died 1915)
Designer, book decorator, writer and lecturer; illustrated books for children; designed interior furnishings, mosaics, tapestries, friezes as well as pottery and tiles (Wedgwoods, 1867–77, Mintons and Pilkingtons). With William Morris he effected a revival of craftsmanship. First President of the Arts and Crafts Society which he helped to found in 1888. Author of numerous books including *The Bases of Art* ,1898, *Line and Form*, 1900, *Ideals in Art*, 1905, having a considerable influence upon Edwardian ceramic design.

      Personal mark & signature

[W.Crane, *An Artist's Reminiscences*, 1907; P.G.Konody, *The Art of Walter Crane*, 1907.]

Crayons
Ceramic crayons or vitrifiable coloured chalks for decorating pottery were invented about 1865 when they were shown at the Industrial Exhibition of the Potteries Mechanics' Institution in Hanley. Both Joseph Thorley and Francis Joseph Emery claimed they had originated ceramic crayons. The process enjoyed some popularity with professional and amateur china decorators. In recent times they have been effectively used by Susie Cooper R.D.I.

Crazing
A fine network of cracks occurring in the glaze of earthenware (sometimes a long time after manufacture) due to the tension set up in the glaze because of unequal shrinkage of glaze and body. In decorative pottery the effect may not be unpleasant, but crazing in table or kitchen wares is very undesirable because unhygienic.

Cream-coloured Earthenware
A good quality earthenware body manufactured by many Staffordshire potters, mid-eighteenth century onwards, and perfected and popularised by Josiah Wedgwood under the name Queensware. Also made in Leeds.

Crispe, Nicholas
A jeweller and potter at Lambeth who engaged John Bacon to model for him. He is known to have had a warehouse in the City but nothing is known of his products. Alan Cunningham stated that Bacon at the age of 14 was apprenticed 'to one Crispe of Bow Churchyard an eminent maker of porcelain.'

[Alan Cunningham, *Lives of the most Eminent British Painters, Sculptors and Architects*, 1830; R.Cecil, *Memoirs of John Bacon*, 1801; A.G.Toppin, 'Nicholas Crisp, Jeweller and Potter', *Trans. English Ceramic Circle*, 1933.]

Crock Street, Somerset
A hamlet near to Donyat where slipwares decorated in the *sgraffiato* style were made from the seventeenth century onwards. Coarse earthenware only was made in the nineteenth century. The wares made are inseparable from those of Donyat. There is a puzzle jug made at Crock Street in the British Museum.
Plate 104 C.

Crouch ware
The early grey stoneware of Staffordshire with a ferruginous wash is probably the 'crouch' ware mentioned by Simeon Shaw (*History of the Staffordshire Potteries*, 1829) as the earliest Staffordshire salt-glazed pottery. The name is perhaps derived from the Derbyshire Crich clay. Josiah Wedgwood in a letter to Bentley (14 January 1777) says 'My Head Clerk, Swift, is commenc'd Master Potter... He is join'd... with Cobb... in a work of Critch Ware, such as Mr Hayward was concern'd in at Chesterfield.'

[Reginald G. Haggar, *English Country Pottery*, 1950; *Letters of Josiah Wedgwood*, Edited by K.E. Farrer), 1903.]

Crowther, John, Bow
A merchant who became part proprietor of the Bow porcelain manufactory c.1750. He became bankrupt in 1763.

Cuckold cup
A well known caudle cup made of tin-glazed earthenware painted in polychrome with a portrait of a man holding a cup, and wearing horns.

By his side is a Lambeth wine bottle. The inscriptions painted in blue read,

'IᶠM COOK COE 1682' and 'OI WAS BORN TO WARE THE HORN'. It was sold at Sothebys, 14 July 1956.

Cullet

Broken glass for remelting, included in the ingredients of the frit used in the manufacture of early soft-paste porcelain.

[See Donald A.MacAlister, *Burlington Magazine*, Vol 51, 1927, 53, 1928, 54, 1929.]

Curfew (Couvre-feu)

An instrument for extinguishing a fire: 'a cover for a fire; a fire-plate' (S. Johnson, *Dictionary*). William Hone (*The Everyday Book*, Vol. 1, 1825) illustrates a copper example. Two forms recorded in pottery (1) consisting of two slabs of clay placed at right angles to one another (2) in the form of a 3-sided hollow article with a handle. The latter is sometimes called a DUTCH OVEN. Specimens in slipware dated 1692–1758.

Plates 82 A, 87 C.

[J.E. & Edith Hodgkin, *Examples of Early English Pottery*, 1891.]

Curnock, Percy Edwin, M.B.E. (born 1873, died 1956)

Son of a Warwickshire farmer; studied at the Wedgwood Institute, Burslem; worked as flower-painter, specialising in roses, at Doulton & Co. from 1886–1954. M.B.E. 1954.

[*Evening Sentinel*, 1 January 1954, 29 December 1956, 1 January 1957.]

Cut steel mounts

Wedgwood's medallions and plaques were mounted in cut steel as jewellery at the factory of Boulton & Fothergill, later Boulton & Watt, Soho. Adams' wares were sent to Thomas Law of Sheffield.

[W.B.Honey, *Wedgwood Ware*, 1948.]

Cutts, James, Snow Hill, Shelton

Son of John Cutts and famous as a designer and engraver of printed earthenware and china: Flourished 1834 to 1870. Stated to have served his time at the Cauldon Works, Shelton. A distinctive style is associated with his name, not without an element of romance and fantasy, and Geoffrey Bemrose likens him to Ravilious. He died about 1870. He worked for most of the leading firms, including Davenports. Sometimes his signature 'J.Cutts Desr.' appears beneath the bankstamp.

In gold

[G.J.V.Bemrose, *Nineteenth Century English Pottery and Porcelain*, 1953.]

Cutts, John & Sons, Hanley

John Cutts (born 1772 died 1851) ceramic painter of 'free' Derby-type landscapes at Pinxton and elsewhere. According to Jewitt he was manager for some years of the Pinxton concern, and before its closure part proprietor with a Mr Coke. Honey says Coke sold the works to John Cutts in 1804, who reduced the staff in 1808, after which a relatively coarse china of Staffordshire type was made until the final closure of the factory about 1813.

Cutts was in communication with the second Josiah Wedgwood in 1812, at the time when Wedgwoods of Etruria began to make bone china, and he decorated sample teawares for them. An entry in Wedgwood's *Decorators Book*

15 February 1813 gives his price for painting a teaservice: '1 tea set No 673 flower pattern, consisting of 52 pieces to a sett Cutts J. 12 days on the above sett at 5/– per day.' Cutts worked for Wedgwood for a time but his work had little appeal. An adverse traveller's report from Winchester, dated 12 November 1816, confirmed Wedgwood's endorsement of one of Cutts' letters in 1813, 'will not suit as a flower painter and probably not as a landscape painter.'

Leaving Wedgwood, Cutts set up as an enameller and gilder in New Street, Hanley and gradually the business grew and his sons were absorbed into it, so that in 1834 the style of the firm was J.Cutts & Sons (White's *Directory*, 1834). In 1842 the firm was described in a Government Report as manufacturers of pottery figures, and as employing 50 workpeople.

John Cutts married a sister of Edward Rowland the Derby painter. She died in 1837 aged 66 years (*Staffordshire Advertiser*, 11 February 1837).

The sons of John Cutts, all of whom except James Cutts were in the business with him, seem to have died before their father.

Rowland B. Cutts (born 1794 died 1841)
John Cutts (born 1804 died 1848)
Lindley Cutts

A daughter of John Cutts, named Ellen, married a crest-engraver named Morris and became mother of Rowland James Morris the sculptor.

John Cutts died 7 June 1851. An announcement in the *Staffordshire Advertiser*, 17 January 1852, described him as a 'china gilder'.

[*Staffordshire Advertiser*, 1837, 1842, 1848, 1851, 1852; *Pottery Mercury*, 1828; *Poll List*, 1841; *Directories*, 1818–51; *Government Report on the Employment of Children*, 1843; *Letters and Documents*, Wedgwood Museum, Barlaston.]

Cyfflé, Paul Louis (born 1724 died 1806)
French modeller, and porcelain and faience manufacturer who founded the Lunéville factory in 1766 but was financially embarrassed about 1777 when he left Lorraine. In 1780 his factory, stock and moulds were sold, the moulds mostly passing to Niderviller. His modelled work included sentimental subjects such as the boy 'sweep' which was adapted for English earthenware made by Ralph Wood (probably by John Voyez).

[Stuart G.Davis, *The Burlington Magazine*, November 1927.]

Cyples Family, Lane End
The Cyples family potted in Market Street, Lane End, in the second half of the eighteenth century and first half of the nineteenth century. Jewitt says the Market Street works was the oldest in Lane End, was coeval with Wedgwoods, and was originally worked by the Cyples family. JOSEPH CYPLES is recorded as manufacturing general earthenware and Egyptian black in 1787. (Bailey's *Directory* of 1783 makes no reference to any potter of this surname). After Joseph's death the factory was worked by MARY CYPLES (who is listed in 1796), and after her by JESSE CYPLES (born 1772 died 1810). In 1805 Jesse Cyples was listed as a maker of Egyptian black. After Jesse Cyples' death, the business was continued by his widow, LYDIA CYPLES (née Steel, born 1775 died 1845) until her death, her sons, RICHARD CYPLES and WILLIAM CYPLES (born 1804 died 1865) assisting her. The business is not listed in 1851. They made china and Egyptian black, (or basaltes).

Jewitt gives no information about the family and merely records that the Cyples family worked the Market Street works, were succeeded by the firm of CYPLES & BARKER, and later by Thomas Barlow. He says also that the High Street Works, Longton, was worked by CYPLES & BALL until taken over in 1842 by Adams & Cooper.

Chaffers records the mark 'I. C Y P L E S' or 'C Y P L E S' incised .The impressed mark 'C Y P L E S' is also known on a basaltes teakettle.

J CYPLES

[*Directories*, 1783–1851; *Poll List*, 1841; *Parish Registers* Stoke-on-Trent, Norton-in-the-Moors, Bucknall; *Staffordshire Advertiser*, 5 January 1811; *Gravestones*, Longton St. Johns.]

Colour plate 6, COALPORT: *see page vii for caption*

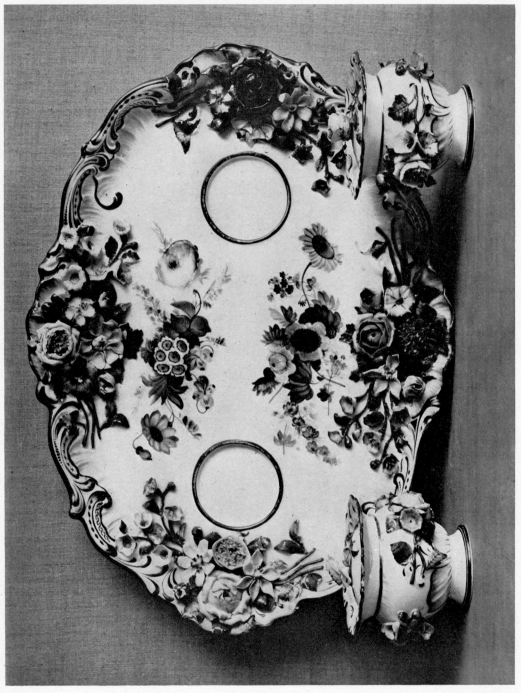

COALPORT tray with pair of toilet-pots and covers, porcelain painted in colours and gilt, c. 1839. Tray, width 12½ inches; pots, height 3 inches.

PLATE 33

COALPORT vase, porcelain *bleu-de-roi* ground with decoration in colours and gilding. Mark, two L's enclosing N, also a torch, in blue enamel. Painted by P. A. Le Quay, middle of nineteenth century. Height 18 inches, width 6¼ inches.

PLATE 34

Top shelf: COALPORT pair of porcelain vases and covers, c. 1850; height 13¼ inches. COALPORT pair of porcelain spill-vases, c. 1830; height 4¼ inches, diameter 2⅜ inches. COALPORT porcelain vase and cover, c. 1865; height 17¼ inches.

2nd shelf: COALPORT tea-pot and sugar basin, 1820; height 6¼ and 4 inches. COALPORT porcelain tazza, c. 1840; width 8½ inches. COALPORT porcelain flower-vase, c. 1830; height 4¾ inches.

3rd shelf: COALPORT plate, c. 1845. Diameter 9¼ inches. porcelain flower-pot, c. 1850; height 6¾ inches, diameter 7½ inches. COALPORT porcelain plate, c. 1850; diameter 9¼ inches.

Bottom shelf: COALPORT porcelain ewer, c. 1840; height 9 inches. COALPORT porcelain flower-vase and cover, c. 1850; height 10 inches, width 12½ inches. COALPORT porcelain ewer, c. 1840; height 9 inches.

PLATE 35

COALPORT

(A) COALPORT mug, probably made at Coalport from Nantgarw receipt, c. 1830; height 4¼ inches.

(B) COALPORT plate, porcelain, painted in enamel colours and gilding. Mark, 'Coalbrookdale' in red; early nineteenth century. Diameter, 9⅛ inches.

PLATE 36

DAVENPORT and other Staffordshire porcelain vases and plates, flower-pots and stands and two jugs, 1810–30.

PLATE 37

Top shelf: DERBY mug, c. 1830; height 4⅜ inches. DERBY porcelain flower-pot and stand, c. 1820; height 7½ inches. DERBY porcelain jug, c. 1830; height 4⅛ inches. *2nd shelf:* DERBY porcelain coffee-cup and saucer, c. 1825; cup height 2½ inches, saucer diameter 5¼ inches. DERBY porcelain tray, c. 1820; width 7 inches, length 9 inches. DERBY tea-cup and saucer, c. 1830; cup height 2¼ inches, saucer diameter 5½ inches. *3rd shelf:* DERBY porcelain tea-cup and saucer, c. 1825; cup height 2⅛ inches, saucer diameter 5½ inches. DERBY porcelain fruit dish, c. 1840; height 2¼ inches, diameter 9⅛ inches. DERBY porcelain tea-cup and saucer, c. 1810; cup height 2⅛ inches, saucer 5⅝ inches. *Bottom shelf:* DERBY porcelain plate, c. 1820; diameter 9¼ inches. DERBY porcelain inkstand, c. 1810; height 5¼ inches. DERBY porcelain plate, c. 1830; diameter 10 inches. DERBY porcelain bell-pulls, c. 1800; length 2¾ inches. DERBY porcelain basket, c. 1840; height 3½ inches.

PLATE 38

(B) DERBY. One of a pair of figures of pedlars selling maps, porcelain painted in colours and gilt. Height 6⅝ inches.

(A) DERBY figure of a musician, porcelain painted in colours, c. 1755. Height 5⅜ inches.

PLATE 39

(A) *Top shelf:* DERBY porcelain tea-cup and saucer, c. 1810; cup height 2⅛ inches, saucer diameter 5½ inches. DERBY scent-bottle, c. 1820; height 4½ inches. DERBY porcelain plate, c. 1840. DERBY counter-box and cover, porcelain, c. 1820; height 5¼ inches. DERBY scent-bottle and stopper, c. 1820; height 4¾ inches. DERBY porcelain coffee-cup and saucer, c. 1820; cup height 2½ inches, saucer diameter 5¼ inches. *Bottom shelf:* DERBY porcelain porringer, cover and stand, c. 1810; porringer height 4⅜ inches, diameter 5¼ inches, stand diameter 7 inches. DERBY porcelain inkstand with three covers, c. 1830; length 11½ inches. DERBY porcelain scent-bottle and stopper, c. 1820; height 4⅛ inches. DERBY porcelain pastille-burner and cover, c. 1820; height 5⅝ inches.

(B) DERBY plate, porcelain, painted in colours, probably by William Duesbury. Mark, a crowned 'D' and crossed batons in purple, c. 1790. Diameter 8 inches.

(C) DERBY cup and saucer, porcelain painted in colours. Probably by J. Banford, c. 1790. Cup height 2½ inches, saucer diameter 5¼ inches.

PLATE 40

(A) DERBY vase, c. 1820. Marks, 'D' under a crown and crossed batons with six dots, also 2 and 58 in blue. Height 8¾ inches.

(B) DERBY ewer, porcelain painted in colours and gilt by William Billingsley, c. 1790. Height 13⅝ inches.

(C) DERBY ewer and basin, porcelain painted in colours and gilt, 1790–95. Basin, height 5⅛ inches, diameter 12 inches. Ewer, height 9½ inches, diameter 8⅛ inches.

PLATE 41

DERBY group of lovers with a clown, porcelain painted in colours, c. 1755. Adapted from a Meissen group modelled by Kaendler, c. 1750. Height 7¼ inches.

PLATE 42

(A) DERBY group, white biscuit porcelain. Mark, a crowned 'D' with a cross, also no: 396 and a triangle. Modelled by W. T. Coffee, late eighteenth century. Height 13¾ inches.

(B) DERBY pair of figures of parrots, porcelain painted in colours, c. 1760. Height 8⅞ inches.

(C) DERBY Mrs. Cibber as a Vivandiere, porcelain figure painted in colours and gilt, c. 1765. Height 8⅝ inches.

(D) DERBY figure, Dr. Syntax landing at Calais. Porcelain painted in colours, c. 1830. Mark, no: 11 incised. Height 4⅝ inches.

PLATE 43

(B) DERBY group of the Virgin Mary, St. Mary Magdalen and St. John the Evangelist, porcelain painted in colours, c. 1760. Height 10½ inches.

(A) DERBY group, porcelain. Virgins distressing Cupid. From a model by J. J. Spengler after Angelica Kauffmann, c. 1795. Height 14 inches.

PLATE 44

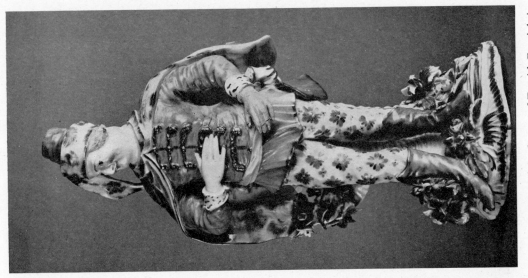

(B) DERBY porcelain figure of David Garrick in the character of Tancred in Thomson's 'Tancred and Sigismunda', c. 1760. Height 8⅞ inches.

(A) DERBY candelabrum, porcelain painted in colours and gilt, 2nd quarter of the nineteenth century. Marks, crossed swords in underglaze blue and no: 280 incised. Height 8¼ inches.

PLATE 45

DEVON posset-pot, reddish earthenware covered with white slip under a yellow glaze. Probably 18th century. Height 8⅛ inches.

PLATE 46

(A) FULHAM figure of Neptune, brown salt-glazed stoneware by John Dwight, c. 1680. Height 12¼ inches.

(B) FULHAM, a lady as 'Flora', stoneware figure by John Dwight. Height 11¾ inches. *(British Museum)*.

(C) FULHAM bust probably of Charles II, white salt-glazed stoneware, by John Dwight, c. 1680. Height 7 inches.

(D) FULHAM, Prince Rupert. Stoneware bust by John Dwight of Fulham. *(British Museum)*.

PLATE 47

(B) FULHAM mug, stoneware, made by John Dwight, mounted with a silver rim on which is engraved 'SS' and date 1682. Height 2¾ inches.

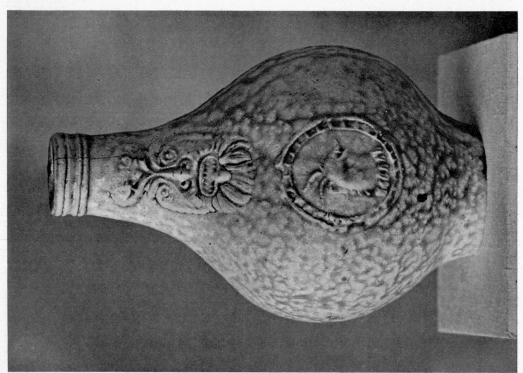

(A) FULHAM bottle, made by John Dwight, yellow-brown salt-glazed stoneware, c. 1680. Height 8½ inches.

PLATE 48

D

Dakin, Thomas, Shelton, Staffordshire

Slipware potter, Shelton; Stoke parish registers under Baptisms, 1710 March 3, records 'Tho. Dakin, f. Tho. & Maiae, de Shelton' A slipware posset-pot in the Victoria and Albert Museum is inscribed TOMAS DAKIN MADE THIS CUP FOR MARY SCULL THARP 1710 HER FRIEND. (Dakin is an early rendering of Deakin).

Dale, John, Burslem, Staffordshire

Engraver and pottery figure maker, Burslem, whose mark,

J.DALE   impressed
BURSLEM

occurs on figures representing the four elements (in the Victoria and Albert Museum) and on a bust of John Wesley. The *Pottery Mercury*, 23 1825, recorded his marriage to Sarah Walker at Astbury Church, Cheshire.

[Reginald G.Haggar, *Staffordshire Chimney Ornaments,* 1955.]

Dale, William, Hanley

Toy and ornament manufacturer, Marsh Street, Hanley, 1851.

Dalmazzoni, Angelo, Rome

Responsible for Wedgwood bas-relief of a 'Roman Procession' and 'The Nereides', etc. Worked in Rome for Wedgwood from 1787 until 1795.

[E.Meteyard, *Life of Josiah Wedgwood,* 1865–1866; W. Mankowitz, *Wedgwood,* 1953.]

D'Alva bottles

Bellarmines; named from Fernando Alvarez de Toledo, Duke of Alva (1508–1583), responsible for a reign of terror in the Netherlands 1567–1573.

[R.Plot, *Natural History of Oxfordshire,* 2nd ed. 1705.]

Dancing hours

One of a pair of blue-and-white jasper plaques, $18^3/_8$ inches long by $5^5/_8$ high, with relief decoration of dancing figures, originally modelled by John Flaxman in the nude, 1775. Draperies were added by William Hackwood.

There is a fine jasper tablet of this subject in the Jordan collection, Detroit, marked Wedgwood & Bentley.

[W. Mankowitz, *Wedgwood,* 1953.]

Daniel family, North Staffordshire

The Daniel family was among the oldest connected with the pottery industry of North Staffordshire and made many important contributions to its development, namely:

1. The introduction of plaster of paris moulds by Ralph Daniel, c.1745.
2. The development of on-glaze enamelling c.1760 by the Daniel family in Hot Lane.
3. The use of raised gilding at Spode's factory in 1802 by Henry Daniel.
4. The introduction of gold lustre effects by James Daniel of Pleasant Row, Stoke-on-Trent.
5. Groundlaying of colour by Henry Daniel in 1826.

The first specific reference to a potter of this name occurs in the Tunstall Court Rolls in 1616. 'Richard Middleton demises to Thomas Danyell of Burselem senior, potter, a pasture called Brownehills and another pasture called The Hill in Burslem containing three acres with right to dig clay.' Thomas Daniel's son, also called Thomas, was listed as an inhabitant of Burslem in 1671 *(Tunstall Court Rolls, Transactions N.Staffs Field Club).* He was probably the potter whose impressed mark, a circle with the name THOMAS DANIEL, was found on a butter

Colour plate 7, DERBY: *see page vii for caption*

pot excavated in Burslem in 1929.

Josiah Wedgwood's MS list of potters in Burslem in 1710–15 included a Robert Daniel who made black and mottled wares at the Hole House, and Ralph Daniel of Hot Lane or Co-bridge, who was probably the potter who introduced plaster of Paris moulds into the potteries about 1745.

Other members of this family were potting later in the eighteenth century. John Daniel, a salt-glaze potter who signed the agreement concerning selling prices in 1770; another potter of the same name became manager of Hollins, Warburton, Daniel & Co., New Hall; Thomas Daniel made earthenware in Burslem from 1770–87 or later; and a Timothy Daniel who was listed as a manufacturer of cream-coloured and red earthenware. Thomas and Timothy Daniel were brothers of Walter Daniel, whom see.

[*Directories*: S. Shaw, *History of the Staffordshire Potteries*, 1829; G. E. Stringer, *New Hall Porcelain*, 1949; *Transactions, N. Staffs. Field Club*.]

Daniel, Henry and Richard, Shelton and Stoke

Henry Daniel (born 1765 died 1841) was the son of Thomas Daniel, potter (who had been an apprentice of Warner Edwards, pioneer enameller and potter). He started as an enameller of pottery and porcelain and is recorded as having introduced the technique of raised gilding at Spode's factory in 1802. Elsewhere he is described as Spode's chief enameller. Shortly afterwards he was in partnership with John Brown in a concern as 'Potters, Enamellers and Gilders, Stoke and Shelton', which was dissolved 4 June 1806 (*Staffordshire Advertiser*, 14 June 1806). It is not known precisely when the firm of H. & R. Daniel came into existence, but factories for the production of high quality china in Shelton and Stoke existed for many years, the former in 1834 being under the style of Henry Daniel & Co., the latter H. & R. Daniel. The Shelton business was in Bedford Row; the Stoke at London Road. A prosperous business was developed, based largely upon Henry Daniel's 'very superior talents in the embellishment of porcelain' (obit. *Staffordshire Advertiser*, 17 April 1841). Henry Daniel introduced the highly dangerous process of groundlaying in 1826, and thereby made possible richer ground colours for the gilders (Shaw, *History of the Staffordshire Potteries*, 1829). The Prince and Princess Borghese, who were staying at Alton Abbey, revisited the factory, 13 September 1840, and ordered extensive services to be decorated *en suite* with views of Alton and scenes of their estates in Rome, Tuscany and Paris. (*Staffordshire Advertiser*, 15 September 1840). A Government visitor to the factory at the time when Henry Daniel was a very old man said that he employed 109 men and boys and 131 women and girls. Although the factory was celebrated and visited by important patrons 'the rooms and the buildings' were described as 'old and dilapidated, small, close, dirty, mostly damp and uncomfortable', and 'never or rarely whitewashed' (*Government Report on the Employment of Children in Factories*, 1842–43).

A relative named Thomas Daniel managed the Stoke and Shelton factories for a time, but he seems to have been a wanderer and got into financial difficulties. A notice concerning insolvent debtors describes him as a glass and china dealer and auctioneer in Nottingham and Winthorpe as well as a pottery manager in North Staffordshire (*Staffordshire Advertiser*, 27 February and 27 March 1841).

Henry Daniel died in 1841 and the business was carried on in Stoke (the Shelton company was apparently wound up) by his son Richard Daniel until 1851 or later. After the failure of this business Richard Daniel became manager of the 'Hill Pottery Co. late S. Alcock & Co. Burslem (L. Jewitt, *Ceramic Art in Great Britain*, 1878).

Daniel, John (born 1756 died 1821)

Son of Ralph Daniel; partner and manager of the firm of Hollins, Warburton, Daniel & Co., New Hall, Shelton, Staffordshire. When he died 'his mortal remains were conveyed in a hearse... to Endon... and interred in a piece of ground at the village belonging to him... he was committed to the "House appointed for all living" without the observance of the offices of religion in any shape, conformably with the opinions of the Free Thinkers to which it is understood he had long been a disciple'.

[*Staffordshire Advertiser*, 27 January 1821; G. E. Stringer, *New Hall Porcelain*, 1949.]

Daniel, Ralph, Cobridge, Staffordshire

Ralph Daniel of Cobridge was said to have introduced from France c.1745 casting from plaster of paris moulds.

Daniel, Walter (born 1749 died 1818)

Walter Daniel was the son of Thomas and Mary Daniel and member of a family long famous in Staffordshire pottery history. He is recorded as manufacturing cream-coloured earthenware and red pottery in Burslem during the closing decades of the eighteenth century (Bailey's *Directory*, 1783, *Tunnicliff's Survey*, 1787). He is stated to have built his factory at Newport in 1793 and is known to have taken his sons into the business which traded as Walter Daniel & Sons until 1801 when the partnership was dissolved. Walter Daniel, junior, carried on under the style Walter Daniel junior & Company (*Staffordshire Advertiser*, 31 October 1801). The partners in the business were Walter Daniel and William Daniel. This business did not last long and in 1804 the house and factory at Newport, Burslem, were offered for sale, (*Staffordshire Advertiser*, 25 February, 1804). Walter Daniel senior retired to Hassall Hall where died 28 July 1818. (*Gravestone*, St John's Churchyard, Burslem.)
[*Directories*.]

Daniell, London

Nineteenth century dealer's mark on Coalport and other fine porcelains.

Davenport family, Longport, Staffordshire

John Davenport, who had served his apprenticeship to Thomas Wolfe at Stoke and worked in partnership with him as a manufacturer of china at the Islington Works, Liverpool, took over Brindley's factory at Longport in 1793. In 1801 he added glass manufacture to his other interests. He retired about 1830, the business being continued by his sons, Henry Davenport and William Davenport who enlarged and added to the factory buildings. When Henry Da-

venport died, the style of the business changed to W. Davenport & Co. and so it passed eventually, when William died, to his son Henry in 1869, who continued until its closure in 1882.

MARKS

DAVENPORT   DAVENPORT
LONGPORT   LONGPORT
STAFFORDSHIRE

Printed

ARTISTS

Cristall, Joshua. Water colour painter who is said to have served his time here.

Cutts, James. Designed patterns for Davenport.

Fletcher, W. Figure painter.

Holland, James. (1799–1870) Water colour painter stated to have been apprenticed to Davenports.

Marsh, James. Modeller.

Mountford, Jesse. Landscape painter.

Slater, William. (1784–1864) Painter.

Slater, William. (1807–1865) Designer 1833–1865.

Steele, Edwin. Painter of flowers in the Rockingham style.

Steele, Thomas. Fruit painter.

WORK

In the earlier years of the firm earthenware only was made including cream-coloured, painted, and transfer-printed wares. Openwork rims are said to have been typical. Good blue-printed earthenware was made and 'flown' blue was extensively used. Wares painted with designs in a peasant style were popular in the period 1815–1835. Monochrome painted landscapes over a coloured ground strike a more distinctive note. Stone china with heavy 'sumptuous' Imari decorations in colour and gold followed the vogue of the 1830s.

China (which was made from the early years of the nineteenth century) was mostly derivative in character. The paste varied from a translucent and white body reminiscent of Nantgarw to something much more grey in tone. New Hall, or what might be called the 'cottage' style of decoration, was used in the early days, but with an influx of Derby artists, heavier ornate wares with lavish gilding and colouring in the Derby styles became general. 'Pictorial' porcelain was characteristic of the factory's output in the mid-nineteenth century, with elaborate topographical landscapes, or still-life pictures.
Plate 37.
[L. Jewitt, *Ceramic Art of Great Britain*, 1878.]

Davis, William (died 1783), Worcester

Apothecary, chief 'arcanist', first manager, and a large subscriber to the original 'Worcester Tonquin Manufacture'.

Dawson, John, Sunderland

Early nineteenth century manufacturer of pottery table-ware, sometimes decorated with coloured transfers and pink lustre. 'D A W-S O N' is found as an impressed mark.

Day, Joseph

A plaque modelled with two lions in relief in the Ernest Allman collection is incised: Joseph Day.

A similar plaque is illustrated in R. Nicholl's *Ten Generations of a Potting Family* (1932) incised in the paste
WILLIAM ADAMS, STOKE, 1818

Deakin & Son, Lane End

Manufacturers of china, earthenware, stone china and pottery figures at Waterloo, Stafford Street, from 1834 until 1851.

Decarle, R.B, Staffordshire

Chaffers refers to this name, found on highly modelled brown stoneware jugs.

Delamain, Henry (died 1757)

Delftware potter at Dublin from 1753 who introduced the use of coal for firing his wares. After his death Mrs Delamain continued the business until her death in 1760. Her executors carried on until 1763.
[L. Jewitt, *Ceramic Art of Great Britain*, 1878.]

Delftware

Earthenware coated with a lead-glaze made opaque by the addition of tin ashes, named after the town of Delft in Holland which, in the seventeenth century, became an important centre for the manufacture of this type of pottery. It was, of course, manufactured in England much earlier. The industry in fact appears to have been started in Norwich in 1567 by Jasper Andries, and continued there by other potters until 1696 or later. The chief centres of delftware manufacture were:

London	from 1571	Glasgow	from 1748
Bristol	from c.1650	Dublin	from 1737
Liverpool	from 1710	Limerick	from 1761

[F. H. Garner, *English Delftware*, 1948.]

De Morgan, William Frend (born 1839 died 1917), Fulham, Middlesex

Potter and novelist. Studied at Royal Academy. From 1864 until 1869 engaged on stained glass, but from 1872 commenced to reproduce Syrian pottery of the sixteenth and seventeenth centuries at 40 Fitzroy Square, London. Later he removed to the Orange House, Cheyne Row, Chelsea where he rediscovered the process of reduced lustre decoration. He took land and built workshops at Merton Abbey, Surrey, in 1882 where he worked until 1888. From 1888 until 1898 he was in partnership with Halsey Ricardo at Sands End Pottery, Fulham, and from 1898 until 1907 when he retired from potting, with Frank Iles and Charles and Fred Passenger. After his retirement the Passengers continued a pot-decorating trade in Brompton Road until 1911.

ARTISTS

Designers **William de Morgan**
             Halsey Ricardo
             Dr Reginald Thompson
Painters: Eight women and seven men were
employed. The best known, whose initials appear
on their work, were:

             Joe Juster
             Charles Passenger
             Fred Passenger

MARKS

Painted

Painted   Impressed

Impressed

WORK

De Morgan pottery is characterised by rich surface
decoration and skilful execution and is perhaps
the outstanding ceramic illustration of the
influence of William Morris and the Arts and
Crafts movement. The tile decoration of the
walls of the Bishop Selwyn mortuary chapel
in Lichfield Cathedral is a good example of his
public work.
Plate 64 B.
[A.M.W. Stirling, *William de Morgan and his Wife*, 1922;
May Morris in *The Burlington Magazine*, Vol. 31, 1917;
Reginald Blunt, *The Wonderful Village*, 1918; Victoria &
Albert Museum, *Catalogue of Works by William de Morgan*,
1921.]

Denby, near Derby

The Denby Pottery, seven miles from Derby
was commenced by a man named Jager in 1809,
but passed into the hands of Joseph Bourne in
1812 whose descendants have continued the
business. The salt-glazed stonewares manufactured
here included Reform Spirit flasks, hunting
jugs with relief ornament and other decorative
wares, as well as stonewares for domestic
requirements.
    See under BOURNE AND SON.
Plate 159 B.
[L. Jewitt, *Ceramic Art of Great Britain*, 1878.]

Dendritic

Having tree-like markings as on Mocha ware.

Derby, Porcelain manufactory

HISTORY AND OWNERS

The date when porcelain was first made in Derby is not certainly known. André Planché was making it by 1751 probably at Cockpit Hill, and Duesbury is known to have decorated in London 'Darby' or 'Darbyshire figures'. A cream jug dated 1750 is believed to be the earliest dated specimen.

By 1756 a flourishing business had been built up and the enameller William Duesbury and John Heath had become proprietors. In 1770 the Chelsea factory was acquired.

Heath failed financially in 1779 and in consequence Duesbury became sole owner. He died in 1786, his son of the same name continuing the factory until his death in 1796. In 1795 he had taken as partner Michael Kean who married his widow, and remained in control until 1811.

The works were bought in 1811 by Robert Bloor. He became insane in 1826, and the factory was managed until its closure in 1848 by James Thomason and Thomas Clarke.

The present Royal Crown Derby Porcelain Company was formed in 1876.

MARKS

| 1750 | 1780 | 1795 | 1830 |

Chelsea Derby

| 1760 | 1770-80 | 1784 | 1784-1810 |

| 1795-6 | | Imitation |

ARTISTS

William Duesbury	painter and enameller
John Bacon	modeller
Zachariah Boreman	landscape painter
Nicolas Gauron	
Edward Withers	flower painter
Richard Askew	painter of figure subjects
J. J. Spengler (or Spangler)	modeller
Pierre Stephan	modeller
William Coffee	modeller
George Cocker	modeller
Edward Keys	modeller
Samuel Keys	modeller
John Whitaker	foreman modeller 1830–1847
Samuel Keys, sen.	gilder
William Billingsley	painter of naturalistic flowers
William Pegg	painter of botanical flowers
Thomas Hill	landscape painter
James Banford	painter of figure subjects
John Brewer	landscape painter
Robert Brewer	landscape painter
George Complin	fruit and bird painter
Cuthbert Lawton	painter
William Longdon	painter of 'Chantilly Sprigs'
Thomas Steele	painter of fruit
Edwin Steele	painter
Horatio Steele	painter
Leonard Lead	painter of flowers
Moses Webster	painter of flowers
George Robertson	landscape painter
Jesse Mountford	landscape painter
Daniel Lucas	landscape painter
William Corden	painter
Fidele Duvivier	painter

Extended lists are given by John Haslem and Llewellyn Jewitt

WORK AND CHARACTERISTICS

The paste of the earliest phase of Derby porcelain was nonphosphatic, and the wares produced rather heavy and of a creamy warm white. Some cream jugs identified by date and inscription, correspond to the 'goat-and-bee' jugs of Chelsea. Lively rhythmical Chinese figure groups, figures representing 'Old Age' and 'The Seasons', and models of boars and goats contrast with the stiffly posed florid later Derby types. The next phase of Derby was characterized by the use of pale delicate colours, large flat flowers and scrolls picked out in colour or mounds with flowery reliefs. The figures themselves were generally of Meissen origin, Derby setting up claims to be 'the second Dresden'. At this period figures seemed to have had precedence over useful wares, upon which the styles of the 'Cotton Stalk' painter (Meissen sprays with thread-like stems) and the 'Moth' painter, (birds, fruit, flowers, landscapes with one or two large moths) may be noted.

The third phase of Derby is distinguishable by the dirty patches (three or four) underneath the wares caused by the wads of clay upon which they were rested during firing. Wares of this kind are referred to frequently as belonging to the 'Patch' family. Figures become more sophisticated and static, rather larger in size, and tend to over-elaboration. The lissom-limbed 'Leda and the Swan' of this period is an outstanding work by an anonymous modeller of tall graceful figures. More conventional are the models of Shakespeare after Scheemakers.

Useful wares were sometimes decorated with blue-and-white Chinese landscapes upon plates with lattice borders with floral intersections. Other Chinese decorations were in crimson and gold over underglaze blue. Transfer-printing was rarely used.

More importance seems to have been attached to useful wares in the Chelsea-Derby period. A creamy bone paste was used, set off by vigorous shapes, neo-classic in form, and decorations of aristocratic severity, of urns and swags.

Figure groups took on a note of sentiment and tended to fussiness in the leafy backgrounds, The dominant influence was Sèvres. Biscuit-porcelain figures simulating marble statuary are typical of the Neo-classic style about 1780.

Ground colours used at Derby did not achieve the beauty of those of Chelsea, but ambitious painting was done by the notable decorators. The floral convention of Withers contrasted the fashionable naturalistic style initiated by Billingsley and the more formal single blooms of Pegg. Figure painting was done on straight-sided coffee cans intended for display rather than for use. Zachariah Boreman and 'Jockey' Hill executed landscapes in a style carried forward into the early nineteenth century by George Robertson and Jesse Mountford, and the two drawing masters, the brothers Brewer.

Showy 'Japans' became popular in the Bloor period with heavy colour and lavish gilding. The fruit and flower painting of the Steeles reached a hard high standard of accomplischment but lacked sensibility. Figures were re-issued from earlier moulds.

Examples in the Victoria and Albert Museum, London; British Museum, London; Metropolitan Museum of Art, New York and the Art Institute of Chicago.
Colour plate 5, and 8 and Plates 29–32 and 38–45 and 160B.

[John Haslem, *Old Derby China Factory*, 1876; Frank Hurlbutt, *Old Derby Porcelain and its Artist Workmen*, 1925; Mrs D.MacAlister, 'The early Work of Planché and Duesbury', *Trans. English Porcelain Circle*, 1929; W.B.Honey, *Old English Porcelain*, 1928; new ed. 1948.]

Derbyshire

Extensive manufactures of pottery and porcelain have flourished in Derbyshire including slipwares at Bolsover and Tickenhall; brown salt-glazed stonewares at Chesterfield, Brampton, Denby, Codnor Park and Belper; cream-colour of Staffordshire type at Cockpit Hill; and porcelain at Derby.

The clay of Crich in Derbyshire (from which the name 'Crouch' ware is probably derived) was used not only by Derbyshire potters but also by those of Nottingham and Staffordshire.

[S.Shaw, *History of the Staffordshire Potteries*, 1829; J.Aiken, *A Description of the country...round Manchester*, 1795; Stephen Glover, *The History, Gazetteer and Directory of...Derby*, 1829; S.Lewis, *A Topographical Dictionary of England*, 7th Edition 1848.]

Devonshire

Several important slipware potteries existed in North Devon working from the early seventeenth century until the end of the Victorian era, notably at Barnstable and Bideford, exploiting the resources of the Fremington clay beds.

Jugs and other presentation wares decorated in *sgraffiato* style with mariner's compasses, Royal arms, country scenes, or birds and foliage are typical. They may be distinguished by the coil (sometimes multiple coils) at the base of the handle and the crude zig-zag or chevron incised round the neck. Trailed slip decoration was also used.

Crude country pottery made at Honiton gave place in the twentieth century to 'art' pottery. At Bovey, pottery of Staffordshire type was, and is made extensively. Important terra cotta works flourished at Watcombe near Torquay in the second half of the nineteenth century.

Examples of Devonshire slipware may be seen in Museums at Exeter and Stoke-on-Trent, and the Fitzwilliam Museum, Cambridge. *Plate 46*.

[Charbonnier, 'Notes on North Devon Pottery,' *Transactions, Devonshire Association*, 1906; L. Jewitt, *Ceramic Art of Great Britain*, 1878.]

Devonshire clay

West country clays are generally stated to have been first used in the Staffordshire Potteries from about 1720. John Astbury is alleged to have been responsible for their introduction. North Devonshire clay was being exported as far as Chester in small quantities as early as 1691 but was evidently intended for use by local pipe-makers (see under Chester). This trade grew and in 1730 three times the quantity was sent to Chester and (while still a relatively small amount) it is reasonable to assume that some of it was sent overland to the potteries of North Staffordshire. The Bideford (N. Devon) export trade declined after about 1730 with the rise of the South Devonshire Clay business from the Port of Exeter (which included Teignmouth). This became a dominant factor in the mid-eighteenth century after road improvements and canal transport made possible the use of the Port of Liverpool for the reception of cargoes. Thus we notice a steady rise in the number of cargoes of ball clay sent to Liverpool from South Devon between 1741 when there were only two until 1770 when they numbered 29. The year 1770 was a year of slump as we know from Wedgwood's correspondence. It was reflected in the number of cargoes shipped to Liverpool in 1772, which was only five. A swift and steady rise within the next thirteen years increased its total to 77. This trade made possible the cream-coloured earthenware body for which Staffordshire became famous. The china clay deposits of South Devon were not worked until the 1830's.

[*Port Books*, Bideford and Exeter (Public Record Office), quoted in *Transactions Devonshire Association*; W.G. Hoskins, *Devon*, 1954.]

Dewsbury, David (flourished 1870-1919)

Ceramic artist, who was trained at Burslem from 1872 and worked at Doultons from 1889 until 1919 as a flower painter on porcelain, specializing in orchids which he rendered in a free 'painterly' style.

[J.Adams, 'Potters Parade' in *Pottery and Glass*, March 1950.]

Dicker, Sussex

Slip-decorated red earthenware of a somewhat rude type was made at this centre, in the nineteenth century. The workshops were continued in operation until comparatively recent times.

'DICKER WARE'

Dillon, Francis and Nicholas, Cobridge

Francis and Nicholas Dillon are recorded as manufacturing earthenware at Cobridge in 1818, but the partnership was dissolved, 1 November 1825 (*Staffordshire Advertiser*, 24 November 1832). Apparently they afterwards engaged with John Blackwell of the Grange in a similar manufactory but this was also dissolved, 28 February, 1828 (*Staffordshire Advertiser*, 24 November 1832). Subsequently Francis Dillon continued on his own account until 1843 when his fixtures and materials were sold (*Staffordshire Advertiser*, 28 January 1843).

Dillwyn, Lewis Weston

Botanist and porcelain manufacturer; chief proprietor of the Cambrian Pottery at Swansea from 1802 until 1836; fellow of the Linnaean Society and author of books on plants and shells, including *The British Conferva*, and with Dawson Turner of *The Botanist's Guide through England and Wales*; member of Parliament for Glamorganshire 1832 to 1835. A notebook in the handwriting of L.W.Dillwyn, containing recipes for porcelain bodies and glazes dated 1815-1817 was presented to the Victoria and Albert Museum Library in 1920, reproduced in H.Eccles and B.Rackham, *Analysed Specimens of English Porcelain*, 1922.

Dimmock & Co, Hanley

This firm, first of all as Thomas Dimmock & Co. and later as John Dimmock & Co., flourished throughout the major part of the nineteenth century. In 1842 it was working two important factories in Hanley and a gilding and enamelling workshop in Shelton near the 'King's Head' Tavern (opposite Shelton Church and now demolished). Good quality earthenware was made. The following marks were used:

'Dipped' Pottery

This class of wares seems to have been first made in Fenton by Thomas Heath from about 1750. In the nineteenth century its manufacture was widespread within and outside the Staffordshire Potteries. William Evans (writing in 1846) described three sub-divisions of 'dipped' pottery: 1. marbled slipware, 2. 'Mocha' and 3. banded wares. The more important manufacturers were:

William Adams	Tunstall
Copeland & Garrett	Stoke
John Tams	Longton
Malings	Newcastle-on-Tyne
J. & R. Riley	Burslem
Broadhurst	Fenton
Greens	Church Gresly
William Chambers	Llanelly

[Reginald G.Haggar, *Concise Encyclopaedia of Antiques*, 1955; W.Evans, *Art and History of the Potting Business*, 1846.]

'Dishevelled Birds', Painter of

An artist employed by James Giles whose touch is recognisable on Worcester, Longton Hall, Bow and Plymouth porcelain, and who evidently decorated a vast quantity and variety of wares. He may have been James Giles himself.

[W.B.Honey, *Transactions, English Ceramic Circle*, 1937; *Old English Porcelain*, 1928, new ed. 1948; J.L.Dixon, *English Porcelain of the 18th Century*, 1952.]

Distressed Mother, The

Memorial to Elizabeth Warren in Westminster Abbey by Sir Richard Westmacott R.A. (1816), copied in parian by Minton & Co. for 'Felix Summerly Art Manufactures'.

[Sir Henry Cole, *Fifty Years of Public Work*, 1884.]

Doctor Syntax

The *Tours of Doctor Syntax in Search of the Picturesque* was written by William Combe (1741–1823) and illustrated by Thomas Rowlandson, first issued in the *Poetical Magazine* from 1809 and separately published in 1812. It was followed in 1820 by Dr. Syntax *In Search of Consolation*, and in 1821 by Dr Syntax *In Search of a Wife*. These appear to have been a burlesque upon the works of the Rev. William Gilpin (1724–1804) whose numerous writings on the Picturesque from 1768 until the posthumous work of 1809 did much to formulate eighteenth century English taste in scenic appreciation. Rowlandson's illustrations were the inspiration of 27 scenes transfer-printed in blue underglaze on earthenware made by James and Ralph Clews, of Cobridge; of painted decoration of a series of Chamberlain Worcester jugs; and of Staffordshire pottery figures of the Walton Salt type.

Dodson, Richard, Derby

Bird painter at the Derby factory after 1810, whose work was said by Haslem to be 'somewhat heavy in colour'.

[John Haslem, *Old Derby China Factory*, 1876.]

Dogs

These have always been popular in earthenware and porcelain. Salt-glazed pug dogs were made, mid-eighteenth century, and repeated in porcelain of reputed Longton Hall manufacture, (marked specimens in Hanley Museum, Stoke-on-Trent). They also occur in Chelsea (sometimes as miniature scent-bottles) and Derby porcelain of the eighteenth century.

Dogs of various kinds and sizes were commonly made in the nineteenth century particularly at Swinton. 'China' dogs usually of the Spaniel type were made as flat-back chimney ornaments, sometimes extremely large in size, by Sampson Smith, Kent, Dudson, and others in common Staffordshire earthenware from 1840 until 1914. Many figures from old moulds of this type are being made today.

Donaldson, John (born 1737 died 1801)
Enameller and miniaturist

John Donaldson was born in Edinburgh, and from an early age showed ability as a portraitist. When he came to London he became a member of the Incorporated Society of Artists and executed a considerable number of commissions as a miniaturist. In 1760 he was living in London. James Boswell, who knew him in Edinburgh, described him as a 'speculative being (who) must forsooth controvert established systems', who 'defended adultery' and 'opposed revealed religion'. He became one of the most notable outside porcelain decorators, executing some work for Sprimont at Chelsea, and some extremely fine classical pictures on Worcester porcelain about 1770. High prices have been paid for his authentic work. A set of vases belonging to the Worcester Works Museum are painted with 'Leda and the Swan', 'The Birth of Bacchus' and 'Europa and the Bull', one of which is signed in monogram. He exhibited at the Royal Academy and the Free Society, 1761–1791.

[S. Redgrave, *Dictionary of Artists of the English School*, 2nd ed. 1878; R.L.Hobson, *Worcester Porcelain*, 1910; F.A.Barrett, *Worcester Porcelain*, 1953; *Boswell's London Journal, 1762–1763*, 1950.]

Donovan, James, and Son, Dublin

Outside enamellers whose establishment was in Poolbeg Street, Dublin. Jewitt states that they purchased 'both English and Continental white wares' for decoration. Their mark 'DONOVAN' or 'Donovan Dublin' occurs on wares decorated in their workshop. Examples may be seen in the British, and Victoria and Albert Museums.
[L. Jewitt, *Ceramic Art of Great Britain*, 1878.]

Don Pottery, Swinton, Yorkshire

John Green manager of Swinton Old Pottery started this factory c.1790, which was probably rebuilt in 1800–1801. In 1807 the firm was known as Greens, Clark & Co., and in 1822 as John William Green & Co. with perhaps Sam-

Painted	Impressed

Transfer-printed

muel T. Lunn as manager. It remained with the Greens until the late 1830's when Samuel Barker of Mexborough took over. It traded from 1852 until 1893 when it was finally closed as Samuel Barker and Son. It was a large factory employing between 200 and 300 workmen.

WORK

Good quality white and cream-coloured earthenware was manufactured, green glazed wares, and much painted and transfer-printed pottery, as well as Egyptian black and other stonewares. About 1812 some china of good quality is said to have been made.

An engraved pattern book similar to that of Leeds was issued.

[L. Jewitt, *Ceramic Art of Great Britain*, 1878; A. Hurst, *Catalogue of the Boynton Collection of Yorkshire Pottery*, 1922.]

Dontil

A Worcester porcelain painter mentioned by Binns.

[R. W. Binns, *A Century of Potting in the City of Worcester*, 1865.]

Donyat, Somerset

An extensive slipware industry flourished here from the seventeenth century and continued well into Victorian times. Three potworks were working in 1848. Earlier specimens which include inscribed mugs, fuddling-cups with intertwined handles, puzzle jugs, pitchers, money boxes and the usual useful farmhouse crockery were vigorously made and attractive in appearance. The *sgraffiato* technique of decoration was used. The lead glaze was freely spattered with copper oxide giving the wares a pleasantly irregular appearance. Dated examples are not uncommon.

Examples in Taunton and Stoke-on-Trent Museums and Fitzwilliam Museum, Cambridge.

Door Furniture

Finger plates, key escutcheons, knobs, bell pulls. These were made by Wedgwood, Turner and others in the eighteenth century. The manufacture of door furniture became a specialised branch of the pottery industry in mid-Victorian times. In 1875 MacIntyre & Co., Washington Works, Burslem and Gaskell, Son & Co, Crown Works, Burslem specialised in this field. (Keate's *Gazetteer*, 1875), William Wood and Co. made door furniture 1889.

Dorset Clay

Poole Clay, that is clay shipped from Poole Harbour, but raised in the area surrounding Wareham in Dorset is generally known in Staffordshire as blue clay. It is not known when it was first worked. An Order in Council (1666), arising out of a dispute between Wareham and Poole, directed that no dues were to be paid on tobacco-pipe clay, which term was again used in an Act of Parliament obtained at the instigation of Poole in 1756.

It was the chief article of export from the quay at Wareham in the 1770's, being dug up at Norden, Heneger Hill and Arne Hill, and exported to London, Hull, Liverpool, Glasgow, and the more considerable part to Staffordshire or to Selby for the Leeds potteries. Some 10,000 tons were exported annually in 1796, the price having dropped from 50s. to about 14s. or 15s. per ton. In 1892, 80, 103 tons were sent from Poole.

[J. Hutchins, *History of Dorsetshire*, 1774, 1796.]

Dossie, Robert

The alleged author of an anonymous treatise entitled *The Handmaid of the Arts* in which the use of calcined bones in porcelain manufacture was described.

Doulton, Lambeth and Burslem

HISTORY

John Doulton (born 1793 died 1873) was a skilled thrower who served his time at the Fulham factory. In 1815 with John Watts he acquired an interest in a potworks in Vauxhall Walk, Lambeth, where they made bottles, mugs and jugs in salt-glazed stoneware with relief decorations of topers, windmills, hunting scenes, etc. The firm was known as Doulton & Watts and its business prospered. In 1820 the partners became owners of the factory and in 1826 moved to more spacious premises in Lambeth High Street.

The history of the Doulton business is one of continuous response to social and economic pressures and adaptation to circumstances. Between 1820 and 1860 new factories were built to answer the requirements of the chemical industry; the demand for salt-glazed drainpipes which resulted from agitation for healthier living and sanitation; and the demand for insulators, stoneware filters and terra cotta statuary and vases. The Reform Flasks, with demi-effigies of prominent politicians were a popular feature following the Reform Bill of 1832.

John Watts retired from the business in 1854 and the firm became known henceforth as Doulton & Co.

The closing years of John Doulton's life (he died at the age of 80 in 1873) saw the development of an important decorative art department at Lambeth as the result of Henry Doulton's association with Lambeth School of Art and its master, John Sparkes. Decorative stonewares of individual quality were made from 1870 onwards.

In 1877 the earthenware factory of Pinder, Bourne & Co., Burslem, was acquired for the production of good class domestic pottery, and in 1884 a new wing was added to it for the manufacture of bone china. This factory soon acquired a reputation and made distinctive contributions in the field of ceramic painting and decorative pottery and porcelain.

The subsequent history of Doultons is one of constant development; of the acquisition of fresh factories for special purposes; of plant renewal and factory rebuilding; and finally of reorganisation and regrouping in face of contemporary economic problems.

MARKS

DOULTON LAMBETH

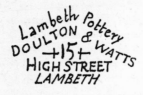

Before 1836

DOULTON ARTISTS (Lambeth)

Barlow, Arthur Bolton 1871–1878	Vegetable forms of décor	
Barlow, Florence c.1873	Animal decorations	
Barlow, Hannah Bolton c.1870	Incised animal décor	
Broad, John 1873–1919	Figure modeller	
Butler, Frank A. c.1873	(deaf and dumb)	
Davis, Louisa c.1873		
Dunn, W.E. c.1873		
Eyre, John c.1885		
Edwards, Louisa E. c.1873		

Eggleton, Frank	1935
Harradine, L.	Modeller of Dickens subjects
Huskisson, W.	c.1878 Decorator
Hoy-Bohrer, Agnete	c.1953
Huggins, Vera	1932–1950

Hastings, W.G.	c.1880
Lee, Francis E.	c.1875
Lupton, Edith D.	c.1879
Marshall, Mark Villars	1876–1912 Figure modeller & decorator
Mitchell, Mary	c.1874
Parker, William	c.1880
Pearce, Arthur E.	1873
Pope, Frank C.	1880–1923 Modeller
Roberts, Florence C.	c.1879
Rowe, William	c.1883
Simmance, Elise	c.1873
Tabor, George Hugo	c.1878
Thompson, Margaret E.	1900
Simeon, Henry	1896
Tinwith, George	1867–1903 Modeller
Wilson, Edgar W.	

DOULTON ARTISTS (Burslem)

Art Directors:

Slater, John	(Painter)	1877–
Noke, Charles John	(Modeller)	1889–1941
Noke, Cecil J.	(Designer)	1941–1954
Ledger, J.	(Designer)	1955–

Designers and Artists:

Hancock, Fred
Fish and game   1879–1913

Mitchell, Henry
Animals and landscapes   1893–1908

Slater, Walter
Flowers   1880–1910

Brown, Wilmot
Flowers   1879–1930

Raby, Edward
Flowers   1892–1919

Allen, Harry
Flowers, birds, landscapes   1900–1950

Price, John   c1912–1950
Flowers

Wilson, Sam
Fish, flowers, landscapes   1880–1909

Nunn, Walter
Landscapes and figures   1900–1910

Tittensor, Harry
Landscape and figures   1900–1925

Curnock, Percy
Flowers (roses)   1885–1954

White, George
Figures   1885–1912

Birbeck, Joseph (senior)
Landscape, game, fish   1900–1926

Brough, Charles
Flowers   1903–1911

Hart, Charles
Flowers, fish, game   1880–1927

Hopkins, C.B.
Landscape   1895–1922

Johnson, Leslie
Portraits and figures   1905–1937

Dewsbury, David
Orchids   1889–1919

Eaton, Arthur
Barbotine painter, figures and
landscape   1889–1932

Noke, Cecil Jack
Designer   1920–1954

Nixon, Harry
Flowerpainter and flambé glaze   1900–1950

Woodman, W.S.
Designer   1939

Hayward, Walter
Designer

Modellers:

Noke, Charles John   1889–1941
Fenton, Harry
Henk, Max

Outside the products of chemical, sanitary and other social science industries and the excellent table wares which they make, the important products of Doultons include:

(1) LAMBETH

A. Relief decorated stoneware – jugs, bottles, Tobys, character pieces (Nelson etc.) in style with other contemporary stoneware manufactures of 1810–35, but rather more ambitious in character. These derive from the Fulham tradition.

B. Salt-glazed stonewares with incised decorations by individual artists and craftsmen who were allowed to sign their pieces, c.1870 onwards. The Barlow sisters did admirable free sketches on pots of animals and foliage. Painted naturalistic decoration was also popular.

C. Salt-glazed stonewares, overloaded with carved decoration or ornamental excrescences in blue, purple or grey Rhenish styles.

D. Figures modelled in naturalistic style by Tinworth, Marshall, Broad etc., ranging from miniatures a few inches in height to monumental statues, altarpieces etc.

E. Contemporary stoneware by Vera Huggins, Reco Capey, Agnete Hoy-Bohrer.

(2) BURSLEM

A. China painting in a free, vignetted, naturalistic style (Dewsbury's orchids and Curnock's roses).

B. Development of strong colour glaze effects – Rouge flambé, Sang de bœuf, 'Sung' and 'Veined Sung'.

C. The Doulton naturalistic figure, Toby jug and character jug.
Plates 49 B, 159 A.

[Desmond Eyles, in *Doulton News* 1946–1951; L. Jewitt, *Ceramic Art of Great Britain*, 1878.]

Doulton, Sir Henry (born 1820 died 1897)

Second son of John Doulton, founder of the firm of Doulton & Watts. Entered his father's business in 1835. Built a special factory to make salt-glazed sewage pipes on the Albert Embankment, Lambeth, 1846. Started additional works at Rowley Regis, Smethwick and St Helens 1846–49. The introduction of the electric telegraph brought a demand for ceramic insulators which Doulton manufactured as well as stoneware water filters, terra-cotta vases and statuary, and acid-resisting chemical plant. In 1877 he bought Pinder & Bourne's factory in Nile Street, Burslem, for the manufacture of earthenware and in 1884 built a new wing to it for bone china. Awarded the Albert Medal of the Royal Society of Arts 1885; knighted 1887.

[Desmond Eyles, 'Doulton Potteries' in *Ceramics for Art and Industry*, 1953.]

Dresser, Christopher (born 1834 died 1904)

A designer who produced special shapes and decoration for Linthorpe, Yorkshire and Ault faience, Swadlincote, 1894. Dresser also designed furniture and interior fittings.

Chr Dresser

Dressler, Conrad (born 1856 died 1940)

Sculptor who became acquainted with De Morgan: designed schemes for wall tiling and figures for glazed architectural faience for various public buildings: lectured 1896 to Liverpool Ruskin Society on *The Curse of Machinery*, but later became interested in kiln construction for ceramics, and designed the first successful commercial tunnel kiln at the tile works of J.H. Barrett & Co., Stoke-on-Trent, 1910. Died in Paris 3 August 1940.

[J.Adams, 'Potters Parade' in *Pottery and Glass*, December 1949.]

'Dry' Blue

A characteristic lapis-lazuli used as an enamel at the Worcester factory, and imitated at Caughley

Dry Bodies

Non-porous stoneware bodies, completed by the first bisquit firing and not requiring the addition of glaze, such as Egyptian black, Jasper, Rosso Antico, Cane, Bamboo, Parian. [W.Mankowitz, *Wedgwood*, 1853.]

Dublin, Ireland

Delftware potteries existed in Dublin from about 1737 until 1776. At Dublin the wares resembled in form those of French faience, although decorations followed Liverpool and Bristol trends.

Duck Egg Porcelain

A much sought after variety of Swansea soft-paste porcelain showing a greenish translucency made about 1816–17.

Dudley Vases

A set of seven Chelsea vases of elaborate *rococo* form with contorted handles, elaborate piercings and sumptuous paintings in the manner of Boucher; so called because formerly in the possession of Lord Dudley. Said to have been made for King George III to present to Lady Liverpool. Examples are illustrated in *Chelsea Porcelain* by William King (1922).

Dudson, James, Hanley

Commenced manufacturing earthenware at Hope Street, Hanley, in 1835. From the first he made 'china dogs' and figures and other ornaments; later other wares were added – ironstone china, teapots, stoneware jugs with popular relief decorations and parian. The firm became Dudson Bros. and as such still continues.

[*Government Report*, 1842; *Directories*, 1835–89; Information per H.S.Dudson, 1949.]

Duesbury, William (born 1725 died 1786)

Independent decorator in London 1751 to 1753 (his account book has been preserved and published). He obtained controlling interests in various porcelain factories in England: Derby 1756–1786, possibly Longton Hall about 1760, Bow in 1763, and Chelsea 1770–1784. His son, William Duesbury (II) (born 1763 died 1796/7) owned the Derby factory from 1786 until his death.

Plate 40 B.

Duke, Sir James, and Nephews

Manufacturers of bone china dinner, dessert, breakfast and tea ware of fine quality, parian statuary, majolica, jet and terra-cotta vases, stoneware jugs and transfer-printed earthenware. Successors to Samuel Alcock & Co. 1860. Chief artist – George Eyre (born 1818 died 1887). Parian statuary modelled or from designs by

Giovanni Meli	G. Abbot
W. C. Marshall	William Beattie

[*Catalogue* 1862 *Exhibition.*]

Dunbibin, John & Co, Liverpool

Manufactured from 1766 until 1768 when the firm became bankrupt (Gore's *Directory, Liverpool Advertiser*). John Lathorn was a partner in this concern.

Duvivier Family

Porcelain painters at, or for, several English factories.

WILLIAM DUVIVIER (died 1755) born at Liège; came to England about 1743 with his son Henri Joseph Duvivier; worked as porcelain painter at Chelsea for Sprimont, died in 1755 and buried at St. Ann's, Soho, 9 March 1755. His property included 250 etchings by Rembrandt and 400 prints of Smith and Lens, as well as pictures by Italian and Flemish masters. It has been suggested that he instructed O'Neale.

HENRI JOSEPH DUVIVIER (born 1740 died 1771) born at Tournai. Worked at Chelsea until 1763 when he returned to his birthplace, died 1771. His work has not been certainly identified.

FIDÈLE DUVIVIER, cousin of Henri Joseph; painter at Chelsea from 1764 until 1769, Derby 1769–1773, and subsequently as an outside decorator of Worcester, Derby, Pinxton, and New Hall porcelain. He was living in Newcastle-under-Lyme and practising as a china-painter and drawing master in 1799, giving instruction at schools in Stone and Newcastle.

[L. Jewitt, *Ceramic Art of Great Britain*, 1878; G. Savage, *Eighteenth Century English Porcelain*, 1952.]

Dwight, John (born c. 1633 died 1703), Fulham Middlesex

Son of an Oxford gentleman of the same name; educated at Oxford and described variously as B.C.L. and M.A. of Christ Church College, 29 June, 1661; chaplain and registrar to four successive Bishops of Chester, from 29 June 1661 to 1670. Moved to Wigan in Lancashire, probably in 1662 (when George Hall, Rector of Wigan, succeeded to the Bishopric) but certainly sometime before 1667. His children were baptised at Wigan Parish Church; Lydia, 24 July 1667, Samuel 18 December 1668, and Philip, 6 March 1670 (New Style 1671). In the entries for the first two children Dwight was described as 'Secretary to the Bishop of Chester' of the latter 'Of Millgate'.

Dwight commenced his experiments in the art of pottery (possibly in Lancashire) using local clays found in the Kennel pits at Haigh near Wigan. His first patent for making 'transparent earthenware commonly called porcellane or china' was granted for 14 years from April 1671, in which year he probably moved to Fulham. In 1676 he was in partnership in a 'Pottworks' at Fulham, with Windsor Sandys of St Martin's-in-the-Fields, and agreed to supply the Glass Sellers Company with bottles. Sandys' name is omitted from the subsequent agreement of 1677. Lydia Dwight, his daughter, died in 1673. In 1684 he took out a further patent which was the subject of lawsuits in 1693 and 1697 for infringement by potters in London Southampton, Nottingham and Staffordshire. He died in 1703. See also FULHAM.

Plates 47, 48.

[R. Plot, *Natural History of Oxfordshire*, 1676, 2nd ed. Charles Leigh, *Natural History of Lancashire, Cheshire and the Peak of Derbyshire*, Oxford, 1700; D. Lysons, *Environs of London*, 1792; S. Young, *The History of the Worshipful Company of Glass Sellers of London*, 1913; *Dictionary of National Biography*; J. F. Blacker, *A.B.C. of Salt-Glaze Stoneware*, London, 1922; A. J. Hawkes, *Notes and Queries*, 7 April 1923; Thomas Pape, 'Early Life of John Dwight' in *Staffordshire Evening Sentinel*, 21 May 1944.]

E

Eardley, James and Herbert, Hanley

Both James and Herbert Eardley are listed separately as toy and ornament manufacturers in New Street, Hanley in 1834 and 1835 respectively. Nothing further is known of them.

Earth potter

Maker or manufacturer of earthenware – 'John Daniell, earthpotter', Tunstall Court Rolls 1693 (*North Staffordshire Field Club, Transactions,* 1931–32).

Eastwood, Hanley, Staffs. Earthenware Manufactory.

The pottery was established in 1720 and worked from c.1750 by William Baddeley who manufactured cane and brown wares. He was succeeded by his son of the same name who continued the productions of the factory with cream ware and black Egyptian added.

The mark was probably adopted to distinguish articles made by Wm Baddeley from those made by the Baddeleys of Shelton. Under his ownership many imitations of Wedgwood were made here in the late eighteenth and early nineteenth centuries.

MARK

EASTWOOD
impressed

SUBJECTS

A typical example is in the Schreiber Collection, Victoria & Albert Museum; a vase and cover in cane-coloured ware, decorated with reliefs in white of classical figures. The mark EASTWOOD on the plinth.

Eccles, John, Park Lane, Liverpool

Black-glazed earthenware and Salt-glazed stoneware were made at the Park Lane Pothouse, Liverpool by John Eccles & Company in 1756. An advertisement in the *General Evening Post,* 22 July 1756 and *Williamson's Liverpool Advertiser,* 16 July 1756 stated that they make and sell 'all sorts of black and white earthenware being the first of the black and white colours ever brought to perfection in Liverpool and offered to sale at such low prices'. They sold also 'all sorts of blue and white earthenware in the newest china taste...' The factory was subsequently worked by Richard Thwaites and Robert Wilcock.

[*General Evening Post,* 22 July 1756; *Williamsons Liverpool Advertiser,* 16 July 1756; H.B.Lancaster, *Liverpool and her Potters,* 1936; C.T.Gatty, *The Liverpool Potteries,* 1882.]

Edge, Daniel and Timothy, Burslem

Manufacturers of fine china toys at a potworks in Waterloo Road, Burslem from 1818 to 1868. Timothy Edge the elder married Martha Holland, the mother of the well-known watercolour painter, James Holland (born 1799 died 1870), whose birth and parentage have always been recorded incorrectly, and by her had several children, including sons named Timothy (baptised 25 December 1805) and Daniel (born 19 December 1803 and baptised 25 December 1805). They are recorded as toy-makers at various dates subsequently. Daniel Edge's business came to a close in 1842 when his factory – 'The very eligible FREEHOLD BUILDINGS and PROPERTY in Waterloo Road, Burslem, belonging to and now occupied by Mr Daniel Edge as a Toy manufactory, comprising three Hovels with other suitable buildings...' was offered for sale by auction (*Staffordshire Advertiser,* 5 November 1842). The elder Timothy Edge died before 1847. His widow Martha died in 1847 at the age of 70 (*Staffordshire Advertiser,* 30 January 1847) The younger Timothy Edge was still potting in 1851 but was later recorded merely as a beer-seller.

Edge, Joseph

Born 14 July 1805, son of a Burslem trader. Started life as a confectioner, a line of business

Colour plate 8, DERBY: *see page vii for caption*

which he did not abandon until 1864. Entered the pottery business in 1847 when he became partner with Benjamin Cork (Cork and Edge) as earthenware manufacturers, Queen Street, Burslem. They made Egyptian black, lustred wares and fancy coloured stonewares. In 1864 the style of the firm was altered to Cork, Edge and Malkin; an additional factory was opened at the New Wharf. By 1875 the firm had become Edge, Malkin and Co. and had abandoned pottery for tiles. Died 21 May 1893.

[Obit. *Staffordshire Advertiser*, 27 May 1893; *Directories*.]

Edge & Grocott
See GROCOTT.

Edwards, Werner (or Warner) (died 1759)
Shelton, Staffordshire

Edwards owned the Bell Bank in Albion Street, Shelton, in the first half of the eighteenth century. There he made lead ore glazed pottery, and introduced some fine enamels for its decoration. T. Daniel of Stoke was later the recipient of his formulas for enamels and some of his designs. Edwards was partner to the Rev. John Middleton. Shaw gives the date of his death incorrectly as 1753.
[*Stoke Parish Registers; S. Shaw, History of the Staffordshire Potteries*, 1829.]

Edwards, William, Lane Delph, Staffordshire

Edwards was a potter reputed to have made coloured earthenware of good quality at this manufactory from about 1750 until 1785. Chaffers describes two plates of his making as green lead glazed, partly washed to show white markings, with basket-work borders and painted with flowers and musical instruments.
[Bailey's *Directory*, 1783.]

Egg shell porcelain
Porcelain of extreme thinness, finished on the lathe, made at Mintons, Belleek, and other factories in the nineteenth century in emulation of Chinese hard-paste porcelain.

Egyptian Black
The popular name in Staffordshire for the 'dry' black stoneware named by Josiah Wedgwood BASALTES. Also called BLACK EGYPTIAN. See BASALTES.

Elers, David (born 1656 died 1742)
Elers, John Philip (born 1664 died 1738)
The Elers are stated by Jewitt to have come to England in 1688 in the wake of William III but there is contemporary evidence that David Elers was already in London in 1686. (*London Gazette*, 26 December 1686, quoted by Prof. Garner, *Trans*. E.C.C. 1948.)

David Elers was born in Amsterdam, 13 June 1656. He is stated to have been a good chemist and widely travelled, having been to Moscow. (George Elers, *Memoirs* 1837). Coming to London with his brother he commenced making pottery at Fulham about 1690, and in 1693 he was cited, with others, for an infringement of John Dwight's patent. He appears to have worked a potworks at Vauxhall in Surrey from 1693 until 1700 (which will be referred to again later) and kept a shop in the Poultry, London. In 1700 the two Elers became bankrupt. David Elers subsequently continued as a merchant, and died in London, unmarried.

John Philip Elers is rather more fully documented. He was a younger brother of David Elers and claimed descent from a baronial family of lower Saxony. Born at Utrecht, he too was silversmith and chemist, and learnt the secret of stoneware in Cologne, and of levigating and refining clay in Holland.

With his brother he was associated in the manufacture of 'brown muggs and theapotts' in England from about 1690, and was cited by Dwight for an infringement of his patent and for enticing from his service a workman named John Chandler. The brothers then opened the factory at Vauxhall, Surrey, where it was stated there was clay suitable for making 'all sorts of *tea* Pots' (John Houghton, *Collections for Improvement of Trade and Husbandry*, 1693). This factory was in operation until the Elers' bankruptcy in 1700. Many red teapots were made there.

The first reference to Elers in Staffordshire occurs in the Newcastle-under-Lyme Corporation Minutes, 1691 – 'Ordered that a present be made to my Lord Chiefe Justice Holt at his cominge to this Burrough from Lancaster Assizes of some of Mr David Elers' earthen ware to the vallew of three pounds or thereabouts.' (Quoted by T. Pape, *Evening Sentinel*, 2 February 1944). There is unfortunately no indication *where* this purchase was made.

About 1693 one or both of the Elers came to North Staffordshire and started to make red teapots. It is unlikely in view of the continuity of the London factory that both brothers would venture north, and as David Elers is known to have kept a shop in the Poultry it seems likely that it was John Philip Elers who started up in Staffordshire, probably in their joint names. George Elers said they rented 'Brada Hall' from 'Mrs Sneyd, of Keele'. It was at Bradwell Wood that Elers made 'Red China'. Simeon Shaw mentioned two sites, Bradwell Hall and Dimsdale Hall, which were connected by a speaking tube said to have been used to give warning of approaching people. This Staffordshire venture lasted five years. Celia Fiennes visiting Newcastle in 1698 to see the manufacture of red teapots was disappointed. The potters 'comeing to an end of their clay... was removed to some other place where they were not settled... so could not see it'. About this time or shortly after, the factory closed down and David and Philip Elers became bankrupt.

The contemporary fame of their products was attested by Dr Martin Lister in 1693 and 1698 and again by Dr Charles Leigh in 1700. Dr Leigh's record in *The Natural History of Lancashire, Cheshire and the Peak, in Derbyshire* (Oxford 1700) is the only one which couples the factories in London and Staffordshire.

John Philip Elers was married 26 August 1699 to Elizabeth Banks of Uttoxeter. In 1700 he with his brother were declared bankrupt and J. Brinley, glass seller at the corner of Fleet Street and Fetter Lane, became their Assignee. (*London Gazette*, December 1700, quoted by Aubrey Toppin.) J. P. Elers found a friend in Lady Barrington who helped him out of his difficulties and set him up as a china and glass dealer in Dublin, where in 1700 his son Paul was born. J. P. Elers died in Dublin in 1738.

PRODUCTS

There is no evidence that the Elers made salt-glazed stone-ware other than 'brown muggs' or that they introduced the salt-glazing technique into Staffordshire. They were justly famous for red stonewares which vary in colour from a rich red-brown to vermilion, are close in texture, and are thinly potted and fine in workmanship. The precision finish of the Elers products was a portent of industrial standards set up by Josiah Wedgwood sixty years later. The Elers decorations comprised beautifully spaced plum blossom sprigs in relief; countersunk relief chinoiseries, and moulds of merry-andrews and wyverns. There are examples in the British Museum, Victoria and Albert Museum, and the Fitzwilliam Museum, Cambridge.

MARKS

None of Elers' ware was marked in an identifiable manner. Imitation Chinese marks were stamped underneath their products, but the square stamps enclosing English initials written pseudo-Chinese fashion occur only on later Elers-type red pottery, some probably by Greatbach for Wedgwood (who produced a jasper cameo medallion of J. P. Elers.)

[*Memoirs of Richard Lovell Edgeworth*, 1820, 3rd ed. 1834, (Edgeworth married J. P. Elers granddaughter); *Memoirs of George Elers*, edited by Lord Monson and G. Leveson Gower, 1903, (G. Elers was J. P. Elers, great-grandson); L. Jewitt, *The Wedgwoods*, 1865: Jewitt had his information from Georgina Elers-Napier, J. P. Elers great-great-granddaughter); Dr Martin Lister, *Philosophical Journal*, 1693, 1698; Dr Charles Leigh, *The Natural History of Lancashire, Cheshire and the Peak in Derbyshire*, 1700; Houghton's *Collections for Improvements of Husbandry*, 1693, 1695; *The Journal of Celia Fiennes;* S. Shaw, *History of the Staffordshire Potteries*, 1829; *Letters of Josiah*

Wedgwood 1762—80 (1903); John Aiken, *A Description of the Country round Manchester*, 1795; *Transactions, English Ceramic Circle*; W. Mankowitz, *Wedgwood*, 1953.]

Elers pedigree, showing sources of information

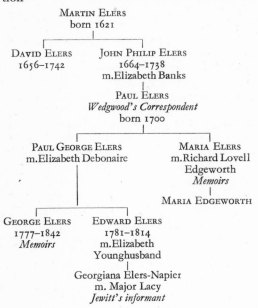

MARTIN ELERS
born 1621

DAVID ELERS
1656–1742

JOHN PHILIP ELERS
1664–1738
m.Elizabeth Banks

PAUL ELERS
Wedgwood's Correspondent
born 1700

PAUL GEORGE ELERS
m.Elizabeth Debonaire

MARIA ELERS
m.Richard Lovell
Edgeworth
Memoirs

MARIA EDGEWORTH

GEORGE ELERS
1777–1842
Memoirs

EDWARD ELERS
1781–1814
m.Elizabeth
Younghusband

Georgiana Elers-Napier
m. Major Lacy
Jewitt's informant

Elizabethan ware

Sometimes applied erroneously to saltglazed stoneware of eighteenth century manufacture.

Elkin, Knight & Bridgwood, The Foley, Fenton, Staffordshire

The Foley Pottery was built in 1820 for the manufacture of earthenware and china, the original partners being George and Thomas Elkin, John King Knight and John Bridgwood. Thomas Elkin withdrew in 1833 (*Staffordshire Advertiser*), the others continuing the business as earthenware manufacturers, china *dealers*, colour grinders and farmers.

When Bridgwood retired the firm traded as Elkin & Knight, and eventually Knight worked the factory on his own.

WORK

The factory produced Egyptian black, shining black, cream-coloured earthenware and blue printed earthenware, including versions of the 'Willow' and 'Broseley' patterns.

Elkin, Richard, Burslem

Earthenware toy manufacturer, High Street, Burslem 1834.

Elland, Yorkshire. Earthenware Manufactories

It is known from an advertisement in the *Leeds Mercury* 1792 that black, brown and cream-coloured earthenware were manufactured at potteries at Blackley near Elland at the end of the eighteenth century.

Ellis, James

Modeller, 1818, and earthenware toy manufacturer, Shelton, 1830.

J. ELLIS & Co

[*Directories*.]   Impressed

Ellis, John, Hanley

Manufacturer of butter pots at the beginning of the eighteenth century, mentioned in Josiah Wedgwood's Ms. list.

Ellis, John, Bristol

His impressed mark occurs on a cream-coloured earthenware mug of early nineteenth century date. Moulded with figural relief decoration.

Elstead, Surrey

A potworks was worked here by Absalom Harris 1860–72.

[H.J.Massingham, *The Curious Traveller*, 1950.]

Ely, Cambridgeshire

Inlaid pottery was made at Ely by Jabez Lucas at the end of the eighteenth century.

Email Ombrant

An illusionist style of decoration like lithophane but the intaglio decoration was filled with coloured glaze (usually green) which produced a monochrome picture in a variety of tones. Developed at the Rubenes factory by Baron A. du Tremblay in the 1840's.

Emery, Francis Joseph, Cobridge

Cashier to T.Furnival & Sons, Cobridge: Introduced the process of decorating bisquit pottery with ceramic crayons; took out patent in conjunction with Derbyshire and Furnival for 'improvements in manufacture' (1859) and for decorating (1865).

[L.Jewitt, *Ceramic Art of Great Britain*, 1878.]

Enamel colours

Low-firing over-glaze ceramic pigments derived from metallic oxides such as copper, manganese, iron or antimony used singly, or combined with an opaque white and lead, zinc or some special flux, were extensively used from the middle of the eighteenth century. A fine pink, crimson or crimson-purple was obtained from gold.

En Camaieu

Monochrome painting in several tones.

Encaustic

A word meaning baked or burnt, frequently applied to medieval inlaid tiles and the imitations made in the nineteenth century; and in consequence identified not with the firing process but erroneously with the technique of manufacture. Wedgwood decorated some of his black basaltes with white and red 'encaustic' enamels after the style of Greek vases, and in 1769 he took out a patent for 'ornamenting earthen and porcelaine ware with an encaustic gold bronze, together with a peculiar species of encaustic painting in various colours in imitation of the antient Etruscan and Roman earthenware'.

[W.Mankowitz, *Wedgwood*, 1953.]

Engine-turning

Decorative process involving the turning of an unfired pot in the leather hard state, upon a specially designed lathe having an eccentric motion to produce geometrical, diced, fluted or similar patterns. Used from c. 1764–65, by Wedgwood and other later potters.

Engine-turning Lathe

According to Simeon Shaw, Thomas Greatbach, the best turner at Palmer's factory, Hanley, suggested the idea to John Baddeley of Eastwood who made the first engine-lathe about 1765. Shaw must have meant William Baddeley, as his son, John Baddeley, was then only eleven years old. (Jewitt gives the inventor's name as William Baddeley.) Josiah Wedgwood is stated to have attempted to obtain control by offering '*eighty guineas* each for six, provided Mr B. would not sell any under that price to other persons'. (Simeon Shaw). In 1764, however, Josiah Wedgwood himself was experimenting with 'Engine-turning'. He wrote to his partner, Bentley, 28 May 1764, 'have sent you a sample of one hobby-horse (engine turning)' and mentioned the acquisition of a book on the subject in French and Latin and the urgent need of an accurate translation. The treatise was probably Plumier's *L'Art de Tourner* (Lyons 1701; Paris 1749) mentioned by Miss Meteyard in her *Life of Josiah Wedgwood* (1865–66). Miss Meteyard said that Greatbach, Baddeley and Wedgwood improved the lathe independently but implied that Wedgwood enjoyed priority. Arthur Young attributed the first application of the tool to Wedgwood but he appears to have visited but few factories, mentioned only one potter by name, and may therefore have been 'inspired'.

[S. Shaw, *History of the Staffordshire Potteries*, 1829; L. Jewitt, *Ceramic Art of Great Britain*, 1878; Arthur Young, *A six Months Tour, of the North*, 1770; E. Meteyard, *Life of Josiah Wedgwood*, 1865–66; *Letters of Wedgwood*, 1903.]

Engobe

A thin coating or layer of clay applied to pottery in the liquid form of slip.

Epergne

An ornamental centrepiece for the dinner table, sometimes of branched form, each branch supporting a dish or vase of flowers – '... elegant Epergnes and other ornamental and useful porcelain' (advertisement concerning Longton Hall, *Public Advertiser*, 12 April 1757).

Epping, Essex

Pottery was made here, mid-nineteenth century, by the firm of Harvey and Davis, brickmakers. [White's *Directory of Essex*, 1848.]

Etruria, Stoke-on-Trent, Staffordshire

In 1766 Josiah Wedgwood purchased the Ridge House Estate and planned to build a new factory, a house for himself, and a village for his workpeople. He appointed Joseph Pickford of Derby as his architect and the factory and Etruria Hall were completed by 1770. He gave the name Etruria to the village because he wished to revive the lost art of the Etruscans. This factory was in operation continuously until 1940 when Josiah Wedgwood & Sons finally transferred to Barlaston. The first of the Wedgwood cottages was demolished in June 1956. [E. J. D. Warrilow, *History of Etruria*, 1951; *Evening Sentinel*, 1956; *Letters of Josiah Wedgwood to Thomas Bentley, 1772-1780*, 1903.]

Etui, etwee

A case to hold small articles such as toothpicks, needles, bodkins, surgical implements.

Evans, David

A painter of wild flowers who worked at Swansea and possibly taught Pollard. [W. B. Honey, *Old English Porcelain*, 1928, new ed. 1948.]

Ewenny, near Bridgend, Glamorgan

Slipwares including covered wassail bowls with many loop handles, decorated in the *sgraffiato* technique for use in the Welsh custom of Mari Lwyd were made here and at the Claypits Pottery in the nineteenth century.

Excise Marks

Royal cyphers and crowns and various numerals indicating town and date where marked, applied standard measures of capacity either upon applied pads of clay, or by stamping the mark upon the plugs of metal inserted into the handle, wall or base, or upon metal encircling bands. Marks applied by stencilling or etching with acid.

Eyre, George (born 1818 died 1887)

Student of the Government School of Design, Somerset House, 1845-47. He was brought to the Potteries in 1847 by Herbert Minton and assisted in the development of the 'encaustic' tile process. Many pavements for public and private buildings were designed by him. He became a notable ceramic painter and designer working for Samuel Alcock & Co., and Sir James Duke and Nephews. [*The Art Union Journal*, 1845; Reginald G. Haggar, *A Century of Art Education in the Potteries*, 1953.]

Eyre, John (died 1927)

Son of George Eyre. National scholar, designer, painter, foreman and kiln superintendent of Minton's London studio. He worked also for Doulton's of Lambeth, and became well known as an illustrator and water colour painter, exhibiting at the R. A., the Paris *Salon*, and the Royal Institute of Painters in Water Colours. [G. W. and F. A. Rhead, *Staffordshire Pots and Potters*, 1906.]

'Fable' painter

An unidentified Chelsea artist, working c. 1750-55, who decorated table wares with illustrations derived from the folio edition of Aesop's Fables (1687) by Francis Barlow. J. L. Dixon suggests there have been as many as three 'Fable' painters of whom one was J. H. O'Neale. Landscape subjects are attributed to this artist. [H. Bellamy Gardner, *The Connoisseur*, 1922; J. L. Dixon, *English Porcelain of the Eighteenth Century*, 1952; W. B. Honey, *Old English Porcelain*, 1928, new. ed. 1948; G. Savage, *Eighteenth Century English Porcelain*, 1952.]

Faience

A French word applied to tin-glazed and other earthenwares, adopted in England in the nineteenth century to describe the larger units employed in architectural ceramics.

Faience Fine

Fine cream-coloured or white earthenware.

'Fair Hebe' jug

A jug in the form of a tree with spreading base modelled in relief with figures of seated girl to whom a youth is offering a nest full of eggs, above which (on a paper) are the words 'FAIR HEBE' on one side; on the other a man holding a glass above which occur the words 'A BUMPER'. Sometimes signed and dated 'Voyez 1788.'

A blue-and-white version has also the impressed mark ASTBURY. The mark R. M. A. (Richard Meir Astbury) has been recorded. Modelled by John Voyez.

Plate 149 B.

[J.W.Glaisher, *Proceedings, Cambridge Antiquarian Society*, 1904; H.Read, *Staffordshire Pottery Figures*, 1929; Reginald G. Haggar, *Staffordshire Chimney Ornaments*, 1955.]

Faraday, Samuel Bayliss (born 1797 died 1844)

Born in Birmingham 17 December 1797. Came to Staffordshire and worked for C. J. Mason as continental traveller from about 1825, and became his partner in 1840.

[*Register of St. Martin's, Birmingham; The Pottery Mercury* 1825; *Staffordshire Advertiser*, 1839–44; Information per Mrs Hollingsworth, a direct descendant.]

Fareham, Hampshire

Slipware is believed to have been made at Fareham in the seventeenth and eighteenth centuries. Inscriptions in white, red or green, with rope-pattern impressed, are characteristic. An example dated 1706 is in the British Museum, but there are no known marked pieces.

Farnborough, Hampshire

A pottery existed here from the end of the eighteenth century. A 'Mr Callaway' sold the stock-in-trade in 1809 to William Smith for £19, and William Smith worked the factory until his death in 1858 when it was continued for a time by his son, of the same name. Pipkins, venisons, money-boxes, pitchers, bowls, bed-pans and stoolpans were made.

[George Bourne, *William Smith, Potter and Farmer*, 1919.]

Farnsworth, Isaac

A 'repairer' at the Derby porcelain factory who is said to have used, as his mark, an incised star, on the figures which he touched up.

[J.Haslem, *Old Derby China Factory*, 1876.]

Fawkener, Sir Everard, (born 1684 died 1758) Chelsea

A proprietor of the Chelsea factory.

[G. Savage, *Eighteenth Century English Porcelain*, 1952.]

Fazackerley, Thomas, Liverpool

Delftware decorated with bold floral ornament in polychrome – green, dark blue, brick red and bright yellow – has been identified as of Liverpool origin, on the traditional evidence supplied by a mug with the initials and date 'T.F. 1757 said to have been made by Thomas Shaw of Liverpool for Fazackerley.

Feathering

See under COMBED WARE.

'Felix Summerly Tea Service'

Designed by Sir Henry Cole and made by Minton & Co. for Felix Summerly Art Manufactures 1846; awarded silver medal by Society of Arts 1846. The tea cups 'being *deep* rather than *wide* offer least scope for the radiation of heat and will keep the tea warm', the 'milk pot has three lips... enabling the liquid to be poured at both angles, right and left, which requires only a motion of the wrist, while the usual method needs the lifting of the arm.' (Cole, *Fifty Years of Public Work*, 1884).

[*Journal, Royal Society of Arts*, 11 March 1949.]

Thomas Fell & Co, Newcastle-on-Tyne

Thomas Fell & Co. made earthenware at St Peter's Pottery in Newcastle in the nineteenth century. His earthenware was exhibited at the International Exhibition of 1861.

Marks are Fell & Co., or F. & Co., sometimes with anchor and cable, or the arms of Newcastle, in blue.

FELL

A dessert-basket and stand of about 1820 is in the Victoria and Albert Museum.

Felspar China

A Felspathic china made by the younger Josiah Spode c.1820 which was marked 'Felspar Porcelain' within a wreath beneath the name SPODE, transfer-printed in purple.

[W.B.Honey, *Old English Porcelain*, 1928, new ed. 1948.]

'Female Archer'

See TOXOPHILITE

Fenton, Staffordshire

The sixth town which Arnold Bennett omitted from his famous 'Five Towns', situated between Stoke and Longton. It comprises the townships of Fenton Vivian, Fenton Culvert, and Lane Delph. Several manufacturers operated at Fenton in the eighteenth century, the most celebrated being Thomas Whieldon of Fenton Low. Since the beginning of the nineteenth century earthenware and china have been manufactured here. The more important firms were F. & R. Pratt, C. J. Mason, Bourne, Baker & Bourne, Thomas and John Carey.

Ferruginous

Rust-coloured; containing iron rust, and therefore a brownish red in appearance.

Ferrybridge, near Pontefract, Yorks. Earthenware manufactory

DATE

The works were established in 1792 as the Knottingley Pottery, by William Tomlinson. The name was later changed to Ferrybridge Pottery.

OWNERS

In 1796 Tomlinson took into partnership Ralph Wedgwood, who had traded previously as an earthenware manufacturer at Burslem, Staffs., under the style Wedgwood & Co., and failed. The firm was known successively as Edwin Tomlinson & Co., Wigglesworth & Ingham, Reed, Taylor & Company until 1851. Other firms followed.

MARKS

Those recorded for this firm, such as

WEDGWOOD & CO.
(impressed)

Wedgwood & Co.

almost certainly applied to Ralph Wedgwood's company in Burslem. The large figure of 'Two Cupids struggling over a heart' cited by Chaffers was almost certainly a Staffordshire piece.

Authentic marks are

FERRYBRIDGE
(impressed)

TOMLINSON & CO.
(impressed)

WORK

White and cream-coloured earthenwares made here, as well as cane, blue-and-white jasper in Wedgwood styles, green-glazed earthenware and white stoneware. See also RALPH WEDGWOOD.

[L.Jewitt, *Ceramic Art of Great Britain*, 1878.]

Fifield, William (born 1777 died 1857)

A pottery decorator who executed porcelain-like rose bouquets and landscapes with buildings in the current water-colour style on cream-coloured earthenware manufactured at Ring's factory in Bristol, 1820–50.

[L. Jewitt, *Ceramic Art of Great Britain*, 1878.]

Fine stone ware

A material which resembles ivory in tint, produced extensively by Turner, Adams and other potters, used for the manufacture of tankards, jugs, goblets, mugs, wine coolers, ice pails, etc. and usually decorated in relief with drinking, coursing, and hunting subjects. The inside of the wares was usually glazed. On earlier productions the coloured bands, which were adopted round the neck and occasionally the base also, were the only portions which were glazed.

Firmin, Samuel

Partner with William Jenkinson and William Littler in the porcelain manufactory at Longton Hall, Staffordshire.

Fishley Family, Fremington, Devon

Five generations of the Fishley family have potted at Fremington in Devon. GEORGE FISHLEY, son of a potter, set up a potworks at Muddlebridge at the end of the eighteenth century, but later removed to Combrew where a potworks already existed. He was the first of the Fremington potters to fire with coal. George Fishley gave greater colour to his wares by the use of manganese as a glaze stain. The Fishleys made not only ordinary wares for farm houses and kitchens, butter-pots, ovens, pilchard pots for Cornish fisherman, but watch stands, chimney ornaments, busts of Wesley, harvest jugs with rolled handles to commemorate sheep shearings and harvest-homes, decorated in the *sgraffiato* technique, and figures in variegated clays. The Fremington clay was used for the body, Bideford pipe clay for the slip decoration.

George Fishley was succeeded by his son, EDMUND FISHLEY in 1839, who continued the business until his death in 1861. The Directory of 1850 lists him at Bickington, Fremington. His name occurs on a jug in Exeter Museum dated 1839.

ROBERT FISHLEY occurs incised upon a jug in Hanley Museum dated 1834. An undated jug in Exeter Museum is inscribed 'R. Fishley jug'.

Edmund Fishley was succeeded by EDWIN BEER FISHLEY (born 1832 died 1912) whose name incised on a jug dated 1851 is in Hanley Museum. According to Jewitt, E. B. Fishley marked his wares

E. B. FISHLEY
FREMINGTON

W. Fishley Holland, grandson of E. B. Fishley, established and built the Braunton and Clevedon Potteries in Somerset.

[Charbonnier, 'Notes on North Devon Pottery' *Trans. Devonshire Association*, 1906; W. F. Holland, 'Memoirs of Fremington', *Pottery Quarterly*, 1955; White's *Devonshire*, 1850; Jewitt, *Ceramic Art of Great Britain*, 1878.]

Flambé glazes

The monochrome copper-red glazes of the Chinese were successfully imitated in the closing decades of the nineteenth century by Bernard Moore and the Burtons. These glazes were designated *Sang de Boeuf* and 'Flambé'. Similar reds were later produced at Doultons of Burslem under the name 'Sung' or 'Veined Sung'.

Flasks

Spirit flasks shaped like fish, potatoes, mermaids, highwaymen's pistols and constable's batons, barrels, shoes were commonly made in brown stoneware and earthenware covered with purple brown 'Rockingham' glaze in the early nineteenth century. Flasks in the form of demifigures of politicians and royalty were made at the time of the Reform Bill. Chief centres of manufacture were Chesterfield, Denby, Brampton, Lambeth.

Plate 49 B.

Flaxman, John, R.A. (born 1755 died 1826)

Born at York, son of a moulder of plaster casts, with premises in Covent Garden, London. He exhibited models at the Free Society of Artists in 1767 and 1769, and in 1770 won a silver medal at the Royal Academy. From 1775 until 1787 he modelled reliefs for Wedgwood's jasper wares such as the well known 'Dancing

Hours' and 'Apotheosis of Homer', and figures, the best known being

Neptune	Faun
Mercury	Cybele
Ganymede	Ceres
Venus (2 versions)	Morpheus
Polyphemus	Apollo
Bacchus (3 versions)	Tritons

He married in 1787, settled in Wardour Street, and executed numerous monumental sculptures including the portrait bust of Josiah Wedgwood (Stoke St. Peter's Church) and monuments of Collins and the Rev. T. Ball (in Chichester Cathedral). He spent seven years in Italy from 1787, studying art, and while there he executed designs for Dante's *Divina Commedia* (1797) Homer (1793) and Aeschylus (1795), marble groups of 'The Fury of Athamas' and 'Cephalus and Aurora', and works for Wedgwood. He was elected R.A. in 1800, and Professor of Sculpture to the Royal Academy in 1810. His later monuments include

Nelson (St Paul's)	Lord Mansfield (The Abbey)
Howe (St Paul's)	Montagu (The Abbey)
Reynolds (St Paul's)	St Michael (Petworth)

[W.G.Constable, *Flaxman*, 1927; W.Mankowitz, *Wedgwood*, 1953.]

Fletcher, Thomas, Shelton

Black-printer in partnership with Sampson Bagnall the Younger from 1786 until 1796, and on own account at Booden Brook, Shelton, from 1796 until about 1810. Subjects printed by him include medallions of the four seasons, Amorini, Conjugal Felicity and Rustic Amusement, 'Come Box the Compass', Hunting Scenes, The Farmer's Arms, Diana, etc. These are signed

T. Fletcher Shelton or

T. FLETCHER, SHELTON

[*Directories*, 1787–1818.]

Flint

An important ingredient of the earthenware body. The properties of ground and calcined flint are alleged to have been discovered by accident about 1720 or 1730, and to have been subsequently exploited in the staple wares of Staffordshire earthenware and stoneware.

Shaw, who attributed the discovery to Astbury, says that the correct proportion of flint to clay was determined by William Bird of Cliff Bank, who was known in consequence as the 'Flint Potter'.

Flint toughens the body and increases the refractoriness of the clay. Flints were imported to the Midlands from the Sussex and East Anglian coast and the North of France.

[S.Shaw, *History of the Staffordshire Potteries*, 1829.]

Flint Mug Works, Liverpool

Said to have been operated by Okill & Company from the middle of the eighteenth century. In 1773 the following advertisement appeared in the *Liverpool Advertiser* (29 October 1773) 'To be sold, the assignment of a term in a lease (14 years whereof are unexpired) of a valuable established Pottery... together with the stock-in-trade... and also a large assortment of cream colour or Queen's ware, manufactured at the said work...' The factory stood at the corner of Flint Street and Parliament Street.

Flower, Joseph, Bristol

Joseph Flower, who was apprenticed to Thomas Frank, started a delftware manufactory at Redcliff Backs in 1743, which continued until 1785. He himself was an artist, and he employed as decorators John Niglett, John Bowen, Michael Edkins, and Thomas Lindslee.

Several different types have been attributed to Flower, but apart from a bowl inscribed 'Joseph Flower Sculp' and another dated and initialled 'J F 1751' none have been certainly identified.

Joseph Flower is also known to have had a crock shop in Bristol.

[W.J.Pountney, *Old Bristol Potteries*, 1920; F.H.Garner, *English Delftware*, 1948.]

Flowering

Method of decorating ware 'with drawings of flowers etc. traced with the point of an iron nail which cut through the thin coat of slip in which the ware had previously been dipped'. (Pitt, *Topographical History of Staffordshire, 1817.*); 'hired little Bet Blowr to learn to flower' (Whieldon's *Notebook*, 1752).

Flown Blue

An underglaze transfer-printed effect in which the design melts into the surrounding glaze with a kind of coloured halo, caused by firing in an atmosphere containing volatile chlorides. Flown blue effects were popular in mid-Victorian times. Other colours, such as brown, green and yellow are subject to the same treatment but have been little used.

[W. White, *The Complete Practical Potter*, 1847].

Floyd, Henry, Cobridge

Toy manufacturer, Cobridge 1834.

Folche, Stephen, Stoke-on-Trent

Manufacturer of ironstone china, Stoke-on-Trent, from 1820 until 1828 when his utensils and raw materials were announced for sale (*Pottery Mercury* 9 February 1828). His potwork a four-oven factory, described as 'lately in the holding of' Stephen Folche was offered to be let in 1829 (*Pottery Mercury* 14 March 1829). Chaffers gives his mark as

FOLCHE'S GENUINE
STONE CHINA

Font

A Wedgwood black basaltes bowl on a high base 11½ inches high and 16½ inches in diameter was used as a font in St Margaret's church, Moreton, Shropshire, from 1785 until 1865 (Lady Lever Art Gallery, Port Sunlight).

Food Warmer

A composite article of pottery or porcelain, usually from 9 inches to 12 inches high, consisting of a hollow pedestal into which a covered bowl with a projecting flange nests. Within the pedestal, which has an arched open-ing at the bottom on one side, there is a cup or container (godet) which fits into a raised verge on the base. Food warmers were made in delft-ware, salt-glazed stoneware, and earthenware, at Leeds, Swansea and in Staffordshire, eighteenth and nineteenth centuries. Described and figured in Wedgwood's *Catalogue*, 1774, as 'Night Lamps, to keep any Liquid warm all night', and clearly developed from the NIGHT LIGHT or VEILLEUSE. Used in sick-rooms or nurseries.

Plate 18 D.

Ford, Lane End

Manufactured 'common stone earthenware and brown ware' at a factory near the Lower Market Place in Lane End which had been built by Roger Wood of the Ash in 1756. Cream-colour was also made here. (Shaw, *History of the Staffordshire Potteries* 1829).

In 1805 the firm of William Ford & Co. was working here, the partners being Singleton, Barlow, and Ford. In consequence of Singleton's death in 1815, the business became that of Hugh Ford. (*Staffordshire Advertiser* 11 and 23 December 1815; *Directory* 1818.)

Forgeries

Forgeries fall into two categories: 1) those which were made for the purposes of fraud; and 2) those which have, by alteration, erasure, or addition, been made to appear to belong to an older, or more desirable, or more valuable, class of wares, although manufactured without fraudulent intention.

Porcelain has been more subject to forging than earthenware. Chelsea, Lowestoft, Derby, and Plymouth have all been faked in one way or another. Paste, marks, or decorations at variance with period form are tell-tale signs. Some forgeries in hard-paste of Derby figures (which were formerly ascribed to Chelsea) are given a gold anchor mark! A hard-type of porcelain used for faking Lowestoft is supplied with authentic Lowestoft inscriptions taken from recorded specimens. Imitations of Chelsea were made at Coalport c.1850 in bone china, and at Tournai in a similar soft-paste although sup-plied with decorations incompatible with the period.

Marks have been forged; sometimes unmarked pieces have been made more 'important' by the addition of marks. This is specially true of Nantgarw porcelain to which etched or painted marks are sometimes added. The eagerness of collectors to acquire marked pieces has led to the demand being supplied.

The faking of earthenware is perhaps less common.

Salt-glaze figures of important subjects are not likely to turn up nowadays and should always be held suspect. There are faked pew groups. Lead-glazed image toys have been copied but are usually heavier in weight and clumsier in appearance. Ralph Wood figures being desirable have excited the fakers' attention. An 'important' piece with figures which are clearly from two distinct and dissimilar moulds has been illustrated. The popularity of the 'Vicar and Moses' resulted in numerous versions by other potters and some of inferior quality with spurious inscriptions.

The dispersal of moulds has led to their 'innocent' re-use at a later date. Turner moulds were used by Bates, Walker & Co. Some of Clews' engravings passed into the hands of Adams. This happened many times. Moulds for flat-back chimney ornaments have been re-worked extensively in recent years, as also the engravings for pot-lids.

Castle Hedingham has taken in some collectors when the mark has been chipped away. The genuine wares of Mafra, Caldas, Portugal are similar to those of Whieldon but rather brighter in colour, and heavier.

Slipwares of known origin were listed in the Catalogue of the Solon Sale as imitations, but he is frequently said to have been taken in by spurious examples. This is not easy to believe as he was an experienced practical potter as well as a connoisseur, a combination of qualities not possessed by his debunkers.

Some doubt has been cast upon elaborate Toft dishes although it is not easy to conceive of any contemporary potter with the technical control necessary for their execution.

Lustre ware is easy to fake, but it was in production throughout the nineteenth century (being made in enormous quantities in the 1860s and 1870s).

Tell-tale re-firing dirt is sometimes mentioned as a clue to added decoration, but any undecorated ware that has stood in the warehouse for a considerable length of time, as may happen when trade is slack, is subject to this hazard. This feature is mentioned in the modern enamelling of old salt-glaze. We know from contemporary sources that salt-glaze ware was in decline from the 1760s, and stocks therefore probably accumulated. This fact should be borne in mind.

The alleged Voyez imitations and forgeries of Wedgwood have never been identified.

Forrester, John, Lane End

He is mentioned in a *memo* dated 26 May 1800 of a grant of an annuity from the Marquis of Stafford which is now in Birmingham Reference Library. John Forrester is listed as an earthenware manufacturer at Lane End in 1805. In 1818 the firm was George Forrester, Market Place, Lane End.

Forrester & Meredith, Lane End

Made 'Queen's Ware, Egyptian Black, Red China and various other wares' at Lane End in 1787 (Tunnicliff's *Survey*). Later the firm was Forrester & Harvey, and subsequently George & John Forrester.

(*Directories* 1787-1818.)

Forster, John

Bernard Rackham recorded a figure in the Glaisher Collection, Fitzwilliam Museum, Cambridge, of a naked boy astride a dophin, inscribed 'John Forster made this Hanley Agust (sic) the 29 1820.' His name has not occurred in local sources.

Forsyth, Gordon Mitchell (born 1879 died 1952)

Pottery craftsman, designer and teacher: studied at Aberdeen and South Kensington: art director of Minton Hollins Ltd, Stoke-on-Trent, 1903–05, and of Pilkingtons, Manchester from 1906–19, where he produced finely painted lustre pottery. From 1920–44 he was

Principal of City of Stoke-on-Trent Art Schools but during that time designed pottery shapes and decorations for Brains of Longton, Pountneys of Bristol and other firms. From 1944 he worked for Grimwades, executing a large number of finely gilded and lustred pieces. His signature was four interlacing scythes or the initials G.M.F., incised. His daughter MOIRA FORSYTH about 1935–1937 modelled an extensive range of individual figures in the Ralph Wood tradition. Examples in Hanley Museum, Stoke-on-Trent.

Incised

[Reginald G. Haggar, *English Country Pottery*, 1950.]

Fowke, Sir Frederick, Bart, Lowesby, Leicestershire

Fowke established a terra cotta works at Lowesby in 1835, using local clays. Some of his pieces were decorated with classical figures and ornaments in black, more rarely with colours and gold. The factory lasted a few years only. There is a black basaltes dish enamelled in colours with flowers and butterflies in the British Museum.

MARK

An impressed mark is given by Jewitt.

The London agent of the firm was Purden of King William Street.

[L. Jewitt, *Ceramic Art of Great Britain*, 1878.]

Franceys & Spence, Liverpool

T. Franceys and W. Spence made portrait busts and plaques of political celebrities in a hard black biscuit stoneware, at Pleasant Street, Liverpool from about 1820 until 1830. These were incised as follows:

Pubd March 1820	Pubd. by
T. Franceys & Spence	W. Spence
Liverpool	1829
W. Spence fecit	

S. and T. Franceys executed a number of marble mural monuments in churches in Staffordshire, notably in St Johns Church, Longton, and Broughton Church.

[H. Boswell Lancaster, *Liverpool and her Potters*, 1936.]

Frank, Thomas, Bristol

Thomas Frank was successor to Edward Ward at Brislington, which he worked as a delftware factory from 1697 until about 1706, when he removed to Redcliff Back. There he and his family potted over an extended period of time.

[W. J. Pountney, *Old Bristol Potteries*, 1920.]

Franklin, George and Alec, Leafield

Made red earthenware honey-jars, money-boxes, jugs and other articles at Leafield for local use, late nineteenth century. Examples in Ashmolean Museum, Oxford.

Freckled Ware

A type of pottery mentioned in Wedgwood's MS list of Burslem potters about 1710–15, and believed to have been an earthenware 'freckled' in imitation of stoneware.

Frit Porcelain

A soft-paste porcelain composed mainly of a glassy, vitreous compound of silica and alkali, called a frit, which is ground and mixed with white clay and a certain amount of lime. Early Chelsea porcelain was of this type.

'Frog' Service

A celebrated service of cream-coloured earthenware manufactured by Josiah Wedgwood in 1773 for Empress Catherine of Russia. Each piece of this enormous service was painted at Chelsea with individual landscapes and mansions of England, and a leaf border with the crest of a green frog in purple black. The service was so named because it was intended for the Grenouille Palace.

There were more than 900 pieces: the ware cost £ 51. 8s. 4d: the decorations nearly £ 2,450: Josiah Wedgwood received for it £ 3,000.

It is now in the Hermitage, Leningrad.

[G.C.Williamson, *The Imperial Russian Dinner Service*, 1909.]

Frye, Thomas (born 1710 died 1762)

Born in Ireland near Dublin, studied art and came to London about 1729. He painted portraits in oils and became proficient as a miniature painter. In 1734 Frederick, Prince of Wales, sat to him. Became interested in the idea of manufacturing porcelain and in December 1744 took out a patent, in conjunction with Edward Heylyn, which specified the essential ingredient as *unaker;* 'the product of the Cherokee nation in America'. Another porcelain formula was patented by Frye in 1749 which included, under the curious and deceptive euphemism 'virgin earth', calcined, ground and washed bone. In 1750 with the aid of two London merchants a factory was established at Bow, called 'New Canton'. Sales, which in the first year are said to have been £10,000 were nearly doubled by 1755. A lot of Bow porcelain must therefore be in existence today.

Frye retired from the management of the Bow factory in 1759 when his health gave way. He toured in Wales for a time and then settled in London as a mezzotint engraver. He died in 1762.

Fulham, Middlesex. Stoneware Manufactory

John Dwight of Fulham took out a patent in 1671 for the manufacture of 'transparent earthenware' and stoneware, then sometimes known as Cologne ware. Dwight was followed by Margaret Dwight, and thereafter the works remained in the family for many years. In 1862 the factory came into the possession of Messrs MacIntosh & Clements: in 1864 it was disposed of to a Mr Bailey. It is still in existence as the Fulham Pottery and Cheavin Filter Co.

MARKS

Fulham
Pottery

This mark is found on a flask of brown-glazed stoneware decorated with a watch, c.1811, in the British Museum.

No other marks are known to have been used.

WORK

John Dwight contributed to the progress of pottery manufacture in England. He was the first maker of a semi- translucent stoneware, the link between earthenware and the fine porcelain produced later. He also made a successful copy of Cologne ware, a greyish durable earthenware used for pots, mugs, etc. imported from Germany in great quantities. Many such articles for domestic use, in various qualities, were made at Fulham in the seventeenth and eighteenth centuries.

Some beautifully modelled statues and busts in salt-glazed stoneware were made by Dwight. S. K. Greenslade suggested that these were the work of the carver, Grinling Gibbons (1648–1721). Red ware of the Elers type was probably also made at Fulham. Between 1693 and 1696 Dwight instituted several lawsuits to defend his patent rights for the manufacture of this and other types of ware. The brothers Elers were cited in one of these cases.

In the eighteenth century only the coarser wares were produced, beer jugs, tankards for the most part crudely decorated with reliefs of convivial and other subjects, and later marked with name of owner or inn for which they were intended.

Excellent examples of Dwight stonewares, including some finely modelled figures and busts, and some later wares may be seen at the British Museum, The half-length figure of a child inscribed 'Lydia Dwight, died March 3rd, 1673' is an outstanding achievement.

Plates 47, 48.

[See also DWIGHT, JOHN.]

Fuddling-cup

A cup with 3, 5, 6 or more conjoined compartments communicating internally, made in *sgraffiato* slipware at Donyat and Crock Street, Somerset. Dates recorded from 1697 to 1770. Similar vessels were made in tin-glazed earthenware at Bristol. Earliest dated piece 1633.

[J.E. and E.Hodgkin, *Examples of Early English Pottery*, 1891; F.H.Garner, *English Delftware*, 1948.]

G

Galena

Native lead sulphide: the common lead ore.

Gallipot

Originally pots brought in galleys; subsequently applied to pottery glazed with tin enamel, especially a small, glazed earthenware pot such as is used by apothecaries for ointments. 'Gallipot maker' (1669) and 'galley pot maker' (1682), occur in Bristol archives.

[W.J.Pountney, *Old Bristol Potteries*, Bristol, 1920.]

Gally Paving Tiles

Glazed tiles, usually earthenware covered with tin glaze used for wall decorations: the name was derived from imported wares brought from the Mediterranean in galleys. 'About the year 1567, *Jasper Andries* and *Jacob Janson*, Potters, came from *Antwerp* and settled themselves in Norwich; where they followed their Trade, making Gally Paving Tiles, and vessels for the Apothecaries.' (John Stow, *A Survey of the Cities of London and Westminster and the Borough of Southwark*, 1598, 6th ed. London, 1755.)

Gally Ware

An old English name for clayware: 'Gally Ware or White Ware is made here in almost equal perfection with what is made in Holland, but that the Dutch undersell us.' (Dwight, 1698.)

Garner, Charles (born 1772),
Lane End Staffordshire

Potter at the Foley, Lane End, late eighteenth century. He was imprisoned in Lichfield Gaol as an insolvent debtor in 1797, but resumed potting and was still in operation in 1818.

[*Staffordshire Advertiser*, 1797; *Directories*.]

Garner, Matthew, Southwark

A potter who is recorded as working at Southwark at the end of the seventeenth century.

[*Catalogue, Burlington Fine Arts Club*, 1913.]

Garner, Robert

Of Penkholl and Hanley; married, 3 January 1732, to Jane Glass; probably the potter of this name employed by Thomas Whieldon, 28 February 1749. Garner established a factory at Fenton about 1750 in conjunction with John Barker, at which he made black ware, white salt-glazed stonewares, and later cream-coloured pottery.

[Whieldon's *Notebook*; S.Shaw, *History of the Staffordshire Potteries*, 1829.]

Garner, Robert (born 1733 died 1789)

Potter, Lane End. Originally manufactured white, salt-glazed stoneware and shining black ware, but later made Queen's ware; married Margaret Astbury.

[S.Shaw, *History of the Staffordshire Potteries*, 1829; Bailey's *Directory*, 1783 and Tunnicliff's *Survey*, 1787.]

Garner, Robert (born 1766)

Potter, Lane End; successor to Robert Garner (1733–89): married Elizabeth Middlemore (1769–1838).

Described by Jewitt as 'a potter in a large way of business and excellent in Queen's or cream-coloured ware'.

Garrett, Thomas (born 1785 died 1865)

Partner in the firm of Copeland & Garrett, Stoke-on-Trent.

[Obit. *Art Journal*, Vol. 4. 1865.]

Garrison Pottery, Earthenware Manufactory, Sunderland

Established early in the nineteenth century by Phillips and Co. for the manufacture of Queen's ware, and printed, lustred and sponged ware.

PHILLIPS & CO.
Sunderland (date)

or

PHILLIPS & CO.
Sunderland Pottery

are usually found on the border of transfer-printed wares. The firm was subsequently carried on by Dixon, Austin Phillips and Company whose marks were

DIXON, AUSTIN & CO.
Sunderland Pottery

DIXON & CO.
Sunderland Pottery

Similar wares were made including jugs decorated with a view of the Wear Bridge, or representations of the Farmers' Arms. Figures were made in some quantity and were of a distinctive type. The toad surprise mug was a North Country speciality.

Gerverot

A modeller cited by Simeon Shaw in his *History of the Staffordshire Potteries*, 1829, but possibly an error for Mongenot.

Gestingthorpe, Essex

Incised pottery with a purple-brown glaze was made at Gestingthorpe, near Halstead, seventeenth and eighteenth centuries. Jugs with cylindrical necks, narrow tubular spouts and three handles have survived. Dates range from 1685–1770. An earthenware factory was still being worked here by Elizabeth Mayer, 1848 (White's *Directory of Essex*).

[B. Rackham and H. Read, *English Pottery*, 1924.]

Gibbons, Grinling (born 1648 died 1721)

Wood carver and sculptor. It has been suggested by S. K. Greenslade that Grinling Gibbons, as a young man, produced the figures which give such celebrity to the productions of Dwight's factory at Fulham.

Notable examples of Gibbons' work (for comparison) are the bronze statue of James II in Trafalgar Square, his font in St. James's Church, Piccadilly, and wood work in many London Churches.

[For his wood carving see H. A. Tipping, *Grinling Gibbons and the Woodwork of his age*, 1914.]

Gibson, John R.A. (born 1790 died 1866)

An eminent Victorian sculptor who sensed the possibilities and the popular significance of the parian paste produced in the late 1840's and produced works which were reproduced in it. He described parian as 'decidedly the best material next to marble' (*Art Journal*, 1848).

Gibson was the son of a North Wales market gardener, educated in Liverpool, and apprenticed to a cabinet-maker. Having started to carve wood, he exhibited at the R. A. in 1816, went to Rome in 1817 and became an assistant to Canova and Thorwaldsen. The rest of his life was spent in Rome apart from occasional visits to England.

His attempt to revive polychrome decoration of sculpture, by colouring his 'Venus Victrix' in 1862, caused something of a sensation.

[T. Matthews, *John Gibson*, 1911.]

Gibson, John and Solomon, Liverpool

H. Boswell Lancaster cited a plaque in Liverpool Museum of a dog in low relief marked 'John Gibson Liverpool 1813' and a figure of 'Mercury' incised 'Solomon Gibson 1816'.

[H. B. Lancaster, *Liverpool and her Potters*, 1936.]

Gilding

Various relatively impermanent forms of gilding were employed on salt-glazed stoneware, earthenware and porcelain in the 18th century, either by means of an emulsion composed of linseed oil and mastic, jappanners' size, amber varnish, or honey. These were fixed by firing at an extremely low temperature. Honey gilding was used at Chelsea and Worcester. It was rather dull in appearance but could be applied with enough thickness to allow for chasing. It was much more durable than size gilding.

Mercury gilding was introduced about 1785, raised gilding in 1802, liquid gold about 1855, bright burnished gold in 1860, and acid gilding in 1863.

Gold has been applied by pencilling, by transfer-printing, and with rubber stamps.

Giles, James (born 1718 died after 1780)
Kentish Town and Cockspur Street, London

An enameller of Bow, Worcester and other porcelains from before 1760 until c.1780. Many unusual styles of decoration came from his workshop. He was born in 1718, and apprenticed to a jeweller, before becoming a ceramic artist. By 1760 he was well established and advertising that he was prepared to 'procure and paint for any person Worcester porcelain to any or in any pattern', and in 1771 hired a room in Cockspur Street from which he advertised wares 'curiously enamelled in figures, birds and flowers' and ornamentated with mazarine blue, and gold.

He was financially embarrassed in 1777 and appealed to Duesbury for a loan, and when he ultimately failed Duesbury took on his premises and stock.

The gilding on wares decorated in Giles' workshop is said to have been thick and crudely chased.

Various styles of enamelling have been ascribed to him, the dishevelled birds, Chelsea landscapes drawn in black and coloured in green, some Chelsea fruit painting, etc. O'Neale may have been employed by him.

MARKS

Chaffers suggested that the red seal mark occurring over the Worcester crescent in underglaze blue may be an indication of his work. Honey put forward the suggestion that the dagger and another mark on Bow was Giles' sign.

[W.B.Honey, *Old English Porcelain*, 1928, new ed. 1948; G. Savage, *Eighteenth Century English Porcelain*, 1952; W. 5. Honey, 'Work of James Giles' *Transactions English Ceramic Circle*, 1937.]

Gillbody, Samuel (died 1762), Liverpool

Recorded first of all in St Peter's Registers in 1736 as a potter. It appears that in 1714 Samuel Gillbody and Thomas Morris took over a potworks in Shaw's Brow. In 1737 however, he was described as a 'dealer in earthenware'. Very little is known about him.

Ginder & Hulse, Lane Delph

Earthenware manufacturers at Lane Delph 1818 until 1834. Samuel Ginder, partner in this concern, died at Stapenhill, Burton-on-Trent, 30 July 1849 aged 72 years.

[*Directories*; *Staffordshire Advertiser*, November and December, 1831, 4 August 1849.]

Girandol

A branched candlestick or candelabrum. ('A pair of girandols with three branches each.')
[*Chelsea Catalogue*, 1756.]

'Girl-in-a-swing' family

A group of porcelain figures manufactured at Chelsea c.1751; so-named from a figure of a girl in a swing in the Victoria and Albert Museum London. The figures are of primitive simplicity and show some affinity to Staffordshire wares of similar date.

[J.L.Dixon, *English Porcelain of the 18th Century*, 1952; G. Savage, *Eighteenth Century English Porcelain*, 1952.]

Glasgow, Scotland, Earthenware manufactories.
The manufacture of tin-glazed earthenware was started at Delftfield by Robert Dinwoodie in 1748 and continued until about 1770 when the Glasgow potters changed over to cream coloured earthenware. Only one identifiable piece of Glasgow delftware is known, a punch bowl painted in blue with the arms of the City of Glasgow (People's Palace Museum, Glasgow).

Various types of pottery were made at a number of factories in Glasgow throughout the nineteenth century, including porcelain at the Verreville and Glasgow (J. and M.P.Bell) factories.

See also BELL, (J. & M.P.), VERREVILLE, NORTH BRITISH POTTERY.

Glass, John, Hanley, Staffordshire
Manufacturer of common earthenware and Egyptian black, Hanley, 1787–1834.

His mark was

GLASS
HANLEY
impressed

Glass, Joseph, Hanley, Staffordshire

He was described in Josiah Wedgwood's Ms. list of potters at work in Hanley (1710–1715) as a manufacturer of 'cloudy sort of dishes painted with Difft color'd slips, and sold at 3s. and 3s.6d. a doz'.

The name occurs with date 1703, on a slipware cradle (Fitzwilliam Museum, Cambridge); on an undated posset-pot (British Museum); and on a dish sold at Sotheby's, 18 April 1947.

On the 8 June 1681 a Joseph Glass was married to Anne Meer. The burial of two of the name Joseph Glass is recorded in *Stoke Parish Register*, 28 February 1717 and 5 April 1730.

Glazing

The application of a glassy material to earthenware or porcelain renders it impervious to liquids and smooth to the touch. Glazes may be dull or matt or brilliant, translucent or opaque, or they may be shot through with brilliant colour. They may be hard and resistant to a knife edge or they may be soft and easily scratched.

Glaze has been applied by dusting powdered lead ore upon the ware, throwing common salt into the kiln so that it volatilizes and forms a thin film of salt-glaze, or by dipping in a liquid glaze solution.

Lead glazes were general until the end of the 19th century except for salt-glazed stoneware and hard-paste porcelain. John Rose invented a leadless glaze for porcelain in 1820 which was awarded the Isis gold medal of the Society of Arts, and Job Meigh a leadless glaze for red earthenware in 1822.

Glider, Glidder

To cover with a glaze. A Bristol delftware punch bowl (dated 1731) carries the following inscription:

John Udy of Luxillion / his tin was so fine / it gliderd this punch bowl / and made it to shine / pray fill it with punch / lett the tinners sitt round / they never will budge / till the bottom they sound

Figured in J. E. and Edith Hodgkin's *Examples of Early English Pottery*, 1891.
Plate 19 C.

'Goat and Bee' jug

A jug decorated in relief with goats and a bee, incised in the base with the word Chelsea, a triangle, and a date, generally 1745, which is regarded as an important documentary piece in respect of the Chelsea factory. A specimen dated 1743 has been recorded by Dr. Severne Mackenna (*Apollo*, December 1944).

The shape is known in variations and unmarked, and was derived from a silver prototype (G. Savage, *18th Century English Porcelain*, 1952). Goat-and-Bee jugs were made at Coalport, c.1850.

Goddard, Thomas (born 1791 died 1872)

A remarkable man who pursued a number of various interests and made a considerable fortune. He was surgeon and man-midwife in Longton, registrar of births and deaths, master potter, colour-maker and flint grinder, colliery proprietor and ironmaster. Born at New Mills, Derbyshire 19 Sept 1791, he came to Staffordshire in 1814 and settled in Longton. Founded the firm of Thomas Goddard and Son, earthenware manufacturers in Commerce Street, Longton, 1826, the business continuing until 1849. Thomas Goddard & Son manufactured medium quality cream-coloured earthenware and employed 96 work-people. Thomas Goddard became Chief Bailiff of Longton in 1853 and died at Park Hall 14 June 1872.

[*MS Diary of John Hackett Goddard;* Goddard family papers; Obituary, *Staffordshire Advertiser* 22 June 1872; Government Reports; Directories.]

Godet

A cup.

Godwin, Thomas and Benjamin, Cobridge and Burslem

A number of potworks at Cobridge and in Navigation Road (or New Basin as it was originally called), Burslem, were operated by Thomas Godwin (born 1752 died 1809) and Benjamin Godwin (born 1754 died 1814) from 1783 and 1809 respectively. Their descendants continued these factories until c.1865. In 1787 T. and B. Godwin were described as manufacturers of Queen's ware and china-glazed earthenware.

[Numerous and very complicated references to this family of potters may be traced in *Directories* 1783 until 1864; *Government Reports; Poll Lists; Parish Registers* of Burslem and Stoke; *Staffordshire Advertiser*, 1806, 1809, 1813, 1814, 1815, 1833, 1834 and 1851.]

Goldenhill, Staffordshire

This village to the extreme north of the Potteries about 2 miles from Tunstall was the site of coarse pottery manufactory in the sixteenth century. Several important factories existed here from the end of the eighteenth century, producing Egyptian black, cream-coloured and banded wares. The latter was the speciality of Thomas Tunstall.

Coarse earthenware was manufactured here well into the nineteenth century by Daniel Vawdrey, and the Collinson family, The latter flourished over 75 years although eventually forced from pottery manufacture to flower pots and from flower pots to bricks.

[S.Shaw, *History of the Staffordshire Potteries,* 1829.]

**Goodwin, John Edward
(born c. 1867 died 1949)**

Designer and art director, Josiah Wedgwood & Sons 1904–34.

Goodwin, Liverpool

Came from Lane End in Staffordshire and set up an earthenware manufactory at Seacombe in 1851 which he operated for about twenty years, making ware with a light blue glaze, and using a 'throwing table' to save labour and expedite production.

Gordon, William, Chesterfield, Derbyshire

Modern studio potter who has successfully produced salt-glazed stoneware at the Walton Pottery Co. since 1946. He began experiments at Chesterfield in 1939.

MARK

WORK

Figures, and useful pottery cast from moulds (not thrown), to the designs and models of William Gordon himself, who is a sculptor.

[G.W.Digby, *The Work of the Modern Potter in England,* 1952.]

Gorhambury, near St. Albans

Two tiles (one in the Victoria and Albert Museum) came from this house, and have been tentatively attributed to Andries and Janson.

They are decorated with the arms and crest of the Bacon family. Gorhambury was completed in 1568 shortly after Andries and Janson are said to have come to Norwich and started the manufacture of tin-glazed earthenware.

[W.B.Honey, *English Pottery and Porcelain,* 2nd ed. 1945.]

Gorsty Hill, near Halesowen, Worcestershire

A slipware pottery producing marbled and solid agate wares existed in the late eighteenth and early nineteenth centuries. Examples are in the Victoria and Albert Museum, London.

**Goss, William Henry, F.G.S.
(born 1833 died 1906)**

Born London, 30 July 1833; started to make ivory porcelain in Stoke-on-Trent 1858; died 1906. Contributed papers on geology and pottery to various journals, including *The Reliquary.* Author of *The Life of Llewellyn Jewitt F.S.A.* (Hanley, 1889). Goss's Armorial China enjoyed great popularity in the seaside holidays trade, but is artistically worthless. In the third quarter of the nineteenth century more interesting products were made including floral jewellery, 'jewelled' vases, 'illuminated' scent-vases, parian statuary and busts. W.W.Gallimore from Belleek modelled for him.

W H GOSS COPYRIGHT

Impressed

Gotch

An East Anglian term for a large handled stoneware jug: 'a gotch of milk' – Robert Bloomfield (1766–1823).

Gouyn, Charles

Silversmith and part-proprietor in the Chelsea factory at its inception.

Graham, John (born 1729 died 1808),
Burslem, Staffordshire

'Manufacturer of white stone earthenware, enamelled white and cream colour' in Burslem 1787. Not recorded in other directories.

[Tunnicliffe's *Survey of the Counties of Stafford, Chester and Lancashire,* (1787); *Burslem Parish Registers.*]

Grainger, Thomas (died 1839), Worcester

Founder of a porcelain factory at Worcester in 1801, which at first decorated 'white' obtained from Caughley and elsewhere, but subsequently made porcelain of a fine translucent kind and later, when the mark was 'Ganger Lee & Co.', porcelain in the style of Chamberlains. Thomas Grainger was a nephew of Humphrey Chamberlain and served his time as a painter to him. Lee was his brother-in-law. When T. Grainger died the business was continued by his son, George Grainger, who introduced 'semi-porcelain' at the factory. The firm was absorbed into the Royal Worcester concern in 1889.

MARKS

GRAINGER LEE & CO
WORCESTER
1801–62

GRAINGER
& CO.

Grainger Lee & Co
Worcester
Printed in red

George Grainger
Royal China Works
Worcester
in red 1801–62

ROYAL CHINA CHINA
G&Co
1801
ENGLAND
Printed after 1823

WORK

Jewitt illustrates extravagantly pierced parian vases and ornamental wares; jugs shaped with the leaves of lily of the valley, the lotus and the waterlily; and a honeycomb coffee service. Parian statuary was made, as well as lithophanes.

Granite ware

Hard, durable and cheap white earthenware, made extensively for the American market in the middle of the nineteenth century. Not to be confused with the greyish, mottled glazed earthenware made by Josiah Wedgwood in imitation of granite. Also called GRANITE CHINA.

Grave insets

Comprising panels with figures and masonic emblems, oval plaques representing Charity, floral bouquets, fruit and flowers, vases and flaming urns; were made by Jonathan Harmer

in terra cotta at Heathfield, near Hailsham, Sussex, early nineteenth century. There is a representative collection in the Sussex Archaeological Museum, Lewes, at Brighton, and at Hastings. Grave insets, still *in situ* are recorded at Hailsham, Brighton and Hastings.

[Reginald G. Haggar, *English Country Pottery*, 1950.]

Grave slabs

Earthenware slabs as substitutes for brasses, iron grave memorials or grave-stones, were made in the seventeenth and early eighteenth centuries in various parts of England. Early Tudor slabs decorated *sgraffiato* are recorded at Lingfield, Surrey. Inlaid earthenware slabs occur at Great Malvern (1640) and Effingham in Surrey (1693). In Staffordshire grave slabs made of earthenware are recorded at Burslem (dates from 1728–1755) and Wolstanton (some still survive in the church porch). Sepulchral monuments in terra cotta were exhibited at the International Exhibition 1862 by Thomas Grimesley of Oxford, who intended them for churchyards.

[Arthur Lane, *A Guide to Tiles*, 1932, pp. 28, 30; Eliza Meteyard, *Life of Josiah Wedgwood*, Vol 1, 1865.]

Gray, A.E., and Company, Stoke-on-Trent, Staffordshire

A pottery decorating business was founded by A.E. Gray in 1912, first in Hanley and later at Whieldon road, Stoke, upon wares bought 'in the white' from other manufacturers such as Johnson Bros.

ARTISTS

Susan Vera Cooper. Later established her own factory.

S. C. Talbot

MARK:
A lithographic transfer-print, in colour, of a sailing ship.

Transfer

WORK

Good hand-painted wares, and painted 'resist' lustre.

Greatbach, William (born 1735 died 1813)

Modeller and potter, son of a farmer at Berry-hill; worked for Whieldon and came into contact with Josiah Wedgwood; manufactured biscuit pottery, particularly fruit and pineapple wares to be sent to Wedgwood's factory to glaze, at Lane Delph 1760–1770; his cream-coloured teapots decorated with black transfer-prints of 'The Prodigal Son' (engraved by Radford) are well known. He was ruined by a bad debt; worked for other potters, producing a good 'china' glaze for the Baddeleys of Shelton; in 1788 employed by the Turners of Lane End; and from 1788–1807 worked for the Wedgwood factory receiving a pension for life on his retirement. A teapot in the British Museum bears his name. He also used the Chinese Seal mark.

[Obit. *Staffordshire Advertiser*, 1 May 1813; W. B. Honey, *Wedgwood Ware*, 1948; S. Shaw, *History of the Staffordshire Potteries*, 1829; W. Mankowitz, *Wedgwood*, 1953.]

Great Totham, near Maldon, Essex

Earthenware was manufactured here in 1848 by William Butcher.

[White's *Directory of Essex*, 1848.]

Green, Aaron

Ceramic decorator and gilder; worked at Mintons 1860–98.

Green Brothers, Leeds, Yorkshire

Proprietors of the Leeds factory 1760–1774. See LEEDS.

Green family, Burslem and Fenton

The Churchyard Works, Burslem, was worked by Thomas Green in the closing years of the eighteenth and opening years of the nineteenth centuries (*Directories*, 1796–1805) as an earthenware factory. He became bankrupt in 1811 and went to Somerset, where he was accompanied by his son of the same name.

Thomas Green the younger (born 1798 died 1859) after working as a traveller, returned to the Potteries in 1822 and worked for Mintons and Copelands before setting up with his brother-in-law (an architect named Richards) as a china manufacturer at the Minerva works, Fenton, in 1833. After Thomas Green's death in 1859 the business was continued by his widow and sons under the style of M. Green & Co. Margaret Green (née Richards) died in 1877, the firm subsequently trading as T. A. & S. Green (Thomas Allen Green and Spencer Green) 1877 until 1897. In 1903 the firm became Crown Staffordshire Porcelain Co. Ltd. It is still operated by the Green family.

[*Directories*, 1796–1889; *Parish Registers*, Burslem; L. Jewitt, *Ceramic Art of Great Britain*, 1878; 'Bone China from Town Six' *Pottery Gazelle*, 1952; *British Bulletin of Commerce Survey*, 1954.]

Green glaze, see under WEDGWOOD.

Green, Guy, Liverpool

Partner in the firm of Sadler and Green and probably co-inventor of the process of transfer-printing on pottery. His signature 'Green, Liverpool' appears on some subjects. He continued in business ten years after Sadler's death, retiring in 1799.

Green, Stephen, Lambeth

Stephen Green made salt-glazed stoneware at the Imperial Pottery in Lambeth during the first half of the nineteenth century. The factory passed by purchase in 1858 into the hands of John Cliff but was closed in 1869. Pieces are marked Stephen Green, Imperial Potteries, Lambeth (impressed) or

The firm specialised in stoneware pistol flasks and other similar articles.

There is an example in the British Museum.

[G. Bemrose, *Eighteenth Century English Pottery and Porcelain*, 1952.]

Green, T.G. and Company, Church Gresley, Staffordshire

A pottery manufacturing coarse earthen washing basins and the like was built at Church Gresley, and passed successively through the hands of W.Bourne, Edwards of Burton-on-Trent, Shaw and Harrison, and Henry Wileman.

T.G. Green took the premises when Wileman died in 1864.

MARKS

Numerous marks have been used, usually with name of firm, type of ware, or pattern.

WORK

Greens made general pottery including yellow ware, Rockingham, black lustre, and 'dipped' pottery. Mocha was made here as well as sponged and lined wares.

[L.Jewitt, *Ceramic Art of Great Britain*, 1878.]

Greenock, Scotland

White and cream-coloured earthenware was manufactured from the second decade of the nineteenth century at several factories here, including the Clyde Pottery, 1816–1903 where cream-colour 'Fancy-coloured Edge' and printed earthenware was made. Punch-bowls are said to have been a speciality. The Greenock Pottery has operated from 1860 onwards.

Greenwich

R. Campbell in *The London Tradesman* (1747) writing of porcelain manufactures, stated 'there is a house at Greenwich and another at Chelsea'. Nothing more is known of this factory nor has its porcelain been identified.

[J.E.Nightingale, *Contributions towards the History of Early English Porcelain*, 1881.]

Greenwood, S., Fenton Staffordshire

A pottery owned by Greenwood is believed to have been in existence at Fenton from about 1780–1790.

A black basalt vase in the Wedgwood style with raised ornament and stamped S.GREENWOOD is in the British Museum.

Gresley, Sir Nigel Bowyer

Founder of the experimental Church Gresley porcelain factory, 1794.

Greybeard

A large earthenware spirit jar or jug; a Bellarmine. Possibly named from the greyish stoneware from which it was made and the fact that it usually was decorated with a bearded relief mask. 'We will give a cup of distilled waters… and ye may keep for the purpose the grounds of the last greybeard.' – Sir Walter Scott (1771–1832) *The Monastery*, 1820.

Griffith and Morgan, Lambeth.

It is known that this firm was manufacturing in 1776, perhaps making delftware.

Griffiths, Thomas

Figure manufacturer, Furnace Road, Longton, 1850.

Grisaille

Painting in grey monochrome.

Grocott, Samuel, Tunstall

Manufacturer of earthenware toys and figures at Liverpool Road, Tunstall, 1822–1828, and possibly the partner in the firm of Edge & Grocott which is known to have made tree-background figure groups in the Walton style with the impressed mark

EDGE & GROCOTT

[*Directories*, 1822, 1828; Reginald G. Haggar, *Staffordshire Chimney Ornaments*, 1955.]

Grog

Pulverised pottery introduced into some pottery bodies to reduce shrinkage during firing.

Groundlaying

A process of covering pottery with an even coating of colour by dusting powdered pigment upon a ground of oil made even by dabbing it with a fine white silk boss; stated to have been introduced by Henry Daniell c.1826 (S. Shaw, *History of the Staffordshire Potteries*, 1829).

Grubbe plates

Four plates presented to the Victoria and Albert Museum London by Mrs Dora Grubbe, a descendant of James Giles, the independent London porcelain decorator; used as a means of identifying wares decorated in Giles's workshop either by himself or his assistants.

Gruitt, Thomas

Name of modeller or maker of a bust of Empress Josephine, dated 1809.

[Reginald G. Haggar, *Staffordshire Chimney Ornaments*, 1955.]

H

Hackwood, Josiah

Toy and figure maker, Upper Hanley, first half of nineteenth century; his factory, offered to let (rent £ 20 per year) comprised one oven and three kilns. His stock of toys and figures 'Biscuit and finished' with moulds etc. offered for sale 1844.

[*Staffordshire Advertiser*, 24 February, 2 March 1844.]

Hackwood, William (died 1836)

Modeller to Josiah Wedgwood and his successors at Etruria from 1769 until 1832; modelled excellent portrait medallions and bas-reliefs, including one of Josiah Wedgwood 1779. By many regarded as the ceramic equal of Flaxman.

[W. Mankowitz, *Wedgwood* 1953; E. Meteyard, *Life of Josiah Wedgwood*, 1865–66.]

Hackwood (William) and Son, Earthenware Manufactory

William Hackwood was potting in Shelton from 1818 until 1853, (from 1842 until its closure, at the New Hall Works). The sale of his figures, utensils and stock of pottery was announced in the *Staffordshire Advertiser*, 10 December 1853, and included 'ornamental articles, gilt earthenware figures and richly enamelled table services. His mark was

  transfer-painted

William Hackwood died in 1849, his son Thomas continuing the business.

Haile, Sam (died 1948)

Teacher and potter. He studied at the Royal College of Art, South Kensington, 1931 until 1934 under Staite Murray, and held teaching posts at Leicester, Kingston and Hammersmith, 1935–36. In 1937 the Brygos Galleries staged a one-man show. He married the potter Marianne de Trey in 1938 and went to America.

In 1943 he enlisted in the army, and after the end of the war worked for a time at the Bulmer Brickyard, Sudbury, Suffolk (1945–1947), and finally from 1947–1948 at Shinners Bridge, Dartington.

[A.C.Sewter, *Apollo*, December 1946; G.W.Digby, *The Work of the Modern Potter in England*, 1952.]

Hales, T, Cobridge, Staffordshire

T. Hales and W. Adams owned a pottery at Cobridge from about 1769 until after 1787. At the beginning of the nineteenth century, Adams alone is mentioned in connection with the pottery. Voyez did work for Hales about 1771.

A cream-coloured vase in the British Museum bears the mark 'VOYEZ & HALES Fecit'.

[P.W.L.Adams, *The Adams Family*, 1914.]

Hall, John and Ralph, Burslem and Tunstall

John and Ralph Hall made blue-printed earthenware and figures at Swan Bank, Tunstall from the early years of the nineteenth century (Holden lists them in 1805), and also at the Sytch Pottery, Burslem. The partnership was dissolved 1 January 1822 (*Staffordshire Advertiser*, 5 February 1831).

Ralph Hall continued the Tunstall pottery. In 1846 it was under the name of Hall and Co., or Hall & Holland (James Holland being the other partner), who were followed by Podmore, Walker & Co., in 1849 (*Staffordshire Advertiser*, 30 June 1849).

John Hall continued at the Sytch, Burslem, taking his sons Joseph and Thomas into the business with him but they became bankrupt in 1832 (*Staffordshire Advertiser*, 20 October 1832, 12 January 1833). Both firms made blue-printed earthenware for the American market and enamelled figures, the latter being sometimes impressed HALL in large capitals at the back. Ralph Hall produced an engraved series of 'English Views', 'Pictoresque Scenery', and 'Italian Views'. His moulds at the final sale (11 July 1849) included a new table service 'designed and executed by Scragg unsurpassed for beauty of form'.

Impressed

[*Staffordshire Advertiser*, various dates; *Directories*.]

Hall, Samuel, Shelton

Potter and figure-maker, New Hall Street, Shelton from 1818 until 1834.

Hallam, Ephraim

Manufacturer of toys and ornaments at a small factory at Bourne's Bank, Burslem in 1851.

Hallam, Thomas (born 1812 died 1850)

Earthenware manufacturer at Longton, fl. 1840–1850.

[*Staffordshire Advertiser*, 30 April 1850.]

Hammon, Clement, Jersey?

In the Jermyn Street Collection, Victoria and Albert Museum, there is a stone china cup transfer-printed in black, marked 'Clement Hammon Jersey Stone'.

Hancock, George

Ceramic painter: son of John Hancock. He worked in the Staffordshire Potteries, at Mansfield, for the Ridgways, of Cauldon Works Shelton, then at Derby (1819–1835). For a brief period he is said to have managed a factory at Burton, after which he went to Lyons (1839). He died at Wordsley in South Staffordshire after 1850.

[J. Haslem, *Old Derby China Factory*, 1876.]

Hancock & Sheldon, Burslem

Earthenware manufacturers at the Hole House, Burslem 1818–1820. The house and potworks in the holding of Hancock and Sheldon with a considerable area of building land was announced for sale in the *Staffordshire Advertiser*, 14 October 1820. In 1818 John Hancock, potter, lived in Rotten Row, Burslem.

Hancock, John (born 1757 died 1847)

Ceramic decorator, born at Nottingham. He is said to have worked at Swansea and for Turner of Lane End (before 1800); claimed to have invented gold, silver and steel lustres which were first used at Spode's factory, Stoke; from 1816 he worked for Wedgwoods, Etruria; d. Etruria 18 July 1847.

[S. Shaw, *History of the Staffordshire Potteries*, 1829; J. Hancock, letter, *Staffordshire Mercury*, 1846.; W.D.John & Warren Baker, *Old English Lustre Pottery*, Newport, 1951.]

Hancock, Robert (born 1729/30 died 1817)

Engraver; son of John Hancock; the tradition that he was born in Burslem 1730–31 is not confirmed by the parish registers; apprenticed to George Anderton, Birmington 1746; working at York House, Battersea, 1753 as engraver for enamels, and associated with S.F. Ravenet, L.P. Boilard and John Brooks; possibly learnt the technique of mezzotint engraving from Brooks or Thomas Frye; probably at Bow 1756 for a brief period before moving to Worcester where he served as engraver, becoming partner in the business 1772–74; his pupils included Valentine Green (d. 1813) James Ross (1754–1821) John Lowick and probably Thomas Turner. Hancock joined Turner at the Caughley factory 1775. He was at Oldbury 1780 (and possibly did some engraving for Bilston enamels); Tividale, Nr Dudley 1781; Birmingham 1791; Bristol 1796; and London 1808. Died 14 October 1816 and buried at Brislington, Bristol.

R. Hancock fecit

RH. Worcester

RH Worcester

R. H. f.

[C. Cook, *The Life and Work of Robert Hancock*, 1948, contains an extensive bibliography; A.R. Ballantyne, *Robert Hancock and his Works*, 1885; W. Turner, *Transfer Printing on Enamels, Porcelain & Pottery*, 1907; *Transactions, English Ceramic Circle*, 1932–35, 1937, 1942, 46, 48; Cyril Cook, *Supplement to the Life and Work of Robert Hancock*, 1956.]

Hancock, Sampson, Derby

Successor to Stevenson and Hancock who worked the small china factory started by William Locker, Bloor's clerk, in 1848.

In red

Hand-and-Cup vase

'A little flower vase of 'Biscuit' or Parian ware, in the shape of a human hand, modelled *au na-*

turel, holding a narrow cup', popular in the 1860's. Said to have been manufactured in large quantities.

[C.L. Eastlake, *Hints on Household Taste*, London 1868, 4th ed. 1878.]

Hanley, Staffordshire

Slipware potters are believed to have worked in Hanley from the seventeenth century. Josiah Wedgwood however only listed seven potters as working here at the beginning of the eighteenth century, and it is evident from the accounts of Richard Pococke 1751, and the Hon. John Byng (Torrington Diaries), that Hanley was a comparatively recent growth in the mid and late eighteenth century. Important manufactures flourished here from 1750 onwards, those of Birch, Glass, Mayer, Palmer, Neale and Baddeley being of considerable interest to collectors. In the nineteenth century Keeling, Wilson, Salt, Shorthose, Meigh, and Ridgway occupied factories in the town, and produced a large variety of wares.

Hard paste porcelain

True porcelain manufactured from china clay and china stone, glazed with china stone made fusible with a flux. It shows a shining fracture when broken and is completely vitrified and dense. Only three factories made it, Plymouth, Bristol and New Hall in its early days. New Hall advertised its production as 'Real China'.

[H. Eccles and B. Rackham, *Analysed Specimens of English Porcelain*, 1922.]

Harding, W. & J., Shelton, Staffordshire

Successors to Cockson and Hackwood, previously Hackwood and Son at the New Hall factory, where they manufactured general pottery.

MARKS

Transfer painted

WORK:

Cream-coloured and transfer-printed wares were made as well as druggists' fittings, Egyptian black and 'Rockingham' glazed pottery.

Harley, Thomas (born 1778 died 1832), Lane End

Started in partnership with John, George and William Weston as manufacturer of earthenware at Lane End in 1799. The parnership lasted until 1801 when it was dissolved by mutual consent on 9 December. From 1801 Thomas Harley worked on his own account as an enameller, black printer and earthenware manufacturer. He was of some importance locally, and his name occurs in connection with a meeting for the abolition of the Slave Trade in 1814 and as a member of a committee of manufacturers protesting against the unfair incidence of the Window Tax in 1815. In 1818 the firm is styled Harley and Seckerson, earthenware manufacturers. Chaffers gives two marks:

T. Harley Lane End HARLEY

The name is impressed on a painted jug bearing a caricature of Napoleon, about 1809, and an earthenware plate transfer-printed with brown leaves.

A pale blue glazed earthenware milk jug in the British Museum also bears this mark impressed.

Harley also owned a pot-work on the canal at Greenbank, St. Helens, and a shop in Thomas Street, Dublin. He died at St. Helens in August 1832 and his will was proved at Chester 4 February 1833.

[*Staffordshire Advertiser*, 1801–1832; *Directories*, 1805–1818; T.C. Barker and J.R. Harris, *A Merseyside Town in the Industrial Revolution; St Helens 1750–1900*, 1954.]

Harmer, Jonathan, Heathfield, Sussex

A Sussex potter who manufactured terra cotta insets for gravestones and tombs c.1800–1820 at Heathfield, near Hailsham. In colour they vary from warm buff to orange-red, and were very capably modelled. They comprise oval plaques decorated with floral bouquets, or groups of fruit and flowers in relief, vases, torches and flaming urns. Some are signed

HARMER FECIT

There is a representative collection in the Sussex Archaeological Museum at Lewes; they also are found *in situ* in churchyards at Brighton, Hastings and Hailsham.

Harper, Thomas

Master potter, Montague Close, Southwark late seventeenth century, who possibly made stoneware of the Rhenish type.

[R.L. Hobson, B.F.A.C. Catalogue, 1913; B. Rackham and H. Read, *English Pottery*, 1924.]

Harris, Absalom

A country potter who established a factory at Elstead, Surrey, in 1860 but removed to Wrecklesham in 1872, where it was continued by his family.

Harrison, George, Fenton, Staffordshire

Jewitt cited an invoice dated 1793 (August 20) which included tureens, root dishes, 'Sallad bowls', tureen ladles and ewers. He evidently made blue-painted and printed earthenware and cream-colour.

[L. Jewitt, *Ceramic Art of Great Britain*, 1878.]

Harrison, John (born 1716 died 1798)

Partner with Thomas Alders (or Aldersea) and Josiah Wedgwood in a potworks at Cliff Bank, Stoke-on-Trent manufacturing agate and marble knife-hafts; cloudy, tortoiseshell and black wares; and salt-glazed stoneware, 1752–54. Later he continued at same factory. His son, John Harrison, continued the trade until he became bankrupt.

[L. Jewitt, *The Wedgwoods*, 1865; S. Shaw, *History of the Staffordshire Potteries*, 1829; W. Mankowitz, *Wedgwood Staffordshire Advertiser*, 1798.]

Harrison, John

Son of John Harrison (born 1716 died 1798) of Stoke-on-Trent; earthenware manufacturer at Cliff Bank, Stoke, from 1783 or earlier until 1802 when he became bankrupt. His two factories were offered for sale in 1802 and again in 1804 when his assignees were stated to be John Baddeley of Shelton, Miles Mason of Lane Delph and William Booth of Hanley. Further announcements concerning his bankruptcy were made from 1805 until 1814.

[Bailey's *Directory*, 1783; *Jurors Book*, Salt Library, 1784; *Staffordshire Pottery Directory* n.d. but c. 1796; *Staffordshire Advertiser*, 1802, 1804, 1805–1814.]

Harrison, John, Tunstall

Manufacturer of china toys and blackware at Tunstall 1829.

[*Directories.*]

Harrison, Lawrence (died 1794), Liverpool

Harrison is listed as a victualler and potter in Williamson Street, (Gore's *Liverpool Directory*, 1769).

Hartley, Greens & Co, Leeds

A firm which flourished from 1783 until 1820. See LEEDS.

Harvey, Charles and Sons, Longton.

Charles Harvey built the factory in Stafford Street, Longton, in 1799 where he traded with his sons until the firm was taken over by Hulme & Hawley. It was returned to the Harvey family about 1840, and in 1841 they were working three factories in Longton. The partners at this time were Charles Harvey, junior, and W.K. Harvey, both sons of the founder. The firm closed down in 1853. They manufactured china, earthenware, gold lustre, and later 'granite', and painted earthenware.

Transfer-printing

Haslem, John (born 1808)

Derby flower painter; author of *The Old Derby China Factory*, 1876.

Hassall, Thomas (born 1878 died 1940)

Studied at Stoke Art School; joined W. T. Copeland & Sons as pottery painter 1892, became art director 1910, and Company director 1932; died 7 April.

[Obit. *Evening Sentinel*, April 1940.]

Hastings, Sussex

Henry Richardson of Brede had an interest in a potworks in Hastings in the eighteenth century, and on January 30 1773, appealed against a rate

assessment in connection with it. It was in St. Clement's Parish where another potter, John Sargent at a later date probably worked the same factory (1794).

In the nineteenth century a potworks called variously the Tivoli and Silverhill pottery was built by King Eldridge and worked by various potters until 1886. It was demolished 1895.

[J.M.Baines, *Sussex Pottery*, 1948.]

Hawley, Thomas

The impressed mark of THO HAWLEY occurs on a bust of John Wesley, coloured in green and blue underglaze but is not otherwise recorded. Honey records a mark HAWLEY for the Kilnhurst pottery, Yorkshire, but potters of this name were working both in Yorkshire and Staffordshire in the nineteenth century.

Hawley of Kilnhurst Old Pottery also held the Rawmarsh pottery. In 1818 and 1822 the style of the firm was Turner & Hawley. The factory was bought from them by the Bramelds.

THO HAWLEY

Impressed

Hayes, Joseph (born 1756 died 1842), Flint

Earthenware manufacturer at Buckley Mountain, Flint, early decades of the nineteenth century.

[Obit., *Staffordshire Advertiser*, 23 April 1842.]

Hayward, Chesterfield

Josiah Wedgwood writing to his partner, Bentley, 14 January 1777, refers to a manufacture of 'Crich' ware at Chesterfield of which Mr Hayward was the proprietor.

'Hearty-good-fellow'

A Toby jug in the form of a swaggering standing figure, first made late eighteenth century by Lakin and Poole, and in nineteenth century by Walton.

Heath, Job (born 1678)

A slipware potter whose name occurs on a posset-pot dated 1702, in the Ashmolean Museum,

Oxford. *Stoke Parish Registers* record the marriage of Job Heath, potter, to Elizabeth Taylor, 28 April 1701.

Heath, John, Burslem

China and figure manufacturer at the Sytch, Burslem, 1810–1823 *(Directories)*. The name occurs occasionally on pottery figures.
[*Staffordshire Advertiser*, 15 Sept. 1810.]

Heath, Thomas, Lane Delph, Staffordshire

A potter, described by Simeon Shaw as manufacturing 'dipped' ware, a type of pottery popular in the eighteenth century. He is said to have flourished c.1710 and to have married off his daughters to three celebrated potters, Neale Palmer and Pratt. Shaw's vague description of the process led Solon and others to assert that Heath introduced the delft technique into Staffordshire.
[S. Shaw, *History of the Staffordshire Potteries*, 1829.]

Heath, Thomas (born 1762 died 1828)

Pottery artist, Shelton; died at Hanford.
[Obit. *Pottery Mercury*, 5 April 1828.]

Heath, William, Longton

Manufacturer of china toys in the High Street, Longton, 1860.

Heath & Son, Burslem, Staffordshire

The impressed mark HEATH & SON is thought to be that of a Burslem firm manufacturing white earthenware, late in the eighteenth century and in the early years of the nineteenth century. It is listed as HEATH & SONS in the *Staffordshire Pottery Directory*, (c.1796).

Heathcote, C. and Co, Longton

Made good quality blue-printed earthenware (sometimes from Turner's engravings) as well as painted and gilded wares, early nineteenth century. Mark used consisted of the Prince of Wales feathers with the name C. HEATHCOTE & Co. in an arc above.

Hempel, F. C, Chelsea

Tablewares and ornamental pottery, as yet unidentified, were made at Chelsea by F.C. Hempel, and later by his widow from about 1774–1797. It is suggested that a vase marked 'F. Muller Chelsea 1789' may have originated here (Victoria and Albert Museum).

Henk, John (born 1846 died 1914)

Modeller, student Stoke Art School 1863–68; worked for Mintons, Stoke, 1863–1914.
Plate 68 B.
[Reginald G. Haggar, *A Century of Art Education in the Potteries*, 1953.]

Henshall & Williamson, Longport

Successors to William Clowes & Company, earthenware manufacturers and makers of black basaltes, Longport, Burslem, from c.1800. The partnership between Hugh Henshall Williamson and Robert Williamson was dissolved 31 December 1830 after which the business was carried on under the name Henshall & Williamson, but by Robert Williamson only.
[*Directories*, 1805, 1818; *Staffordshire Advertiser*, 13 August 1831.]

Herculaneum, Liverpool

A potworks near the site of the present Herculaneum Dock in Liverpool was founded by Richard Abbey & Graham in 1793. It was sold to Worthington, Humble & Holland three years later. Employed there were forty men, women and children brought from Staffordshire in 1796. Archibald Mansfield, a thrower from Burslem who afterwards potted on own account in Liverpool, was foreman or manager. The company was enlarged in 1806 and continued to operate until 1833 when the partnership was dissolved and the property sold to Ambrose Lace and others for £25,000. Among those who were in partnership at this time was John Mort, son of the Rev. James Mort and nephew of John Mort master potter of Cobridge. Lace leased the premises to Thomas Case, gentleman, and John Mort, potter, who operated until 1836. Subsequently the firm traded as Mort and Simpson until the works were closed down in 1841. Apart from the

Herculaneum Pottery the company was also in occupation of an earthenware factory on the Sankey Canal, St Helens (1 biscuit, 2 gloss ovens). The advertisement of the sale of stock in the *Staffordshire Advertiser*, 14 November 1840, stated that the Herculaneum Pottery was 'now about to be pulled down for the erection of docks'. An 'Unreserved sale of valuable copper-plate engravings Blocks and Cases, superior Figure Moulds' to be held at the Leopard Inn, Burslem, was advertised in the *North Staffordshire Mercury*, 23 January 1841. The products of the factory included blue-printed earthenware, cream-coloured stoneware jugs, drab stoneware, busts, earthenware figures, and from 1801 porcelain of the Staffordshire type.

MARKS

HERCULANEUM in a semi-circle above a crown; a crown enclosed by a garter inscribed HERCULANEUM; the word HERCULANEUM impressed; HERCULANEUM POTTERY impressed: a scroll enclosing the so-called 'liver' bird was sometimes used, as also a 'liver' bird surrounded by a floral wreath with the word HERCALUNEUM in an arc above and a scroll inscribed LIVERPOOL beneath (printed in red) on porcelain.

HERCULANEUM
Impressed

[*Staffordshire Advertiser*, 1833, 1840, 1841 numerous advertisements; *Staffordshire Mercury*, 1829; *North Staffordshire Mercury*, 1841; H.B.Lancaster, *Liverpool & her Potters*, 1936; Mayer, *History of the Art of Pottery in Liverpool*, 1855; L. Jewitt, *Ceramic Art of Great Britain*, 1878.]

Herefordshire

A number of medieval pottery sites existed in this county; in the late seventeenth and early eighteenth centuries wares similar to those made in Staffordshire were produced at a number of workshops at Whitney-on-Wye, Boresford, Upton Bishop and various sites in Deerfold Forest. Tygs, posset-pots (occasionally with applied pads of clay impressed with a coat-of-arms), costrels, pitchers, dishes and candlesticks were made. A crude *sgraffiato* zig-zag appears on the plates. The glaze effects ranged from copper-green to pale straw colour.

[Marshall, *Woolhope Transactions*, 1946.]

Hicks, Richard (born 1765 or 9 died 1844)

Engraver and manufacturer; born Shrewsbury, son of Richard Hicks (1740–1815); apprenticed to Thomas Turner at Caughley; partner of Joseph Boon (Boon & Hicks, Shelton) 1805–1808, and of Job Meigh (Hicks & Meigh, later Hicks, Meigh & Johnson) 1810–1835; made stone china and blue-printed earthenware; married Lydia Meigh 1801; died White House Shelton, 2 March 1844.

[Obit. *Staffordshire Advertiser*, 9 March 1844; *Register of Deaths*, Bethesda Chapel, Hanley; Jewitt, *Ceramic Art of Great Britain*, 1878; R.G.Haggar, *The Masons of Lane Delph*, 1952.]

Hicks & Meigh, Shelton, Staffordshire

Successors to the Baddeleys of Shelton, and manufacturers of good ironstone china from 1810 until 1835. The partners were Richard Hicks, Job Meigh, and from 1822 a man named Johnson, when the firm was Hicks, Meigh & Johnson.

WORK

Transfer-printed and enamelled ware were extensively manufactured. A fine specimen attributed to this factory is the large Bellringers' jug in the Newcastle-under-Lyme Museum, which is painted with the Borough coat of arms.

MARKS

Printed

Hilditch died 22 September 1843, aged 51 years, and his son William, who was also in the business, on 1st January 1850, aged 21 years. The firm however continued under the same style until 1858 when Hopwood died. It was subsequently continued by his executors until May 1867 when the stock and plant, including moulds and copperplates as well as the business, were purchased by Dale, Page & Co. The mark H & S within a wreath and underneath a crown, or within a square frame beneath an eagle are recorded by Honey and Chaffers.

[*Gravestones* in St Johns and St James Churchyards, Longton; *Directories*, 1818–75; *Government Report*, 1843; *Staffordshire Advertiser*, 1813, 1817, 1851; *Pottery Mercury*, 1826; *Poll List*, 1841; L.Jewitt, *Ceramic Art of Great Britain*, 1878.]

High Halden, Kent

A country pottery existed here in the nineteenth century, using slip decoration and the inlaid technique. Geoffrey Bemrose in *Nineteenth Century Pottery and Porcelain* (1952) illustrated a money-box with the inlaid name, J.G. DUDEN, marked 'HALDEN POTTERY'.

A small rectangular plaque with a relief representation of the Kentish Siamese Twins, Eliza and Mary Chulkhurst, of Biddenden illustrated in *Apollo* 1943, attributed to this factory, appears to have been an imitation of the Biddenden Cake which William Hone illustrated in *The Everyday Book* Vol 2, 1827.

Hilditch, Lane End & Lane Delph

There were many potters of this name working at Lane Delph and Lane End in the eighteenth century whose products cannot now be identified. The firm of Hilditch & Co. made bone china at Lane End from about 1805 until 1813 when the dwelling house and set of potworks 'used as a china manufactory and occupied by Messrs Hilditch & Co.' were offered for sale (*Staffordshire Advertiser*, 23 July 1813). In 1818 the firm is listed as Hilditch & Martin (*Parson & Bradshaw's Directory* 1818). In the 1820's the firm was known as Hilditch & Son. In 1830 John Hilditch was joined in partnership by William Hopwood and the firm became known as Hilditch and Hopwood (Jewitt). John

Hill, Thomas (born 1753 died 1827)

Son of a Battersea enamel painter of the same name. He worked at Chelsea, 1779, where he had contact with and was influenced by Z. Boreman: he possibly took lessons with Paul Sandby. There is a gap in his career between 1784 and 1794 when he went to Derby. He painted landscapes, often of swift-moving mountain streams with stepping-stones, using a bright palette of colours including a prominent yellow and green. He was in London in 1800 and died 1827. He was popularly known as 'Jockey' Hill.

Hobbs, Henry, Bristol

Potter at the Limekiln Lane potworks from 1706 until 1715. He died in 1724.

[W.B.Pountney, *Old Bristol Potteries*, 1920.]

Hobson, Ephraim, Cobridge

Manufacturer of earthenware toys and Egyptian Black, 1800–1818.

Holdcroft, Joseph, Longton

Parian, majolica and lustre ware manufactured by Joseph Holdcroft at the Sutherland Pottery, Daisy Bank, Longton, from 1870. Holdcroft had learnt the trade at Mintons. A 'Wren' vase with well-modelled birds and foliage was a speciality of the factory.

MARK

impressed

Holdship, Richard and Josiah, Worcester

Engravers and part-proprietors of the original porcelain works at Worcester, from 1751 until 1759. Richard Holdship went to Derby, and in 1764 offered to impart information concerning the Worcester porcelain formula, and to teach 'Printing in Enamell and Blew'.

Rivalry existed between Josiah Holdship and Robert Hancock, and a couplet printed in *The Gentleman's Magazine*, (20th December 1757), 'Inscribed to Mr Josiah Holdship' was reprinted in the *Worcester Journal* (January 1758) with a rejoinder. It reads

'What praise is thine, ingenius Holdship, who
On a fair porcelain the Portrait drew.
Hancock, my friend, don't grieve tho'
    Holdship has the praise,
'Tis yours to execute, 'tis his to wear the bays.'

MARK

Some Worcester engravings carry not only the signature of Hancock in full, but a rebus design of R H in monogram and an anchor

These marks are traditionally regarded as those of Holdship who was believed to have been in charge of the printing department. This mark however may stand for Robert Hancock who later added his signature in full because the monogram was confused with that of Holdship. Much confusion has arisen from the initials of Hancock and R. Holdship being the same. The monogram with the reversed 'R' has been described as RJH and believed to represent Richard and Josiah Holdship.

Holdsworth, Peter, Ramsbury, Wiltshire

The Holdsworth Potteries were started in 1945 at Ramsbury near Marlborough.

MARK

Holland, Thomas (born 1748 died 1807)

'Manufacturer of black and red china ware and Gilder'. Commenced make pottery in Burslem c. 1785. First recorded in 1787 in Tunnicliff's *Survey of the Counties of Stafford, Chester and Lancaster*. Married Ann Hill (born 1773) on 5 August 1801 but died a few years later and was buried in St John's Churchyard, Burslem, 17 July 1807. The business was carried on at Liverpool Road, Burslem by his widow until 1841 or later. Mrs Ann Holland died 9th December 1847, aged 74 years.

[*Burslem Parish Registers*; Tunnicliff's *Survey*, 1787; *Staffordshire Advertiser*, 11 Dec. 1847; *Directories*.]

Holland, Thomas, Burslem

Born c.1778–79, baptised 17 January 1779. Son of Thomas and Thomasine Holland. Recorded variously as a potter at the Sytch, Burslem, 1818; a potter's presser in 1822–23; as a manufacturer of earthenware toys and figures in Church Street, Burslem, 1828 and 1834; and as a pottery modeller in 1834. He was uncle of James Holland (born 1799 died 1870) the water colour painter.

[*Directories*, 1818–34; *Parish Registers, Burslem;* Reginald G. Haggar, 'The Birth and Parents of James Holland' in *Apollo*, 1948.]

Holland, W. Fishley, and G. T.

Studio potters at Clevedon, Somerset, whose marks are the signatures of the potters written cursively.

Hollins, Michael Daintry (born 1815 died 1898)

Born in Manchester, 22 March 1815, son of Thomas Hollins, merchant, of Cheetham Hill and Sarah Clegg his wife. He was the grandson of Samuel Hollins, partner in the New Hall concern. He qualified as a surgeon but in 1838 abandoned the scalpel for potting and became partner to his uncle Herbert Minton of Stoke-on-Trent in 1845. The firm was known as Minton, Hollins & Co., manufacturers of china and earthenware, stone and parian wares, and mosaic and encaustic pavements, and situated at Elden Place and Church Street, Stoke. Hollins was closely connected with the development of the tile business and when in 1868 the business was divided he took over the tile works and shortly afterwards built a new factory in Stoke-on-Trent, specially designed for tile manufacture.' The firm still continues. Gordon Forsyth was art director 1903–1905.

[Furnival, *Leadless Decorative Tiles, Faience and Mosaic*, 1904; Rupert Simms, *Bibliotheca Staffordiensis*, 1894; J.C. Wedgwood, *Staffordshire Pottery and its History*, n.d. (1914); *British Bulletin of Commerce Survey*, 1954–55.]

Hollins, Samuel (born 1748 died 1820), Shelton, Staffordshire

Son of Richard Hollins (born 1702 died 1780) of Far Green, Hanley; manufacturer of earthenware and 'red china' at a factory on the Caulden Canal, Vale Pleasant, Shelton, from c.1780 until c.1815. He was one of the original partners in the New Hall concern which traded as Hollins, Warburton & Co., and by a codicil to his will dated 27 April 1820 he left his interest in the Company (valued at his death £5,975), to his son Thomas Hollins of Cheetham Hill, Manchester.

Hollins gave money for the building of Hanley Church in 1787 and the Parsonage House in 1813. He died in 1820 and was buried in Hanley Churchyard where there is a plain table-tomb to his memory.

About 1815 he must have made over his earthenware business to Matthew Mare, his son-in-law (who manufactured earthenware on the Cauldon Canal and is listed in Parson and Bradshaw's *Directory* 1818).

Samuel Hollins made excellent unglazed dark green and dark red stonewares with relief decoration. In 1825 the earthenware factory 'which may easily be converted into a silk or any other factory...' with 45 acres of land and 28 houses in Shelton, Etruria and Bucknall 'the property of the late SAMUEL HOLLINS Esq.' was offered for sale by private contract (*Pottery Mercury*, 8 June 1825). Matthew Mare who remained in occupation until 1826 probably declined business in that year since a further advertisement in the *Pottery Mercury*, 26 July 1826, says the china and earthenware works may be entered upon immediately.

A bowl and teapot in brown stoneware marked 'S. Hollins' are in the British Museum.

[*Parish Registers*, Stoke and Bucknall; *Jurors' List*, 1784; *Directories*, 1783–1805; *The Pottery Mercury*, 1826; A. Huntbach, *Hanley, Stoke-on-Trent*, 1910; G. E. Stringer, *New Hall Porcelain*, 1949.]

Hollins, T. & J., Far Green, Hanley, Staffordshire

The pottery at Hanley was established about 1750 by Richard Hollins, who was succeeded by his sons, T. & J. Hollins.

Samuel Hollins, brother of Richard Hollins, occupied a factory at Shelton at about the same period (see Samuel Hollins).

T. & J. Hollins made good-quality stonewares in the Wedgwood style, in the characteristic colours of blue, red, green and maroon, usually with raised cameo figures, or other decoration, sometimes in white. Their mark was

T. & J. HOLLINS
(impressed)

Hollins & Ford, Red Street, Wolstanton, Staffordshire

William Hollins and George Ford manufactured earthenware at Red Street, Wolstanton until 22 August 1799. Red Street was the home of North Staffordshire red-ware potters.

Holmes, George, Derby

An inscription 'George Holmes did this figer 1765' is recorded upon a Derby figure formerly in the Leverhulme Collection but nothing is known of this modeller, except that he may have been the repairer cited by Jewitt in a list of factory hands in 1787.

[L. Jewitt, *Ceramic Art of Great Britain*, 1878; W.B. Honey, *Old English Porcelain*, 1928, new ed. 1948.]

Homeric Vase

Regarded by Josiah Wedgwood, next to the Portland Vase, as his greatest achievement. The cameo subject, 'The Apotheosis of Homer' was modelled by Flaxman c.1776.

Homeric vases were made in blue solid jasper, black, and perhaps in grey. They were often later mounted upon ornamental bases with gryphon angles, or circular drums. A companion vase ornamented with 'The Apotheosis of Virgil' was also made.

The first Homeric vase was given by Wedgwood to the British Museum. There is a fine specimen in Nottingham Castle Museum. Another example in the Metropolitan Museum, New York.

[W. Mankowitz, *Wedgwood*, 1953.]

Honiton, Devonshire

A coarse earthenware pottery was established at Honiton in the early years of the eighteenth century but was totally destroyed by fire in May 1756 (London *General Evening Post* 10 June

1756). *Sgraffiato* decorated slipware was made here although the manufactures were not very extensive (Lewis, *Topographical Dictionary of England* 1848; White's *Directory of Devonshire* 1850). In 1850 Susan Hussey was making brown earthenware but the business declined and finally closed down. James Webber reopened the 'old pottery' before 1881 but moved to a new site in that year. His manufacture included flowerpots, bread pans and baking dishes which the maker hawked in and around Exeter every Saturday. Foster & Hunt succeeded Webber; and C. Collard took over the business in 1918 and started to make 'art' pottery which has been the staple ever since. Collard sold the business in 1947 to the present proprietors.

COLLARD
HONITON
ENGLAND

NORMAN HULL
POTTERY
N.T.S. Hull

[Coxhead, *The Romance of Wool, Lace and Pottery Trades in Honiton*, 1953.]

Hood, George, Tunstall and Burslem

Identified as the 'Geo. H' whose ramshackle, backstreet potworks was described in '*When I was a Child*' by 'An Old Potter' (1903). Hood is first listed as an earthenware toy manufacturer in 1822. His business prospered and in 1831 he acquired land at Brownhills and built the Highgate Pottery. In 1835 he also took over John Walton's figure and toy factory in Navigation Road, Burslem. In 1834 his son Henry died and in 1837 his wife. The Walton factory was offered for sale in June 1838 and in July of the same year the factory equipment at Brownhills including a valuable set of engravings 'under an execution from the Sheriff' was put up for auction. But the Walton factory apparently was not sold for George Hood continued in occupation until 1841. The *Staffordshire Advertiser*, 16 January 1841, reported a serious calamity at George Hood's warehouse in Burslem (Waltons Old Factory) when the warehouse floor holding nearly ten tons of ware collapsed upon 20

workers underneath seriously injuring three women. In 1841 the Highgate Factory was offered for sale. Afterwards George Hood started up again in a small way on Bourne's Bank where he employed 12 workpeople making figures and dogs.

[Reginald G. Haggar, *Staffordshire Chimney Ornaments*, 1955; *Staffordshire Advertiser*, 1831, 1834, 1837, 1839, 1841; *N. Staffordshire Mercury*, 1841.]

Horrobin, Richard (born 1765 died 1830)

Joiner, carpenter and organ builder, and evidently a ceramist of resource for his obituary notice in the *Staffordshire Advertiser* (27 November 1830) describes him as 'the reviver of gold lustre on china and earthenware'.

Hot Lane, Burslem

A road leading from Smallthorne to Cobridge and the scene of the commencement in North Staffordshire of on-glaze enamelling of stoneware and earthenware about 1750. Two Dutchmen are stated to have been responsible for its introduction. The Warburtons and the Daniels became active in this branch of the pottery industry which was at this time worked separately from pottery manufacture. Enamellers purchased ware 'in the white' for decoration, or decorated wares to manufacturers' instructions. The most celebrated eighteenth century enamelling establishments were those of 'Widow' Warburton, and Warner Edwards.

Hounslow, Middlesex

Combed slip dishes and other country pottery were made in the eighteenth century. From 1830, for a short period, wares similar to those made at Isleworth were made here.

Hubble, Nicholas, Wrotham

There were two slipware potters of this name, the elder dying in 1689. The initials 'N H' occur on slipware tygs and other vessels from the 1640's until 1687.

[J.W.L.Glaisher Appendix to B.Rackham and H.Read, *English Pottery*, 1924.]

Hudibras

An equestrian figure made by Ralph Wood of Burslem after an engraving by William Hogarth for an illustrated edition of Butler's satire, published in 1726 (B. Rackham, *Animals in Staffordshire Pottery* 1933). Popular over a long period of time and made in earthenware with glaze colours and enamel colour effects from about 1770 until 1800.

Plate 146.

Hughes, Thomas (born 1686 died 1758)

A china painter of St Pancras, Middlesex, who had two apprentices, John Gabriel Jorney at Clerkenwell in 1749 and James Bouskell at St Pancras in 1751. Hughes died in April 1758.

[A. J. Toppin, *English Ceramic Circle Transactions*, 1933; W.H.Tapp, *ibid* 1939.]

Hugheson class of slipware

This class is notable for the use of (1) a green slip or a copper green stain in the lead glaze, (2) strapwork ornament, and (3) treatment of handles somewhat like those of Wrotham Pottery. It comprises jugs with the name SAMUEL HUGHESON dated 1677 and 1678 in the Fitzwilliam Museum, Cambridge; posset-pots lettered JOHN HUGHESON dated 1690 and 1691 in the same collection; and allied pieces such as the JOHN WENTER 1686 jug in the British Museum, and a posset-pot (ANN BENOM F K 1687) and a jug (RICHARD DENNIS) in the Ashmolean Museum at Oxford.

The provenance of this class is difficult to determine. Rackham and Read in *English Pottery* 1924 attributed the class to Staffordshire, but Rackham omitted all reference to it in his more recent *Early Staffordshire Pottery* 1948. The name Hugheson does not occur in the Parish Registers of Stoke, Wolstanton and Burslem at these dates. The only possible reference is a mutilated entry under marriage at Stoke, 8 November 1689 ('... Hughson de Civitate Cestrae & ... Dresser de Dilhorn.') which refers to a Mr Hughson of the City of Chester.

Hull, Belle Vue Pottery

A potworks was started here by James and Jeremiah Smith, Job Ridgway of Shelton and

Colour plate 9, LOWESTOFT: *see page vii for caption*

Josiah Hipwood in 1802. In 1806 the factory passed to Job and George Ridgway who, after working it for a few years, closed it down. In 1825 William Bell purchased the pottery and used it until 1840.

Much cream-ware, usually painted or transfer-printed in blue or brown with landscapes, etc., was exported to Germany, together with various potter's materials and colours. The factory was a large one with a depot in Hamburg.

Specimens are in the British Museum, and marked thus

Impressed

Transfer-printed

Hulme, Jesse (born 1789 died 1852)

Portrait artist, designer and engraver; before 1816 he was at Swinton, Yorkshire and presumably connected with the Swinton Factory; moved to New Hill Old Hall (5 miles north of Rotherham) 1820; came to Staffordshire 1825 and attempted to make porcelain; became ceramic decorator and worked as engraver for Wedgwoods 1842–44; died Albion Street, Shelton 16 April 1852.

[L.Jewitt, *Ceramic Art of Great Britain*, 1878; *Art Journal*, 1858; obit. *Staffordshire Advertiser*, 23 April 1852.]

Hulme, John (born 1771 died 1831)

Earthenware manufacturer at Lane End and principal in the firm of John Hulme & Sons (*Staffordshire Advertiser*, 16 July 1831). His son, H. Hulme, who was associated with his father's business, died in 1829 (*Pottery Mercury*, 26 September 1829).

Humble, Green & Co, Leeds, Yorkshire

Proprietors of the Leeds Pottery 1774–1783. See LEEDS.

Hunslet, Leeds, Yorkshire.

Several potteries manufacturing coarse pottery existed at Hunslet Moor in the first half of the nineteenth century.

Hunslet Hall, Leeds, Yorkshire

Cream-coloured and blue-printed earthenware of good quality was made at Hunslet Hall Pottery by Petty and Rainforth from c.1792. The factory was continued until 1880 or later under various names.

1818 Pettys & Co.   1825 Samuel Petty & Son
1822 Petty & Hewitt   1847 John Mills

MARKS

RAINFORTH & CO.

(impressed)

was used in the 1790's. As much of this factory's output was unmarked it is thought to pass for that of the Leeds Factory.

[A.Hurst, *Catalogue of a Collection of Yorkshire Pottery*, 1922.]

Hürten, Charles Ferdinand (born 1818 died c. 1897)

Born in Cologne; went to France in 1836, became a painter of flowers, and worked for the Sèvres works. His work at the 1858 Paris International Exhibition attracted the interest of Copelands whose service he entered in 1859, remaining with them until 1897. He became well-known as a ceramic flower painter excelling in realist groups painted either from water-

colour sketches or direct from nature. He exhibited in London in 1865.
[A. Hayden, *Spode and his Successors*, 1924.]

Hyatt & Harrison, Fenton

Manufactured earthenware at a 'newly erected
Set of Potworks' at Lower Lane, Fenton, from
c.1796 to c.1805. The factory was offered 'to be
let' in 1801 (*Staffordshire Advertiser*, 9 May 1801).
The partners were William Hyatt of Newcastle-
under-Lyme, attorney, and George Harrison of
Fenton.

I

Images, Image Toys

Earthenware, stoneware or porcelain figures.
The word occurs in an advertisement of Wil-
liam Littler & Company – 'Beautiful Essence
Pots, Images, Flowers, Vases etc.' in *Aris's Bir-
mingham Gazette*, 12 June 1758.
Plates 1, 2 B and C, 3, 94, 95.

Imari

A familiar name for the porcelains exported by
Japan from Arita in the province of Hizan
during the first half of the eighteenth century.
'Brocaded Imari' in blue, red and gold were the
inspiration of later English china and earthenware patterns made at Derby, Worcester, Spode,
Mintons and Masons. These were generally
known as 'Japans'.
Plates 12 C, 133 A and B.

Incised decoration

Decoration cut into the paste or body with a
sharp pointed instrument. Much used by country potters for names, inscriptions and dates.
See also SGRAFFIATO.

Independent decorators

In the eighteenth and early nineteenth century
porcelain was often bought 'in the white' for
decoration by outside firms of enamellers and
gilders, the most notable of whom were Giles,
Duesbury, Baxter (who embellished Coalport
China), T. M. Randall & R. Robins (who from
Spa Fields, London, decorated Swansea, Nantgarw and Coalport for London dealers).

Salt-glazed stoneware was similarly decorat-
ed by Duesbury, and cream-coloured ware by
Mrs Warburton at Cobridge, Robinson &
Rhodes at Leeds, and Absolon at Yarmouth.

Other outside decorators were Fidèle Duvivier, Allen of Lowestoft, John Cutts & Sons of
Shelton.

Initialist 'I.B.'

The initials I.B. occur with some frequency,
either alone or in combination with other initials on slipwares of Staffordshire type, includ-
ding jugs and posset-pots (dates 1690–1700). It
has been suggested that these stand for the
name Izaac Ball, whom see.
[Reginald G. Haggar, in *Apollo*, December 1953.]

Initialist 'I.S.'

Possibly John Simpson of Chell, who made
mottled and black wares at Rotten Row, Burslem, 1710–1715, or Joseph Simpson of Newcastle-under-Lyme, who made red dishes and
pans in the same locality. The initials occur
mostly on dishes with relief decoration of
pomegranates and fleur-de-lis, perhaps inspired
by stump work pictures.

Initialist 'I.W.'

See JOHN WRIGHT.

Initialist 'R.F.'

The initials R.F. which occur with some frequency on slipwares of late seventeenth and
early eighteenth centuries, in conjunction with
others, may stand for Ralph or Richard Fletcher

who are both listed among the inhabitants of Burslem in the *Tunstall Court Rolls* 1671. The initials occur on pieces dated 1682, 1686, 1688, 1696 and 1697.

Intaglio

Decoration which is incised or sunken, as opposed to that in relief.

Ipstones, Staffordshire

Site of a coarse earthenware pottery which was excavated at Hay House Farm, Belmont in this parish in 1950. Pitchers, vinegar kegs, mugs, bowls, settling pans and the like were made. One piece of slipware decorated with trailed decoration was found and was evidently of eighteenth century date. An advertisement announcing 'A coarse POTTERY to be let... between Leek and Cheadle, Staffordshire' in the *Staffordshire Advertiser*, 16 September 1797 clearly referred to this potworks.

[Information per W.D. Johnsone who excavated the site.]

Ipswich, Suffolk

Slipware pottery was made in the Rope Walk, Ipswich, from the late eighteenth century or earlier. A dish with combed and feathered slip treatment is recorded by Rackham and Read, marked 'W. BALAAM Rope Lane Pottery IPSWICH'.

In 1844 Mary Ann Schulen and John William Schulen worked pottery factories in Rope Lane (known as Rope Walk) Mill Place and Back Street. Lewis in his Topographical History described the manufacture as 'extensive'.

[White's *Directory of Suffolk*, 1844; Lewis, *Topographical Dictionary of England*, 1848; Rackham and Read, *English Pottery*, 1924.]

Ireson, Nathaniel

A delftware potter connected with the factory at Wincanton, Somerset, from 1737 until 1748.

[G. Sweetman, *Nathaniel Ireson, a West Country Potter*, 1900; Hugh Owen, *Two Centuries of Ceramic Art in Bristol*, 1873; W. J. Pountney, *Old Bristol Potteries*, 1920; F. H. Garner, *English Delftware*, 1948.]

Ironstone China

A hard, durable white earthenware alleged to contain slag of ironstone as one of its ingredients, patented by Charles James Mason in 1813. The patent specification was false and unworkable. Other firms have used the name, notably Ridgway & Morley and Geo. L. Ashworth & Bros.

Plates 4 B, 65 A, C and D.

[Reginald G. Haggar, *The Masons of Lane Delph*, 1952.]

Isleworth, Middlesex. Earthenware manufactory.

The factory here was established about 1760 by Joseph Shore. Richard and William Goulding later owned it. It closed down about 1825.

A type of porcelain akin to that of Worcester was formerly ascribed to this factory in error, although porcelain may have been made at Isleworth prior to 1800.

'Welsh' wares, useful domestic articles decorated with zig-zag patterns in brown and yellow slip, were probably the main products of the factory.

Red, green and buff terra cotta teapots and ornamental pieces with relief decoration and of nineteenth century manufacture, marked 'S. & G', have been wrongly ascribed to this factory. Its mark was:

S & G

Islington china manufactory, Liverpool

This manufactory was operated by Thomas Wolfe of Stoke-on-Trent in partnership with John Davenport from 1792 until 1796; then as Thomas Wolfe & Company from 1796 until 1800 (his partners being Miles Mason and John Lucock); from 1803 until 1808 in conjunction with his son-in-law, Robert Hamilton, and finally from 1808 until his death in 1818, with Robert Hamilton and William Arrowsmith who had married another daughter.

[*Staffordshire Advertiser*, 1801; *London Gazette*, 1800; *Williamson's Liverpool Advertiser*, 1800; *Gore's Liverpool Directory*.]

Italian comedy figures

The Chelsea Catalogue (1755) refers to 'Figures of the Italian Theatre'. These subjects from the Italian *Commedia dell' Arte* were frequently copied by the porcelain modellers of Bow and Chelsea from Meissen adaptations of Callot and other designs in Luigi Riccoboni's *Histoire du Théâtre Italien*, (1728). Some became extremely popular; Pierrot, Harlequin and Columbine; Pantaloon; the Captain, the Doctor and the Advocate; Isabella and Cynthio.

The better known re-appeared in Staffordshire salt-glaze, and later in almost unrecognisable versions in the work of the Staffordshire earthenware figure makers.

A second edition of Riccoboni's book appeared in 1731 and it was translated into English as *An Historical and Critical Account of the Theatres of Europe* in 1741.
Plate 7 B.
[Herbert Read, 'Staffordshire Salt-glaze in the collection of Mr J. Henry Griffith... *The Connoisseur* 1924; W.B. Honey, *Old English Porcelain*, 1928, new ed. 1948; George Savage, *Eighteenth century English Porcelain*, 1952.]

J

Jackfield, Shropshire. Earthenware Manufactory

Earthenware is said to have been made at Jackfield in the sixteenth century, but nothing is known with certainty until Richard Thursfield from Stoke began to manufacture there at the beginning of the eighteenth century. He was succeeded by his son who carried on the business until about 1780, when it was taken over by John Rose from Coalport.

No marked examples are known, but there is reason to believe that a type of black-glazed red earthenware, usually decorated with oil-painting over the glaze, was made here from about 1760–1775. But this kind of ware was produced in some quantity throughout Staffordshire at that time, so that no pieces can definitely be attributed to Jackfield.

Two jugs decorated in this manner with oil-paint and oil-gilding are in the British Museum.

Jackson, Job and John, Burslem

Job and John Jackson worked the two lower factories at the Churchyard in Burslem for a short period before getting into financial difficulties. Announcements in *Staffordshire Advertiser*, 14 November 1835, and 23 January 1836, concerned the sale of their property and equipment which included 'valuable and modern engravings'. J and J. Jackson produced an extensive range of American views with a floral rose border, as well as scriptural subjects.

Jackson, Joseph, Shelton

Probably succeeded to the business of Charles Tittensor, as he is listed as an earthenware toy manufacturer in Queen Street, Shelton, in 1834.

Jacobite pottery

Occasional inscriptions and emblems on salt-glazed stoneware, earthenware and Jackfield ware indicate Jacobite sympathies. Portraits of Bonnie Prince Charlie are not uncommon on salt-glazed stonewares. Inscriptions and emblems on contemporary glass such as 'May the tenant be ready when the steward comes', a stricken and burgeoning oak, oak leaf, bee, butterfly, jay, Jacob's Ladder foliage, carnation, fritillary, thistle, triple ostrich plume, and the 6-petalled rose of the House of Stuart with one or two buds, all of which are considered Jacobite emblems have few echoes on pottery.

A punch-bowl inscribed 'May all true gentlemen have a true steward and may the tenant be ready when the steward comes. God bless P.C. and down with the rump', is recorded by Rackham and Read *English Pottery*, 1924.

Jahn, Louis (died 1911)

Painter of figure subjects on porcelain. Born at Oberweisbachin, Thuringia, he came to Staffordshire in 1862 and worked for Mintons as a porcelain painter. He was art director of

Brownfields from 1872 until 1895, and of Mintons 1895 to 1900. He was Curator of Hanley Museum 1900–1911.

'Japans'

A loose term covering a wide variety of patterns and styles derived from oriental sources, employed in decorating English porcelain in the eighteenth and nineteenth centuries, including Chinese *famille verte* and *famille rose* patterns; the Imari of Arita with showy floral or brocaded effects in underglaze blue and enamel colours with added gilding; and patterns in the Kakiemon style enamelled in turquoise, red, green, yellow and blue.

The 'Japans' became very popular in the 1820's, and were extensively used at Derby, and in Staffordshire on bone china made by Spode, Minton and Davenport, as well as for decorating stone or ironstone china (Masons for example). 'Japans' were sometimes given special names, as with Mintons' 'Amherst Japan' which took its name from William Pitt, Lord Amherst (b.1773–d.1857) who, when sent on an embassy to China refused to 'Kow-Tow' to the Emperor.

See IMARI, KAKIEMON.

Jasper

A fine close-grained stoneware body of unusual composition including in its ingredients barytes and barium carbonate, dense and hard enough to stand polishing on a lapidary's wheel and capable of being stained throughout its substance with metallic oxides to fine shades of blue and lavender, sage and olive green, lilac, ochreous yellow (a rare tint) and a peculiarly velvety black. It was the culmination in 1774 of an extended series of experiments by Wedgwood 'over a long period of time'. Wedgwood himself described it as 'a white porcelain *bisque* of exquisite beauty and delicacy'. To be distinguished from the less valuable 'Jasper Dip' (which see).

Manufacturers of Jasper ware:

Josiah Wedgwood
Humphrey Palmer
John Turner
James Neale

Robert Wilson
David Wilson & Sons
William Adams
Daniel Steel
J. Adams & Company
Colour plate 14 and Plates 110, 113, 124, 126, 127.

Jasper dip

Coloured solution applied to white jasper body by dipping; name also of ware made of white jasper covered with a surface colouring.

Jeannest, Emile (born 1813 died 1857)

Modeller; pupil of Delaroche; came to London c.1845; brought into Staffordshire by Herbert Minton as modeller to the Minton Factory; modelling instructor at the Potteries Schools of Design 1848–52; went to Elkingtons of Birmingham as designer 1852. Many of his designs were reproduced in the *Art Union Journal*.
Plate 67.
[*Art Union Journal*, 1857; Reginald G. Haggar, *A Century of Art Education in the Potteries*, 1953.]

Jelly mould

A pottery 'former' of various patterns used for shaping jellies and blancmanges. Eighteenth century examples conform outwardly to the pattern of the interior mould. Modern moulds are smooth outside.

Jet-enamelled ware

One of the most celebrated productions of the Worcester porcelain factory in the eighteenth century consisting of wares transfer-printed in black. Giles purchased 'jet-enamelled' services from Worcester in 1769.

Johnson Bros, Hanley and Tunstall, Staffordshire

Founded in 1883 by four brothers, Henry, Robert, Alfred and Fred Johnson. The business was at first on a modest scale, but in the last 70 years has expanded until today Johnson Bros. is probably the largest firm of earthenware manufacturers in the world, controlling a number of factories in England and abroad. The present head of the firm is Sir Ernest Johnson.

MARKS

WARES

Starting with the production of 'Granite' for overseas markets, the firm has developed in the twentieth century fine self-coloured bodies, Grey dawn in 1929, followed by Rose, Green and Golden dawn. A new shape has been made each year. Finely engraved table wares are a speciality, 'Old Britain Castles' engraved by Fennell being one of the most notable.

The potting of this firm is distinguished by uncommon lightness and finish.

[Anonymous, *Pottery and Glass*, March 1946.]

Johnson, James

A Toft-style slipware dish, decorated with a head beneath a crown, dated 1694, in Nottingham Castle Museum, is inscribed with this name. Nothing is known of him.

Johnson, Moses

Master potter, Southwark, 1690.

[R. L. Hobson, *B.F.A.C. Catalogue*, 1913.]

Johnson, Reuben and Phoebe, Shelton

Reuben Johnson is recorded as a manufacturer of lustred china and fancy earthenware at Miles Bank, Hanley, in 1818. In 1834 the factory is listed under the name of his widow, Phoebe Johnson. Phoebe Johnson and Son were members of the first North Staffordshire Chamber of Commerce in 1836. She apparently gave up business about 1840. An announcement of the sale of her household furniture (*Staffordshire Ad-*

vertiser, 14 November 1840) said she was 'leaving the neighbourhood.'

MARK

Johnson, Thomas and Joseph, Fenton

This firm is said to have made white salt-glazed stoneware and 'crouch' ware at Fenton in the second half of the eighteenth century, the factory at a later date being taken over by Mayer & Newbold. Their wares were made from clay obtained in Brickhouse field. Not listed after 1783.

[S. Shaw, *History of the Staffordshire Potteries*, 1829.]

Johnson, William and Madin, Aaron, Chesterfield Derbyshire

The stone bottle works, Whittington Moor, was established by Wm. Johnson and Aaron Madin in 1818, and carried on afterwards by Johnson's son-in-law, Samuel Lancaster. They made domestic crockery in fireclay stoneware; salt-glazed and lead glazed blackware was made from common brick clay.

[L. Jewitt, *Ceramic Art of Great Britain*, 1878.]

Johnson & Brough, Lane End

Richard Johnson potted first of all with a man named Bridgwood at Lane End until 1796, then with Jonathan Brough who died in 1804, and subsequently on own account. He became bankrupt in 1814.

[*Directories*, 1796–1805; *Staffordshire Advertiser*, 1814–15.]

Jones, Hannah, Hanley

Manufacturer of earthenware dogs at the Market Place, Hanley, 1830.

Joney Grig

A dialect term used in North Staffordshire and still occasionally heard for a chimney ornament in the form of a dog, sometimes shortened to Joney or Jona.

[Reginald G. Haggar, in *Connoisseur Concise Encyclopaedia of Antiques*, Vol 2. 1955.]

K

'Kakiemon' style

A name given to a distinctive asymmetrical style of enamel decoration on Japanese porcelain, extensively imitated or copied in eighteenth century by English porcelain painters at Bow, Chelsea and Worcester, both directly, or indirectly from Meissen copies or adaptations; named after the Japanese potter Kakiemon (fl. c.1650), who used enamel colours at Arita. *Plates 10 A, 22 C, 133 C.*

Kean, Michael, Derby

Miniature painter, and from 1795 until 1811 part-proprietor of the Derby factory.

Keeling, Anthony (born 1738 died 1815), Tunstall, Staffordshire

Original partner in Hollins, Warburton & Co., hard-paste porcelain manufacturers in 1781, but withdrew after a dispute.

He manufactured pottery at Tunstall from 1783 until 1810. He was married to Ann Booth 22 August 1760, built Calver House, 1793, and retired and moved to Liverpool 1810, where he died 14 January 1815. (*Staffordshire Advertiser*, 21 January 1815).

In 1802 Anthony and E. Keeling were operating two factories in Burslem and used the mark:

A. & E. KEELING

In 1787 Keeling was described as a 'Manufacturer of Queen's Ware in general, blue painted and enamelled, Egyptian black, etc.'

[Stoke and Wolstanton, *Parish Registers: Directories, 1783–1805*; S. Shaw, *History of the Staffordshire Potteries*, 1829; Tunnicliff's *Survey*, 1787.]

Keeling, James, Hanley, Staffordshire

Earthenware manufacturer, New Street, Hanley, recorded from c.1795 until c.1830. He is not listed as a potter in 1834 but is given under private addresses in White's *Directory* as a Gentleman, and had evidently retired. He made dinner and tea wares transfer-printed underglaze. *The Pottery Mercury*, 22 November 1828 recorded that James Keeling had issued a dinner service transfer-printed with views from Buckingham's *Travels in Mesopotamia*, and intimated that other potters were about to put on the market wares with Turkish and oriental scenery. He patented improvements in decorative processes in 1796, and improvements in pottery ovens and firing processes in conjunction with Valentine Close.

[S. Shaw, *History of the Staffordshire Potteries*, 1829.]

Keeling, Joseph and Edward, Hanley, Staffordshire

Manufactured general earthenware at a factory in Keeling's Lane, Hanley, from 1787 or earlier until 1804. The factory described as particularly suitable for the production of Egyptian black was offered 'to be let or sold' in 1804 because Joseph Keeling was 'declining business on account of ill health'. (*Staffordshire Advertiser*, 8 and 15 December 1804). Edward Keeling, who in 1804 was living in the house adjoining the works, died 4 November 1833 aged 81 years. His obituary described him as formerly an earthenware manufacturer (*Staffordshire Advertiser*, 9 November 1833).

[*Directories*.]

Keeling, Toft & Co, Hanley, Staffordshire

This company was in production from 1806 until 1824, making Egyptian black and other contemporary earthenwares. Toft & May were successors, continuing the business until 1830.

MARKS

KEELING, TOFT & CO.
(impressed)

'Keep within Compass'

A transfer-printed decoration used by John Aynsley (1752–1829) of Lane End, on earthenware, c.1800. The picture shows a young woman holding a book inscribed 'The Pleasures of Imagination Realised' beneath a pair of compasses, and standing in a landscape with a dog at her feet and an open box of jewellery, lettered 'The Reward of Virtue', beside her. Above the compasses are the words 'Fear God', round the picture 'Keep within Compass and you shall be sure to avoid many troubles which others endure', and at the bottom 'Prudence brings Esteem'. At the corners are four scenes showing a woman (1) playing cards, (2) drinking and neglecting her children, (3) arrested, and (4) beating hemp in prison – a morality sequence probably suggested, particularly scene 4, by Hogarth's engravings of the Harlot's Progress. Further inscriptions 'Attend unto this simple fact As through this life you rove', and 'That virtuous and prudent ways Will gain esteem and love', complete the design.

Plates transfer-printed and coloured with this decoration are said to have been given by Aynsley to his apprentices on leaving the factory (G.W. Rhead, *The Earthenware Collector*, 1920). An example of this decoration is in the Victoria & Albert Museum.

See AYNSLEY, JOHN.

[B. Rackham, *Catalogue of the Schreiber Collection*, 1930.]

Kemp, Dorothy, Felixstowe, Suffolk

Studio potter; studied potting at Shinner's Bridge Dartington, and at St. Ives, Cornwall under Bernard Leach. She teaches at a Girls High School in Ipswich.

Lead-glazed earthenware, slip decorated pottery and stoneware are marked:

Kensington, London

References to potworks and to a site known as the Potteries occur in maps, engravings and old records of Kensington, but apart from coarse horticultural pottery the output of the factory is unknown.

[G. Wills, 'The Kensington Potteries' *Apollo*, 1956.]

Kent, James, Old Foley, Longton

This firm of general domestic potters, Old Foley, Longton, was founded by James Aloysius Kent (born 1864 died 1953) with five workmen from the firm of Barker & Kent (including Arnold Bennett's brother, Septimus Bennett, modeller) in 1897.

Kent, William

Founder of the firm of William Kent Ltd, Burslem. Started in partnership with Gaskell and Parr in Burslem, and on the dissolution of the partnership in 1878, built a factory on the present site, Auckland Street, Burslem. From the first, pottery figures from old moulds were manufactured by the traditional method of pressing. Most of the figures and dogs were of the flat-back' type made in Staffordshire from c.1840 onwards, as well as some earlier types on square plinths, such as 'St Sebastian'.

[Reginald G. Haggar, *Staffordshire Chimney Ornaments*, 1955.]

Kent

During the nineteenth century a group of potteries in Kent – at Brabourne, Deal, Sevenoaks and also in other districts – made a type of coarse pottery from red or pink clay found in the county. Crude designs in slip were usually the only decoration. The best examples are reminiscent of the well-known Wrotham, Kent, slipware made in the seventeenth and eighteenth centuries.

[Geoffrey Bemrose, *Nineteenth Century English Pottery and Porcelain*, 1952.]

Keyes, Phyllis, Bloomsbury, London

Made decorative pottery at Bloomsbury. Her early shapes were designed by Graham Bell and Stephen Tomlin, and were based on natural forms and cast in moulds. Decorations were drawn or painted swiftly in bright colours upon the tin-enamel glaze by Jane Bussy, Simone Bussy, Angelica Garnett, Duncan Grant and Vanessa Bell.

[Reginald G. Haggar, *English Country Pottery*, 1950; Lucien Myers 'Phyllis Keyes' in *Pottery and Glass*, 1946.]

Keys, Edward (born 1798)

Ceramic modeller. He was the son of Samuel Keys, senior, and trained as a modeller at the Derby works which he left in 1826 for the Potteries. In 1835 he was living at Stoke Lane, and working at Mintons (obit. Mrs Mary Keys, *Staffordshire Advertiser*, 8 November 1834) where he stayed until 1842, his wages averaging 30/- per week (Report, *Commission on the Employment of Children in Factories*, 1842). He tried to manufacture porcelain in 1842 but failed and became bankrupt (*Staffordshire Advertiser*, 14 May 1842). From 1845 until 1853 he worked for Wedgwood, Etruria.

[J. Haslem, *Old Derby China Factory*, 1876.]

Keys, Samuel (born 1771 died 1850)

China gilder at Derby where he had been apprenticed in 1785. After working upwards of 60 years at the Derby Factory, he retired. He died at Bridge Street, Derby, 8 October 1850 (*Staffordshire Advertiser*, 19 October 1850).

[J. Haslem, *Old Derby China Factory*, 1876.]

Keys, Samuel, Derby and Stoke, Staffordshire

Figure modeller at the Derby factory; came to the Potteries 1830; recorded at Upper Cliffe Bank, Stoke in 1834 and at Liverpool Road, Stoke in 1842; he was one of the original members of the North Staffordshire Society of Arts, 1842.

He went into partnership with John Mountford (Keys and Mountford) as parian manufacturers, John Street, Stoke, and exhibited at the 1851 exhibition where they were awarded an Honourable Mention. In John Street he kept the 'Cock' Inn, 1851–1864. Keys modelled ornamental and useful wares, using the drawings of his brother John Keys (born 1797 died 1825), for terra cotta, majolica and other types of pottery. In 1862 the partnership was Keys &

Briggs, Stoke, and they exhibited jet, mosaic, and majolica at the International Exhibition, 1862.

[J. Haslem, *Old Derby China Factory*, 1876; *Directories*, 1834–1860.]

Killigrew

Stoneware potter, Chelsea, for whom John Stearne worked before being engaged by Dwight & Sandys, c.1675.

[R. L. Hobson, *B.F.A.C. Catalogue*, 1913.]

Kilnhurst pottery, Swinton, Yorkshire

Kilnhurst Old Pottery was established in 1746 by William Malpas. It passed through various hands until taken over by Joseph Twigg & Brothers in 1839. Members of the Twigg family worked it until 1881, using the impressed marks:

White and ivory earthenware decorated in various styles was made, including painted, printed, 'sponged', banded, and mosaic.

Another factory near the Kilnhurst railway station produced common earthenware from c.1818 until 1860.

[A. Hurst, *Catalogue of the Boynton Collection of Yorkshire Pottery*, 1922.]

Kiln waster

Ware coming from the kiln spoilt, and therefore to be thrown away as useless. Kiln wasters discovered in excavation afford good evidence of factory production.

Kingswinford, Staffordshire

Potters have worked in this Black Country district over a long period of time. John Onions of Thorns is mentioned in a deed dated 13 January

1801 which is in Birmingham Reference Library. He was still at Thorns in 1834. Lewis in his *Topographical Dictionary of England* in 1848 remarked 'Some potteries of stoneware and earthenware of every kind'. The industry still survives. Potters here were:

Benjamin Green, Brierley Hill, 1818–1834
T. Parish, Brierley Hill 1818
Joh Barnbrook, Brierley Hill 1834
Samuel Edge, Brettell Lane 1834
Richard Evans, Moor Lane 1834
John Onions, Thorns 1801–1834
William Read, Thorns 1834
Smith & Sons, Brettell Lane 1834
Smith & Hodnett, 1851–1860
Thomas Southall, Brierley Hill 1834
Westwood, Moor & Rider, Brierley Hill 1834
Westwood & Moore, Moor Lane 1851
James Green, Brettell Lane 1851
Joseph Handley, Brettell Lane 1851
Thomas Meese, Brettell Lane 1851–1860
Charles Wassall, Brettell Lane 1851
George Carder, Ley's Pottery, Brettell Lane 1860–1896
Mrs J. Green, Delph Brierley Hill 1860
J. Hampton, Brettell Lane 1860
Christopher Wassall & Co., Moor Lane, Brierley Hill 1860
Thomas White, Delph Pottery, Brierley Hill 1860–1896
Wright & Co., Moor Lane (Stoneware), 1896
[Documents, Birmingham Reference Library; *Directories.*]

Kirkcaldy pottery, Fifeshire, Scotland. Earthenware manufactory.

Originally known as the Links Pottery and founded in 1714 using local clay, it passed in the early years of the nineteenth century into the control of the Methven family, who traded as David Methven & Sons. David Methven died in 1861, and soon after the business was taken over by Andrew Young, who became sole proprietor. Methven's mark was:

Originally brown wares were made, but under Methven ownership white earthenware was made from Devon and Cornwall clays. Printed ware including a popular 'Verona' design was also made, as well as Mocha, dipped, and pottery decorated with 'designs cut out of the roots of sponges'.
[J.A.Fleming, *Scottish Pottery*, 1923.]

Kishere, Joseph, Mortlake
Salt-glazed stoneware of the familiar late Fulham type was made by Joseph Kishere at Mortlake until 1811. They are found marked:

'Kishere Pottery, Mortlake Surry'
(impressed)

Knottingley, Yorkshire
See FERRYBRIDGE.

Knottingley, Holes, Yorkshire
The Masterman family for several generations made chimney ornaments and toys at this potworks, flourishing c.1838 to c.1881.
[A.Hurst, *Catalogue of the Boynton Collection of Yorkshire, Pottery*, 1922.]

L

Lace work designs
Formed by impressing lace or fern fronds upon soft clay shapes, or by dipping lace fabric in porcelain slip, allowing it to dry and firing it so that a porcelain or pottery imitation of the pattern results. First tried at Meissen and Strasburg, it was adopted at Derby and in Staffordshire (early nineteenth century). Charles Toft used the process at his factory, High Street, Stoke, about 1889 (Specimens in Newcastle-under-Lyme Museum).

Lafayette at the Tomb of Washington

Underglaze blue transfer-print used for decoration of plates and dishes by Enoch Wood & Sons, Burslem. Adapted from a drawing prepared by D. W. Jackson for the New York firm of china importers, Harris & Chauncey.

La Fécondité

A subject representing a naked reclining woman with five children, modelled in relief upon oval dishes, perhaps intended as 'marriage platters', copied from similar dishes attributed to the French potter Bernard Palissy (c.1510–1589): made at Lambeth in tin-enamelled earthenware, the earlier specimens decorated in polychrome, the later in blue-and-white: some bear the arms of the City Companies of London: dates from 1633 to 1697 recorded.

Lakin & Poole, Burslem, Staffordshire

Thomas Lakin and John Ellison Poole (born 1766 died 1829) entered into partnership in 1791. In February 1795 Thomas Shrigley became a partner, the style of the firm becoming Poole, Lakin & Shrigley. Soon after Lakin withdrew, and in 1797 Poole & Shrigley became bankrupt. This firm is stated by many writers erroneously to have worked in Hanley. Their mark is:

LAKIN & POOLE (impressed)

Blue-printed earthenware, painted cream-colour Egyptian black in the Wedgwood manner, and figures often on lofty square bases were made. The group representing 'The Assassination of Marat' is well-known. Enamelling is rather tight and unadventurous.

After the bankruptcy Poole potted for a short time on his own account, hence the impressed mark:

POOLE

Thomas Lakin after leaving the firm operated a factory on Bourne's Bank, Burslem, from 1795–1799. The impressed mark LAKIN is known. He subsequently worked for Davenport, and finally became manager of the Leeds Factory, his son succeeding him in that position after his death (*Staffordshire Advertiser*, 1797,

1799, 1803, 1824). His recipe book *Potting, Enamelling, and Glass Painting* was published posthumously in Leeds in 1824.

[Reginald G. Haggar, *Staffordshire Chimney Ornaments*, 1955.]

Lambeth, London. Earthenware manufactories.

DATES

Certain kinds of delftware and maiolica, the earliest known pieces being of the late sixteenth century, are designated 'Lambeth', although this type of pottery was made not only in the factories there but also at other works in Vauxhall, Aldgate and Southwark, and possibly in other riverside boroughs besides. Work from the various factories of this group cannot be assigned to individual potteries, and some is in fact difficult to distinguish from Dutch tinglazed wares of the early period. Lambeth ware was produced over two centuries, and examples have principally come to light in excavations in the City of London.

WORK AND SUBJECTS

In 1571 two potters from Antwerp, Andries and Janson, settled at Aldgate. Earliest examples of English tin-glazed ware date from about this time, not all these being derived from the Dutch tradition, although many potters from Holland certainly came to London in the late sixteenth and early seventeenth centuries. The Malling jugs, narrow-necked and globular in shape with a mottled glaze in browns and blues, belong to this period. A plate dated 1600, inscribed 'THE ROSE IS RED THE LEAVES ARE GRENE GOD SAVE ELIZABETH OVR QUEENE', and decorated with a view of a town is the first dated English piece known.

From 1614 many more dated pieces are in existence. Italian, Dutch and Chinese styles of decoration are common. Some are initialled for their owners, the letters usually being placed in triangle-form, and many bear the arms of London livery companies. Designs, usually in bright, thick maiolica colours include stylized fruit and foliage, star-shaped flowers, birds and sphinxes, and, towards the end of the seventeenth century, portraits of kings, family groups, biblical subjects, inn signs and verses or inscriptions appear more frequently and colours become more various. Chinese subjects were copied from imported oriental wares and often greatly improved upon by simplification and freedom of treatment. Articles for domestic use formed a large part of the manufacture of the potteries; these included tiles, plates, mugs, jars, jugs, wine-bottles, posset-pots, punch-bowls, wall-pockets and plaques.

The Lambeth ware factories were still in existence at the beginning of the nineteenth century. They were in decline, however, in 1800 and as regards work after that date no examples of decorated wares are known.

DISTINGUISHING CHARACTERISTICS

As no marks were used on these wares, their origin is ascertained by comparison with delftware known to be from Holland, inscriptions on various commemorative pieces, and names of owners sometimes incorporated in the design. In articles made at a later date, a more distinctively English form of decoration is apparent.

These later productions are sometimes difficult to distinguish from contemporary Liverpool and Bristol tin-glazed earthenware; in general, Lambeth potters produced a neatly-drawn design and more finished effect, but often lacked the vigour and individuality of the best examples from Bristol.

The glaze on early Lambeth pottery is usually white. In later pieces a blue-green tint becomes apparent, fairly easily distinguishable from the bluish-purple of Bristol glaze. The first *bianco* decoration is believed to have been used at Lambeth.

Many specimens of Lambeth ware of all periods are in the Fitzwilliam Museum, Cambridge, the British Museum, and the Victoria and Albert Museum.

Plates 50–51.

[F.H.Garner, *English Delftware*, 1948.]

Lamprey Pots

Richard Marsh of Hanley, working c.1710, is listed in the Wedgwood MSS as a maker of mottled and black wares including lamprey and venison pots. Lampreys were formerly regarded as palatable food.

[E.Meteyard, *Life of Josiah Wedgwood*, 1865–1866.]

Landing of Lafayette

Underglaze blue transfer-print engraved from a drawing by Samuel Maverick. Used by James & Ralph Clews as decoration for dinner ware, 1824. Lafayette (1757–1834) French general and politician, landed at Castle Garden, New York, 16 August 1824.

Plate 4 A.

[Illustrated in Reginald G. Haggar, *English Country Pottery*, 1950.]

Landore pottery, Swansea, South Wales

Built by John Forbes Calland on the Swansea Canal at Landore, one mile from Swansea, in 1848, for the manufacture of table and toilet wares in earthenware, but closed down in 1856. Its copperplates were transferred to the South Wales Pottery at Llanelly.

MARKS

J F CALLAND & CO

LANDORE POTTERY

CALLAND

SWANSEA

Lane Delph, Staffordshire

The name Delph means a digging, such as a claypit or quarry. 'Drowned in a delph' occurs in Staffordshire parish registers; the name therefore has no reference to any special type of pottery manufacture.

There were numerous factories for the manufacture of earthenware here in the latter part of the eighteenth century, and for earthenware and bone china in the nineteenth century.

Lane End, Staffordshire

The township around St. Johns Church incorporated within the town of Longton, which see.

Lane, Rev. Obadiah, Longton Hall

Lord of the Manor of Longton before it was taken over by Heathcote in 1777. The Lanes of Longton Hall occur continuously in Stoke Parish Registers from 1732 until 1749 after which no further entries have been found, which suggests that at or about this time the Lanes left Longton Hall for some other residence. The year 1750 is the traditional date of the establishment of Littler's factory at Longton Hall. The Rev. O. Lane was Prebend of Gaia Minor, Lichfield, from 1767–80.

[Reginald G. Haggar in *Apollo*, 1952.]

Langley Mill

See LOVATT'S POTTERIES LTD.

Langston, George

Mortgages dated 1 January 1709/10 and eighteenth, twentieth and twenty-first May 1714 in Birmingham Reference Library mention George Langston, potter, of St. Clement Danes, Middlesex.

Lathe

Introduced into Staffordshire Potteries probably by J. P. Elers c.1693. Early eighteenth century pottery turning lathes were made by Randle of Congleton. Improvements by William Baddeley and Josiah Wedgwood, c.1765. See ENGINE-TURNING LATHE.

[S. Shaw, *History of the Staffordshire Potteries*, 1829; E. Meteyard, *Life of Josiah Wedgwood*, 1865–66.]

Lauraguais, Duc de Brancas, Comte de

A French arcanist who possessed the secret of making hard-paste porcelain and in 1766 took the initiative towards an English patent for it, although his specification was never entered. He found kaolin in France at Alençon in 1758 and in Cornwall in 1766. He was in Birmingham in 1766 trying to sell his formula for which he wanted £2,000. Dr. Erasmus Darwin seems to have thought his 'Scientific passion is stronger than perfect Sanity'. Some pieces of French porcelain with monograms LB or LR have been attributed to him. No authentic English porcelains survive, if ever made.

[E. Meteyard, *Life of Josiah Wedgwood*, 1865–66; L. Jewitt, *Ceramic Art of Great Britain*, 1878; Xavier de Chavagnac and A. de Grollier, *Histoire des Manufactures françaises de porcelaine*.]

Lazulite

A blue-tinted parian.

Leach, Bernard, St. Ives, Cornwall

Studio potter: born at Hongkong 1887; studied at the Slade School, London. Returned to the Far East in 1909, and settled in Japan where he learnt Raku and stoneware pottery from the Sixth Kenzan. He returned to England and in 1920 founded the St. Ives Pottery. He taught at Dartington Hall in 1933 and founded a slipware pottery at Shinner's Bridge.

He revisited Japan in 1934, and in 1937 abandoned slipware for stoneware. His workshops were damaged by a land mine in the war. Important exhibitions of Leach pottery have been held at the Berkeley Galleries in London, 1946, and in Sweden, Norway, and Denmàrk 1949. The St. Ives Pottery has developed into a small factory.

Leach's pupils include Cardew, Pleydell-Bouverie, Braden, Kemp, David Leach, Margaret Leach, and Hamada: his writings include *A Potter's Outlook*, 1928; *A Potter's Book*, 1940; and *The Leach Pottery 1920–1946*, 1946. His marks are:

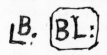

Bernard Leach

David Leach

The products of the Leach workshops include moderately priced useful domestic stonewares of excellent form and workmanship, and individual pieces of consummate craftsmanship. Bernard Leach's style is a highly personal one in which virile decorations are successfully wedded to fine distinctive pottery shapes. He has executed slipwares in the Toft style.

Examples of his wares are in Stoke-on-Trent Museum and the Victoria and Albert Museum, London.

Plates 157 A and B.

[John Farleigh, *The Creative Craftsman*, 1950; G.W. Digby, *The Work of the Modern Potter in England*, 1952; Muriel Rose, *Artist-Potters in England*, 1955.]

Leach, Margaret, Aylburton, Gloucestershire

Studio potter working at the Taena Community. Studied at Liverpool from 1936 until 1940 and at St. Ives under Bernard Leach for a further three years.

In 1947 she started to make pottery at The Barn, Chepstow, where she was assisted by Dorothy Kemp; and joined the Taena Community in 1950.

Her slipware pottery, of vigorous form and decoration, is marked:

Lead, Leonard (born 1787 died 1869)

Flower painter at Derby, son of Leonard Lead of Belper, wood-collier.

[L. Jewitt, *Ceramic Art of Great Britain*, 1878.]

Leadless glaze

A leadless glaze for red earthenware was invented by Job Meigh, for which he received a gold medal from the Society of Arts, 1822 (*The News*, 2 June 1822). For the dangers of lead poisoning in the pottery industry see the postscript 'On the Dangerous Processes...' by Millicent, Duchess of Sutherland, to H. Owen's *Staffordshire Potter*, 1901, and W. J. Furnival's *Leadless Decorative Tiles, Faience and Mosaic*, 1904.

Leaf dishes

Dishes shaped like, or modelled in relief to represent various leaf forms. 'Leaf basons and plates' are mentioned in sale notices concerning the Longton Hall factory in the *London Public Advertiser*, 12 April 1757, and *Aris's Birmingham Gazette*, 20 June 1757.

Leafield, Oxfordshire

The brothers George and Alec Franklin made money boxes, honey jars, mugs and other domestic red wares here in the second half of the nineteenth century. Examples in the Ashmolean Museum, Oxford.

Leak, Jonathan

Manufacturer of earthenware and Egyptian black, Burslem; married at Norton-in-the-Moors 13 November 1798, Mary Wood, of Burslem, paintress, niece of Enoch Wood; in partnership with George Leak until 23 February 1813 and afterwards potted on own account at Commercial Street, Burslem (advertisement *Staffordshire Advertiser*, 9 July 1814); the *Directory* for 1818 lists him as a potter at 20, Row, Burslem; Jewitt says he was a clever potter; sailed for Sydney, New South Wales in the Brig 'Recovery' 1819; in 1820 commissioned by the N.S.W. Government to make a cast of the head of Martin, the Bushranger *(New South Wales Gazette)*; his wife and children followed him 1822 and 1825; in Australia Jonathan Leak set up as a 'potter and brickmaker' in Market Lane, off Elizabeth Street, Sydney, where he was still working in 1840.

[W. Jewitt, *Ceramic Art of Great Britain*, 1878; Reginald G. Haggar, in *Apollo*, March 1950; H. G. S. Baker, letter in *Apollo*, July 1950; Reginald G. Haggar, *Staffordshire Chimney Ornaments*, 1955.]

Leeds, Yorkshire (The Old Pottery). Earthenware manufactory

DATES AND OWNERS

The Old Pottery at Hunslet (as distinct from the later factories of Hunslet Hall and Rothwell in the same district) was established about 1760 by two brothers named Green; at an early date in its history it was known as Humble, Green and Co. and later, when William Hartley joined the firm, it became Hartley, Greens & Co. It was at that time producing its finest work, and from 1820 may be said to have been in decline. The factory was sold in 1825 to Samuel Wainwright and was known for a time as S. Wainwright & Co. Subsequently it was the Leeds Pottery Co. and Warburton, Britton & Co. It closed in 1878.

Thomas Lakin formerly of Burslem managed the Leeds Pottery before he died in 1824.

MARKS

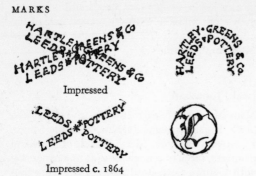

Impressed

Impressed c. 1864

Some comparatively modern Leeds productions are marked 'Leeds Pottery' (impressed). The wares which sometimes make use of old patterns and old moulds are easily distinguishable from earlier pieces, for the mark is impressed in very even lettering and has none of the irregularity of the type used in marking earlier pieces.

WORK

Early earthenware made at Leeds is notable for its colour, a rich cream with a deep fine glaze, sometimes of a slightly greenish tinge rather more hard and brilliant than Wedgwood but less even. Queen's ware of this sort was made in quantity in many Staffordshire potteries at about this time, but that made at Leeds has a particularly delicate and highly-finished appearance. From about 1780 until 1820 it formed the largest part of the production of the factory and was exported to several European countries. Pierced or basket-work was popular and made with great skill.

Plates bordered with interwoven twigs, all fashioned by hand; centrepieces of complex design and making use of figures; dishes with twisted handles; small, well-modelled figures; all these are characteristic subjects in Leeds cream-ware. Transfer-printing was also used to decorate some pieces. Red, black, lilac and green were colours most frequently used, together with the underglaze blue popular throughout Staffordshire at that time. Enamelled decoration was usually in subdued colours.

Certain types of agate wares were made, often having reserved panels painted with flowers.

At a later date, the factory also produced black Egyptian and lustred wares, and a white ware with a bluish glaze.

DISTINGUISHING CHARACTERISTICS

In early unmarked pieces attributed to Leeds, the perfection of finish and glassy smoothness of glaze are the most distinctive features. This glaze is supposed to have contained arsenic, which in a short time undermined the health of the workmen in the pottery and so had to be discontinued. Flower designs in black and red, though not peculiar to Leeds, are especially characteristic. In later monochrome painting a green enamel of a particularly lustrous appearance was used.

IMITATORS

Several factories in the Leeds district made ware in imitation of those made at the Old Pottery; amongst these are Hunslet Hall, Rothwell and, more recently, Slee's Modern Pottery. Some wares from these factories were impressed with the Leeds mark.

Examples of Leeds wares to be seen at the British Museum, Victoria and Albert Museum, Temple Newsam House, Leeds, and The Yorkshire Museum, York; also in the Metropolitan Museum of Art, New York; and the Boston Museum of Fine Arts.

Plates 52–55.

[Donald Towner, *Handbook of Leeds Pottery*, 1951; W.B. Honey, *English Pottery and Porcelain*, 1933; later editions; A. Hurst, *Catalogue of the Boynton Collection of Yorkshire Pottery*, 1922.]

Leeds, Hunslet

See HUNSLET and HUNSLET HALL, for other factories.

Lees, G. and R, Cobridge

Manufacturers of blue-printed earthenware. The factory utensils were offered for sale in 1841 and the manufactured stock including 'a very large quantity of fine well-assorted EARTHENWARE... of Willow and approved patterns'.

[*Staffordshire Advertiser*, 31 July and 28 August 1841.]

Lees, Thomas, Sneyd Green, Staffordshire

Manufacturer of pottery figures at Sneyd Green 1822–23.

Lessore, Émile (died 1876)

Painter of ceramic figure subjects: said to have studied in the studio of Ingres and worked in

Colour plate 10, SCOTTISH: *see page vii for caption*

(A) Earthenware and stoneware money-boxes: *(left to right)* front, cottage penny bank, c. 1825, Staffordshire, height 3⅜ inches. Two-tier box, Belper, Derbyshire, 1834, height 6¾ inches. Staffordshire slipware box, early eighteenth century, height 3½ inches. Back, slipware 'hen and chickens' Burton-in-Lonsdale, c. 1840, height 5¼ inches. 'Hen and chickens' Yorkshire, early nineteenth century, height 7½ inches. Salt-glaze box inscribed and dated 1791, Nottingham, height 6 inches. *(Hanley Museum)*.

(B) DOULTON salt-glazed stonewares: *(left to right)* flask 'Mr and Mrs Caudle', c. 1846; spirit flask 'William IVths Reform Cordial', c. 1832; 'Silenus' jug; and character mug in the form of Napoleon.

PLATE 49

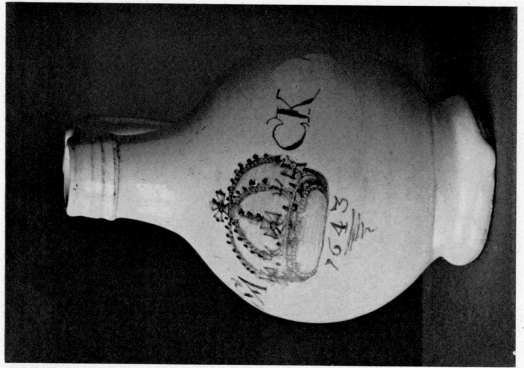

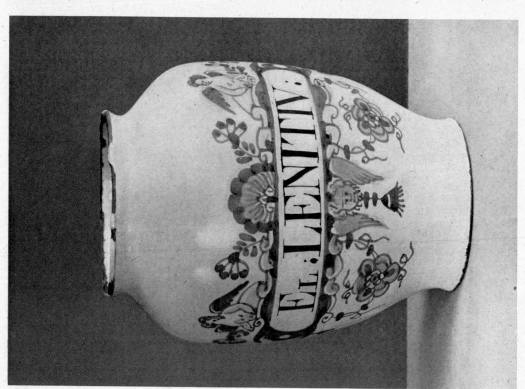

(A) LAMBETH drug-vase of tin-enamelled earthenware '(delft') painted in blue and manganese-brown. On the front is a label with the name of the drug. Mark, a cross in manganese. Second half of seven

(B) LAMBETH wine bottle, tin-enamelled earthenware, painted in blue. Dated 1643. Height 6¼ inches.

PLATE 50

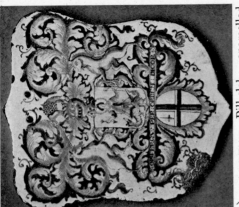

(C) LAMBETH Pill-slab, enamelled earthenware, painted in blue with the arms of the Apothecaries' Company and of the City of London. Second half of 17th century. Height 11⅞ inches; width 10⅛ inches

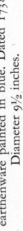

(B) LAMBETH barber's bowl, enamelled earthenware painted in blue. Dated 1738. Diameter 9½ inches.

(D) LAMBETH cups, tin-enamelled earthenware painted in blue, c. 1700. Heights 3 inches.

(A) LAMBETH candlestick-salt, tin-enamelled earthenware painted in colours. Dated 1657. Height 8 inches.

PLATE 51

LEEDS vase, cream-coloured earthenware, c. 1790, height 9¾ inches. Pair of candlesticks, cream-coloured earthenware, probably Leeds of c. 1790, height 10 inches.

PLATE 52

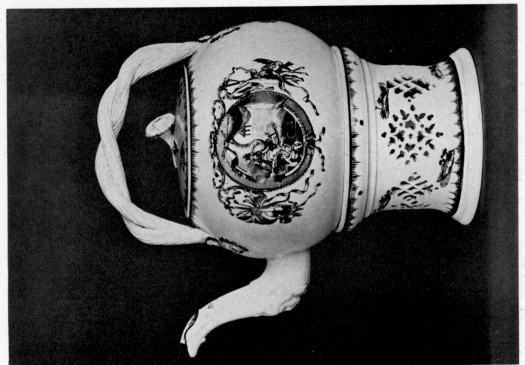

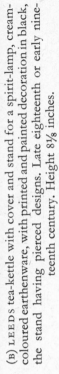

(B) LEEDS tea-kettle with cover and stand for a spirit-lamp, cream-coloured earthenware, with printed and painted decoration in black, the stand having pierced designs. Late eighteenth or early nineteenth century. Height 8⅛ inches.

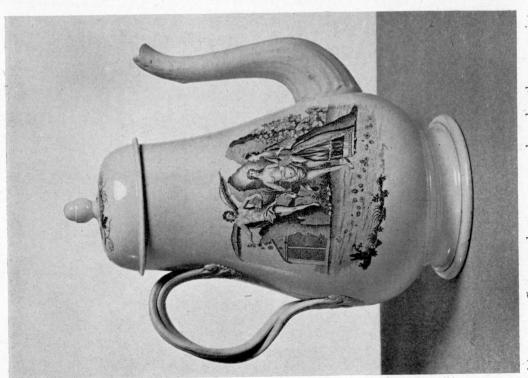

(A) LEEDS coffee-pot and cover, cream-coloured earthenware printed in black. Mark, 'Leeds Pottery,' printed on one side. Late eighteenth or early nineteenth century. Height 9½ inches.

PLATE 53

(B) LEEDS bust of a man, emblematic of Air
earthenware painted in colours. Mark 'Leed
Pottery'. c. 1780. Height 6½ inches.

(A) LEEDS flower-pot and stand, cream-coloured earthenware painted in green and black, c. 1800.
Height 7½ inches, width 6 inches.

(C) LEEDS jug, earthenware painted in colours, early
nineteenth century. Height 5⅝ inches.

PLATE 54

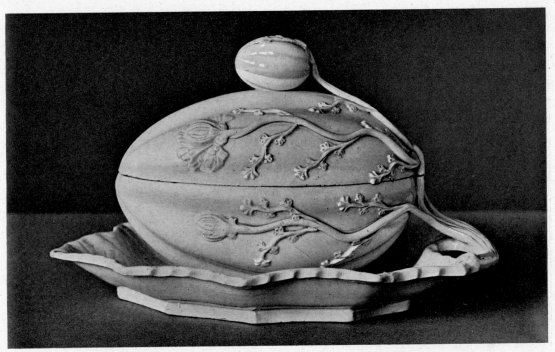

(A) LEEDS tureen with cover and stand, cream-coloured earthenware, c. 1790.
Height 5 inches, length 8½ inches, width 6½ inches.

(B) LEEDS chestnut bowl with cover and stand, cream coloured earthenware, with pierced decoration. Mark, 'I' impressed.
Late eighteenth or early nineteenth century. Height 8⅝ inches.

PLATE 55

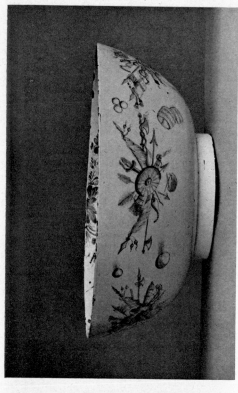

(B) LIVERPOOL punch-bowl, earthenware enamelled and painted in blue, red and green, mid-eighteenth century. Height 8⅝ inches, diameter 20⅜ inches.

(D) LIVERPOOL punch-bowl. Herculaneum Pottery, white earthenware printed and painted in colours, c. 1800.

(A) LIVERPOOL punch-bowl, earthenware, painted in blue underglaze: about 1760. Diameter 14½ inches.

(C) LIVERPOOL punch-bowl. Herculaneum Pottery, cream-coloured earthenware painted in colours, c. 1800.

PLATE 56

(A) LIVERPOOL porcelain coffee-pot and cover, printed in black, c. 1760. Height 7½ inches.

(B) LIVERPOOL barrel-shaped jug, cream-coloured earthenware printed in black. c. 1795. Height 7 inches, diameter 5¼ inches.

(C) LIVERPOOL stoneware. Herculaneum Pottery. Bust of Adam, Viscount Duncan of Camperdown. Mark, 'Herculaneum' impressed. c. 1800. Height 8¾ inches.

(D) LIVERPOOL. Drinking-cup, cream-coloured earthenware, printed in black and painted over in colours. Herculaneum Pottery, c. 1800. Height 3½ inches, Diameter 3⅜ inches.

PLATE 57

(A) LONGTON HALL figure of a musician, porcelain painted in colours, c. 1755. Height 5¼ inches. Porcelain group, two boys feeding a goat, painted in colours, c. 1755. Height 5⅛ inches. Porcelain figure of a market-woman selling butter, painted in colours, c. 1755. Height 5⅞ inches.

(B) LONGTON HALL porcelain pair of figures, painted in colours and gilt, c. 1755. Height 4⅞ inches, 4⅜ inches.

(C) LONGTON HALL porcelain figure, painted in colours, a girl seated with a basket of grapes in her lap, c. 1755–60. Height 4¾ inches.

PLATE 58

(A) LONGTON HALL porcelain sauce-boat, painted
in underglaze blue, c. 1755.
Length 7½ inches, width 3½ inches.

(B) LONGTON HALL porcelain tea-pot and cover,
painted in enamel colours, c. 1755.
Height 4½ inches, diameter 3½ inches.

(C) LONGTON HALL porcelain vase and cover
painted in colours, c. 1755.
Height 10⅞ inches.

(D) LONGTON HALL porcelain figure of a goatherd,
painted in colours and gilt, c. 1755.
Height 10⅛ inches.

PLATE 59

(A) LOWESTOFT porcelain tea-pot painted in colours on a yellow ground, dated 1767. Height 5½ inches.

(B) LOWESTOFT porcelain bowl painted in colours and gilt, c. 1765. Height 3 inches.

(C) LOWESTOFT porcelain cup and saucer painted in colours, c. 1770; cup, height 2 inches, saucer diameter 4⅞ inches. Porcelain cream-jug painted in colours, c. 1770, height 3½ inches. Porcelain mug painted in colours, c. 1770, height 4⅜ inches. Porcelain vase painted in colours, c. 1770, height 6¼ inches.

PLATE 60

(B) LOWESTOFT porcelain bowl painted in underglaze blue, dated 1773. Mark, 'S' in blue inside foot-ring. Diameter 7 inches.

(A) LOWESTOFT porcelain toilet-tray, perhaps painted in colours by William Absolon of Yarmouth, late eighteenth century. Diameter 4½ inches.

(C) LOWESTOFT porcelain dish painted in underglaze blue, c. 1770; width 7⅜ inches, length 9½ inches. Porcelain cup and saucer painted in red and blue, c. 1770; cup height 1½ inches, saucer diameter 4⅝ inches. Porcelain cup and saucer painted in underglaze blue, c. 1770; cup height 1¾ inches, saucer diameter 4⅞ inches. Porcelain cup and saucer painted in underglaze blue, c. 1770; cup ht 1¾ inches, saucer diam. 4⅛ inches.

PLATE 61

MARKS (A) Bristol, c. 1775; (B) Imitation of Chelsea-Derby, c. 1775, made in mid-nineteenth century; (C) Bristol, c. 1780; (D) Swinton, c. 1825; (E) Spode, c. 1830; (F) Copeland, c. 1840; (G) Chelsea, c. 1775; (H) Worcester, c. 1815; (I) Chelsea, c. 1760; (J) Minton, c. 1820; (K) Minton, c. 1825; (L) Worcester, c. 1760; (M) Worcester, c. 1810; (N) Spode, c. 1820; (O) Worcester, c. 1855.

PLATE 62

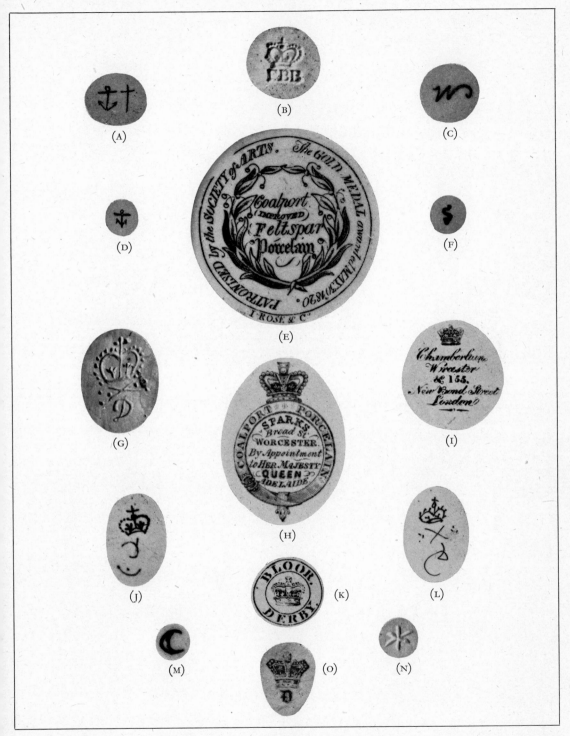

MARKS (A) Bow, c. 1770; (B) Worcester, c. 1815; (C) Worcester, c. 1770; (D) Chelsea, c. 1765; (E) Coalport, c. 1825; (F) Caughley, c. 1790; (G) Derby, c. 1790; (H) Coalport, c. 1825; (I) Worcester, c. 1820; (J) Derby, c. 1780; (K) Derby, c. 1825; (L) Derby, c. 1820; (M) Worcester, c. 1765; (N) Derby, c. 1790; (O) Derby, c. 1840.

PLATE 63

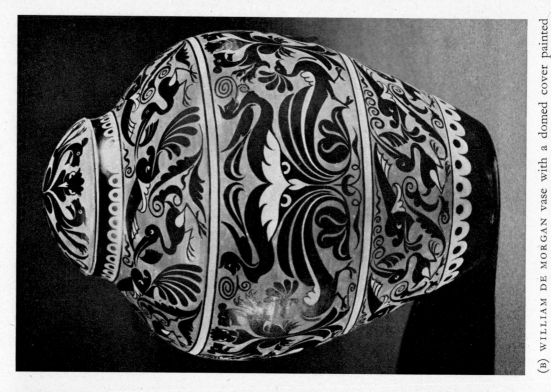

(B) WILLIAM DE MORGAN vase with a domed cover painted in lustre. 13½ inches high.
(Mrs. Frank Nasmyth)

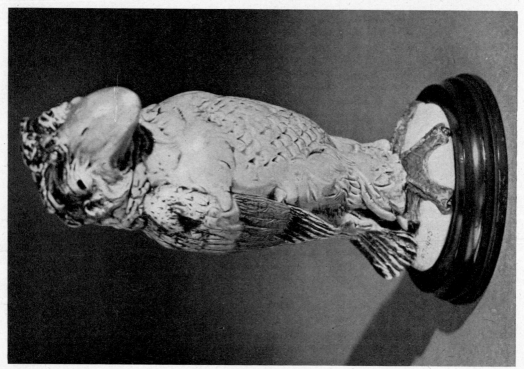

(A) MARTIN BROTHERS salt-glazed stoneware owl. Mark, R.W. Martin and Bros. London and Southall, 10–7–1905, incised. 10¾ inches high. (Mrs. Frank Nasmyth)

PLATE 64

the porcelain factory of Sèvres where his success attracted the jealousy of his colleagues. Came to England in 1858, worked for a few months at Mintons, and moved on to Wedgwoods of Etruria where he achieved a great reputation as a ceramic painter. He remained at the factory until 1863 and then went back to France, to Marlotte at Fontainebleau where he died in 1876. He kept up connections with the Wedgwood factory until the end. He was the greatest of the ceramic figure painters of the nineteenth century, sparing as a colourist, and perhaps owing something to the painters of Barbizon in his feeling for light and tone and rustic sentiment, yet wedded indissolubly to the great French classic tradition looking back beyond Boucher and Watteau to the Renaissance. His touch, however, was very individual, loose and spontaneous in quality. He signed his work 'E. Lessore' or with initials.

MARKS

Emile Lessore

E Lessore

L3

E Lessore

Plates *114 C, 122 A.*

[W. Mankowitz, *Wedgwood*, 1953.]

Lewis, Thomas (born 1783 died 1833)
Ceramic artist, Windmill Hill, Hanley.
[Obit. *Staffordshire Advertiser*, 27 July 1833.]

Limehouse
A London porcelain factory of short duration was situated here, near Dick Shore, as early as 1746 (*Daily Advertiser*, 1 January 1747), but was in difficulties in 1748 (*Daily Advertiser*, 3 June 1748) and probably wound up shortly after. Richard Pococke stated that Lowris's

China House, Bristol, was established by one of the principals of this Limehouse concern, and that another workman set up in Staffordshire near Newcastle-under-Lyme (*Travels through England* ... 1750–51, 1888). It has been suggested that the Limehouse factory was run by William Tams or William Ball financed by the Rev. John Middleton, all Staffordshire men (Mrs Donald Macalister 'Early Staffordshire China': *Transactions, English Ceramic Circle*, 1933). Nothing is known of its products.
[G. Savage, *18th Century English Porcelain*, 1952.]

Limerick, Ireland
A centre for the manufacture of tin-glazed earthenware from 1762 until 1768, producing wares similar in style to those of Liverpool.

Lindslee, Thomas
Apprenticed to the Limekiln Lane Delftware Pottery, Bristol, in 1725; later connected with the short-lived factory at Wincanton, Somerset, but probably returned to Bristol after its closure.
[Pountney, *Old Bristol Potteries*, 1920.]

Linthorpe, Yorkshire
This factory established by John Harrison in 1879 produced 'Art' pottery of extravagant form with speckled or flown glazes, flowers applied in coloured slips, and imitation Japanese pottery. The factory closed when Harrison died in 1889. Christopher Dresser worked here. Marks include 'LINTHORPE Chr. Dresser' impressed, or LINTHORPE superimposed upon a vase.

Impressed

Liphook, Hampshire
An earthenware potworks called the Milland Pottery was started in 1948 and uses the mark of a windmill between the words MILLAND/POTTERY.

Colour plate 11, SPODE: *see page vii for caption*

Lithophane, Lithophany

A porcelain or bone china transparency moulded thinly in *intaglio* to produce monochrome
illusionist pictures (portraits, figure groups,
landscapes) by transmitted light. The process
was invented in 1827 by Baron de Bourgoing,
and used by Mintons, Copelands, and Grainger
& Lee of Worcester, working under licence
from Griffith Jones of London who acquired
the right to use the process. Lithophanies are
sometimes called transparencies.

Lithography

A process for reproducing pictorial effects, in
colour or monochrome, invented by Aloys Se-
nefelder (1771–1834) about 1796, using the
grease-holding and water-repelling properties
of oölitic limestone.

Ducoté appears to have been the first to attempt to apply the process, in conjunction with
etching, for the production of ceramic transfers
in 1839. Francis Morley, used this technique at
the Broad Street Works, Shelton, in the 1840's.
Some of the lithographic stones have survived.

The first litho-transfers, properly so-called,
were made by Day & Son in 1863 and submitted
to Josiah Wedgwood & Sons, Etruria, but they
were extremely crude.

In the 1890's several firms including Booths
of Tunstall and Pountneys of Bristol experimented with litho-transfers, but little progress
was made until the invention of Duplex paper.
A pioneer in this field was Leonard Grimwade.

Later developments include the substitution
of metal plates for stone, (although still there
are more stones used than in the rest of the
country) Harry Taylor of the Universal Transfer Company being the first to do this. He also
introduced the first dusting machines and the
offset process. In the 1940s Harry Taylor and
Frank Dearden experimented with photo-lithography.

Among artists who have designed effectively
for the process are Eric Ravilious, Harry Tittensor, Victor Skellern, and Albert Wagg.

Littler, William (born 1724 died 1784)

Salt-glazed stoneware manufacturer, in partnership with Aaron Wedgwood at Brownhills, and
porcelain manufacturer at Longton Hall trading
as Littler and Co. from 1752 until 1760. Later
manager to the firm of Baddeley & Fletcher at
Shelton.

Littler's blue

A brilliant 'royal' blue or lapis-lazuli found on
porcelain attributed to Longton Hall, and on
salt-glazed stoneware believed to have been
made by William Littler & Aaron Wedgwood,
c.1750.

This salt-glazed blue was achieved by dipping
the wares in a solution of flint and clay stained
with ground zaffre and sometimes also a little
manganese. Simeon Shaw says that Wedgwood
and Littler invented the process.
[S. Shaw, *History of the Staffordshire Potteries*, 1829.]

Livermore, Nicholas (died 1678),
Wrotham, Kent

A potter who is recorded in the parish registers
of Wrotham, Kent.
[J.W.L.Glaisher, Appendix to *English Pottery* (Rackham and Read), 1924.]

Liverpool, Lancashire. Delftware, earthenware
and porcelain manufactories

DATES

It is said that the manufacture of delftware in
Liverpool began about 1710 when some potters
from Southwark settled in the district, but potteries certainly existed in the city at an earlier
date and some faience bowls painted with ships
and inscriptions and made early in the seventeenth century are assigned to Liverpool. By
1780 the manufacture of delftware had almost
ceased and many of the best potters had departed
to work in Staffordshire.

Little is known of individual potteries in Liverpool, marks are rare, and only certain features common to wares from the district single
them out for identification.

The date at which the manufacture of porcelain began in the Liverpool factories (of which
there were about a dozen in 1760) is also uncertain; it is likely that potteries already producing
delftware turned to porcelain manufacture to

compete with the Staffordshire firms.

The industry in Liverpool was in decline in 1780–90, but some cream and white wares were produced after that period.

(1) *Delftware* – Pot painters and enamellers.
Baxter, John. fl. 1732–1779; died 1779
Coventry, Ralph. fl. 1726–1761.
Evans, George. fl. 1730–1734.
Heyes, Henry. fl. 1730.
Hughson, George. fl. 1769.
Rimmer, William. (Enameller).
Stringfellow, William. (Enameller).
Thier, Robert. fl. 1727.
Tillinor, Thomas. fl. 1725.
Weever, Edward. fl. 1720.
Williams, John. fl. 1727–1769.
Williams, Samuel. (Landscape painter).

WORK AND SUBJECTS

Alderman Thomas Shaw is known to have been a potter in Liverpool in the early eighteenth century, and a panel dated 1716, crudely painted with a landscape, is from his kiln. Potters named Chaffers, Christian, Pennington, Barnes, Harrison and Drinkwater are listed as potters or painters working there in the latter half of the eighteenth century.

About 1750, John Sadler, another Liverpool potter, introduced (possibly invented) transfer-printing. In partnership with Guy Green he developed the process with such success that wares were imported from other parts of the country to be decorated at Liverpool in this way. A large export trade, mainly to America, grew up and by 1760 articles of all kinds both useful and decorative came in a steady flow from the factories.

Punch-bowls, made largely for ships and often bearing the name of the vessel and paintings of ships or marine subjects, form a large class of Liverpool ware. Many are very attractive, but some later examples are of enormous size and grotesque design. A characteristic example of the earlier type is in the Liverpool Museum, dated 1760 and inscribed 'Success to the Monmouth'.

Flower painting of a bold and rather crude type is seen at its most distinctive on a mug made for a man named Fazackerly in 1757, and this kind of decoration, making use of *bianco*, is known by his name.

Vases and jugs (especially ones of large size with curved sides), wall-pockets, trinket-trays, 'bricks' (rectangular flower vases), were all made in quantity in Liverpool.

A large and attractive class of earthenware consists of tiles printed with such subjects as actors and actresses of the day etc., usually in black or red but occasionally in polychrome.

DECORATION AND DISTINGUISHING CHARACTERISTICS

Liverpool is at times difficult to distinguish from Bristol (to which it is generally inferior in design and workmanship) and occasionally from Lambeth. A clue to Liverpool origin can however be found in some details of design and decoration.

Chinese subjects popular in the eighteenth century were used at Liverpool as elsewhere, usually on a plain cream ware, painted or printed in blue under the glaze. In articles decorated in polychrome, a greyish-green, purple, bright blue and reddish-brown were much employed. The 'Fazackerley' design of a flower in the shape of a Tudor rose, outlined in *bianco*, is distinguishable with certainty as Liverpool, and is found on a considerable number of plates and dishes. Armorial designs were often used, as were river-scenes and marine views. Flower decorations in reserved panels on a mottled ground of blue or purple were copied from imported oriental wares.

With the popularity of transfer-printing, a fashion grew up for reproducing illustrations from contemporary books, prints and paintings of the period. These are often well engraved and usually printed on plain cream wares in monochrome. Subjects from Hogarth and his school are characteristic.

Marks are almost unknown: a prunus blossom on the base of articles decorated in the Chinese manner is sometimes found, but this was also used at Bristol and, less frequently, at Lambeth. Numerals occur on various types of delftware; the numbers used are said to be higher at Liverpool than at either Bristol or Lambeth. A border of reddish-brown on plates is reputed to be a Liverpool characteristic.

(2) *Porcelain.*

A considerable variety of porcelain is attributed

to the Liverpool factories, some of which seems to have been experimental and some of good quality and pleasing design. None can be assigned to individual factories, and it is possible that some pieces attributed to Liverpool may have been of Staffordshire manufacture.

The paste used is soft, heavy and somewhat coarse, with a bluish glaze often deepening in colour at the base of the article. Some pieces are reminiscent of Worcester, especially in their shape. Tall jugs and coffee-pots, and barrel-shaped mugs, are especially characteristic.

The flower decoration used is similar to that found on Liverpool earthenware, and is usually in rather bright colours with the flowers outlined in black. Transfer-printing is of rather indifferent quality; it is often found in a dark shade of red which seems to be peculiar to Liverpool wares.

Examples of Liverpool delftware and porcelain can be found at the Victoria and Albert Museum, the British Museum, and the Liverpool Museum.

Plates 56–57.

[C.T.Gatty, *The Liverpool Potteries*, 1882; J.Mayer, *History of the Art of Pottery in Liverpool*, 1885; B.Rackham and W.B.Honey, 'Liverpool Porcelain', *Transactions, English Porcelain Circle*, 1929.]

Liverpool, Herculaneum Pottery
See HERCULANEUM, Liverpool.

Livesley, Cotter & Co, Liverpool

Gore's *Directory* for 1777 describes this firm as potters and gives its address as 24 Haymarket, Liverpool. In the Mayer MSS there is a plan of what is described as 'Messrs Livesley's Mug Works, near the Dog Kennels', 1779.

[H.B.Lancaster, *Liverpool and her Potters*, 1936.]

Livesley, Powell and Company, Hanley, Staffordshire

William Livesley & Co. manufactured china and earthenware of all kinds at Old Hall Lane, Hanley, from about 1850. In 1851 they had two factories, the second standing on Miles Bank, Hanley. The partners were William Livesley and Edwin Powell. The firm continued until comparatively recent times under various styles:

WM. LIVESLEY & COMPANY
LIVESLEY, POWELL & COMPANY

POWELL & BISHOP (from 1865)
POWELL, BISHOP & STONIER
BISHOP AND STONIER

MARK

Impressed

White or cream earthenware of durable quality decorated both simply, and in 'the most elaborately and gorgeously enamelled, painted, gilt and jewelled varieties', was made. The firm of Powell & Bishop possessed a patent for gold and colour printing acquired from 'some Austrians'.

[L. Jewitt, *Ceramic Art of Great Britain*, 1878.]

Llanelly, South Wales

The earthenware factory, known as the South Wales Pottery was set up here in 1839 by William Chambers, junior, of Llanelly House. White and cream-coloured ware was made, also 'dipped' pottery, coloured bodies and for a short time parian.

In 1854 the business was taken over by Messrs. Coombs & Guest. W.T.Holland became sole proprietor in 1858 and continued it until 1869, when D.Guest became a partner and the style of the firm became Holland & Guest. The engraved plates of other factories in Wales – Landore, Ynisymudw, and the Cambrian Pottery at wansea – were bought and used by them.

Lloyd, John (born 1805 died 1850) and Rebecca, Shelton

Earthenware and china toy manufacturer first of all in Market St. and later in Marsh St., Hanley, from about 1834 until after 1851. His china figures were of the 'flatback' variety and included shepherds and shepherdesses. Marked specimens are in Hanley Museum and the Fitzwilliam Museum, Cambridge.

MARK

Impressed

within a frame impressed at the back or underneath the piece. Examples marked in both places are known.

[Reginald G.Haggar, *Staffordshire Chimney Ornaments*, 1955.]

Lochee, John Charles
Modeller of portrait medallions for Josiah Wedgwood from 1784–1797.

Locker, John, Tunstall
An early Staffordshire toy manufacturer recorded at Tunstall in 1802, but not otherwise known.

Lockett, John & Sons, Longton
The firm is first listed in 1802 as J. & G. Lockett, and a little later in 1805 as George Lockett & Co. By 1818 the firm was styled John Lockett & Co. and continued as such until the 1830's when it became John Lockett & Son, the address being Chapel Street. This firm manufactured Egyptian black, stoneware and lustred earthenware. John Lockett died 24 October 1835 aged 62. (*Staffordshire Advertiser*, 31 October 1835). In 1851 the firm was styled John & Thomas Lockett, Market Street. In 1864 the firm was operating two factories, in King Street and Market Street, the partners being John Lockett and John William Lockett. In 1875 they advertised a wide range of china and earthenware, including black lustre, gold lustre, turquoise, sage drab teapots, stoneware jugs, Egyptian black, etc. In 1889 the firm was once more John Lockett & Co., and as such continued.

[*Directories*, 1802 until 1889.]

Lockett, Timothy and John, Burslem, Staffordshire. Earthenware manufacturers
Timothy and John Lockett manufactured earthenware in Burslem from 1786 until about 1802

when the Locketts moved to Lane End. In 1805 the firm was listed as George Lockett & Co. Later it became John Lockett & Sons (whom see).

Early members of the family appear to have made salt-glazed stoneware; a large cask or barrel in white salt-glaze, surmounted by a figure of Bacchus, bears the impressed mark

J. LOCKETT
A teapot of black jasper with reliefs in white, in imitation of Wedgwood, and marked as above, is in the British Museum.

[*Directories*, 1787–1822.]

Lockett, William, Nottingham
One of the best known Nottingham manufacturers of brown salt-glazed stoneware whose name is first mentioned in the Borough records in 1739, and who is known to have been in production until 1777 or later. Incised and dated specimens from 1755 until 1777 are known. Characteristic is a tea-caddy in Nottingham Castle Museum inscribed 'Wm and Ann Lockett 1758'.

London slipwares
See under METROPOLITAN SLIPWARES.

'Long Elizas'
Curiously elongated renderings of Chinese women occurring upon Worcester porcelain in the 1770s. The name is an anglicized version from the Dutch *Lange Lyzen*.

Longport, Burslem, Staffordshire
Longport situated in the valley between Burslem and Wolstanton became of some importance after the cutting of the Trent and Mersey Canal as one of the landing places or wharves for potters' materials – Middleport and Newport (New Basin originally) springing up later. Factories were constructed here in the second half of the eighteenth century, the most notable being Brindley's. The firm of Davenport flourished here from 1793 until 1882, manufacturing porcelain, earthenware and glass.

Longton, Staffordshire

The latest of the Staffordshire Potteries' towns to grow to importance, its expansion at the beginning of the nineteenth century coinciding with the rapid development of the bone china industry. Earthenware and fine stonewares were also made here in the second half of the eighteenth century; and from c.1750 to c.1760 it was the scene of the first manufacture of porcelain in Staffordshire, namely that of Littler at Longton Hall.

The most notable potters of Longton and Lane End were:

John Turner	John Aynsley
Chetham & Woolley	Benjamin Plant
Thomas Harley	Mayer & Newbold
William Littler	Hilditch & Sons
Sampson Smith	Sampson Bridgwood

Longton Hall, Staffordshire. Porcelain manufactory

DATE AND OWNERS

Little is known definitely of the history of Longton Hall, the first porcelain factory in Staffordshire. It is believed on the basis of documents recently discovered to have been established about 1750 (the date given by Pitt in his *Topographical History of Staffordshire*, 1817), and certainly before October 1751. It was first worked independently by William Jenkinson who had 'obtained the art... of making a certain porcelain ware in imitation of china ware', but in 1751 in partnership with William Littler (whom see) and Aaron Wedgwood. From 1752 until 1760 the style of the firm was Littler and Company (advertisements in Aris' *Birmingham Gazette*) but other partners are known to have been admitted, including Samuel Firmin, button maker, in 1753, and Robert Charlesworth whose summary repudiation of the partnership brought the business to a sudden and untimely end in 1760. William Duesbury appears to have had some associations with the factory. Evidently the story of this factory is still far from complete.

The factory site was determined early in 1955 by Dr Bernard Watney and Dr Blake. Further excavations have been made by Mr A.R. Mountford for Hanley Museum. The finds, some of considerable importance, include fragments of porcelain, kilnwasters and kiln furniture. These are in the Stoke-on-Trent and Victoria and Albert Museums.

MARKS

In blue

Crossed L's appear in several forms and these may stand for Littler, Longton. Marks are usually in blue under the glaze.

WORK AND DISTINGUISHING CHARACTERISTICS

The name of Wm. Littler is associated with that of the factory almost from its foundation: his work there included much which seems to have been experimental. A deep blue glaze seen on some wares is supposed to have been his invention. He was later said to be manager at the works of Baddeley & Fletcher, Shelton. The produce of this factory, apart from one piece, has never been identified.

Two types of porcelain are attributable to Longton Hall. The more usual is a crude rather heavy porcelain of peculiar translucency for its thickness, the body appearing a pale green or blue with 'moons' of white when seen by transmitted light. The basic colour is a rather cold glassy white in natural light.

The wares include leaf-dishes similar to those made in Staffordshire salt-glazed stoneware, various articles in fruit and vegetable form often with twig-handles painted green, vases and basketwork dishes. Plates and dishes with moulded borders are frequent.

Decoration is in bright and rather crude colours, notably a deep underglaze blue, yellowish-green, dull pink and a rather thick red. Gilding was used sparingly.

The second Longton Hall type is a rather finer porcelain, in imitation of Meissen, often making use of the same subjects: vases decorated with applied double flowers, plates painted with birds, and bouquets of flowers, etc. There is some similarity to Chelsea in many of the pieces, but most are of inferior quality.

Figures were made at Longton Hall probably from the beginning. It is now known, as the result of recent excavations on the site, that the 'Snow-man' type of figure was made here. Later figures have the merits of vigorous execution and individuality, but are usually roughly modelled and give the appearance of being unfinished. Scrolled bases picked out in red are a distinguishing characteristic of these figures, together with the Longton Hall palette of yellows, blues and paintlike deep red. Subjects include 'Britannia', 'Turkish Actors', and 'Samson rending the Lion'.

Examples are in the British Museum, Victoria and Albert Museum, and Stoke-on-Trent Museum.
Plates 58–59.

[Bernard] Watney, *Transactions, English Ceramic Circle;* W.B.Honey, *Old English Porcelain*, 1928; new ed. 1948.]

Lovatt's Potteries Ltd, Langley Mill, New Nottingham Earthenware manufacturers.
Manufacturers of Brown ovenware and earthenware of quality.

MARKS:

Also the words 'LANGLEY Pottery' superimposed upon a windmill.

Lowdin's Bristol factory
The earliest Bristol Porcelain was made at a glass-house, and was so-named because the premises were occupied until 1745 by William Lowdin. Richard Pococke in 1751 referred to the building as 'Lowris china House'.

See BRISTOL (PORCELAIN).

Lowesby, Leicestershire
Factory started by Sir Frederick G. Fowke in 1835 for the production of terra cotta and stoneware picked out in enamel colours.

See FOWKE.

Lowestoft, Suffolk. Porcelain factory

DATES

A factory manufacturing soft paste porcelain was established in Bell Lane (now Crown Street), Lowestoft in 1757. The original partners were Robert Browne, Philip Walker, Obed. Aldred, and John Hickman (Gillingwater, *An Historical Account of the Ancient Town of Lowestoft*, 1790). The firm lasted until 1802 and produced unpretentious coloured and blue-and-white ware of attractive quality. In spite of many ancient claims that it was, hard-paste porcelain was never made here. The Lowestoft wares did not excite much contemporary admiration. Silas Neville, visiting the factory 26 August 1772 said 'most of it is rather ordinary'. In 1770 the firm was styled Robert Browne & Co., and had a London warehouse in Queen Street, Cheapside. Robert Allen was the best known painter although Neville asserted that most of the painting was done by women.(Silas Neville *Diary* 26 August 1772).

MARKS

No mark was consistently used, but numerals up to 28 often in underglaze blue inside the footring are found on some pieces. Factory marks of Worcester, Meissen and other factories were sometimes imitated.

$$W \quad \mathbb{C} \quad \cancel{\mathbb{X}} \quad \big($$

ARTISTS
The most famous is Robert Allen who was employed at the works from the age of twelve until the factory closed, as painter and eventually manager. Chaffers also gives the names of the following:
John Sparham
John Bly
Abel Bly
Joseph Bly
John Redgrave
Margaret Redgrave
James Redgrave
Richard Powles
Mrs Stevenson and daughter
Mrs Simpson
James Balls

James Mollershead
Mrs Cooper
William Hughes (modeller)
John Stevenson (modeller)
Thomas Rose

WORK

Many pieces made at this factory are dated or inscribed and a fairly complete sequence from the earliest to the last years of the factory can be established. Tea-caddies, inkstands, and other small pieces intended for visitors were often lettered 'A Trifle from Lowestoft'. Dates from 1761 until 1795.

The Lowestoft porcelain paste was very similar to that of Bow, although the glaze was generally thinner and rather absorbent. Patches of discoloration are to be found in Lowestoft teacups.

Table wares and numerous small articles were most frequently decorated in underglaze blue, the colour being usually darker than that of the Bow or Worcester. Porcelain moulded in relief was made in some quantity and can be identified from surviving moulds. A wicker-work design of rough character was much used. Openwork baskets and cabbage-leaf jugs were also made.

Oriental designs of figures in landscapes or flowers are common; marine views and inscriptions were popular, some being in distinctive colours, for the most part bright browns and reds. A similarity to Delft ware of the period is sometimes observable.

In the later articles the designs become more elaborate, Chinese influence being dominant. Commemorative pieces such as punch-bowls ('Success to the Jolly Farmer, 1774'), jugs, and plaques, often inscribed and frequently painted with local views, were made. Amongst other pieces there are mugs with double-twisted handles; teapots of globular form and toy tea services. Recently a few figures have come to light, but no larger groups. They are cats, swans sheep, and *putti*. Printing, usually of indifferent quality, and always under the glaze, was adopted for some articles.

Sprig decorations were popular in the closing years of the factory.

Examples of the original moulds are preserved in Lowestoft Public Library and Norwich Castle Museum. Casts in the British Museum. *Colour plate 9 and Plates 60–61.*

[W.W.R.Spelman, *Lowestoft China*, 1905; F.A.Crisp, *Lowestoft China Factory*, 1907; A.J.B.Kiddel 'Inscribed and dated Lowestoft Porcelain' *Transactions* E.P.C. 1931; A.E.Morton, *Lowestoft China*, 1932; Silas Neville, *Diary*; J.L.Dixon, *English Porcelain of the 18th century*, 1952.]

Lowndes & Beech, Tunstall, Staffordshire

Abraham Lowndes and James Beech established an earthenware manufactory at Sandyford, Tunstall about 1820, which was continued by James Beech alone until 1845.

[*Directories.*]

Lucas, Daniel

Daniel Lucas (died 1867) was one of the most celebrated painters of landscape on porcelain in the nineteenth century. His sons, John Lucas, William Lucas and Daniel Lucas were all apprenticed under him at Derby. Daniel Lucas, after working at the Derby factory, returned to the Staffordshire Potteries and worked for various manufacturers. He was an original member of the first North Staffordshire Society of Arts in 1841 (*Prospectus and Catalogue*, Newcastle-under-Lyme Museum). In 1841 when he was living at the Sytch, Burslem, he sold his furniture, which included 'valuable oil paintings by Rhodes, Price, and Lucas in handsome gilt frames, BARREL ORGAN capable of playing fifty tunes, etc.' (*Staffordshire Advertiser*, 10 July 1841). An excellent example of his work is illustrated in Geoffrey Bemrose's *19th Century English Pottery and Porcelain*, 1952. His manner was hard and topographical, in emulation of contemporary landscape painting.

[L. Jewitt, *Ceramic Art of Great Britain*, 1878.]

Lucas, Jabez

Slipware potter working at Ely, Cambridgeshire, late eighteenth century.

Lunn, Dora (Mrs Hedges)

Pioneer studio potter, specialising in matt glaze effects, Ravenscourt Park, London; established 1916; still operating 1936.

[*Studio Year Book*, 1919; G.M.Forsyth, *Twentieth Century Ceramics*, 1934.]

Lusterer, Lustrer

A manufacturer of earthenware or china decorated with metallic lustres: a person who decorates pottery with metallic lustres; 'Enamellers, Lustrers and Gilt Ornamenters...' (White's *Gazetteer*, 1834).

Lustre decoration

Decoration by means of thin films of metal. Josiah Wedgwood experimented with lustre decoration from about 1790 and his successors made commercial use of silver, pink (gold) and 'moonlight' lustre from about 1805. John Hancock claimed to be the first to produce lustre effects in Staffordshire while employed by Henry Daniel & John Brown, enamellers of Hanley (*Staffordshire Mercury*, 1846). Hancock sold the recipe to various persons for small sums of money and its use soon became widespread. The earliest commercial use of silver lustre is stated to have taken place at Wolfe's factory in Stoke by John Gardner (Simeon Shaw, *History of the Staffordshire Potteries*, 1829). Others also had a hand in its early development and application. The obituary notice of Richard Horrobin, organ builder and carpenter, said that he might be considered 'the reviver of gold lustre on china and earthenware' (*Staffordshire Advertiser*, 27 November 1830). John Aynsley was 'the first lusterer' at Lane End (*Staffordshire Mercury*, 28 February 1829). G. Sparkes, enameller, Slack's Lane, Hanley, also helped to develop and popularise the process. Various methods of application were used: pencilled, 'resist', banded, or in conjunction with transfer-printing and enamelling. It enjoyed popularity in Staffordshire and the Out-Potteries (i.e. South Wales, Yorkshire, Tyneside, Scotland) from about 1805 until 1875. The export factors Burgess, Dale & Goddard did an extensive trade in lustre wares with the U.S.A. in the 1850's (Goddard MSS *Diaries*, 1851–60). The subjects used for lustre decoration cover the whole field of public and domestic life, religious, political, sporting, travel and sensational events, – the humours of every day life accompanied sometimes by pious quatrains, or sentimental and licentious doggerel.

Lustred pottery may be seen in the Sunderland Museum, and Hanley Museum, Stoke-on-Trent, and in the Lucy Mand Buckingham Collection, Art Institute of Chicago.

Colour plate 18 and Plates 120 B, 151 B and C, 152 C.

[W. D. John and Warren Baker, *Old English Lustre Pottery*, 1951; S. Shaw, *History of the Staffordshire Potteries*, 1829.]

Lustres

Vases with prismatic glass pendants; chandeliers; 'a Most beautiful Lustre, richly embellished with flowers etc. and a fine figure of a woman, sounding a trumpet' – Item 80, 7th Day's sale Monday, April 5, *Chelsea Catalogue*, 1756; Wedgwood's jasper ware was used for these.

Lustrosa ware

Trade name for decorative pottery with oriental transmutation glaze effects, made by Geo. L. Ashworth & Bros, c.1913.

[*The Connoisseur, Vol 35, 1913.*]

Lyes, John

A workman who had knowledge of the composition of the Bristol Porcelain; when he was taken on at Worcester he was given a special bonus to secure his loyalty.

'Macaroni sportsman'

A transfer-print used on Staffordshire cream-coloured earthenware c.1775–80; copied from Darly's *Comic Prints Characters, Caricatures, Macaronis etc.* 1772, showing a sportsman with attendant, accidentally shooting his own dog.

Machin, Arnold, R.A.

Modeller in terra cotta; painter of figures on porcelain at Mintons 1925–29, and Derby 1931; studied at Stoke, Derby and South Kensington; modelled pottery figures, animals, and a set of chessmen for Wedgwoods from 1940, notably 'Taurus', 'Ferdinand the Bull,' 'Penelope', 'Country Lovers', 'Bridal Group', and 'Madonna & Child'. Elected A.R.A. 1947 and R.A. 1956.

Plate 121.

[Reginald G.Haggar, 'Arnold Machin', in *Studio*, 1947, and *Pottery & Glass*, 1945 and 1947.]

Machin, Joseph (born 1770 died 1831)

Enameller and black-printer, Old Croft, Nile Street, Burslem, 1800–1831; died 7 July 1831 (*Staffordshire Advertiser*, 9 July 1831).

Machin & Potts, Hole House, Burslem

Earthenware and china manufacturers Hole House, Burslem, from 1818 until 1834, when their factory was offered for sale. Oliver Potts took out a patent for printing in 1831. At this factory the first steam press for transfer-printing was used.

Drab stonewares with relief ornament were made in addition to blue-printed earthenware.

MARK

PUBLISHED
AS THE ACT DIRECTS
June 20th, 1834, by
Machin & Potts
Burslem, Staffordshire

(stamped upon an octagonal panel)

Example in the British Museum.

[S.Shaw, *History of the Staffordshire Potteries*, 1829.]

Machin, William

One of the last of the Staffordshire figure makers whose works in Percy Street, Hanley, and later in George Street, flourished from 1875 until 1912. Jewitt said he made 'ordinary earthenware and common coloured figures'. These were of the 'flat-back' type.

[L.Jewitt, *Ceramic Art of Great Britain*, 1878; W. Scarratt, *Old Times in the Potteries*, 1906; Reginald G. Haggar, *Staffordshire Chimney Ornaments*, 1955.]

Madeley, Shropshire. Porcelain Manufactory

A factory for the manufacture of soft-paste porcelain is said to have been established at Madeley about 1826 by a potter who had previously worked at Coalport, T.M.Randall, who later moved to Shelton.

No mark was used, but good quality imitations of Sèvres are said to have been made here until about 1840.

[L.Jewitt, *Ceramic Art of Great Britain*, 1878.]

Mafra

A potter of this name was working at Caldas da Rainha in Portugal producing pottery animals, figures and anthropomorphic jugs of the Toby type from about 1853 onwards, usually with brilliant 'Whieldon' tortoiseshell glazes. These were generally marked, but might easily be passed for authentic Whieldon wares if the marks were removed.

Magnus

Mixture of lead and manganese used by seventeenth century Staffordshire potters to produce a dark, red-brown, glazed effect – 'all the *colours* being chiefly given by a variety of *slips*, except the *Motley colour*, which is procured by blending the *Lead* with *Manganese* by the *Workmen* called *Magnus*'. (Dr Robert Plot, *Natural History of Staffordshire*, 1686).

Maiolica and Majolica

The name given to tin-glazed earthenware made in Spain and Italy from the fourteenth century, being the Italian form of the place-name Majorca, whence ships engaged in transporting Valencian lustred pottery from Spain traded. First applied to Spanish lustred wares, the term was gradually extended to cover Italian lustred wares executed in the Spanish technique, and ultimately to any kind of earthenware with painted decoration on tin glaze. The technique of the Italian *maiolica* potter is described in *The Three Books of the Potters Art* by Cipriano Piccolpasso, c.1556, translated by Bernard Rackham and A. van de Put. Should not be confused with MA-JOLICA – the name absurdly given by Victorian potters to earthenware decorated with coloured glazes, introduced at Mintons about 1850, for decorative pottery, but applied extensively to domestic wares, to architectural pottery intended for facing pillars, walls, staircases, balconies, and to flower-pots and umbrella stands.

[Geoffrey Bemrose, *Nineteenth Century English Pottery and Porcelain*, 1952; L. Arnoux, 'Pottery', *British Manufacturing Industries*, 2nd Ed. 1877.]

Malachite

A name given to a parian paste coloured to resemble the green of malachite stone.

Maling, John and Robert, Sunderland and Newcastle-on-Tyne

In 1762 Christopher Thompson and John Maling erected factories at North Hylton near Sunderland. The business was transferred to the Tyne by their successor Robert Maling in 1817, who made white and printed earthenware for the Dutch market. He was succeeded by his son C. T. Maling in 1853, and in 1854 the Ford Pottery was built where marmalade, jam and meat-extract pots were made by machinery.

Various kinds of pottery were made in the earlier period, including wares transfer-printed with views, enamelled and embellished with pink lustre, and mocha ware.

MALING

Malkin family, Burslem

A number of potters apart from the more celebrated Samuel Malkin worked in Burslem in the eighteenth century. Wedgwood's MS list of manufacturers working about 1710–15 included:

Thomas Malkin, maker of black and mottled wares at the Hamel.

Richard Malkin, making similar wares at the Knole (or Knowle).

Isaac Malkin, producing mottled and black pottery at Greenhead.

The Knowle Works had evidently been in the hands of the Malkin family for about 70 or more years (P. W. L. Adams, *Notes on some North Staffordshire Families*, 1930).

Tunnicliff's *Survey* of 1787 mentions the firm of Bourne and Malkin at Burslem as 'manufacturers of china glaze, blue painted, enamelled, and cream-coloured earthenware', and cites Burnham Malkin separately as a potter.

Malkin, Samuel (born 1668 died 1741)

Slipware potter, Burslem, flourished 1710 to 1730. He is not listed in Wedgwood's MS list of potters working in Burslem about 1710–1715, but his name occurs as member of a select vestry which met 22 May 1707 (*Book kept with Parish Registers of Burslem*). He died in 1741. The record of his burial describes him as 'The old parish clerk of Burslem'.

His wares comprise dishes with notched edges and bold designs in light and dark slip separated by raised outlines which are frequently milled with a roulette. The subjects are generally religious or proverbial ('Adam and Eve', 'Remember Lot's Wife', 'We Three Loggerheads', 'Keep within Compass', etc.) and generally they are signed on the face S. M. Formerly this class of slipware was ascribed to a potter named S. Meir of Tickenhall, but excavations at Massey Square, Burslem in 1939 which brought to light fragments of this type of pottery and the survival of a fully signed fragment dated 1712 discovered by Mr Ernest Allman finally determined their origin. This piece was presented to the British Museum in 1956. Examples dated 1726 are known. Examples, Fitzwilliam Museum, Cambridge and Hanley Museum, Stoke-on-Trent.

Plate 87 A.

MARK

[*Parish Registers of Burslem;* Geoffrey Bemrose, *Report, Hanley Museum and Art Gallery,* 1940; Hugh Tait 'Samuel Malkin and the "SM" Slipware Dishes', *Apollo,* 1957.]

'Malling' jugs

English tin-glazed pottery jugs splashed or mottled with metallic oxides in imitation of Rhenish 'Tigerwares', and similarly mounted. Dates recorded from 1549 until 1618. Some of these wares have been attributed to a Sandwich-Maidstone potter, working c.1582, and derive their name from a specimen formerly in West Malling church, Kent. Also called 'TIGERWARE' or 'LEOPARDWARE'.

[W.B.Honey, *English Pottery and Porcelain,* 1933; F.H. Garner, *English Delftware,* 1948.]

Manganese oxide

A powerful colouring oxide used from the end of the seventeenth century for staining earthenware bodies (it enters into the composition of most blacks) and glazes yielding tints varying from brown to violet-purple.

Mansfield, Nottinghamshire

About 1800 William Billingsley the porcelain ceramist and decorator had a decorating workshop here. Among his employees was a gilder named Tatlow.

Mansfield, Archibald

Thrower who came from Burslem and acted as foreman or manager at the Herculaneum Pottery, Liverpool in 1796. He subsequently set up as an earthenware manufacturer, making common earthenware at Canning Street, Bevington Bush, Liverpool, which was continued until his death. An advertisement announcing 'To be SOLD or LET – the well known MANUFACTORY, built and occupied by the late Mr Archibald Mansfield' appeared in the *Staffordshire Advertiser,* 20 March 1841.

Marbling

Decoration by working together various coloured slips with a wire comb and sponge in emulation of marbled papers or natural stones. Common on Staffordshire, Swansea, Leeds and Don pottery in the 18th century.
Plate 88.

'March to Finchley'

Hogarth's engraving of this subject (dated 1749) was painted upon a set of tiles acquired near Maidstone, and now in the Fitzwilliam Museum, Cambridge. Tin-enamelled tile pictures of this character were apparently made in London.

[Arthur Lane, *Guide to Tiles,*1939.]

Mare, Hugh and John, Hanley

Early eighteenth century manufacturers of 'Black and motled' earthenware in Hanley.

Mare, John and Richard
Mare, John and Matthew

John and Richard Mare, earthenware manufacturers, Hanley, signed the agreement concerning earthenware selling prices in 1770 which Simeon Shaw included in his *History of the Staffordshire Potteries,* 1829, and continued in partnership until after 1787. In 1796 the firm is listed as John Mare only and this is repeated in 1802 and 1805. Subsequently John Mare took into partnership Matthew Mare. This partnership was dissolved 2 February 1814 when Matthew Mare took over his father-in-law's factory (Samuel Hollins') at Vale Pleasant, Shelton (*Staffordshire Gazette,* 7 February 1814). John Mare then took over a potworks adjoining the Kings Head Inn, Piccadilly, Shelton, and worked it until 1826 when he became bankrupt (*Pottery Mercury,* 1 March 1826). In 1827 the factory was offered for 'peremptory sale by auction' (*Pottery Mercury,* 4 April 1827).

Marks, Henry Stacey, R.A., R.W.S. (born 1829 died 1898)

Painted Shakespearean subjects, landscapes, etc. Exhibited R.A. 1853–97. Designed pottery decorations for Mintons.

Markus, Lili

Studio potter; commenced work in Hungary in 1932 making table sets, vases and relief decorations as well as figures; came to England and worked for a time at a studio at Grimwades, Stoke.

[G.M.Forsyth, *20th Century Ceramics*, 1934; G.M.Forsyth 'Lily Markus; Artist Potter' in *Pottery & Glass*, January 1946.]

Marsh Family, Burslem, Hanley and Longton, Staffordshire

Potters named Marsh are recorded in Staffordshire records over a long period of time. Wedgwood's MS List of Potters working c.1710–15 included Moses Marsh, who made stoneware in the middle of Burslem; and Richard Marsh who manufactured lamprey pots and venison pots, and mottled and black wares in Hanley. A working potter named William Marsh was engaged by Thomas Whieldon for 3 years in June 1753 for a wage of 7/– per week plus 10/6 each year as earnest, and 'an old coat or something abt 5s value' (Whieldon's *Notebook* in Hanley Museum).

Jacob Marsh is stated by Simeon Shaw, writing in 1829, to have been the last surviving member of a family long engaged in the manufacture of all kinds of pottery and salt-glazed stoneware. His first factory was in the centre of Burslem but he transferred to the Lane Delph Pottery near the entrance of Lane End in 1806. His Burslem factory was then offered to be Let (*Staffordshire Advertiser*, 3 May 1806). He is listed among the earthenware manufacturers of Lane End and Longton in 1818. In 1834 the factory in Church Street, Lane End, was in the name of John Riley Marsh.

[*Directories; Staffordshire Advertiser* 3 May 1806; S.Shaw, *History of the Staffordshire Potteries*, 1829; J.C.Wedgwood, *Staffordshire Pottery and its History*, n.d.]

Marsh and Co. (Samuel), Burslem, Staffordshire

Earthenware manufacturers at Burslem in the early part of the nineteenth century. Samuel Marsh was in Pleasant Street in 1818. He was joined in partnership by William Goodwin, John Dean and William Handley until 29 June 1829 when the partnership was dissolved and Marsh and Goodwin continued alone, (*Pottery Mercury*, 11 July 1829). This partnership lasted less than three months. Goodwin left the business 26 September 1829 (*Pottery Mercury*, 3 October 1829). Subsequently, the company consisted of Samuel Marsh and William Willatt who continued in Silvester Square, Burslem as manufacturers of Egyptian Black until about 1840.

At Brownhills in Tunstall, Joseph Marsh made china from about 1805, and was apparently succeeded by the firm of Marsh & Heywood, as china and earthenware manufacturers about 1818, the partners being Samuel Marsh and Richard Heywood.

Marsh-Balden, Oxfordshire

Coarse peasant pottery made here was referred to by Dr Robert Plot in his *Natural History of Oxfordshire* (2nd Edition 1705).

Marsh, James F.

One of the most celebrated modellers of the nineteenth century. In the 1851 Exhibition he exhibited a terra cotta wine-cooler in the revived renaissance taste. He was a modeller at Davenport's factory, Longport, for many years, but later served the industry as a designer-modeller on his own account. He helped Rowland Morris on the Wedgwood Institute sculptures 1865–69. At the 1865 Industrial Exhibition in Hanley he exhibited terra cotta wares and an 'adaptation of a medieval jug'.

[L.Jewitt, *Ceramic Art of Great Britain*, 1878; *Minute Book, Wedgwood Institute.*]

Martha Gunn

A female Toby jug, modelled in the likeness of Martha Gunn (1727–1815) the celebrated

Brighton bathing-woman who is alleged to have dipped the Prince of Wales in the sea.

[Reginald G.Haggar, *Staffordshire Chimney Ornaments*, 1955.]

Martin, Anne, Lane Delph, Staffordshire

Manufacturer of earthenware at Lane Delph 1793. She made 'blue grey jugs and mugs' and the usual general earthenware of the time, including 'blue painted mugs' and 'dipd bosed jugs". The latter were probably a type of mocha ware.

[L. Jewitt, *Ceramic Art of Great Britain*, 1878.]

Martin Bros, Southall, Middlesex

Between 1873 and 1915 salt-glazed stoneware in a variety of styles was made by Robert Wallace Martin, Walter Martin and Edwin Martin at Southall, Middlesex. The background to their wares was Doulton's traditional salt-glazed stoneware. Robert Wallace Martin, who was a modeller, was trained at Doulton's. Quizzical animals and birds, face jugs and other objects of similar character were modelled and produced at this workshop. Vases in the form of gourds and other vegetables produced after seeing the Paris Exhibition of 1900 are among the most satisfying of their wares. Good use was made of surface texture, restrained colour, and form in relation to productive technique. A shop in Brownlow Street, London, rented from F. J. Nettlefold an early collector of Martin ware, was run by Charles Martin, the commercial head of the business, from 1878 to 1909.

A large collection of Martinware is exhibited at the Public Library and Museum, Southall, Middlesex.

Mark used

3-1898

*Martin Bros
London & Southall*

Incised

Plate 64 A.

[C.R.Beard, *Catalogue of the Collection of Martinware formed by F.J.Nettlefold*, 1936.]

Martin, William, Lane End

China manufacturer at Lane End, first of all in partnership in the firm of Hilditch and Martin 1818 and subsequently at a small factory near the Market Place (one biscuit, one gloss hovel, and a warehouse used as a painting shop), on his own account until 1834 when the factory was put up for auction.

[*Directories; Staffordshire Advertiser*, 14 June 1834.]

Maskery, Maria

Toy manufacturer, Piccadilly, Hanley 1834.

[White's *Gazetteer*, 1834.]

**Mason, Charles James
(born 1791 died 1856)**

Inventor and patentee of Mason's Ironstone China: partner, with his brother G. M. Mason, as manufacturer of ironstone china, 1813–1829; and later on own account or in partnership with Samuel Bayliss Faraday (1797–1844) his continental representative: bankrupt 1848: started up again at the Daisy Bank Longton, but finished in 1854; died 5 February 1856. Introduced a steam press to increase output and reduce labour in the printing department of his factory, and in 1844 a machine for making plates and saucers which was withdrawn because of certain mechanical defects and the opposition of the workers: married Sarah Spode (1788–1842). For marks see below.

[Reginald G.Haggar, *The Masons of Lane Delph*, 1952; *The Potters 'Examiner and Workman's Advocate* 1844; Harold Owen, *The Staffordshire Potter*, 1901; *Staffordshire Advertiser* 1836, 1839, 1844, 1848.]

**Mason, George Miles, M.A.
(born 1789 died 1859)**

Son of Miles Mason: educated privately and at Brasenose College, Oxford: in partnership with his brother, C. J. Mason 1813–1829; contested the 1832 election for the newly formed borough of Stoke-on-Trent, unsuccessfully: lived successively at High Croft, Stoke-on-Trent, Wetley Abbey, and after 1848 at Green Lane, Small Heath, Birmingham: married Eliza Hemming. Father of the landscape painter George Hemming Mason, A.R.A. (born 1818 died 1872).

[Reginald G.Haggar, *The Masons of Lane Delph*, 1952.]

Mason, Miles (born 1752 died 1822)

Born at Dent, Yorkshire and baptised 3 January 1753; trained in London under his uncle John Bailey; acquired in 1782 the business (Fenchurch Street, London) and property of Richard Farrar (d.1775) chinaman and glass seller, and married his daughter Ruth Farrar (1767–1834); Master of the Worshipful Company of Glass Sellers of London, 1793; partnership with Thomas Wolfe (1751–1818) and John Lucock in the Islington China Manufactory, Liverpool 1796–1800, and with George Wolfe, earthenware manufacturer, at Lane Delph 1796–1800; manufacturer of hard porcelain and bone china, Victoria Works 1800–1806, and Minerva Works Lane Delph 1807–1813; retired to Liverpool 1813; died at Newcastle-under-Lyme 26 April 1822. In 1804 he advertised an extensive matching business. Miles Mason made bone china, a hard porcelain and earthenware. Indifferent workmanship.

MARKS

M. MASON or MILES MASON impressed. A square seal with the name MILES above and MASON below. The pseudo-Chinese seal also occurs alone on willow pattern services.

Transfer-printed in blue on bone China

[Williamson's *Liverpool Advertiser* 17 June 1800; *Staffordshire Advertiser* 19 June 1800, 9 November 1805 11 April 1807; *London Morning Herald* 15 October 1804; *Gentleman's Magazine* 26 April 1822; Reginald G.Haggar, *The Masons of Lane Delph*, 1952.]

Mason, William (born 1785 died 1855)

Partner of his father Miles Mason from 1806–1811; pottery dealer at No 1, Smithy Door, Manchester, and manufacturer of blue-printed earthenware, Lane Delph 1811–1824.
MARK W. MASON (transfer-printed in blue).

[*Staffordshire Advertiser* 6 and 9 March 1811; *Pottery Mercury*, 15 and 22 November, 1828; Reginald G.Haggar, *The Masons of Lane Delph*, 1952.]

Masons of Lane Delph, Staffordshire

Miles Mason, after some years of experimental potting in Liverpool (in partnership with Wolfe and Lucock as a china manufacturer) and in Fenton (with George Wolfe as earthenware manufacturer) started to make porcelain at a factory in Market Street, Fenton, in 1800. He advertised an extensive 'Matching' business in the London *Morning Herald*, 15 October 1804, claiming his ware 'to possess superior quality to Indian Nankin China'. In 1807 he moved to the Minerva works, Fenton, where he continued to make porcelain and bone china in conjunction with his eldest son, William Mason. When he retired in 1813 the business was continued by G.M. and C.J. Mason, the other son, William, having taken over a separate factory. George Miles Mason withdrew from the business about 1829, leaving Charles James Mason to continue on his own account, or for a short period in partnership with Faraday until he became bankrupt in 1848. Charles James Mason started up again at the Daisy Bank, Longton in 1851, exhibited at the great Exhibition in that year but closed down in 1854.

MARKS

Transfer-printed

Variations in crown

No 306

Transfer-printed

WORK

Early types of porcelain made by Miles Mason were of an extremely hard consistency and rather opaque; a translucent bone paste was also made. Blue printed decorations were popular, and painted landscapes, Chinese subjects, border patterns of Regency type.

G. M. and C. J. Mason made showy Imari patterns with massed effects of colour and gold, often rather crudely applied. Very large pieces were made in ironstone china, including fireplaces, bed-posts, vases five feet high, some in a revived rococo style, others with pseudo-Chinese decorations. Blue-printed earthenware was extensively made.

Mason's moulds and engravings were acquired by Francis Morley.

Examples of Miles Mason's bone china and porcelain are in Hanley Museum, Stoke-on-Trent, and the British Museum and Victoria and Albert Museum, London. Mason's ironstone china, including a fireplace and other large pieces is well represented at Hanley.

Good examples of Miles Mason's porcelain and the later products of the family, including another fireplace, are in Geo. L. Ashworth & Bros Works Collection.

Plate 4 B, 65.

[Reginald G. Haggar, *The Masons of Lane Delph*, 1952; Alfred Meigh, *The Masons of Lane Delph: Master Potters* 1937, an unpublished typescript in possession of Geo. L. Ashworth & Bros.]

Massey, John

Manufacturer of Egyptian Black, Goldenhill, Tunstall 1805–1809.

[*Holden's Triennial Directory*, 1805–1809.]

Massey, Nehemiah (born 1803)

A well-known potter who made Egyptian Black, lustred earthenware, and pottery figures, Waterloo Road, Burslem, from about 1830 until 1868. The firm was styled Massey & Son in 1864. Parian was added to the firm's products about 1860.

Massey, Richard (born 1765 died 1830)

Enameller and manufacturer of lustred earthenware, Castle Street, Burslem 1818–1830.

[*Directories: Staffordshire Advertiser*, 13 November 1830.]

Massey, William (born 1770 died 1839), Lane End

Modeller for the younger Turners of Lane End. His obituary stated that 'many works of great beauty now extant in the Potteries were executed by him'.

[*Staffordshire Advertiser*, 1839; S. Shaw, *History of the Staffordshire Potteries*, 1829.]

Masterman family

Manufacturers of earthenware toys and figures at Knottingley Holes, Yorkshire from 1838 until 1881 or longer.

Matt glaze

A glaze with a dull, non-reflecting surface.

Matthews, William, Lane Delph, Staffordshire

Manufacturer of 'mottled and cloudy pottery, eighteenth century.

[S. Shaw, *History of the Staffordshire Potteries*, 1829.]

Mayer & Newbold, Lane End (now Longton) Staffordshire Porcelain Manufactory

Thomas Mayer (born 1762 died 1827) and

Colour plate 12, SPODE: *see page vii for caption*

(A) MASONS OF LANE DELPH. G.M. and C.J. Mason, ironstone china dessert dish painted in red, green and gold. Mark, MASON'S PATENT IRONSTONE CHINA impressed, c. 1815–20. Width 9⅝ inches (*J. V. Goddard*).

(B) MASONS OF LANE DELPH. Miles Mason, bone china plate painted with pseudo-Chinese decoration in colours. Mark, M. MASON impressed, c. 1805. Diameter 7⅜ inches.

(C) MASONS OF LANE DELPH. G.M. and C.J. Mason, ironstone china plate transfer-printed in blue and coloured. Mark, MASON'S PATENT IRONSTONE CHINA impressed, c. 1815–20. Diameter 10 inches (*J. V. Goddard*).

(D) MASONS OF LANE DELPH. G.M. and C.J. Mason, ironstone china plate decorated in colours and gold. Mark, MASON'S PATENT IRONSTONE CHINA impressed, c. 1825. Diameter 10⅛ inches (*J. V. Goddard*).

PLATE 65

METROPOLITAN jug, red earthenware with white slip decoration under a yellow glaze, found at Wittington Park, Buckinghamshire, sixteenth century. Height 10 inches.

PLATE 66

MINTON porcelain comport painted and gilded, supported by Parian ware figures modelled by
Émile Jeannest, c. 1851. Height 17½ inches.

PLATE 67

(A) MINTON bone porcelain plate. Mark, 'M' between curved strokes and 816 in blue. c. 1810–1815. Diameter 8⅞ inches.

(B) MINTON earthenware egg-basket decorated with majolica colours. Modelled by John Henk. c. 1870. Height 14 inches.

(C) MINTON earthenware bottle transfer-printed in black under a turquoise glaze, 1871. Height 10¼ inches. (R. G. Haggar).

(D) MINTON bone porcelain plate transfer-printed with 'Gothic' pattern designed by A. W. N. Pugin. Exhibited at the 1851 exhibition. Diameter 9¼ inches.

PLATE 68

(A) NANTGARW porcelain plate painted in colours and gilt. Mark, NANT-GARW. 'C.W.' impressed. Diameter 9½ inches. Plate painted in colours and gilt with a view of Esher place and other small views. Mark NANT-GARW. 'C.W.' impressed. Diameter 9¾ inches.

(B) NANTGARW porcelain plate, the figure subject probably painted in colours and gilt in London. Diameter 8¼ inches.

(C) NANTGARW porcelain plate (probably decorated in London). Mark, NANT-GARW. 'C.W.' impressed. Diameter 10 inches.

PLATE 69

(B) NEWCASTLE-ON-TYNE jug, earthenware, moulded in low relief, painted in colours and purple lustre. Mark, SEWELL impressed. Early nineteenth century. Height 9½ inches.

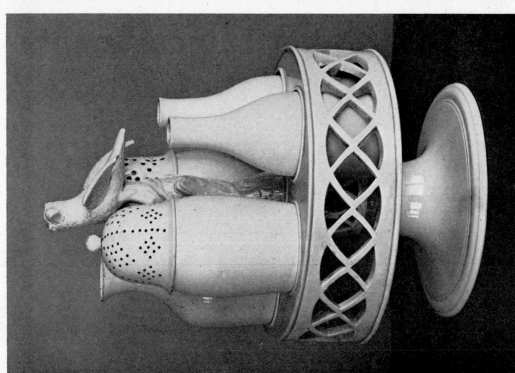

(A) NEWCASTLE-ON-TYNE cruet, cream-coloured earthenware. Mark, SEWELL & CO., and a star impressed. Early nineteenth century. Height 10¼ inches. Diameter 7¼ inches.

PLATE 70

(B) NEWCASTLE-ON-TYNE fruit dish, earthenware, painted in colours on a green ground. Mark, FELL NEWCASTLE impressed. Early nineteenth century. Length 9⅞ inches.

(D) NEWCASTLE-ON-TYNE plate, cream-coloured earthenware probably decorated in colours in Holland. Mark SEWELLS & DONKIN impressed. Dated 1819. Diameter 10¼ inches.

(A) NEWCASTLE-ON-TYNE plaque, earthenware, moulded in relief and painted in colours. Dated 1816. Size 10⅝ inches × 9½ inches.

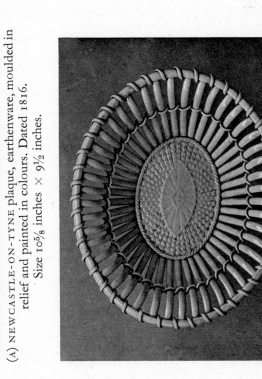

(C) NEWCASTLE-ON-TYNE fruit basket, cream-coloured earthenware, moulded in low relief. Mark, FELL impressed. Early nineteenth century. Length 10⅞ inches.

PLATE 71

(A) NEW HALL tea-pot, porcelain, painted in colours. Mark, 354 in red. Dated 1803. Height 6 inches.

(B) NEW HALL tea-cup and saucer, porcelain, painted in colours and gilt. Mark on the saucer, NEW HALL within a double circle, printed in red. c. 1810. cup, height 2¼ inches, diameter 3½ inches. saucer, diameter 5⅝ inches. NEW HALL jug, porcelain, painted in colours. c. 1790. Height 6¼ inches. NEW HALL tea-cup and saucer, porcelain, painted in colours. c. 1790. cup, height 2 inches, diameter 3½ inches. saucer, diameter 5¼ inches.

PLATE 72

(A) NOTTINGHAM loving-cup, brown salt-glazed stoneware with incised decoration. Dated 1740. Height 6¾ inches, diameter 6⅝ inches.

(B) NOTTINGHAM punch-bowl, brown salt-glazed stoneware with incised and impressed decoration, dated 1750. Height 12¾ inches, diameter 22¼ inches.

PLATE 73

NOTTINGHAM lion, brown salt-glazed stoneware. Length 12 inches. (*Mrs Bruce George*).

PLATE 74

(A) PARIAN WARE MINTON figure 'Dorothea' (Don Quixote). Exhibited at the 1851 exhibition. Height 14 inches.

(B) PARIAN WARE MINTON figure 'Psyche' modelled by Albert Carrier-Belleuse. Mid-nineteenth century. Height 17 inches.

(C) PARIAN WARE COPELAND copy of the Portland vase. Exhibited at the 1851 exhibition. Height 8¼ inches.

(D) PARIAN WARE COPELAND figure 'Innocence' by J. H. Foley, R.A. Exhibited at the 1851 exhibition. Height 16⅜ inches.

PLATE 75

(A) PINXTON ice-pail and cover, porcelain. Painted in colours by William Billingsley. c. 1800. Height 9⅝ inches.

(B) PINXTON goblet, porcelain, painted in colours and gilt. Mark G impressed. c. 1800. Height 5½ inches, diameter 5 inches.

(C) PINXTON tea-pot and cover, porcelain, painted in colours and gilt. c. 1800. Height 6⅞ inches, length 10¾ inches.

PLATE 76

(A) PLYMOUTH porcelain group, painted in colours. About 1770. Height 7¼ inches.

(B) PLYMOUTH porcelain hare, painted in colours. c. 1770. Height 6¼ inches.

(C) PLYMOUTH mug, porcelain, painted in colours. Mark, the sign for tin in red. c. 1770. Height 4⅞ inches.

(D) PLYMOUTH sauce-boat, porcelain, painted in colours. c. 1770. Length 5½ inches.

(E) PLYMOUTH salt-cellar, porcelain, painted in colours. c. 1770. Width 4 inches.

PLATE 77

(A) SCOTTISH carpet balls, white earthenware printed in colours. Early nineteenth century.
Diameter 2½ inches.

(B) SCOTTISH PORTOBELLO plaque, brown earthenware with blackened surface, moulded in relief with a profile portrait of Louis XVI. Late eighteenth century. Size 6⅞ × 5¾ inches.

(C) SCOTTISH PORTOBELLO plaque unglazed red terra-cotta, moulded in relief with a bacchanalian scene. Late eighteenth century. Size 6⅝ × 8⅝ inches.

PLATE 78

SPODE tea-cup and saucer, porc. Mark, SPODE 3157 in red. c. 1815. Ht 2¼ in. SPODE spill-vase, porc. Mark, SPODE 711 in red. c. 1820. Ht 4¾ in. SPODE plate, porc. Mark, SPODE in red. c. 1815. Diam. 8⅜ in. SPODE vase and cover, porc. c. 1810. Ht 4⅛ in. SPODE vase, porc. Mark, SPODE 1166 in red. c. 1820. Ht 4¼ in. SPODE tea-cup and saucer, porc. Mark SPODE 1926 in red. c. 1815. Ht 2¾ in.

SPODE vase, porc. Mark SPODE 868 in red. c. 1820. Ht 6⅛ in. SPODE vases, porc. Mark, SPODE 1166 in red. c. 1820. Ht 3 in. SPODE dish, porc. Mark SPODE 557 in red. c. 1810. Length 11 in. SPODE vase, porc. c. 1820. Ht 5¼ in.

SPODE plate, porc. Mark, SPODE 2974 in red. c. 1820. Diam. 8⅜ in. SPODE pot-pourri bowl and cover, porc. c. 1815. Ht 5⅛ in., diam. 6 in. SPODE tea-cup and saucer, porc. c. 1820. Ht 2¼ in. SPODE plate, porc. Mark SPODE 2089 in red. c. 1815. Diam. 9¼ in.

SPODE coffee-cup and saucer, porc. Mark SPODE in crimson. c. 1820. Ht 3 in. SPODE porringer, cover and stand, porc. c. 1820. Porringer, Ht 4 in. Stand, diam. 8½ in. SPODE candlestick with extinguisher, porc. Mark, SPODE 4618 in gold. c. 1825. Ht 3 in.

PLATE 79

(B) SPODE porcelain plate painted in colours and gilt. Mark SPODE FELSPAR PORCELAIN printed in purple. c. 1830. Diameter 9⅛ inches.

(A) SPODE coffee-pot, porcelain painted in colours and gilt. Mark SPODE 4896 in gold and SPODE FELSPAR PORCELAIN printed in purple. c. 1830. Height 9½ inches.

(C) SPODE chocolate-cup, cover and saucer, porcelain with stipple-printed decoration in black. c. 1810. Cup, height 4⅜ inches, diameter 5½ inches. Saucer, diameter 5⅝ inches.

PLATE 80

Richard Newbold (born 1758 died 1836) were in partnership as china and earthenware manufacturers in Lane End at the Lower Market Place from about 1817 until 1833. Richard Newbold also worked a manufactory for china, Egyptian black, lustre and earthenware at Green Dock, Lane End, which was sold in 1836.

The factory made porcelain of good quality and their jugs were in great demand. Flower painting on coloured grounds and the considerable use of gilding are characteristic. Their marks were

M & N

M & N

[*Staffordshire Advertiser*, 26 January, 14 September, 5 October 1833, 6 August 1836; *Gravestones*, St John's Churchyard, Longton; S. Shaw, *History of the Staffordshire Potteries*, 1829; Parson and Bradshaw's *Directory*, 1818; White's *Directory*, 1834.]

Mayer, Elijah (born 1750 died 1813)

Son of Elijah Mayer of High Carr (who was drowned by the incoming tide when crossing the sands near Ulverston) and Elizabeth his wife; merchant in Holland 1773; letter from Mayer to Bagnall dated 1773, de Haarlemerdyke, Amsterdam, is quoted by Stringer (1949); married Jane Mayer 5 March 1773 at Bucknall; manufacturer of Queen's, cane, 'Brown Line Ware' and Black Basaltes of fine quality, High St., Hanley; died 9 January 1813.

[Obit. *Staffordshire Advertiser*, 16 January, 1813; tombstone, Hanley Churchyard; S. Shaw, *History of the Staffordshire Potteries*, 1829; G. E. Stringer, *New Hall Porcelain*, 1949.]

Mayer, Elijah junior

Commission agent and china manufacturer; later ironmonger and potter; subsequently commission agent of various addresses, Shelton and Hanley; was a prisoner in the Kings Bench Prison, Surrey, 1827 (*Pottery Mercury*, 6 June 1827). Not to be confused with the previous entry.

Mayer, John

Manufacturer of china and earthenware, Fenton, 1834.

[White's *Gazetteer*, 1834.]

Mayer, Joseph (born 1775 died 1860)

Son of Elijah and Jane Mayer; in partnership with his father from about 1805–1813; continued the business until about 1840; died Hanley 28 June 1860, leaving a fortune of upwards of £200,000 which was the subject of an action in the Probate Court, London and which, even today, is the subject of speculative enquiry.

[*Personal Recollections of Leonard James Abington*, Hanley 1868.]

E. Mayer & Son, Hanley, Staffs. Earthenware Manufactory

A factory was established by Elijah Mayer about 1773; from 1805 it was known as E. Mayer & Son. The works are believed to have closed about 1840. The following impressed marks are found:

E. Mayer

E. Mayer & Son

Fine quality cream ware, black basalt and other kinds of earthenware were made. Two examples of about 1800, marked, are in the Victoria and Albert Museum.

See also ELIJAH MAYER and JOSEPH MAYER.

Mayer, Joseph and John, Longport, Burslem, Staffordshire

Earthenware manufacturers, Longport, 1845. A stoneware jug adapted from Rossi's Collection of Antique Vases, illustrated in *The Art Union*, January 1845; White's *Gazetteer*, 1851 lists the firm as Thomas, John and Joseph Mayer, Furlong and Dale Hall Pottery, Burslem, china and earthenware manufacturers.

Polychromatic biscuit printing was developed by the Mayers and continued by their successors

Liddle, Elliot & Co. Vitreous stoneware, cane, parian, and ordinary earthenware were made. A jug with an 'oak pattern in relief was illustrated by Jewitt. Products were marked: T. J. & J. MAYER or MAYER BROS.

[*Art Union Journal*, 1845; L. Jewitt, *Ceramic Art of Great Britain*, 1878.]

Mayer (Samuel) & Company, Tunstall and Burslem, Staffordshire

Earthenware manufacturers, Tunstall and Burslem: the partners comprised Samuel Mayer, Joseph Mawdesley, Ralph Lees, and Jesse Bridgewood: bankrupt 1840.

[*Staffordshire Advertiser*, 11 July 1840, 23 November 1841; *North Staffordshire Mercury*, 23 January 1841.]

Mayer, Samuel, Shelton and Hanley, Staffordshire

Manufacturer of fine earthenware toys, Piccadilly, Shelton 1830–34; Old Hall Street, Hanley, 1835 to 1841.

[Reginald G. Haggar, *Staffordshire Chimney Ornaments*, 1955.]

Mayer, Thomas, Shelton, Staffordshire

Manufacturer of figures in china and earthenware, Shelton 1834–41. In 1835 his potworks was announced as 'to let' (*Staffordshire Advertiser*, 9 May, 25 July, 8 August, 3 October 1835).

Mazareen, Mazarine blue

A dark rich blue frequently used for the decoration of porcelain, less frequently for earthenware. The origin of the name is unknown, but thought to be an attributed use of the name Cardinal Giulio Mazarine (1602–1661) jurisprudent, diplomat and Cardinal, or the Duchesse de Mazarin (died 1699). The name is mentioned in the Chelsea *Catalogue* 1756.

Meakin, J. & G, Hanley, Staffordshire

Earthenware manufacturers, Hanley; founded by James Meakin at Lane End 1845; transferred to Cannon Street, Hanley 1848 or 50; removed to Market Street where it was continued by

James Meakin, junior, and George Meakin; made hard 'granite' earthenware, chiefly for American market; in 1859 the Eagle Pottery was built; the Eastwood Pottery, Joiners Square was acquired 1887 (it had been established by Charles Meakin, son of James Meakin, senior); a scheme of reconstruction, including gas-faired tunnel kilns for bisquet and glost, warehousing, canteens, machinery was started 1936; the output on 1951 was stated to be 1,000,000 pieces a week, 80 % for export (*Evening Sentinel*, 28 May 1951).

MARKS

[Bernard Hollowood, *The Story of Meakins*, 1951.]

Mearne, Edward, Bristol

A potter who is listed as working in Bristol in 1673.

Medieval Pottery

Between the Roman occupation and the Reformation, English pottery shows little technical development. Potters were satisfied with relatively coarse local clays, an uneven lead glaze, and simple ornamentation by means of applications of slip, incisions with a sharp tool, or modelled clay reliefs. The Cistercian wares and the inlaid tiles represent more refined types of English medieval ceramics.

Shapes were generally bold, capacious, and generously formed. Decorations often show an appropriateness lacking in recent industrial pottery. Anthropomorphic and zoomorphic forms occur frequently.

The wares were distributed widely throughout the country. Aquamaniles in the form of mounted figures or of animals have been found at Scarborough and elsewhere (examples in museums at Scarborough, Salisbury, Lewes, Warrington, Norwich, and the British and Victoria & Albert Museums). They have been attributed to the thirteenth century by Bernard Rackham and Sir Herbert Read but are thought by W.B.Honey to be archaic fourteenth century productions. Mask-mugs and jugs with applied relief masks again were made in widely dispersed areas, (Ashmolean Museum, Oxford; Yorkshire Museum, York; Cambridge Museum of Archaeology; London Museum; Guildhall Museum, London; Nottingham Castle Museum; etc.).

Apart from jugs other vessels have not survived in any quantity and probably were not so extensively made.

The evolution of the pitcher follows style-development in Gothic from a graceful spindle or baluster shape, becoming gradually full-bellied and ending with a sturdy rotund body surmounted by a cylindrical neck in Tudor days.

The origin of pots on the thrower's wheel is often clearly indicated by the horizontal wreathing or ribbing of the walls and the thumb marks which attached the clay to the wheel-head. Handle attachments often show the same manipulative skill and inventiveness.

Ornament by means of stamps (heraldic devices, animals, etc.); applied clay imbrications; ribs, masks, and roulette ornament; incisions; painted, trailed and *sgraffiato* slip was used extensively in the fourteenth century.

More refined pottery made at the close of the Middle Ages includes red earthenware covered with a dark treacle-brown or near-black glaze generally known as 'Cistercian' ware because specimens have been recovered from Yorkshire Cistercian Abbey sites. Jugs and other vessels covered with a good copper green-glaze were also made.

Important medieval kiln sites have been excavated at Cheam (Surrey), Rye (Sussex), Sneyd Green (Staffordshire) and Nottingham.

See also CHEAM, SNEYD GREEN, CISTERCIAN WARE.

[G.C.Dunning, *London Museum Medieval Catalogue*, 1940; B.Rackham, *Medieval English Pottery*, 1948; B.Rackham and Herbert Read, *English Pottery*, 1924; W.B.Honey, *English Pottery and Porcelain*, 1933; Leopold Vidler, 'Medieval Pottery Kilns found at Rye', *Sussex Archaeological Collections*, 1933; Frank Stevens, 'Old Sarum Pottery', *Wiltshire Archaeological and Natural History Magazine*, 1933; R.L.Bruce-Mitford, 'The Archaeology of the Site of the Bodleian Extension in Oxford', *Oxoniensia*, 1939; Charles Marshall, 'A Medieval Pottery Kiln at Cheam', *Surrey Archaeological Collections*, 1924; G.J.V.Bemrose, 'Notes' *Transactions North Staffordshire Field Club*, 1954-1955.]

Medieval Tiles

Sometimes inappropriately called 'encaustic' tiles, medieval tiles were extensively made by itinerant craftsmen moving from site to site carrying their wood-blocks with them. Patterns may therefore recur at places widely separated. Tiles were made in various techniques, stamped, inlaid, and slip-decorated. The inlaid process consisted of impressing a tile (generally made of plastic red clay with a woodblock upon which a pattern has been carved) and filling in the impression made by the block with white-firing clay. Patterns were foliate, heraldic or pictorial in character, and were so designed as to be self-contained, or capable of arrangement in sets of 2, 4, or more units.

The earliest tiles decorated with finely stylised heraldic or animal motifs are best – the Chertsey Abbey tiles illustrating the exploits of Richard Coeur de Lion, and the story of Tristram, being famous. They were made, as proved by repetition at Halesowen where they occur with an inscription, about 1270. An earlier tile floor comprising hunting scenes, portraits, shields-of-arms, and animals was laid down in the Chapter House at Westminster Abbey between 1253 and 1259 and has survived almost unaltered.

The tiles used in parish churches were generally much simpler in character and often of poorer workmanship. Blocks would appear to have been used over a lengthy period of times: patterns therefore reveal little stylistic development and were sometimes defective in execution.

An innovation of the fifteenth century was the smearing of the tiles with a contrasting white slip before impressing the surface with the wood block. Tiles of this period were sometimes decorated with patterns reminiscent of the crocketed pinnacles of Perpendicular Gothic architecture, notably at Great Malvern priory.

Some fourteenth century tiles found at Tring Church, Hertfordshire illustrate apocryphal scenes from the infancy of Jesus, executed in the *sgraffiato* slip technique.

[A.Lane, *A Guide to Tiles*, 1938; L.Haberly, *Medieval Paving-tiles*, 1937; P.T.B.Clayton,' The Inlaid Tiles of Westminster', *Journal, Archaeological Institute*, 1912; M.R.James, 'Rare Mediaeval tiles and their story' *Burlington Magazine*, 1923; W.R.Lethaby, 'The Romance Tiles of Chertsey Abbey', *Walpole Society Annual*, 1913.]

Medway, Joseph

Recorded as a thrower of 'porcelain' at a pottery in Rotterdam, Holland, in 1649.

[B. Rackham and H. Read, *English Pottery*, 1924.]

Meigh family, Shelton and Hanley, Staffs.

Several members of this family were manufacturing pottery from the late eighteenth century. See under HICKS & MEIGH, OLD HALL.

Meigh, Job (born 1784 died 1862), Shelton, Staffordshire

Manufacturer; son of Job Mee or Meigh (1750–1817); partner of Richard Hicks from 1810–35; awarded Gold Medal by the Society of Arts for a leadless glaze for red earthenware (*The News*, 2nd June 1822); died Ash Hall, Bucknall.

[Reginald G. Haggar, *The Masons of Lane Delph*, 1952.]

Meir, John

Occurs on a slipware cradle decorated with a crowned head, and inscribed 'JOHN MEIR 1708 MADE THI…' A John Meir and Joyce Asson were married at Stoke-on-Trent, 23 September 1672.

Meir or Meer, Richard

This name is recorded on Staffordshire slip wares of various dates from 1682 until 1708, but nothing is known of the craftsman. The name MEIR seems a variant of MARE which occurs frequently later in the eighteenth century. A Richard Meer was married at Stoke on 2 August 1675 to Maria Pilsbury.

Meir, Richard (born 1685 died 1762), Lane Delph, Staffordshire

Manufacturer of 'red china and other bodies, from whom Josiah Wedgwood occasionally bought. An invoice dated 4 June 1762 (Wedgwood Museum, Barlaston) gives an idea of his products.

Bought of Richd. Meir

2½ dozen carved teapots att 16/–	2. 0. 0	
2 dozen of cut feet teapots att 5/–	10. 0	
½ dozen plain bottom teapots att 4/6	2. 3	
	£ 2.12. 3	

Richard Meir died in 1762 and was buried in Stoke churchyard (grave near old church ruins). He bequeathed his 'Buildings Potworks Lands Tenements' to his daughter Sarah Meir who carried on the business. She continued to supply Josiah Wedgwood with teapots (invoice dated 9 June 1763). In December 1763 she married Thomas Smith of St. Faith's, London.

[*Stoke Parish Register; Gravestone*; P. W. L. Adams, *Notes on Some North Staffordshire Families*, 1930.]

Meir, Samuel

Slipwares decorated with Sun-faced flowers and proverbial subjects and inscriptions with raised outlines and notched edges, frequently with initials 'S. M.' as part of the decoration, were formerly attributed to Samuel Meir, but the discovery of shards of a similar type at a site in Burslem, and the survival of a fully signed fragment, proves they were made by Samuel Malkin parish clerk of Burslem, whom see.

Meli, Giovanni, Stoke-on-Trent

A native of Sicily who came to Staffordshire about 1849 where he was employed as a modeller and designer, and later set up as a parian manufacturer. He appears to have worked for Adams of Tunstall, Sir James Duke & Nephews, Burslem, Copelands, Stoke-on-Trent, and many other firms. In 1864 he was manufacturing parian statuary near the Stoke Town Hall, but Robinson & Leadbeater bought him up in 1865. Meli then went to Italy with the intention of starting a terra cotta works, but unable to find clay finally emigrated to the U.S.A. Meli's exhibits at the 1862 Exhibition included parian statuary ranging in size from 2 to 25 inches in height and from religious to poetical subjects in character, butter-tubs, ornamental jugs and vases and dessert pieces.

[L. Jewitt, *Ceramic Art of Great Britain*, 1878.]

Mellor, William, Hanley, Staffordshire

Manufacturer of Egyptian black in Hanley in the closing years of the eighteenth century. The firm is listed under his name in 1796 but by 1802 was in the name of Mrs. Mellor, who was succeeded by Keeling, Toft & Company.

'Merryman'

An inscription, variously spelt, extended over a set of six plates made in tin-glazed earthenware in London from last quarter of seventeenth century until 1750 (dates recorded range from 1684–1742). The uncertain orthography was taken by W. B. Honey as an indication of manufacture by a Dutch potter working in England, if not of actual Dutch manufacture. Louis Gautier claimed the class for a Dutch potter working in England named James de Pauw. Prof. F. H. Garner regards them as English. The rhyme reads (1) 'What is a mery man, (2) Let him doe all what he kan (3) To entertayne his gess (4) With wyne and mery jests (5) But if his wyfe doth frown (6) All meryment goos downe.' Other rhymes extended over a series of plates are recorded, such as the 'Servant and 'Grace' series. The 'Servant' series (dated examples 1711) has the following rhyme: (1) 'I am a servant unto all, (2) Both rich and poor, grate and small, (3) Who uses me with diligence (4) Will be on me at small expense. (5) But when by servants I am ended, (6) My grate fault is I can't be mended'. The 'Grace' extended over a series of six plates, dated 1697, reads (1) 'When thou sit down to meat, (2) Give thanks before thou eat, (3) Be sure that thou conceive (4) The mercies thou receive, (5) That such favours may be (6) Repeated unto thee'.

[W. B. Honey, *English Pottery & Porcelain*, 1933; F.H. Garner, *English Delftware; Catalogue B.F.A.C.*, 1913; Reginald G. Haggar, *English Country Pottery*, 1950.]

Metropolitan slipware

The name given to a class of red earthenware decorated with white trailed slip, most of which has been found in the London area and probably originated there; characterised by commonplace shapes and inexpertly applied inscriptions often of a puritan religious character. Examples dated from 1638 to 1659 are recorded. Articles made included jugs, mugs, bowls, chamber-pots. There are numerous examples in the British Museum. A chamber pot in Hanley Museum is lettered, EARTH I AM ET TES MOST TRU DISDAN ME NOT FOR SO ARE YOU.
Plate 66.

Mexborough, Yorkshire. Earthenware Manufactories

Several factories for the manufacture of cream and cane colour wares for domestic use were in operation at Mexborough from the end of the eighteenth century, including Mexborough, or Rock Pottery which was operated successively by Bevers & Ford; Ford, Simpson & Bevers; Reed & Taylor; James Reed; John Reed and his executors until c.1873; and finally by Sidney Woolfe & Co. Closed down 1883.

MARKS

Impressed   Transfer printed

Mexborough Old Pottery. Established in 1800 by Sowter & Bromley, but taken over in 1804 by Peter Barker and worked by the Barker family until it closed in 1844. Printed earthenware was made here chiefly.

MARK

SOWTER & CO. (impressed)
MEXBRO

Incised   1838

A James Emery made earthenware at Mexborough from 1837 to 1861.

[A. Hurst, *Catalogue of the Boynton Collection of Yorkshire Pottery*, 1922.]

Middlesbrough pottery, Middlesbrough, Yorkshire. Earthenware Manufactory

The firm was started in 1834; from 1844 until

1852 it traded as the Middlesbrough Earthen-ware Co., and from 1852 until it was closed down as Isaac Wilson & Co. It made painted and printed earthenware.

Examples in Yorkshire Museum, York, and British Museum. (Plate with Blue 'willow and another copper lustred.)

Impressed

[A. Hurst, *Catalogue of the Boynton Collection of Yorkshire Pottery*, 1922.]

Middlesex

D. Lysons' statement that in 1795 a 'china' factory existed at Isleworth cannot be substantiated, but earthenware of various kinds was certainly made from the mid-eighteenth century.

A potworks flourished at Brentwood during the later years of the eighteenth century. In 1774 it was making 'sugar-loafs' and 'tun pots'.

At Wood Green a pottery factory in White Hart Lane which had existed from the seventeenth century, turned over in more recent times to the manufacture of flower pots and horticultural wares. Recent factories exist at New Southgate.

[D. Lysons, *Environs of London*, 1795 and 1811; M. Yearsley, *Diary of John Yeoman*, 1934; H. Clay, 'Isleworth Potteries' *Burlington Magazine*, 1926; Michael Robbins, *Middlesex*, 1953.]

Middleton, John (died 1744)

Potter at Shelton, Staffordshire; father of Rev John Middleton. On May eighteenth, 1719 James Shettell of Stoke-upon-Trent was apprenticed to him for a fee of £10. John Middleton died in 1744 leaving his freehold tenement in Stoke parish, known as 'The Goat's Head', upon trust to his executors (William Pope alias Miles of Shelton, potter, and his son James Middleton) 'to dispose of ye overplus (if any) betn his youngest son Stephen Middleton and his daut. Hannah Middleton'. He gave the rest of his estate to James Middleton, chargeable with £100 each to be paid to Stephen and Hannah within a year of his death. His eldest son fared less well – 'I give to my eldest son John Middleton one shilling'.

Middleton, Rev. John, B.A. (born 1714 died 1802)

Son of John Middleton who, because of a quarrel, cut him off with a shilling; curate of Hanley 1737–1802; secret partner of Warner Edwards in a potworks in Shelton; called in to arbitrate on behalf of Palmer in his dispute with Josiah Wedgwood. He was a man of singular views who disapproved of the contemporary system of annual hiring of factory labour. An enamelled, salt-glazed jug in Hanley Museum is inscribed 'To my worthy friend John Walter of Checkley this pitcher is presented, as a Testimony whereby I wou'd shew how much I respect and hon'r him, on account of that Skill which (with great Pains & too moderate Profit) he hath so successfully employed for the Good of the Publick in general & in particular of his affectionate Friend, J. Middleton.' It has been suggested that he financed a porcelain manufacture at Limehouse in London. The Rev. John Middleton married Lydia, daughter of Joshua Heath, master potter. Percy Adams noted that Lydia was left an annuity by her father 'free of interference of her husband.'

[Rupert Simms, *Bibliotheca Staffordiensis*, 1894; Simeon Shaw, *History of the Staffordshire Potteries*, 1829; E. Meteyard, *Life of Josiah Wedgwood*, 1865–66; Mrs McAlister, 'Early Staffordshire China' *Transactions English Ceramic Circle*, 1933; Ward, *History of Stoke-upon-Trent*, 1843; Henry Wedgwood, *Romance of Staffordshire*, n.d.; P.W.L. Adams, *The Adams Family*, 1914.]

Midhope, Yorkshire

Slipware pottery of various kinds, including combed ware was made here in the eighteenth and nineteenth centuries.

Miles, Thomas, Shelton, Staffs

Miles Bank, Hanley (in the eighteenth century the boundary between Shelton and Hanley) marks the site of a potworks worked by Thomas Miles for the manufacture of brown stoneware, for which he used a mixture of sand from Baddeley Edge and 'Can marl obtained from the coal pits.' Another potter of the same name, in Shelton, is stated to have made a 'rude kind of white stoneware.' Nothing more is known about these potters.

[S. Shaw, *History of the Staffordshire Potteries*, 1829.]

Milk pans

Wide spreading basins used in the dairy and known in Devon according to size as 'narrow bottoms', 'wide bottoms', 'cawderns', 'washing pans', and 'eighteen pennies'.

[W. Fishley Holland, *Pottery Quarterly*, 1955.]

Mills, George

Toy manufacturer, Hanley, 1846.

[Williams *Commercial Directory*, 1846.]

Mills, Henry (born 1802 died 1850)

Toy manufacturer, Shelton.

[White's *Directory of Staffordshire; Staffordshire Advertiser*, 10 August 1850.]

Minton, Herbert (born 1793 died 1858)

Son of Thomas Minton and eventually his successor as head of the Minton business. The great expansion of the Minton concern in the 1830s and 1840s was due largely to his vision and enterprise. Artists were brought to the factory from Derby and Davenports and new decorative styles were developed. The manufacture of tiles by die-pressing from dust was successfully carried out, and excellent (if somewhat mechanical) copies of medieval inlaid tiles were made with the help of his friend A.W.N. Pugin, whose designs were admired. Parian, majolica, and Sèvres style porcelains were produced in quantity, and of remarkable craftsmanship. When he died in 1858 it was said that 'his firm employed 1500 workpeople, a number which has never been exceeded by any ornamental factory before or since'. He was a keen educationist and advocated and supported the Potteries Schools of Design. He drew the attention of the authorities of South Kensington Museum in 1856 to the magnificent collection of bronzes and maiolica formed by M. Soulanges which resulted in its ultimate purchase, piece by piece and belatedly for the nation. He brought the first of the foreign artists to Mintons – Arnoux, Jeannest, Carrier, Lessore and Protât – and gave liberal support to the Great Exhibition of 1851 which was a triumph for Mintons. Hartshill and Penkhull churches were built by him.

[M.D. Wyatt, 'On the Influence (of) Herbert Minton', *Journal, Society of Arts*, 28 May 1858.]

Minton, Thomas (born 1766 died 1836)

Born at Wyle Cop, Shrewsbury and apprenticed to Thomas Turner of Caughley. Worked in London and Stoke (for Spode) as engraver, and then set up as a manufacturer in Stoke-upon-Trent in 1793, in partnership with Joseph Poulson and William Pownall of Liverpool, manufacturing blue-printed earthenware, and eventually bone china and felspar china.

Mintons (Mintons Ltd.), Stoke-on-Trent, Staffs

DATE AND OWNERS

Founded by Thomas Minton in 1793, in partnership with William Pownall and Joseph Poulson. Minton had previously worked as an engraver, and for Spode. After Poulson's death in 1808 Thomas Minton continued the business on his own account and in 1817 he took his sons into partnership and traded as Thomas Minton & Sons. After Thomas Minton's death the firm was continued by Herbert Minton and John Boyle until 1841. During this period tiles and buttons were manufactured under patents of Samuel Wright 1830 and Richard Prosser 1840. Michael Daintry Hollins became a partner in 1845 and the style of the firm was Minton & Hollins, or Minton Hollins & Co., and so continued until the tile business was separated from the china and earthenware trade in 1868. Herbert Minton died in 1858 and his nephew Colin Minton Campbell became head of the firm which was known as Minton & Co. In 1883 it became Mintons Ltd.

MARKS

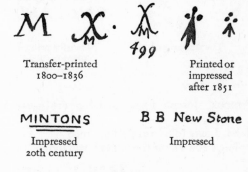

Transfer-printed 1800–1836

Printed or impressed after 1851

MINTONS

Impressed 20th century

B B New Stone

Impressed

MINTON

Impressed 1861 onwards

1822–1836

Transfer-printed
1860–1880

Transfer-printed

Transfer-printed
M – 1822–30
M & Co – 1841–44
M & H – 1845–68

Transfer-printed

Transfer-printed
uranium glaze
1918

ARTISTS

Art Directors

Arnoux, Joseph François Léon (1816–1902) 1849–95
Jahn, Louis (died 1911) 1895–1900
Solon, Leon Victor (born 1872, still living) 1909

Wadsworth, John William (1879–1955) 1909–14
Woodman, Walter Stanley 1914–30
Haggar, Reginald George, R.I. 1930–35
Wadsworth, John William 1935–55

Staff Designers

Bourne, Samuel, 1828–63
Eyre, George (1818–87) c.1847
Reuter, Edmund G. (1845–after 1912) 1875–95

External Designers

Cole, Sir Henry, C.B. (1808–82) 1846
Crane, Walter, R.W.S. (1846–1915)
Marks, Henry Stacey, R.A. (1829–1898)
Moody, Thomas Wollaston (1824–86)
Pugin, Augustus Welby Northmore (1812–52)
   1849–52
Smith, J. Moyr
Stevens, Alfred (1817–75) c.1860

Staff Modellers

Carrier-Belleuse, Albert, sculptor and figure
   modeller

Cocker, George (1794–1868). Modeller of bis-
   cuit figures
Comolera, Paul (1875) Modeller of birds and
   animals
Henk, John (1846–1914) 1863–1914
Jeannest, Émile (1813–57) 1847 Figure modeller
Key, Edward (1798–   ) 1826–45
Owen, Eric Raymond 1922–47
Protât, Hugues, Figure modeller
Toft, Charles (1832–1909)

Painters, Gilders and Decorators

Allen, Thomas (1831–1915) Figure painter
Boullemier, Antonin (1840–1900) Figure painter

Boullemier, Lucien (1876–1949) Figure painter
Buxton, Samuel Fruit, flowers and butterflies

Bolton, Samson (born 1800) 1811-after 1842 Overlooker, painting dept 1842

Bancroft. Painter of flowers and fruit

Birks, Alboin (1861–1941) 1876–1937. Pâte-sur-pâte

Birks

Coleman, Helen Cordelia A.R.W.S. (1847–84)

Coleman, William Stephen (1829–1904). Figure painter

Clark, Obadiah (born 1785) 1827-after 1842. Gilder

Dean, Edward J. (1884–1933). Painter of fish and game

JEDean

Colclough, Joseph 1925–35. Flower painter

Eyre, John, R.I. (died 1927). Director of Minton's London studio

Evans, John. Landscape painter

Foster, W.H. Figure painter

Green, Aaron (1860–98). Gilder

Henk, Christian (died 1905). Figure painter

Hancock. Painter of flowers and fruit

Kirkby, Thomas. Painter of figure subjects

Lessore, Êmile

Leroy, Désiré. Painter of birds and flowers and worker in white enamel

Lucas, Daniel. Landscape painter

Mussill, William (died 1906). Flowers and birds and underglaze

Machin, Arnold, R.A. (1925–33). Enameller

Mitchell, Henry, (1860). Animal painter, pupil of Speight

Elden, Matthew. Director of Minton's London studio

Pilsbury, Richard (1830–97) 1866–92. Flower painter

Pratt, Henry Lark (1805–73) 1830. Landscape painter

Rouchard. Worker in the Barbotine technique

Rischgitz, Edward. (1864–67). Figures and cattle

Randall, George (1862). Birds and flowers in Sèvres style

Rivers, L. Flowers and butterflies

Roberts, Ellis (1860–1930) 1874–82. Figure subjects

Solon, Marc Louis (1835–1912) 1870–1904. Pâte-sur-Pâte

Smith, Jesse. Rose painter

Simpson, John (1837–47.) Principal flower painter Simpson, William, son of John Simpson, painter of birds and animals

Smith, Joseph (born 1789) 1804-after 1842. Gilder

Smith, Joseph (born 1804) 1842. Painter

Steele, Thomas (1772–1850) 1825–43. Painter of flowers and fruit

Wright, Albert. Fish and flowers

A.H.Wright   A.H.Wright

WORK

Early earthenware made at the Stoke factory is usually white decorated in blue, often in pseudo-Chinese manner. These productions were of good quality and careful finish, owing much to Thomas Minton's early experience at Spode's. In 1798 porcelain manufacture was started but at first did not prove profitable, and was not made in any quantity until about 1825 when artists from the Derby factory brought new talent to Minton's. The body of the porcelain is from that time of a lighter and purer colour, and the glaze finer.

Some delightful patterns, evidently the work of one artist, are characterised by flecks, dots, circles, used to texture patterns of original and sometimes fantastic character.

Table wares figure largely among Minton's productions from the first. Early pieces have a mark which is sometimes confused with Sèvres. Dark blue grounds, medallions of flowers, Chinese landscapes and much gilding are all characteristics.

But painting of finely engraved shells and similar subjects occur on early pieces.

Inlaid or so-called encaustic tiles were made in the 1840's, sometimes from drawings by A.W.N.Pugin.

After Arnoux became Art Director and other foreign artists came to the factory, Sèvres styles and colours were faithfully imitated. Parian was

MINTONS (DATE MARKS)

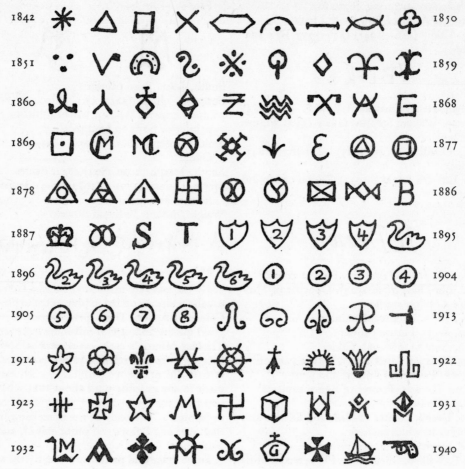

From 1824 onwards marks, as above, impressed in the paste were used on China and sometimes on earthenware to denote years of manufacture

made from 1845; majolica glazes were introduced in 1850 and used for table wares, toilet wares, figures and architectural faience. M. L. Solon brought to the factory the pâte-sur-pâte technique. Alfred Stevens designed ornamental pieces, and the Henry Deux wares were meticulously copied by Charles Toft. Block printing was used on tiles and other wares.

With the employment of distinguished French and English artists and modellers, and the already well established technical excellence of the factory, Minton's became the foremost firm in the country for the manufacture of porcelain, and a great profusion and variety of wares were issued by it. These were often greatly influenced by Sèvres, both in subjects and treatment, and certainly rival the productions of that firm.

Good examples in the British Museum and the Victoria and Albert Museum and in the Minton's Works Collection, Stoke-on-Trent. A small choice selection may be seen in Manchester Art Gallery. *Plates 67–68.*

[L. Jewitt, *Ceramic Art of Great Britain*, 1878; Geoffrey Bemrose, *Nineteenth Century English Pottery and Porcelain*, 1952; W.B.Honey, *Old English Porcelain*, 1928, new ed. 1948; *Government Report on Employment of Children in Factories*, 1842; *Tile Pattern Book*, Hanley Reference Library.]

Mist, Fleet Street, London

Mist is named as an agent in London for various earthenware manufacturers in the Potteries (possibly for Turner amongst others). The name is found on some black basalt wares, perhaps made to his order. The mark 'Abbott and Mist' is also used.

A white stoneware jug in the British Museum is marked 'MIST', impressed.

Mitchell, John, Burslem, Staffs. Potter

John Mitchell was engaged principally in the manufacture of salt-glazed stoneware in the early eighteenth century. His factory seems to have been of some size, and from 1743 until 1750 he employed Aaron Wood as a block-cutter.

Mocha ware

A form of 'dipped' pottery decorated with coloured bands into which tree, moss or fern-like effects have been introduced by means of a diffusing agent, a drop of which 'ramifies' the coloured bands to produce the pattern. 'Mocha' occurs under the heading 'DIPPED WARE' along with Banded, blue banded and common cable in the working-price list appended to *The Declaration... Chamber of Commerce* for the Potteries, June 1836. Undoubtedly many pottery firms whose names were appended to the list were making it. Simeon Shaw in *Chemistry of Pottery,* 1837, mentions 'mocha dip', but does not define its application. The process is plainly described by William Evans, *Art and History of the Potting Business,* 1846, as an effect produced by letting fall a drop 'of a saturated infusion of tobacco in stale urine and turpentine, and it ramifies into the resemblance of trees, shrubs, etc'.

The process was used from about 1780 until 1914. The earliest dated example, in Christchurch Mansion Museum, Ipswich, is lettered 'M. Clark 1799'. Chiefly used for ale, shrimp and nut measures, less frequently for kitchen and table wares. An old working potter (1955) identified the ware as 'Tobacco-spit' ware.

[Geoffrey Bemrose, *Nineteenth Century English Pottery and Porcelain,* 1952; Reginald G. Haggar, 'Cottage Pottery and Popular Art' in *Companion to the Connoisseur Concise Encyclopaedia of Antiques,* 1955; J.A.Fleming, *Scottish Pottery,* 1923.]

Moco, Moko

Buff or red ware mottled by spattering various coloured slips over the surface before glazing. A cheap nineteenth century substitute for MOCHA which was extensively exported. 'Black Jack Moco' mentioned by Evans 1846.

[Reginald G.Haggar, *Companion to the Connoisseur Concise Encyclopaedia of Antiques,* 1955; W.Evans, *Art and History of the Potting Business,* Hanley, 1846.]

Money boxes

Made at most country potworks as well as in industrial centres of pottery manufacture from early times; usual forms – houses, chests of drawers, globes, fir cones, pigs, hens, hens and chickens, cushions.

Associated with the ancient custom of the 'Christmas box' and referred to in such expressions as 'he doth exceed in receiving, but is very deficient in giving; like the Christmas earthen boxes of the apprentices, apt to take in money, but he restores none till he be broken, like a potter's vessell, into many shares'. (Humphrey Browne, *Mass of the Microcosme or a Moral Description of Man,* 1642), 'An apprentice's box of earth' (Masons' *Handful of Essaies,* 1621). *Plates 49 A, 154 B.*

[Reginald G. Haggar, *English Country Pottery,* 1950.]

Mongenot, Joseph (born 1769 died 1814)

A Swiss modeller and designer who worked for Adams of Tunstall and other potters. He was the son of an officer in the French Service prior to the French Revolution who was guillotined at Montpellier. He came to England in 1788 and practised as an engraver, modeller and designer in London, Birmingham and other towns. The last two years of his life were spent in Tunstall, Staffordshire. For William Adams of the Greengates Factory he designed bas-reliefs of the Sacrifices to Apollo, Diana and Pomona, Aphrodite, etc.

[Obit. *Staffordshire Advertiser,* 5 March 1814; *Staffordshire Gazette,* 7 March 1814.]

Monkey orchestra

'Monkies in different attitudes playing on musick' are listed in the *Chelsea Catalogue,* 1756.

They were copied from a series of Meissen figures modelled by Johann Joachim Kaendler, considered by some to be caricatures of the Court Orchestra of Saxony.

Monteith, Monteth, Monteigh

A punch-bowl with a scalloped edge; a vessel used for cooling or carrying glasses; said to have been named after a Monsieur Monteigh (Anthony à Wood, 1632–95).

'Moonlight' lustre

A marbled lustre effect produced by mixing gold, pink, grey and other colouring stains, used by the Wedgwood factory, early nineteenth century, and the Turners of Lane End.

[W.Mankowitz, *Wedgwood*, 1953.]

'Moons'

Small areas of greater translucency observable by transmitted light in some early porcelains such as Chelsea, the cause of which is not known for certain. Honey attributed it to the presence of an excess or aggregate of frit: Savage to the imprisonment of air in the body. The presence of 'moons' was first noticed in Chelsea porcelain by Dr Diamond.

[W.B.Honey, *Old English Porcelain*, 1928, new ed. 1948; George Savage, *Eighteenth Century English Porcelain*, 1952.]

Moorcroft, William (died 1946)'
Cobridge, Staffordshire

Master potter: trained at the Wedgwood Institute, Burslem, from 1886 until 1895; experimented with decorative pottery at MacIntyres, Burslem; founded the firm of W.Moorcroft Ltd., Cobridge, in 1913 where he produced 'powdered' blue effects, raised outline decorative pottery, and fine wares with flambé glazes.

MARK

[Geoffrey Bemrose 'William Moorcroft: A Critical Appreciation' in *Pottery and Glass*, June 1946.]

Moore, Bernard (born 1853 died 1935),
Stoke-on-Trent, Staffordshire

In 1870 Bernard Moore in conjunction with his brother Samuel Moore took over his father's business as a china manufacturer, St Mary's Works, Longton, continuing it until 1905 when the business was sold. Bernard Moore then took premises at Wolfe Street, Stoke-on-Trent, specialised in glaze effects, practising as a ceramic consultant, his son Bernard Joseph Moore joining him in 1906. Bernard Moore became celebrated for his researches into the glazes of the Far East, producing remarkable examples of *flambé, sang de boeuf* and lustre effects, Persian blues and aventurine and crystalline glazes. He was an admirer of the French potter Théodore Deck (born 1823 died 1891). Between 1905 and 1914 he employed a number of artists who executed individual decorative pieces for exhibition purposes. Bernard Moore's exhibits at the Brussels Exhibition 1910 were destroyed by fire.

ARTISTS

John Adams (born 1882 died 1953)

Hilda Beardmore

Dora Billington

George Allen Buttle (born 1870 died 1925)

Gertrude Jackson

Hilda Lindop

Annie Ollier

Reginald R. Tomlinson

Edward R. Wilkes

FACTORY MARKS

BERNARD
MOORE
≈ 1904

Painted

BM   BERNARD
MOORE   BM

[John Adams, 'Potters' Parade' in *Pottery & Glass*, 1949;
Obit., *Pottery Gazette*, May 1935.]

Moore Brothers, Longton, Staffordshire

The firm of Hamilton and Moore (partners, Sampson Hamilton and Samuel Moore) made china in a factory in the High Street, Longton from 1830 until 1859 when Samuel Moore became sole proprietor. Samuel Moore carried on the business at the St. Mary's Works until 1870 when his sons, Bernard Moore and Samuel Moore succeeded him, trading as Moore Brothers. An advertisement in 1889 describes them as 'manufacturers of art porcelain'. The business was sold in 1905. Moore Bros employed good artists and produced wares of excellent quality for the period.

ARTISTS

Rowland James Morris (died 1909) figure modeller from 1885–1890.

Richard Pilsbury (born 1830 died 1897) Art Director and Chief Designer 1892–1897

George Allen Buttle (born 1870 died 1925) ceramic painter

E. R. Wilkes, specialist on flambé glazes

Annie Ollier, ceramic painter.

[Jones and Keates' *Directories;* John Adams in *Pottery and Glass*, November 1949.]

Moorstone

Alternatively growan-stone or china-stone.

Morley, Francis, Hanley

Born at Sneinton Hall, Nottingham, son of Richard Morley (joint founder of the hosiery firm of J. & R. Morley). He married Emma, daughter of William Ridgway of Northwood, and became a partner in the firm of Ridgway, Morley, Wear & Co. Broad Street, Shelton (now Hanley). He became sole proprietor of the business in 1845, and continued either under own name, or as Morley & Co. (1850–1858) or Morley & Ashworth (1858–1862). Retired to Breadsal Priory, Derbyshire in 1862.

Morley purchased the Mason moulds and engravings, experimented with Ducoté's lithographic process, produced wares in the style of Mason and Hicks & Meigh.

MARKS

Printed

Morley family, Nottingham. Potters

The Morley family were engaged in the manufacture of brown stoneware from the closing years of the seventeenth century until 1780 or

157

later. The more important members of it were:

James Morley, Apprenticed to Thomas Harper of Montague Close, Southwark, 'to learn earthen potts of Divers sorts'; cited by Dwight for an infringement of his rights in 1693. His name appeared in Nottingham Burgess lists in 1697.

John Morley, Burgess of Nottingham 1695; nominated for sheriff 1725.

Thomas Morley, Obtained lease of land at Crich in Derbyshire, probably to get clay for pot-making.

Joseph Morley, Burgess 1721–22.

Charles Morley, Senior burgess 1722–23. Chamberlain 1735 and sheriff 1737.

Charles Morley, junior; Burgess 1754; owner of the potworks as late as 1799.

See NOTTINGHAM.

[*Transactions, Thoroton Society*, 1933; Thomas Bailey, *Annals of Nottingham*, 1853.]

**Morris, Rowland James
(born c. 1847 died 1909)**

Ceramic sculptor; studied at Hanley Art School under Protât, awarded National Scholarship to South Kensington; sculptor of the figure panels 'Labour of the Months' and 'Processes of the Pottery Industry' Wedgwood Institute, Burslem, 1865–73; later became modeller to the trade, working for Bernard Moore, St Mary's Works, Longton, c.1885–90, and J.S.Wilson, parian manufacturer, St Gregory's Works, Longton.

R J Morris

Incised

[Reginald G.Haggar, *A Century of Art Education in the Potteries*, 1953; *Minute Book Wedgwood Institute* 1861–1873, in Hanley Reference Library.]

**Mort, John (born 1768 died 1806),
Cobridge, Staffordshire**

Manufacturer of china and earthenware, Cobridge, from about 1800 until his death in 1806, in partnership with Barker and Chester under the title of Mort, Barker and Chester. The business was continued after his death under the style Mort & Co. until 1825 when the stock of 'manufactured china, in biscuit, gloss, plain white, blue-printed and burnished gold' was sold 'under a distress for rent.'

[*Staffordshire Advertiser*, 17 March 1804, 1 March 1806; *Pottery Mercury*, 5 January 1825; Holden's *Triennial Directory*, 1805–07.]

Mortlake, Surrey, Earthenware Manufactory

The date of the establishment of the first pottery at Mortlake is unknown; earthenware for domestic use was probably made during the eighteenth century, but manufacture of brown stoneware, in imitation of the white stone ware made by Turner, was started by Joseph Kishere in 1800. Mugs, jars etc. were among the chief of his products. Some examples of this stoneware are marked 'Kishere Mortlake'.

Wagstaffe & Co. are said to have manufactured delftware in Mortlake at about this period, but no work from this manufactory has been identified.

W.B.Honey, *English Pottery and Porcelain*; Geoffrey Bemrose, *Nineteenth Century Pottery and Porcelain*, 1952.]

Mortlock, John, Oxford Street, London

An agent who bought undecorated porcelain from various manufacturers in the early nineteenth century (including Swansea, Nantgarw and Coalport) to be painted to his order by Randall, Robins and other artists. His name is found on various articles, including Rockingham brown-glazed 'cadogan' teapots.

See ROCKINGHAM.

Morton, Andrew

A Scotsman who is recorded as working as foreman-potter at a factory in Rotterdam in 1629.

[B.Rackham and H.Read, *English Pottery*, 1924.]

Moseley, John, Burslem and Cobridge

The name first occurs in an advertisement (*Staffordshire Advertiser*, 14 November 1801) recording the dissolution of partnership with William Dale of Stoke-on-Trent, 9 November 1801. The partners had potted at Cobridge under the style Moseley & Dale. A potworks at Cobridge belonging to Adams was leased for a time to a 'Mr Moseley' sometime later, and in 1818 John Moseley (there may have been two potters of this name) is listed twice as an Egyptian Black manufacturer at the Churchyard Works, Burslem, and as an earthenware manufacturer at Cobridge (Parson and Bradshaw's *Directory*). The Cobridge potworks was offered for sale in 1834 (*Staffordshire Advertiser*, 26 April 1834).

Chaffers records the following mark:

Moulding

Process of shaping an article either by 'pressing' a bat of clay upon a 'form' or in a 'mould', or by 'casting' with liquid slip.

Moulds

The introduction of porous plaster-of-Paris moulds, attributed to Ralph Daniel who had seen them in use in Paris c.1745, made possible a wide variety of shapes of irregular form and decoration.

Some form of mould had been in use in Staffordshire for a long period, probably 'formers' made of wood, fired clay (pitcher moulds) or alabaster. Metal moulds were used for fine sprig decorations.

After the porous plaster mould had been adopted the process was to cut a model or block in alabaster (Aaron Wood was described as a 'block-cutter') make impressions from it in clay, assemble them and fire them to form 'pitcher' moulds from which working moulds in plaster could be run off as required. Later a model was made in clay, 'blocked and cased' by the mould-maker from which working moulds were prepared.

Many old moulds exist, some dated and inscribed, thus affording valuable evidence of factory or individual style. Dated and inscribed moulds include the following:

A.W.   Aaron Wood

R.W. with dates 1748, 1749, 1750, 1763. Ralph Wood

'Ralph Wood 1770'

J.B. 1763. John Baddeley

'William Bird made this mould', etc. 1751

Examples of moulds in British Museum, Victoria and Albert Museum, Hanley Museum.

Mountford, Jesse (died 1861)

Brother of John Mountford; ceramic landscape painter at Derby until 1821 when he left to go to Longport.

Mountford, John

Claimed to be the inventor of parian. Derby figure maker, who worked for Copelands at the time when parian was first made, and subsequently in partnership with Samuel Keys as manufacturer of parian. In 1864 he was working on his own account in Stoke. Parian statuary occurs incised 'J. Mountford – Stoke'.

[*Staffordshire Advertiser*, 20 September 1851; *Directories*; J. Haslem, *Old Derby China Works*, 1876.]

Moustache-cup

A cup with a screen or arrangement to protect the moustache from moisture when drinking, popular in Victorian times, introduced by Harvey Adams and Company, china and earthenware manufacturers, Sutherland Road Longton.

[L. Jewitt, *Ceramic Art of Great Britain*, 1878.]

'Mr & Mrs Caudle'

A relief decoration popular on brown, salt-glazed stoneware spirit flasks made about 1846 by Doulton of Lambeth and other potters. Based upon Douglas Jerrold's *Punch* papers – 'Mrs Caudle's Curtain Lectures'. One side depicts 'Mr and Mrs Caudle in bed', the other 'Miss Prettyman'.

[Reginald G. Haggar, *English Country Pottery*, 1950.]

Muffin

A flat, spongy cake usually eaten toasted and buttered, hence an earthenware or china plate of small dimensions for holding a muffin.

Mugworks

A pottery factory: '...the late Mr Joseph Brook's Mug Works in Brownlow Hill Lane, plan'd 19 June 1788, on lease.'

Similar expressions such as 'mug dealer' and 'mug-man' occur in Liverpool directories and parish records.

[Mayer MS, quoted H. Boswell Lancaster, *Liverpool and her Potteries*, Liverpool, 1936.]

Murray, Keith, R.D.I., A.R.I.B.A.

Architect and designer of pottery, glass and furniture; designed decorative wares for Josiah Wedgwood & Sons from 1933 and planned, with his partner C. S. White F.R.I.B.A., the Barlaston Factory, the foundation stone of which was laid in 1938. In 1940 the earthenware works was completed.

[J. M. Graham & H. C. Wedgwood, *Wedgwood*, 1948.]

Murray, William Staite, Bray, Berkshire

Studied at Camberwell Art School and started up as a potter at Yeoman's Row, South Kensington, in 1919. Influenced by Hamada whom he met at St Ives c. 1920–21; moved to Brockley in Kent, firing his wares in Bermondsey. Later he went to Bray in Berkshire where he built a kiln and workshop.

He taught at the Royal College of Art from 1925 until 1940 and had many pupils, including Haile, Heber Matthews, H. F. Hammond and Victor Shellern.

Went to Southern Rhodesia in 1940.

Murray made stonewares strongly influenced by Chinese wares of the Sung Dynasty. His forms are sculpturesque and 'imbued with a mystical and suggestive mood'. His mark is:

[Muriel Rose, *Artist Potters in England*, 1955; E. Marsh, in *Apollo*, April 1944.]

'Muses modeller'

An unidentified craftsman, so-called because he modelled a set of figures of the Muses and others in a similar style at the Bow factory c. 1752. Tentatively identified by F. Severne Mackenna as 'Mr Tebo'. George Savage has listed 27 figures which can be attributed to this modeller.
Plate 8 B.

[G. Savage, *Eighteenth Century English Porcelain*, 1952.]

Muss, Charles (born 1779 died 1824)

Painter at the Caughley manufactory and later worked independently in London. He employed John Martin (born 1789 died 1854) an apocalyptic visionary, who painted the picture of 'Paradise Lost' on the specimen of Flight & Barr Worcester porcelain in the Allen Collection, Victoria and Albert Museum.

[B. Rackham, *Catalogue of the Herbert Allen Collection*, Victoria and Albert Museum 1923.]

Musselburgh, Scotland

Earthenware was made at Musselburgh. See under PORTOBELLO. Porcelain was not, as erroneously stated, made here in the eighteenth century.

Mussill, William (died 1906)

A flower painter who came to Mintons about 1870, from Paris. He was born at Altrohalm in Bohemia. An avid student of nature, he spent most of his spare time in conservatories at Trentham piling up innumerable sketches of birds and flowers executed in *gouache* upon tinted paper. As a ceramic painter he was at his best on large pieces where his dexterous rich painting was effective. His ceramic painting was all 'once-fired work' (as his pupil, Penson, has reported) and in consequence vivid and lively in quality.

Myatt family, Bilston, Staffordshire

About 1830 George Myatt succeeded Abraham Bruiton at the Shropshire Row Potworks, Bilston, where he manufactured blue-and-white earthenware. There is a record in 1834 of Benja-

Colour plate 14, STAFFORDSHIRE: *see page viii for caption*

min Myatt, manufacturer of yellow wares at the Bradley Pottery where he had succeeded the Wildes. Decorative pottery of excellent quality was developed at that factory using feathery slip or incised decorations and warm ochre and olive green glazes. The impressed mark MYATT occurs. Before 1851 Robert Bew, a pot-dealer, took over, although the factory remained under Myatt management. Robert John Myatt, beer-seller and manager of the Bradley Lower Pottery, Bilston, is listed in White's *Staffordshire*, 1851 and Melville's *Wolverhampton Directory*, 1851.

Myatt, Richard, Benjamin and Joseph, Lane End

Richard Myatt is listed in Bailey's *Directory* 1783 as a potter at Lane End. He evidently made, the 'red china' of the Elers type because his mark MYATT impressed occurs on engine-turned pieces of this kind. Richard Myatt died in 1804. Before his death the factory must have been taken over by Joseph Myatt who is listed in the local directory for 1796. In 1818 Benjamin and Joseph Myatt were manufacturing lustred pottery in the High Street, Lane End. Joseph Myatt died in December 1852 aged 67 years.

[*Directories*, 1783, 1796, 1818; *Staffordshire Advertiser*, 14 July 1804, 18 December 1852.]

Nadin, W.

Purchaser of the Church Gresley Factory 1800.

[W.B.Honey, *Old English Porcelain*. Jewitt, *Ceramic Art of Great Britain*, 1878.]

Nankin

Chinese seaport and chief town in the province of Kiangsu and the ancient capital of China. Large quantities of porcelain decorated in blue were exported through this town, hence the term 'Nankin Blue' or 'Nankin China' or simply 'Nankin' became a synonym for blue-and-white porcelain.

Nantgarw, Glamorgan. Porcelain manufactory

DATES AND OWNERS

William Billingsley who had been a well-known flower painter at Derby founded the factory in November 1813, in partnership with his son-in-law, Samuel Walker. After exhausting his capital, William Weston Young advanced sums amounting to nearly £600 and eventually became partner in the venture. This proved inadequate and the three partners appealed for financial assistance to the Government with the result that their endeavours were brought to the notice of L.W.Dillwyn who arranged for the transference of the business to the Cambrian factory at Swansea.

Billingsley stayed at Swansea until 1816 when he returned to Nantgarw, there to be rejoined by Walker in 1817. With new capital supplied by W.W.Young and some country gentlemen, the Nantgarw concern was operated until the end of 1819, but, their capital exhausted, Billingsley and Walker were compelled to vacate Nantgarw in the spring of 1820. In November the moulds and plant with some decorated and a lot of undecorated china were offered for sale and taken over by Young, who became sole proprietor. No further ware was made, although much of the undecorated porcelain was painted by Pardoe. Further sales took place in 1821 and 1822 when it was said that Rose of Coalport bought up the plant and moulds.

MARKS

NANT GARW
G.W.

ARTISTS

Billingsley himself decorated some of the Nantgarw products: he was assisted by his daughter and two other women. Billingsley also employed for short periods William Pegg of Derby, John Latham from Coalport and Thomas Pardoe of Swansea. All the above were flower painters.

A much larger proportion of Nantgarw porcelain was sent undecorated to London to various independent enamellers. This was more ambitiously decorated and is usually fairly easily distinguishable from the simpler local designs used at Nantgarw. The agent Mortlock sent pieces to Moses Webster (a Derby painter of repute) and Sims for painting, these being afterwards fired in the kiln of Robins and Randall.

WORK

During its short life the Nantgarw factory produced some fine porcelain of quite exceptional translucency. Billingsley himself compared it to that of Sèvres, and the decoration used was often in the French manner. Extremely white and at times almost glasslike, the porcelain unfortunately did not always stand firing and much was lost in the kiln. These losses led to the financial difficulties which eventually forced Billingsley to leave Nantgarw. He was never successful in finding a soft-paste of comparable quality which could be fired reliably.

Few shapes were made at Nantgarw and these are generally simple in character. Table wares comprising tea and dessert services were the chief productions of the factory. A distinguishing feature of the plates was a fine embossed scroll and flower pattern, although, of course, plain shaped plates were also used.

Less frequent are such decorative pieces as spill holders, taper stands, specimen and cabinet cups and saucers, pen trays and pot-pourri vases.

Work from Nantgarw and Swansea may be seen in the National Museum of Wales, Cardiff, the British Museum, the Victoria and Albert Museum and the Glynn Vivian Art Gallery, Swansea.

Plate 69.

[Isaac J. Williams, *Guide to the Collection of Welsh Porcelain*, National Museum of Wales, 1931; *Nantgarw Pottery and its Products*, 1932; W. D. John, *Nantgarw Porcelain*, 1948.]

Nappey, Nappie

An oval baking dish, – 'Nappeys and Baking Dishes' – (Agreement, dated 1770).

[S. Shaw, *History of the Staffordshire Potteries*, 1829.]

Nash, Margere

Name recorded on a Staffordshire slipware dish decorated with a doubleheaded eagle (British Museum).

Neale & Bailey, London

The firm of James Neale, merchant, was established about 1761 at St Johns Wapping. From 1780 until 1790 the firm was Neale, Maidment & Bailey, St Paul's Churchyard, and from 1790 until 1814 (when Neale died) Neale and Bailey. They were agents for Staffordshire pottery and Swansea porcelain, and the name NEALE & BAILEY is sometimes found on articles produced or decorated to their order. After Neale's death, Thomas Bailey (born 1751 died 1828) a native of Newcastle-under-Lyme, Staffs, became sole proprietor (*Pottery Mercury*, 15 March 1828).

[A. V. Sutherland-Graeme, 'James Neale, Potter' in *The Connoisseur*, 1947.]

Neale, James (born 1740 died 1814),
Church Works, Hanley, Staffordshire
Earthenware Manufactory

DATES AND OWNERS

James Neale, who had been Humphrey Palmer's London agent, took over Palmer's business in Hanley after his failure in 1778. Robert Wilson was made a partner in 1786 and for a time the firm was known as Neale & Wilson. The style Neale & Co. seems to have been adopted when other partners were admitted. Robert Wilson succeeded Neale, and when he died in 1801 he was in turn followed by David Wilson who took his sons into partnership and traded as David Wilson & Sons. David Wilson and the sons who were in the business, except John, had died before 1817 when John Wilson became bankrupt and the factory passed to other hands.

MARKS

NEALE & Co

NEALE & Co

NEALE

Impressed

NEALE & CO

G

NEALE & WILSON

Impressed

WORK AND SUBJECTS

The firm made good quality cream-coloured wares, blue-painted and lustred table ware, jasper, black Egyptian, marbled vases etc. many pieces in close imitation of Wedgwood. Designs from Wedgwood were not infrequently copied, and classical shapes and decoration figured largely in work from the pottery.

Figures made by Neale & Co. are often of considerable merit. Usually small in size, they are modelled, and coloured in a neat restrained manner (a turquoise blue is notable for its frequent use) in fine, clear enamels. The figures were generally made for easy delivery from moulds, and were sometimes gilded in a porcelain style.

Marked examples may be seen in the British Museum, Victoria and Albert Museum, Fitzwilliam Museum, Cecil Higgins Museum, Bedford, and Hanley Museum, Stoke-on-Trent.

See also PALMER.

[Reginald G. Haggar, *Staffordshire Chimney Ornaments*, 1955; A.V.Sutherland-Graeme, 'James Neale, Potter' in *The Connoisseur*, 1947; B.Rackham, *Early Staffordshire Pottery*, 1951.]
Colour plate 14.

The Newbottle Pottery, Sunderland, Co. Durham. Earthenware Manufactory

A pottery said to have been established about 1755; white earthenware of indifferent quality was made there in the first half of the nineteenth century. At that time it was owned by Anthony Scott, whose descendants succeeded him in the business.

See also SUNDERLAND (Southwick Pottery).

Newcastle-under-Lyme, Staffordshire

Famous for its clay pipes in the seventeenth century, notably those made by Charles Riggs (died 1676). From about 1730 until 1754 Samuel Bell (died 1754) and Joseph Wilson made brown glazed Astbury-type teapots at a potworks in Lower Street. Examples may be seen in Newcastle Museum. The names of thirty potters are given in the Newcastle Poll Lists between 1774 and 1792. In 1837 the names of forty potters are listed. In the closing years of the eighteenth century J.Bulkeley and William Bent manufactured in Newcastle, but dissolved partnership 11 November 1797. Robert Bath, variously described as earthenware manufacturer, saggar maker and licensed retailer of beer and tobacco, had a potworks at Halmerend near Newcastle but became bankrupt in 1840.
Plate 71.
[Robert Plot, *Natural History of Staffordshire*, Oxford, 1686; *Newcastle-under-Lyme Poll Lists*, 1734–1837.]

New Forest ware

Dark earthenware decorated with slight abstract motifs in light coloured slipware made by Roman potters in the New Forest area during the third and fourth centuries A.D.

New Hall, Shelton, Staffordshire

In 1780 Richard Champion approached Josiah Wedgwood seeking his advice and assistance in disposing of his patent for the manufacture of hard-paste porcelain. The outcome was the formation of a company which operated first of all in Tunstall at the factory of Anthony Keeling, comprising master potters of repute, which bought Champion's patent and commenced the manufacture of hard paste porcelain in 1781.

The members of the Company were:

Samuel Hollins (born 1748 died 1820)
Anthony Keeling (born 1738 died 1816)
Jacob Warburton (born 1741 died 1826)
William Clowes
Charles Bagnall (born 1748 died 1814)
Richard Champion (died 1791)
John Turner (born 1738 died 1787)

It is possible that Joshua Heath was also a

partner. Tunnicliff styles the firm Heath, Warburton & Co, but he is by no means always accurate and reliable.

A dispute arose among the partners shortly after the enterprise was launched, and Keeling and Turner withdrew. Champion also, having obtained the position of Deputy Paymaster of the Forces, went to London in 1782. The business was transferred to Shelton.

Upon the withdrawal of Champion, John Daniel became a partner and manager of the firm which was styled Hollins, Warburton, Daniel & Co.

Between 1804 and 1810 Jacob Warburton and Charles Bagnal dropped out of the business and Peter Warburton became a partner. In 1810 Peter Warburton took out a patent for transfer-printing in gold and silver, and in the same year Samuel Hollins, Peter Warburton, John Daniel and William Clowes purchased the New Hall Estate on behalf of the Company. Much of the land was subsequently laid out for building sites, and in all probability the purchase was in the nature of land speculation. Peter Warburton died in 1813.

Samuel Hollins died in 1820 and John Daniel in 1821. Daniel's place as manager was taken by John Tittensor who managed the business until it finally closed down in 1835. In 1831 the estate and factory were offered for sale. In 1832 they were announced to be let, but the business was not finally wound up until the sale of manufactured stock in 1835.

As well as earthenware, two grades of porcelain were made at this factory: hard-paste porcelain until about 1810, and bone china subsequently. The firm also traded in potters' materials, being able to supply Cornish clay and Cornish stone for local use.

The 'Sprigged muslin' type of pattern is chiefly associated with New Hall, but elaborate painted and gilded wares were produced, with chinoiseries and picturesque printed landscapes washed over in crude bright colours. Fancy jugs with relief hunting scenes were made as well as chimney ornaments, although the latter have never been identified. The Neo-Classic mode is evident in some of the handles, but not stressed. A distinctive silver-shape teapot is peculiar to this factory.

Little has been recorded about the personnel of this factory.

OFFICE STAFF

Charles Tittensor (died 1815) not to be confused with the figure maker of the same name, traveller,

John Tittensor, traveller 1815 until he became manager in 1821.

ARTISTS AND CRAFTSMEN

Francis Emery, decorating manager.

James Wantling (died 1848) decorator.

Fidéle Duvivier, painter.

Henry Bone, R.A. (born 1755 died 1834) painter (mentioned by Jewitt).

Charles Sheen, thrower and presser 1791. (Formerly of Worcester, later went ot Derby.)

There are few good collections of New Hall wares, perhaps the most complete being that of the New Hall Pottery Company (brought together by G. E. Stringer). There are representative pieces at the Victoria & Albert Museum, South Kensington, Christchurch Mansion, Ipswich, and Hanley Museum.

MARKS

Pattern numbers prefaced by a letter 'N' or 'No' in cursive style occur on hard paste porcelain: a double circle enclosing the words 'New Hall' on bone china. Earthenware is usually unmarked.

Initials and pattern number printed before 1812; circular mark transfer-printed 1812-1835

After the closing down in 1835 of the porcelain company the premises were occupied by:

William Ratcliff, manufacturer of earthenware	1837–1840
Vacant or uncertain	1840–1846
William Hackwood & Son, earthenware and jet	1846–1850
Thomas Hackwood, earthenware	1850–1856
Cockson & Harding, earthenware	1856–1862

Vacant or uncertain 1862–1864

W. & J.Harding, cream colour, printed, Egyptian black, Rockingham ware etc. 1864–1869

Thomas Booth & Sons, earthenware 1875

Ambrose Bevington, earthenware 1889

Plant & Gilmore 1892–1899

New Hall Pottery Co. earthenware 1899–1956
Plate 72.

[G.E.Stringer, *New Hall Porcelain*, 1949; Reginald G. Haggar, 'New Hall, the Last Phase', *Apollo*, 1951; T.A. Sprague, 'Hard Paste New Hall Porcelain' *Apollo*, 1949–50; L. Jewitt, *Ceramic Art of Great Britain*, 1878; Simeon Shaw, *History of the Staffordshire Potteries*, 1829; G.E. Stringer, 'Two Hundred Years of Bas Reliefs' *Pottery Gazette*, 1954; *Staffordshire Advertiser*, 10 November 1804, 30 January 1813, 21 January 1815, 22 July 1815, 14 May 1814, 15 July 1820, 11 September 1830, 5 March 1831, 25 August, 1 September 1832, 24 November 1832, 5, 12, 26 September 1835; *Pottery Mercury*, 30 March 1825; *Staffordshire Mercury*, 19 December 1829; *Staffordshire Gazette*, 28 June 1814; *Directories*, 1787, 1796, 1802, 1805, 1818, 1822, etc.]

Nightingale jewel

A decoration on Staffordshire pottery mugs copied from a jewel stated to have been given by Queen Victoria to Florence Nightingale after her return from the Crimea. According to another source the name was given to china mugs distributed by Lady Nightingale to the employees of Empress Eugénie (1826–1920) on the death of the Prince Imperial, who was killed in the Zulu War, 1879.

Niglett, John, Bristol

Pot painter at Lime Kiln Lane and Redcliff Backs to whom delftware painted with elongated Chinese figures and other features derived from K'ang Hsi *famille verte* is attributed because there is in Bristol Museum a plate painted in this manner bearing the initials JNE said to be those of John Niglett and Esther his wife. It is dated 1733.

[F.H.Garner, *English Delftware*, 1948; W.G.Pountney, *Old Bristol Potteries*, 1920.]

Noggin

A small drinking vessel. NOGGIN-BOTTLE, a small bottle holding a small quantity of liquor, usually a $^1/_4$ pint. 'The Ingenious *John Dwight*... hath discovered the *Mystery* of the Stone or Cologne Wares (such as D'Alva Bottles, Jugs, Noggins)'.

[R.Plot, *Natural History of Oxfordshire*, 2nd Ed. 1705.]

Norfolk

Several slipware pieces in the Glaisher Collection (such as the tyg with an impressed ornament in green, dated 1632, and another with raised openwork decoration simulating metalwork, dated 1684) are said to have come from Norfolk, but no slipware factory is recorded here.

Delftware was made in Norwich in the sixteenth and seventeenth centuries. Absalon's decorating business in Yarmouth is well known.

There may have been manufactures of coarse crockery at Downham and Thetford about 1836 (Thomas Scales, Bridge Street, Thetford).

See ABSOLON, DELFTWARE, NORWICH.

[W.White, *History Gazetteer and Directory of Norfolk*, 1836.]

Northamptonshire

Chaffers recorded a potworks at Potters Pury, apparently of eighteenth century date, and cited a jug of coarse earthenware, inscribed 'Robin Woodward, Yardley Gobion 1761' as likely manufacture, Yardley Gobion being near by.

North-British Pottery, Glasgow, Scotland. Earthenware manufactory

The original pottery was built c. 1810 and called the Osley Pottery. After passing through various hands the Potworks were bought by Alexander Balfour, in 1874, who later took into partnership Robert Cochran, junior.

Earthenware egg hoops, cowmilk jugs, six sided jugs with handles and relief ornament modelled from the vine are typical of the products of this factory, which also produced gay painted wares with African mottoes for export to the West Coast of Africa.

[J.Fleming, *Scottish Pottery*, 1923.]

Northwood, John, Stourbridge

The first craftsman to make an exact replica of the Portland vase in glass. Wedgwoods commissioned him in 1877 to polish a pottery edition of the Vase of which 15 copies were sold by W.P. & G. Phillips of Oxford Street London by subscription.

Northwood's monogram

incised occurs on the white relief above the Wedgwood impressed mark, accompanied by a Greek letter.

[W.Mankowitz, *The Portland Vase and the Wedgwood Copies*, 1952; D.R.Guttery, *From Broad-Glass to Cut Crystal*, 1956.]

Norton-in-the-Moors, Staffordshire

John Aiken in his *Description of the Country... around Manchester* published in 1795 mentions a manufacture of coarse earthenware here. Nothing more is known of it.

Norwich, Norfolk

Jasper Andries and Jacob Janson, potters from Antwerp, settled in Norwich in 1567 and started a delftware pottery whose products have not been identified. They removed to London in 1570 but the factory continued in operation until 1696. Some white-ware posset-pots, different in character from those of known Lambeth origin which came from Norfolk, and an uncertain class of puzzle jugs with a flower (often a tulip) on the front which may be of English origin should be considered in relation to this factory.

[John Stow, *A Survey of the Cities of London*, etc., 1598, 6th Edition 1755.]

Nottingham, Earthenware Manufactory

DATES AND POTTERS

Pottery was made in Nottingham from the thirteenth century (as excavations in the district have shown) and its production continued along characteristic lines until about 1800. The manufactories making Nottingham wares are unidentified, but occasionally the name of the potter appears on the article. James Morley, one of the defendants in the action for protection of his patents brought by Dwight of Fulham late in the seventeenth century, certainly worked here as did other members of the Morley family. The name of William Lockett is found on pieces made about 1755, and William Woodward is listed as a maker of slipware in the eighteenth century. As Nottingham began to decline as a centre for pottery, neighbouring towns (Denby, Chesterfield and Swinton amongst others) began to produce wares similar in style. The last authenticated piece from Nottingham is dated 1799.

SUBJECTS AND DISTINGUISHING CHARACTERISTICS

Earliest pieces made in Nottingham were of lead-glazed earthenware. Many handled tygs etc. date from the sixteenth century. It is believed that stoneware began to be made in the second half of the seventeenth century. About 1690 the most productive period in Nottingham began. Wares made during that time are remarkable for their fineness of finish, precise decoration making use of limited varieties of pattern, and extremely pleasing shapes. The ferruginous clay which overlaid a very hard body gave a rich brown colour and a faint metallic lustre to the surface of the article. The grain of this surface is much finer than that of other stonewares of the period, and the pieces are light and usually very thin. Posset-pots, some teapots (now rarely seen), mugs and small jugs – all were made, apparently in some quantity, in Nottingham. The decoration often consists only of lines incised round the piece; formal flowers, sometimes reserved in a lighter colour, or alternately painted in slip of a darker colour, bands of roughened clay, small stamped patterns and, more ambitiously, the piercing of an outer layer of clay (called 'carving') were all common forms of decoration. Inscriptions were often incised. Very much later some designs in relief were produced in the Fulham manner, but these entirely lack the charm of the simpler designs.

Nottingham wares are nearly always distinguishable from other stonewares made at rival factories by their superior design and finish. Nowhere at this period were salt-glazed articles made with such precision and sureness of touch.

'Nottingham' is sometimes marked, often as part of an inscription or in shortened form – a jug in the Victoria and Albert Museum is marked 'Nott'. 1703.

A useful guide to style and treatment is provided by the illustrated advertisement sheet of James Morley in the Bodleian Library, Oxford – 'Such as have Occation for these sorts of Pots commonly called Stoneware, or for such as are of any other Shape not here Represented may be furnished roth them by the Maker James Morley at ye Pot-House in Nottingham', – which shows a decanter (necked jug) a carved teapot, a mogg, a Flower-Pot, a carved jug and a capuchine (or small cup).

Examples of Nottingham stoneware may be seen in the Victoria and Albert Museum, British Museum, Nottingham Castle Museum, Hanley Museum, Stoke-on-Trent.

Plates 73–74.

[Alfred Parker, *Transactions, Thoroton Society of Nottingham*, 1933; C. Deering, *Nottinghamia vetus et nova*, 1751; T. Bailey, *Annals of Nottingham*, 1855; Daniel Defoe, *A Tour through England and Wales* 1724–1726.]

Nuneham Courtney, Oxfordshire

Pottery made here in seventeenth century (Plot, *Natural History of Oxfordshire*, 2nd ed. 1705).

Oade, Nathaniel, Southwark, London. Potter

A potter at Gravel Lane, Southwark, whose four sons attempted to take over the business in 1718, by force.

Obsidian

A dark coloured volcanic rock imitated in parian which was so-named.

Oeil-de-Perdrix

Partridge eye: a decoration consisting of an even ground of small circles usually upon a coloured background.

Oil-gilding

Gilding of a non-permanent character by means of japanner's size, used in the eighteenth century before the method of firing gold became known.

Okill & Company, Liverpool

See FLINT MUG WORKS.

Old Hall Pottery, Hanley, Staffordshire. Earthenware manufactory

Built on the site of the Old Hall, Hanley (hence its name) by Job Mee or Meigh in 1790 who worked it in partnership with Peter Walthall until 1802. In 1812 the business was styled Job Meigh & Son (his second son Charles having entered the business). Job Meigh died in 1817 but Charles Meigh continued the business under the old style until 1835. From 1835 until 1847 the firm traded as Charles Meigh. In 1850 Charles Meigh enlarged the company to include his son, also named Charles, and a man named Pankhurst, trading as Charles Meigh, Son & Pankhurst. From 1851 until 1860 the business was known as Charles Meigh & Son. The Old Hall Earthenware Co. Ltd (the first pottery limited company in N. Staffordshire) was formed in 1862 and traded under this name until 1887. From 1887 until its closure in 1902 the firm traded as Old Hall Porcelain Works Co. Ltd. The factory was subsequently demolished. The most typical products of the factory were the elaborately modelled relief jugs made in a hard whitish porcellanous stoneware under Gothic Revival inspiration c. 1845. Other specimens are classical in subject matter but executed without grace and with monstrous lumpy handles. Numerous marks were used, those on the transfer-printed wares being included in or placed underneath floral or ornamental cartouches enclosing the pattern name.

J.M. & S. (italics)   MEIGH'S
M. & S.   CHINA
    C.M.   C.M.S. & P.

Job Meigh & Son 1812–1834

Charles Meigh 1835–1847

Charles Meigh & Son & Pankhurst 1850

CM&S
Charles Meigh & Son Printed

Charles Meigh & son 1851–1860

[Information per Alfred Meigh; L. Jewitt *Ceramic Art of Great Britain*, 1878; *Directories*, 1805–1889.]

Oldfield & Co, Brampton, Nr Chesterfield, Derbyshire. Earthenware manufactory

A firm of stoneware manufacturers, Messrs Oldfield, Madin, Wright, Hewitt & Co. established an earthenware factory at Brampton in 1810, which by 1838 had passed into the sole ownership of John Oldfield, by whom it was continued.

The firm made brown salt-glazed stoneware, including bowls, bottles, meat pots, pitchers, pancheons, nappies, porringers, 'Welsh' trays, spirit flasks and vinegar kegs; jugs embossed with hunting and rural scenes, Toby jugs and reform spirit flasks. The marks used were:

MARKS

OLDFIELD & CO   J. OLDFIELD
MAKERS

Impressed   Impressed

[L. Jewitt, *Ceramic Art of Great Britain*, 1878.]

Omega workshop

Roger Fry, art critic, opened the Omega Workshop in 1913, in an attempt to revive 'joy in craftmanship'. He received instruction in pottery technique at Poole but while his wares revealed taste and sensibility they had little effect and the workshop closed down in 1919.

[Thomas Hennell, *British Craftsmen*, 1943.]

On-glaze, Over-glaze

Decoration applied after the ware has been glazed and fired, literally decorated on top of the glaze.

O'Neale, Jeffrey Hamet (born 1734 died 1801), Artist

O'Neale's signature, O.N.P. is found on Worcester and Chelsea porcelain. Animals, illustrations from the Fables of Aesop, figures in landscape were among the subjects he used. It has been suggested that he also worked for James Giles of Kentish Town, London. Signed Worcester pieces are to be found in the British Museum.

O'Neale, miniaturist, book illustrator and ceramic artist, was born in Ireland, worked at Chelsea soon after 1752 and later for Worcester and Josiah Wedgwood as an outside decorator. From the latter he received three guineas a week which Wedgwood considered excessive, although he acknowledged that 'O'Neale works quick' (1771). In 1765 he was a member of the Incorporated Society of Artists.

O. N. P

[W.H.Tapp, *Jeffrey Hamett O'Neale*, 1938; K.E.Farrer (Ed.), *Letters of Josiah Wedgwood*, 1903.]

Opaque china

Trade name for a fine white porcellanous earthenware used by Swansea, Ridgway & Morley and others, nineteenth century.

'Orange-jumper'

A local decoration recorded on Yorkshire cream-coloured earthenware made at the Don Pottery c.1808, depicting a coarse-featured local horse-breaker who, in the election of 1807, acted as a messenger for Lord Milton. He is clothed in orange, the 'colour' of Lord Milton, and is accompanied by the following rhyme: 'The Figure there is no mistaking It is the famous man for... breaking; Oh that instead of horse and mare He had but broken crockery ware Each grateful potter in a bumper Might drink the health of Orange Jumper.' Tawny-orange, incidentally, was considered the colour appropriate to the lower classes.

[Reginald G.Haggar, *English Country Pottery*, 1950.]

Osland, John

This name is recorded upon a large slipware dish decorated with head of Charles II (?) and the initials T.T., and might have been made for John Osland by Thomas Toft. The name Osland does not occur in local Registers, but a 'Mr Osland' was listed in the Hearth Tax Rolls for Amblecoate, South Staffordshire, in 1666. This dish is in the British Museum.

Overhouse works, The, Burslem, Staffordshire

A manufactory inherited in 1756 by Thomas Wedgwood, an elder brother of Josiah. His son Thomas succeeded him at his death in 1772. Cream and blue-painted wares were made there about 1786. In 1809 the works passed out of Wedgwood hands.

Owl jugs

Jugs with detachable heads made in slipware in Staffordshire late seventeenth and early eighteenth centuries, and white salt-glazed stoneware from 1730 to 1770, sometimes with brown slip enrichment. Examples in Fitzwilliam Museum, Cambridge.

P

Paint Chest

A water colour painter's outfit: 'The *Paint-Chest* contains sets of large and small vessels, and neat palats, for the use of those who paint in Water Colours.' (Wedgwood *Catalogue*, 1779).
[W.Mankowitz, *Wedgwood*, 1953.]

Palin & Co.

An unknown form of pottery manufacturers whose mark, on blue-and-white earthenware of Staffordshire type made in the late eighteenth or early nineteenth century (in Victoria and Albert Museum, London) has been recorded. The name Palin is known in Staffordshire but no factory or firm is listed.

Palin, John

This name occurs in yellow underneath the base of a figure of Venus in a private collection.

Palmer, Humphrey, Church Works, Hanley, Staffordshire. Earthenware manufactory

DATES

Palmer was a rival and imitator of Wedgwood from about 1760. Financial difficulties caused his failure in 1778 and the business was subsequently carried on with the help of J. Neale. Enoch Wood served his apprenticeship to Palmer.

MARKS

PALMER

ARTISTS

Thomas Rothwell. A designer and engraver employed at Hanley until 1778 and afterwards at Swansea.

John Voyez. The celebrated modeller who formerly worked for Wedgwood was employed by Palmer from 1769.

WORK AND SUBJECTS

Palmer's work was mainly in imitation of that of Wedgwood (a court case arising at one time over his infringement of Wedgwood's patents). It was of excellent quality: Wedgwood himself remarked of it in a letter to a friend, 'The body is very good, the shape and composition very well.'

Black basaltes decorated with reliefs were the first wares imitated by Palmer, evidently with some success. Agate vases, jasper seals and medallions, red wares with lathe-made patterns were copied at a later date. Mrs Palmer took an active part in the management of her husband's business. She ordered new wares from Wedgwood for copying as soon as they were delivered to the London warehouse.

Specimens are in the British Museum, the Victoria and Albert Museum, and the Holburn of Menstrie Museum, Bath.

See also NEALE, J. and VOYEZ, John.

[Reginald G. Haggar, *Staffordshire Chimney Ornaments*, 1955; M.H.Grant, *The Makers of Black Basaltes*, 1910.]

Pancheon

A large shallow bowl with sloping sides used for settling milk.

Pap-dish

A shallow boat-shaped vessel with a tubular spout for feeding infants or invalids.

Pardoe, Thomas (born 1770 died 1823)

An artist who worked for Derby, Worcester and Swansea from about 1785 until 1809 when he removed to Bristol and worked as an independent enameller until 1821. Thereafter he decorated porcelain at Nantgarw.

Principally a flower painter, much of his work is found on all the above porcelains and also Coalport. Plates copied from botanical magazines were seen in his earliest work. Later his painting is inclined to be careless.

His signature in gold is quite often found on various pieces.

Pardoe, Fecit Bristol.

His son, W.H.Pardoe, opened the earthenware manufactory at Nantgarw in 1833.

There is a signed example of Thomas Pardoe's work in the Victoria and Albert Museum, London.

[W. J. Pountney, *Old Bristol Potteries*, 1920; William Turner, *The Ceramics of Swansea and Nantgarw*, 1897.]

Parian

A special kind of porcelain *bisque* used for statuary and intended to replace the famous Derby *bisque* porcelain, and stated in the *Art Union*, Vol 10, 1848, to have been invented at Copeland & Garretts, Stoke-on-Trent, about 1845, with the active encouragement of Thomas Battam (1810–1864) who was art director. Elsewhere Spencer Garrett is credited with its invention, which was disputed, however, by John Mountford, by Minton, and by T. & R. Boote. John Mountford stated (*Staffordshire Advertiser*, 20 September 1851) 'I am prepared to prove that in the latter part of 1845 I discovered that material known as 'statuary porcelain', that I gave to Mr S. Garrett (then of the firm of Messrs Copeland & Garrett) the receipt for its production, John Mountford was then employed at the Copeland factory. T. & R. Boote claimed that Thomas L. Boote first made the body in 1841, 'when learning the art of pottery with Mr E. Jones, and he produced a further specimen from the same receipt in the year 1842 when with Mr Maddock'. Mintons claimed they produced it in

1845. By 1846 it was in commercial production and by 1850 numerous firms were making the body. Wedgwoods called their parian Carrara. Until about 1849–50 the body was generally known in the trade as Statuary Porcelain. Parian tinted to various shades was popular in 1870's and 1880's.

Plate 75.

[*Staffordshire Advertiser*, 26 July, 11 October, 8 November 1851; *Cassell's Illustrated Exhibitor*, July 1851; *Art Union*, Vols 8 & 10, 1846–48; John Haslem, *The Old Derby China Works*, London 1876.]

Parker, Daniel (born 1633 died 1696)

Master potter, Southwark. Other potters named Parker who were employed by Dwight included Henry and Nathan. The latter was working in 1677.

[R.L.Hobson, *B.F.A.C.Catalogue*, 1913.]

Parr family, Burslem

Specialised in the manufacture of earthenware toys, nest eggs, taws and marbles. Several potters of this name, probably all related, were engaged in this business between 1828 and 1875, among them, Richard, Edward, John, Thomas and W.Parr. It is likely that Kent of Burslem took over their plant and moulds in 1878.

[Information from descendants; *Directories*, 1828–75; *Poll Lists*.]

'Parson and Clerk'

A figure group produced in earthenware showing a drunken parson being conducted home by his clerk, after a night's carousal; first made by Enoch Wood c.1790 as a sequel to the 'Vicar and Moses'. This popular satire on the squarson type of incumbent was also used with appropriate verses as a transfer-print on cream-coloured earthenware in Staffordshire and Leeds. The design was possibly suggested by the fourth plate, 'Night', in Hogarth's series 'Four Times of Day' (engraved and dated 25 March 1738) which shows a reveller being led home after celebrating Restoration Day.

Parting-shards

Bits of fired pottery used to separate pots after they have been glazed to prevent them sticking together: 'Their *flat ware* though it be *leaded*, having only *parting-shards* i.e. thin bits of old pots put between them, to keep them from *sticking* together.' (R.Plot, *Natural History of Staffordshire*, 1686).

Pastille-burners

Box-like containers, often made in the shape of cottages, summer-houses and churches, with detachable perforated lids for burning cassolette perfumes, made in china and earthenware eighteenth and nineteenth centuries, but very popular 1820–1850. Cassolette perfumes consist of finely powdered willow-wood charcoal, benzoin, fragrant oils and gum arabic.

[Reginald G.Haggar, in *Apollo*, 1950.]

'Patch' family

Porcelain figures made at Chelsea and Derby, so named from the presence of three or four dark unglazed patches left on the under-surface by the pads or wads of clay upon which the wares were rested during the glost-firing. First noted by Bernard Rackham.

[W.B.Honey, *Old English Porcelain*, 1928, new ed. 1948.]

Pâte-sur-Pâte

Literally clay on clay. A French technique known as *pâtes d'application*, involving the building up of translucent white or tinted reliefs on coloured parian or porcelain by means of modelling and painting. First employed at Sèvres, and introduced into England at Mintons in 1870 by Marc Louis Solon (1835–1912) the ceramic craftsman and historian. Solon never repeated any of his subjects which were all entirely hand-done. His pupils, Frederick Alfred Rhead and Alboin Birks (1861–1941) exploited the process, the last named carrying on the technique with modifications until his retirement in 1937, particularly on service plates. But nearly all the pieces which he decorated in this process were mould-made repetitions of a stock design, extensively touched up by hand. Birks' designs were continued for a short period by his assistant, Richard Bradbury, whose signature occurs on late examples. The process was discontinued in 1939.

[Information from Alboin Birks.]

171

Pattison, James, Lane End

Earthenware toy manufacturer in the High Street, Lane End, from about 1818 until 1830 (*Directories*, 1818–30). The name John Pattison and date 1825 have been recorded on a figure of Venus (Reginald G.Haggar, in *Apollo*, 1950, and *Stafford-shire Chimney Ornaments*, 1955).

MARK

Painted

'Pearl' ware

White earthenware containing a larger proportion of flint and white clay than cream-coloured earthenware; made by Josiah Wedgwood 1779 but not much used by him. Also a dry body made by Chetham & Woolley, Lane End, c.1795 and used like jasper for the manufacture of ornaments.

[W. Mankowitz, *Wedgwood*, 1953; S.Shaw, *History of the Staffordshire Potteries*, 1829.]

Pearson, John and Edward, Burslem and Cobridge, Staffs

John Pearson originally worked as a member of the firm of Buxton, Room & Pearson, which dissolved partnership 20 July 1831 (*Staffordshire Advertiser*, 30 July 1831) the business being continued by A.B.Buxton and J.Pearson.

By 1834 John Pearson had become sole owner and was potting in Newcastle Street, Burslem. He was succeeded by Edward Pearson, who in 1851 had moved to Liverpool Road. Later still he took the Abbey Works at Cobridge where he made ironstone china and earthenware.

[*Directories*, 1834–64.]

Peasant style

Ornament derived from folk art; specifically, earthenware painted in the 'resist' lustre style with a restricted palette of colours; made in Staffordshire from 1800–1850; but rarely marked. Jugs lettered with initials within a heart and a date are recorded.

[Geoffrey Bemrose, *Nineteenth Century English Pottery and Porcelain*, 1952.]

Peever

A piece of slate or stone used in the game of hopscotch, also a flat disc of pottery used for the same purpose, and coloured and lettered with the name of the owner. Made at Alloa, Scotland, nineteenth century.

[J. A. Fleming, *Scottish Pottery*, 1923.]

Pegg, William (born 1775 died 1851)

Born of poor parents and educated at Shelton in Staffordshire. He heard an itinerant Calvinist preacher in 1796 and became deeply religious and his subsequent life as a craftsman was coloured by his religious convictions. He took up pottery painting in 1788, went to Derby in 1796, became a Quaker in 1800 and abandoned ceramic painting from religious scruples in 1801. Followed various trades, returning to porcelain painting again at Derby 1813 until 1820 when he finally abandoned it. He took a shop in Derby where he died in 1851. Pegg was a flower painter in the botanical style, and often added to the ware the name of the plant or bloom.

Pellat & Green, London

A dealer's name which occurs as a mark on English porcelain, c.1815–20, notably Swansea.

Pencoed, nr Bridgend, South Wales

Slipware, including large harvest jugs in *sgraffiato*, puzzle jugs and wassail bowls, made at Pencoed in the eighteenth and nineteenth centuries.

A marked example is in the British Museum.

Penkhull, Stoke-on-Trent. Staffordshire

Simeon Shaw, writing in 1829, states that 'at Penkhull in 1600 were three manufactories for coarse brown pottery, one of which belonged to Mr Thomas Doody'.

[S.Shaw, *History of the Staffordshire Potteries*, Hanley, 1829.]

Pennington, James

A painter of excellent monochrome figure subjects and portraits on Worcester porcelain.

Pennington, Seth, James and John

Seth Pennington, one of three brothers who all worked in Liverpool, owned a delftware factory in the city from about 1760, which he operated in partnership as Pennington & Part.

Wares from this pottery are noted for the use of a particularly bright, thick blue enamel; a tin-glazed porcelain with blue and manganese decoration also comes from his kiln. A drug-pot decorated in blue, marked 'P' under the base, is probably his and can be seen in the British Museum. In Hanley Museum is a large punch-bowl inscribed 'Success to the African Trade', decorated by John Robinson, an artist employed by Seth Pennington.

In 1788 Pennington & Part mortgaged their property for £500, and in 1799 the 'China Works' were offered for sale (*Staffordshire Advertiser*, 10 August 1799) Later (before 1810) Pennington & Part dissolved partnership.

James Pennington is listed as a potter in Liverpool from 1761 until 1774 at the China Works, Copperas Hill.

John Pennington owned a pottery in Islington which he sold later to Thomas Wolfe of Stoke-on-Trent, where he also made punch-bowls.

[Gore's *Directory of Liverpool*, 1766–74; J.Mayer, *On the Art of Pottery, with a History of its Progress in Liverpool*, 1873.]

Penny bank

A money-box of earthenware, in the form of a house or chest of drawers.
Plate 49 A.

Perkins, Mary

Name occuring on a trailed slipware dish, dated 1704, in the British Museum.

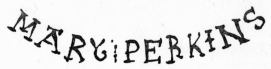

'Pew' group

Figure group representing a man and woman (more rarely two men and a woman) seated upon a high-backed settle; made in white salt-glazed stoneware, Staffordshire, about 1730–1740; more rarely in earthenware. There are 'Pew' groups in the Fitzwilliam Museum, Cambridge and the British Museum, London. The name was probably derived from Sir Arthur Church's description in *English Earthenware* 1884 – 'a man and a woman… are seated on a high-backed bench or pew'.

[Illustrated in H. Read, *Staffordshire Pottery Figures*, 1929; Reginald G. Haggar, *Staffordshire Chimney Ornaments*, 1955; B.Rackham and H.Read, *English Pottery*, 1924; Reginald G. Haggar, *English Pottery Figures*, 1947; B.Rackham, *Catalogue Glaisher Collection*, 1934; *Catalogue… Earley English Earthenware*, B.F.A.C., 1914.]

Phillips, Lane Delph

Simeon Shaw mentions this potter at Lane Delph c.1760, but was probably alluding to Thomas Philips of Lane End, earthenware manufacturer who is recorded in 1783. In 1791 the firm was William and John Philips. Jewitt says the firm worked first of all at Lane Delph where it made salt-glazed earthenware but moved subsequently to Green Dock, Lane End, and produced cream-colour.

[S.Shaw, *History of the Staffordshire Potteries*, 1829; *Directories*, 1783, 1787, 1796; L.Jewitt, *Ceramic Art of Great Britain*, 1878.]

Phillips, G, Longport, Staffs. Potters

The following marks are found on blue-printed earthenware:

PHILLIPS
LONGPORT
(Impressed)

G. PHILLIPS
LONGPORT
(Impressed)

Edward and George Phillips are listed as manufacturers at Longport about 1822.

Phillips & Bagster

Successors to David Wilson & Sons, cream-colour and white earthenware manufacturers, High Street, Shelton. The partnership between Jacob Phillips and John Denton Bagster (died 1825) lasted from 1818 until 1825. The firm closed down in 1828. Leonard J. Abington was modeller to the firm. The stock of moulds included 'an excellent assortment of bas-relief figures'.

[Announcements in *The Pottery Mercury*, 12 July, 13 September and 4 October 1828; *Records of the Ancient Corporation of Hanley*.]

Photo ceramics

The word 'decal', short for 'decalcomania' was originally applied to the process of transferring pictures from prepared paper to the surface of pottery and porcelain. It was popular 1862–64 and was an early application of the photographic process for the decoration of pottery. (The word, decal, is now almost exclusively used for lithographic transfers.) Photographic decorations were occasionally used by Wedgwoods of Etruria in the 1870's. The popularity of the process is attested by the publication in 1896 of a book written by W. E. Henry and H. S. Ward entitled *Photo Ceramics*, giving 'instruction in photography applied to the decoration of plaques, pottery and other ceramic... surfaces'.

Pie-crust ware

Pottery pie dishes of buff stoneware with covers simulating pastry were made during the flour tax by the firms of Wedgwood, Turner, etc. ('After Brummel's retirement, viz., in July 1800, the scarcity was so great that the consumption of flour for pastry was prohibited in the Royal Household, rice being used instead; the distiller left off malting, hackney coach fares were raised 25 per cent, and Wedgwood made dishes to represent pie-crust.' Capt. Jeffs, *Life of George*

Brummel Esq. 1844, Vol 1, p. 49.) 'About 1780 he (Turner) discovered a vein of fine clay... at Green Dock... From this he obtained all his supplies for manufacturing his... *Stone Ware Pottery* of a cane colour... some of them represent different kinds of pastry...' (Simeon Shaw, *History of the Staffordshire Potteries*, 1829, pp. 172–173).

Pierced Decoration

Decoration formed by hand-piercing the walls of vessels in the leather-hard state with punches shaped like leaves, hearts, trefoils, quatrefoils, etc., arranged to form intricated lacelike designs. It was extensively employed at Leeds where the designs were executed with remarkable precision and delicacy. The process was also used to admirable effect by Wedgwood and others in Staffordshire.

Piggin

A small milk pail, hence CREAM PIGGIN ('piggins', Whieldon's *Notebook*).

Pilchard pots

Large earthenware vessels made in North Devon, Cornwall and South Wales for the use of West country fishermen, and known by size as 'gallons', 'bussas', 'great crocks'. 'Great crocks' were also known as large stones.

[W. Fishley Holland, 'Memories of Fremington,' *Pottery Quarterly*, 1955.]

Pilkington's Lancastrian Pottery

The Pilkington Tile and Pottery Company at Clifton Junction, Manchester started as a glazed tile and brick works in 1892. The manufacture of pottery with pressed and cast shapes was commenced in 1897. These early wares were self-coloured or covered with flecked or crystalline glaze effects. In 1903 William Burton developed splendid scarlet and tangerine orange glaze effects from the use of uranium. Gordon Forsyth joined the firm in 1906 and a good thrower (T. Radford) was engaged. Designs by Walter Crane and Lewis F. Day were commissioned and some elaborately enriched individual lustred pottery was produced. Gordon Forsyth left the factory in 1919 to become Principal of Stoke-on-Trent Schools of Art but lustre-painting was continued until 1927. The production of decorative pottery ceased in 1938.

ARTISTS

A. Barlow

A. Burton
Charles E. Cundall (later R.A.)

J. Chambers
Walter Crane (born 1846 died 1915)

D. Dacre
Lewis F. Day

E. Dent
T. Evans
Gordon M. Forsyth (born 1879 died 1952)
A. Hall
J. Jones

W. S. Mycock

Gwladys Rodgers

Richard Joyce

Each artist signed his work with a distinctive signature or mark.

FACTORY MARK

Pill-slabs

Apothecary's pill-slabs were made in tin-glazed earthenware at Lambeth, and were decorated frequently with the arms of the Apothecaries Company, or the City of London.

Pilsbury, Richard (born 1830 died 1897)

Ceramic flower painter; born Burslem; apprenticed as ceramic artist to Samuel Alcock & Co., Burslem: studied Burslem School of Design under W. J. Muckley; instructor, School of Design, London; returned to potteries and worked at Mintons, Stoke, 1866–92, and as Art Director, Moore Bros, Longton, 1892–97.

[Obit. *Art Journal*, 1897; G.W. and F.A. Rhead, *Staffordshire Pots and Potters*, 1906.]

Pinxton, Derbyshire. Porcelain Manufactory

DATES AND OWNERS

A small porcelain factory was established at Pinxton about 1796 by William Billingsley and John Coke. Billingsley left the concern in 1801 and his partner Coke carried on the works until they were sold to a landscape painter named John Cutts in 1804. The factory is believed to have been closed about 1812.

MARKS

ARTISTS

Billingsley himself decorated some of the wares, and in addition the following are known to have worked at Pinxton:

John Cutts. Landscape painter
Richard Robins. Later a partner of Randall of Spa Fields, independent enamellers.
Edward Rowland. Landscape painter.

Artists named Slater, Marriott, Musgrove and Mellor are also listed.

WORK AND DISTINGUISHING CHARACTERISTICS

Billingsley brought to Pinxton from Derby a

staff of workmen, and the soft-paste porcelain produced while the factory was under his management was made to his own formula: it is of that peculiarly translucent quality characteristic of Swansea and Nantgarw. Simple shapes were decorated in the Derby manner, not, however, making use of the raised flowers and leaves characteristic of Derby. The best known designs from Pinxton are those using only a small sprig – a cornflower or forget-me-not – on a white ground. Plates and dishes were most often edged with gold, or with a dark red or blue.

Landscapes washed with a yellow green colour are fairly common. Ground colours are exceedingly rare on most flower decorated pieces, but occasionally a canary-yellow is seen.

Billingsley left the factory, taking his recipes for soft-paste porcelains with him; and thereafter a much coarser and more opaque type of ware was made, not unlike Derby of a poor quality.

Examples are in the British Museum and the Victoria and Albert Museum.

See also JOHN CUTTS.
Plate 76.

[W.B.Honey, *Old English Porcelain*, 1928, new ed. 1948; L.Jewitt, *Ceramic Art of Great Britain*, 1878.]

Pipe-clay

A fine white clay used in the manufacture of tobacco-pipes. According to Dr Pococke, pipe-clay was imported into Staffordshire from Poole Dorset, but earlier local white firing clays were used by the Newcastle-under-Lyme pipe-makers.

[R.Pococke, *Travels through England*, 1750. Edited by J.J.Cartwright, 1888.]

Pipkin

An earthenware cooking vessel: 'this little pipkin fits this little jelly' (Robert Herrick, *A Ternary of Littles*). 'pots and pipkins' (Wedgwood to Bentley 27 February 1780).

Pitcher, Pitchar, Pitchard

An earthenware or stoneware vessel with a handle; a coarse earthenware jug or vessel with

one or more ears or handles; often the word is applied to defective or broken crockery; a piece of fired clay. Pitchers were used extensively for road making ('Item, for Tho Keeling for getting and filling Robish & pitchards 3 days) 2s.6d'. (*Churchwardens' Accounts*, Stoke-on-Trent, 1656, *North Staffs Field Club Transactions*). In North Devon they were known according to size as 'penny jugs' or 80's, 'pint-and-a-halfs' or 60's, 'tuppennies' or quarts, 'pinchguts' (3d), 'gully-mouths' (4d) 'thirty tales (5d) and 'Long Toms' (holding 2 gallons and costing 7d).

Pitcher mould

A pottery mould made of clay and fired, commonly used in the eighteenth century before the discovery and popular application of the properties of plaster-of-Paris.

Place, Francis, Manor House, York. Potter, d.1728.

Francis Place is reputed to have made a kind of marbled stoneware and experimental types of early porcelain towards the end of the seventeenth century. A coffee-cup marbled in grey, black and brown in the Victoria and Albert Museum is stated on the authority of Horace Walpole to be Place's work.

Place does not appear to have made pottery in any quantity for sale, but it is said that a potter named Clifton of Pontefract in Yorkshire made use of the results of his experiments and 'made a fortune by it'.

[Sir. A.H.Church, *English Earthenware*, 1884, quoting from the *Journal of Ralph Thoresby*, 1714.]

Plant, Benjamin

Master Potter at Lane End late eighteenth and early nineteenth centuries. In 1784 he bought 612 yds. of land upon which to build his factory, where he made teapots, table-wares, and lustred and enamelled figures. A teapot dated 1814 and marked B.Plant is in the possession of Mr H.J. Plant of Longton, who also owns Plants *Diary*. In 1818 Benjamin Plant was listed as a potter, living near the Baptist Chapel, Lane End. His son, Thomas Plant (born 1801 died 1853) was

(A) STAFFORDSHIRE SLIPWARE earthenware posset-pots decorated with slip *(left)* with initials I.B. (Isaac Ball) and R.F. (Robert Fletcher) and 1696; *(right)* with the name 'ROBBORT WOOD' (Robert Wood) c. 1700. Sizes 8½ and 9⅛ inches respectively. *(Hanley Museum)*.

(B) STAFFORDSHIRE SLIPWARE earthenware cradles decorated with slip: *(left)* red earthenware with white slip, early eighteenth century, 9 inches long; *(centre)* cream earthenware cradle with notched edges dated 1839, 10 inches long; *(right)* inscribed 'Made by Ralph Shaw October the 31 Cobridg: gate' and 'M.T 1740', 10¾ inches long. *(Hanley Museum)*.

PLATE 81

(A) STAFFORDSHIRE SLIPWARE *(left)* Dutch oven in brown earthenware decorated in white slip with tulip motifs, late seventeenth century or early eighteenth century. Height 10 inches; *(right)* Brown earthenware dish with white slip decoration, c.1700. Diameter 12½ inches. *(Hanley Museum)*.

(B) STAFFORDSHIRE SLIPWARE jug, buff earthenware, covered with dark brown slip and decorated in white slip under a yellow glaze, late seventeenth century. Height 5⅜ inches.

(C) STAFFORDSHIRE SLIPWARE cup, buff earthenware, decorated with white and dark slips under a yellow glaze, dated 1701. Height 4¼ inches.

PLATE 82

STAFFORDSHIRE SLIPWARE posset-pot, buff earthenware with decoration in white and brown slips under a yellow glaze, late seventeenth century. Height 6 inches.

PLATE 83

(A) STAFFORDSHIRE SLIPWARE dish, red earthenware, with slip decoration signed Ralph Simpson, late seventeenth century. Diameter 17 inches.

(B) STAFFORDSHIRE SLIPWARE dish, red earthenware with decoration in light brown and white slips under a yellow glaze inscribed 'W.R' (for William III), late seventeenth century. Diameter 16¾ inches.

PLATE 84

(A) STAFFORDSHIRE SLIPWARE dish, red earthenware, with slip decoration, signed Thomas Toft, c. 1670–1680. Diameter 18 inches.

(B) STAFFORDSHIRE SLIPWARE dish, red earthenware, with slip decoration, signed Thomas Toft, c. 1670–80. Diameter 17¼ inches.

PLATE 85

(A) STAFFORDSHIRE SLIPWARE dish decorated in coloured slips with Royal Arms and initials C.R., the name Thomas Toft in a panel beneath. Diameter 22 inches. (*Hanley Museum*).

(B) STAFFORDSHIRE SLIPWARE dish, red earthenware with bird incised *(sgraffiato)* through a coating of white slip. Eighteenth century. Diameter 12½ inches.

PLATE 86

(A) STAFFORDSHIRE SLIPWARE dish, earthenware, decorated with sunflowers and birds and the initials S.M. (Samuel Malkin, of Burslem), 1st half eighteenth century. Diameter 17 inches.

(B) STAFFORDSHIRE SLIPWARE red earthenware posset-pot decorated with green, white and brown slip, late seventeenth or early eighteenth century. Height 5⅜ inches.

(C) *(left)* STAFFORDSHIRE SLIPWARE red earthenware Dutch oven decorated in slip with birds and flowers, late seventeenth or early eighteenth century. Height 10 inches. *(Hanley Museum).* (D) *(right)* STAFFORDSHIRE SLIPWARE red earthenware mug with decoration incised *(sgraffiato)* through a coating of white slip, dated 1747. Height 6⅞ inches.

PLATE 87

STAFFORDSHIRE SLIPWARE marbled dish with a notched edge, late seventeenth or early eighteenth century. Diameter 13¾ inches.

PLATE 88

(A) STAFFORDSHIRE SALT-GLAZED STONEWARE loving-cup, dated 1761, with scratch blue decoration. Ht 8½ inches. Diameter 10¼ inches. *(Mrs Frank Nagington)*.

(B) STAFFORDSHIRE SALT-GLAZED STONEWARE mug with scratch blue decoration, dated 1752. Height 5 inches.

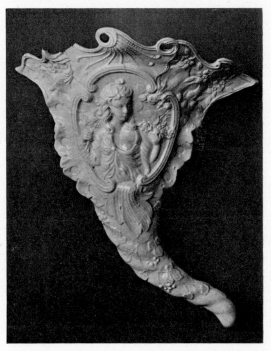

(C) STAFFORDSHIRE SALT-GLAZED STONE-WARE wall flower-holder, with moulded relief ornament, c. 1760. Height 8¾ inches.

PLATE 89

STAFFORDSHIRE SALT-GLAZED STONEWARE water-bottle and basin, painted in enamel colours, c. 1750. Height of bottle, 9⅛ inches; diameter of basin, 9½ inches

PLATE 90

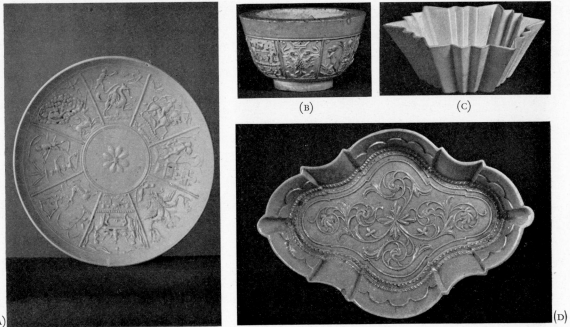

(A) STAFFORDSHIRE SALT-GLAZED STONEWARE saucer with decoration moulded in relief, c. 1745. Diameter 5 inches. (B) STAFFORDSHIRE SALT-GLAZED STONEWARE block for making moulds for tea-cups, dated 1749. Height 2 inches. (C) STAFFORDSHIRE SALT-GLAZED STONEWARE jelly mould, c. 1750. Height 1¼ inches, diameter 3¾ inches. (D) STAFFORDSHIRE SALT-GLAZED STONEWARE pickle tray, middle of eighteenth century. Length 6¼ inches.

(E) STAFFORDSHIRE SALT-GLAZED STONEWARE jug enamelled in colours and dated 1764. Height 8 inches.

(F) STAFFORDSHIRE SALT-GLAZED STONE-WARE cream-jug decorated with touches of blue. c. 1750. Height 3 inches.

PLATE 91

(A) STAFFORDSHIRE SALT-GLAZED STONE-WARE tea-pot, painted in enamel colours, mid-eighteenth century. Height 4½ inches.

(B) STAFFORDSHIRE BLACK-GLAZED STONE-WARE teapot, red with relief decoration under a black glaze, c. 1750. Height 3¾ inches. (*Mrs Frank Nagington*).

STAFFORDSHIRE SALT-GLAZED STONEWARE teapot and cover painted in purple-black enamel, c. 1760. Height 4⅜ inches.

PLATE 92

STAFFORDSHIRE SALT-GLAZED STONEWARE coffee-pot, painted in enamel colours, c. 1765.
Height 9½ inches.

PLATE 93

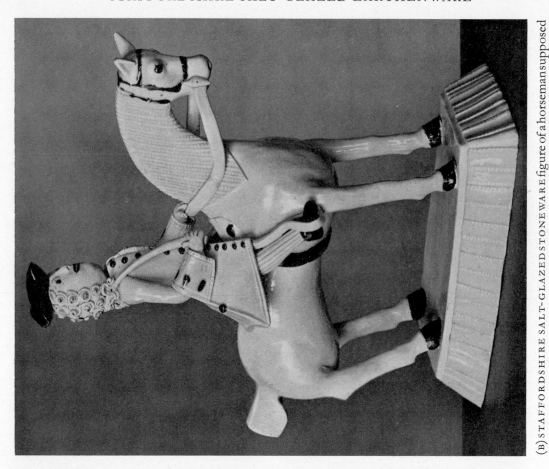

(B) STAFFORDSHIRE SALT-GLAZED STONEWARE figure of a horseman supposed to represent George II, decorated in brown slip, c. 1745. Height 9¼ inches.

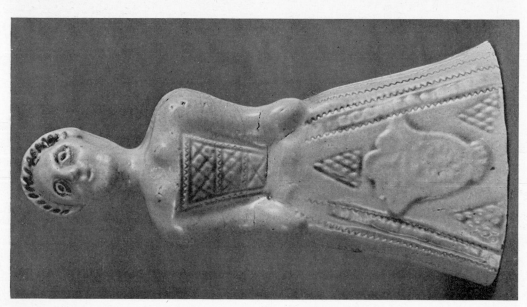

(A) STAFFORDSHIRE SALT-GLAZED STONEWARE figure of a woman, white with touches of blue, c. 1745. Height 6 inches.

PLATE 94

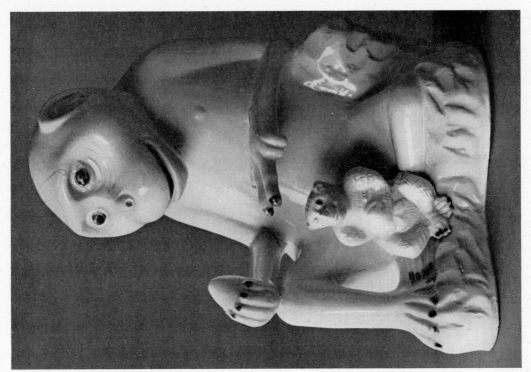

(A) STAFFORDSHIRE SALT-GLAZED STONEWARE bust of Empress Maria Theresa (one of a pair), c. 1745. Height 7½ inches.

(B) STAFFORDSHIRE SALT-GLAZED STONEWARE figure of a monkey with a young one, c. 1740. Height 7½ inches.

PLATE 95

(A) STAFFORDSHIRE SALT-GLAZED STONEWARE teapot in the form of a camel, c. 1745. Height 4½ inches.

(B) STAFFORDSHIRE SALT-GLAZED STONEWARE teapot, decorated in enamel colours with a portrait of Frederick, King of Prussia, c. 1765. Height 4½ inches.

PLATE 96

also a pottery figure maker.

MARKS

*B Plant
Lane End*

TP

Painted

[Parson & Bradshaw's *Directory*, 1818; *Staffordshire, Evening Sentinel*, 5 April 1955.]

Plaster of Paris

A fine white plaster consisting of calcined gypsum which swells and sets rapidly when blended with water. Used in the pottery industry for making moulds and stated to have been introduced into Staffordshire by Ralph Daniel of Cobridge c.1745, who had seen them used in a porcelain manufactory in France (Simeon Shaw, *History of the Staffordshire Potteries*, 1829, p.163. *Chemistry of Pottery*, 1837, p. 417).

Platter

A circular dish: 'dined in an earthen platter' (Pepys, *Diary*, 6 September 1666).

Plymouth, Devon. Earthenware manufactory

Coarse earthenware (brown and yellow) was manufactured here in the eighteenth century, but gave way about 1810 to the production of painted or printed cream colour. In 1815 three factories were operating in Plymouth.

The Plymouth Pottery Company founded by William Alsop made common blue transfer-printed white earthenware.

Jewitt gaves its mark as 'P.P.Coy.L, Stone China' with the addition of the Royal Arms.

[L. Jewitt, *Ceramic Art of Great Britain*, 1878.]

Plymouth, Devonshire. Porcelain manufactory

DATES AND OWNERS

This, the first English factory to make hard-paste porcelain' was established in 1768 by William Cookworthy, who in that year patented his formula for the manufacture of hard-paste. He was aided in the founding of the works in Coxside, Plymouth, by a company of Quakers: in 1770 the factory was moved to Bristol, and in 1773 the patent rights were sold to Champion who assumed control of the business. The factory was known as the Bristol China Manufactory. In 1775, in the face of intense opposition from potters in Staffordshire under Wedgwood's leadership, Champion obtained a modified renewal of the patent, but crippled financially was compelled to sell out to a company of potters in Staffordshire in 1781.

MARKS

A number of different marks were used, and some of these were certainly employed after the factory had been moved to Bristol.

$$2\!\!\!\downarrow$$

ARTISTS

Henry Bone. Enameller, apprenticed at Plymouth.

Saqui (sometimes referred to as Le Quoi or Soqui) a painter of birds, etc. in the Sèvres manner, who also decorated Bristol and Worcester porcelain.

Certain pieces, notably shell-shaped articles and figures, are marked TEBO or T°., a modeller or repairer of this name being in the service of Champion, and possibly earlier of Cookworthy at Plymouth.

SUBJECTS

Tablewares, figures and statuettes, vases and other ornamental pieces were made at Plymouth. Early porcelain was often decorated in Oriental styles in underglaze blue. Applied decoration in relief was used for shell and rock-work pieces such as salt-cellars, small dishes etc., these proving very popular. Sets of the 'Seasons' and the well-known 'Continents' are typical of the figures produced at Plymouth and later at Bristol.

Colour plate 15, STAFFORDSHIRE: *see page viii for caption*

DISTINGUISHING CHARACTERISTICS

Much of the early porcelain made at Plymouth is clearly of an experimental nature. Flaws, fire-cracks and discolourations are common, and a smoky tint affects nearly all the colours used. The glaze is rather thick and dull in appearance. In pieces decorated in underglaze blue the blue is of a greyish tone, often according pleasantly with the body of the ware which is semi-translucent and has a grey, faintly brown tint by transmitted light.

Figures made at an early date at Longton Hall clearly served as models for those made later at Plymouth. The resemblance is so marked that it has been suggested that Cookworthy acquired some of the actual moulds used there when the Longton Hall factory closed down.

Generally there is little originality in forms of decoration, and most designs are derivative, Derby and Worcester influences being apparent in many cases. Work in the Sèvres style by Saqui is of a higher quality, some of his birds and landscapes being very well executed.

Figures have scrolled, hollow bases, picked out in dull crimson.

Transfer-printing is extremely rare and does not seem to have been used with any success.

Examples are to be found in the Victoria and Albert Museum and the British Museum.

See also COOKWORTHY and BRISTOL.

Plate 77.

[J.L.Dixon, *English Porcelain of the Eighteenth Century*, 1952; W.B.Honey, *Old English Porcelain*, 1926, new ed. 1948; Hugh Owen, *Two Centuries of Ceramic Art in Bristol*, 1873.]

Podmore, Robert, Worcester

A Robert Podmore is mentioned as being in the secret of the manufacture of porcelain and as receiving a special bonus 'the better to engage his fidelity' at Worcester from 1751 onwards. A man named Podmore was working at Liverpool before 1756 and at Wedgwoods in 1755.

Polesworth, Warwickshire

Slipware pottery was manufactured at this pot-works during the eighteenth and nineteenth centuries. In the Glaisher Collection, Fitzwilliam Museum there is a dated example (1801).

[B.Rackham, *Catalogue of the Glaisher Collection*, 1935.]

Polito's menagerie

A popular figure group, probably made by Obadiah Sherratt of Hot Lane; Polito's Menagerie was in Staffordshire in 1808 – 'Just arrived and will be exhibited during the Fair at Wolverhampton indisputably the largest menagerie in Europe. S.POLITO, the celebrated collector of Living Curiosities, etc. etc.' (*Staffordshire Advertiser*, 9 July 1808). S.Polito died April 1814 at Manchester, (*Staffordshire Advertiser*, 20 April 1814), and his widow a few months later, (*Staffordshire Advertiser*, 30 July 1814). His Menagerie was purchased by Mr Cross, who for 20 years had been its superintendant (William Hone, *Everyday Book*, Vol 2. London, 1827). Later the same model was made to do service for Wombwell's Circus. Examples in Museums at Newcastle-under-Lyme, Brighton, and Hanley, Stoke-on-Trent.

[Reginald G.Haggar, 'Obadiah and Martha Sherratt of Hot Lane' in *Apollo*, Vol 50, November 1949; Reginald G.Haggar, *Staffordshire Chimney Ornaments*, 1955.]

Pollard, William (born 1803 died 1854)

Worked as porcelain painter for the Bevingtons at Swansea, and noted for loosely arranged flower sprays in which the gaps between the blossoms are filled with a dusky purple-black.

Poole, John Ellison (born 1766 died 1829)

Pottery manufacturer; partner in the firm of Lakin & Poole from 1791 to 1795; Poole, Lakin & Shrigley 1795; and Poole & Shrigley 1795–1797. In 1797 he was adjudged bankrupt. He appears to have potted on his own account as the mark POOLE has been recorded.

[*Parish Registers*, Burslem; *Staffordshire Advertiser*, 20 May 1797, 21 October 1797, 10 October 1801, 4 June 1808.]

Poole, Dorset

Poole has been a centre for the manufacture of pottery and tiles over a long period of time because of the rich clay deposits in the Wareham and Corfe areas. From 1854 tiles were made at Hamworthy by Sanders, and in Poole at the East Quay works from 1861.

Carter & Co. was established by Jesse Carter

at Poole in 1873. He later acquired the East Quay and Hamworthy factories, took his sons into partnership, and made a reputation for decorative wall tiles, faience and floor tiles. Decorative lustre pottery in *L'art Nouveau* style was made in the 1890's as well as in traditional lustre styles in the Edwardian age by Owen Carter. Important large-scale architectural faience in the della Robbia manner was made subsequent to the 1914–1918 war to designs by Harold Stabler and others. Painted tiles are a speciality of Carters.

The Poole Pottery (Carter, Stabler and Adams) was founded in 1921. Other concerns have sprung up since.

Plate 156.

Pope and Devil

A reversible bell-shaped cup showing the Pope in a triple tiara when held one way up, and the head of the Devil when reversed. Sometimes inscribed 'When Pope absolves, the Devil smiles'. Made in earthenware, late eighteenth century. Examples at Brighton and Victoria and Albert Museums.

Porcelain

A word loosely applied in the seventeenth and eighteenth centuries to white wares with oriental designs attempting to simulate imported oriental porcelain, such as delftware, stoneware, etc. Imported Chinese red teapots were called red porcelain, a name which clung to Elers-type red teapots and other wares throughout the eighteenth century.

The term has been used more narrowly and correctly since the eighteenth century to describe translucent wares made in emulation of Chinese and Continental porcelain, but only three factories certainly made true (that is hard-paste) porcelain in England, namely Plymouth, Bristol and Shelton New Hall.

The fine porcelains of the eighteenth century were all soft-paste, either (1) glass, or (2) bone, or (3) soapstone.

The standard Bone China, produced since the time of Spode, is a hybrid porcelain with heavy percentage of bone ash in the ingredients.

See under Bow, CHELSEA, CAUGHLEY, BRIS-TOL, DERBY, COALPORT, NANTGARW, SWANSEA, WORCESTER, etc. Also under BONE CHINA, SOFT-PASTE, HARD-PASTE.

[H. Eccles and B. Rackham, *Analysed Specimens of English Porcelain*, 1922.]

Porphyry

A red-stained parian paste said to resemble porphyry.

Porringer

A child's basin or cup for broth or porridge: sometimes a covered vessel; also known as a POTTINGER.

Portland Vase

A cameo glass vase traditionally but erroneously stated to have contained the ashes of Alexander Severus and his mother, and to have come from his sepulchre at Monte del Grano; probably made at Alexandria c.50 B.C. Before 1642 it passed into the possession of the Barberini family from whom it was purchased by Sir William Hamilton in 1770, who sold it to the Duchess of Portland. Lent to the British Museum 1810 but smashed by an 'inebriated neurotic' named Lloyd 1845, and restored with the aid of Wedgwood's copy. Put up for sale at Christie's 1929 but withdrawn when the bidding reached £29,000. Purchased by British Museum 1946.

The significance of the decoration is obscure. Erasmus Darwin's theory that the vase played some part in a latter-day revival of the Eleusinian mysteries and that its decoration had esoteric ritual significance is recorded and supported by Mankowitz.

Josiah Wedgwood copied the Portland Vase 1786–90, his copy being pronounced accurate in effect and detail by Sir Joshua Reynolds P.R.A. The first edition comprised 29 specimens. William Webber was chiefly responsible for the modelling. There were several subsequent editions, the 1839 being notable because the nude figures are 'decently' draped; the Bellows edition was issued for an American firm in 1909; an ordinary jasper Portland Vase has been issued from 1880 onwards. The finest nineteenth century edition is that undercut and polished by John Northwood of Stourbridge for Wedgwood's in 1877–80, limited to 15 copies, cipher signed N above the Wedgwood impress mark.

[W.Mankowitz, *The Portland Vase and the Wedgwood Copies*, 1952.]

Portobello, Scotland

Several factories are known to have operated here from the eighteenth century, notably:

Scott Bros: Manufacturers of stoneware, red ware and ornamental pottery including birds and animals from about 1786 until 1796. The mark SCOTT BROS. (impressed) is recorded. The factory was later taken over by Cookson and Jardine who reconstructed the works 'on Staffordshire lines'. The business was sold to Thomas Yoole in 1808 and he in 1810 took his son-in-law Thomas Rathbone, a Staffordshire man, into the concern, which then traded as Thomas Rathbone & Co. The products have a distinctively Staffordshire flavour, figures, plaques, animals (including lions copied from the Loggia dei Lanzi, Florence), plaques with printed scriptural texts and lustre borders. Marks:

or T. RATHBONE

The works closed down in 1845 but were reopened in 1856 by a new company founded by Dr. Gray, in which some of the Rathbone family had a small interest. This new company flourished and expanded, purchasing the Newbigging Pottery in 1880.

Waverley Pottery: Erected 1770, occupied by various owners who made stoneware jugs, until acquired by A.W.Buchan & Co.

Westbank Pottery: Said to have been working in the eighteenth century.

Newbigging Pottery, Musselburgh. Established 1820 by John Tough: acquired by Grays 1880.

Rosebank Pottery: Erected in eighteenth century, made domestic pottery.

Colour Plate 10 and plate 78.

[J.A.Fleming, *Scottish Pottery*, 1923; L.Jewitt, *Ceramic Art of Great Britain*, 1878.]

'Portobello' wares

Wares made at Tunstall, Staffordshire in imitation of pottery made at Portobello, Scotland, mentioned by Simeon Shaw, 1829.

[S.Shaw, *History of the Staffordshire Potteries*, 1829.]

Posset

A beverage comprising hot ale, milk, sugar, spices and small pieces of oatcake, toast or bread, said to have been a common supper beverage in Staffordshire and Derbyshire on Christmas Eve, but evidently of widespread popularity. A beverage of similar type, known as 'egged-ale' comprising hot ale, eggs, sugar and spices was still made in Staffordshire (Cheadle area) by old people on Christmas Eve as recently as 1935. 'Hot ale' was a North Staffordshire remedy for a cold.

Posset-pot

Straight-sided or bell-shaped vessel with multiple loop handles and spouts, generally covered with a slanting or dome-shaped lid, and occasionally 'crowned' with an elaborate knob and series of handles. Used for carrying or drinking posset, and made in the seventeenth and eighteenth centuries in slipwares, delftware, stoneware, etc. A favourite inscription on Staffordshire slipware specimens was 'THE BEST IS NOT TOO GOOD FOR YOU'. Also called a spout-pot.

Plates 81 A, 83, 87 B, 104 B.

Pot Bank (Potbank)

A potworks: Staffordshire name for a pottery factory.

Pot-Howcans, Nr Halifax, Yorkshire

A well known family of gipsy potters, the Hallidays, was settled at Howcans for many years. Lead-glazed slipware, dark brown in colour, was made from the seventeenth century onwards.

[G.Bemrose, *Nineteenth Century English Pottery and Porcelain*, 1952.]

Pot-lids

Polychrome colour-printing on pottery was developed by F. & R. Pratt of Fenton, and Mayer of Burslem, from 1848 and Brown, Westhead, Moore & Co., Shelton, later, and was used extensively for the decoration of pot-lids. Subjects were taken frequently from early nineteenth century narrative pictures, battle-pieces, animal subjects etc.

[Harold George Clarke, *Colour Pictures on Pots lids* (with Frank Wrench), London 1924; Clarke, *The Pot Lid Recorder*, 1950; Clarke, *Under Glaze Colour Picture Prints on Staffordshire Pottery*, 1949, 1955.]

Pottery

Opaque fired earthenware.

Pottery, The

Name given to the pottery manufacturing district of North Staffordshire extending from Goldenhill to Longton and including Tunstall, Burslem, Longport, Cobridge, Hanley, Etruria, Shelton, Stoke, Fenton, Longton: 'I went to see the Pottery villages' (Richard Pococke, *Travels through England*, 1750–51) 'They are all of them already ranked under the general name of The Pottery'. (J.Aiken, *A Description of the Country... round Manchester*, 1795). 'At Lane End the population of the Pottery commences' (Hon. John Byng, *The Torrington Diaries*, 1792): more frequently rendered The Potteries: 'I had the pleasure of viewing the Staffordshire Potteries', (Arthur Young, *A Six Months Tour through the North of England*, 1770).

Pottery making machines

In 1844 John Ridgway introduced a machine for manufacturing patchboxes (*Potters Examiner*, 3 August 1844). Wall's patent self-acting hand or steam operated machine for making dishes, plates, cups, saucers and bowls, was introduced at C.J.Mason's factory, Fenton, November 1844 (*Potters Examiner*, 9 November 1844) but was withdrawn because of a mechanical defect and the opposition of the workers. A machine for hollow-ware pressing was tried out by Smith & Co., Stockton-on-Tees, 1845 (*Potters Examiner*, 8 February). Machinery, tried out by

Mason at Fenton, Chapels of Leeds and Barkers of Leeds was abandoned early in 1845 (*Potters Examiner*, 1 March 1845). Messrs Copeland introduced a similar machine known to the workers as the 'Scourge' but this was withdrawn because of the approaching general election of 1847, at which Alderman Copeland was a candidate for Stoke-on-Trent. The hand-operated 'jolley' was not- re-introduced until about 1870. Multiple semi-automatic 'jolleys' were first put into use in England in 1946, and the completely automatic plate-making machine in 1947.

[*The Potters' Examiner*, 1844–45; J.C.Wedgwood, *Staffordshire Pottery and its History*, n.d.; Harold Owen, *The Staffordshire Potter*, London, 1901; W.Evans, *Art and History of the Potters Business*, 1846; Reginald G.Haggar, *The Masons of Lane Delph*, 1952.]

Poulson, Joseph (born 1750 died 1808)

'Eminent manufacturer of china and earthenware', Stoke-on-Trent; partner with Thomas Minton in firm of Minton, Poulson & Pownall 1796–1808.

[Obit. *Staffordshire Advertiser*, 10 December, 1808.]

Poulson, William, Fenton Low

Only two potters in Stoke itself were recorded in Wedgwood's MS List of early eighteenth century North Staffordshire potters, Ward and Poulson. The latter was probably William Poulson of Fenton Low buried 15 July 1746. It is possible that Thomas Whieldon took over his factory.

[*Parish Registers, Stoke-on-Trent.*]

Pounce pot

A small box with a perforated lid for perfumes; a powder box or jar; a pierced-topped jar for sprinkling powdered pumice used to dry ink (before the popularity of blotting paper).

Pountney & Company, Bristol. Earthenware Manufacturers

The factory which Joseph Ring established in Water Lane, Temple Street, Bristol, in 1786 for the manufacture of Queen's and other Staffordshire-type earthenware, was eventually owned by Pountney & Co.

Elizabeth, widow of Joseph Ring, junior, formed a Company in 1813 with Henry Carter and John D. Pountney. The other partners had either died or retired in 1835, leaving J. D. Pountney as sole owner. In 1836 he took Gabriel Goldney into the business. John Pountney died in 1852, but the factory was worked by his widow under the style Pountney & Co. until her death in 1872. The firm still survives.

MARKS

Chaffers records the following mark.

| Impressed | en bleu | modern mark |

ARTISTS

William Fifield (d.1857) and **John Fifield**.

WORK

White and blue-printed earthenware, parian statuary, and imitations of Etruscan wares were typical of Pountney's early Victorian and mid-nineteenth century products.

[L. Jewitt, *Ceramic Art of Great Britain*, 1878.]

Powder blue

A rich granulated ground-colour effect used at Worcester; achieved by blowing powdered pigment on to the surface of the ware, prepared with a coating of oil.

Pownall, William (born 1754 died 1814)

Partner and financier in the firm of Minton, Poulson & Pownall, Stoke-on-Trent, from 1796 probably until the death of Poulson in 1808. Pownall died at Leipsic House, near Liverpool, in 1814 (*Staffordshire Gazette*, 29 November, 1814).

[*Rate Books* Entries per A. Meigh; *Directories*.]

Pratt, Felix (born 1780 died 1859),
Lane Delph, Staffordshire

Felix Pratt was the son of William Pratt (born 1753 died 1799) master potter at Lane Delph from 1783 or earlier until his death in 1799. The

business was then continued by his widow (nee Ellen Edwards born 1760 died 1815) with the help of her sons who eventually started up seperate businesses in Fenton, F. & R. Pratt, as china and earthenware manufacturers from 1812, and John as an earthenware potter only. Both these firms flourished throughout the nineteenth century.

The name PRATT which occurs impressed on some eighteenth century wares is that of William Pratt. The name Felix Pratt is associated with a class of toby jugs, relief-decorated jugs and figures coloured with a distinctive palette including orange-ochre, brown, pale yellow, blue and olive green; but these were also made in widely distributed areas outside Staffordshire, notably in Scotland. F. & R. Pratt specialized in multi-colour printing from contemporary narrative paintings, on pot-lids and on table wares. The engravings were often excellent in quality. Jesse Austin executed some of the more important. They also made red terracotta picked out in enamel colours, and 'Etruscan' ware. Examples in the Victoria and Albert Museum.

MARKS

PRATT
FENTON

1830–1840 Transfer-printed

[*Parish Registers; Directories*, 1783–1889. Poll Lists; Gravestones. *Govt. Report*, 1842; *Staffordshire Advertiser*, 9 February 1799, 8 December 1810, 23 July 1813, 7 January 1815, 22 February 1840, 28 February 1852 referring to various members of the family; *Evening Sentinel*, 24 December 1916; This family has been very inaccurately recorded.]

See also PRATT TYPE.

'Pratt' type

Wares made at the end of the eighteenth and beginning of the nineteenth centuries, decorated with a distinctive palette of high temperature colours, including a drab blue, yellow, ochre, dirty orange, dull green, brown, etc. Relief decorations are common. Figures also were decorated in this range of pigments. The type is usually associated with Felix Pratt of Fenton, and the name 'PRATT' is occasionally found on them, but it is unlikely that the earlier pieces were made by Felix Pratt, who was not born until 1780 and died 1859. William Pratt (1753–99) and his wife Ellen Edwards (1760–1815) who succeeded him, may have been responsible for some of these wares which are, however, known to have been made by potters in other parts of England and Scotland over a long period of time.

Plates 153 A, 154 B.

[Reginald G. Haggar, *Staffordshire Chimney Ornaments*, 1955; *Directories; Parish Registers*.]

Pratt, Henry Lark (born 1805 died 1873)

Landscape painter on porcelain who served his apprenticeship at Derby, but subsequently worked at Mintons' factory Stoke from 1830. As an oil painter he is said to have been patronised by the nobility, and is known to have executed extremely dull topographical works.

[J. Haslem, *Old Derby China Works*, 1876; obit. *Staffordshire Evening Sentinel*, 8 March 1873; Gravestone, *Stoke Parish Churchyard*.]

Presser

A person who forms pattery vessels by pressing bats of clay into moulds or upon 'forms'. Mentioned by Arthur Young, 1770. HOLLOW-WARE PRESSER, a maker of vegetable dishes, tureens etc. FLATWARE PRESSER, a maker of plates, dishes and saucers.

[A. Young, *A Six Month Tour through the North of England*, London 1770.]

Prestonpans, Scotland

One of the most important centres of pottery production in Scotland and evidently of considerable antiquity. There are records of pottery manufacturers here in the early part of the seventeenth century. In 1754 there were two potworks employing a total of 70 potters, in 1796 there were four (two of them small) with 256 workpeople. Considerably expansion took place in the nineteenth century.

FACTORIES

Gordon's: said to be of early eighteenth century origin. Started as a small manufactory with two ovens only. In early nineteenth century made blue-printed earthenware, jugs with embossed figures painted in brown, orange and green and round or oval in section, terra cotta and jet with 'smear' glaze. The factory was wound up in 1832.

Watson's: Started about 1750 with three kilns and employing 80 workers: made figures (sturdy fishwives with striped petticoats and spotted bodices), punch-bowls and commemoration pottery (given to incoming tenants of farms) as well as the usual useful wares. When the Watsons got into difficulties, John Fowler, the Edinburgh brewer, stepped in, eventually becoming proprietor. Later the firm was Fowler and Thomson (with Charles Belfield as Works Manager). Manufactures at this time included plates, 'grey beards', bottles and other articles. Firm closed down c. 1840. The mark WATSON (impressed) occurs occasionally on figures.

Newhalls: Small works, making common wares.

Cuttle: Yellow ware crockery made here.

High Street, Prestonpans: Rombach's works for manufacture of domestic pottery, closed about 1820.

High Street, Prestonpans: Adam Cubie's manufactory for production of jugs, salt-buckets, butter tubs, for farm houses. Said to have closed down 1797.

Belfields: Founded by Charles Belfield after the failure of Watson's pottery, and flourished throughout the nineteenth century. See CHARLES BELFIELD.

[J. A. Fleming, *Scottish Pottery*, 1923.]

Price, John Frederick (born 1898 died 1943)

Designer of table wares in the 'modern' style for Pountney's of Bristol, and of tiled fireplaces etc. for Thynnes of Hereford. For several years President of the Society of Industrial Artists.

Prince, John, Lane Delph

At Lane Delph, near Fenton Lane, John Prince manufactured 'red porcelain' and white, salt-glazed stoneware, realising from his business a large fortune. Prince's daughter married one of his turners, John Stirrup, of Cinderhill, near Lane End.

[S. Shaw, *History of the Staffordshire Potteries*, 1829.]

Processes

The processes of pottery manufacture have become more complex with the change over from country craft conditions to factory production during the Industrial Revolution. The chief processes are:

Casting: formation of pottery shapes by pouring slip into plaster moulds. When sufficient thickness of clay has been formed the spare slip is poured away and the mould left to dry after which the article may be removed from it. Telltale seam marks are indications of cast or pressed wares. Casting came into use about 1745.

Dipping: glazing ware by immersing it in glaze solution.

Enamelling: decoration of ware overglaze with bright colours.

Engraving: cutting patterns on copper plates for transfer-printing; incising ware in the leather-hard condition.

Firing: transforming soft clay into hard potshard by burning or baking in a potters oven; pottery may be subject to 4 firings for biscuit, for glaze (glost firing), for 'hardening-on' (under glaze transfer-printed wares are hardened-on, to burn out the printers' oil before glazing), and for on-glaze decoration in colour or gold.

Glazing: applying the glaze solution to the ware which when fired gives its surface quality. Originally done by dusting, subsequently by dipping, and nowadays quite frequently by spraying.

Modelling: preparing the original form of a vessel from which the master mould is made. Allowance for shrinkage has to be nicely calculated.

Mould making: preparation of moulds from an original model.

Ornamenting: application of relief ornament to pottery in the plastic state.

Printing, transfer-printing: application of tissue transfers printed from engraved copper-plates.

Throwing: making ware upon the fast-revolving potters' wheel. A ball of clay is thrown upon the revolving wheel head, centred, and drawn up by the hand to the required shape.

Turning: adding finish to the thrown article, by paring away unnecessary clay to make it light and smooth. The ware is turned in a leather-hard state by placing it on a chum or hollow drum which holds it in place.

Prosser's patent

Richard Prosser of Birmingham took out a patent, dated 17 June 1840, for making buttons, knobs, tiles and bricks by solidifying clay 'in a state of powder, by pressure between hard surfaces, either plain or figured, into solid articles, without any water being used'. This process was' taken up by Mr. Minton, of Stoke-on-Trent, and at the beginning of the year 1842, a make of 5,000 gross (of buttons) per week was found insufficient to meet the demand'. Patents for improved machinery taken out by M. Baptirosse, a Parisian manufacturer, and cheap French labour destroyed this English manufacture. Richard Prossers a civil engineer and inventor was born in 1804 and died 21 May 1854.

[W. J. Furnival, *Leadless Decorative Tiles, Faience and Mosaic*, Stone 1904; Richard B. Prosser, *Birmingham Inventors and Inventions*, 1881.]

Protât, Hugues

Sculptor, modeller and designer, at Mintons of Stoke and for Wedgwoods of Etruria: Modelling Instructor at Hanley and Stoke Schools of Design, 1850–1864. He designed and modelled vases and other ornamental pieces for Wedgwoods in 1870–71 from 14 Great Smith Street, Westminster, including the Protât Vase and a jardinière for which he was paid £25.

[Reginald G. Haggar, *A Century of Art Education in the Potteries*, 1953; Letters from Protât to Wedgwood in the Wedgwood Museum, Barlaston, 1870–71; Government Reports.]

Pugin, Augustus Welby Northmore (born 1812 died 1852)

Architect and designer of ecclesiastical furnishings. Designed so-called 'encaustic' tiles for Herbert Minton, whose friend he was. Minton's 'Gothic' pattern, an underglaze blue-print, is said to have been designed by Pugin.
Plate 68 D.

[M. Trappes-Lomax, *Pugin, A Mediaeval Victorian*, 1933, contains Pugin-Minton correspondence.]

Punch

A beverage consisting of spirits (originally aqua vitae or arrack) blended with hot milk or water, sweetened with pure loaf sugar, and flavoured with spice and lemon. Introduced about 1625. In the seventeenth century it was a recognised sailor's drink ('a drinke very special among those who frequent the sea' – Thomas Worlidge, 1675). Served in seaport taverns and known as 'puntz'. It became fashionable in high society when taken up by William III, punch clubs were formed, and a 'ritual' of blending and serving was evolved. Punch-bowls, kettles and barrels became essential items of equipment in the 'punchery'. Taverns and Coffee houses became 'punch houses', and Punch itself became known by a specific title, such as Brandy Punch, Rum Punch, etc.

Punch Barrel

A large barrel or urn-shaped container for blending punch, popular second half of eighteenth century. Mentioned in sale announcements of Chelsea (1778) and Chelsea-Derby porcelain (1784).

Punch bowl

A basin, made in tin-enamelled earthenware, salt-glazed stoneware or porcelain, ranging in size from half-pint to twelve quarts, used for serving punch. Sometimes called a JORUM.
Plate 56, 73 B, 97 A.

Punch Kettle

A vessel like a gigantic tea-pot used c.1750 for blending, carrying and serving hot punch.

Punch mugs

Punch was usually served in stem glasses, but apparently about 1755, mugs were used for drinking this beverage: 'punch bowls and mugs' – sale advertisement, William Littler (*Aris's Birmingham Gazette*, 20 June 1757).

'Purple Landskips'

Airy landscapes painted on Chelsea porcelain, 1753–58, in a monochrome purple-crimson, referred to in the factory catalogues.
[J.L. Dixon, *English Porcelain of the 18th Century*, 1952.]

Puzzle jug

A pitcher or jug made in earthenware, stoneware or delftware usually with a capacious globular body and pierced, cylindrical neck offering a challenge to the uninitiated drinker. 'From Mother Earth I take my birth/ Am made a joke for man;/ And am here filled with good cheer/ Come taste it if you can', or 'Here gentlemen come try your skill/ I'll hold a wager if you will;/ That you drink not this liquor all/ Without you spill or let some fall'. The rim of the neck usually consisted of a hollow tube connected with the inside by the hollow tubular handle, and this rim tube generally issued into a number of spouts or apertures, frequently three but sometimes five or even seven. Almost invariably there was a hidden hole underneath the top of the handle. To meet the challenge the drinker had to block all the openings excepting the one from which he intended to imbibe the contents, and drain the jug by suction. Commonly made in the seventeenth and eighteenth centuries, particularly at Liverpool. Prof. Garner points out that the perforations and proportion of neck to body in delftware offers a clue to origin; those made at Liverpool generally being pierced with 4 hearts and ellipses arranged circularly; those of Bristol with intersecting circles; and those of Lambeth with narrow necks.
Plate 104 C.
[F.H.Garner, *English Delftware*, 1948.]

'P.V.' mark

This incised mark occurs on earthenware figures of Shakespeare (after Scheemaker's statue in Westminster Abbey) and Milton, of late eighteenth century date. The initials may possibly stand for 'Palmer: Voyez' but there is no conformatory evidence.

P·V

[Illustrated and discussed Reginald G. Haggar, *Staffordshire Chimney Ornaments*, 1955.]

Pyrometer

An instrument for measuring the heat of kilns, invented by Josiah Wedgwood, F. R. S., and the subject of explanatory pamphlets: *Description and use of a thermometer for measuring the higher degrees of heat from a red heat up to the strongest that vessels made of clay can support* (1784) and *Additional observations on making a thermometer for measuring the higher degrees of heat* (1786). William Evans stated that Wedgwood's pyrometer 'was invented by Thomas Massey (a Bailiff in Mr. Wedgwood's manufactory)'.

[William Salt Library, Stafford; W.Evans, *Art and History of the Pottery Business*, 1846.]

Q

Quail patterns

Sometimes called PARTRIDGE PATTERNS. Drawn and enamelled in a simple Kakiemon style, incorporating, with foliage and rocks, a pair of quails. Used on Bow, Chelsea and Worcester porcelain, on Delftware of the eighteenth century, and on earthenware of the twentieth century, where it has been adapted as an underglaze transfer-print in blue (Furnivals Ltd.).

Queen Charlotte's pattern

A design comprising radial floral panels in blue with gilding, selected during a visit to the Worcester Factory by Queen Charlotte and King George III in 1788.

Queen's pattern

A counterchanged pattern consisting of alternate radiating whirling bands of red-on-white

and white-on-blue ornament with gilded embellishments used at Worcester from c.1770 onwards, and continued into the Flight and Barr, and Chamberlain periods.

Also known as the 'Catherine wheel', 'Whorl', or 'Spiral' pattern.

[W.B.Honey, *Old English Porcelain*, 1928, new edition 1948.]

Queen's Vase, The

Made to commemorate the coronation of Queen Elizabeth II and presented to the Queen by the British Pottery Manufacturers Federation. It was designed by John W.Wadswarth (born 1879 died 1955). This elaborate piece is really a silversmith's shape and unlike and unsuitable to pottery. It stands 25 ½ inches high and 11 ½ inches wide. It is ten-sided and includes ten niches in which are placed models of the Queen's Beasts. Below the shoulder are the Royal Arms and floral emblems of the countries of the Commonwealth. The vase is surmounted by the Royal Crown. Replicas were sent to each of the Commonwealth countries. The moulding, decoration and production of the vase were shared by Mintons, Wedgwoods, Copelands, Derby, Doultons and Worcester.

[Illustrated in *British Bulletin of Commerce*, November 1954.]

Queensware

The name given by Josiah Wedgwood to his perfected cream-coloured earthenware, after he had obtained for it the royal patronage and title 'Potter to the Queen'; subsequently adopted for this staple product of the earthenware industry throughout Staffordshire.

Quintal flower Horn

A five 'fingered' flower-holder made at the Leeds factory: a three 'fingered' flower-horn was also produced.

R

Raby, Edward, Bristol

Maker of porcelain panels with applied relief decorations, at the Water Lane Pottery, Bristol c.1845–1850.
Plate 19 B.

Randall, Thomas Martin (born 1786 died 1859)

Independent enameller in partnership with Richard Robins, with a workshop at Spa Fields, London, who decorated much English porcelain for London dealers. He was responsible also for decorating in elaborate Sèvres styles white Sèvres porcelain bought up in Paris by Baldock & Jarman in the early nineteenth century, and for stripping slightly enamelled Sèvres porcelain by etching away the colour, and replacing with more costly forms of ornamentation.

He is stated to have started a soft paste porcelain factory at Madeley, Shropshire c.1825 in imitation of Sèvres.

T M R
Madeley
S

Painted

Ratcliff, William, Hanley

Moved to the New Hall Factory (after the closure of the porcelain manufactory) in 1837 and potted there until about 1840 making white and transfer-printed earthenware. His mark was a circle enclosing an R, surrounded by Sun's rays.

Rattle

A hollow ball containing a marble or pellet used to amuse infants: an instruments used to make a rattling noise: a stoneware rattle, of Nottingham make, in Hanley Museum is dated 1760. Hodgkin illustrates a specimen inscribed 'Elizabeth Clarck December ye 25th 1769'.
[J.E. and E. Hodgkin, *Examples of Early English Pottery* 1896.]

Rattlesnake seal

Basaltes seal made by Wedgwood and Bentley 1777, showing a coiled rattlesnake about to strike, surmounted by the legend, 'Don't tread on me' adapted from a description of the first American flag. Wedgwood in letter to Bentley, 17 August 1777, wrote 'One rattlesnake is in hand. I think it will be best to keep such unchristian articles for *Private Trade*'. Distributed by Wedgwood to the friends of the American cause.
[*Letters of Josiah Wedgwood*, 1903.]

Ravilious, Eric (born 1903 died 1942)

Designer and book illustrator: studied at Eastbourne and Brighton Art Schools and Royal College of Art, London; influenced by Paul Nash; mural paintings, Morley College, London, 1930, and Morecombe 1932; wood-engravings for numerous books, including publications of the Golden Cockerel Press, The Cresset Press, Golden Hours Press; from 1937–41 designed table ware decorations for Josiah Wedgwood & Sons Ltd; painted numerous water colours; designed some glass and furniture; official war artist 1941; married Tirzah Garwood, engraver, 1930, and lived in Essex.
[J.M. Richards, *Catalogue, Eric Ravilious Memorial Exhibition*, 1948–49; R.Y. Goodden, in *Architectural Review*, 1943.]

Ray, George, Longton

Known to have modelled a bust of William Turner of Lane End (now in Hanley Museum) which is inscribed with his name, 'G. RAY, LANE END', and is believed to have worked for the younger Turners.

Ray & Tideswell, Longton

The firm of Ray & Tideswell manufactured china and earthenware at the Daisy Bank, Longton, from 1831 until 1837 when the firm was listed as Richard Ray. In 1851 Moses and Richard Ray are separately listed as china and earthenware manufacturers at Longton.

Read, George (born 1770 died 1847)

Artist and modeller; married, Burslem, 1 January 1811, to Sarah Whalley (he is described as modeller and widower); in Stafford gaol for debt 1813 (*Staffordshire Advertiser*, 18 December 1813) d. Bleakhill, 31 December 1847 (*Staffordshire Advertiser*, 8 January 1848). A George Whieldon Read, modeller, was in prison for debt, 1839 (*Staffordshire Advertiser*, 2 March).

'Real' China

Name given to the hard-paste porcelain made by the New Hall concern 1781–1812; 'Hollins, Warburton, Daniel and Co. manufacturers of real china, Shelton' (Holden's *Triennial Directory* 1805).

Red China

Fine red stoneware of the type introduced into Staffordshire by Elers, made from about 1693 until end of eighteenth century. A similar body was made by Josiah Wedgwood which he called Rosso Antico, but Wedgwood was aware that it differed little from wares then in current production in Staffordshire. He wrote to Bentley, 3 March 1776, 'I am afraid we shall never be able to make the *Rosso Antico* otherwise than to put you in mind of a *red-Pot-Teapot*'.

Red gloss pottery

Roman Red Gloss Pottery was made at various places in England, notably at Colchester, Essex.

Red Street, Wolstanton, Staffordshire

Simeon Shaw says that a hundred years before the time of Dr Plot's visit to Staffordshire (i.e. about 1577) the potters of Red Street were producing 'considerable quantities of all kinds of vessels then used' (*History of the Staffordshire Potteries*, 1829). During the eighteenth century the potters of Red Street, Elijah Mayer (who perished near Ulverston) and Moss 'fabricated greater quantities of pottery than any others of the whole district'. Probably the stabilising of the cream-coloured earthenware body killed the trade in the Red Street country crockery. The Moss family were the last in Red Street to make crockery, but abandoned it about 1845 for bricks and tiles which they had been making from the eighteenth century. Thomas and Henshall Moss are listed as early as 1796 as manufacturers of earthenware, bricks and tiles. Henshall Moss also kept the 'Wheat Sheaf' in Red Street. He died in 1833 at the age of 78 (*Staffordshire Advertiser*, 3 March 1833) and was succeeded by other persons of the same name who made bricks and farmed land in this area until 1889 or later. Richard Moss made earthenware and Egyptian black at Red Street where he also kept the 'Crown Inn' in 1834. He died in 1847 aged 64 (*Staffordshire Advertiser*, 4 November 1847).

Samuel Riles, potter, occupied a potworks in Red Street until 1815 when it was offered for sale (*Staffordshire Advertiser*, 11 February 1815). It was stated to be 'on the line of a road which cannot fail to command and ensure an excellent ready Money Retail Trade from Travellers'. This factory was probably taken over by Benjamin Myatt who is recorded here in 1818.

[*Staffordshire Advertiser; Directories*; S. Shaw *History of the Staffordshire Potteries*, 1829.]

Redrich and Jones

Jewitt says a patent for marbling earthenware was taken out by these in 1724 and describes the process as 'staining, clouding and damasking'.

[L. Jewitt, *Ceramic Art of Great Britain*, 1878.]

Reid W. & Co., Liverpool, Lancs.

Makers of blue-and-white wares in the mid-eighteenth century. A type of bone porcelain was possibly also manufactured by this firm. In 1759 the works were closed owing to bankruptcy. Their mark was:

REID & CO.

Wedgwood gave the ingredients of their paste as Purbeck Clay, Isle of Wight Sand, Chalk and Bone Ashes.

[Williamson's *Liverpool Advertiser*, 24 September, 19 November 1756; A.T. Green, 'Contributions of Josiah Wedgwood...' *Ceramic Society Transactions*, 1930].

Regency style

An architectural and decorative style associated with the Prince Regent (extending from 1811) and marked by some extravagance of form and ornament as shown in Brighton Pavilion. Revealed in over-ornate pseudo-oriental styles popular on pottery and porcelain from 1815 to 1830.

'Regent China'

A very translucent china body, resembling that of Nantgarw, but harder, introduced in 1811 for occasional use during the Regency at Chamberlain's Worcester factory and marked specially:

> Chamberlains
> Regent China
> Worcester
> E 155
> New Bond Street
> London

Registration marks

Wares marked with the following lozenge mark are decorated with patterns or designs registered with the British Patent Office between 1842 and 1883 inclusive:

Class (i.e. earthenware and glass)   Year
Month Day Parcel 1842-1867

Year letters 1842–1867:

X 1842	P 1851	Z 1860
H 1843	D 1852	R 1861
C 1844	Y 1853	O 1862
A 1845	J 1854	G 1863

I 1846	E 1855	N 1864
F 1847	L 1856	W 1865
U 1848	K 1857	Q 1866
S 1849	B 1858	T 1867
V 1850	M 1859	

Month letters:

C January	E May	D September
G February	M June	B October
W March	I July	K November
H April	R August	A December

Class Day Year Month   1868-1883

Year letters 1868–1883:

X 1868	U 1874	J 1880
H 1869	S 1875	E 1881
C 1870	V 1876	L 1882
A 1871	P 1877	K 1883
I 1872	D 1878	
F 1873	Y 1879	

Month letters:

C January	E May	D September
G February	M June	B October
W March	I July	K November
H April	R August	A December

There was a slight variation in the year 1878 when from 1st to 6th March, the registration letters for month and year were G and W respectively.

Resist process

An onglaze decorative process used generally with silver lustre.

The decoration is painted upon the glazed surface of the ware in a 'resist', covered with metallic solution and fired, the infusible resist portion firing away during the process leaving a white decoration reserved against a bright metallic background.

Plates 120 B, 152 C.

Reuter, Edmund (born 1845 died after 1912)

Ceramic designer and watercolour painter; son of a botanist, born at Geneva; went to Paris 1864; visited Egypt 1868; came to London in 1870 and made some contact with William Morris; assistant designer, Minton's, Stoke 1875–95; returned to Switzerland 1895; still living 1912; executed fine illuminated addresses, illustrations and imaginative water-colours.

[Prof. Robert Mobbs 'A Swiss Artist'; Edmund G. Reuter, *Studio*, Vol. 55, 1912.]

Rhead, Frederick Alfred (born 1856 died 1929)

Ceramic designer and craftsman. Studied at the Potteries and Newcastle Schools of Art, and worked as apprentice to Marc Louis Solon. Went to Wedgwood where he executed a vase in pâte-sur-pâte for the Paris Exhibition 1878. Art Director successively at Bodleys, Brownfields Pottery Guild (for whom he executed the Gladstone Vase 1888), Wileman & Co. Longton, and Wood & Sons Burslem. Joint author with his brother G. W. Rhead of *Staffordshire Pots and Potters*, 1906.

Rhinoceros vase

A large, ungainly, covered porcelain vase surmounted by a rhinoceros, made for Earl Fitzwilliam, Marquis of Rockingham, at Swinton, c.1826. The original is preserved at Wentworth House; a companion is in the Victoria and Albert Museum. It was painted by Edwin Steele.

[Illustrated W.B. Honey, *Old English Porcelain*, 1928, new ed. 1948.]

Rhodes, David (died 1777), Painter

In 1760 Rhodes is believed to have been in partnership with John Robinson of Leeds, an independent enameller. About 1769 he was taken into the service of Wedgwood, remaining with the firm until his death. An early Worcester dish in the Victoria and Albert Museum is marked 'Rhodes pinxit', and may have been decorated by him.

Richardson, George (born c. 1620 died 1687)

Slipware potter at Wrotham, Kent: married February 1643/4, to Mary Hubble (died 1687). The initials G R are found on tygs, candlesticks, jugs and other pieces from 1642 until 1675.

[J.W.L. Glaisher, Appendix to B. Rackham and H. Read, *English Pottery*, 1924.]

Riddle & Company, Lane End

China and lustre manufacturers. In 1835 the original partnership was dissolved, John Hartshorne and William Edwards withdrawing from the concern (*Staffordshire Advertiser*, 7 November 1835). In 1840 George Bryan also withdrew, leaving John Riddle and Arthur Lightfoot to continue the business in Union Square, Longton. The firm is listed under their name in 1851.

[*Staffordshire Advertiser*, 10 October 1840; *Directories*, 1851.]

Ridgway, Job (born 1759 died 1813)

Younger son of Ralph Ridgway master potter of Chell, who failed in 1766 and left Staffordshire for Swansea. He returned to Burslem c.1780 but after six months moved on to Leeds where he was converted; returned once more to Staffordshire 1781 and became a Wesleyan preacher and journeyman potter; started up as master potter in partnership with his brother George Ridgway (c.1758–1823) in 1792 at the Bell Works, Shelton, where he made 'blue-printed' earthenware; left his brother 1802 and built the Cauldon Works and house where in 1808 he started the manufacture of china; married Elizabeth Mayer (1755–1810) sister of Elijah Mayer; in 1797 he helped to found the Methodist New Connexion.

[Henry Wedgwood, *Job Ridgway*, n.d. (pamphlet).]

Ridgway family, Shelton and Hanley, Staffs. Earthenware and porcelain manufactories.

DATES AND PRINCIPALS

The family of Ridgway had extensive connections in the potteries from the end of the eighteenth century. In 1792 Job Ridgway and his brother George acquired the Bell Bank Works at Hanley, Staffordshire, and the partnership continued until 1802, when Job Ridgway established a separate factory at Cauldon Place. Job's two sons, John and William Ridgway, succeeded their uncle at the Bell Bank. In 1830 John Ridgway left to follow his father at the Cauldon works, while his brother William carried on and extended the Bell Bank.

Several other firms came under Wm. Ridgway's, and his son E. J. Ridgway's, ownership, including those formerly owned by Geo. and Thomas Taylor, Elijah Mayer, Palmer and Wilson, Toft and May, and Hicks, Meigh and Johnson. The whole concern, known as W. Ridgway & Son, was dissolved in 1854, and shortly afterwards the Bell works were purchased by Joseph Clementson.

John Ridgway owned the Cauldon works until 1859; later they were taken over by Brown, Westhead, Moore & Co.

Other members of the Ridgway family were in business in potteries in Poole and Hull.

WORK

In the various factories owned by the Ridgways all kinds of pottery and porcelain were made. In the time of Job Ridgway, blue-printed wares were produced, and also a type of porcelain akin to Swansea. Bone china of excellent quality was made at the Cauldon factory in the first half of the nineteenth century; designs used at the end of this period are very similar to those of Minton with whom Ridgway's seem to have been in competition.

Wm. Ridgway's son, E. J. Ridgway, is noted for his introduction of jasper wares which were manufactured with considerable success in the early and mid-nineteenth century. Stoneware articles of excellent design and finish were also made. The Ridgways pioneered several decorative processes, including the application of photography.

Specimens of works from the various factories are in the British Museum and Hanley Museum, Stoke-on-Trent.

[L. Jewitt, *Ceramic Art of Great Britain*, 1878.]

MARKS

Transfer-printed
1814-1830

Ridgway Pedigree

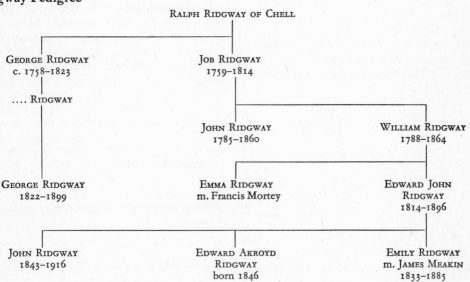

[*Staffordshire Advertiser* 30 January 1813, 5 September 1835; *Evening Sentinel* 20 May 1916; *Staffordshire Gazette*, 7 June 1814; Monuments, Bethesda Chapel, Hanley; J. C. Wedgwood, *Staffordshire Pottery and its History*, n.d.]

Rie, Lucie

Studio potter who produces stoneware, tin-glazed earthenware and porcelain characterised by bold striking forms, and rather austere decoration.

She was trained at the Kunstgewerbe-Schule, Vienna, under Michael Powolny. Came to London in 1938 and opened a studio at Albion Mews. Hans Coper has worked with her since 1947. Their marks are:

Hans Coper   Lucie Rie

[G.M. Forsyth, *Twentieth Century Ceramics*, 1934; G.W. Digby, *The Work of the Modern Potter in England;* 1952; Muriel Rose, *Artist Potters in England* 1955.]

Riley, John and Richard

Manufactures of china, stoneware, black lustred pottery, figures, cream-coloured tablewares, blue-printed and 'dipped' ware at Nile Street, Burslem from 1802 until 1814 and at Hill Works, Burslem from 1814 until 1828. John Riley died about 1827 and Richard Riley (who was born in 1770) in 1828. The manufactured stock which included 'a number of rich burnished sets of tea, dinner and dessert services' in bone china was announced to be sold on the 13 and 14 April 1831 in the *Staffordshire Advertiser* (2 April 1831).   *Plate 5.*

[*Staffordshire Advertiser*, 18 September 1830, 29 January, 5 February, 2 April 1831; *Pottery Mercury*, 18 October, 1 November 1828; S. Shaw, *History of the Staffordshire Potteries*, 1829; *Directories*, 1802–23; *Parish Registers, Burslem*.]

Rivers & Clews, Shelton, Staffs. Earthenware manufacturers

This firm was manufacturing in 1818. The impressed mark RIVERS appears upon lustred cream coloured ware in the Victoria and Albert Museum.

Robinson & Leadbeater, Stoke-on-Trent

The firm of Robinson & Leadbeater, parian manufacturers and modellers, Stoke-on-Trent, was started in Wharf Street and swiftly prospered. In 1865 they bought up Giovanni Meli's business in Glebe Street and in 1870 Leveson Hill's in Wharf Street. The partners in the concern were Edward James Leadbeater (born 1837 died 1911) who served his apprenticeship at Thomas Worthington's factory, Hanley, and James Robinson. The firm turned out a vast amount of decorative parian wares of good quality, including portrait busts, figures, etc. They used the mark:

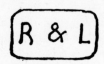

Impressed

[Obit. *Staffordshire Sentinel*, 28 March 1911; L. Jewitt, *Ceramic Art of Great Britain*, 1878; *Directories*.]

Robinson, Wood & Brownefield, Cobridge

John Robinson, John Wood and William Brownfield took over the Cobridge Pottery after the failure of Clews, in 1836. John Robinson died soon afterwards, but the firm continued under the same title until March 1841 when the partnership between 'Dorothea Robinson of Cheadle... widow and John Robinson, late of Lane End... manufacturers of earthenware, and John Wood and William Brownfield, both of Cobridge... manufacturers of earthenware under the style or firm of Robinson, Wood and Brownfield has been and stand dissolved, determined, and put an end to, upon and from the 12th day of March now last past'. (*Staffordshire Advertiser*, 31 July 1841). John Wood and William Brownfield continued the business until 1850 when John Wood died and William Brownfield became sole proprietor.

[*Directories*.]

Rockingham, Swinton, Yorks. Earthenware and porcelain manufactory.

DATES AND OWNERS

The Swinton Old Works or the Rockingham

Colour plate 16, STAFFORDSHIRE: *see page viii for caption*

(A) SUSSEX punchbowl, red earthenware with decoration inlaid in white clay under a yellow glaze, dated 1809. Height 4¼ inches, diameter 10 inches.

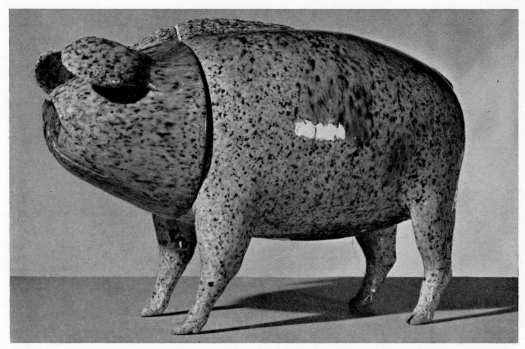

(B) SUSSEX earthenware jug and cup in the form of a pig, covered with a brown and yellow glaze, early nineteenth century. Rye (Cadborough). Height 6¾ inches, length 10⅛ inches.

PLATE 97

SUSSEX red earthenware jar with inlaid leaf decoration in white slip, 1811. Made at Chailey, Sussex. Height 8⅞ inches. *(Hanley Museum).*

PLATE 98

(A) SWANSEA dish, porcelain painted in colours, c. 1820, mark 'Swansea' impressed.
Length 20⅝ inches, width 15 inches.

(B) SWANSEA sugar-bowl, cover and stand, porcelain painted in colours and gilt. Mark (on stand) 'Swansea' printed in red, c. 1820. Bowl height 4⅝ inches, stand diameter 7¾ inches.

(C) SWANSEA plate, white earthenware, painted by W. W. Young. Marks 'P. Aegeria, P. Justina. P. Cardui' in black, c. 1802–10. Diameter 7½ inches.

PLATE 99

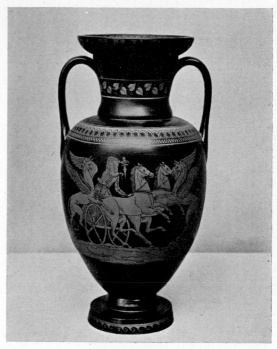

(A) SWANSEA food-warmer and cover with spirit-lamp, porcelain painted in colours and gilt, c. 1820. Height over-all 8⅞ inches.

(B) SWANSEA amphora, after the Greek, earthenware, nineteenth century. Height 14¾ inches, diameter 8⅜ inches.

(C) SWANSEA pot-pourri vase and cover, porcelain painted in colours and gilt, c. 1820. Height 9⅝ inches.

(D) SWANSEA spill-vase, porcelain, painted in colours by Thomas Baxter, c. 1820. Height 5 inches.

PLATE 100

SWINTON pair of vases, porcelain, painted by Edwin Steele, about 1825. Ht 10⅜ in. MINTON candlestick, porcelain painted in colours and gilt, c. 1840. Ht 8⅛ in.

SWINTON milk jug, porc., painted in colours and gilt, c. 1840. Ht 9⅞ in. Plate, porc., moulded, painted in colours and gilt. Mark 'B' incised and a griffin and 'Rockingham Works, Brameld', printed in red, c. 1825. Diam. 9¾ in. Sugar-basin cover and stand, porc., painted in colours and gilt. Mark 457 in red, c. 1830. Length 6⅝ in.

Two of a set of three spill-vases, porc., painted by Edwin Steele. Mark, a griffin and 'Rockingham Works, Brameld Manufacturer to the King' printed in crimson, c. 1830. Hts 4⅝ in. and 3¼ in. Spill-vase, porc., painted in colours and gilt, c. 1830. Ht 4½ in. Fruit dish, porc., painted in colours and gilt, c. 1830. Length 11 in. Spill-vase, porc., painted in colours and gilt, c. 1830. Ht 3⅛ in.

Inkstand, porc., painted in colours and gilt, c. 1830. Width 8 in. Vase and cover, porc., painted in colours and gilt, c. 1830. Ht 10½ in. Cup and saucer, porc., painted in colours and gilt, c. 1830. Ht, cup 2¾ in. diam. of saucer 5½ in.

PLATE 101

SWINTON (Rockingham Works) vases, porcelain, painted in colours and gilt by Edwin Steele, c. 1825. Height 8⅞ inches, and 13 inches.

PLATE 102

(A) TURNER stone china soup plate transfer-printed in blue under-glaze. Mark, 'TURNER' impressed, c. 1800–05. Diameter 9¼ inches. (*Arthur M. Moorby*).

(B) TURNER stone china dish, decorated with a 'Japan' pattern in colour and gold. Mark, Turner's patent, in red. c. 1800. Length 12 inches, width 8½ inches. (*Mrs Frank Nagington*).

PLATE 103

(A) WEST OF ENGLAND tyg, eleven handled, in brown-glazed red earthenware, dated 1682.
Diameter 10¼ inches.

(B) WEST OF ENGLAND (Wiltshire) posset-pot, earthenware with stamped and applied decoration under a dark
brown glaze, seventeenth century. Diameter 10⅛ inches.
(C) SOMERSET puzzle-jug, red earthenware with decoration incised through white slip under a yellowish glaze
splashed with green. Crock Street, dated 1791.
Height 7½ inches.

PLATE 104

WHIELDON WARE coffee-pot, with relief ornament under a mottled (tortoiseshell) glaze, c. 1760.
Height 8½ inches.

PLATE 105

(A) WHIELDON ware bowl and octagon dish., c. 1760. Bowl: dull brown and cream with irregular flecks and streaks, ht 4¾ inches. Dish. deep purple-brown, width 15 inches. *(Mrs Frank Nagington)*.

(B) WHIELDON figures of birds, earthenware, decorated with grey, slate-blue and yellow glazes, c. 1755–60. Heights, 7⅛ inches and 8½ inches.

PLATE 106

WHIELDON Staffordshire earthenware figure of a mounted soldier, coloured yellow, green and purple-brown. Possibly by Thomas Whieldon, c. 1750–60. Height 10 inches. *(Hanley Museum)*.

PLATE 107

(A) WHIELDON ware agate-handled knife and fork with blue, green and brown
veining, and agate-ware jug, c. 1750.
Fork 8 inches, haft 3⅛ inches; knife 9⅞ inches; haft 3½ inches; jug height 9 inches *(Mrs Frank Nagington)*.

(B) WHIELDON ware teapot with relief ornament and mask feet under a glaze stained with metallic
oxides, c. 1750. Length 6⅜ inches, height 4⅛ inches. *(Mrs Frank Nagington)*.

PLATE 108

ADAMS (Greengate Pottery) Tunstall, blue jasper-dip with white relief representing Ganymede and the Eagle. Mark, 'ADAMS' impressed, c. 1800. Height 6¼ inches, width 5 inches.

PLATE 109

(A) TURNER blue-grey and white jasper medallion, 'Cupid and the Eagle'. Mark, 'TURNER' impressed, c. 1785. Height 3¼ inches, width 4¼ inches. (*Arthur M. Moorby*).

(B) TURNER cream-jug, blue-jasper with white cameo decoration. Mark, 'TURNER' impressed, 1785 Height 2½ inches.

PLATE 110

NEALE & CO. cups and saucer decorated in old gold and green with Wedgwood pattern. Mark, 'Neale and Co.' impressed. c. 1790. *(Mrs Frank Nagington).*

(B) BARKER, black-basaltes ware cream-jug, mark 'BARKER' impressed, early nineteenth century. Height 4⅛ inches.

(C) CASTLEFORD cream-coloured earthenware plate, painted in black, made by David Dunderdale and Co., Mark, 'D.D. &.Co. CASTLEFORD', late eighteenth century. Diameter. 8½ inches.

PLATE III

(A) STAFFORDSHIRE cream-coloured earthenware tureen, made by Turner at Lane End, mark 'TURNER' impressed. Late eighteenth century. Width 17 inches.

(B) Cream-coloured earthenware jug, painted in enamel colours by William Fifield, probably Bristol, dated 1794. Height 6 inches.

(C) LEEDS cream-coloured earthenware plate with pierced rim and painted in green enamel, late eighteenth century. Diameter 9¼ inches.

PLATE 112

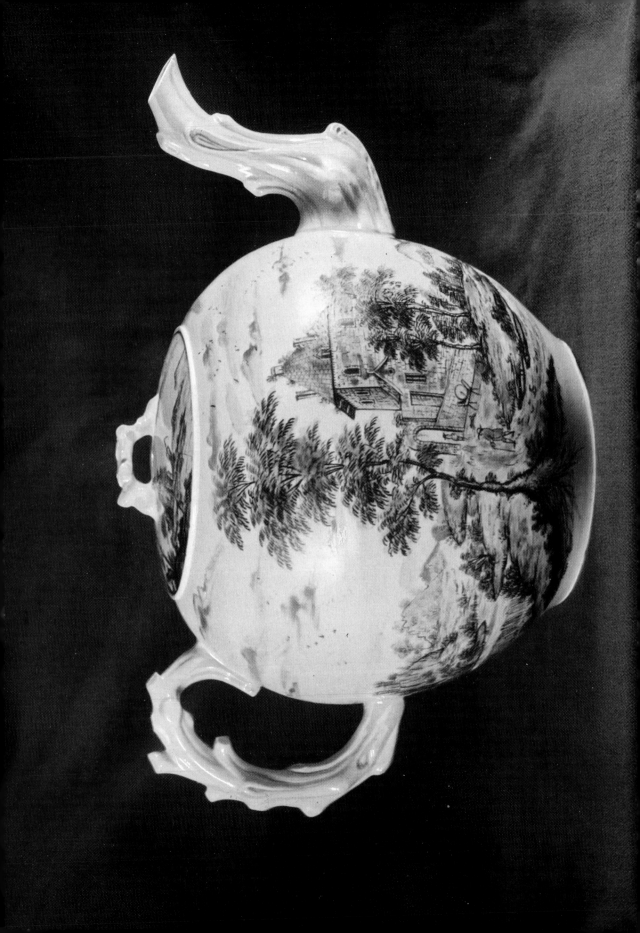

Works was founded about 1745 by Edward Butler. William Malpas made white and brown wares here in 1765, and later in the early 1780's Thomas Bingley & Co. made various types of earthenware.

From 1787 until 1806 the factory was linked to Leeds first as Greens, Bingley & Co. (1787–1800) and then as Greens, Hartley & Co. (1800–1806). Its wares are probably inseparable from those of Leeds or Staffordshire. In 1806 William Brameld took over, trading as Brameld & Co. and when he died in 1813, his three sons continued the factory producing earthenware of all kinds including the well-known manganese-brown Rockingham glaze, and the equally celebrated 'Cadogan' type teapot. About 1820 they started to make bone china of the Staffordshire type, got into financial difficulties, and in 1826 became bankrupt. The *Pottery Mercury* (15 March 1826) carried an announcement that the Swinton Pottery 'Late in the occupation of Messrs Brameld & Co., against whom a commission of bankrupt hath lately been awarded and issued' was to be let. The proprietors, according to Jewitt, appealed to Earl Fitzwilliam who granted them the financial resources to carry on, and the right to use the griffin passant crest as a trade mark. From 1820 until 1842 a large quantity of excellent china was made, usually in a florid, rococo taste.

MARKS

Painted in red   Impressed

ARTISTS

John Wager Brameld. Painter

Thomas Steele. (1771–1850). Fruit painter.

William Corden. (1797–1868). Landscape and figure painter.

John Speight.

Brentnall. Fruit and flower painter.

Collinson. Fruit and flower painter.

Llandig. Fruit and flower painter.

Tilbury. Landscape painter

Isaac Baguley. Foreman painter

John Cresswell.

Bailey. Butterfly painter.

John Speight, junior.

William Eley. Figure modeller.

WORK AND DISTINGUISHING CHARACTERISTICS

None of the earthenware known to have been made at Rockingham before 1765 has been identified, but after that date a type of brown stoneware, frequently indistinguishable from that made in Nottingham at the time, was produced.

Wares manufactured in the early years of the Brameld family's ownership are very similar to Leeds: cream-ware, stonewares including black basalts, marbled and 'tortoiseshell' articles were all made in the factory. A peach-shaped hot-water pot filled from the base and originally copied from a Chinese design became famous as the so-called 'Cadogan', and the brown manganese glaze used on these pieces was well-known as the 'Rockingham glaze'. The London dealer Mortlock ordered large numbers of Cadogans. The tea and coffee pots made at Rockingham were likewise extremely popular. They were most often glazed in a chocolate colour and lined with white.

From 1820 onwards the characteristic types of Rockingham porcelain were manufactured. Pieces made at this period are often over-ornate, decoration being extravagant, technically extremely skilled, yet lacking by excessive use of gilding, flowers in full relief, etc., the charm which some of the factory's simplest pieces possess. Amongst the latter are some biscuit figures and certain tablewares decorated with flowers on pale ground colours. A resemblance to Derby is noticeable, this being due to the fact that a number of Derby workmen and artists also worked at Rockingham.

Great vases such as the 'rhinoceros' vase in the Victoria and Albert Museum can hardly be paralleled as examples of the potter's skill in modelling and firing, but nearly all such large and elaborate productions are tasteless in their excess of ornament and are of interest simply as curiosities.

Colour plate 17 STAFFORDSHIRE: *see page viii for caption*

Dinner and dessert services were made to order, and in 1832 a most ambitious dinner service was made for King William IV. This was decorated with views of castles and country seats of the nobility, etc., and the expense of its production is said to have caused the firm considerable loss.

Examples are in the Victoria and Albert Museum, the British Museum, and Yorkshire Museum, York.

See BRAMELD, the DON POTTERY, and MORTLOCK.

[L. Jewitt, *Ceramic Art of Great Britain*, 1878.]

'Rockingham' glaze

A lustrous, purple-brown lead glaze (stained with manganese) made at the Rockingham factory, Swinton, early nineteenth century, and in Staffordshire.

Rococo style

An extravagant and vivacious style marked by use of scrolls, rockwork, seaweed, and other irrelevant motifs arranged capriciously. It flourished in England in mid-eighteenth century, and is more particularly associated with the porcelain houses (for example Chelsea), and factories manufacturing salt-glazed stoneware.

The style was revived during the first half of the nineteenth century by English porcelain factories when full relief modelling of flowers and other features, accompanied by florid painting and gilding, became the rule.

Rogers, John and George, Dale Hall, Burslem. Earthenware manufacturers

The brothers John Rogers (1760–1816) and George Rogers (1763–1815) potted at Dale Hall from 1780 (when they built the factory), until 1815 when George Rogers died. John Spencer Rogers joined his father at this time and the firm became John Rogers & Son.

John Rogers died in 1816 leaving large sums of money to charity, including £1,000 to the North Staffordshire Infirmary, but the firm continued under the same title until Spencer Rogers failed in 1842. The pottery was then purchased by James Edwards.

MARK

The usual mark was the name Rogers impressed sometimes with the addition of the sign for Mars or Iron:

WORK

The firm made good quality cream-coloured earthenware and blue-printed for the American trade, including engravings of Boston State House with an elaborate rose and forget-me-not border, and sentimental subjects such as 'The Adopted Child' and 'Love in a Village'. Well painted naturalistic sprays occur on cream-coloured plates in the Victoria and Albert Museum. *Plate 152 B.*

[*Staffordshire Advertiser*, 22 April 1815, 26 March 1842; *Directories*, 1818–1834; *Parish Registers*, Burslem; L. Jewitt, *Ceramic Art of Great Britain*, 1878.]

Roman Charity

One of the finest groups produced at the Chelsea porcelain factory c. 1769, modelled from an engraving by William Panneels after a picture of Rubens in the Prado, Madrid. It stands 16½ inches high and shows Pera offering her breast to the bearded Cimon who is bound with gilded chains. Fine examples in the British Museum, London, and the Irwin Untermyer Collection, New York.

[Y. Hackenbroch, *Chelsea and other English Porcelain in the Irwin Untermyer Collection*, 1957.]

Roman Lead-glazed Pottery

Glazed wares were manufactured by Roman potters during the 2nd century A.D. at a kiln at Holt in Denbighshire which has been excavated.

Rose de Barry

A popular misnomer for Rose Pompadour.

Rose-engine-turning

Basketwork patterns produced on the engine-lathe.

Rose, John (died 1841)

Founder of the Coalport factory. Rose purchased the Caughley Factory in 1799, and the moulds and stocks of Swansea and Nantgarw 1822–1823. He was awarded the 'Isis' Gold Medal of the Society of Arts for a leadless felspathic glaze in 1820 which was commemorated by one of the Coalport factory marks. The business was continued after his death by his nephew, William F. Rose (died 1864).

[L. Jewitt, *Ceramic Art of Great Britain*, 1878.]

Rose Pompadour

A colour introduced at Sèvres in 1757. The Chelsea Claret ground is believed to have been an imitation, introduced c.1760. The advertisement of 1768 cited by Nightingale mentioning 'Mazarean and Pompadour Sets' probably refers to this colour. Coalport produced a passable Rose Pompadour in nineteenth century.

[J. E. Nightingale, *Contributions towards the History of Early English Porcelain from Contemporary Sources*, Salisbury, 1881.]

Ross, James (born 1745 died 1821)

Engraver; apprenticed to Robert Hancock 1765. His signature appears on a number of Worcester porcelain specimens.

J Ross Vigorniensis sculp

[C. Cook, *The Life and Work of Robert Hancock*, 1948.]

Rossi, John Charles Felix, R.A. (born 1762 died 1839)

An associate of Bacon at Coade's factory. Studied at Rome. Patronised by Lord Egremont for whom he executed important commissions. A number of monuments by him may be seen in St. Paul's Cathedral, London.

Rosso Antico

The name given by Josiah Wedgwood to his red stoneware, which was a variation on the 'red porcelain' introduced into Staffordshire by Elers: 'We shall never be able to make the *Rosso Antico* otherwise than to put you in mind of a *red-Pot-Teapot*.' (Wedgwood to Bentley, 3 March 1776).

[*Letters of Wedgwood*, 1903.]

Roubiliac, Louis-François (born 1695 died 1762)

Son of a banker in Lyons: studied sculpture under the sculptor to the King of Saxony, Balthazar: returned to France and worked with Nicholas Coustou in Paris: came to England in 1720 and worked here for the rest of his life, leaving it only for a brief visit to Rome in 1752. He enjoyed the esteem of Walpole and became the most celebrated sculptor in England, his statue of Handel making him popular. Other and perhaps better works are his George I in Golden Square, and the Nightingale monument in Westminster Abbey.

His connection with the Chelsea porcelain factory has been the subject of considerable speculation. He belonged to the Soho circle of French expatriates, and Nicholas Sprimont was godfather of his daughter. The white royal busts have been attributed to him, as also have three large figures representing the senses of 'Sight', 'Smell' and 'Truth'. Roubiliac died in 1762.

Rowland, Edward

Landscape painter on porcelain at Pinxton. He was brother-in-law to John Cutts, of Pinxton and Shelton, Staffordshire

Rowley & Jervis, Stoke-on-Trent

Earthenware manufacturers at the close of the eighteenth century. The partnership between Josiah Rowley and Hugh Lucy Jervis was dissolved 14 January 1796 and the business continued in the name of Josiah Rowley. Hugh Lucy Jervis died in 1809, (*Parish Registers*, Stoke-on-Trent).

[*Staffordshire Advertiser*, 13 February 1796; *Directory*, 1796.]

Rowley, William (born 1785 died 1832)

Toy and figure manufacturer, Shelton.

Ruel, James, Fulham, London. Potter

A late eighteenth century maker of stoneware dishes, mugs, etc., for domestic use.

Ruscoe, William, Exeter

Artist potter with wide industrial and teaching experience in Stoke-on-Trent and Exeter. Author of *English Porcelain Figures 1744–1848* (1947) and *A Manual for the Potter* (1948).

Responsible, with Gordon Forsyth, for a revived interest in schools in early Staffordshire image toys. His marks are

Produced stonewares and slipwares, including figures in terra cotta, and images in the eighteenth century style.

Rye, Sussex. Earthenware manufactories

Two factories are known, the Cadborough Pottery and Belle Vue Pottery.

CADBOROUGH POTTERY

About 1807 a potworks was established at Cadborough brickyards by James Smith, which was continued by his son Jeremiah Smith (b. 1794 d. 1864), flockmaster, hop-grower and seven times Mayor of Rye. Country pottery was produced. Dated examples of early Rye pottery are uncommon. A canister in Brighton Museum inscribed 'G. and E. Chapman, Rye, Sussex, April 22, 1808' is ascribed to the factory. From about 1827 William Mitchell acted as manager of the works and in 1840 took over the business. In 1859 Mitchell took his son Frederick Mitchell into partnership and traded as Wm. Mitchell & Son. Henry also came into the business. About 1850 Fred. Mitchell experimented with applied decoration. Dated moulds with his initials show flower or leaf forms (verbena, oak, etc.).

In 1869 Fred. Mitchell obtained the lease of land in Udimore Road and started the Belle Vue Pottery. Country crockery continued in production at Cadborough, under William Mitchell (d. 1871) and his son Henry.

Manufactures included butter-pots, bowls, meat-pans, bottles, pitchers, etc. The well known 'Sussex Pig' was a speciality.

BELLE VUE POTTERY

Opened by Fred. Mitchell (d. 1875) for the production of rustic pottery with applied decorations. Jugs and other pots wreathed with hops are characteristic. After 1875 the business was continued by Mrs Mitchell and her nephew Frederick Thomas Mitchell (1864–1920). Realistic decorations were attempted. Pseudo-Palissy wares embellished with crawling reptiles were made and apparently enjoyed some popularity. 'Folding' jugs made by twisting the clay when soft indicate the taste of the factory.

MARK

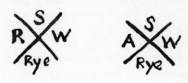

S

Sadler, John (Sadler & Green), Liverpool, Lancs. Transfer-printers

John Sadler, b. 1720 (son of Adam Sadler, a printer in New Market, Liverpool) invented a process by means of which pottery already glazed could be decorated with designs first engraved on copper plates, thence transferred to paper and finally on to the wares. The colours were then fired in a muffle kiln for fixing. This method of transfer-printing made possible the accurate reproduction of complex designs. Guy Green was Sadler's partner in an extensive business carried on in Harrington Street from the middle of the eighteenth century.

It is said that the process was actually invented by Sadler about 1750; not until 1756 was a form of patent contemplated (but never finalised) as Sadler and Green decided to keep the invention secret.

The firm is believed to have manufactured pottery, but its wares have not been identified with certainty. They decorated large quantities of Staffordshire and Liverpool earthenware; Wedgwood's Queen's ware was sent regularly to them for printing. Oriental patterns, portraits, illustrations from Aesop, tiles showing figures of actors and actresses – all these were printed at the factory. Much of the earlier work was in black, or black and red.

Sadler retired about 1770, and Green continued the business until 1799.

MARKS

SADLER   1756
             SADLER & GREEN

ARTISTS

Harry Baker. Engraver
J. Robinson. Engraver (also at Burslem)
Marked specimens are in the Victoria and Albert Museum.

See also TRANSFER PRINTING.

Sagger, Segger, Shrager

A baked fire proof clay box used by potters to enclose and thus protect fine ceramic wares during the firing process: 'they put them in the shragers to keep them from sticking to one another... and to preserve them from the vehemence of the fire...' (Plot, 1686); 'piles of seggars' (*Chambers' Edinburgh Journal*, 23 November 1839). SAGGER CLAY – clay from which saggers are made.

St Helen's, Lancaster

Several factories operating in St. Helens in the nineteenth century were all called 'mugworks'.
(1) The one with which the Herculaneum Pottery was connected, had been owned by Thomas Harley (died 1832) who shipped wares from here to a shop which he owned in Thomas Street, Dublin. Mort & Simpson of Herculaneum leased the factory in 1836. Thomas Bayley from Burslem was manager.
(2) Lightfoot's Potworks, Gerards Bridge, was founded by Thomas Lightfoot and carried on by his three sons after his death until it got into difficulties and closed down in the 1870's.
(3) Ravenhead Pottery was worked from 1830 until 1884. Benjamin Blake was at this factory in the later years.
(4) Sutton Heath was known as Swaines Pottery, and leased to Thomas and Francis Grace of Marshalls cross.
(5) Marshalls Cross was worked by Thomas Grace.

[T.C.Barker & J.R.Harris, *A Merseyside Town in the Industrial Revolution: St Helens 1750–1900*, 1954; Quoting *St Helens Newspaper; Wigan Gazette; Liverpool Mercury*, etc.]

Salisbury, Wiltshire

A type of slipware was made in or around Salisbury for about 200 years. Christening goblets in a dark red ware, manganese glazed and with incised decoration, bear dates from 1603. W. Zillwood is named as a potter in the district in the seventeenth century and some early pieces are marked W.Z.

Tableware decorated with views of Salisbury Cathedral and Stonehenge are sometimes marked with the name of a Mr Payne, who ordered various articles to be printed for sale at his warehouse in Salisbury, nineteenth century date.

Salopian

Mark used at Caughley: see Caughley.

Salt, Ralph (born 1782 died 1846), Marsh Street, Hanley

Worked from 1812 first as a lusterer and enameller on Miles Bank, and from 1828 as a manufacturer of figures and 'porcelain tablets' in Marsh Street. He made groups, individual figures and animals with bocages in the manner of Walton, enamelled in bright colours, sometimes lustred. They are frequently marked at the back SALT in large letters.

Impressed

Examples in Hanley Museum, Stoke-on-Trent.

His son Charles Salt (born 1810 died 1864) was a modeller, and is said to have continued the business, and modelled a bust of Wesley and introduced the manufacture of parian at his factory.

Plates 153 B.

[Reginald G. Haggar, *Staffordshire Chimney Ornaments*, 1955.]

Salt-glazed stoneware

Stoneware in which the glaze is formed by throwing salt into the kiln when it reaches the maximum temperature. The salt decomposes, forming sodium oxide and hydrochloric acid, the former combining with the alumina and silica of the surface of the wares to form a thin coating of glaze. Chief centres of salt-glazed stoneware manufacture were Fulham and Lambeth, Nottingham and Staffordshire.

Examples may be seen as follows:

Fulham and Lambeth: Victoria & Albert Museum and British Museum

Derbyshire: Derby Museum

Nottingham: Nottingham Castle Museum, Hanley Museum, Stoke-on-Trent, Victoria & Albert Museum

Staffordshire: Hanley Museum, Stoke-on-Trent, Victoria & Albert Museum, British Museum, City Art Gallery, Manchester, Fitzwilliam Museum, Cambridge, Ashmolean Museum, Oxford, Cecil Higgins Museum, Bedford.

Colour plate 13 and 17, and plates 89 A, B and C 90, 91, 92, 93, 94, 95, 96.

Salt Kit

A dome-shaped jar, surmounted by a knob and loop handle with a wide, circular opening at one side, used for storing salt, etc. Made in slipware in Yorkshire and in Weatherigg's Pottery, Penrith, and in stoneware at Portobello, Scotland.

Sandbox or Sand-Dredger

A box with a pierced top for sifting sand upon wet ink to dry it, used before the invention or popularity of blotting paper, c.1820.

See also POUNCE-POT.

Sandford, Moses, Hanley

Country potter producing 'Milk pans and Small Ware' in Hanley at 'the beginning of the eighteenth century'.

[E. Meteyard, *Life of Josiah Wedgwood*, 1865–1866.]

Sandys, Windsor

Gentleman, St Martin-in-the-Fields, London. Partner of John Dwight in the potworks at Sands End, Fulham, 1674–1676. His name is cited in an agreement of the Glass Sellers Company, London, concerning the manufacture of bottles.

[*Records of the Worshipful Company of Glass Sellers of London.*]

Sans, William, Staffordshire

The name is said to be found on certain dishes of about 1670 similar to those made by Thomas and Ralph Toft.

[S. Shaw, *History of the Staffordshire Potteries*, 1829.]

'Scale' ground

A distinctive Worcester decoration, sometimes referred to as 'fish-scale' design, but possibly derived from Meissen *Mosaik border*. George Savage suggests it may owe something in its origin to peacock's feather ornament seen on Italian maiolica and Near Eastern faience. Used at Worcester as early as 1761 in pink, and in 1763 in blue. The Chelsea *Catalogue* 1756 frequently cites wares decorated with 'Mosaic Border'.

[W. B. Honey, *Old English Porcelain*, new edn. 1948; G. Savage, *Eighteenth Century English Porcelain*, 1952.]

Schulen, Mary Ann and John William

Manufacturers of earthenware at Rope Lane and Bank Street, Ipswich in 1844.

[White's *Directory of Suffolk*, 1844.]

Scotland

A large number of factories manufactured earthenware in Scotland since the eighteenth century, the chief centres of production being Glasgow, Portobello and Prestonpans.

Colour plate 10 and plate 78.

'Scratch blue'

A class of white salt-glazed stoneware decorated with free floral, bird or other ornament and inscriptions incised upon the wares in the unfired 'green' state; into which a mixture of clay and cobalt, (the exact proportions of which were determined by experiments made by Gordon

Forsyth c.1922), was rubbed. Specimens dated from 1724-76 recorded. The majority of the dated pieces were made between 1745 and 1755.
[B.Rackham and H.Read, *English Pottery*, 1924.]
Plates 89 A and B.

'Scratch brown'

A type of salt-glazed stoneware decorated with incisions into which brown pigment or clay was introduced: Specimens dated 1723-24. Used on settles of 'Pew' Groups c.1730–40. Superseded by 'Scratch Blue'.
[Reginald G.Haggar, *English Country Pottery*, 1950.]

'Scratch cross' family

A group of porcelain wares, marked with an incised cross or one or two knife incisions on the inner surface of the footring, including pear-shaped jugs and cylindrical mugs, regarded by Bernard Rackham as indications of an experimental early Worcester paste (*Catalogue, Herbert Allen Collection of English Porcelain*, 1923). George Savage says they are probably workmen's marks and states that they also occur on 'indubitable Bow mugs' (*18th century English Porcelain*, 1952). F.A.Barrett records them as occurring possibly on Liverpool and Bristol porcelain also (*Worcester Porcelain*, 1953).

Scroll salt (Pully salt)

A form popular in Lambeth delftware of the seventeenth century based upon a silver prototype. F.H.Garner says the three projecting arms were used 'to support a napkin'. Penzer (discussing silver) says the arms were used to 'provide a stand for a flat porcelain fruit bowl'.
[F.H.Garner, *English Delftware*, 1948; N.M.Penzer 'Scroll Salts' *Apollo Annual*, 1949.]

Selman (Seltman) J & W, Tunstall, Staffordshire

Manufacturers of bronzed and earthenware toys, Gritten Street, Brownhills, Tunstall c.1865. Their figures became well known, and Scarratt in his *Old Times in the Potteries*, 1906, includes, Selman of the Flash in his short list of more important manufacturers.

Their mark was:

SELMAN
Impressed
[Reginald G.Haggar, *Staffordshire Chimney Ornaments*, 1955.]

Semi-China, Semi-Porcelain

Durable porcellanous earthenware: stone-china.

Sewell & Donkin, Newcastle-on-Tyne. Earthenware Manufactory

Sewell and Donkin manufactured Queen's Ware, pink lustred wares, pierced baskets like those of Leeds, etc. from about 1780. An attractive type of decoration combining transfer-printing with washes of colour was used on some pieces.

Articles are usually marked with the name of the firm, and some with the name of Sewell alone.

SEWELL

Sgraffiato

Cutting away, incising or scratching through a coating of slip to expose the colour of the underlying body. A technique popularly used in Devonshire, Somersetshire, South Wales, Staffordshire and Sussex, seventeenth to nineteenth centuries.
Plates 86 B, 87 D.

Shakespeare

The monument of William Shakespeare (1564-1616) in Westminster Abbey, London, sculptured in 1740 by Peter Scheemaker (1690-1771?) after a design by William Kent (1684-1748) became a popular model for Staffordshire pottery figures made by Enoch Wood, Aaron Wood and others from 1760 to 1840. The subject was engraved by Robert Hancock, 1770-75, and used on Worcester bell-shaped tankards.
[Reginald G.Haggar, *Staffordshire Chimney Ornaments*, 1955; C. Cook, *The Life and Work of Robert Hancock*, 1948.]

Sharpe, Thomas, Swadlincote, Burton-on-Trent, Staffordshire

Thomas Sharpe erected the Swadlincote potteries in 1821 and from 1821 until 1838 when he died they were worked by him alone. Subsequently the business was carried on by his brothers as Sharpe Bros & Co.

Marks used were:

T. SHARPE   THOMAS SHARPE
(impressed)   (impressed)

Manufactures included the usual cane or yellow wares, fireproof crockery, black lustre pottery, 'Rockingham' wares, and blue-printed earthenware. The 'Snufftaker' toby jug with Rockingham glaze was made here.

Shaw, Aaron, Burslem, Staffordshire
Manufacturer of stoneware and 'dipped' pottery about 1710.

Shaw, Amos and Kitty, Lane End, Staffordshire
Amos Shaw was listed as a potter at Steele Street, Lane End, in 1818; he died 2 May 1829 'upwards of 50 years' of age, and was described as a china manufacturer (*Pottery Mercury*, 9 May 1839).

Mrs Kitty Shaw continued the business until 1855 when the factory which, according to the sale advertisement 'had been in full work for many years past' and was in Chancery Lane, was put up for sale by auction.
[*Directories*. *Pottery Mercury*, 9 May 1829; *Staffordshire Advertiser*, 3 January 1835.]

Shaw, Moses, Burslem, Staffordshire
Recorded as making stonewares and freckled wares at the beginning of the eighteenth century.

Shaw, Ralph
A mid-eighteenth century potter at Cobridge who attempted to patent a kind of *sgraffiato* technique in 1732; described as 'litigious and overbearing'; name occurs on a documentary trailed slipware cradle (Hanley Museum) 'Made by Ralph Shaw October 31, Cobridge gate M T 1740 (or 46); died between 1754–59; said to have worked in France.

Ralph Shaw

[S. Shaw, *History of the Staffordshire Potteries*, 1829; W. B. Honey, *English Pottery and Porcelain*, 1933, later editions.]

Shaw, Simeon (born 1784 or 86 died 1859)
Born in Manchester; died in County Lunatic Asylum, Stafford; principle of an Academy for young Gentlemen, first in Hanley, later in Tunstall, Staffs, 1818–51; author of various works, including *History of the Staffordshire Potteries*, Hanley, 1829, an unreliable and inaccurate treatise but containing much information not to be found elsewhere and *The Chemistry of Pottery-* 1837. Supplied John Ward with information for his *Stoke-upon-Trent*. Shaw is still the chief published source for eighteenth century Staffordshire pottery history.
[MS copy of the Enumerator, Thomas Cooper, *Tunstall Census* 1841; S. Shaw, *History of the Staffordshire Potteries*, 1829; (the reprint of 1891 gives notes on the author) *Directories*, 1818–1851.]

Shaw, Alderman Thomas, Liverpool. Potter
Thomas Shaw owned a pottery in Liverpool at the beginning of the eighteenth century. A large plaque from this pottery dated 1716 was in the Liverpool Museum for many years. Other identified pieces are dated 1722 and 1756.
See also LIVERPOOL.

Shelley family, Lane End, Staffordshire. Potters
In 1783 Thomas and Michael Shelley are recorded as potters at Lane End, the former alone being listed in 1796. In 1798 the Upper Works formerly occupied by Thomas Shelley, deceased, was announced as to let (*Staffordshire Advertiser*, 1 December 1798).

Another Thomas Shelley (born 1773, still living 1842) and perhaps son of one of these earlier potters, stated that he 'commenced china-making' about 1798 but was obliged to abandon it 'from Misfortunes' after two or three years (*Government Report*, 1842).

Thomas Shelley of Lane Delph became bankrupt in 1804 (*Staffordshire Advertiser*, 11 February 1804).

Shelley, Susannah & Company, Hanley, Staffordshire

Susannah Shelley is first recorded in partnership with John Yates as a china manufacturer at the beginning of the nineteenth century. The partnership ceased 22 October 1803 (*Staffordshire Advertiser*, 29 October 1803), but the business was continued by Susannah Shelley & Co. In 1804, however, ovens, kilns, utensils were offered for sale (*Staffordshire Advertiser*, 29 and 22 December 1804), and in 1806 the buildings described as 'lately in the occupation of Yates & Shelley but now of Mr. James Greatbach' (*Staffordshire Advertiser*, 6 December 1806). Her china has not been identified.

Sheriff Hill Pottery, Newcastle-on-Tyne

This potbank was worked by George Patterson successor to Jackson & Patterson, supplying white earthenware to Norway.

Lewins and Parsons also had a factory for common earthenware here.

[L. Jewitt, *Ceramic Art of Great Britain*, 1878.]

Sherratt, Obadiah and Martha, Hot Lane, Burslem, Staffordshire

Started to manufacture figures and toys in Hot Lane, Burslem about 1815, but moved to Waterloo Road in 1828. After his death the business was continued by his son Hamlet about 1846, and subsequently by his widow Martha (née Vernon, born 1784). The firm closed down between 1851 and 1860.

Sherratt's figures are never marked.

A distinctive type of figure, boldly and sometimes crudely modelled, often of large size and usually mounted upon a table base with four or six legs is attributed to him. Characteristic are Bull Baiting Groups, Politos Menagerie, and the 'Death of Monrow'. Examples in Brighton, Newcastle-under-Lyme and the Stoke-on-Trent Museums.

Plate 155 A.

[Reginald G. Haggar, *Staffordshire Chimney Ornaments*, 1955.]

Shinner's Bridge, Dartington, Devonshire

A pottery started in 1947 and worked by Sam Haile and Marianne de Trey (his wife). See HAILE.

Shirley, William and Jesse, Hanley, Staffordshire

Little is known about these manufacturers of earthenware and bone china. The firm of William and Jesse Shirley was working at the Old Hall Works, Hanley until they failed in 1817 (*Staffordshire Advertiser*, 29 March, 20 September). 'Mr Shirley Senior, late Manufacturer of earthenware' died at Deptford 23 January 1827 (*Pottery Mercury*, 31 January).

Apparently Jesse Shirley then set up as a china manufacturer until his untimely death at the age of 37 in 1828 (*Pottery Mercury*, 11 October). The stock of manufactured goods offered for sale afterwards included 'an excellent assortment of BURNISHED GOLD CHINA... comprising 5 sets of blue and gold chimney ornaments; 12 sets of enamelled ditto. quantity of burnished gold china toys', and 'china chimney ornaments' (*Pottery Mercury*, 13 December 1828). For 16 years Jesse Shirley had been clerk of St John's Chapel, Hanley.

Shorthose, John (born 1768 died 1828)
Earthenware manufacturer.
Hanley, Staffordshire

A manufactory, variously known as Shorthose & Co., Shorthose & Heath, was founded in the second half of the eighteenth century and continued until 1823 when the firm became bankrupt. John Shorthose died in Brussels during a business trip. Cream-coloured wares, blue-printed, and black basaltes (possibly porcelain at a later date) were manufactured here. Some marks used are identical with those employed by other potteries, so that some pieces are difficult to ascribe to Shorthose with certainty.

The firm specialised in transfer-printing of a high quality, often with added enamel colouring, for the export trade.

The following marks were used:

Shorthose & C°

C C

Examples in Hanley Museum, Stoke-on-Trent.
[*Directories*, 1796–1818; *Pottery Mercury*, 2 and 16 February 1825, 14 June 1828; *Staffordshire Advertiser*, 24 December 1831.]

'Siamese Twins'

The 'monstrous' birth in Somerset, 19 May 1680, was recorded both on slipware – dish decorated in the *sgraffiato* technique – and Bristol delftware. The Kentish Siamese twins, Eliza and Mary Chulkhurst (who died in 1734 at the age of 34) were apparently made in redware in imitation of the 'Biddenden' cake.
[*Apollo*, Vol. 37, 1943; W. Hone, *The Every-Day Book*, Vol. 2, 1827.]

Sidney Cove medallion

Circular relief representing Peace, Art, and Labour attending upon Hope, designed by Henry Webber, modelled by William Hackwood, and 'MADE BY JOSIAH WEDGWOOD OF CLAY FROM SIDNEY COVE', New South Wales, 1789. The clay was sent by Governor Phillip to Sir Joseph Banks to be forwarded to Wedgwood.
[E. Meteyard, *Life of Josiah Wedgwood*, 1865–66.]

Simpson, Charles (born 1753 died 1827)

Manufacturer: confidential clerk to John Turner, the elder, and witness to his will in September 1785; continued in employment of younger Turners; advertised his willingness to accept post as book-keeper or partner 1802 (*Staffordshire Advertiser*, 9 January); married, 23 May 1793, Mrs Sarah Clive, mother of John Henry Clive; partner in firm of Turner, Glover & Simpson 1803–06 (*Staffordshire Advertiser*, 8 September, 17 November 1804, 27 March, 19 April, 5 July, and 13 September 1806); took a potworks at Sandyford, Tunstall, where he made cream-coloured earthenware, 1809–17, (P. W. L. Adams, *John Henry Clive*, 1947); factory announced for sale 1814 and to let 1817 (*Staffordshire Advertiser*, 29 January 1814, 20

September 1817); died Newfield Hall 11 November 1827; Mrs Simpson died 3 June 1833 (tombstone, Newchapel Churchyard).

Simpson, John, Burslem

In 1671 the Tunstall Court Rolls record a John Simson (sic) as one of the inhabitants of Burslem, and according to Wedgwood's MS List of potters working in Burslem about 1710 John Simpson was making 'Red dishes & pans' at Rotten Row. It has been suggested that the moulded octagonal slipware dishes decorated with pomegranates and the initials 'I.S.' were probably made by him (Reginald G. Haggar, *English Country Pottery*, 1950). Round dishes with two gauntlet gloves in the centre, and four fleur-de-lis and four lions alternating occur with the same initials. These were probably inspired by stumpworks pictures.

Other John Simpsons, recorded in Wedgwood's list, made different kinds of ware, for example, John Simpson of Chell 'black and mottled wares', also in Rotten Row; and another John (nicknamed 'Double Rabbit') wares of uncertain category at the West end of the town.

Simpson, Moses, Hanley

Shaw records this potter at Hanley, but apart from stating that he belonged to the family of Bulky Simpson' is unable to describe his work. The initials, M.S. which occur on some slipware pieces may refer to this potter.
MARK

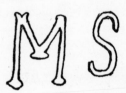

Simpson, Ralph, Staffordshire. Potter

The name of Ralph Simpson is found on various pieces, and may be that of a potter born 1651 died 1724. A dish of a kind similar to Toft ware, marked with Simpson's name and decorated with a pelican, is in the Victoria and Albert Museum. In the British Museum there is a dish with a portrait of King William III, and in the Fitzwilliam Museum, Cambridge, another with a bust of a king, possibly Charles II, which may be Simpson's work. But since wares of this type were made by a number of potters in the seventeenth and eighteenth centuries, it is extremely difficult to ascertain accurately either date or maker.

Colour plate 16 and plate 84.

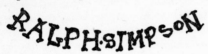

Simpson, Richard, Burslem

Richard Simpson is one of two makers of 'Red dishes' listed in the Wedgwood MS as potting at the beginning of the eighteenth century. His potworks was near the pump, at the West end of Burslem.

Simpson, William

Name recorded on slipware posset-pot, dated 1685. A William Simpson is recorded in the Tunstall Court Rolls 1671, and occurs also in Josiah Wedgwood's MS list of potters working 1710–15, as making cheap earthenware at Stocks, Burslem. Another William Simpson made 'clowdy and mottled' in Hanley at the same period. William Simpson, potter, of Hanley, died in 1748.

[*Parish Registers; Tunstall Court Rolls;* J.C.Wedgwood, *Staffordshire Pottery and its History,* n.d.]

Sims, John

Proprietor of a porcelain decorating establishment at Five Fields Row, Pimlico, in 1792. Zachariah Boreman joined this establishment in 1794 and painted 'Derby' landscapes for him. James Turner, flower painter and James Plant, figure and landscape painter, worked for Sims.

Slater family

A well known family of pottery decorators and designers extending over four generations. The most important were:

WILLIAM SLATER (born 1784 died 1867) who was born at Normanton, Derby, and worked at Derby, in London, at Derby again as decorating manager, and finally in Staffordshire for Davenports: died in Burslem.

WILLIAM SLATER (born 1807 died 1865) designer at Davenports, 1833–65.

JOSEPH SLATER (born 1812 died 1896) designer, gilder and crest painter at Derby, S. Alcock & Co. Burslem, and Mintons Stoke until 1875. Later he was head of the majolica dept. of Brown, Westhead, Moore & Co., Shelton.

ALBERT SLATER, son of Joseph: flower painter at Mintons', subsequently worked for Pinder, Bourne & Co., and Minton Hollins & Co.

JOHN SLATER, another son of Joseph: Art Director of Doultons of Burslem.

FREDERICK SLATER, son of Albert: modeller at Belleek Pottery, Fermanagh, Ireland.

[W.Scarratt, *Old Times in the Potteries,* 1906.]

Slave Emancipation Society Seal

Modelled by Hackwood and produced by Josiah Wedgwood for the Slave Emancipation Society 1787. Wedgwood was a member of its committee and organised County Meetings in Staffordshire in support of the cause. Seals and cameos were made in large quantities and in various bodies, showing the kneeling, chained slave. Inscription 'Am I not a man and a brother'.

[E.Meteyard, *Life of Josiah Wedgwood,* 1865–66.]

Slee's Pottery, Leeds, Yorkshire

Commenced in 1888 for the manufacture of cream-coloured ware to the patterns of the Leeds Pottery. The body is said to be inferior to that of the earlier factory, but the moulded and pierced designs are well executed. Marks used are those of the original factory.

Slip

Clay reduced to a liquid batter, used for making, coating, or decorating pottery; 'these (clays) mixed with water they make into a consistence thinner than a syrup, so that being put into a bucket it will run out through a quill; this they call slip, and is a substance wherewith they paint their wares'.

Plate 16.

[R.Plot, *Natural History of Staffordshire*, 1686.]

Smalt (Smalts)

The deep blue of cobalt oxide, also sometimes known as smales.

Smear glaze

A thin deposit of glaze upon the surface of pottery produced by smearing the inside of the saggar in which the ware is to be fired with the glaze solution. This vaporises in the heat of the oven and forms a surface deposit upon the wares within the saggar. Sometimes mistaken for salt-glaze.

Smethwick, near Birmingham

Site of the Ruskin Pottery founded by W.Howson Taylor. See TAYLOR (HOWSON).

Smith, Joseph, Tunstall, Staffordshire

Manufacturer of earthenware at Tunstall in the second half of the eighteenth century. He is recorded as potting in Tunstall in 1784 (*Jurors Book*, Salt Library, Stafford) and 1796. The factory was announced for sale or to let in 1802 (*Staffordshire Advertiser*, 3 July).

A firm called Smith & Steele was listed in *Holden's Directory*, 1805.

Smith, Sampson (born 1813 died 1878), Longton, Staffordshire

'Manufacturer of all kinds of burnished and ENAMELLED CHINA GOLD AND SILVER LUSTRES and FIGURES IN GREAT VARIETY' (advert. Jones's *Mercantile Directory of the Pottery District*, 1864); starting in 1846 as a pottery decorator, from about 1850 until 1859 he made earthenware figures of the 'flat back' type at the Garfield Pottery, High Street, Longton, and from 1859 until his death at the Sutherland Pottery. His figures are often large in size and comprise 'China Dogs' of all kinds and sizes, celebrities, cottages, toby jugs and castles. The business was continued after his death until 1888 by his executors; from 1888–1912 by Adderley & Tams; from 1912 by John Adderley and W.H. Davies until 1918 when figure making was abandoned; from 1918 until today by Barker Bros, who revived the manufacture of figures about 1948 using some of the original moulds. The factory still operates under the style Sampson Smith Ltd.

Figures were of simple type, modelled for easy delivery from 3 part moulds, and sparingly coloured. Some were decorated with a rich oven blue and bright enamels. Others with flesh tints, a few accents of colour and touches of gold. Marks used are:

In relief underneath dogs

[Reginald G. Haggar, *Staffordshire Chimney Ornaments* 1955.]

Smith, William (born 1790 died 1858), Farnborough, Hampshire

Farmer-potter at Farnborough, Hampshire, 1819–58; made country pottery for farmhouses and articles for use in hospitals and prisons, also some earthenware toys.

[G.Bourne, *William Smith, Farmer and Potter*, 1919.]

William Smith & Co, Stockton-on-Tees, Yorkshire. Earthenware manufacturer

An earthenware manufactory founded by William Smith in 1824. In 1826 the firm became Wm. Smith & Co.

They were chiefly imitators of Wedgwood wares. About 1848 they were restrained by an injunction applied for by Wedgwoods from using the latter's name on their productions (spelt WEDGEWOOD on Smith's ware). White and cream-coloured earthenware was made.

A marked example – a saucer with a faint blue glaze and ridge pattern painted in blue – is in the British Museum. Other examples in the Yorkshire Museum, York.

W.S. & Co's
WEDGEWOOD QUEEN'S WARE

W.S. & Co's
STOCKTON

experimental porcelain factory at Newcastle-under-Lyme, but now known (because of excavations made on the site) to be the production of William Littler of Longton Hall, or of Jenkinson at the same works.

Most of the models are known in salt-glazed stoneware or Whieldon-type earthenware

[R. Pococke, *Travels in England*, 1750–51; Mrs D. Mac-Alister, *Transactions, English Ceramic Circle*, 1933 and *Apollo*, 1927; G. Savage, *18th Century English Porcelain*, 1952.]

Sneyd Green, Burslem, Staffordshire

Three medieval kilns were excavated at a site near the medieval trackway from Hulton Abbey to Rushton Grange in 1953–54. A large quantity of pitcher fragments were recovered from these sites comprising jugs and dishes. Some complete oval hand-made dishes found here would seem to have been used for cooking fish. Most of the pottery from these kilns was of thirteenth and fourteenth century date.

During investigations important types of white on red slipware were brought to light. These date from c.1650–c.1730.

[Geoffrey Bemrose, *Transactions, North Staffs. Field Club*, 1954–5.]

Sneyd, T, Hanley, Staffordshire

Name found upon red and other coloured jugs in crude imitation of the Portland Vase. Probably early nineteenth century:

T. SNEYD
HANLEY

Snizer, Lambeth

Snizer is named as a potter in Lambeth, and is said to have been the last maker of delftware. Nothing is known, however, about the dates and exact nature of his work.

'Snowman' figures

Porcelain figures heavily glazed with a thick, opaque, glassy glaze, obscuring the modelling, sometimes identified as the production of an

Snufftaker

A form of standing toby jug shaped like an ugly hunch-back, taking a pinch of snuff. Usually made in earthenware covered with a lustrous brown 'Rockingham' glaze. Made at Rockingham and in Staffordshire from c.1795.

Soapstone (Soaprock)

Soapstone or steatite was first used as an ingredient of the English soft-paste porcelain paste at a Bristol factory, and was adopted as the basis of early Worcester porcelain. Benjamin Lund, the Bristol Quaker brass-founder, was licensed to quarry soaprock or soapstone at Gew Graze near Mullion 7 March 1748. Other prospectors for porcelain-making materials are recorded, including Baddeley & Yates from Staffordshire, who on 1 January 1760 were granted a soaprock licence from the Lord of the Manor of Erisey in the Lizard Peninsula.

[E. Morton Nance, 'Soaprock Licenses', *Transactions, English Ceramic Circle*, 1935.]

Soft-paste porcelain

Porcelain which is both softer as a material than true or hard-paste porcelain, and less refractory and therefore requiring a less intense heat to fuse it. It differs also from hard-paste in that the glaze of hard-paste is closely allied to the nature of the body and may be fired with it, whereas soft-paste porcelain is given a lead glaze which is fired at a second (glost) firing at a lower temperature in the glost-oven.

Solon, Leon Victor (born 1872)

Son of Marc Louis Solon: the foremost ceramic exponent of *L'Art Nouveau* styles: studied at Hanley and South Kensington; Art Director and Chief Designer at Mintons, 1900–1909. Much influenced by the decorative designs of Mucha. Went to America in 1909 and set up as an interior decorator.

[Reginald G. Haggar, *Art Education in the Potteries*, 1953; *Evening Sentinel*, 8 May 1954.]

Solon, Marc Louis (born 1835 died 1912)

Ceramic artist of great resource and originality; worked at the Sèvres factory, where he developed the technique known as *pâte-sur-pâte*, or in France *pâte d'application*, c.1859; came to England 1870 and was employed by C. M. Campbell at Minton's as an artist in pâte-sur-pâte until 1904; wrote extensively on ancient pottery, notably *Art of the Old English Potter*, 1885; *Brief Account of Pâte-sur-pâte* (originally published in *Studio*, 1894), 1906; *Brief Account of Old English Porcelain*, 1903, etc.

Solon never repeated his decorations. Each vase or plaque is therefore a unique creation of the artist.

Alboin Birks and F. A. Rhead were his pupils.

His signature is found:

Soqui (Saqui)

Monsieur Soqui, a bird-painter alleged to have come from Sèvres, was described as an 'excellent painter and enameller'. He worked at Plymouth and Bristol in a style characteristised by thickly stippled strong colour with faint suggestions of remote foliated landscapes and first identified by Bernard Rackham.

[*Burlington Magazine*, Vol. 25, 1914.]

Southampton, Hampshire

Symon Wooltus and his son are known to have made stoneware in Southampton from about 1660 until 1671. Their wares were probably of Rhenish type, closely resembling the imported stoneware of the period.

Spa Fields, Islington, London

Site of Randall & Robins' enamelling establishment, early nineteenth century.

Spängler, Jean Jacques

Son of the Director of the Zürich porcelain factory, at which factory he learnt the craft of ceramic modelling. In 1790 Spängler signed an agreement to work at Derby for three years, but appears to have been of a restless temperament, and after attempting to return to the Continent in 1792 was arrested and imprisoned at Ramsgate. He returned for a short time to Derby afterwards, but little more is known of him. A few Derby models can be attributed to Spängler with certainty.

Plate 44 A.

Spode, Josiah, Stoke-on-Trent, Staffordshire. Earthenware and porcelain manufacturer.

DATES AND OWNERS

The Spode factory was founded by Josiah Spode (born 1733 died 1797) in 1770; first apprenticed to Whieldon of Fenton in 1749, he became manager of the works owned by Turner and Banks at Stoke at the age of twenty-nine. On the death of Banks in 1770, Spode took over the factory on mortgage. By 1776 he was making earthenware in his own name, trade was increasing, and he was engaged on extensive pioneer work to improve his productions. He died in 1797, leaving a prosperous business to his son, Josiah Spode (b. 1754, d.1827). A grandson of the founder, Josiah Spode III, succeeded him, and the factory was carried on under his ownership until his death in 1829. The firm was bought from his executors in 1833 by Wm. Taylor Copeland, already a partner in the business in the time of the third Josiah Spode. During the period 1833–1847 the title was Copeland & Garrett. Thereafter, and up to the present day, the firm has been known by Copeland's name alone – sometimes as Copeland, late Spode – and is still owned by descendants of Wm. Taylor Copeland.

MARKS

Printed in purple

Stone China

Printed in blue

SPODE $Spode\ L.518$

in red

COPELAND
& GARRETT

ARTISTS

Artists did not usually sign their work on Spode pieces, and only very few are known by name. Thomas Lucas, an engraver, and a painter named James Richards, came to Spode's from Caughley. Henry Daniel, a gilder and enameller who joined the firm in 1802, invented a process for decorating porcelain in raised unburnished gold. Many fruit and flower painters were employed at the factory. Later artists include Thomas Battam, Robert F. Abraham, C.F. Hürten, Lucien Besche, and Thomas Hassall.

WORK

The first Josiah Spode inherited a tradition of earthenware manufacture to which he adhered in the early years of his ownership of the factory; the favourite oriental designs of the period were used and improved, the transfer-printing in blue underglaze being especially successful. His work to improve the quality of transfer-printing greatly affected the future use of this process: formerly designs had been printed in hard outline, filled in afterwards with enamel colours. Spode introduced a softer outline in colours blending with the enamels afterwards used, achieving a harmony of design and colour never before obtained. In later patterns much of the transfer-print is left unpainted, only small portions of the design being enamelled afterwards. This improved method of printing enabled attractive tableware to be made comparatively cheaply. He also made jasper, black Egyptian and black-printed wares of good quality.

Josiah Spode soon turned to the manufacture of porcelain. After the expiry date of Cookworthy's patent for making porcelain from Cornish china-clay and china-stone, Spode took this basic recipe (on which he had been experimenting for several years), adding to it calcinated bone, which combination of ingredients produced a bone-china of fine quality, transparent and durable. This bone-china, or bone-porcelain, was to become the basic formula for china made by future generations of potters, and still remains a standard for present-day manufacturers. His son is credited with the introduction of Spode felspar and stone-china, the former akin to porcelain in its hard transparent body.

In the first half of the nineteenth century the Spode and Minton factories were rivals in both artistry and output. Copeland, and later his son, managed the commercial side of the firm, and the alliance of Spode and Copeland resulted from the outset in a highly successful manufactory. Much of the ware made from 1785 onwards was sold through the firm's London warehouse.

Advances in mechanisation owed much to Spode's initiative. Steam engines of a then advanced type were used to drive grinding pans and turner's lathes early in the factory's history. At the same time new kilns were installed to enable heat to be regulated more exactly.

Spode was appointed potter to the Prince of Wales in 1806.

SUBJECTS AND DISTINGUISHING CHARACTERISTICS

Early earthenware is usually easily distinguishable, as is most Spode work, and all pieces were almost invariably marked from 1800 onwards. Some reproductions of Meissen and early Worcester have had their marks removed by grinding, but identification is still possible: Spode's paste was considerably softer than that of Meissen, and the colours used in Worcester reproductions are on the whole brighter than those of the originals. Chelsea colours and types of design were used from time to time.

In the early years, the most popular Spode pieces were in the Chinese style or so-called Imari patterns. These were produced at an earlier period than those in a similar manner afterwards made in vast quantities at Worcester and Derby. The peacock pattern and other designs originating in *famille rose* porcelains were also highly successful.

In porcelain plates and dishes of unusual form were made as a departure from the circular and oval shapes traditionally used. Ground colours – dark blues, reds, yellow, green and lavender amongst others – of very rich appearance are characteristic, and most often found in conjunction with motifs of flowers and fruit, birds, etc. Designs became more and more ambitious and the demand for extravagant decoration grew with a growing industrial prosperity in the country at the time. Gilding was profuse and often detracted from the charm of the design itself. Stippled or solid gold grounds are frequent. Designs reminiscent of Sèvres and other continental porcelain were extensively used.

At the same time a form of decoration traditionally English is found; landscapes were painted in panels surrounded by coloured borders, garlands of flowers etc., some of these pieces being extremely effective.

This latter kind of ornamentation has a charm inclined to be lost in more pretentious Spode pieces which are often over-decorated and too extravagant to appeal to present-day taste. In all their productions, however, the technical skill and quality of Spode work is unsurpassed.

Specimens are in the Victoria and Albert Museum, the British Museum and the Spode-Copeland Museum, Stoke-on-Trent.

Colour plates 11 and 12 and plates 79–80.

[L. Jewitt, *Ceramic Art of Great Britain*, 1878; S.B. Williams, *Antique Blue and White Spode*, 1948; Arthur Hayden, *Spode and his Successors*, 1924; S. Shaw, *History of the Staffordshire Potteries*, 1829.]

Spode, Samuel (born 1758 died 1817),
The Foley, Lane End, Staffordshire

Stated to have been the last of the salt-glaze potters in Staffordshire. He is known to have manufactured earthenware from about 1790 until 1807 or later.

[*Directories; Staffordshire Advertiser*, 1 February 1817.]

'Sponged' ware
A crude, easily-recognised, peasant style of decoration achieved by free painting and by dabbing the ware with a sponge impregnated with pigment; originally made by William Adams of Tunstall, and because of its 'bright fancy character' extensively exported. James Beech of Tunstall made similar wares.

[L. Jewitt, *Ceramic Art of Great Britain*, 1878.]

Sporting subjects
The adoption of sporting subjects for the decoration of earthenware, stoneware, and porcelain provides many clues to changing social habits. Earlier such decorations were severely conventionalized to meet the requirements of sprig-moulded relief decorations, but the development of painting techniques and of transfer-printing made possible more realistic and graphic representations of such subjects.

COURSING: A popular subject for relief ornament upon mugs and tankards made in stoneware at Fulham throughout the eighteenth century. It was less frequent as a transfer-print.

FOX HUNTING: Common on late eighteenth and early nineteenth century printed wares.

COCK FIGHTING: A view of a cockpit after an engraving by Hogarth was used as a transfer-print on cream-coloured earthenware c.1780. A realistic printed-and-enamelled representation of each sequence of a cock-fight was popular in Staffordshire in the first half of the nineteenth century. Dated and inscribed jugs and bowls are known. Many were made by Elsmore & Forster of Tunstall.

BEAR-BAITING: Jugs in the form of bears hugging a dog are typical products of Staffordshire and Nottingham manufacturers of salt-glazed stoneware.

SHOOTING:

BULL-BAITING: Popular as a chimney orna-

Colour plate 18, STAFFORDSHIRE: *see page viii for caption*

WEDGWOOD vase of dark blue jasper-ware with reliefs in white, copied from an ancient Roman glass vase in the British Museum known as the 'Portland Vase'. Made at Etruria, Stoke-on-Trent, first half of the nineteenth century. Height 10 inches, diameter 7½ inches.

PLATE 113

(A) WEDGWOOD vase, agate ware. Made at Etruria, 1770–80. Mark 'Wedgwood & Bentley Etruria'. Height 12¾ inches.

(B) WEDGWOOD tripod incense-burner, red earthenware, covered with gold ('copper') lustre. Mark 'Josiah Wedgwood Feb 2. 1805'. Etruria. Height 5¾ inches.

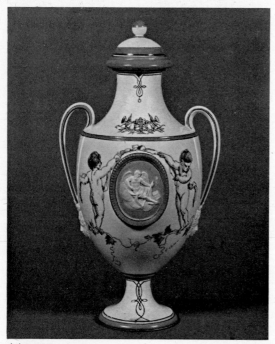

(C) WEDGWOOD vase and cover, cream-coloured earthenware enclosing two medallions of blue jasper-ware. Signed by Emile Lessore, mark 'Wedgwood' & 'WUQ', 1862. Height 9¾ inches.

(D) WEDGWOOD vase of black-basaltes ware. Mark 'Wedgwood' impressed. Etruria, c. 1785. Height 9 inches.

PLATE 114

(A) WEDGWOOD teapot and cover, red stoneware. Mark, imitation Chinese seal-mark, impressed. Etruria, c. 1760–70.
Height 5¼ inches, width 6¼ inches.

(B) WEDGWOOD teapot and cover, red stoneware. Mark 'Wedgwood' impressed.
Etruria, late eighteenth or early nineteenth century.
Height 3¼ inches, width 6¼ inches.

(D) WEDGWOOD teapot and cover, sage-green jasper dip with white reliefs. Mark 'Wedgwood' impressed. Late eighteenth century.
Height 5 inches.

(C) WEDGWOOD coffee-pot, black-basaltes ware, painted in enamel colours. Mark 'Wedgwood' impressed. Etruria, c. 1815. Height 6½ inches, diameter 4½ inches.

PLATE 115

(A) WEDGWOOD cup and saucer, cream-coloured earthenware, printed in purple. Etruria, printed at Liverpool, c. 1775. Cup, height 1¾ inches, diameter 3 inches; saucer, diameter 5 inches. WEDGWOOD milk-jug and cover, cream-coloured earthenware, printed in purple. Etruria, printed at Liverpool, c. 1775. Mark 'Wedgwood' impressed. Height 6½ inches, diameter 3¼ inches.

(B) WEDGWOOD dish, cream-coloured earthenware, painted in colours. Etruria, c. 1780. Diameter 11⅝ inches. WEDGWOOD dish, cream-coloured earthenware. Etruria, c. 1780. Height 5¾ inches. WEDGWOOD milk-jug, cream-coloured earthenware, painted in brown. Etruria, c. 1780. Ht 5½ inches.

PLATE 116

(A) WEDGWOOD dessert-plate, earthenware, moulded in low relief and covered with a green glaze. Mark 'Wedgwood' impressed. Etruria, c. 1860. Diameter 8⅜ inches.

(B) WEDGWOOD plate, porcelain, painted in colours and gilt. Mark 'Wedgwood' printed in red. Etruria, c. 1815. Diameter 8⅜ inches.

(C) WEDGWOOD plate, porcelain, painted in colours with a view of 'Saltram, Devon' and gilt. Etruria, c. 1815. 'Mark, Wedgwood' printed in red. Diameter 8½ inches.

(D) WEDGWOOD plate, earthenware, painted in colours. Mark, 'Wedgwood' impressed. Etruria, c. 1840. Diameter 8⅝ inches.

PLATE 117

(A) WEDGWOOD cruet. Cream-coloured earthenware. Mark 'Wedgwood' impressed. Etruria, c. 1770. Stand, length 11¼ inches, width 6¾ inches. Bottles, height 5½ inches, diameter 2 inches.

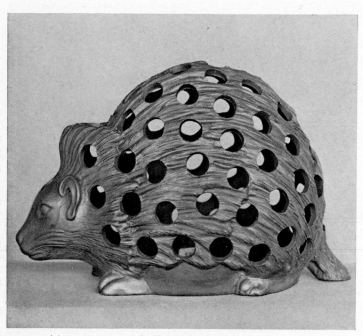

(B) WEDGWOOD bulb-pot in form of a porcupine, black-basaltes ware.
Etruria, late eighteenth century.
Height 6¾ inches, length 10⅛ inches.

(C) WEDGWOOD piggin, red stone-ware. Probably made at Burslem, c. 1765. Height 2½ inches, diameter 2¾ inches.

PLATE 118

(left) (A) WEDGWOOD tureen and cover, cream-coloured earthenware, painted in blue enamel and gilt. Mark 'Wedgwood' impressed. Etruria, c. 1790. Height with cover, 6½ inches. *(right)* (B) WEDGWOOD cup, cover and saucer, cream-coloured ware, painted in red and brown. Mark 'Wedgwood' impressed. Etruria, late eighteenth century. Cup, height 4 inches, diameter 3¼ inches. Saucer, diameter 5⅜ inches.

(C) WEDGWOOD basin, earthenware, printed in dark brown, painted in red, blue, green, and gilt. Mark 'Wedgwood' impressed. Etruria, 1st half nineteenth century. Height 2⅞ inches. Diameter 5¾ inches.

(D) WEDGWOOD cup and saucer, porcelain with decoration painted in colours and gilt. Mark 'Wedgwood' printed in red. Etruria, c. 1815. Cup, height 2⅝ inches, diameter 3 inches. Saucer, height 1⅛ inches, diameter 5 inches. (D)

PLATE 119

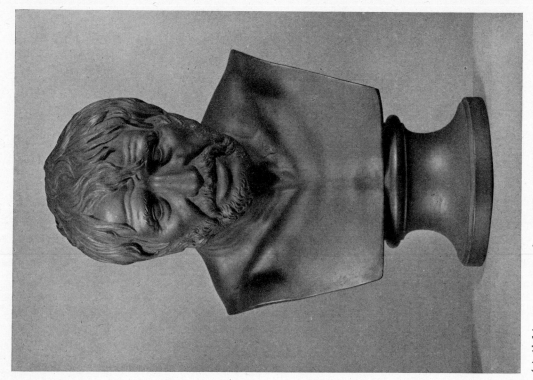

(A) (*left*) WEDGWOOD bust of Seneca, black-basaltes ware. Etruria, c. 1785. Height 17½ inches, width 11½ inches. (B) (*right*) WEDGWOOD candlestick, earthenware, covered with 'silver lustre' (platinum) with a pattern reserved by the resist process. Mark 'Wedgwood' impressed. Etruria, early nineteenth century. Height 6 inches.

PLATE 120

WEDGWOOD bridal group, earthenware, modelled by Arnold Machin, R.A. Height 10¼ inches.

PLATE 121

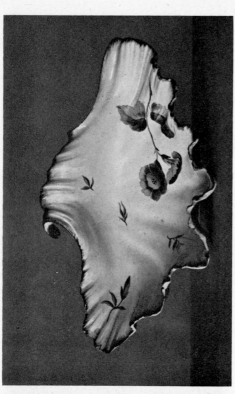

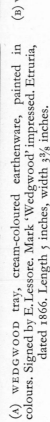

(A) WEDGWOOD tray, cream-coloured earthenware, painted in colours. Signed by E. Lessore. Mark 'Wedgwood' impressed. Etruria, dated 1866. Length 5 inches, width 3⅜ inches.

(B) WEDGWOOD tray, cream-coloured earthenware, painted in crimson. Mark 'Wedgwood' impressed. Etruria, c. 1770. Height 2¼ inches, length 7¾ inches.

(C) WEDGWOOD pair of porcelain flower bowls and covers. Etruria, c. 1815. Height 2½ inches, width 3⅜ inches. WEDGWOOD porcelain coffee-cup and saucer. Etruria, c. 1815. Cup, height 2½ inches, diameter 2⅝ inches. WEDGWOOD porcelain sugar-bowl with cover and stand. Etruria, c. 1815. Bowl, height 4¾ inches, width 6¼ inches. Stand, length 8⅝ inches. WEDGWOOD porcelain tea-cup and saucer.

PLATE 122

WEDGWOOD medallion, biscuit-coloured stoneware, a group in high relief of a centaur and bacchante. c. 1770–1775. Diameter 15¼ inches.

PLATE 123

WEDGWOOD plaque, blue jasper-ware with white relief decoration. Mark 'Wedgwood & Bentley' impressed. c. 1775–80. Height 8½ inches, width 5⅞ inches.

PLATE 124

(A) WEDGWOOD medallion. Portrait of Thomas Bentley, blue jasper-ware. From a model by Joachim Smith. Mark 'Wedgwood' impressed. Etruria, c. 1775–85. Height 5¼ inches, width 4 inches.

(B) WEDGWOOD medallion, blue and white jasper-ware. Mark 'Wedgwood' impressed. Etruria, c. 1785. Diameter 2⅝ inches.

(C) WEDGWOOD plaque, black-basaltes ware. Bust of Jean-Jacques Rousseau (b. 1712, d. 1778). Mark 'Wedgwood & Bentley' impressed, c. 1775–80. Height 2 inches, width 1½ inches.
WEDGWOOD plaque black-basaltes ware. Bust of François-Marie Arouet de Voltaire (b. 1694, d. 1778). Mark 'Wedgwood & Bentley' impressed, c. 1775. Height 2 inches, width 1½ inches.

PLATE 125

WEDGWOOD plaques and medallions of blue jasper and jasper dip ware with white cameo relief. Etruria, late eighteenth century. With one exception all are marked 'Wedgwood' impressed. Width of the largest 10 inches.

PLATE 126

WEDGWOOD medallions of blue jasper-ware with white cameo figures, mounted in chased brass frames. Mark 'Wedgwood & Bentley' impressed. 'THE NINE MUSES'. Etruria, c. 1775. Ht of each 3¼ inches.

PLATE 127

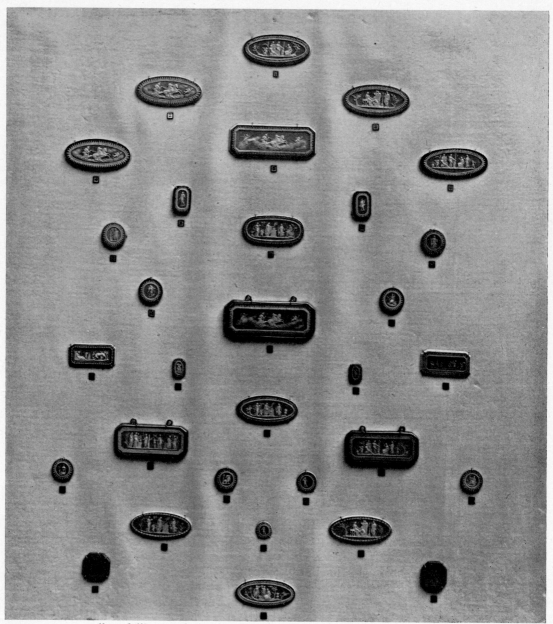

WEDGWOOD small medallions and plaques of jasper dip ware of various colours combined with white cameo figure subjects. Etruria, late eighteenth century. Except where decorated on both sides, all have 'Wedgwood' impressed.

PLATE 128

ment from the late eighteenth century until about 1840.

HORSE-RACING: Occurs as a nineteenth century tranfer-print and as relief ornament on stone-wares. Models of celebrated horses ('Eclipse') or jockeys became popular in the nineteenth century.

FISHING:

PRIZE-FIGHTING: One of the best prints shows Humphries and Mendoza fighting at Odiham, 1788; other well known fights depicted upon pottery or represented as a chimney ornament include:

> Spring and Langan at Chichester
> Tom Sayers and Heenan
> Johnson and Perrins at Banbury
> Molineux and Cribb

Individual figures of prize fighters are known.

WRESTLING: A rather uncommon subject for pottery decoration.

STAG-HUNTING:

ARCHERY: A popular subject for figures, jugs with relief ornaments and transfer-printed ware, early nineteenth century.

CRICKET: Mugs with relief decorations of Lilly-white bowling, Pilch batting and Box keeping wicket are known: flat-back chimney ornaments of celebrated cricketers were modelled by Sampson Smith: some transfer-prints of special cricket matches are recorded.

Sprigged Decoration

Application of relief ornament, often in a contrasting colour by 'sprigging' from a metal or hard-plaster mould, as on Jasper ware.

Sprimont, Nicholas (born 1716 died 1771)

Born at Liége, nephew of the silversmith Nicholas Joseph Sprimont, to whom he served an apprenticeship. Came to England where he appears to have worked as a silversmith, and in 1742 married a Kensington girl, Ann Protin. In 1745 became factory manager and part proprietor with Charles Gouyn and Thomas Briand (died 1784) of the Chelsea porcelain factory. After breaking with his partners he ob-

tained for Chelsea the secret patronage of William Augustus, Duke of Cumberland, second son of George II. He was ill in 1758 and again in 1763. In 1769 the factory equipment was sold, and in 1771 he died.

Spur Marks

Rough marks formed by spurs or stilts upon which the glazed wares rest during the firing process. These are distinct from and smaller than the marks left by the bit-stones used earlier. A factory for the manufacture of spurs and stilts was built by Charles Ford of Hanley in 1840.

[J. G. Wedgwood, *Staffordshire Pottery and its History*, n.d.]

Stabler, Harold, R.D.I. (born 1872 died 1945)

Silversmith, designer and studio potter; partner in the firm of Carter, Stabler and Adams, 1920–45; executed notable architectural sculptures in coloured faience (including memorials at Rugby and Durban, South Africa) in conjunction with Phoebe Stabler.

Statuary porcelain

The original name of Parian (which see).

Stearne, John, Lambeth

A Lambeth potter who worked successively for Killigrew of Chelsea, and Dwight & Sandys at Fulham. About 1684 he attempted to start a pot-works in Kent, (in conjunction with Sir Humphrey Miller, Bart., of Oxenheath), in the parish of Little Peckham, but was thwarted by Dwight. Originally he had been a painter of 'porcellane', a common name at that time for delft, c.1656.

[R. L. Hobson, *Burlington Fine Arts Club Catalogue*, 1913.]

Steatite, see under SOAPSTONE

Steel, Daniel, Burslem, Staffordshire. Earthenware manufacturer

Daniel Steel (b. 1766) made jasper and ornamen-

Colour plate 19, SWANSEA: *see page viii for caption*

tal earthenware in the Wedgwood style. Two vases in the British Museum are impress-marked STEEL. The works closed in 1824.

Examples in Hanley Museum, Stoke-on-Trent.

Steel, Moses, Burslem, Staffordshire

Moses Steel is listed as a maker of cloudy ware in Burslem in 1715, and in 1750 a potter named Thomas Steel is said to have made moulded ware in the same district.

Steele, Thomas (born 1772 died 1850)

Fruit painter at Derby working in a careful, highly coloured style. For a time he appears to have worked at Swinton; later in Staffordshire for Davenports, and from 1825 to 1843 for Mintons.

[G. Haslem, *Old Derby China Works*, 1876; *Staffordshire Advertiser*, 2 November 1850.]

Steen

An earthenware vessel with two ears, used for liquids, but often used for bread, meat or fish.

Stephan, Pierre

A French modeller who worked for the Chelsea factory, and then for the Derby factory from 1770–1795. His agreement with Duesbury, dated 17 September 1770, described him as a 'modeler (sic) and China or Porcelaine Repairer'. He was in Shelton, Staffordshire, in 1795. In 1802 he was listed as Peter Stephan, 'modeller and carver'. Jewitt states that he removed to Jackfield and started a small earthenware and encaustic tile factory, using as his mark an anchor with cable, (impressed), or his name and an anchor and torse printed. For Derby Stephan is said to have modelled sets of figures representing 'the Elements', 'Antique Seasons', a group of four boys and a 'Pastoral Group'. His name occurs incised upon figures representing British Generals and Admirals. He is also stated to have done work for Wedgwood.

Pierre or Peter, Stephan's son, of the same name, was modeller at Coalport as late as 1878 (Jewitt).

[L. Jewitt, *Ceramic Art of Great Britain*, 1878; *Staffordshire Directories*, 1800–1802.]

Stephenson, John, Hanley

Toy and ornament manufacturer, Bethesda Street, 1851.

Stevens, Alfred (born 1817 died 1875)

Sculptor, painter, designer. Studied in Italy from 1833 until 1842; assistant to Thorwaldsen 1841–42; designed schemes of interior decoration, firebacks, cutlery, lamp-posts, maiolica, and mural decorations in Renaissance styles. The Wellington Memorial, St Paul's Cathedral, (completed after his death), is his greatest achievement. In 1860 he produced designs for maiolica for Mintons Ltd.

[Hugh Stannus, *Alfred Stevens and his Work*, 1891.]

Stevenson, Andrew, Cobridge, Staffordshire

Younger brother of Ralph Stevenson. He traded at Cobridge in partnership with a potter named Bucknall, in the firm of Bucknall & Stevenson from about 1805; and later on his own account.

He made excellent blue-printed earthenware primarily for America, until 1819 when his business closed down. Good series of 'English Views' and 'American Views' are known by this potter – the latter from drawings by Wall.

[*Parish Register;* Hudson Moore, *Old China Book*, 1903, reprint 1936.]

Stevenson, Ralph, Cobridge, Staffordshire. Earthenware manufacturer

A firm named Stevenson and Dale produced earthenware at Cobridge in 1802. In 1805 it traded as Stevenson & Godwin. In 1815 the factory was known by Ralph Stevenson's name alone. The firm became bankrupt in 1835.

Stevensons made blue-printed wares, especially commemorative pieces. American and other views, portraits of eminent men of the

time, etc. are typical

MARKS

Specimens are in the British Museum.

[*Staffordshire Advertiser* 26 April 1834, 26 December 1835, 30 January 1836; *Directories*, 1815–1834.]

Stevenson, Sharp & Company, Derby. Porcelain manufacturers

Successors to the business established by William Locker after the closing down of the old Derby Works in 1848. They were followed by Stevenson & Hancock, and finally by Sampson Hancock alone.

'Sticky' blue

A bright-blue used at the porcelain factory of Seth Pennington, Liverpool, first noted by Bernard Rackham.

Stirrup cup

A drinking vessel in the form of a foxes head, made in earthenware by Whieldon, Ralph Wood, John Turner and others, and in soft-paste or bone porcelain at Chelsea, Derby, Rockingham and Coalport.
Other animals' heads were sometimes used.

Stoke-on-Trent

The Pottery towns of North Staffordshire, Tunstall, Burslem, Hanley, Stoke, Fenton and Longton which takes its name from the ancient ecclesiastical parish of Stoke St Peter's.

Stoke itself has been the site of important pottery and porcelain manufactories since the end of the eighteenth century, the more important firms being those of Mintons, Copelands, Adams, H. & R. Daniels, Wolfes, and Geo. Jones.

Stouker

One who 'stouks' or affixes handles or ears to pottery vessels: a handler: 'when they are dry they stouk them' 1686; Whieldon uses the word 'handleing' – 'Feby 20, 1749 Hired Wm Cope for handleing and vineing'.
[R. Plot, *Natural History of Staffordshire*, 1686; T. Whieldon's *Notebook*, Hanley Museum.]

Stourbridge

Richard Pococke visiting the glasshouses at Stourbridge in 1751 recorded, 'they had also a manufacture of China with a contract to sell it only to the promoters of it in London, but I found it not carried on' (*Travels in England*, 1750–51). W. B. Honey regarded this as a confused reference to opaque white glass (*Old English Porcelain*, 1928), but in view of the abundance of fine clays in the area, the frequent contacts between Bristol and Stourbridge, and the general reliability of Pococke's observations, this record of an apparently abortive attempt at porcelain manufacture should not be too lightly dismissed.

For other manufactures in the district see under KINGSWINFORD.

Stratford-le-Bow, see Bow.

Street, John, Marsh Street, Shelton
China figure manufacturer, 1846.

Stretton, Samuel, Lane Delph
An earthenware toy manufacturer of this name is recorded at Lane Delph in 1828.

Stubbs, Benjamin and Joseph, Longport, Burslem, Staffordshire
Benjamin Stubbs is listed in 1818 as an earthenware manufacturer at Longport but may have been in occupation from an earlier date. The firm later became Joseph Stubbs who retired from business in 1834. Joseph Stubbs, died in 1836. The announcement of sale of engravings, moulds, etc. (*Staffordshire Advertiser*, 1 Novem-

ber 1834) described the engraved plates as of 'most-modern and approved patterns suitable for the American and Home trade'. Stubbs made a series of 'American Views' with a showy border of eagles, scrolls and flowers, printed in dark blue, as well as 'English Scenes'.

Stubbs, George, A.R.A. (born 1724 died 1806)

The greatest English *animalier*. Josiah Wedgwood manufactured for his use some large cream-ware plaques to be painted in enamel colours: Stubbs executed for Wedgwood a number of wax models from which jasper tablets were made, including 'The Frightened Horse' and 'The Fall of Phaeton'. Important examples of Stubbs' painting upon cream-ware plaques are in the Lady Lever Art Gallery, Port Sunlight – 'Portrait of Wedgwood', (1782), and 'Haymakers', and 'Haycarting' (1794), and 'The Farmer's Wife and the Raven', exhibited at the R.A. in 1782.

Stubbs, William, Hanley

Jewitt dismisses Stubbs as a manufacturer of common china and earthenware services and of 'smaller and commoner classes of china toys and ornaments'. He contributed to the large output of unidentified chimney ornaments of late Victorian date. Working first of all in partnership in the firm of Stubbs & Bird (1851), he subsequently for thirty or more years manufactured at the Eastwood Vale Works, Hanley.

Studio Pottery

Name applied to pottery made by artist craftsmen working outside the centres of the pottery industry, and made, decorated, glazed and fired by, or under the direct control of the craftsmen themselves. The studio pottery movement originated in France with the work of Cazin and Carries in the 1870's, and in England with the pottery of the Martin Bros. 1878, and William de Morgan in 1872. Studio potters are often referred to now as artist potters.

[May Morris, *Burlington Magazine*, Vol. 31, 1917; Reginald Blunt, *The Wonderful Village*, 1918; Victoria & Albert Museum, *Catalogue of Works by William de Morgan*, 1921; Charles R. Beard, *Catalogue of the Collection of Martin Ware formed by Frederick John Nettlefold*, 1936; Bernard Leach, *A Potter's Book*, 1940; R. G. Cooper, *The modern Potter*, 1947; R. G. Haggar, *English Country Pottery*, 1950; G. W. Digby, *The Work of the Modern Potter in England*, 1952; John Adams, *Pottery & Glass*, 1949–51; Also for illustrations, G. M. Forsyth, *Twentieth Century Ceramics*, 1934; Victoria & Albert Museum, *English Pottery Old and New*, 1936; Muriel Rose, *Artist Potters in England*, 1955.]

LIST OF STUDIO POTTERS (The more important ones are treated individually and are marked*)

*Billington, Dora
Barron, Paul

Bell, Muriel
Bradley, Norah
Brown, Percy
*Bouverie, Katherine Pleydell-

*Cardew, Michael
Cottrell, John
Coper, Hans
Crofts, Stella (figures)
Dunn, Constance

Davis, Harry

Davis, May
Epton, Charlotte
Finch, Raymond

*Fry, Roger
*Forsyth, Gordon Mitchell (1879-1952)
Forsyth, Moira (figures)
Foy, Peggie (figures)

Gregory, Christine (figures)
Hoy, Agnete
Green, Harding
*Gordon, William
Hamada, Sjohi
Harding, Deborah
Haile, Thomas Samuel
Hammond, H. F.

Horsman, Kathleen F.
Kemp, Dorothy
*Leach, Bernard
Leach, David
Leach, Margaret
Marlow, Reginald
Mathews, Heber

Mills, Donald
*Murray, W. Staite
Murray, Kenneth
Melbourne, Colin
Keyes, Phyllis
Odney Pottery (John Bew and A.F.Spindler)
*Parr, Harry (figures)
Parnell, Gwendolen (figures)
Potts, Ann (figures and pottery)
Queensbury, The Marquis of
Rushton, James
Rey, Margaret
Rie, Lucie

Stabler, Phoebe
*Stabler, Harold, RDI
Scott, G.
Trey, Marianne de

Thomas, Gwylim
Wadsworth, Philip
Washington, R.J.

Wells, Reginald (figures and pottery)
Worrall, William
Walker, Agatha (figures)

'19 ḥ 21

Sudell, Richard

A name occurring on a red and white agate mug
or tankard in Hanley Museum. It is covered
with a strong, orange-coloured glaze and inscribed 'Pertineo Richardo Sudell de Shelton in
parochia de Stoke super Trent, in comitatu
Staffordiae tricesimo die Novembris Anno
Domini 1738 Richardus Sudell armiger'.

The name Richard Sudell of Shelton occurs in
Stoke-on-Trent *Parish Registers* in 1740.

Sunderland, County Durham

Several manufactories of a coarse type of cream-
coloured ware, for the most part transfer-printed and frequently pink-lustred, existed in the
Sunderland area in the late eighteenth and the
nineteenth centuries. The following are the best
known of these firms:

NORTH HYLTON POTTERY, Sunderland:
Founded by Christopher Thompson and John
Maling in 1762. Later the firm was known as

Dixon, Austin & Co., and subsequently as Dixon, Phillips & Co. (owners of the Garrison Pottery in the same district).

MARKS

DIXON & CO.
DIXON, AUSTIN & CO.
SUNDERLAND
(impressed)

Wares decorated with transfer-prints (Wear Bridge), sentimental inscriptions and splashes of pink lustre were popular.

FORD POTTERY, South Hylton, Sunderland

The pottery was founded in 1800 and was owned by John Dawson & Co. The Dawson family worked it until 1864 when it closed down.

MARK

D AW S O N (impressed)

WEAR POTTERY, Sunderland;

Founded in 1803 by Brunton & Co., and known soon after by the name of Samuel Moore and Co. Popular subjects – views, commemorative inscriptions etc. – decorate their wares.

MARKS

MOORE & CO.
SOUTHWICK
MOORE & CO. (impressed)

A plate of about 1820, decorated with a steamship and marked, is in the British Museum. SOUTHWICK POTTERY, Sunderland:
In 1789 the pottery was owned by Anthony Scott, owner of another pottery at Newbottle. Combed slipware was included in the productions of this factory.

MARK

SCOTT (impressed)

Other factories in the area, making similar wares, were the SOUTHWICK UNION POTTERY, the NEWBOTTLE POTTERY, CARR'S HILL POTTERY, FELL of Newcastle-on-Tyne.

See also LUSTRE.
Plate 151 B and C.

Sussex

Crude types of slipware were made at various places in Sussex – Brede, Chailey, Rye, Wiston, Dicker and Burgess Hill amongst them – in the late eighteenth and early nineteenth centuries. Articles for domestic use such as jugs, plates and flasks formed the chief of their productions.

A better-finished and more interesting variety of slipware was produced at this period in Rye, Chailey and Brede, and also at Bethersden in Kent. This was made by inlaying with white clay incised or stamped designs (often inscriptions first impressed with printer's type) on the body of the ware. Formal patterns, foliage, stars, etc., are found on articles made in this way. At Burgess Hill an agate ware was made.

Sussex wares are often distinctive by reason of a streaked glaze used with pleasant effect on many pieces. A glaze speckled with manganese is also common. Jugs in the form of a pig, the head forming a lid or cover, and flat pocket flasks, seem to be peculiar to the Sussex potteries.

The Rye pottery, still in existence at the present time, made some interesting pieces in a red ware in the nineteenth century. These were experimental and not made commercially.

Examples of various types of Sussex slipware are in the British Museum, the City Museum and Art Gallery, Stoke-on-Trent, The Sussex Archaeological Museum, Lewes, and Hastings Museum. *Plates 97–98.*

[J.W.Baines, *Sussex Pottery: East-Sussex*, 1948; G. Savage, Early Sussex Pottery, *Apollo* 1956; Mrs. Celia Hemming, 'Sussex Pottery', *The Connoisseur* 1909 and 1912.]

Swadlincote, Burton-on-Trent, Staffordshire

Site of Thomas Sharpe's stoneware and earthenware manufactory and of Ault Potteries Ltd. (founded 1887).

See SHARPE (Thomas) and AULT FAIENCE.

Swansea, Glamorganshire, Wales. Earthenware and porcelain

CAMBRIAN POTTERY

DATES AND OWNERS

The Cambrian Pottery at Swansea was founded about 1764. Little is known of the factory's first few years, but William Coles is believed to have been the proprietor during the early period. Coles died c.1778–79 leaving the pottery to his three sons. Coarse red wares were manufactured in the early days. By 1790 John Coles was joined by George Haynes and the firm became Coles & Haynes.

In 1802 William Dillwyn purchased from Haynes the lease of the pottery together with a preponderance of shares in the concern on behalf of his son Lewis Weston Dillwyn (born 1778 died 1855). Haynes remained as manager, the firm being Haynes, Dillwyn & Co. On Haynes departure in 1810 (to form the Glamorgan Pottery two years later) he was succeeded by Timothy Bevington a Staffordshire potter, and his son John Bevington, the company trading as Dillwyn & Co. In 1817 the Bevingtons and others formed a company, rented the Cambrian Works from Dillwyn, and traded as T. &. J. Bevington & Co. Their lease expired in 1824 when the potworks reverted to Dillwyn, who in 1831 took his son Lewis L. Dillwyn into partnership.

David Evans and a man named Glasson took over the pottery in 1850. Shortly after it passed to Evans's son, D. J. Evans. The works were closed down in 1870 and later dismantled.

MARKS

SWANSEA **DILLWYN & Co**

SWANSEA **SWANSEA**

Swansea **Pardoe Cardiff** *Swansea*

ARTISTS

Baxter, Thos. (1782–1821) Originally an independent enameller in London, he went to Worcester as a painter in 1814. In 1816 he left to work at Swansea, returning to Worcester three years later. Subjects from natural history, figures, shells etc. are amongst his work.

Beddow, George. Painter of birds, landscapes and figure subjects, about 1815.

Billingsley, Wm. (1760–1828) Decorated a small number of Swansea pieces. He excelled as a painter of roses.

Colclough, Matthew. Painter of birds.

Evans, Evan. A flower painter and follower of Pollard.

Morris, Henry (1799–1880). A pupil of Billingsley and painter of flowers and fruit at Swansea from about 1815.

Pardoe, Thomas (1770–1823). A well-known flower painter working at Swansea from about 1797 until 1809. He also painted birds, animals and some local landscapes. Many Swansea plates were decorated by him.

Pollard, Wm. (1803–1854) A painter of wild flowers working at Swansea from about 1819.

Rothwell, Thos. A designer and engraver employed at Swansea from 1785–1790.

Wood, Isaac. Modeller.

Young, Wm. Weston (1776–1847) Painter of Swansea and Nantgarw earthenware and porcelain. An illustrator of a volume on natural history, his subjects were mainly birds, butterflies, flowers and plants.

Bentley, George. Modeller from 1791 until c.1798.

WORK

The Swansea factory in its early years made wares similar to those produced in Staffordshire at the period – cream wares, blue-printed, black basalts, marbled wares and articles decorated with enamels and with lustre. Much of this work is indistinguishable from its Staffordshire counterparts. The quality is variable, but some pieces are very well modelled and flower decoration was already being used extensively in the factory.

In 1814 Billingsley and Walker, then occupying the factory at Nantgarw, joined Dillwyn at Swansea with the intention of collaborating in the production of a porcelain stronger in body and less subject to flaws in firing than that previously made at Nantgarw to Billingsley's formula. After experiments lasting nearly two years, a more stable composition was produced and manufactured commercially until September 1817. There are at least three distinct varieties of this paste, the most successful being that known as 'duck-egg' because of its greenish translucency by transmitted light. Later a more opaque type of porcelain was made; this has a yellowish tinge and a thin, rather dull, glaze. A third type is much harder, white and glassy in appearance.

After 1817 a porcelain incorporating soapstone and much inferior to the earlier kinds was made. This has not the same interest for collectors as the 'duck-egg' variety, now much sought after.

SUBJECTS AND DISTINGUISHING CHARACTERISTICS

Porcelain made during Billingsley's period at Swansea is sometimes hard to distinguish from Nantgarw. Composition and decoration are very similar. The shapes and designs used at Swansea were often more ambitious, the resources of the factory being greater, and in the period 1814–17 many of the productions owe much to French porcelain of the period. Designs taken from natural history, particularly flowers reproduced from the rather stiff botanical prints of the time or more attractively in sprays or scattered groups, are characteristic of Swansea. Thomas Pardoe and Wm. Pollard were probably the most influential decorators at the factory

Table ware, and especially plates, form the largest part of existing Swansea pieces. Vases and other decorative objects were also made, but not in such quantity. Classical forms are usual in the latter.

Fakes are not uncommon – some marked with a Swansea mark – and were usually made in France. These, however, are mostly distinguishable from true Swansea as the style of decoration and often the forms and shapes are quite dissimilar.

Specimens bearing various marks and some signed by the artists are in the British Museum, Victoria and Albert Museum, the National Museum of Wales, Cardiff, and the Glynn Vivian Art Gallery, Swansea.

See also NANTGARW, BILLINGSLEY.
Colour plate 19 and plates 99–100.

Swansea, Glamorgan Pottery
Set up as a rival to the Cambrian Pottery about 1813 by George Haynes, his son-in-law William Baker, and others. In 1838–39 the Dillwyns acquired the factory and having no need of its premises closed it down.

Production was similar in character and quality to that of the Cambrian Pottery. Transfer printing was extensively used, as also printing and enamelling. Specialities were Cow Milk jugs and plates with wickerwork borders.

MARKS
The name BAKER, BEVANS & IRWIN forming nearly a circle with the word SWANSEA impressed and enclosing Prince of Wales Feathers. Transfer-printed marks include the firms, initials.:

B B & I   or   B B & Co

Swift & Cobb, Burslem, Staffordshire
Josiah Wedgwood's head clerk, Swift, entered into partnership with one of Wedgwood's former warehouse men, named Cobb in 1777 in a manufacture of 'Crich Ware such as Mr Hayward was concerned in at Chesterfield'. Swift became landlord of the Leopard Inn, Burslem at the same time. (Letter, Wedgwood to Bentley, 14 January 1777). Salt-glazed stoneware was evidently made. The venture failed in 1778, and Wedgwood loaned Swift the money, about £100, necessary to clear his debts.
[K.E.Farrer, *Letters of Josiah Wedgwood*, 1903.]

Swill Hill (or Soil Hill), Yorkshire
A slipware pottery existed here in the eighteenth and nineteenth centuries.

Swinton, Yorkshire
A number of earthenware factories flourished here in the eighteenth and nineteenth centuries: see under DON, KILNHURST, MEXBOROUGH, and ROCKINGHAM.
Plates 101–102.

Sword Hilts
Occasionally sword hilts were fitted with ceramic insets, as on the sword reputed to have belonged to Beau Brummel (1778–1840) in Nottingham Castle Museum. This is fitted with Wedgwood jasper ware cameos set in cut steel probably by Matthew Boulton.
[Illus. *Concise Encyclopaedia of Antiques*, Vol. 2, 1955.]

T

'The Excelsior Government Stamped Earthenware Measure' for which he had taken out a patent, and undoubtedly many 'mocha' ware capacity mugs were made by him. John Tams was succeeded by his son, John Edmund Tams (born 1875 died 1952) who took out a patent for the use of talc in the manufacture of earthenware.

[Keates *Directories*, 1875, 1889; *Staffordshire Evening Sentinel*, 17 November 1952.]

Talbott, Luke

Master potter, in partnership with R. White and Matthew Garner, Gravel Lane, Southwark, manufacturing stoneware, c.1695.
[R. L. Hobson, B.F.A.C. *Catalogue*, 1913.]

'Taluf faience'

Ornamental pottery made by James MacIntyre & Co., Burslem, decorated mechanically in *sgraffiato* slip, the ornamental effect being produced by placing the article on an eccentric lathe which brought the pot alternately against a stationary tool, thus removing portions of slip to show the underlying 'body'.
[*Catalogue of the Exhibition of Decorative Pottery*, Imperial Institute, 1894.]

Talor (Tallor), William

Name recorded on large Toft-style slipware dishes with the Boscobel Oak, Royal Arms, Coronation, etc. One piece is dated 1700. Examples in British Museum, Temple Newsam, Leeds, Brighton Museum, and Manchester City Art Gallery.

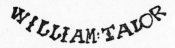

Tams, John (died 1919)

A general earthenware business was founded by John Tams at Crown Pottery, Stafford Street, Longton, before 1875, manufacturing among other things lustre, Egyptian black, drab, printed wares and 'mocha'. In 1889 Tams advertised

Tassie, James (born 1735 died 1799)

Celebrated modeller and moulder of wax portraits. He supplied casts of portrait-reliefs and gems to Josiah Wedgwood from 1769 until 1791.
[J. M. Graham and H. C. Wedgwood *Wedgwood* 1948.]

Tatlow, Joseph

A gilder of porcelain who worked at Derby, Pinxton, and with Billingsley at Mansfield, and to whom a covered cup enriched with gilding only (Cardiff Museum) which is signed 'Billingsley, Mansfield' has been tentatively attributed.

Taws

Small balls or marbles made of earthenware or stoneware used in game of carpet bowls, made in Staffordshire, Yorkshire and Scotland.

Taylor, George

Name occurring on slipware posset-pot, dated 1692, and a dish decorated with a representation of a coronation. Stoke Registers record the marriage of George Tayler to Ellinor Tayler 29 April 1687.

Taylor, Harry (born 1871 died 1956)

Pioneer in the field of lithography and photo-lithography as applied to manufacture of ceramic transfers. Experimented at Doultons in 1898 and founded the Universal Transfer Co. in 1901.
[Obit. *Pottery Gazette* May 1956.]

Taylor, Howson (died 1935)

Potter; founded the Ruskin Pottery, Smethwick, in 1898, with the help of his father, Edward Richard Taylor, (1838–1911), principal of the Birmingham School of Art. The business was closed down in 1935. Made vases and bowls in plain and broken colours, with lustre decorations against coloured grounds, and with high temperature flambé glazes.

[L.B. Powell, *Howson Taylor, Master Potter n.d.*]

Taylor, John Duncombe

Taylor painted a service of Chamberlain's Worcester porcelain in 1807 with 'Scenes from the Arabian Nights' which he signed and dated. Nothing is known of him, and he may have been an outside decorator.

[F.A. Barrett, *Worcester Porcelain*, 1953.]

Taylor, Thomas and George, Bristol, Gloucestershire. Potters

Owners of Taylor's Factory, Redcliff, from 1739 until 1768.

[W.G. Pountney, *Old Bristol Potteries*, 1920.]

Taylor, William and John, Burslem, Staffordshire. Potters

The following mark is found on a mug of white glazed earthenware in the British Museum:

W. T. & Co. (impressed)

This has been ascribed to William and John Taylor, working at Burslem about 1750. They are said to have been makers also of salt-glazed stoneware. Shaw mentions red porcelain and black-glazed teapots as part of their output.

[S. Shaw, *History of the Staffordshire Potteries*, 1829.]

Taylor, William, Bristol, Gloucestershire. Potter

Proprietor of the Temple Back Pottery, June 1756 until 1777.

[W.G. Pountney, *Old Bristol Potteries*, 1920.]

Tea and Coffee Equipage

'A compleat tea and coffee equipage, containing 8 tea and 8 coffee cups, a teapot and stand, a slop bason, a sugar bason, a cream ewer and plate'. (*Catalogue of the Chelsea Sale* 1756.)

Tea Caddy

A rectangular jar with cylindrical neck and cover. Made in delftware, cream-coloured earthenware, salt-glazed stoneware, porcelain and bone china, often with relief decorations and sometimes lettered with the name of the tea, such as 'Herb Tea' or 'Bohea'. Erroneously called a teapoy.

Teapot

The form of a teapot used in England was determined by imported oriental teapots at the end of the seventeenth century. The discovery of the properties of plaster-of-Paris made possible the production of teapots of more complicated shapes or with special features. These have been frequent since the beginning of the nineteenth century.

FANCY-SHAPED TEAPOTS: in the form of a camel, ship, house, chinaman, cauliflower, pineapple, or cottage occur in salt-glazed stoneware, and earthenware in the eighteenth century.

BREWSTER SHAPE: oval straight-sided teapot with lid fitting into an oval collar, c.1780.

CADOGAN: a lidless teapot, see CADOGAN.

'NARROW BOAT': teapots specially made in brown encircled with coloured, or coloured and lustred flowers, for canal narrow boats and regarded as part of their traditional equipment. Many were made at the Midway Pottery near Burton-on-Trent.

ROYLE'S SELF-POURING TEAPOT: patented 1887. A globular teapot with tall cylindrical neck worked on a suction pump system. The spout enters the body through a grating. The metal lid, fashioned like a piston three inches in depth, runs up and down the neck, and when plunged down spurts the tea into the cup. Royle claimed that his self-pouring pot would 'supercede the present antiquated and laborious action in serving tea'.

DOUBLE TEAPOT: the Leeds Factory made a double teapot with double intertwined handles and spouts. An example in Leeds City Art-Gallery is inscribed, Green Tea Bohea Tea'.

TOBY TEAPOT: an ugly type formed in the shape of a man and made in earthenware in the nineteenth century.

Features of teapots to which special attention has been given are the lock of the lid, and the pouring of the spout which have been the subject of numerous patents.
Plate 96 A.

Teapoy

A name frequently but incorrectly used for a tea caddy or tea canister.

Tebo

Probably the French name Thibaud anglicised. Very little is known about this craftsman who has been the subject of speculation. A 'Mr Teboe, jeweller' is recorded as living at Fetter Lane, London, in 1747, (*Daily Advertiser*, 13 November 1747). There is evidence of a repairer at Bow from about 1750 who signed his work T°. Severne Mackenna suggested that he might have been the 'Muses Modeller'. Sometime between 1760 and 1768 the same workman was at Worcester, and his mark also occurs on Plymouth porcelain of the Cookworthy period. From about 1775 Mr Tebo was working for Josiah Wedgwood who formed a poor opinion of his ability, (Josiah Wedgwood to T. Bentley 3 July 1775, 11 July 1775, and 28 October 1775). Subsequently he went to Dublin and passed into obscurity.

$$T^{o} \quad T$$

[*The Burlington Magazine*, Vol. 25, 1914; *Letters of Wedgwood* 1903; W.B.Honey, *Old English Porcelain*, 1928, later editions; G.Savage, *Eighteenth Century English Porcelain*, 1952.]

Tellor (Taylor), James

A dated slipware cradle with royal portraits is lettered JAMES TELLOR 1673 (Greg Collection, Manchester Art Gallery).

Terra Cotta

Red biscuit earthenware varying in colours according to firing, from a warm soft pink to a rich purple-red.

Theed, William, R.A. (born 1764 died 1817)

Sculptor and designer; studied at Royal Academy Schools from 1786 and became a painter of neo-classical subjects which he exhibited at R.A. in 1789. Went to Rome, became known to Flaxman and returned to England 1794. Worked for Rundell & Bridge, goldsmiths, on his return, and for Wedgwoods of Etruria 1799–1814. He was in Staffordshire advertising as a drawing master in Newcastle-under-Lyme in 1803, (*Staffordshire Advertiser*, 10 and 17 December 1803). His address at that time was Wolstanton. Later he moved to Trentham, where William Theed the younger, (also R.A.), was born in 1804. William Theed the elder designed large-scale memorials, was elected A.R.A. 1811, and R.A. 1813.

[*Parish Registers*, Wolstanton and Trentham; *Staffordshire Advertiser*, 10 and 17 December 1803; *Dictionary of National Biography*; Wedgwood records.]

Thetford, Norfolk

Thomas Scales is described as 'a glass and china dealer and earthenware manufacturer', 1836 (White's *Gazetteer of Norfolk*, 1836).

Thompson, Joseph, Hartshorne, Derbyshire

Joseph Thompson established the Hartshorne Potteries in 1818 and these were continued by his sons, Richard and Willoughby Thompson, trading as Thompson Bros.

Derbyshire brown stonewares were made, yellow wares lined with white, reform flasks of politicians, etc. Marked thus:

J. THOMPSON (impressed)

Joseph Thompson
Wooden Box
Pottery
Derbyshire
(impressed)

Thrower

One who spins, forms or 'throws' pottery vessels by hand upon a revolving wheel or jigger: '1372, Thomas le Thrower takes up land in Thursfield' *(Tunstall Court Rolls)*. A thrown pot is one spun on the wheel, and frequently reveals the marks of its origin, noticeably in the wreathing or horizontal ribbing of the surface, or the thumbing of the foot.

Tickenhall (or Ticknall), Derbyshire. Earthenware manufactory

A pottery existed at Tickenhall in the sixteenth century at which a hard red ware, decorated with slip or applied reliefs, was made over at least two centuries. Tickenhall was one of a group of potteries making this type of ware, others being at Cockpit Hill, Wrotham, Hanley and in other districts. From excavations carried out in the neighbourhood, Tickenhall seems to have been a manufactory of some size.

It is rarely possibly to ascribe individual pieces to the various potteries: a very large class of domestic articles in similar lead-glazed earthenware exists. Posset-pots, puzzle jugs, tygs, candlesticks etc. are all commonly found. The body is usually red in colour, (or very occasionally buff), glazed in streaky colours derived from copper, iron or manganese. Some black ware of this type is probably of a later date.

Simple patterns, scratched or applied on pads of clay to the finished body, are characteristic.

Many slipwares formerly ascribed to this factory are now believed to be of Staffordshire origin.

Examples of this type of ware are to be found in the British Museum.

'Tigerware' jug

A big-bellied pitcher with a cylindrical neck made in German salt-glazed stoneware, imported into this country in the sixteenth century. Examples are found mounted with Elizabethan silver or gilt embossed and engraved neckbands, covers, handles and footrims. Imitated in English tin-enamelled earthenware. See 'MALLING' JUG. Also called 'LEOPARD' WARE.

Tin glaze

A lead glaze made opaque by the addition of tin ashes. Sometimes called tin-enamel. Used in England from c.1570 until early nineteenth century.

Tinworth, George (born 1843 died 1913)

Modeller at Doulton's Lambeth factory from 1867. He was a regular exhibitor at the Royal Academy. Three large terra cotta panels 'Gethsemane', 'The Foot of the Cross', and 'The Descent from the Cross' exhibited at the Royal Academy in 1874 attracted considerable attention. He executed many commissions for large-scale religious works including altarpieces at York Minster and Shelton Church, Staffordshire, and mural panels now at Trentham and Sandringham. Many miniature figures were executed by him. Samples in Brighton Museum. Signature:

Incised

[D. Eyles, *Doulton News*, 1950.]

Tittensor, Charles

Figure-maker and black-printer, Shelton. Born 1764 and christened at Stoke 15 January. In 1802 entered into partnership with Robert Pope in a small potworks in Hanley. The partnership was dissolved in 1803. From 1803 until 1807 Charles & John Tittensor continued the business and in 1807 the firm became Tittensor & Simpson, continuing as such until 1813. Later Charles Tittensor potted on his own account and he is recorded in Queen Street, Shelton in 1818 and 1823. He made Walton-type figures with tree backgrounds decorated with enamel colours with impressed mark, TITTENSOR. A cream-coloured mug transfer-printed in black with 'GRETNA GREEN or the RED HOT MARRIAGE', signed TITTENSOR, has been recorded.

Impressed

[R.G.Haggar, 'More Light on the Tittensor Family' in *Apollo*, 1950; 'Charles Tittensor; Figure-maker and Blackprinter' in *Apollo*, 1950; Also *Staffordshire Chimney Ornaments*, 1955; *Staffordshire Advertiser*, 29 March 1800, 27 February 1802, 15 October 1803; *Directories*, 1818–1828.]

Tittensor, Jacob

Name found inscribed on a bucolic plaque modelled in relief in the Voyez style, dated 1789; the name occurs in Stoke parish registers, 1780 and 1791.

Jacob Tittensor

T   **T**

Incised   In relief

[H.B.Lancaster, 'An unrecorded Family of Potters,' in *Apollo*, Vol. 37, 1943; See also Reginald G.Haggar, in *Apollo*, Vol. 51, 1950, Vol. 52, 1950.]

Tittensor, John

Partner to Charles Tittensor, potter, Shelton, 1803; traveller, New Hall concern 1815–21, and manager in succession to John Daniel 1821–35. Member of select vestry, Stoke, 1836, Poor Law Guardian 1842; described as a gentleman, Bucknall 1845.

[*Staffordshire Advertiser*, 15 October 1803; 25 August 1832, 24 November 1832; 26 March 1836; 2 April 1842; *North Staffordshire Mercury*, 23 January 1841; *Potter's Examiner*, 22 March 1845; *Directories*, 1818, 1822.]

Tittensor, William (born 1733 died 1803)

Earthenware manufacturer, Shelton, and owner of property in Hanley, Longton, Lichfield and London.

[*Staffordshire Advertiser*, 27 February 1802, 1 December 1804; Stoke, *Parish Registers*, Document in Hanley Library.]

Toad mugs

Commonly made in the North Country in the nineteenth century, but also more rarely elsewhere. They consisted of drinking mugs with a large toad inside which can be seen only when the pot is emptied, causing surprise and consternation because of folk superstitions concerning the use of toad poison. The inscription 'Tho' malt and venom seem united...' is not uncommon.

Toby Jug

A jug in the form of a man holding a mug of beer and a clay pipe, adapted from an engraving issued by Carrington Bowles with the verses of a song 'The Metamorphosis, or Toby Reduc'd' said to have been translated from the Italian by Rev. Francis Fawkes. The brim of the three-cornered hat formed the lip of the jug, and the crown a detachable cover or cup. Female Toby jugs are known, as well as other variants.

Made by Ralph Wood, James Neale, Lakin & Poole, Spode, Davenport and others in Staffordshire, Yorkshire and other areas.

Variants include:

Toby Fillpot	Shield Toby
Admiral Howe	Bluff King Hal
The Black Man	The Collier
Martha Gunn	The Thin Man
The Gin Woman	The Farrier
The Parson	The Unfrocked Parson
The Welsh Country	(sometimes called
Gentleman	Dr Johnson)
The Convict	The Night Watchman
The Hearty Good	The Sailor
Fellow	Paul Pry (19th century)
The Snuff Taker	The Royal Bargeman
The Planter	The Fiddler
Punch (19th century)	Judy (19th century)
John Bull	The Woodman
(19th century)	(19th century)
Pickwick (19th century)	

All the early variants are represented in the Elizabeth Marianne Wood Collection, Stoke-on-Trent Museum; others may be seen in the Victoria and Albert Museum, British Museum and the Fitzwilliam Museum, Cambridge. *Plate 148.*

[Richard Aldington, *The Times Literary Supplement*, 8 March 1923; R.K.Price, *Astbury Whieldon and Ralph Wood Figures and Toby Jugs*, 1922; Sir Harold Mackintosh, *Early English Figure Pottery*, 1938; Desmond Eyles, *Good Sir Toby*, 1955; Reginald G.Haggar, *Staffordshire Chimney Ornaments*, 1955.]

Toft & May, Hanley, Staffordshire

Thomas Toft (b. 1767 d. 1834) manufactured earthenware in Charles Street, first of all in partnership with a man named Keeling (Toft & Keeling) and later with Robert May who continued the business on his own account after Toft's death in 1834, (*Staffordshire Advertiser*, 1 March 1834).

Toft, Charles (born 1832 died 1909)

Ceramic decorator, modeller and potter. Studied at Stoke School of Design and worked at Mintons where he executed careful copies of inlaid *Henri Deux* wares and parian statuary. His bust of the Duke of Wellington in Hanley Museum is signed and dated 1853. He left Mintons and went to Birmingham to work for Elkngtons, but returned to the Potteries to become chief figure modeller at Wedgwood's of Etruria 1872–89. He executed for them a medallion bust of Gladstone in 1877, and the 'Peace and War' vase for the Paris Exhibition 1878 (for which he was paid £30). Also models after designs by Walter Crane. Patented a self-closing jug lid which was taken up by Wedgwoods (who paid him $1/_4$d royalties) and Brown, Westhead Moore & Co. In 1889 he started a pottery manufactory at the Swan Works, High Street, Stoke, where he made rustic wares in brown and white slip (including pieces decorated in slip with fern and lace motifs) exhibiting remarkable ingenuity and lack of taste. Toft died at Burton-on-Trent in 1909. His son, Albert Toft (born 1862 died 1949), was a celebrated sculptor.

[Obit. *Manchester Guardian*, 6 May 1909; *Daily Mail*, 6 May 1909; Information concerning works done for Wedgwoods per Mr. Tom Lyth; *Stoke School of Design Registers*.]

Toft, Cornelius

A 2-handled incised white salt-glazed loving cup in Northampton Museum is inscribed:

W B Marthar Barber C T
Cornelius Toft 1727/8 hand
C Martha Barber T
1727/8

Cornelius Toft, the son of Thomas Toft was born in 1677 and died in 1728. Thomas Toft's grandson Cornelius (the son of Matthias Toft) was born in 1703.

[*Catalogue, Burlington Fine Arts Club*, 1914.]

Toft, James (born 1673)

Son of Thomas and Ellena Toft and probably the maker of Toft-style dishes bearing his name. Dishes dated 1695 and 1705 are known.

IAMES TOFT

[*Stoke-on-Trent Parish Registers*.]

Toft, Ralph (born 1638)

Probably the brother of Thomas Toft. Married Christabell Hatton (died 1693) at Stoke 19 December 1669. The name occurs on many typical large Toft-style dishes decorated with a double-headed eagle, cavaliers and ladies, or with a mermaid, two being dated 1676 and 1677. A posset-pot in Bedford Museum is dated 1683. Signed examples in National Museum of Wales, and Museums at Salford, Hanley and Bedford.

RALPHOFT

[*Stoke-on-Trent Parish Registers*.]

Toft, Thomas (died 1689)

A name occurring on numerous large round dishes and more rarely on hollow-wares. It is not known for certain whether the name is that of maker or recipient, but it would seem that the traditional view that Thomas Toft made these pieces is justified for it is unlikely that any collector would have wished to have 35 or more such outsize dishes sometimes decorated with the same subjects. The Royal Arms occur on Toft dishes at least five times. Tofts are recorded in the Parish Registers of Stoke-on-Trent (from 1638) and Burslem; and in Hearth Tax Rolls for Shelton, Bucknall, Fenton and Stanley in 1666. The name Toft also occurs in Hearth Tax Returns for Rushton Spencer and Leek.

Simeon Shaw refers to 20-inch dishes made by Thomas Toft in 1650, and there are numer-

Toft Pedigree

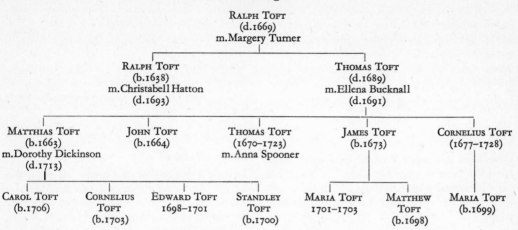

RALPH TOFT
(d.1669)
m.Margery Turner

RALPH TOFT
(b.1638)
m.Christabell Hatton
(d.1693)

THOMAS TOFT
(d.1689)
m.Ellena Bucknall
(d.1691)

MATTHIAS TOFT
(b.1663)
m.Dorothy Dickinson
(d.1713)

JOHN TOFT
(b.1664)

THOMAS TOFT
(1670–1723)
m.Anna Spooner

JAMES TOFT
(b.1673)

CORNELIUS TOFT
(1677–1728)

CAROL TOFT
(b.1706)

CORNELIUS TOFT
(b.1703)

EDWARD TOFT
1698–1701

STANDLEY TOFT
(b.1700)

MARIA TOFT
1701–1703

MATTHEW TOFT
(b.1698)

MARIA TOFT
(b.1699)

ous references to Thomas Toft in Stoke-on-Trent Parish Registers. He married Ellena Bucknall 21 April 1663 and died a pauper in November 1689 (buried 3 December). Their children Matthias (born 1663) John (born 1664) Thomas (born 1670) James (born 1673) and Cornelius (born 1677) were all christened at Stoke. A fragment of supposed Toft ware inscribed 'Thomas Toft I made it Tinkersclough 166–' cited by M. L. Solon is now generally regarded as a fake foisted upon Solon by hoaxers. Three tiny fragments of Toft pottery including a shard inscribed '...OFT' were found three feet below ground at the corner of Stafford Street and Trinity Street, Hanley in 1953. (*Evening Sentinel*, 25 November). 35 large dishes, 2 jugs and a posset-pot are recorded with Thomas Toft's name. They are decorated with 'trailed slip', the dishes having trellis rim borders interrupted by panels enclosing the name. More rarely a border of fleur-de-lis or heads was used. The centre decorations comprised Royal Arms, (incorrectly rendered), Arms of the Cordwainers, Company, the Boscobel Oak, Pelican-in-her-Piety, lions rampant, double-headed eagles, figures of cavaliers and ladies, a man smoking, and foliage. Dated examples are known – 1671, 1674, 1677, and 1689.

Examples in following Museums:

Victoria & Albert Museum, London
Hanley Museum, Stoke-on-Trent
Temple Newsam, Leeds
Manchester City Art Gallery
Fitzwilliam Museum, Cambridge
Nelson Gallery of Art, Kansas City
Metropolitan Museum of Art, New York
British Museum, London
Grosvenor Museum, Chester
Yorkshire Museum, York
Ashmolean Museum, Oxford
National Museum of Ireland, Dublin

Colour plate 16 and plates 85, 86 A.

thomas:toft

THOMAS TOFT

thomas TofT

A A A a

Variations in letter A in
Toft signature

[R.G.Haggar, *English Country Pottery*, 1950; Ronald Cooper, *Pottery of Thomas Toft*, Leeds, 1952; *Parish Registers, Stoke-on-Trent*; Hearth Tax Returns, William Salt Library; G.W.Rhead, *The Earthenware Collector*, 1920; W.B.Honey, *English Pottery and Porcelain*, 1933.]

Tooth & Co. Ltd, Bretby Art Pottery, Burton-on-Trent

Established in 1883 during the vogue for 'Art' wares produced under the influence of the aesthetic movement.

MARK

Torksey, Lincolnshire

It has been stated that William Billingsley made porcelain here about 1802–1803 but none has been identified with certainty. Billingsley probably decorated porcelain bought from elsewhere.

Tortoiseshell ware

Cream earthenware covered with a lead glaze stained with mottlings of blue, brown and green from oxides of cobalt, manganese, and copper. Made by Whieldon and other potters, c.1750. *Plate 105.*

Toxophilite, The Fair

Female Archer, or alternatively 'Fair Toscopholite'. A popular subject 1790–1820 or later, for engraved transfers, for relief decoration, and as a model for figures made in earthenware particularly by Salt of Hanley.

Transfer-printing

The application of decorations from engraved copper plates to pottery or porcelain by means of bats of gelatine (bat-printing) or later (c.1800) by paper tissues. It was effected overglaze at Bow (1756) and Worcester 1756/7 by Robert Hancock, and at Liverpool by J. Sadler c.1756. Printing in blue underglaze was practised at Worcester c.1759 and popularized during Hancock's employment at Caughley 1775, and adopted soon after at Liverpool, Lowestoft, Bristol and in Staffordshire.

Other colours were used during the nineteenth century including pink, puce, orange-brown and green. Gold-printing was patented by Peter Warburton in 1810. Multi-colour, and block-printing were used from the 1840's in Staffordshire.

See also BLACK PRINTER.

Transparencies

'Bought some transparencies in china 10/–' (*Diary, John Hackett Goddard,* 6 October 1858). See LITHOPHANE.

Truro, Cornwall

Truro alone survives as a centre for the manufacture of country pottery out of the dozen or so which formerly made pancheons and pitchers in the Duchy of Cornwall. Samuel Lewis (*A Topographical Dictionary of England,* 7th ed. 1848) records 'two small potteries for the coarser kinds of earthenware'. W.T. Lake manufactures earthenware and red ware at Chapel Hill pottery using the following mark:

LAKE'S
CORNISH
POTTERY
TRURO

Trusty Servant, The

A composite figure in porcelain with pig's head and deer's feet, made early nineteenth century, said to be based upon a painting of this title at Winchester College. The doggerel explains its significance

> The Trusty Servant's portrait would you see
> This emblematic figure well survey.
> The porker's snout not nice in diet shows;
> The padlock shut no secret he'll disclose.
> Patient the ass his master's rage will bear.
> Swiftness in errand the stag's feet declare.
> Loaded his left hand apt to labour saith,
> The Vest his neatness, open hand his faith.
> Girt with his sword, his shield upon his arm,
> Himself and master he'll protect from harm.

Copelands produced a version in 1858.

Tunnicliff, Michael, Tunstall, Staffordshire

Manufacturer of earthenware toys and figures,

Colour plate 20, WEDGWOOD: *see page viii for caption*

WORCESTER *(top shelf):* pair of porc. mugs, stipple-printed in black with a view of the Severn at Worcester, c. 1810, ht 3⅜ in.; pair of porc. vases, c. 1810, ht 5⅞ in.; porc. ewer, 1859, ht 10⅜ in. *2nd shelf:* porc. pastille-burner and cover, mark '5' incised, c. 1820, ht 4½ in.; pair of porc. candlesticks, c. 1840, ht 8¼ in.; porc. plate, c. 1800, diam. 9⅝ in.; porc. teacup, c. 1800, ht 2¼ in., diam. 3½ in. *3rd shelf:* porc. bowl, c. 1845, ht 3 in., diam. 4⅞ in.; porc. tray, c. 1810, height 2⅝ in., length 9¼ in.; porc. jug, c. 1840, ht 4¼ in. *Bottom shelf:* porc. soup-plate, c. 1820, diam. 9½ in.; porc. bottle and stopper, c. 1845, ht 9½ in.; porc. plate from a service made for Queen Victoria and decorated by Thomas Bott, 1861, diam. 9½ in.

PLATE 129

(A) WORCESTER jug, painted in colours, probably by Humphrey Chamberlain, junior, c. 1810. Mark, 'Chamberlains Worcester', written in red. Ht 5½ in. WORCESTER vase and cover, painted with a distant view of Magdalen College, Oxford, c. 1820. Mark on cover, 'Chamberlains Worcester & 155 New Bond Street London', written in red. Ht 8¾ in. WORCESTER jug, painted with a view of Worcester, c. 1810. Ht 5 in.

(B) WORCESTER vase, c. 1820. Mark, 'Flight Barr and Barr Worcester London House 1 Coventry Street', and 'Royal Porcelain Works', written in red. Ht 5 in. WORCESTER pot-pourri vase, c. 1810. Mark 'Barr Flight and Barr Royal Porcelain Works Worcester London House N.1. Coventry Street' written in red. Ht 8⅜ in. WORCESTER toy ewer, c. 1820. Mark, 'Flight Barr and Barr Worcester', written in black. Ht 3½ in.

PLATE 130

(A) WORCESTER beaker, c. 1795. Height 3¾ inches, diameter 3⅜ inches. WORCESTER chocolate cup with cover and saucer, c. 1800. Mark on all three pieces 'B' incised. Cup, height 5¼ inches; saucer, diameter 6⅜ inches. WORCESTER mug painted with a figure of Poetry, after a painting by Angelica Kauffmann, c. 1783. Height 3¼ inches.

(B) WORCESTER mug, printed in black from copper-plate by Handeck, c. 1760. Height 4¾ inches. WORCESTER jug, printed in black with a foxhunting scene adapted from a painting entitled '*In Full Chace*' by James Seymour, c. 1780. Height 7 inches. WORCESTER mug, printed in black with a bust of Queen Charlotte from a plate by Hancock, c. 1765. Height 4¾ inches.

PLATE 131

WORCESTER vase, decorated on either side with the arms of the Honourable East India Company, c. 1830. Mark, 'FBB' under a crown, impressed. Height 15 inches.

PLATE 132

(A) WORCESTER jug, decorated in imitation of Japanese Imari porcelain, c. 1800. Height 7 inches. WORCESTER inkstand, decorated in imitation of Japanese Imari porcelain, c. 1800. Mark, 'Chamberlains Worcester' partly obliterated, written in gold. Height 4¼ inches, length 9¼ inches. WORCESTER jug, decorated in imitation of Japanese Imari porcelain, c. 1810. Height 6¾ inches.

(B) *Left:* WORCESTER vase and cover, decorated in imitation of Japanese Imari porcelain, c. 1800. Mark, on the vase 'T' incised, on the cover 'Chamberlains Wors No. 276' written in red. Ht 19¼ inches. (C) *Right:* WORCESTER vase, decorated in the style of Japanese Kakiemon porcelain, c. 1770. Ht 11¼ inches.

PLATE 133

(A) WORCESTER mug, porcelain, painted in colours, c. 1780. Height 3½ inches.

(B) WORCESTER beaker, painted by Thomas Baxter, c. 1820. Mark 'Chamberlains Worcester' written in gold. Height 3⅜ inches.

(C) WORCESTER mug, porcelain, printed in black, c. 1765. Height 5⅞ inches.

(D) WORCESTER mug, c. 1760. Mark, an open crescent in blue. Height 5 inches.

(E) WORCESTER mug, porcelain, printed in red, c. 1761. Height 6 inches.

(F) WORCESTER mug, porcelain, decorated with prints in lilac washed over with enamel colours, c. 1765. Height 3½ inches, diameter 2⅞ inches.

PLATE 134

(A and B) WORCESTER jug, porcelain, painted in colours, c. 1760. Height 10½ inches, width 7¼ inches.

(C) WORCESTER goblet, porcelain, printed in black and gilt, c. 1775.
Height 3½ inches, width 4⅝ inches.

(D) WORCESTER cup and saucer, porcelain, painted in colours and gilt, c. 1802.
Cup height 3 inches, saucer diameter 6½ inches.

PLATE 135

(B) WORCESTER tea-pot, porcelain, painted in colours and gilded, c. 1765. Height 5½ inches.

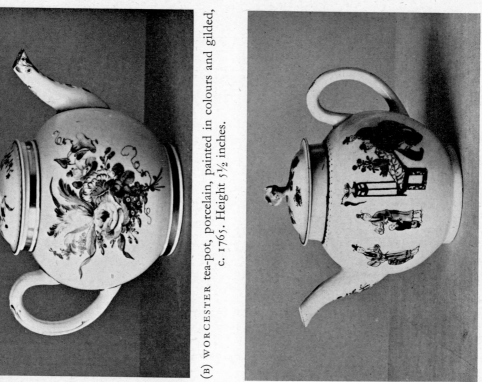

(D) WORCESTER tea-pot and cover, decorated in imitation of Chinese porcelain, c. 1770. Height 5½ inches.

(A) WORCESTER tea-pot, porcelain, painted in colours and gilded, c. 1765. Height 5 inches.

(C) WORCESTER tea-pot and cover, porcelain, painted in colours and gilded, c. 1775. Height 5⅞ inches, diameter 4⅞ inches.

PLATE 136

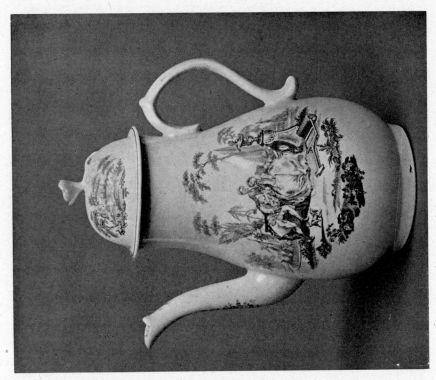

(B) WORCESTER coffee-pot and cover, porcelain, decorated with transfer prints, c. 1765. Height 8¾ inches.

(A) WORCESTER coffee-pot and cover, c. 1760. Height 8 inches.

PLATE 137

(A) WORCESTER plate, Grainger's factory, porcelain printed in colours and gilt. Mark, 'New China Works, Worcester', in red. Diameter 8½ inches.

(B) WORCESTER plate of Chamberlain's Worcester. Painted and signed 'T. Baxter 1808'. Diameter 9⅜ inches.

(C) WORCESTER plate, c. 1775. Diameter 8 inches.

(D) WORCESTER dessert-plate, Flight and Barr, c. 1800. Diameter 9 inches.

PLATE 138

(A) *Left:* WORCESTER Flight and Barr plate, c. 1810. Marks 'BFB' under a crown impressed; 'Barr Flight and Barr Royal Porcelain Works' within an oval surrounded by the words 'Manufacturers to their Majesties, Prince of Wales, and Royal Family. Established 1751', and surmounted by Crown and Prince of Wales' feathers, printed in red. Diameter 8¾ inches. (B) *Right:* WORCESTER dish, porcelain, printed in black and gilt, c. 1775. Width, 8¼ inches.

(C) *Left:* WORCESTER dessert dish, c. 1770. Width 7⅞ inches. (D) *Right:* WORCESTER Chamberlain dessert-dish, painted by Humphrey Chamberlain junior, copied from an engraving by F. Bartolozzi after a design by Angelica Kauffmann, c. 1800. 9 inches square.

PLATE 139

WORCESTER porcelain basket with cover and stand, c. 1770. Basket, height 5½ inches, length 7½ inches.

PLATE 140

(A) WORCESTER Chamberlain's factory, Jardiniere, porcelain painted in colours, c. 1815.
Mark, 'Chamberlains Worcester' in gold. 'Orpheus and Eurydice' probably painted by
Thomas Baxter. Height 8⅛ inches, length 8⅜ inches, width 3¼ inches.

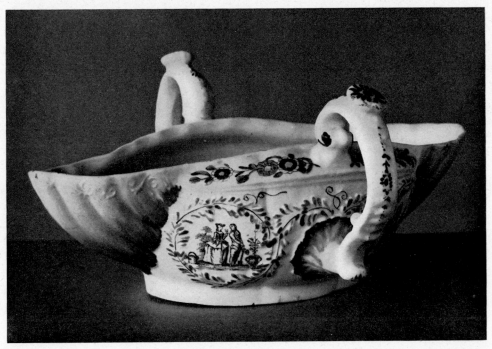

(B) WORCESTER sauceboat, porcelain, printed in black and painted in colours, c. 1756.
Length 7½ inches.

PLATE 141

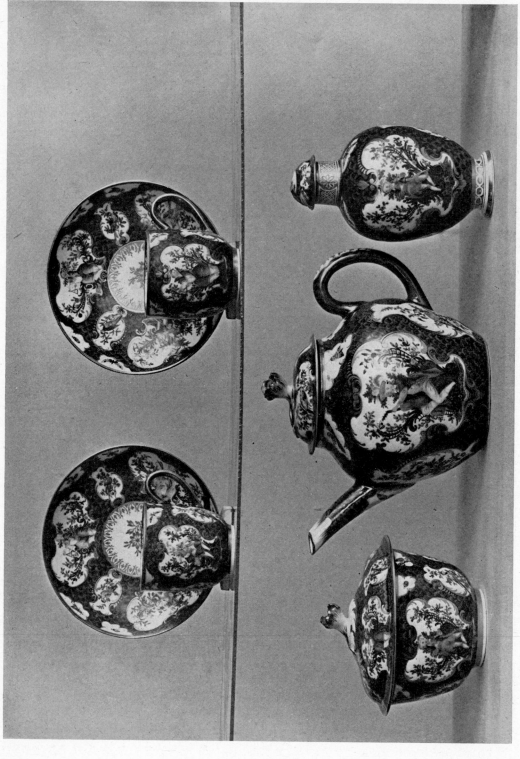

WORCESTER part of a tea service, porcelain painted in colours and gilded. Mark, a fretted square in underglaze blue, c. 1770. Height of tea-pot 6¼ inches.

PLATE 142

WORCESTER part of a tea service, c. 1775. Mark, on all except two saucers, an open crescent in blue. Tea-pot height 5¼ inches.

PLATE 143

(A) WORCESTER bowl, printed in purple and gilt, c. 1765. Height 4 inches, diameter 9 inches.

(B) *Left:* WORCESTER vase and cover, painted with figure subject of which the title 'Reward of Innocence' is written in red on the base of the vase, c. 1820. Height 6½ inches. (C) *Right:* WORCESTER vase, c. 1770. Height 8¾ inches, width 6¼ inches.

PLATE 144

as well as general pottery, High Street, Tunstall 1828–35.

MARK

Impressed

[Reginald G. Haggar, *Staffordshire Chimney Ornaments*, 1955.]

Tunstall, Staffordshire

Seat of important manufactures of various kinds of earthenware from the end of the eighteenth century. Several early 'Sun-kiln' potteries existed in this area. The more important factories are those of Adams, Clive, Child, John Wood, and Ralph Hall.

Turner, John (born 1738 died 1787), Lane End (now Longton) Staffordshire

DATE AND OWNERS

Potter at Stoke from about 1756; then at Lane End from 1762–87; continued by his sons John and William Turner until 1803, when the Company was enlarged to include, John Glover and Charles Simpson (Turner & Co). John Turner withdrew in 1804, and the company was wound up in 1806 when both the younger Turners were declared bankrupt.

MARKS

TURNER   TURNER & CO.
impressed   impressed

Turner's Patent

In red

This mark was adopted for the firm's stoneware, usually painted in red, from 1800–05.

John Turner was, Josiah Wedgwood apart, the most famous Staffordshire potter of his time. Skilful, enterprising and successful in business, much of his work is equal in quality and similar in style to Wedgwood's.

Turner manufactured white stoneware in partnership with R. Bankes at the works of Josiah Spode in Stoke till 1762 when he moved to Lane End to manufacture on his own account, largely cream-coloured wares, stoneware, dry bodies and jasper.

In 1775 Turner was involved with Wedgwood in the opposition of the Staffordshire potters to the extension of Cookworthy's patent, which Champion tried to effect. Together they leased clay-mines at St. Austell and Redruth, and though unable to prevent the renewal of Champion's patent, succeeded in restricting his use of Cornish clay to the manufacture of transparent ware.

In 1786 the firm is described as 'Turner & Abbott, Potters to the Prince of Wales, Lane End'. Abbott (whose name also occurs with that of Mist) seems to have been Turner's partner on the Continent, the firm having a depot in Delft. This Dutch trade was increased by John and William Turner, John's sons, their creamcoloured ware being shipped undecorated to be enamelled in Holland by local painters.

John Turner was a member of the NEW HALL porcelain company from 1781–82. He died in 1787.

William and John Turner succeeded their father, continuing successfully all the styles he had manufactured. But their prosperous business was ruined through its dependence on the Continental trade which was lost to them as a result of the French Revolution and the Napoleonic Wars. Their two factories closed in 1806, John Turner joining Thomas Minton as manager. When the Turner potteries closed William Adams bought some of their models for his jasper and stone-ware, and Heathcote later acquired some of their engravings. William Turner started up again in Longton and worked successfully until 1829.

ARTISTS

John Hancock. Was for sometime prior to 1800 employed by John and William Turner, and introduced the method of gilding with burnished gold.

Colour plate 21, WEDGWOOD: *see page viii for caption*

John Lucock. Principal modeller to William and John Turner.
E. Ray. Modeller of busts and portraits.
William Massey. Modeller.

DISTINGUISHING CHARACTERISTICS

The Turner factory cream-wares, stonewares, and fine blue-and-white jasper are often mistaken for Wedgwood and are frequently equal in quality.

Turner used a fine local clay he discovered at Green Dock, which fired to a light cane colour. Mixed with china clay and china stone it gave a number of fine-grained closely vitreous bodies varying in colour from a light cream to a warm buff or pie-crust colour, all of excellent quality.

Turner's blue-and-white relief-decorated jasper-ware was copied from Wedgwood's and competed with his, although Turner developed his own decorative styles, usually rather less severe than Wedgwood's.

Turner's jasper is different in formation from Wedgwood's, being a fine white stoneware or porcelain intermediate in composition between Wedgwood's and true porcelain, usually vitreous and with a glossier surface and different texture to Wedgwood's jasper, though Turner's blue is nearer to slate than Wedgwood's and the dark blue close to turquoise.

Fine grey stonewares with relief decorations were manufactured by the younger Turners; stone china which was a forerunner of the bodies used by Spode and Mason; and white earthenware transfer-printed in blue underglaze. *Plate 103, 110.*

[*Staffordshire Advertiser*, Numerous references, various dates; S. Shaw, *History of the Staffordshire Potteries*, 1829; *Directories.*]

**Turner, John, the Younger
(born 1766 died 1824),**
Lane End, Staffordshire

Son of John Turner, master-potter. Succeeded to his father's business (with his brother William) but withdrew in 1804. Bankrupt 1806. Entered the service of Minton when Poulson died in 1808. Still in financial difficulties when he moved to Dean's End, Brewood (from which the family came) in 1815. Later moved to Brewood Hall where he died.
Colour plate 14.

[*Staffordshire Advertiser*, 26 November 1803, 2, 9 and 16 August 1806, 17 September 1814, 2, 19 and 26 August, 16 September, 28 October, 4 November 1815, 29 March and 12 April 1817, 3 July 1824; *Pottery Mercury*, 7 July 1824; Reginald G. Haggar, *Staffordshire Chimney Ornaments*, 1955.]

Turner, Thomas, London

A dealer in London who employed William Duesbury and probably others to enamel porcelain bought in the white. He flourished from about 1750 until 1767.

[W. B. Honey, *Old English Porcelain* 1928, new ed. 1948.]

Turner, Thomas (born 1749 died 1809),
Caughley, Shropshire

Son of the Rev. Dr Richard Turner: proprietor of the Caughley porcelain factory 1772 until 1799, and a well-known ceramic engraver.

[L. Jewitt, *Ceramic Art of Great Britain*, 1878.]

Turner, William (born 1762 died 1835)

Son of John Turner of Lane End. Ran his father's business in collaboration with his brother and others until its closure in 1806 when he became bankrupt.

He started up again in Longton using the same shapes and patterns (*Staffordshire Advertiser*, 6 June 1807) but finally closed down in 1829. He is said to have narrowly escaped death in France during the Revolution.

[Obit., *Staffordshire Advertiser*, 13 October 1798, 27 September 1800, 8 September, 10, 17 and 24 November 1804, 5, 12 and 19 April, 5 July, 2, 9, 16 and 30 August, 13 September, 15 and 22 November 1806, 6 June and 17 October 1807, 22 May 1813, 17 October 1829, 11 July 1835; S. Shaw, *History of the Staffordshire Potteries*, 1829; *Staffordshire Mercury*, 10 October and 12 December, 1829.]

Turnor, Ralph, Staffordshire

A name which occurs on a seventeenth century posset-pot in the British Museum with an incomplete date '168'.

Twemlow, Shelton, Staffordshire

The firm of George & Thomas Twemlow was potting in Shelton in 1783. It was followed by

John Twemlow who is recorded in Shelton in 1796. Jewitt cited an invoice, dated 1797, showing that he was a manufacturer of painted earthenware tablewares, and oval and octagonal teapots in Egyptian black.

Twiffler, Twyffler

A pudding plate. The word occurs in a price agreement dated 4 February 1770, cited by Simeon Shaw. In 1842 a 'twiffle-maker' was described as 'a maker of small plates'.

[S. Shaw, *History of the Staffordshire Potteries*, 1829.]

Twigg, see under KILNHURST

Twyford, (Twiford), Joshua

A Shelton potter who is alleged to have insinuated himself into the employment of Elers at Bradwell Wood in order to obtain the secrets of his manufacture. His name is generally given as Joshua and he is stated to have made red and black 'Elers' ware and salt-glazed stoneware. Joshua Twyford, son of William and Margaret Twyford was christened at Stoke St. Peters Church 6 December 1640, and died in 1729 and was buried 8 September. Shaw (who records his name as Josiah in his *Chemistry of Pottery*, 1837), attributes to him the introduction of pipe clay. A black teapot with vine decoration in Hanley Museum, which came from Enoch Wood's collection, is traditionally regarded as of Twyford's manufacture.

Alleged mark of Twyford
on specimen in British
Museum

[*Stoke-on-Trent Parish Registers.*]

Tyg

A word of obscure origin used to describe cylindrical drinking vessels with from one to twelve handles: a multiple-handled beaker. *Plate 104 A.*

U

Unaker

China clay. It is mentioned in the patent specification of Heylyn and Frye, (1744) as 'the produce of the Chirokee nation of America called by the natives Unaker' (specification of patents No. 610, 6 December 1744). It was used with a frit to make early Bow porcelain.

American china clay was known to Cookworthy by 1745. Richard Champion received from his brother-in-law Caleb Lloyd of Charleston, S. Carolina, in 1765 a consignment of China Clay, but the discovery of the fine clays of Cornwall released English potters from any necessity to import the ingredients of their wares.

Underglaze

Decoration (painting or printing) applied to pottery in the biscuit condition before the application of glaze and the glost-firing.

Contrasted to OVERGLAZE.

The colours of course are absolutely permanent.

Uranium Oxide

Used in a lead glaze to produce a brilliant tangerine-orange or vermilion red glaze used by William Burton at Pilkington's c.1903 and at Mintons, for their 'Solar' ware c.1905. The use of uranium is now prohibited.

Useful Wares

Wares intended for use at table or in the preparation of food in contradistinction to 'ornamental' wares, which are intended to provide visual satisfactions.

V

Van Hamme, John Arians
A Dutchman living in England c.1676 who took out a patent dated 27 October 1676 for the manufacture of tiles.
[L. Jewitt, *Ceramic Art of Great Britain*, 1878.]

Vauxhall, London
A factory manufacturing red teapots was worked here by Elers at the end of the seventeenth century. Delftware and lead-glazed earthenware was made at Vauxhall from the early years of the eighteenth century as was noted by Ralph Thoresby in his diary, 24 May 1714. Salt-glazed stoneware was made at Vauxhall by Joseph Kishere and others.

Venables & Morris, Shelton
Earthenware toy manufacturers in New Hall Street, Shelton, from 1830 until 1841.

Vermicelli ground
A ground, usually of gold, formed by covering the surface with a continuous wriggling line. The title is adapted from the long threads of vermicelli.

Verreville Pottery, Glasgow, Scotland
Established in 1777 as a glass house but turned over to earthenware in 1820 during the ownership of John Geddes. Robert Alexander Kidston became proprietor in 1835 and he and his successor, Robert Cochran, improved and extended the production to include china. Workers were brought from Staffordshire and Derby. Robert Cochran died in 1869, but the business was continued by his son and grandson.

The works were eventually sold; and finally demolished in 1918.

The porcelain made here was decorated contemporary style with elaborate floral encrustations, pierced basketwork, floral and landscape paintings. Some figures were made including 'The Seasons'.

Verwood, Dorsetshire
A country pottery which has operated from the nineteenth century and still flourishes.

Vicar and Moses
A popular subject with the Staffordshire figure makers during the second half of the eighteenth century first made by Ralph Wood. It shows a parson in the pulpit asleep, with the parish clerk at the desk below conducting the service. Recorded with Ralph Wood glazes, as a 'white' figure group, and in enamel colours. Extensively pirated. The marks

R. WOOD   Ra Wood
                 Burslem

occur occasionally. The incised mark

Incised

has been noted on a number of examples, some spurious.

Voyez, John (born c. 1735 died c. 1800)
Modeller and manufacturer of French extraction, trained as jeweller, worked in London for Rundell; associated with Capizzoldi in model of George III's state coach; worked at the artificial stone manufactory, 1767; exhibited, Free Society of Artists, London 1767-68; brought to Staffordshire by Wedgwood 1768; quarrelled with him and was imprisoned in Stafford Gaol 1769; worked for Humphrey Palmer on his

release; married, as second wife in 1770 Sarah Woodhouse, who bore him a daughter, baptised Sophia Charlotte 1774; exhibited again at Free Society 1771–72; worked for T. Hale, Cobridge; described 1772 as 'carver and manufacturer of composition at Cowbridge'; issued catalogue of seals and intaglios 1773 and did an extensive trade, undermining that of Wedgwood 1773–76; probably modelled for the Ralph Woods, of Burslem; 'Fair Hebe' jug 1788 made for Richard Meir Astbury, 1788; in London 1791; disappears from record.
Plate 149 B.

[J. T. Smith, *Nollekens and his Times*, 1828; E. Meteyard, *Life of Josiah Wedgwood*, 1865–66; Nightingale, *Contributions... English Porcelain*, 1881; *Letters of Josiah Wedgwood*, 1903; F. Falkner, *The Wood Family of Burslem*, 1912; H. Read, *Staffordshire Pottery Figures*, 1929; Reginald G. Haggar, *Staffordshire Chimney Ornaments*, 1955.]

Vyse, Charles

Stoneware potter and modeller, trained at Burslem Art School and South Kensington where he worked from 1905 until 1909 before proceeding to Italy. From 1919 he began to make pottery figures which were exhibited in Bond Street London. Experimented in the production of wood-ash glazes.

[G. W. Digby, *The Work of the Modern Potter in England* 1952.]

W

Walker

A London dealer in porcelain whose name and address appear on cream-coloured earthenware made about 1800. A pair of dolphin-shaped sauce-boats in the Schreiber Collection, Victoria & Albert Museum, are marked on the foot-rim

Walker Minories
(impressed)

[B. Rackham, *Catalogue of the Schreiber Collection*, 1930.]

Walker, Samuel

Son-in-law of William Billingsley and partner to him at Worcester and Nantgarw.

Walker & Galley, Tunstall, Staffordshire

George Walker and Samuel Galley manufactured shining black and Egyptian black wares at the Chemical works, Tunstall Bridge, for a few years until the partnership was abruptly terminated in November 1841.

[*Staffordshire Advertiser*, 13 November 1841.]

Wall, John (born 1708 died 1776)

Dr John Wall was the son of a one-time Mayor of Worcester and a successful local tradesman. He was the ward of Lord Sandys and married Lord Sandys's cousin. Well-educated locally, he went to Oxford, became a Fellow of Merton, studied medicine at St Thomas's Hospital, London, and did some competent amateur painting. He was one of the original shareholders in the Worcester concern formed in 1751 for the manufacture of soapstone porcelain. He died in 1776. The first period of Worcester Porcelain is known among collectors as the 'Dr. Wall period' and is used to cover wares produced down to the year 1783, seven years after his death.

Walley, William (born 1785 died 1842)

Manufacturer of toys, figures, and animals at a small back-street potworks employing 8 workers in Marsh Street, Shelton.

[*Staffordshire Advertiser*, 31 December 1842; *Govt. Report*, 1842.]

Walthall, Peter

Attorney, Newcastle-under-Lyme; partner with Job Meigh in the firm of Meigh and Walthall, pottery manufacturers, Old Hall Pottery, Hanley, 1790–1802.

[*Staffordshire Advertiser*, 8 May 1802; Information per Alfred Meigh.]

Waltham Abbey, Essex

A potter named Henry Walker worked at Upshere Hamlet, in this parish, 1848.

[White's *Directory of Essex* 1848.]

Walton, John, Burslem

Began his manufacture of pottery figures in the first decade of the nineteenth century and flourished until 1835. His factory was in Navigation Road, Burslem, where he made figures with tree backgrounds decorated with bright enamel colours, and Egyptian black. Often there is a large blue scroll on the base of his figures, which are sometimes marked within a scroll at the back.

Impressed

Occasionally the mark is underneath. He made well modelled toby jugs as well as toys decorated with gay, bright colour. His potworks was taken over by George Hood who probably continued to use the moulds.

Not to be confused with other figure-makers of the same surname:

James Walton, Brunswick Street, Hanley, fl. 1848–51.

Joshua Walton, Piccadilly, Hanley, fl. 1830–35.

William Walton, Hope Street, Shelton, fl. 1846.

Examples in the British Museum; Victoria and Albert Museum; Hanley Museum, Stoke-on-Trent; Temple Newsam, Leeds; and the Fitzwilliam Museum, Cambridge.

Plate 155 B.

[Reginald G.Haggar, *Staffordshire Chimney Ornaments*, 1955.]

Warburton family, Cobridge, Staffordshire

A family of potters working at Fenton Low and Cobridge in the eighteenth and early nineteenth centuries. Joseph Warburton (1694–1752) was one of the most important potters in the early part of the eighteenth century. His factory was in Hot Lane. He was succeeded by his son John (1720–61) who married Ann Daniel (1713–98) the 'Widow' Warburton who decorated pottery for Josiah Wedgwood. Mrs Warburton had her son Thomas (d.1798) as partner and traded as Ann Warburton & Son. Jacob Warburton, another son, had a factory at Cobridge. He was born 1741 and died 1826, and became a principal in the New Hall concern. Other members of the Warburton family had factories at Cobridge: Joseph (d. 1827) as a manufacturer of common earthenware; James, maker of garden pots, saggers, chimney pipes and quarries; and John who made earthenware. Peter Warburton (whom see) made cream-coloured ware at Bleak Hill, Cobridge, and had as partner his younger brother Francis until 1802, when the latter went to France and set up as manufacturer of cream-coloured earthenware at La Charité-sur-Loire.

[Reginald G.Haggar, 'The Warburton Family of Cobridge, *Apollo*, 1955.]

Warburton, John (born 1720 died 1761)
and successors Earthenware manufactory
Hot Lane, Cobridge, Staffordshire

DATES AND OWNERS

The factory worked by John Warburton was in existence in 1710 and was in fact one of the largest in the Potteries at that time. John Warburton's widow carried on the business after his death, and through their son, Thomas Warburton, the firm remained in the hands of the Warburton family for more than a century.

MARK

WARBURTON (impressed)

WORK

Primarily makers of cream-coloured wares. These were much improved during Mrs Warburton's management of the business. The factory was also engaged at this period in independent enamelling, much of it for Wedgwood who sent quantities of tableware to Hot Lane for this purpose. Marked pieces are extremely rare.

A marked two-handled vase decorated with black slip and gilding is in the Victoria and Albert Museum. Another, of white ware decorated in black and gold, is in the British Museum.

Warburton, Peter (born 1773 died 1813)

Manufacturer of cream-coloured earthenware first of all in partnership with Francis Warburton until 29 March 1802 when the partnership was dissolved (*Staffordshire Advertiser*, 3 April 1802) and subsequently on his own account at Bleak Hill Cobridge. Between 1804 and 1810 he became a partner in the New Hall joint stock company. In 1810 he took out a patent for transfer-printing in gold. He died 24 January 1813 (*Staffordshire Advertiser*, 30 January 1813). He married Mary, daughter of Francis Emery, who survived until 6 November 1837. The mark of Peter and Francis Warburton was

Impressed

Wares decorated with gold transfer prints were marked 'Warburton's Patent' beneath a crown, in mauve. Excellent cream-coloured table wares were made as well as figures in the style of Ralph Wood.

[Reginald G. Haggar, 'The Warburton Family of Cobridge' in *Apollo*, 1955; *Burslem Parish Registers*; *Staffordshire Advertiser*.]

Ward, George, Staffordshire

An earthenware potter whose name occurs on an undated early eighteenth century Staffordshire slipware posset-pot inscribed: 'George Ward made this cup and so no more but God bless the Queen and all her parleme'.

[B. Rackham, *Early Staffordshire Pottery*, 1951; J.E. and E. Hodgkin, *Examples of Early English Pottery, named, dated and inscribed*, 1891.]

'Warren Hastings' pattern

A decoration comprising border panels of figures and landscapes, combined with scattered 'Meissen' flowers, which decorated a set of Chelsea porcelain at one time in the possession of Warren Hastings (1732–1818), and sold at Dalesford House in 1818.

Warrington, Lancashire

A pottery was established here about 1797 by two Quaker brothers, James and Fletcher Bolton who took as managing partner, Joseph Ellis of Hanley, a former apprentice of Josiah Wedgwood. Staffordshire workmen were engaged, but the firm did not remain long in existence. Wares of inferior quality usually unmarked were produced including blue-and-white earthenware, black ware, etc. The Boltons became bankrupt in 1812.

[L. Jewitt, *Ceramic Art of Great Britain*, 1878.]

Watcombe, near Torquay, Devonshire

Established in 1869 for the manufacture of terra cotta and 'art' manufactures. Charles Brock of Hanley became art director and manager about 1870.

Statuettes, busts, candlesticks, jugs, tobacco jars, as well as architectural enrichments were made. The business was carried on under the name THE WATCOMBE TERRA COTTA CLAY CO. Among other marks used was:

WATCOMBE
TORQUAY

Wattisfield, Suffolk

A Roman pottery site, evidently worked in medieval times and subsequently. There are records of potters in the parish from 1646 until 1689. Thomas Death leased this pottery site from John Coggisdale in 1754 and he and his descendants apparently continued to work the factory until Thomas Watson took it over in 1808. The Watson family have potted here continuously ever since, producing frying pans, washing bowls, gotches, steens and bread pans for local kitchen use, and when these went out of favour flower pots for the great East Anglian estates and nurseries. Recently the country potter's craft and the slip technique have undergone a revival. A jug in Brighton Museum with a streaky, purple-brown glaze which is lettered 'Nathaniel Mos in Hepworth October the 2nd 1739' is attributed to Wattisfield because of its colours and because Hepworth is a neighbouring village. In 1844 Thomas Harrison was also making brown earthenware in this village.

MARK

SFK

Impressed

[Reginald G. Haggar, *English Country Pottery*, 1950.]

Watts, B.

Name occurring incised upon two glazed yellow earthenware watch stands in the form of castles: 'B. Watts, Ferrybridge, 1839'. (Yorkshire Museum, York). The maker is otherwise unknown.

Watts, John (died 1858), Lambeth

Partner in the firm of Doulton & Watts, Lambeth from 1815 until 1854 when he retired.

Wayte & Ridge, Longton

China, parian, earthenware and lustre were manufactured by this firm at the Waterloo Place Works, Heathcote Road, Longton, in 1864. Figures with their impressed mark

W & R
L
85

Impressed

have been recorded.

Weaver, John (died 1735), Bristol

A potter at Bristol from 1724 until 1735, co-partner with William Pottery of the Limekiln Lane Pottery.

[W. G. Pountney, *Old British Potteries*, 1920.]

Webber, Henry

Modeller and head of the ornamental department, Wedgwood's, Etruria 1782–1801; recommended to Josiah Wedgwood by Sir William Chambers and Sir Joshua Reynolds, and commenced work 2 July 1782 at salary of £ 252 per annum; sent to Rome, July 1787, where he worked in the Capitoline Museum and travelled in Italy with Wedgwood's eldest son; worked on the Portland Vase.

[E. Meteyard, *Life of Josiah Wedgwood*, 1865–66; W. Mankowitz, *The Portland Vase and the Wedgwood Copies*, 1952.]

Wedging

Slicing and kneading together prepared clay to remove pockets or bubbles of air. '...they wage it, i.e. knead or mould it, like bread'. (R. Plot, *Natural History of Staffordshire* 1686.)

Wedgwood Family, N. Staffordshire

Gilbert Wedgwood potted at the Overhouse, Burslem, about 1612. His son Thomas built the Churchyard Works at which two successive Wedgwood generations worked, although the more successful potting branch of the family through this period were cousins, Dr Thomas Wedgwood and his son (1655 to 1717 and 1695 to 1737), whose salt-glazed wares were highly esteemed.

The family achieved international eminence with the rise of Josiah, the quality of whose earthenware products enabled him to establish, between the years 1759 and 1795, the firm which still continues.

[J. C. Wedgwood, *The Wedgwood Family*, 1910.]

Wedgwood, Josiah (b. 1730 d. 1795), Burslem and Etruria, Staffordshire. Potter

HISTORY

Josiah Wedgwood was born in 1730 at Burslem, the youngest and thirteenth child of Thomas and Mary of the Churchyard Works, where Josiah was apprenticed to his brother Thomas in 1744.

Josiah left the Churchyard in 1752 to go into partnership at Stoke with John Harrison and John Aldersea, or Alders, at Cliffe Bank, where he made agate, tortoise-shell and other staple wares until, desiring greater experimental opportunities, he joined Thomas Whieldon for a five-year partnership in 1754.

On leaving Whieldon in 1759 Wedgwood took over the Ivy House Works, which he retained until 1773 for the manufacture of useful wares. In 1764 he rented the Brick House (or Bell Works) to accommodate his expanding trade. In 1766 he bought the Ridge House Estate where he proceeded to erect a house and factory which he named Etruria. The same year he proposed a partnership to Thomas Bentley, a Liverpool merchant with valuable Continental connections, whose taste for classical art accorded with his own. In 1769 Bentley joined him, the partnership lasting until Bentley's death in 1780. The Wedgwood & Bentley Etruria period was responsible for the finest products of the factory.

Wedgwood's business expanded in all wares (except bone-china and porcelain, which he never manufactured) until his death in 1795, when the factory was inherited by his second son Josiah.

MANUFACTURES

Cliffe Bank, 1752 to 1754

Staple wares were made, including agate and marble knife hafts and cloudy, tortoise-shell and black wares with lead or salt glazes. Wedgwood's own work is not determinable.

Whieldon/Wedgwood partnership, 1754 to 1759

Wedgwood improved coloured glazes generally, and in the course of his experimental work devised 'a green glaze to be laid on common white (or cream-colour) biscuit ware'. He subsequently described this glaze as 'the result of many experiments that I made in order to introduce a new species of coloured ware to be fired along with the tortoise-shell or agate ware in our common gloss ovens, to be of an even self-colour, and laid upon the ware in the form of a coloured glaze'. Some green glazed items may have been made in the latter days of the partnership. Since, however, the experiments came to fruition so late in this phase, it is more reasonable to ascribe the finer and purer green glazed wares to Wedgwood's next period of manufacture.

Ivy House, 1759 to 1764

Wedgwood continued the production of staple and Whieldon style wares but added green and, after 1760, yellow glaze, devising such shapes as the cauliflower and the pineapple to use the new colours to advantage. The modelling of these styles was contracted out, principally to William Greatbatch of Lane Delph, Fenton. Other styles jobbed out for modelling to Greatbatch included the leaf and the Chinese, some of the latter in red unglazed ware being marked by a pseudo-Chinese seal. None of these jobbed-out items were, however, marked 'Wedgwood'.

Cream-ware was probably perfected by Wedgwood in 1762 when he presented Queen Charlotte with a caudle and breakfast set. After 1765, in which year Wedgwood was first styled 'Potter to the Queen', the product was known as Queen's ware. The best examples are pale in shade, light in weight, often decorated in coloured enamels, with border patterns often of neoclassical design. Earlier examples are free-hand painted with flowers or with transfers and enamels, the earlier transfer examples being by Sadler & Green, the later by engravers whom Wedgwood employed in Staffordshire. The finest free-hand decorating was carried out under Bentley's supervision at a workshop in Chelsea (e.g. the Catherine service). Most cream-ware and all Queen's ware items are impress marked, the earlier in upper and lower case, the later in upper case only. Manufacture of cream-ware has continued to the present day.

Brick House or Bell Works, 1764 to 1769

Wedgwood concentrated on increasing out-put of useful wares in Queen's ware, though many items, both useful and decorative, were made in basaltes. Items are impressed in upper and lower case, or in upper case; quality is high.

Etruria, opened June 13th 1769

The first day's production consisted of six Etruscan ware vases thrown by Wedgwood while Bentley turned the wheel. They were painted with red classical figures and inscribed 'Artes Etruriae Renascuntur' ('The Arts of Etruria are re-born'), a clear indication of the ambitions and tastes of the partnership and the style which was to dominate its period.

Before 1780 basaltes had been developed as a decorative body applied with endless variation to the manufacture of chimney ornaments, vases and decorative useful ware of the finest quality. The seal and wafer marks were used on vases and larger pieces, and the upper and lower case or upper case *Wedgwood & Bentley* mark impressed on smaller items. Encaustic and enamel decoration, finely finished high reliefs and perfect lapidary polishing, typify the basaltes of this period.

The partnership was formed in regard to the manufacture of decorative wares but Bentley was associated with Wedgwood in all major enterprises of the period, and especially responsible for the decoration of the service commissioned by Catherine the Great of Russia, an undertaking which established Wedgwood's useful wares at the highest point of fashion and the top of the market. Creamware was also, in this period, developed decoratively, the 'surface agates' and other styles emulating polished stone, garnitures or suites of chimney ornaments being the most successful. These are often found with basaltes bases with the wafer or seal mark, or are otherwise impressed Wedgwood & Bentley.

It was also during the partnership that Wedgwood developed his most successful decorative ware. Called at first 'the white body', Wedgwood's intention was to to devise a body with lapidary imitative possibilities, one capable of emulating Graeco-Roman objects in coloured glass or polished natural stone. Through 1773 to 1774 he experimented with 'white spars and earths', many of which had never been used before. By the end of 1774 he had developed a 'fine white terracotta of great beauty and delicacy' with a 'waxen' finish. By 1776 he had improved the body, which he then described as 'a fine white artificial jasper of exquisite beauty and delicacy, proper for cameos, portraits and bas-reliefs'. The two styles of jasper, tinted in various colours, but especially in blues, are described in the 1787 catalogue as;

'a) White porcelain biscuit with a smooth wax-like surface, of the same properties as the basaltes except in what depends on colour'

and

'b) Jasper – a white porcelain biscuit'.

Jasper was used with conspicuous success as a decorative body, a vast range of items being produced in it of great fineness and finish, including tea and chocolate ware, vases, plaques, bas-reliefs, and cameos in all sizes, in light and dark blues, green, black, lilac or lavender, and a peach-pink, usually with white reliefs. The jasper product of the partnership period is, however, largely blue-and-white or solid white, and is usually marked Wedgwood & Bentley, impressed though many smaller items are found unmarked, being units of sets and sold as such.

After Bentley's death the jasper experiments continued, culminating in the immense project of 1786 to 1790, the making of the Portland Vase copies, which items are the finest jasper product Wedgwood ever achieved and represent the peak of the body's success as a fashionable article of commerce.

While basaltes, jasper and Queen's ware are the most successful of Wedgwood wares, other 'dry' or unglazed bodies enjoyed a considerable market in both decorative and useful applications. These were all made from local marls to which various 'ochrous' earths were added to produce colour. There are many variations of colour due to the quantity of admixture and the degree of firing. These wares were described by Wedgwood as

a) Rosso antico; dark red to chocolate
b) Cane ware; buff
c) Terra cotta; light red
d) Drab ware; olive grey
e) White stone ware: pure white

SUBSEQUENT HISTORY OF THE FIRM

Josiah Wedgwood II's conduct of the factory was unsuccessful due to his lack of interest coupled with the damage to trade caused by the Napoleonic Wars – so much so, that in 1811 he wrote 'the business is not worth carrying on, and if I could withdraw my capital from it, I would tomorrow'. Nevertheless, the period is distinguished by ten years of experiment in and production of bone-china (1812 to 1822). Tea and dessert ware was made and painted by John Cutts of Pinxton (principally landscapes) and Aaron Steele (Etruscan styles and birds). There was also a fine fruit painter who is unidentified, and a number of printed designs. Items are found marked in upper case under the glaze, printed in blue, black, red and gold. The ware found no great success.

By 1828 Wedgwood's trade had so declined that the London showrooms were closed, the stock of wares and old moulds and models being sold for £16,000, a considerable disaster to the firm and one from which it was unable to recover for many years.

In 1875 a London showroom was opened again and in 1878 the making of bone-china revived. Emile Lessore is the only artist of this period whose work has high quality. With the opening of the modern Wedgwood factory at Barlaston (started before and completed just after the 1939 War) the firm regained its eminent position and has, in the post-war period, become once again one of the most successful of English pottery and porcelain manufacturers. Contemporary production concentrates on useful wares in bone china and earthenware, but some jasper and basaltes are still made.

WEDGWOOD ARTISTS

Art Directors

Allen, Thomas 1880–1900
Goodwin, John Edward 1900–1934
Skellern, Victor 1934

Resident Designers and Artists

Lessore, Emile 1859–1875
Taplin, Millicent 1927
Wall, Peter
Cholerton, Herbert A. 1901
Hodgkiss, James c. 1900–1925
Holland, Arthur Dale 1908–1940
Steel, Aaron 1784–1812
Wilson, Ralph 1769–1776
Wilcox, Sarah 1769–1776

Outside Designers

Beauclerk, Lady Diana 1789
Crane, Walter, R. W. S. 1867–1877
Holmes, Sir Charles John, K.C.V.O., 1930
Hammersley, J. A. 1844–1845
Murray, Keith, R. D. I. 1932
Powell, Alfred 1910–
Ravilious, Eric 1935–1942
Templeton, Lady 1783–1787
Wedgwood, Star 1930
Zinkeisen, Anna 1930–
Wilson, Norman 1927–

Modellers

Austin, Arnold 1904–1947
Austin, J. A. 1904–1927
Bedson, William 1773–1776
Birks, Joseph 1867–1875
Birks, Simon 1867–1875
Boot, Thomas 1769–1773
Brownsword, Henry 1849–1853
Hackwood, William 1769–1832
Keeling, William 1769
Keys, Edward 1845–1853
Owen, Eric Raymond 1947
Schenk, Frederick 1872–1873
Toft, Charles 1880–1889
Voyez, John 1768–1769
Webber, Henry 1784–1801
Wood, William 1767–1808

Outside Modellers

Bacon, John, R.A.
Coward, John 1765–1769
Dalmazzoni, Angelo 1785–1792
Flaxman, John, R. A. 1775–1800
Mangiarotti, Michelangelo 1788
de Wilde 1777
Pacetti, Camillo 1787
de Vaere, John 1787–1798
Lochee, John Charles 1774–1788
Protât, Hugues 1870–1871
Smith, Joachim 1774–1782
Stephan, Pierre
Stubbs, George, A. R. A., 1780–1790
Tassie, James 1769–1791
Wyon, E. W. 1852–1866
Machin, Arnold R. A., 1938
Skeaping, John 1930
Theed, William, R. A., 1799–1814

MARKS

JOSIAH WEDGWOOD
Feb. 2nd 1805

Wedgwood & Bentley

Wedgwood
& Bentley
356

Wedgwood WEDGWOOD

WEDGWOOD & SONS   WEDGWOOD

Wedgwood
& Bentley

E. Lifsore

Wedgwood & Bentley: Etruria

Wedgwood
& Bentley

WEDGWOOD
WEDGWOOD

Wedgwood
Wedgwood

Wedgwood

WEDGWOOD

W. & B.

WEDGWOOD

Wedgwood wares may be seen at the British Museum where the Portland Vase can be compared with the original, Victoria & Albert Museum, Nottingham Castle Museum, Lady Lever Art Gallery Port Sunlight, Wedgwood Museum, Barlaston, Stoke-on-Trent Museum and Art Gallery, Art Institute of Chicago, Metropolitan Museum of Art, New York, Fogg Museum of Art, Cambridge, (Mass.), and Philadelphia Museum of Art.

Colour plates 20 and 21 and plates 113–128.

[W. Mankowitz, *Wedgwood*, 1953; W. Mankowitz, *The Portland Vase and the Wedgwood Copies*, 1952; E.Meteyard, *Life of Josiah Wedgwood*, 1865–66; L.Jewitt, *The Wedgwoods*, 1865; K.E.Farrer (ed) *Letters of Josiah Wedgwood*, 1903 and 1906; see bibliography.]

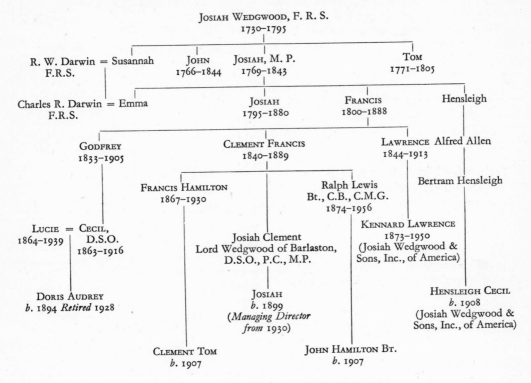

GILBERT WEDGWOOD, at the Overhouse, Burslem (1588–1678)
THOMAS WEDGWOOD, at the Churchyard House, Burslem (1617–1679)
THOMAS WEDGWOOD, at the Churchyard House, Burslem (1660–1716)
THOMAS WEDGWOOD, at the Churchyard House, Burslem (1687–1739)

JOSIAH WEDGWOOD, F. R. S.
1730–1795

R. W. Darwin = Susannah   JOHN   JOSIAH, M. P.   TOM
F.R.S.   1766–1844 1769–1843   1771–1805

Charles R. Darwin = Emma   JOSIAH   FRANCIS   Hensleigh
F.R.S.   1795–1880 1800–1888

GODFREY   CLEMENT FRANCIS   LAWRENCE Alfred Allen
1833–1905   1840–1889   1844–1913

FRANCIS HAMILTON   Ralph Lewis   Bertram Hensleigh
1867–1930   Bt., C.B., C.M.G.
                    1874–1956

LUCIE = CECIL,   KENNARD LAWRENCE
1864–1939   D.S.O.   Josiah Clement   1873–1950
            1863–1916 Lord Wedgwood of Barlaston, (Josiah Wedgwood &
                       D.S.O., P.C., M.P.   Sons, Inc., of America)

DORIS AUDREY   JOSIAH   HENSLEIGH CECIL
b. 1894 Retired 1928   b. 1899   b. 1908
                        (Managing Director (Josiah Wedgwood &
                        from 1930)   Sons, Inc., of America)

CLEMENT TOM   JOHN HAMILTON BT.
b. 1907   b. 1907

Note: Names in Small Capitals connected with the firm.

Wedgwood & Co, Tunstall

Earthenware manufacturers established c.1840 by Enoch Wedgwood (born 1813 died 1879) and Jabez Charles Wedgwood, as E. Wedgwood & Co. Became a limited liability company, 1900.

Not to be confused with the firm of Wedgwood & Co. in which Ralph Wedgwood was concerned. See RALPH WEDGWOOD.

Wedgwood, Aaron (born 1624 died 1700), Burslem, Staffordshire

Stoneware potter, son of Gilbert Wedgwood and father of Thomas and Richard Wedgwood, potters. Cited by Dwight for an infringement of his patent in 1693.

Wedgwood, Enoch (born 1813 died 1879)

Master potter, son of Isaac and Charlotte Wedgwood. Became partner in the firm of Podmore, Walker & Co. c.1835, and head of the firm a few years later when, with his brother, he founded the business of E. Wedgwood & Co. Chief Bailiff of Tunstall 1855 and 1856.

Wedgwood, Ralph (born 1766 died 1837), Burslem and Ferrybridge

Manufacturer of cream-coloured earthenware at Burslem under the style Wedgwood & Company, late eighteenth century. He suffered from the depression in the trade in 1793 and was compelled to part with a number of his work-people (letter of Josiah Wedgwood 22 April 1793) soon after becoming bankrupt (various notices *Staffordshire Advertiser*, 29 April 1797–8 December 1804). He then went to Yorkshire where he entered into partnership with others in the Knottingley (later Ferrybridge) Pottery in 1797 but left about 1800 and went to London to pursue an ineffective but inventive career, producing duplicating apparatus which he called a 'Pennaepolygraph' among other inventions. He died in 1837. The mark WEDGWOOD & Co., impressed frequently recorded as the mark of the Knottingley Company probably refers to Wedgwood & Co., Burslem.

Wedgwood, Richard (born 1668 died 1718)

Stoneware potter, Burslem, cited by Dwight for infringement of his patent 1693.

Wedgwood Society, The

Founded in London, March 1955, by Sir George Barnes and Wolf Mankowitz, to cater for the needs of students, collectors and experts. Issues transactions edited by Geoffrey Wills.

[*Evening Sentinel*, 15 March 1955.]

Wedgwood, Dr Thomas

(born 1655 died 1717), Burslem, Staffordshire Stoneware potter at Ruffleys. He was cited by Dwight for infringing his patent. Succeeded by his son of the same name, who is thought to have made improvements in the body, producing a fine drab- or putty-coloured stoneware.

Wedgwood, Date Marks

A system of marks recording the date of manufacture of earthenware was introduced at the Wedgwood factory in 1860 and consisted of three capital letters representing month, potter and year respectively.

MONTH MARKS FROM 1860 TO 1864

J January	Y May	S September
F February	T June	O October
M March	V July	N November
A April	W August	D December

MONTH MARKS FROM 1864 TO 1907

J January	M May	S September
F February	T June	O October
R March	L July	N November
A April	W August	D December

YEAR MARKS 1860–1930

An Alphabetical cycle starting with O for 1860 and ending with Z for 1871: A 1872, Z 1897; A 1898, Z 1923; A 1924, G 1930.

In 1930 this somewhat confusing method of dating was changed and simplified, a figure being used to indicate the month (1–12 January to December), a letter for the potter, and two figures for the year (thus 35 for 1935, or 50 for 1950).

Wednesbury, Staffordshire

Plot records 'divers sorts of *Vessels* which they paint with Slip, made of a *reddish* sort of *earth* gotten at Tipton' (1686). These wares have not been identified but probably have been attributed to North Staffordshire. The names of Wednesbury potters have not been recorded, but two names survive in Birmingham Reference Library. Thomas Mills of Wednesbury, potter, was creditor in a quitclaim 20 November 1740, while Joseph Perry, potter, is mentioned in documents concerning lands dated 12 September 1749. The 'last potters removed from the parish about fifty years ago, and went to reside in the Staffordshire potteries'. (J.N. Bagnall, *A History of Wednesbury*, Wolverhampton, 1854).

[R.Plot, *Natural History of Staffordshire*, 1686.]

Wells, Reginald

Sculptor and potter; commenced potting at Col'drum Farm, West Malling, in Kent, c.1904, and sold his wares at his own shop in Sloane Street London; in the 1920's he potted at Chelsea.

Welsh Wares

Shallow meat dishes decorated with feathered slip designs. They are shaped like a gardener's trug and were commonly made in Staffordshire, Sunderland and Isleworth under the above name.

Weston, Lane End

The firm of Weston & Hull (George, John and William Weston, James Hull and Thomas Harley) is recorded in Lane End as manufacturing earthenware about 1796. Hull withdrew 21 November 1796, the business continuing under the same style. By 1801 the three Westons were potting alone and continued until 11 November 1804 when John Weston decided to start up on his own, leaving his brothers to continue as George Weston & Co. John Weston was bankrupt in less than 2 years. George Weston & Co. continued until 1829.

[*Directories*, 1796–1823; *Staffordshire Advertiser*, 3 December 1796, 12 December 1801, 15 December 1804, 16 May 1807; *Pottery Mercury*, 14 November 1829.]

Whieldon, Thomas. Potter (born 1719 died 1795),

Fenton Low (or Little Fenton), Staffordshire

DATES

Thomas Whieldon founded his factory in 1740. From 1754 until 1759 Josiah Wedgwood was his partner. He built up an extensive business and made a fortune estimated at £ 10,000 from his trade. He declined potting about 1780, and became High Sheriff of Staffordshire in 1786.

MARKS

No marks were used at his pottery.

WORK

Whieldon, one of the best-known of English potters, had a strong and lasting influence on the tastes of his time and on the work of craftsmen to follow him. His apprentices were many, amongst them Josiah Spode, Aaron Wood the block cutter, Robert Garner, Wm. Greatbach, J. Barker and Uriah Sutton.

Whieldon gave his name to a highly developed type of earthenware distinctive for its wide range of colours made possible by the use of coloured clays in the body and also by means of staining oxides in the glaze. Starting from the agate ware made at an earlier date, Whieldon revived and improved the methods formerly used, producing marbled wares of considerable merit. Simple shapes were customary in plates, dishes and other articles, the pieces relying mainly on colour for their appeal. 'Tortoiseshell' ware was amongst Whieldon's most successful productions. For decoration, applied reliefs often in paler clay are characteristic. Spouts and handles were often made in a lighter-coloured clay, and lead glazes were used.

Josiah Wedgwood became Whieldon's partner in 1754; he was certainly in a great measure responsible for many of the improvements and developments which gave Whieldon his leading place amongst potters of his time. It was Wedgwood who revived the use of a brilliant green glaze, almost unused since the sixteenth century, and put it to service in the making of 'pineapple' and 'cauliflower' pieces which were later to achieve great popularity.

Pieces made of a black ware with gilt decoration were also made by Whieldon from about 1750. A similar body was used by potters at Jackfield in Shropshire at about this time, and the two are often indistinguishable.

Salt-glazed stoneware and earthenware were often made in the same shapes and from the same moulds. The formula for cream-coloured earthenware which formed the basis for many of Whieldon's productions was taken up by Wedgwood when he established his own factory and developed to become the Queen's ware on which his early reputation rested.

Early Whieldon designs and shapes were often taken from those used by silversmiths of the period, being adapted very successfully to the other medium.

About the middle of the eighteenth century Whieldon engaged in making figures, both in salt-glaze and earthenware. The subjects were those familiar to a rural community; musicians, equestrian figures of extremely lively conception, soldiers, gamekeepers etc, all rendered in a simple manner and again relying on colour for their immediate effect. Later, moulds were used for shaping, and a greater variety of colours introduced by means of the glaze. Rather more ambitious subjects were added to the simpler ones which still retained their popularity – portraits of famous men and heroes of myth or legend, reproductions in miniature of buildings, etc.

The makers of such various kinds of Staffordshire wares of the time cannot usually be named with certainty. Many pieces are ascribed to Whieldon or Astbury. Whieldon made almost every type of ware in common use at this period, and added his knowledge and craftsmanship to the development of many of them. His pupils extended his influence, many becoming potters of repute.

Examples of Whieldon ware of many kinds are in the British Museum, the Victoria and Albert Museum, Hanley Museum, Stoke-on-Trent, Brighton Museum, and the Fitzwilliam Museum, Cambridge.
Plates 105–108.

[Obit., *Staffordshire Advertiser*, 28 February 1795; S. Shaw, *History of the Staffordshire Potteries*, 1829; W. Mankowitz, *Wedgwood*, 1953; Reginald G. Haggar, *English Country Pottery*, 1950; Thomas Whieldon's *Notebook*, Hanley Museum, Stoke-on-Trent.]

White, Richard

A late seventeenth century master potter working at Southwark.

(R. L. Hobson, *Catalogue, Burlington Fine Arts Club*, 1913.)

Wibsey, Yorkshire

A brown salt-glazed stoneware was made here in the later part of the eighteenth century not unlike that produced at Nottingham

Wigornia

A Roman form of the name Worcester, which is found embossed underneath a unique cream boat of Worcester porcelain c. 1752. Illustrated by F. A. Barrett in *Worcester Porcelain* (1953).

Willcox, Matthew, Brislington, Bristol

Proprietor of St. Anne's Pottery, Brislington, from 1671 until 1682.

[W. G. Pountney, *Old Bristol Potteries*, 1920.]

Wileman, Foley, Stoke-on-Trent, Staffordshire

Henry Wileman built the Foley China Works in 1860. He was the owner of the Foley Potteries which he worked as a china and earthenware manufacturer. At his death in 1864 the business was continued by his sons, J. F. and C. Wileman for three years, when the business was divided C. J. Wileman taking over the china trade and J. F. Wileman the earthenware.

C. J. Wileman retired in 1870, and the two branches were re-united. Shortly after, J. B. Shelley was taken into partnership under the style Wileman & Co. Good useful wares were made.

MARK

Printed

Wilkinson, A. J., Burslem, Staffordshire

Founded in 1880 by Arthur J. Wilkinson. **Distinctive** earthenware shapes and decorations were made by this firm for an exhibition at Harrods, London, in 1934, the designers and artists being

Dame Laura Knight, R.A.
Duncan Grant
Milner Gray
Vanessa Bell
Eva Crofts
John Everett
Alan Walton
R. Y. Goodden, R.D.I.
Sir Frank Brangwyn, R.A.
Graham Sutherland
Barbara Hepworth
John Armstrong
Dod Procter, R.A.
Paul Nash
Ben Nicholson
Billy Waters

Clarice Cliff is Art Director.

See also BRAIN.

Colour plate 22, WORCESTER: *see page viii for caption*

(A) WINCANTON plate, tin-enamelled earthenware painted in manganese, c. 1740.
Diameter 11⅞ inches.

(B) WROTHAM jug, red earthenware, deep yellow glaze, dated 1674. Height 12⅜ in., diam. 10¼ in.

(C) WROTHAM tyg, red earthenware, decorated in white slip under yellow glaze, dated 1649.
Height 6¼ inches.

(D) YORK cup, grey stoneware, streaked with black and brown. Made by F. Place (d. 1728), c. 1683–94.
Height 2½ inches.

PLATE 145

RALPH WOOD earthenware figure of Hudibras with glaze coloured yellow, green and brown, adapted from an engraving by William Hogarth, c. 1770–80. Mark '41' impressed. Height 11¾ inches.

PLATE 146

(A) RALPH WOOD figure of a stag, white earthenware, with glaze coloured brown, green and blue, c. 1770–80. Mark, '95' impressed. Height 9⅜ inches.

(B) RALPH WOOD figure of a shepherd with a lamb under his arm, white earthenware, with glaze coloured manganese-brown, dark brown, green, yellow and grey. c. 1770–80. Height 8½ inches.

(C) RALPH WOOD group of a shepherd with shepherdess, earthenware, with glaze coloured pale blue, green, yellow and brown, c. 1770–80. Ht 9⅝ inches.

(D) ENOCH WOOD figure emblematic of Eloquence, earthenware, painted in enamel colours, 1790. Height 18½ inches.

PLATE 147

RALPH WOOD toby jug, earthenware, painted in coloured glazes, c. 1770. Height 10⅛ inches.

PLATE 148

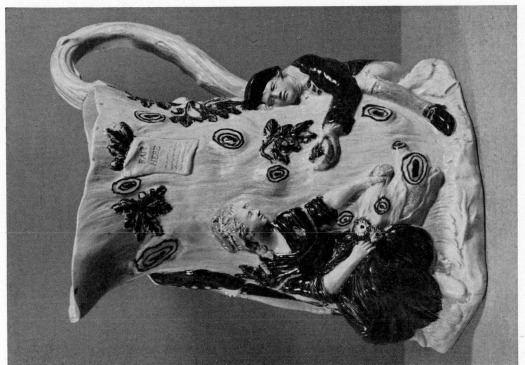

(B) RALPH WOOD jug, earthenware with coloured glazes. Moulded figures and the inscription 'Fair Hebe'. Signed 'J. Voyez 1788', c. 1788. Height 9⅝ inches.

(A) ENOCH WOOD bust of Jean-Jacques Rousseau, earthenware, painted in coloured enamels, c. 1790. Height 6½ inches.

PLATE 149

(A) WROTHAM two earthenware tygs decorated with applied pads of clay and slip. *(left)* with initials G.R. (George Richardson, potter) & date 1653. *(right)* with initial 'J.L. & T.P.E.' and date 1636. *(Hanley Museum)*.

(B) WROTHAM dish, red ware, coated with white slip, through which is scratched various ornamental patterns and the inscription 'IE WE 1699 WRO-THAM'. Diameter 2 inches. *(British Museum)*.

(C) WROTHAM tyg, ornamented with dots, zig-zags and formal plants and medallions. Initials 'JE 1697'. Height 6¾ inches, diameter (with handles) 9½ inches. *(British Museum)*.

PLATE 150

(A) CASTLEFORD teapot and cover, white stoneware, early nineteenth century. Height 4¾ inches, length 7½ inches.

(B) SUNDERLAND, jug, earthenware, painted in pink lustre. Signed 'J. Philips Hylton Pottery', first quarter of nineteenth century. Ht 8⅛ inches.

(C) SUNDERLAND plate, pale green glaze, decorated with pink lustre, printed with a steamship, 'Trident' in black. c. 1820. Diameter 8¾ inches.

PLATE 151

(A) STAFFORDSHIRE earthenware jug, painted in yellow, orange & blue, c. 1800. Height 5¾ inches.
(B) ROGERS, Dale Hall, Burslem. Earthenware plate painted with a floral spray in colours. Marks, 'Rogers' impressed & 'A6' in grey. c. 1830. Diameter 8¾ inches.

(C) STAFFORDSHIRE earthenware jug, decorated 'in resist' with silver (platinum) lustre, early nineteenth century. Height 5½ inches.

PLATE 152

(A) STAFFORDSHIRE figures, nineteenth century, earthenware, painted in underglaze colours in the 'Pratt' style, early nineteenth century. Height 4 inches.

(B) STAFFORDSHIRE, Ralph Salt, Hanley. Earthenware figure of a shepherdess painted in enamel colours. Mark 'Salt' impressed, 1st half nineteenth century. Height 5⅛ inches.

(C) STAFFORDSHIRE, nineteenth century, earthenware figure, 'The Squire' painted in colours, early nineteenth century.
(*Mrs M. Bruce George*).

PLATE 153

(A) STAFFORDSHIRE, earthenware group, Rajah on an elephant, painted in enamel colours c. 1835. Height 8⅞ inches.

(B) STAFFORDSHIRE earthenware money-box in the form of a cottage, decorated in the 'Pratt' style, early nineteenth century. Height 4¾ inches.

(C) STAFFORDSHIRE earthenware group, 'Bull-baiting', painted with enamel colours, early nineteenth century. Length 11⅞ inches, height 7¾ inches.

PLATE 154

(A) STAFFORDSHIRE, earthenware group, 'Teetotal', decorated overglaze with enamel colours. Probably made by Obadiah Sherratt, Hot Lane, Burslem, c. 1835. *(Mrs M. Bruce George)*.

(B) STAFFORDSHIRE, earthenware group, 'Dandies', painted with enamel colours. Walton type, early nineteenth century. *(R. G. Haggar)*.

(C) STAFFORDSHIRE, earthenware figure, 'Orlando', painted and gilded, c. 1840. Height 18 inches. *(Miss Moira Forsyth)*.

PLATE 155

(A) CONTEMPORARY. Poole. New vase shapes painted in the Delft or in-glaze technique.

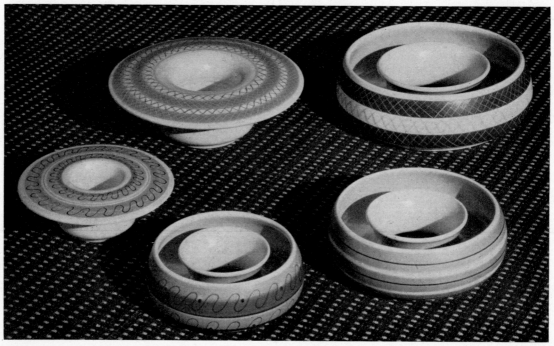

(B) CONTEMPORARY. Poole. Group of posy-holders, earthenware, with hand-painted decorations.

PLATE 156

(A) CONTEMPORARY stoneware bottle in black and rust by Bernard Leach, 1956. Height 14 inches. *(Bernard Leach)*.

(B) CONTEMPORARY stoneware jar, rust-brown on oatmeal, by Bernard Leach, 1955. Height 14 inches. *(Bernard Leach)*.

(C) CONTEMPORARY. Susie Cooper bone china tea service. *(Susie Cooper)*.

PLATE 157

(A) CONTEMPORARY. New Chelsea China plate designed by Edward Ardizzone, R.A. (*New Chelsea China*).

(B) CONTEMPORARY. New Chelsea China cup, saucer and plate in traditional 'Picardy Rose' pattern. (*New Chelsea China*).

(C) CONTEMPORARY. Waistel Cooper bottle and bowls. (*Photo: Heal & Sons, Ltd*).

PLATE 158

(A) CONTEMPORARY. Doulton bone china coffee-pot, plate and coffee cup and saucer, 'Caprice' pattern. *(Doulton Fine China Ltd.)*.

(B) CONTEMPORARY. Derby unglazed jars, pot and jug stone colour with pale green rims and handles and scroll decoration in white relief. *(Photo: Service Advertising Co. Ltd)*.

PLATE 159

(A) CONTEMPORARY. Ashtrays and bowls in earthenware by Elizabeth Duncombe.
(Photo: Heal & Sons Ltd).

(B) CONTEMPORARY. Crown Derby plate, teacup and saucer in bone china.
(Royal Crown Derby Porcelain Co Ltd).

PLATE 160

Willems, Joseph

A modeller who may perhaps be identified as the 'Mr Williams' who exhibited at the Exhibition of the Society of Artists of Great Britain from 1760 until 1765, and who appears to have worked at the Chelsea factory. The 'Roman Charity' adapted from an engraving after Rubens is attributed to him. Also:

Leda and the Swan (after Boucher)
Una and the Lion
Pietà (after Van Dyck)

[George Savage, *18th Century English Porcelain*, 1952.]

Willow Pattern

A popular pseudo-Chinese design first engraved by Thomas Minton, and known in numerous variants. Mintons, Spode, Turner, Davenport, Adams and others in Staffordshire used a version of the pattern, as did the factories of Leeds, Swansea, Liverpool and Sunderland. Dated examples are rare: a plate with this design in Hanley Museum, Stoke-on-Trent is lettered 'THOMASINE WILLEY, 1818'.

Wilson, Robert (died 1801),
Hanley, Staffordshire

Partner with James Neale in firm of Neale & Wilson and eventually his successor; manufacturer of cream-coloured earthenware (tablewares and figures) and 'dry' bodies. He was succeeded by David Wilson & Sons, the partners being David Wilson, sen. (died c.1816), David Wilson, jun. (died 1817), James Wilson, (born 1789 died 1814) and John Wilson. The firm was bankrupt in 1817.

The wares of Neale were continued with the addition of silver lustred tablewares and figures.

MARKS

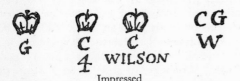

Impressed

[Reginald G.Haggar, *Staffordshire Chimney Ornaments*, 1955; *Staffordshire Advertiser*, 24 January 1801, 10 September 1814, 18 January, 12 July, 30 August, 28 September 1827.]

Wincanton, Somerset

A pottery here worked by Thomas Lindslee (who came from the Limekiln Lane Works, Bristol) and Nathaniel Ireson, made tin-glazed earthenware in the second quarter of the eighteenth century. Pieces dated 1737 to 1748 are known. A typical decoration includes motifs within panels reserved against a speckled manganese ground. The factory was excavated by William Pountney in 1917.

Plate 145 A.

[W.B.Pountney, *Old Bristol Potteries*, 1920; F.H.Garner, *English Delftware*, 1948; G.Sweetman, *Nathaniel Ireson, A West Country Potter*, 1900.]

Winchcomb, Gloucestershire

Site of a country pottery which was taken over by Michael Cardew in 1926 for the production of fine quality slipwares.

Wine Bottles

Tin enamelled globular bottles were made at Lambeth (specimens dated 1629 to 1672) with initials, date, and name of wine in blue such as Sack, 'Whit', Claret, or 'Renish'.

Rackham and Read adopted the suggestion put forward by Frank Falkner that these were made for wine samples, being too small for use in such hard-drinking days, (*English Pottery*, 1924) but they may have been intended for what appears, from contemporary diaries, to have been a customary gift, on January 1st, of a bottle of wine, (F.H.Garner, *English Delftware*, 1948).

Plate 50 B.

Wirksworth, Derbyshire

An obscure factory said to have been producing porcelain in 1770, and again from 1804 until 1808 under William Billingsley's direction: but this cannot be authenticated.

Wasters found at Wirksworth, however, indicate that porcelain was made here, and that the shapes and decorations of New Hall were imitated.

[G.Bemrose, *19th Century English Pottery and Porcelain* 1952; L.Jewitt, *Ceramic Art of Great Britain*, 1878; W.B.Honey, *Old English Porcelain*, 1928, new ed. 1948.]

Witch Bottles

Bellarmines have been so named, because they have been found frequently under the thresholds or hearths of old houses, or in ditches or river beds, usually filled with such things as pieces of cloth pierced with pins, twists of human hair, hand-made nails, finger-nail parings, and bones.

These charms were either intended to ward off the evil effects of witchcraft, or to inflict some injury upon another person by magical processes.

[Christina Hole, *English Folklore*, 1940.]

Withers, Edward

One of the earlier painters at Derby who executed flowers in a conventional style characterised by a distinctive outline and treatment of high lights. He worked also at Caughley and in Staffordshire, and in 1789 once more at Derby under a three-year agreement. He later went to Birmingham and became a painter of japanned tea trays.

Wolfe, George

Earthenware manufacturer in partnership with Miles Mason, Fenton, 1796–1800. (*Staffordshire Advertiser*, 19 July 1800; *Rate Books*, now destroyed).

[P.W.L.Adams, 'Thomas Wolfe', *Transactions, North Staffordshire Field Club*, Vol. 58, 1923–4; Reginald G. Haggar, *The Masons of Lane Delph*, 1952.]

Wolfe, Thomas, the Elder
(born 1720 died 1800)

Potter, Stoke; partner in firm of Bell & Wolfe, potters; married Elizabeth Bell (1726–1807); father of Thomas and George Wolfe, potters.

[Gravestone, Stoke Churchyard; Bailey's *Directory*, 1783; P.W.L.Adams, *The Adams Family*, 1914 and supplements; P.W.L.Adams, *Notes on some North Staffordshire Families*, 1930.]

Wolfe, Thomas the Younger
(born 1751 died 1818)

Manufacturer of Queen's ware, blue-printed earthenware, cane, Egyptian black at the Big

Works, Church Street, Stoke-on-Trent, 1784–1800 on own account; 1800–1811 in partnership with his son-in-law Robert Hamilton (born 1779 died 1828); finally 1811 until his death in 1818 again on his own account. He also made porcelain in Liverpool at the Islington China Manufactory 1792–1818; first in partnership with John Davenport 1792–1796; then with Miles Mason and John Lucock as Wolfe & Company 1796–1800; and with his son-in-law Robert Hamilton 1800–1818. His mark recorded on cream-coloured earthenware was 'Wolfe' impressed.

Wolfe

Impressed

[*Gravestone*, Stoke Churchyard; Bailey's *Directory*, 1783; Tunnicliff's *Survey*, 1787; Gore's *Liverpool Directory* 1818; Announcements in *London Gazette*, 1800, Williamsons' *Liverpool Advertiser*, 17 June 1800; *Staffordshire Advertiser*, 19 July 1800; J. Mayer's *Art of Pottery... in Liverpol*, 1873; Reginald G.Haggar, *The Masons of Lane Delph*, 1952.]

Wood, Aaron (born 1717 died 1785)

The most celebrated block-cutter and modeller of the eighteenth century who worked for nearly all the leading potters of that period, Thomas Wedgwood of Burslem, John Mitchell, Thomas Whieldon and Ralph Wood among them. The 'Pew' groups have been attributed to him: such models as the 'Hudibras' (copied from an engraving by Hogarth), the 'Vicar and Moses' and 'Old Age' are more likely to be his work.

[W.B.Honey, *English Pottery and Porcelain*, 1933, second ed. 1945; F. Falkner, *The Wood Family of Burslem*, 1912.]

Wood, Enoch (1759-1840), Burslem

Enoch Wood was the son of Aaron Wood, the celebrated block-cutter and modeller; received instruction in art from an uncle, William Caddick, in Liverpool, and served his apprenticeship to Humphrey Palmer of Hanley. Several early works, 'Crucifixion', and 'Descent from the Cross' have survived in Burslem (St John's) Church. Started to manufacture pottery in partnership with Ralph Wood about 1784, making useful earthenware, cane ware, Egyptian black, coloured bodies, and seals and cyphers. In 1790 he took into partnership James Caldwell of Linley Wood, and traded as Wood & Caldwell until 1818. Subsequently he took his sons into the business, who continued it under the style Enoch Wood & Sons until 1846 (six years after his death).

MARKS

E. WOOD

ENOCH WOOD
SCULPSIT
(impressed or incised)

WOOD & CALDWELL
There ar several variations.

Impressed

WORK:

Enoch Wood was an accomplished modeller who did portraits of John Wesley from life, which became famous. Other busts were executed by him, notably Whitefield, Handel, King William IV, Emperor Alexander of Russia. Large figure groups such as the 'Ariadne & Bacchus' after a sculpture by Houdon, or 'St Paul preaching at Athens' after Sir Henry Cheere, are characteristic. toby jugs, groups

representing 'The Night Watchman' or 'Parson & Clerk' are more attractive. Many tree background pieces were made by him. These are usually enamelled over glaze, sometimes with the addition of touches of silver lustre.

Excellent blue-printed earthenware was made for the American market. Over sixty American views were produced, usually with an elaborate 'shell' border. English and French views were also made, and religious subjects.

Jasper wares and black basaltes in the style popularised by Wedgwood were made, and some experimental porcelain.

Plates 146-149.
[F. Falkner, *The Wood Family of Burslem*, 1912; Reginald G. Haggar, *Staffordshire Chimney Ornaments*, 1955.]

Wood, Ephraim (born 1773 died after 1830), Burslem

Cousin of Enoch Wood and the younger Ralph Wood; enameller, gilder and lusterer of earthenware, and manufacturer of pottery figures, St John's Square and Nile Street, Burslem, from about 1805 until 1830. A number of hitherto unattributed figures, some of them representing John Liston the actor in various character parts, and marked WOOD impressed without any initial may have been made by this potter.

EW
1788

WOOD

π

Occurs imressed upon a white 'Fair Hebe' jug. May stand for Ephraim or Enoch Wood

Impressed upon early 19th century Staffordshire figures. Possibly mark of Ephraim or Enoch Wood. The bench sign and circles are probably workmen's marks

[Reginald G. Haggar, 'Ephraim Wood and the Wood Family of Burslem', *Apollo*, 1950; *Parish Register; Directories*.]

Wood, George, Hope Street, Hanley
Toy and ornament manufacturer, 1851.

Wood, Isa (born 1682 died 1715)
Salt-glazed stoneware potter at the 'Back of the George', Burslem; son of Robert Wood; mar-

ried at Stoke 24 April 1704 to Maria Sheldon; mentioned in Josiah Wedgwood's list of early eighteenth country potters (recorded by Miss Meteyard in her *Life of Josiah Wedgwood*, 1865–66). The site of his factory was excavated by H. W. Maxwell, J. Cook and Thomas Pape in 1929. Capacity mugs with the Royal Cypher under a Crown and various decorative features were discovered. Examples in Hanley Museum, Stoke-on-Trent.

[*Parish Registers* of Burslem and Stoke.]

Wood, John (born 1746 died 1797)

Manufacturer of cream-coloured earthenware at Brownhills, Burslem; murdered by Dr Oliver, a rejected suitor of his daughter, in 1797.

[H. Wedgwood, *Romance of Staffordshire*, n.d.]

Wood, Ralph, Burslem, Staffordshire

There were three generations of potters of this name; Ralph Wood the elder (born 1715 died 1772), was the son of a miller. He commenced to manufacture salt-glazed stoneware, 'Whieldon' ware, figures and toby jugs in Burslem in 1754 and built up a successful business which was continued by his son, Ralph Wood II (born 1748 died 1795) and grandson, Ralph Wood III (born 1781 died 1801) until 1801.

MARKS:

R. WOOD
(impressed)

Ra Wood
(impressed)

Ra Wood
Burslem

Incised

A rebus mark in the form of a miniature representation of trees occurs on some Wood figures. Many Wood figures were impressed with mould numbers which have been tabulated and identified.

WORK:

Ralph Wood figures and toby jugs of the early period are characterised by skilful modelling in relation to the glaze effects which the elder Ralph Wood introduced. These stained glazes, applied with a brush, were generally rather grey and washy in appearance but richer and deeper where the modelling or tooling was sharp.

Black basaltes figures were made and a number of excellent Toby jugs. John Voyez is believed to have modelled for Ralph Wood. The

Wood Pedigree

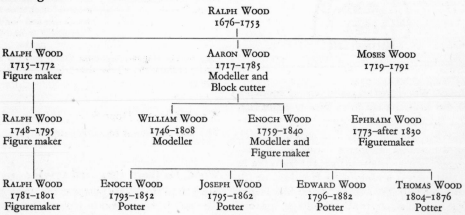

younger Ralph Woods decorated their figures with bright on-glaze enamel colours. Examples in British Museum and Victoria and Albert Museum, London; Stoke-on-Trent Museum and the Fitzwilliam Museum, Cambridge.
Colour plate 15 and plates 146-149.

[F.Falkner, *The Wood Family of Burslem*, 1912; Reginald G.Haggar, *Staffordshire Chimney Ornaments*, 1955; R.K. Price, *Astbury Whieldon and Ralph Wood Figures and Toby Jugs*, 1922.]

Wood, Robert (born 1650 died 1717)

Slipware potter in Burslem. A posset-pot in Hanley Museum is lettered THE BEST IS NOT TOO GOOD FOR YOU ROBBORT WOOD.
Plate 81 A.

ROBBORT WOOD

Slip

[Described by Reginald G.Haggar in *Apollo*, 1952.]

Woodville (or Wooden Box), nr. Hartshorne, Derbyshire. Earthenware manufactory

A pottery making stoneware and earthenware was established here in 1818 by Joseph Thompson. His name is found on pieces from this manufactory, sometimes followed by the place name 'Wooden Box Pottery'.

Other potteries were working in this district early in the nineteenth century.

Wooltus, Symon

Master potter, Southampton, 1666-71, cited by Dwight in his lawsuits 1693; manufacturer of salt-glazed stoneware.
[R.L.Hobson, *B.F.C.A.Catalogue*, 1913.]

Wooltus, Symon, Junior.

Master potter: son of Symon Wooltus; made stoneware for Killigrew of Chelsea before 1693.
[R.L.Hobson, *B.F.A.C.Catalogue*, 1913.]

Worcester, Worcestershire. Porcelain manufactory

DATES AND OWNERS

The Worcester manufactory was established in 1751 by a company of subscribers including Dr John Wall, physician, William Davis, apothecary, Richard and Josiah Holdship, and Edward Cave whose association with the *Gentleman's Magazine* gave the factory products considerable free publicity.

Porcelain manufacture was commenced at Warmstry House, from a formula used at Bristol.

In 1772 the original company was reconstituted and Robert Hancock held (for two years) shares in the business. After the death of Wall in 1776 and Davis in 1783 (end of 'Dr Wall' period) the concern was bought by the London agent Thomas Flight for his two sons, Joseph and John, and Robert Chamberlain left the factory to form a rival company.

John Flight died in 1791, and in the following year Martin Barr joined the company, the successive partnerships being

Flight & Barr	1792–1807
Barr, Flight & Barr	1807–1813
Flight, Barr & Barr	1813–1840

In 1840 Chamberlain's concern was amalgamated with the original business and from 1847 his premises used, in place of Warmstry House as the porcelain manufactory.

Walter Chamberlain and John Lilly became owners of the business in 1848, and in 1850 were joined by W.H.Kerr. From 1852 the style was Kerr & Binns and from 1862 the Royal Worcester Porcelain Company.

A third Worcester factory for porcelain, started by Thomas Grainger in 1801, was absorbed by Royal Worcester in 1889, while a fourth, founded by James Hadley in 1896, experienced a like fate in 1905. See also CHAMBERLAIN and GRAINGER. The Royal Worcester Company continues.

MARKS

About 1755-65

About 1755-65   1760

1760-1795   1755-83   1780

Flight   *Flight*   *Flight & Barr*
In Blue   In red   In red
1783-89   1789-92   1792-1807

B   B
1800   1820

B.F.B.   Incised   F.B.B.
Barr, Flight & Barr   Flight, Barr & Barr
1807-13   1813-40

Printed   Impressed   Printed
Kerr & Binns   1852-1862   James Hadley
                               & Sons 1896-1903

James Hadley & Sons   Since 1862
1896-1903   Impressed

ARTISTS

James Giles. Outside decorator of Worcester porcelain 1760–1780.

John Donaldson. Painter of mythological subjects who signed his work in monogram.

J.H.O'Neale. Animal and figure painter.

Tebo (Thibaud?). Repairer of figures.

James Pennington. Painter of classical subjects *en grisaille* and in colour.

Thomas Baxter. Painter of figures, flowers, birds and shells in a naturalistic style at Worcester 1814–1816 and 1819–1821. Decorated Worcester porcelain in London. Dated examples (1802, 1808, 1809) in Victoria and Albert Museum.

Robert Hancock. Engraver 1757 or earlier, to 1774.

Valentine Green. Apprentice to Hancock 1760–1764.

James Ross. Apprentice to Hancock.

John Lowick. Apprentice to Hancock 1765.

Thomas Turner. Probably an apprentice to Hancock.

George Davis. Painter of exotic birds, c.1815.

Fidèle Duvivir. A signed and dated teapot (1772) is painted with rural lovers beside urn. Exhibited at Worcester Exhibition in London 1951.

C. Hayton. Views of gentleman's houses in Herefordshire and Derbyshire painted on a set of plates signed and dated 1821–1822 are mentioned by Chaffers.

James Taylor, left Worcester 1771.

Extended lists of craftsman and artists are given by the older authorities, Binns and Chaffers, but quite a lot of their works remained unidentified. The influx of Chelsea artists about 1768 and its influence upon style should be noted, as also the extensive decoration of Worcester porcelain by outside enamellers.

WORK AND DISTINGUISHING CHARACTERISTICS
Early Worcester: 1751–1752
Early Worcester porcelain was a soapstone paste, almost indistinguishable from that of Bristol of preceding years, thin and hard-looking, at first a creamy white, but soon somewhat greyish in tint, and finished with glaze which tended to shrink or recede from the foot-ring.

Useful wares were made, teapots, cream jugs, cups and saucers, as well as other items; shapes were often derived from silver. Sauce-boats, which sold at 16s a pair in 1751, were made in some quantity.

Underglaze blue *chinoiseries* in imitation of imported 'Nankin' china, sometimes by a painter who used fine brush strokes, were among the earliest decorations. Sometimes the underglaze blue of early Worcester is blurred. Other pseudo-Chinese decorations were done in a brilliant palette of enamels, (turquoise, citron, brick-red, pale purple and black), with delicate drawing and a nice sense of relation of pattern to form.

Dr Wall Period: 1752–1783

The settled conditions of production resulted in a much wider range of wares and decorations, marked by excellent potting. Shapes of useful wares are generally dominated by silver forms. A thin glaze tending to shrink from the footring is still characteristic: it is never crazed.

Landscape and figure subjects in the European style; fantastic crimson landscapes in reserved panels against yellow grounds; red landscapes painted upon relief scrolls superimposed upon leaf dishes; flower painting in the style of Meissen; transfer-printing in black, brown, purple or red, occasionally washed over in colour; all these may be found in the early Wall period.

After Chelsea artists had been taken on at the factory about 1768, decoration became more elaborate and Meissen influence gave place to Sèvres.

Workmanship was always of the highest quality although decorations tended to hide the quality of the paste. The looser Kakiemon patterns were replaced with brocaded Imari all-over designs, panelled with fan-shaped and circular patches.

Coloured grounds (apple-green, mazarine blue, turquoise, lavender, claret, yellow) were extensively used in combination with reserved panels enclosing exotic birds, or foliage and figure subjects framed in gold. Sometimes grounds were diapered with patterns, such as the imbricated dark-blue ground generally known as 'Scale blue'. A powder-blue ground was also used. Gilding was generally lacelike in quality and of excellent workmanship. Much Worcester porcelain in this period was outside-decorated at Giles's workshop in London. Vases with large reserved panels were supplied to Donaldson to be filled with figure subjects, such as 'Leda and the Swan' after Boucher; or to O'Neale to be painted with animals or long-limbed graceful mythological figures.

Fluted jugs with rococo handles, and 'cabbage-leaf' jugs, elegant candlesticks, rococo flower holders, jugs with mask or foliated lips, flanged bottles, and leaf dishes of many kinds were made from the 1760's.

Pear-shaped jugs with spreading footrings, and cylindrical mugs are sometimes found incised with a cross or other incisions on the inner surface of the footring (scratch-cross family). By some these marks have been thought to indicate an experimental paste: by others merely workmen's tallies.

Black-pencilled Chinese subjects of a rather attenuated kind contrast with precise imitations of the oriental in colour.

Transfer-printing at Worcester was extensively used, the subjects being taken from fantastic *chinoiseries* by Jean Pillemont, engravings by Hubert Gravelot such as 'Aeneas and Anshises' and 'Children's Games', C.N.Cochin's 'L'Amour', or rustic subjects by Gainsborough, Hayman and Luke Sullivan. Portraits of contemporary notabilites were engraved after Ramsay, Reynolds and Van Loo.

From 1760 blue-and-white decoration, transfer-printed or painted was characterized by a deep strong tone almost like indigo blue.

Figures in Worcester porcelain have a certain rarity value but are lacking in accomplishment. The poses are awkward and stiff. Subjects which have been identified include A Sportsman, Turk, and Gardener, as well as the Chelsea model 'La Nourrice'.

Later wares: 1783 onwards

Interest in paste diminishes towards the end of the eighteenth century, and decoration becomes of supreme importance. Landscapes of a topographical kind were adapted from contemporary engravings usually of local or near-local subject in the finished style popularized at Derby. Classical subjects, shells, feathers, portraits, executed in colour, or grey, or brown monochrome by such skilful executants as Pennington or Baxter are typical of the neo-classic phase of Worcester production.

Armorial services, in this, as in earlier periods were extensively produced. In the nineteenth century 'Japans' in the style of Derby or Spode became common; new ground-colours were brought into use covered with seaweed and vermicelli patterns in bright mercury gilding.

Later Worcester porcelain of the nineteenth century has often distinctive, if not aesthetically satisfying qualities. The almost miraculous pierced wares of George Owen, emulating Japanese ivory carving, or the styles derived from Japanese export Satsuma ware are typical.

The white enamel painting of Thomas John Bott is more attractive.

FORGERIES AND FAKES

Undoubtedly Worcester, whose output over the years has been enormous, has been more extensively imitated than any other factory, such imitations occurring in soft and hard-paste porcelain and in Staffordshire pottery.

Colour plates 22-24 and plates 129-144.

[F.A.Barrett, *Worcester Porcelain*, 1953; F.Severne Mackenna, *Worcester Porcelain*, 1950; R.W.Binns, *A Century of Potting in the City of Worcester*,1877; W.B.Honey, *Old English Porcelain*,1928, new ed. 1948; Geoffrey Bemrose, *Nineteenth Century English Pottery and Porcelain*,1952; R.L. Hobson, *Worcester Porcelain*, 1910; Wallace Elliot 'Worcester Porcelain Figures', *Transactions*, *English Ceramic Circle*, 1934; Geoffrey Wills, 'John Flight of Worcester', *The Connoisseur*, 1947; C.Cook, *The Life and Work of Robert Hancock*, 1948.]

Wrecclesham, Surrey

A potworks was established by Absalom Harris in 1872 and continued by his family.

Wright, John

A name recorded on large Toft-style slipware dishes (dates recorded from 1705 to 1707). Possibly also the potter who inscribed his initials on a slipware posset-pot in the British Museum, inscribed 'ANN DRAPER THIS CUP MADE FOR YOU AND SO NO MORE I.W. 1707'. There are references to John Wright in Stoke and Burslem Parish Registers. See also 'INITIALIST I.W'.

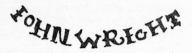

Wright, William

Recorded on Toft-style slipware dishes, one of which is dated 1709.

Wrotham, Kent

Slipware was made at Wrotham and in the neighbourhood in the seventeenth and eighteenth centuries, when the pottery there was extensive. A Wrotham pottery was in existence in 1612; no dated pieces are known after 1739. Owners are unknown, but it is suggested that

Thomas Jull, whose initials appear on some Wrotham pieces, may have been one of them. Similar wares were being made in Staffordshire at this period making identification difficult in some cases, but many pieces are marked 'WROTHAM', often in conjunction with the initials of potter or eventual owner.

Wares for domestic use formed a large part of the production of Wrotham. Cups, jugs, tygs and posset-pots were all made there, though dishes seem to have been comparatively rare. Most examples now in existence were probably made for presentation or other special purpose, and much of the more common domestic wares must have perished in course of time. Candlesticks, unusual elsewhere, were made at the pottery, and a pair dated 1649 are in the Victoria and Albert Museum.

The body of the ware was usually of lead-glazed red clay, decorated with white or yellow slip in simple patterns; these were inscriptions, in either applied or in trailed slip, pads of white clay bearing initials or designs in relief. Some applied decoration is edged with an imitation of stitching, and other types of ornament derived from embroidery are used. Handles often bear a groove throughout their length which is filled with a twisted cord of white and red clay. Stars, masks and rosettes occur frequently as motifs. Many of the jugs are reminiscent of Rhenish stoneware.

Potters at Wrotham included George Richardson (c.1620–87) and Nicholas Hubble (d. 1689). John Ifield (d. 1716) and Nicholas Livermore (d. 1678) are listed as having worked there.

Later slipware made at Brabourne, High Halden and other places in Kent seems to have been derived from Wrotham productions.

Representative collections of Wrotham and similar wares are in the Victoria and Albert Museum, British Museum, Maidstone (Kent) Museum, some pieces bearing the name Wrotham.
Plate 145 B, C and D.

[J.W.L.Glaisher, Appendix to B.Rackham and H.Read, *English Pottery*, 1924.]

Y

wares of various sorts, mostly of a coarse brown ware, green-glazed. The pottery continued in existence into the eighteenth century.

[L. Jewitt, *Ceramic Art of Great Britain*, 1878.]

Ynisymudw, South Wales

An earthenware factory existed at this place (about 10 miles from Swansea) from 1850 until 1859 and was worked by William Williams and Michael Martyn Williams who owned a brickworks here. The copperplates were sold to the South Wales Pottery.

[L. Jewitt, *Ceramic Art of Great Britain*, 1878.]

Yarmouth, Norfolk

Delftware and pottery of various kinds have been wrongly ascribed to a factory at Yarmouth. A decorator named Absolon working in the town, who added his signature to pieces sent to him or bought by him for decoration from various manufacturers in the country, caused some confusion over the place of manufacture of such items.

See ABSOLON.

Young, William Weston

Ceramic painter of botanical subjects at Swansea from 1803 until 1806, and draughtsman of many of the plates which illustrate L. W. Dillwyn's *The British Conferva*. He became proprietor of the porcelain factory at Nantgarw.

Yates, John and his successors, Hanley

The elder John Yates is recorded as an earthenware manufacturer in Hanley from 1770 until 1796. His sons, William (died 1825 aged 58), and John (died 1828 aged 68) had a factory in Shelton which was operated by members of the Yates family until 1834 or later, and which in 1843 was trading as Yates & May.

[*Staffordshire Advertiser* and *Pottery Mercury*, 4 May 1825, 21 June 1828; *Directories*, 1783–1834; J. Ward, *The Borough of Stoke-on-Trent*, 1843; Monument, Hanley Church.]

Z

Zaffre

An impure oxide of cobalt used as a blue colouring for pottery.

Yearsley, Yorkshire. Earthenware manufactory

At the beginning of the eighteenth century a member of the Wedgwood family worked at a pottery established on the estate of Sir George Wombwell. The manufacture included useful

Zillwood, W.

A potter working in the Salisbury area whose initials are sometimes found incised in wares.

Appendix 1

Names of potters, pottery firms, pot-dealers and agents, and outside decorators taken from Directories

Introduction

The following appendix to the main text of the Encyclopedia consists of a series of classified entries from 18th. and 19th. century directories which provide useful information concerning potters, pottery firms, potters' agencies, and outside decorators.

This series should be regarded merely as a token of the enormous wealth of untapped ceramic historical material awaiting exhaustive analysis.

In using these entries ceramic students should be mindful (1) of the possible errors of transcribers; (2) that in directories issued in frequent editions entries may be repeated without checking or revision; (3) of the evident incompleteness of some directories, due either to negligence of compilation, or to policy; (4) of piracy; and (5) that some firms may have gone out of business between time of compilation and publication.

A few examples of errors may be useful. Errors of the first kind may easily arise out of names such as Clewes, Clews, Clowes; Baggeley and Baddeley; Seltman and Selman. The entry, Heath, Warburton & Co., in *Bailey's Western Directory* 1784, may be an error for Hollins, Warburton & Co. It is repeated in Tunnicliff's *Survey*, 1787 and may have been the original style and partnership of the New Hall concern, but Heath's association with the firm is not otherwise known. Examples of the second kind are less easy to specify, but in considering the entries in the numerous editions of Pigot's directories during the troublous 1830s possibility of unchecked repetition should not be excluded.

National directories afford many examples of the third feature. Important firms were often included to the exclusion of back-street potters with the result that the picture of industrial development offered is false both as to extent and nature.

Two flagrant examples of piracy must suffice. Tunnicliff's *Topographical Survey of the Counties of Stafford, Chester and Lancaster*, (1787), repeats substantially the North Staffordshire entries in *Bailey's Western Directory* (1784), and these are inaccurate, incomplete and unsatisfactory. Bailey's errors are duly incorporated even to placing Josiah Wedgwood's factory in Fenton! Another example is the repetition in T. Allbut's *The Staffordshire Pottery Directory* (published in Hanley, 1802) of information issued in John Tregortha's *A View of the Staffordshire Potteries*, (Burslem 1800). This is less serious because the interval of time was short, and because too most of the firms survived and their location was accurately reported.

These lists may be supplemented by lists of potters whose names appear under public notices in contemporary newspaper advertisements, or in apprenticeship deeds, transcripts of local census records, jurors lists and poll books.

Information is provided in Appendix III of books giving classified lists of ceramic craftsmen or products.

For those who wish to pursue researches among directories and newpapers the following reference books will be found indispensible:

Goss, C. W. F., *The London Directories, 1677–1855,* 1932.

Norton, Jane E., *Guide to the National and Provincial Directories of England and Wales, excluding London, published before 1856,* Royal Historical Society, 1850.

A Tercentenary Handlist of English and Welsh Newspapers, The Times, 1920.

Catalogue of Printed Books. Newspapers published in Great Britain and Ireland 1801–1900, British Museum, 1905.

Bristol

PIGOT'S DUBLIN & HIBERNIAN PROVINCIAL DIRECTORY, LONDON, 1824

Bristol China Enamellers

Pardoe, Thos. Long Row, Thomas St.
Wild, John. 1 Horse Fair,

Potters

Bright John (stone water pipe maker) 131 Avon St.
Duffett Jas. (red ware) Barton Hill
Duffett J. Pipe Lane, Temple Back
Flood & Co. (red ware) Temple Back
Hassall J. & Co. (stone ware) 12 Merchant St.
Machin B. (red ware) Wilder St.
Milson & Melson, Temple St.
Oland John, (stone) 2 Langton Terrace
Pountney & Allies, (manufacturers of all sorts of plain and ornamental earthenware) Temple Back.

Powell Wm & Thos. (brown stone ware) Thomas St.
Price Chas. & Son, (stone ware) Temple & Thomas St.
Sheppard Mrs. (and brick and tile) Avon St. St. Philip's
Yabbicomb Henry (sugar, chimney and garden pot manufacturers) Temple Back.
Yabbicomb H. & T. (stone ware) Avon St. St. Philip's.

PIGOT'S DUBLIN AND HIBERNIAN PROVINCIAL DIRECTORY MANCHESTER 1826–7

Bristol China Enamellers

Pardoe, Thos. Long-Row, Thomas St.
Wild, John, 1 Horse-fair.

Potters

Bright, John (stone water pipe maker) 131 Temple Street

Cox, G. Avon St.
Duffett, Jas. (red ware) Barton-Hill
Duffett, J. Pipe-Lane, Temple Back
Flood & Co. (red ware) Temple-bk
Hassall, J. & Co. (stone ware)
    12 Merchant Street
Machin, B. (red ware) Wilder St.
Milsom and Melsom, Temple St.
Oland, John (stone). 2 Langton Ter.
Pountney, & Allies (manuf. of all sorts
    of plain and ornamental earthen-
    ware) Temple-back
Powell, Wm. and Thos. (brown stone-
    ware) Thomas St.
Price, Chas. & Son (stone ware)
    Temple and Thomas St.
Sheppard Mrs. (stone ware) Avon St.
    St. Phlilip's
Spokes, John (stone ware) Avon St.
    St. Philip's
Yabbicomb, Henry (sugar, chimney
    and garden pot manufacturer)
Yabbicomb H. & T. (stone ware)
    Avon St. St. Philip's.

PIGOT'S LONDON DIRECTORY, 1826
Bristol Potters
Bright John (stone water pipe maker)
    131, Temple-st.
Cox G. Avon-street.
Duffett Jos. (red ware) Barton-Hill
Duffett J. Pipe-Lane, Temple Back.
Flood & Co. (red ware) Temple-bk.
Hassall & Co. (stone ware) 12, Mer-
    chant Street.
Machin B. (red ware) Wilder Street.
Milsom & Melsom Temple Street
Oland John (stone) Langton ter.
Poultney & Allis (Manufacturers of all
    sorts of ornamental earthenware)
    Temple back.
Powell Wm. & Thos. (brown stone
    ware) Thomas Street.
Price Chas & Son (Stone-ware)
    Temple & Thomas Street.
Sheppard Mrs (and Brick & Tile) Avon-
    street, St. Philip's.
Spokes, John (stone-ware)
Yabbicomb Henry (sugar, Chimney
    and garden pot manufacturers)
Yabbicomb H & T. (Stone ware)
    Avon-street. St. Philips.

Derbyshire, Leicestershire, Nottinghamshire, and Rutlandshire

KELLYS POST OFFICE DIRECTORY
    OF DERBYSHIRE, LEICESTER-
    SHIRE, NOTTINGHAMSHIRE
    AND RUTLANDSHIRE 1848
Potters
Bourne J. Pottery, Codnon Park,
    Alfreton.

Briddon Samuel & Henry, Brampton,
    Chesterfield
Evans R. Canal Bridge, Ilkeston,
    Nottingham.
Hall, J. Sutton Bonnington,
    Loughborough.
Johnson. Mrs. Catherine, Whittington
    moor Pottery Chesterfield.

Madin A. Whittington Moor Pottery, Chesterfield.

Pearson J. J., Whittington Moor, Chesterfield

Proudman & Co. Lount. Ashby-de-la-zh.

Samforth Mrs M., Stone Gravels, Chesterfield.

Schofield, G.Eaton East Retford

Synyard T. Clayworth, Bawtry.

Straw W., Farnsfield, Southwell.

Devonshire

WILLIAM WHITE'S HISTORY, GAZETTEER AND DIRECTORY OF DEVONSHIRE, 1850

Barnstaple

Bannam Thos. North Walk.

Rendell Elias D., Litchdon st.

Bideford

Ching Bryant, East-the-Water.

Crocker Saml., Strand.

Cole John, East-the-Water.

Green George, High Street.

Tucker John & Son, Potters' Lane.

Fremington

Fishley Edmund, pot and tile maker, Bickington.

Honiton

Hussey Susan, potter.

Bovey Tracey

Bovey Tracey Pottery Co., earthenware, drain pipe, &c. manufacturers.

Plymouth

Alsop, William, Earthenware manufacturer Coxide Pottery.

Leeds and Sheffield

LEEDS DIRECTORY FOR 1798

Dixon, Joseph, Tea, china, glass and staffordshire ware man, Briggate.

King John tea dealer, and glass and china man (?) Market Place.

Knowles A. china and glass man Briggate.

HISTORY DIRECTORY OF YORK 1822

Earthenware Manufacturers. Leeds

Allison Joseph Hunslet.

Brown S. Hunslet mon side.

Clark J. Holbeck Lane End.

Hartley Green & Co. Leeds Pottery.

Petty's & Hewitt Hunslett Hall.

Russel William, Meadow Lane.

Taylor William, Hunslet.

PIGOT'S DUBLIN & HIBERNIAN PROVINCIAL DIRECTORY LONDON, 1824

Leeds Earthenware Manufacturers

Allison Joseph, Hunslet.

Brown Samuel, Hunslet Moor Side.

Cartledge Thomas, Hundet Pottery.

Clark J. Holbeck Lane End.

Hartley, Greens & Co. Leeds pottery.

Pettys & Hewitt, Hunslet hall Pottery.

Russell Wm. Medow Lane.

Taylor Wm. Hunslet.

Leeds Earthenware manufacturers

Allison Joseph, Hunslet.
Brown Samuel, Hunslet-moor-side.
Cartlidge Thomas, Hunslet.
Clark, H. Holbeck-lane-end.
Hanson George, Hunslet.
Hartley Greens, and Co. Leeds Pottery.
Pettys & Hewitt, Hunslet-hall.
Russell Wm. Meadow Lane.
Taylor Wm. Hunslet.

PIGOT & CO'S DIRECTORY OF
SCOTLAND 1837, APPENDIX

*Sheffield Earthenware Manufacturers
& Potters.*

Barker Samuel. Masbro.
Green George, Rawmarsh.
Hanley Eliza, Rawmarsh.
Taylor Thos. & Co. Rawmarsh.

PIGOT'S LONDON DIRECTORY,
1836

Leeds Earthenware Manufacturers

Allison Joseph, Hunslet.
Brown Samuel, Hunslet-moor-side.
Cartlidge, Thomas. Hunslet.
Clark J. Holbeck-lane-end.
Hanson, George, Hunslet.
Hartley, Green & Co. Leeds Pottery.
Pettys & Hewitt, Hunslet Hall.
Russell Wm. Meadow-lane.
Taylor Wm. Hunslet.

Liverpool

BAILEY'S NORTHERN DIRECTORY
1781

Liverpool

Barnes & Cotter, china manufacturers
and potters. Hay market.
Bramwell & Breeze, Earthen warehouse
Cornhill.
Penninnington John, china
manufacturers Folly Lane.
Pennington & Part. china
manufacturers Shaws-brow.
Stokes Joseph, earthen warehouse
Georges Dock.
Skellhorn William, earthen warehouse
South Dock.

THE LIVERPOOL DIRECTORY
1766.

Chaffers Richard & Co. china makers,
Shaw's-brow.
Christian Philip, potter, Lord street.
Cotter James & Co. potters,
Haymarket.
Drinkwater George & Co. potters,
Duke-street.
Dunbibin John. potter. Shaw's-brow.
Fisher Frederick. potter. Harrington-
street.
Poole Samuel, potter. Dale-street.
Roberts Berry & Co. potters. Dale-
street.

Roscoe John, potter, Shaw's-brow.
Stringfellow William, enameller,
     Park-lane.
Tyer Robert, potter Shaw's-brow.
Thwaites Richard, potter, Park Lane.
Willcock Robert & Co. potters,
     Park lane.
Williams John, potter Shaw's-brow.

PIGOT & CO'S DIRECTORY OF
SCOTLAND, 1837 APPENDIX
Liverpool Earthenware Manufacturers
Baker William & Co. 49 Castle Street,
     Thomas France Bennett, agent.
Davenport Wm. & Co. 36,
     Canning Place South.
Herculaneum Co. Tohteth Park & 5,
     South John Street.
Ingleby Thos. & Co. Orford Street.

Mansfield Archibald, Canning Street.
Swaine Thos. & Robert. (stone and
     black ware) 19, College-lane.
Webster Bros. (stone and black ware)
     Salthouse dock East.
Yates George & William C.
     (stone ware) 22, Hanover Street.

PIGOT & SLATER'S DIRECTORY OF
LIVERPOOL, MANCHESTER, 1843
Liverpool Earthenware Manufacturers
Baker, William & Co. 20 Castle Street
     and Fenton, Potteries, Staffordshire.
Herculaneum Pottery Company,
     4 Hanover Street, James Mort agent.
Swain, Thomas and Robert,
     14 College Lane.
Yates, Geo. & Wm., 27 Hanover
     street.

London & Home Counties

HENRY KENT'S LONDON DIRECTORY, 1736.

Grove Richard, potter, Tooly Street, Southwark.
Sherwill Benjamin, Potter, Little Tower-street.
Wilkinson Samuel, Potter, St. Mary Overs, in Southwark.

MORTIMER'S THE UNIVERSAL DIRECTOR, LONDON, 1763.
China Manufacturers
The different Manufactories of English China, which have been brought to any tolerable degree of perfection, are here subjoined, with the names of the Proprietors or Managers, and the Places of Sale in London.
Crowther, John, Proprietor of the Bow China Manufactory at Bow in Essex; and in Cornhill.
Sprimont, Nicholas, Proprietor of the Chelsea China Manufactory. Laurence Street, Chelsea; and at the Warehouse in Piccadilly.
Spurling, John, Proprietor of the Worcester China Manufactory. London-house, Aldersgate-street

Potters

It is to be understood that the following are the real Manufacturers of the Blue and White, and Plain White, Earthen wares, except those which are distinguished as Brown Stone Potters, who make only jars, jugs, etc. and do not undertake any part of the White branch. There are a great many Manufactories of Stone and Earthen ware in different parts of the kindom; but the following are the only Manufacturers in or near London.

Addison and Abernethy. Hermitage-street, Wapping.

Bacchus, Thomas. George-yard, Thames-Street.

Dunbibin, John. Coffin's-yard, Margaret's-hill, Southwark.

Griffiths, —, Lambeth.

Grove, Joseph. Horslydown-lane, Southwark.

Jackson — Vauxhall.

Jones, John. Brown Stone Potter, Lambeth.

Sanders and Richards. Vauxhall.

Sanders, William. Mortlake.

Swabey, Samuel. Vauxhall.

White, Henry, Brown Stone Potter. Lambeth.

White, William, Ditto. Fulham.

Giles, James, China and Enamel Painter. Berwick-street, Soho. This ingenious artist copies the patterns of any China with the utmost exactness, both with respect to the Design and the Colours, either in the European or Chinese taste: he likewise copies any paintings in Enamel. He has also brought the enamel colours to great perfection, and thereby rendered them extremely useful to the curious Artists in that branch.

Donaldson, John. Potrait painter. At the lower End of Princes-street, Leicester-Square.

BAILEY'S NORTHERN DIRECTORY 1781.

London

Ansley Thos. potter & glass-seller. 13, Fenchurch-st.

Bacchus, Wm. Potter. 36, Upper Thames-st.

Byard & Co. Pot and Pearl ash manufacturers(?) Wood Bridge Street, Clerkenwell.

Dunbibin Samuel, China and earthenware man. Borough.

Fidler Thos. Chinaman 35, St Paul's Churchyard.

Griffin & Morgan, potters, Lambeth.

Hall, Edward. China & Glassman. 2, Paul's Court, Huggin Lane, Wood St.

Hardess, Mandz & Co. Potters and hardwareman, St Catherines.

Colour plate 24, WORCESTER: *see page viii for caption*

Miles & Co. potash and pearl manufacturers, Woodbridgst. Clerkenwell.

Moore, John, 73, St Paul's Churchyard.

Moss George, potter, Vauxhall, Lambeth.

Swabey Samuel Esq. potter, Vauxhall.

Tidmarsh, John, potter & glass seller, 123, Rosemary L.

Turner & Abbott Staffordshire-potters, china and glass men, 9, Old Fish Street.

Wedgewood & Bentley, Staffordshire-warehouse. 12, Greek St., Soho.

Woods, Henry, chinaman 35, Poultry.

BAILEY'S BRITISH DIRECTORY 1784.

London

Bacchus William, Potter No. 36, Upper Thames Street.

Baker Samuel, Chinaman Portugal-Street.

Balls William, Glass and China Seller, No 52, Fenchurch Street.

Bamford Elizabeth, Staffords Warehouse, Tothill-st., Westminster.

Bardwell John, Chinaman, No 10, Ravenrow Spilthle Fields.

Bell James, Chinaman, No. 105, Oxford Street.

Bestridge & Co., Glass & Staffordshire-warehouse, No 24, Whitechapel Road.

Bigland Thos., Potter, Rotherhithe-street.

Blades John., Glass Manufactory, No 5, Ludgate Hill.

Brumer Mary, Glass China and Earthenware-house, No 142, Whitechapel.

Campbell George., China Manufacturer, No 17, Chiswell Street.

Clarkson Wm., Glass and Chinaman, No 144, St John's St.

Clarkson John, Chinaman Market Street, St James.

Clowes and Williamson, Potters China and Glassmen, Brookes Wharfe.

Cotterell Wm., China and Glassman, No 9, Mansionhouse-st.

Dalton Abraham, Red Potter St Nicholas Deptford.

Darknell Robert. Potter, 173, Tooley-st.

Davis Simon, Chinaman Church Lane, St Martin's.

Edwards John, China and glassman, St James Market.

Elliot, William, Chinaman, No 27, St Paul's Church-yard

Ellwood & Co., Chinaman 36, Ludgate Street.

Fidler Thos. Chinaman 35, St Pauls Church.

Fogg & Son, Chinamen, No 50, New Bond St.

Gurney Geo. & J. B., Potters, Lambeth.

Hardess, Mantz and Co., Potters and Hardwaremen, St Catherines

Hardy Daniel, Chinaman, No 9, High Holborn.

Hayward John, China and glassman, No 206 Oxford-st.

Hewson William, Chinaman, No 86, Aldgate

Hewson William, Chinaman, No 388, Strand.
Hillcock Robert, China and glassman, No 57, Cheapside.
Laggatt Rich, Chinaman Newport Street.
Longmore Benjamin, Chinaman, No 33, Coventry Street.
Malden John, Glassman & Potter, No 72, Wapping Wall.
Mason Miles, China and glassman, 131, Fenchurch Street.
Means Edward, China and glassman, 54, No 139 Leadenhall-Street
Morris Wm., Potter St Paul's Deptford.
Morthock William, Chinaman, No 250, Oxford Street.
Nevell Eben, China & Glassman, 2, Gt Titchfield St.
Newbury Benj. chinaman, No 74, Fleet St.
Parry Isaac, Potter and Sugar Mould Maker, St Pauls Deptford
Philips George, Chinaman, No 135, Oxford Street.
Philipps John, Red Potter Princes-st., Lambeth.
Roberts Jn., Chinaman, No 117, Holborn Hill.
Spode Josiah, Potter, No 46, Fore-st., Chipplegate.
Stevens Thomas, Chinaman, No 201, Upper Shodwell.
Waters Richard Brown, stone and Red Potter Nr. Lambeth Chrch.
Whitling George, Chinaman, No 3, Chiswell Street.
Wilkinson Thos., Potter, No 58, Wapping.
Williams Thos., Chinaman, No 1, St James Street.
Willington Roger., Chinaman, 39, Minories.
Wood Henry, Chinaman Bridge Street, Westminster.
Woods Henry, Chinaman, No 35, Poultry.

GENERAL LONDON GUIDE FOR 1794

Potters   (those with a X are Wholesale Dealers; those with an S are Subscribers)

Abbott & Newberry, 82, Fleet-st.
Bingham H. Princes-st. Lambeth.
Dawson Rob. 31, St. Paul's-Church-Yard.
X Green & Limpus. 62, Up Thames St.
Griffin & Morgan. Lambeth. S.
Hardels Mantz & Co. 277, Wapping.
Moss. Geo. Vauxhall.
Moss. Geo. Princes-street, Lambeth S.
North & Son. 104, Norton Falgate.
Odyin John. 36, Upper Thames Street.
. Pugh & Speck. Booth-st., Spitalfields, S.

Potters

Armstrong Barnabas, Foxes Lane. Shadwell.
Bacchus & Green. 35 & 36, Upper Thames Street.
Bingham Henry, Princes-st. Lambeth.
Bloodworth G. 15, Vauxhall-walk, Lambeth.
Brayne Jno. Nine Elms, Battersea.
Darvill & Bloodworth. Princes-street, Lambeth.
Davies F. Ferry Street, High-street, Lambeth.
Doulton & Watts. 14, Vauxhall-walk, Lambeth.
Green Jas. Princes-st., Lambeth.
Higgins Jno. Princes-st. Lambeth.
Hill & Co. Glasshouse-street, Vauxhall.
Jones S. L. Oliver. Up. Fore-street, Lambeth.
Milner & Morris. 116, Lr. Thames-st.
Moss Thos. Princes-st., Lambeth.
North Wm. 104, Bishopsgate without.
Passenger R. 95, Union-st., Boro.
Pavitt & Davis, Nine Elms Battersea.
Pugh Jas. & Wm. Fore-st., Lambeth.
Scott Anthony, 61, Wapping-Wall.
Waters J. Richard. High-street, Lambeth.
Wilson Henry. 11, Vauxhall-walk, Lambeth, 14, Eastcheap.
Wisker Jno. Vauxhall-bridge.
Yates Jas. (and glass seller) 137, Rosemary Lane.

London China and Glass Manufacturers

Bacchus & Green, 35 & 36 Upper Thames St.
Bloor Robert, (Derby China) 34, Old Bond St.
Chamberlain, H. & R. 155 New Bond St.
Clews, John & Co. 119 Holborn-hill
Davenport Jas. & Co. (& earthenware) 82 Fleet st.
Flight, Barr & Barr, 1 Coventry St. Haymarket.
Spode & Copeland, Portugal St, Lincoln's Inn Fields
Rose & Co. 9 Thanet Pl. Temple Bar.

Potters

(Those marked thus * are Potters' Warehouses only)

* Armstrong Barnabas, Foxes Lane, Shadwell
Bacchus & Green, 35 & 36 Upper Thames St.
Bingham, Henry, Princes St. Lambeth
Bloodworth, Chas. 15 Vauxhall Walk, Lambeth.
Brayne John, Nine Elms, Battersea,
Darvil & Bloodworth, Princes St. Lambeth
Doulton & Watts, 14 Vauxhall Walk, Lambeth
Danès F., Ferry st. Hugh st, Lambeth
Green James, Princes St. Lambeth
Higgins, John, Princes St. Lambeth
Hill & Co. Glasshouse St. Vauxhall
* Hughesden Jos. 65 Wapping Wall.
Jones, Samuel Oliver, Upper Fore-st, Lambeth.
Milner & Morris, Lower Thames St.
Moss. Thos. Princes St. Lambeth
North, Wm. 104 Bishopsgate-without
Passenger R. 95 Union St., Boro.
Pavitt & Davis, Nine Elms, Battersea
Pugh, Jas. & Wm. Fore St. Lambeth
Scott, Antony, 61 Wapping Wall
* Smith, Josh. 8 Tottenhouse Yard.
Wanner, Philip, Kings Rd. Chelsea
Waters, Richard, High St. Lambeth
Wilson, Henry, 11 Vauxhall Walk, Lambeth & 14 Little Eastcheap
Wisker, John, Vauxhall Bridge.
Wood, John 29 Ratcliff – highway.

PIGOT'S LONDON DIRECTORY 1836

China and Earthenware Manufacturers & Glass Dealers

Bloor Robert, 34 Old Bond St. and at Derby
Bradley John & Co. 47 Pall mall
Brameld & Co. 13 Vauxhall bridge Road
Chamberlain W. & Co. 155 New Bond St.
Copeland & Garretts, 5 Portugal St. Lin. Inn.
Davenports & Co. 82 Fleet st.
Fielding Thomas, 69 Sale St. Pad.
Flight. Barr & Barr, 1 Coventry St. Haymarket and at Worcester

Green Jos. & Co 10 and 11 St. Paul's Church ard.
Nash, Andrew John & Co. 75 Cornhill
Peake William, York Road, Waterloo road.
Rose John & Co. 4 Newcastle St. Strand
Tidmarsh & Brown. 4 Rosemary Lane.
Wedgwood, Thos. 40 Dorset St, Spitaflds.

China Painters and Enamellers

Anderson Jno. 16 Gloucester St. St. John St. Rd.
Essex Wm. 32 Compton St., Brunswick Sq.
Higham Jno, 13 Tavistock St. Tavistock Sq.
Myatt Wm. 22 Primrose St. 'Bishopsgate'

Potters

Armstrong, Charlotte (wholesale) 8 Cockhill, Ratcliff.
Blackburn, John. 131 Fenchurch St.
Bloodworth Charles, Vauxhall Walk
Brameld & Co. 13 Vauxhall Bridge Road
Brayne John, Nine Elms, Lambeth
Breillat, Joseph, 61 Blackman St. Borough.
Doulton & Watts, 28 High St. Lambeth.
Green, Joseph & Co. 35 Upper Thames St.
Green Stephen, Princes St. Lambeth
Hale, John, St. Ann's place, Limehouse.
Higgins John, Princes St. Lambeth
Hill, David & Co. Vauxhall Walk
Jones & Sefton, Princes St. Lambeth.
Loder Edward, 43, Lower Shodwell
Marshall Charles, Upper Holloway
Marshall John Upper Holloway
Passenger, Robert, 95 Union St. Borough
Purden, John (and agent for Sir Fred Fowke's ornamental vases and flower pots) 18 King Wm. St. Strand. Manufactory at Lowesly Hall.
Scott, Henry & Co; 61 Wapping Wall & at Sunderland
Smith, Thomas, Princes St. Lambeth.
Waters John Richard, Hugh St., Lambeth
Westwood, Moores & Ryder, 10 North Wharf Rd., Harrow Rd.
Whitton Benj. Read's Alley, Rotherhithe.
Wisker John, High St. Vauxhall
Woolf Lewis & Co. 78 Wapping Wall

Potters-Wholesale

  * Stone Potters   + Brown Stone Potters

   Armstrong Mrs, 8 Cockhill, Ratcliff

+   Bloodworth C. Vauxhall Walk, Lamb.

+* Brayne John, Nine Elms, Vauxhall.

+* Breillat Joseph, 61 Blackman st.

+   Davis E. Fountain Stairs, Bermondsey.

+   Doulton & Watts. 28, High Street, Lamb.

+   Green S. (& White) Princes Street, Lamb.

*   Higgins Hen. Thos. Ferry Street, Lambeth.

+   Hill David & Co. Vauxhall Walk.

+* Kishere Wm. Mortlake, Surrey.

+* Robinson George, Kew Bridge.

+* Sefton Wm. Princes Street, Lambeth.

+   Singer A. & Co. (& Delph) Vauxhall.

+* Waters John Rich. High Street Lambeth.

+   White Charles Edward, Fulham.

China, Glass & Earthenware Manufacturers and wholesale Glass dealers

Alcock & Co. (F. Azemberg: Agent) 89 Hatton Garden.

Bacon James, New Cross.

Beck, Mrs. S. & Son, 59 Crown Street, Finsbury.

Bloor, Robert. 34, Old Bond Street.

Brameld & Co (The Griffen) Piccadilly top of the Haymarket.

Buddrich Geo. W. 104, Bishopsgate without.

Chamberlain W. & Co. 155, New Bond Street.

Cheshire Geo. 3 Wharf, City Road, Basin.

Cooke Charles. 22 & 231, Wapping.

Cullum & Peake, 2, Knightsbridge Terrace.

Davenports' & Co. 82, Fleet Street.

Floyd C. 31 Bartholomew Ter. Goswl rd.

Green J. & Sons. 11 St Pauls Church Yard. & 34 & 35 Upper Thames st.

Jacobs A. 14, Crown Street, Finsbury.

Johnson Owen. 3 Bond Ct. Walbrook.

Kewell B. 13 & 14 Vauxhall Bridge Road.

Lockhead James, 5, High Holborn.

Martin Richd. Weaver. 148, Tooley St.

Newington & Sander, 319, High Holborn.

Pellatt Apsley, Holland St. Blkfrs Road.
Rennick F. Northampton Square 36 Clkwl.
Rose John & Co. 4, Newcastle Street, Strand.
Sharpus T. & Co. 13 Cockspur St. Haymkt.
Solomon. N. 44, Chiswell Street, & Red Lion wf.
Symons E. (& cutler) 32, Bread Street.
Wedgewood T. 5 6 & 7 Crispin st. Spitflds.
Wileman H. Irongate whf. Paddington.

China Painters
Battam T. & Son, 2 Johnson's ct. Fleet st.

Potters
Bacon James, New Cross
Colson Thos, & Wm. Archery Rd., Highgate.
Dawson. Wm. E. Plumstead Common.
Field George. Barnet Common.
Gates Charles. Shooter's Hill.
Gramsby John A. Barnet Common.
Harding & Co. Pibright Guildford.
Harris James, Plumstead Common.
Hatcher John, Beneden Cranbrook.
Hoar Joseph. Nutbrown Emsworth.
Jee James Blackheath-rd., Greenwich.
Jee T. Cottage Pl. South Street Greenwich.
Looker Benjamin Kingston Hill.
Marshall R.H. Mount Pleasant Norwd
Miller John Hellingly Hailsham
Norman Wm. & Richard Chailey, Lewes.
Norman Wm. St John's Comm. Keymer, Lewes.
Pascall Thos. Nowood.
Richardson William, Tonbridge.
Savage William Plumstead Common.
Scales Wm. Green Lanes, Tottenham.
Waghorn Wm. R. Nonsuch Park, Ewell.
White Chas. Edw. High Street, Fulham.
White Edward Rolvenden, Cranbrook.
Wild Henry, Bosham, Chichester.

Potters Home Counties

Bacon James, New Cross.
Colson Thos. & Wm. Archery Rd. Highgate.
Dawson Wm. E. Plumstead Common.
Field George. Barnet Common
Gates Charles, Shooter's hill.
Gransby John A. Barnet Common.
Harding & Co. Pirbright, Guildford.
Harris James. Plumstead Common.
Hatcher John, Benenden Cranbrook.
Hoar Joseph. Nutbourne, Emsworth.
Jee. James. Blackheath Rd. Greenwich.
Jee T. Cottage Pl. South St, Greenwich.
Looker, Benjamin, Kingston Hill.
Marshall R. H. Mt Pleasant Norwd.
Miller John, Hellingly, Hailsham.
Norman Wm. & Richard. Chailey, Lewes.
Norman Wm. St Johns Common, Keymer, Lewes.
Pascall Thomas, Nowood.
Richardson William. Tonbridge.
Savage William, Plumstead Common.
Scales Wm. Green. Lanes, Tottenham.
Waghorn Wm. R. Nonsuch Park. Ewell.
White Chas. Edw. High st, Fulham.
White Edward, Rolvenden, Cranbrook.
Wild, Henry, Bosham, Chichester.

Newcastle-on-Tyne and North Country

BAILEY'S NORTHERN DIRECTORY, 1781

Newcastle

Hillcoat William Potter, Quay side.
Jackson Paul, Potter, Quay side.
Warburton John, Potter, Quayside

WHITE'S BURHAM–NORTHUMBERLAND DIRECTORY 1827

Earthenware Manufacturers. Stockton-upon-Tees

Smith & Whalley, High Street

THE FIRST NEWCASTLE DIRECTORY *Newcastle-upon-Tyne*, 1778 *reptd.* 1889.

Potters

Hillcoat, Wm. Quay side. (also in 1782, 83 and 84)

Jackson, Paul. ditto. (also in 1782, 83, and 84)

Warburton, John. ditto. (also in 1782, 83, 84 and 1787)

THE NEWCASTLE AND GATESHEAD DIRECTORY FOR 1782, 83, AND 84

Smith, Harvey & Co. earthen-ware manufact, near Stepney.

Harris, Jos. china, glass, and Staffordshire warehouse, Biggmarket.

ALEXANDER IHLER'S DIRECTORY OF NEWCASTLE AND GATESHEAD *Newcastle*, 1833

Earthenware manufacturers

Codling & Co., Tyne Pottery, Felling-shore.

Dalton, Burn, and Co. Stepney Pottery. Also 1838

Davies, R., & Co. South-shore. Also 1838

Dryden, John, and Co. Ouseburn. Also 1838

Fell, T. & Co. St. Peter's Pottery. Also 1838

Hepworth, John, 62, Close.

Maling, Robert, Ouseburn, also 1838, 1847

Jackson & Patterson, 37, Quayside. Also 1838

Redhead, Wilson, & Co., Skinnerburn.

Sewell & Donkin, St. Anthony's Pottery. Also 1838, 1847

Thompson, T. & J. Ouseburn. Also 1838

Warburton, Jos. Heworth-shore.

Wallace, Thomas, and Sons, Castle-stairs and Warburton. Also 1838

Wilson, E. & R. Ballast Hill

Wood, Joseph, Felling-shore.

1838

Bagshaw, John, Ouseburn.

Charlton, Ralph, Ouseburn.

Patterson, Dawson, Codling, Heworth-shore, Gateshead.

1847

Newcastle

Bell, Thomas & Co. Stepney Pottery
Carr, & Patton, Ouseburn
Charlton, John, Ouseburn.
Fell, Thomas & Co. St. Peter's Quay.
Gray, George, Ouseburn.
Wallace, Jas. & Co. Forth Bank
Wilson, Rt. Chpr. Tyne Main Ptry

Gateshead

Kendell & Walker, Carr's Hill.
Parker, Benjamin, Carr's Hill.
Patterson, Thomas, Sheriff Hill.
Wilson, Robert, Friars Goose.

Stockton-on-Tees

Harwood T. & Co., Clarence Pottery.
Smith, William & Co. South Stockton.
Smith, Wm. jun. & Co.
    North shr Pottery.

North Shields

Carr & Patten, Low Lights.

South Shields

Armstrong Jno. & Co., Oyston Lane.

Sunderland

Dixon, Phillips & Co. Sunderland
    Pottery, foot of High St.
Marr, Sarah, North Quay.
Moore, Samuel & Co., Bridge & Wear
    Potteries, and low Southwick.
Rickaby & Blakelock, Sheep Fold
    Pottery.
Scott, Brothers, & Co., Southwick
    Pottery.

neighbourhood of Sunderland.
Southwick (High)

Moore, Charles.
Scott, Henry.
Scott, Anthony, jun.

AN ACCOUNT OF NEWCASTLE-
UPON-TYNE, 1787

Alphabetical List of the people in Trade;
    and their residence in Newcastle
    1787.
Backhouse, Hillcoat, & Co. earthen-
    ware pottery, Ouze-burn.
Spearman and Co. skinnerborn pottery,
    Firthbanks.
Warburton, John, pottery-ware house,
    Quayside.

PIGOT & CO'S DIRECTORY OF
SCOTLAND 1837, appendix

Earthenware Manufacturers. Newcastle.

Bagshaw John, Ouseburn.
Charlton Ralph, Ouseburn Flint Mill.
Dalton, Burn & Co. Stepney Pottery.
Davies Richard & Co. Tynemain
    Pottery, Salt Meadows, Gateshead.
Dryden John & Co. (and improved
    economical filters) Phoenix Pottery.
Ouseburn.
Fell Thos & Co. St Peter's Pottery.
Ferry John, Sherriff Hill.
Jackson & Patterson. 37 Quay Side.
Maling John, Ouseburn.
Maling Robt. Ouseburn bridge pottery.
Patterson & Co. Felling Shore.
Russell Frederick (stone) North Shore
    & New-Road. St Ann's.
Sewell & Donkin. St Anthony's Pottery.
Wallace Thos. & Sons. Forth Bank.
Wallace Thos. Skinnerburn.
Wilson Wm Brown St Anthony's.
Wood John. Gateshead & Folly.
Wood, Joseph. Felling shore.

Norfolk

NORWICH DIRECTORY 1782

Croskill Henry Earthenware Dealer No. 2. Maddler Mkt.
Derfley James Wholesale and Retail Potter No. 21, Pottergate Street.

KELLY'S POST OFFICE DIRECTORY OF LONDON AND
NINE COUNTIES 1846

Potters Cambridge Norfolk & Suffolk

Fox J. Swanton Novers, Fakenham.
Rawling S. Bridge Rd. Downham

Scotland

GRAYS ANNUAL DIRECTORY 1834–35 OF EDINBURGH AND
ITS VICINITY

Potters
Cooper W. and stained glass maker to the king. 14, Elm-Row.
Dun. T. Glass cutter 41, Abbey Hill.
Duncan John. Glass cutter 8, MacDowall-st.
Fraser John Glass cutter 36, Queen-street, Leith.
Geddes James. crown & plate glass warehouse 25, Greenside-st.
Glen Robt. glass cutter & dealer 7, North College Street.
Milne, Cornwall & Co. manufactureres of stoneware, Pipe-st, Portebello.
Oliphant Thos. glass cutter 8, Shakespeare Sq.
Ranken John. Flint glass manfuacturers and brassfounder, Leith Walk.
Rathbone & Co. earthenware manufacturer Portobello.
Reid W. & Son. China and earthenware manufacturers, Newbiggin.

PIGOT & CO'S DIRECTORY OF SCOTLAND, 1837

Pottery Manufacturers Glasgow

Kidston Robt. Alexander & Co. Anderston & Verreville Pottery works.
Murray & Co. St Rollox.
Thompson John, Annfield Pottery, Gallowgate.
Wellington Pottery, 602, Gallowgate – Alex Patterson, mangr.
Wilson. Wm. Campbellfield Pottery.

Staffordshire

BAILEY'S NORTHERN
DIRECTORY, 1781

Newcastle under Lyne and Neighbourhood

Adams William & Co., potters Burslem.
Baddley Ralph, potter Shelton.
Bacchus William, potter Fenton.
Barker Thos, potter Lane Delf.
Blackweel John, potter Cobridge.
Booth Hugh, potter Stoke.
Bourne Joseph, potter Hanley.
Boone Edward, potter Longport.
Brindley John, potter Longport.
Bucknall Ralph, & Sons potters
    Cobridge.
Clowes William & Co., potters
    Longport.
Daniel Walter, potter Burslem.
Daniel Thomas, potter Burslem.
Edwards William, potter Lane Delf.
Garner Robert, potter Lane End.
Godwin Thomas & Bery, potters
    Cobridge.
Hales & Adams, potters Cobridge.
Harrison John Jnr., potter Stoke.

Heath & Bagnal, potters Shelton.
Hollins Samuel, potters Shelton.
Keeling Anthony, potter Tunstall.
Mare John & Richard, potters Hanley.
Myatt Richard, potter Lane End.
Neale James & Co., potters Hanley.
Philips Thomas., potter Lane End.
Perry Samuel & Co., potters Hanley.
Pratt William, potter Lane Delf.
Pickance & Daniel, potters Cobridge.
Robinson & Smith, potters Cobridge.
Shelley Thos., potter Lane End.
Shelley Michael, potter Lane End.
Spode Josiah, potter Stoke.
Smith Thos. & Co., potters Burslem.
Turner John, potter Lane End.
Twemlow Geo. & Thos., potters Shelton.
Wedgewood Joseph Esq., potter to
    Her Majesty. Etruria.
Wedgewood Thos., potter Burslem.
Warburton Joseph, potter Stoke.
Wolfe Thos. Jnr., potter Stoke.
Wood John, potter Burslem.
Yates John, potter Shelton.

BAILEY'S WESTERN DIRECTORY, 1784

Potters in Staffs 1) Burslem and Newcastle

Adams William & Co. Manufacturers of cream coloured ware and china glazed
ware painted.
Bagley William Potter.
Bourne John. Manufacturer of china glaze, blue painted, enamelled and cream
coloured earthen ware.
Bourne & Malkin Manufacturers of China glazed, blue, and cream coloured
ware
Cartlidge S & J. Potters.

Daniel Thos. Potter.

Daniel John, Manufacturer of cream colour and red earthenware.

Daniel Timothy, Manufacturer of cream colour and red earthen ware.

Daniel Walter, Manufacturer of cream colour and red earthen ware.

Green John Potter.

Holland Thos. Manufacturer of black and red china ware and Gilder.

Keeling Anthony, Manufacturer of Queen's ware in general blue painted and enamelled Egyptain black (Tunstall Near Burslem)

Lockett Timothy and John, White stone potters Burslem.

Malkin Burnham, Potter.

Robinson John. Enameller and Printer of cream colour and china glazed ware.

Rogers John and George Manufacturers of china glazed wares painted blue and cream colour.

Smith Ambrose & Co. Manufacturers of cream coloured ware and china glazed ware painted blue.

Smith John & Joseph Potters.

Stevenson Charles & Son Manufacturers of cream coloured ware, blue painted.

Wedgewood Thos. Manufacturers of cream coloured ware and china glazed ware, painted with blue etc. Big house.

Wedgewood Thos. Manufacturer of cream coloured ware and china glazed ware, painted with blue etc. Over House.

Wilson James. Enameller.

Wood, John Potter.

Wood Enoch & Ralph Manufacturers of all kinds of useful and ornamental earthenware. Egyptian Black, Cane and various other colours; also black figures, seals and cyphers.

Wood Josiah Manufacturers of black fine glazed, variegated and cream coloured ware and blue.

Cobridge

Blackwell, Joseph, Manufacturers of blue and white stone ware, cream and painted wares.

Blackwell, John, Manufacturer of blue and white stone, ware and cream and painted wares.

Burknall Robert, Manufacturer of Queen's ware blue printed, enamelled, printed etc.

Godwin Thos, and Benj. Manufacturer of Queen's ware and china glazed blue.

Hales and Adams, Potters.

Robinson Smith, Potters.

Warburton Jacob, Potter.

Hanley

Bagnall Sampson, Potter.

Boon Joseph, Potter.

Chatterley C & E., Potters.

Glass John, Potter.

Heath, Warburton & Co., China
Manufacturers.
Keeling Edward, Potter.
Mare, John & Richard, Potters.
Mayer Elijah, Enameller.
Miller Wm., Potter.
Neale and Wilson, Potters.
Perry Samuel, Potter
Taylor Geo., Potter.
Wright Thos., Potter.
Yates John, Potter.

Shelton

Baddeley J. & E. Potters.
Hassells John, Potters.
Heath & Bagnall Potters.
Hollins Samuel, Potter.
Keeling Anthony, Potter.
Taylor and Pope Potters.
Twemlow G. Potter
Whitehead Christopher Charles, Potter.
Yates John, Potter.

Stoke

Bell Sarah Potter.
Boot Hugh Manufacturer of china,
china glaze and Queen's ware in
all its various Branches.
Brindley James Potter.
Spode Josiah Potter.
Straphan Joseph Merchant and factor
in all kinds of earthenware.
Woolfe Thos. Manufacturer of Queen's
ware in general, Blue, Printed
and Egyptian Black Cane etc.

Fenton

Bacchus Wm. Manufacturer of Queen's
ware in all its various branches.
Boon Edward Manufacturer of Queen's
ware

Brindley Taylor Potter.
Clowes and Williamson Potter.
Turner John Potter.
Wedgewood Josiah and Thos. Potters.

Lane End

Barker John Manufacturer of cream
coloured china glaze and Blue Wares.
Barker William Potter.
Barker Richard Potter.
Cyples Joseph Manufacturer of
Egyptian Black and Pottery in general.
Edwards William Potter.
Garner Joseph. Potter.
Forrester and Meredith, Manufacturers
of Queen's ware Egyptian Black,
Red China and various other ware.
Garner Joseph, Potter
Garner Robert. Manufacturer of
Queen's ware and various other
wares.
Shelley Michael Potter.
Shelley Thos Potter.
Turner & Abbott Potters to Prince of
Wales.
Walklete Mark Potters.

Worcester

Davis William & Co., Worcester
Porcelain Manufactory.

THE STAFFORDSHIRE POTTERY
DIRECTORY
Chester & Mort, Hanley and New-
castle, n.d. (published c 1796).
Ralph Baddeley, Shelton.
Bagnall & Boon, Shelton.
Birch & Whitehead, Hanley.
John & Edward Baddeley, Shelton.
Booth & Marsh, Shelton.
William Chatterley, Hanley.

James Greatbatch, Shelton.
John Glass, Hanley.
Hallam & Shelley, Shelton.
Samuel Hollins, Shelton.
Hollins, Warburton & Co., Shelton.
Thomas Heath, Shelton.
Thomas & John Hollins, Shelton.
James Keeling, Hanley.
Edward Keeling, Keeling's Lane,
    Hanley
John Mare, Hanley.
Elijah Mayer, Hanley.
William Mellor, Hanley.
Meigh & Walthall, Hanley.
Richard Poole, Shelton.
Thomas Pope, Shelton.
Stephen Pope, Shelton.
Ridgway, Smith & Ridgway, Shelton.
Stanley & Co., Hanley.
Thomas Broom Simpson, Hanley.
Shorthose & Heath, Hanley.
George Taylor, Hanley.
John Twemlow, Shelton.
Joseph Warrilow, Hanley.
Dorothy Whitehead, Hanley.
James & Charles Whitehead, Hanley.
Robert Wilson, Hanley.
John Yates, Hanley.
John & William Yates, Shelton.
Bagshaw, Taylor & Maier (sic),.
    Burslem
Charles Ball, Burslem.
Edward Bourne, junior, Burslem.
John Breeze, Burslem.
Bedson & Rhodes, Burslem.
William Dawson, Burslem.
Walter Daniel, New Port.
Edward Griffith, Burslem.
Thomas Green, Burslem.

John Gilbert, Burslem.
Heath & Sons, Burslem
Holland & Co., Burslem.
Lewis Heath, Burslem.
Thomas Holland, Burslem.
Timothy & John Locket, Burslem.
Daniel Morris, Burslem.
Marsh & Hall, Burslem.
Poole & Shrigley, Burslem.
Robinson & Sons, Burslem.
Daniel Steel, Burslem
J. Wedgwood & Co., Burslem.
Thomas Wedgwood, Burslem.
Wedgwood & Co., Burslem.
Ralph Wood, Burslem.
Wood & Caldwell, Burslem.
William Adams, Cobridge.
John & Andrew Blackwell, Cobridge
Dale & Co., Cobridge.
Benjamin Godwin, Cobridge.
Thomas Godwin, Cobridge.
John Hamersley (sic.), Cobridge.
Robinson & Smith, Cobridge.
Wedgwood & Byerley, Etruria.
Jacob Warburton, Cobridge.
William Adams, Goldenhill, Tunstall.
Baggaley & Vodrey, Tunstall.
Thomas Baggaley, Tunstall.
John Breeze, Longport.
John Capper, Golden-hill, Tunstall.
Samuel & John Cartlich, Tunstall.
John Collison, Tunstall.
John & Caleb Cole, Newfield.
Mary Colclough, Pitts-hill.
John Davenport, Longport.
Gerrard & Alker, Longport.
Henshall Williamson & Clowes, Long-
    port.
Anthony Keeling & Son, Tunstall.

John Lindop, Green-lane.
Jonathan Machin, Tunstall.
Thomas & Henshall Moss, Red-street.
John & George Rogers, Longport.
Joseph Smith, Tunstall.
Theophilus Smith, Smithfield.
Thomas Tunstall, Tunstall.
John Wood, Brown-hills.
Ephraim Booth & Sons, Stoke.
Buckley & Bent, Newcastle.
John Harrison, Stoke.
Keeling & Co., Stoke-lane.
Minton & Poulson, Stoke.
Josiah Rowley, Stoke.
Josiah Spode, Stoke.
Thomas Wolfe, Stoke.
Allcock & Ward, Lane-end.
Richard Astbury, Lane-delph.
John Aynsley, Lane-end.
Sampson Bagnall, Lane-delph.
Samuel Barker, Lane-delph.
Richard Barker, Lane-end.
Bourne & Baker, Lower-Lane.
Bray & Harrison, Lane-delph.

Chatham (sic) & Wooley, Lane-end.
Mary Cyples, Lane-end.
James Dawson, Lane-delph.
Thomas Forster, Lane-delph.
Forster & Harvey, Lane-end.
Robert Garner, Lane-end.
Harrison & Hyatt, Lower-lane
Samuel Hughes, Lane-end.
Benjamin Jackson, Lane-end.
Sarah Jackson, Lane-end.
Thomas Jackson, Lane-end.
Johnson & Bridgewood, Lane-end.
Ann Martin, Lane-delph.
Joseph Myatt, Lane-end.
William & John Philips, Lane-end.
William Pratt, Lane-delph.
Thomas Shaw, Lane-end.
Thomas Shelley, Lane-end.
Samuel Spode, Folly.
Ghomas Stirrup, Lane-end.
William & John Turner, Lane-end.
Mark Walklate, Lane-end.
Weston & Hull, Lane-end.
Thomas Wolfe, Lower-Lane.

HOLDEN'S TRIENNIAL DIRECTORY, Holden & Co. London 1805

William Adams, china and earthenware manufactory, Cobridge
John and Edward Baddeley, earthenware mfrs. Shelton
William Baddeley, Egyptian black mfr. Shelton
Bagshaw & Meir, earthenware mfrs. Burslem
William Bailey, china gilder, Lane end
Richard Barker, Earthenware mfr. Lane end
George and William Barnes, E'ware mfrs. Lane end
William and Thomas Bathwell, E'ware mfrs. Burslem
John Blackwell, china and e'ware mfr. Cobridge
Robert Becket, e'ware mfr. Lane end
Richard Billington & Sons, e'ware mfrs. Cobridge
Edmund John Birch, e'ware mfr. Shelton

John and William Birks and Co. Egyptian black mfr. Lane end
Boon and Hicks, e'ware mfrs. Shelton
Booth and Bridgewood, e'ware mfrs. Lane end
Hugh and Joseph Booth, 'eware mfrs. Stoke-upon-Trent
William Booth, Egyptian black mfr. Shelton
Edward Bourne e'ware mfr. Burslem
Bourne, Baker and Bourne, E'ware mfrs. Fenton Potteries
Charles Bourne, E'ware mfr. Lane Delph
John Breeze and Son, E'ware mfrs. Tunstall
Samuel Bridgewood, e'ware mfr. Lane end
Samuel and Thomas Cartlich, e'ware mfrs. Tunstall
Cartwright and Wood, Enamellers and printers, Cobridge
Chetham and Wooley, pearl and printed ware, Egyptian black, &c. mfrs.
Lane end
Valentine Close, E'ware mfr. Keeling's Lane
Coomer, Sheridan and Hewit, e'ware mfrs. Green dock, Lane end
Jesse Cyples, Egyptian black mfr. Lane end
Daniel and Brown, enamellers, Hanley
John Davenport, china and e'ware mfr. Longport
William Ford and Co. e'ware mfrs. Lane end
John Forrester, e'ware mfrs. Lane end
George Forrester, e'ware mfr. Lane end
Robert Gardner, e'ware mfr. Lane end
John Glass, e'ware mfr. Hanley
Thomas Godwin, e'ware mfr. Cobridge
Goodwin and Jarvis, china and e'ware mfrs. Stoke-upon-Trent
Edmund Goodwin, e'ware mfr. Shelton
John Goodwin, China and E'ware mfr. Boothenville, near Stoke
Thomas Green, e'ware mfr. Burslem Church yard
James Gridbach, red potter, Shelton
John and Ralph Hall, e'ware mfrs. Burslem
John Hammersley, Corse e'ware mfr. Shelton
Thomas Harley, enameller and e'ware mfr. Lane end
Harrison, Brough and Co. e'ware mfrs. Green dock, Lane end
Harte, Singleton and Co. e'ware mfrs. Lane end.
Charles Harvey and Sons e'ware mfrs. Lane end
Thomas Heath, e'ware mfr. Burslem
Henshall and Williamson, E'ware mfrs. Longport
Hollins, Warburton, Daniel and Co. mfrs. of real china, Shelton

Thomas and John Hollins, E'ware mfrs. Hanley
Peter and Thomas Hughes, E'ware mfrs. Hanley
Hyatt and Harrison E.ware mfrs. Fenton
Johnson and Brough E.ware mfrs. Lane end
Joseph Keeling, E'ware mfrs. Keelings' Lane
Anthony and Enoch Keeling, china and e'ware mfrs. Tunstall
James Keeling, e'ware mfr. Hanley
Keeling, Toft and Co. e'ware mfrs. Hanley
Leigh and Breeze e'ware mfrs. Hanley
Lindop and Taylor e'ware mfrs. Longport
George Lockett and Co. e'ware mfrs. Lane end
Joseph Machin, Enameller, Burslem
John Mare, E'ware mfr. Hanley
Jacob Marsh, E'ware mfr. Burslem
Joseph Marsh, china mfr. Brown Hill
Miles Mason, china mfr. Lane delph
John Massey, Egyptian black mfr. Golden hill
Matthes and Ball, black glaze stone ware and gilt work mfrs. Lane end.
Elijah Mayer and son, china and e'ware mfrs. Hanley
Job Meigh, e'ware mfr. Hanley.
Mellor and Taylor, e'ware mfrs. Burslem
Minton and Poulson, china and e'ware mfrs. Stoke-upon-Trent
Mort, Barker and Chester, e'ware mfr. Cobridge.
Moseley, John, Egyptian black manufacturer, Cobridge
Ralph Pope, coarse ware potter Shelton.
George Poulson, china and e'ware mfr. Cobridge
John Pratt, E'ware mfr. Lane Delph
Ellin Pratt, E'ware mfr. Lane Delph
Rhead and Goodfellow, E'ware mfrs. Burslem
George Ridgeway, china and e'ware mfrs. Shelton
Job Ridgway, china and e'ware mfr. Cauldon place, Shelton
John and Richard Riley, china glaze e'ware manufacturers, Burslem
John Robinson and Sons, e'ware mfrs. Burslem
John and George Rogers, China e'ware mfrs. Longport
George and Thomas Shaw, e'ware mfrs. Lane end
Shorthose and Heaths, junrs. E'ware manufacturers for exportation, Hanley
Smith and Steele, e'ware mfrs. Tunstall
James Smith, e'ware mfr. Stoke-upon-Trent
Josiah Spode, china and e'ware mfr. Stoke-upon-Trent

Samuel Spode, e'ware mfr. Folley House
William Stanley, E'ware mfr. Burslem
Daniel Steele, E'ware mfr. Burslem
Stevenson and Godwin, e'ware mfrs. Cobridge
Thomas Stirrup, e'ware mfr. Lane end
G. Taylor, e'ware mfr. Hanley
William Tellwright, e'ware mfr. Tunstall
Thomas Tunstall, banded ware mfr. Golden hill
Turners, Glover and Simpson, china and e'ware mfrs Lane End
Unett and Brammer, carthenware manufacturers, Lane End
Mark Walklate and Son, e'ware mfrs. Lane end
Peter Warburton, e'ware mfr. Cobridge
Jos. Warrilow, e'ware mfr. Hanley
Jos. Wedgwood and Byerley, potters to her majesty, Etruria
Thomas Wedgwood, e'ware mfr. Bighouse, Burslem
George Weston and Co. e'ware mfrs. Lane end
Charles and James Whitehead, e'ware mfrs. Hanley
Christopher Whitehead, E'ware mfr. Shelton
David Wilson, china and e'ware mfr. Hanley
Wolfe and Hamilton, china and e'ware mfrs.
Stoke-upon-Trent
Wood and Caldwell, china and e'ware mfrs. Burslem
John Wood, e'ware mfr. Brown hills
John and William Yates, E'ware mfrs. Shelton

Appendix 2

Engravers for pottery and porcelain

Adams, James, Furlong, Burslem, 1800–1802.

Adams, Richard, 48, Liverpool Road, Stoke, 1887.

Adams, Stephen, 26 Victoria Street, Basford, 1887.

Allan & Barlow, Bagnall Street, Shelton, 1834.

Allden, Henry, working for Edward Whitehouse, Little Fenton, 1801 (*Staffordshire Advertiser* 19th September, 1801). He had run away from his master's em-

Allen & Green, Vine Street, Hanley, 1837–1851.   [ployment.

Allen, Theophilus, partner in the firm of Wildig & Allen 1834–1837. His address in 1834 was Union Street, Hanley and in 1851, John-Street, Hanley. He was born in 1800 and died in 1851 (Obit *Staffordshire Advertiser* 5th April 1851). From 1837 to 1851 he was partner to John Green in the firm of Allen and Green, successors to Wildig & Allen. His name occurred in the *Poll List*, 1841.

Amos, David, Queen Street, Wolstanton, 1908.

Aston, James, 33, Belgrave-road, Stoke, 1887.

Austin, Jesse, born 1806, died 1879: Engraver and designer; Waterloo Road, Burslem (1846), and later North Terrace, Fenton. His engraved work is referred to in the *Art Journal* 1844. He executed finely engraved plates after narrative paintings for Pratts of Fenton.

Baddeley, Edward Gerard. The first reference to this engraver occurs in a summons against Thomas Heath for non-payment of £5 wages due to him. (*North Staffordshire Mercury* 23 January 1841). Listed from 1834 untill 1889. Address, 35, Wheatley Place, Hanley. 'Mr Baddeley' engraver for Wedgwood of Etruria from 1852 until 1877.

Baddeley & Heath, Liverpool Road, Burslem, 1864–1889.

Baddeley, Thomas, Chapel field, Hanley 1800; Slack's Lane, Hanley 1822; Duke Street, Hanley, 1834.

Baines, Henry, Waterloo Road, Burslem, 1879.

Baines, Thomas, Bleak Hill, Burslem, 1851.

Banks & Bagnall, John Street, Shelton, 1822–1823.

Banks, William, born 1782, died 12th January, 1833, (*Staffordshire Advertiser* 19th January, 1833): Address, Albion Street, Shelton. Possibly partner in firm of Banks and Bagnall, Shelton.

Barbon, William, Edmund Street, Hanley, 1851, to 1865, 51, Church Street,
Barlow, James, Northwood, Hanley, 1861–1865.   [Hanley, 1887.

Barlow, William, Prospect Buildings, Hanley, 1851–1865.

Barrett, Edward, married at Burslem 4th June 1799 to Elizabeth Ellis, of Burslem
    (*Parish Registers* Burslem)

Beard, William, born 1869, died 1950. Address, 13, James Street, Stoke. Worked
    at Mintons from 1882 until 1948.

Beech, Charles, Portland Chambers, Church Street, Longton, 1879–1889.

Beech, John, King Street, Newcastle-under-Lyme 1834–1839.

Bennett, Henry, 2, Old Market Place, Stoke, 1865–1879.

Bentley, Wear & Bourne, Vine Street, Shelton, c 1815–1823.

Bentley & Wear, Vine Street, Shelton, 1823–1833.

Bentley, Wear & Wildig, Vine Street, Shelton, 1833.

Bentley, William, born 1777; married at Stoke 24th December 1801 to Mary Waste;
    died at Bucknall Cottage 30th May 1833: opened a picture gallery at his engraving
    shop in Vine Street 1825: In partnership in the firm Bentley, Wear & Bourne
    from 1815 (or earlier) until c 1823 when the firm became Bentley & Wear. In
    1834 the firm was listed as Bentley, Wear & Wildig but Bentley died between the
    compilation and the publication of Whites 1834 Directory. (*Pottery Mercury*
    1824–1825: *Staffordshire Advertiser* 1815 and 1833: S. Shaw, *History of the Stafford-
    shire Potteries*, 1829).

Blair, William, Stafford Street, Longton, 1899.

Blood, George, Bridge Street, Lane End, 1822–1823.

Bostock, Samuel, born 1808 and died 1834 (*Staffordshire Advertiser*, 28th June 1834).
    Address, Upper Hanley.

Boulton, Frederick A, 20, Cheapside, Hanley, 1889–1908.

Bourne H. head engraver at Mintons for whom he engraved 'Berlin Birds',
    'Delft', and 'Danish Patterns', 1869–1872. Executed engravings for the *Art
    Journal*, 1866–1871.

Bourne, Semei (Simeon), Albion Street, Shelton, 1818, married at Norton-in-the-
    Moors 12th April to Rebecca Ford (*Norton Parish Register*).

Bourne, William, Queen Street, Fenton, 1851–1879.

Bowden, Thomas, Fenton, 1879.

Bradbury, Benjamin, Stafford Row, Shelton, 1818; Tinker's Clough, Shelton, 1834.

Brindley, James, London-Road, Chesterton, 1889.

Brindley, James, Union-Buildings, Burslem, 1818.

Brookes, Ernest, designer and engraver, 5, Harding Terrace, Stoke, 1887: Harding
    House, and Sutherland Chambers, Stoke, 1908.

Brookes, J., Park Terrace, Stoke, 1875–1879.

Brookes, John, born 1792 died 1868: Address in 1818 Hadderage, Burslem: in later life Dale Hall, Burslem. His gravestone in St Pauls Church Yard, Burslem, says that he worked 26 years for Williamson and 37 years for W. Davenport & Company.

Brookes, Philip, designer and engraver: Albion Place, Shelton 1822–1823: Fenton 1834. His son, Philip Henry Brookes, died aged 20, 31st March 1841 (*Staffordshire Advertiser*, 10th April 1841).

Brookes, William, the elder, died 1838 (*Staffordshire Advertiser*, 25th August 1838). In 1818 living at Wolstanton: His business address was Fountain Buildings, Burslem. Simeon Shaw records him as designing for New Hall a pattern based upon wall papers. He executed work for William Adams of Greengate, Tunstall (S. Shaw, *History of the Staffordshire Potteries* 1829). Adams 'Classical Landscapes' based on a picture by Claude was probably engraved by him.

Brookes, William, the younger, Fountain Buildings, Burslem, 1834: worked for Wedgwoods 1811–1839. Engraved illustrations for Ward's *Stoke-on-Trent*. 1843.

Brough, William, High Street, Newcastle-under-Lyme, 1822–23.

Brown, Aaron, High Street, Shelton 1818: partner in firm of Dixon, Brown & Brown & Toft, Bell's Mill, Shelton, 1822-23.   [Toft, later in 1822 Brown & Toft.

Buxton, Samuel, Commercial Buildings, Stoke 1818. His wife died at the age of 40 in July 1827 (*Pottery Mercury* 4th August 1827).

Carr, James, Smallthorne 1879.

Chadwick, Samuel, 8, Richmond Terrace, Hanley, 1887.

Chaloner, W. H., printer and engraver.

Charlesworth, W. J., Church Street, Longton, 1908.

Chatterley, Thomas, Broad Street, Shelton 1818. A tombstone in Stoke Churchyard is inscribed 'Thomas Chatterley Ingraver (sic) of Shelton died 1818 aged 26 years'.

Clive, John Henry, born 1781 died 1853: potter and engraver (P. W. Adams. *John Henry Clive* 1947).

Cockson, Thomas, Fenton Vivian, 1818. Perhaps the same as Thomas Coxon, born 1780 died 1825 (*Pottery Mercury* 25th May 1825).

Cooper, John, Stoke-on-Trent. Married 7th July 1825 to Harriet, eldest daughter of Daniel Greatback of Penkhull (*Pottery Mercury* July 1825), who was also an Engraver.

Copeland, J. & Son, High Street, Hanley, 1851.

Copeland, Theophilus, Hanley, 1865.

Copeland, Thomas, flourished 1865–1889, various addresses given 3, Gate Street, Hanley; Chatham Street, Hanley and 12, Albion Street, Hanley. According to Scarrett *(Old Times in the Potteries)*, he died c. 1900–1905.

Cotton, Thomas, Hanford, 1843. Died in the prime of life, 17th May 1835 (*Staffordshire Advertiser*, 30th May 1835).

Cutts, James, Engraver and designer: worked for many firms including Davenports.

Dale, John, Engraver and toy manufacturer, Burslem. Married at Astbury, Cheshire to Sarah Walker, 14th Feb. 1825 (*Pottery Mercury* 23 February and 30th March [1825]).

Davies, E., worked for Wedgwoods of Etruria, 1903–1932.

Davies, Isaac, Union Street, Shelton, 1818.

Davies, Frederick, worked at Mintons, Stoke-on-Trent.

Dean, Richard, Well Street, Hanley 1834: Edmund Street Hanley (*Poll list* 1841): In partnership with George Procter until 1841 when the partnership was dissolved (*Staffordshire Advertiser* 4th September 1841).

Dennison, T., 18, Market Street, Longton, 1910.

Dickin, William, born 1810 died 1838 at the house of his father in Burslem, 16th April (*Staffordshire Advertiser* 21st April 1838). Address: Fenton.

Dixon, Brown & Toft, Well Street, Hanley, 1818.

Dixon Oliver, Fenton Low, 1796; High Street, Hanley 1802. Possibly the partner in the firm of Dixon, Brown & Toft. Address in 1818, Well Street, Shelton.

Docksey, Ralph, 76, Mount Street, Hanley, 1889–1908.

Doncaster, Henry, Bleakhill, Burslem, 1851–1879.

Doncaster, Samuel, worked for Wedgwood's of Etruria 1806–11. Address: Waterloo Road, Burslem, 1834, 1841 (*Poll list* 1841).

Doncaster, Samuel, Newcastle Street, Burslem, 1887.

Downes, H. J., Cheapside, Hanley, 1908.

Downing, William, Old Hall Lane, Hanley, 1800–1802, worked for Wedgwoods of Etruria, 1806–1811.

Drake, E. Horace, designer and engraver, Fountain Square, Fenton, 1908.

Dulton, Thomas, Heathcote Road, Longton, 1864.

Edge, Samuel, Burslem, 1796.

Ellis, George, Hope Street, Shelton, 1834.

Evans, Evan, Wolstanton: married to Elizabeth Lucy Apperley, at the Wolstanton Church 22 November, 1767 (*Woolstanton Parish Registers*).

Evans, Fred, born c 1865 died 1950. Worked for Johnson Bros. Hanley from 1893 until 1945.

Farrington, Frank, designer and engraver. Manager of Latchford's Workshop, Stoke-on-Trent.

Fennell, Henry, born c 1854, died June 1934. married a daughter of Elisha Pepper, engraver. His engraving workshop was first in Jasper Street, then in Mollart

Street, Hanley. At one time he employed as many as nineteen journeymen and apprentices. Executed many patterns such as 'British Castles' for Johnson Bros. and 'Constable Landscapes' for Grindleys. Archibald Landon became his manager, and subsequent to his death when the firm became a limited company, one of its directors. The business was closed down in 1943.

Fenton, John, near Church Road, Hanley 1818. Firm of T. & J. Fenton.

Fenton T. & J., High Street, Hanley, 1822–1823.

Fenton, Thomas, Church Road, Hanley, 1818. Firm of T. & J. Fenton.

Fletcher, T., Shelton.

Ford, G., worked for Wedgwoods of Etruria 1842–43.

Ford, Hugh, married at Stoke-on-Trent, 6th September 1807 to Mary Poulson. *(Stoke Parish Registers)*.

Ford, Joseph, Albion Place, Shelton 1834: His daughter Emily, died at the age of 7 years in 1842 (*Staffordshire Advertiser*, 23 April 1842).

Forrester, John, Cobridge, 1851: 2, Vale Place, Hanley 1887.

Forrester, Richard, married at Stoke 6th September 1817 to Mary Baker of Hanley *(Stoke Parish Register)*: Address in 1818, Burslem.

Fox, Joseph, Newfield Terrace, Tunstall, 1887.

Freeman, Benjamin, Waterloo Road, Burslem, 1822–23.

Freeman, died at the age of 60 in July 1834, at Shelton (*Staffordshire Advertiser*, 26th, July 1834) (Perhaps same as above).

Gallimore, William, Hanley, 1865'.

Goodwin, John, Mount Street, Tunstall 1879–1887.

Goodwin, Thomas, Fenton 1834–1879 (*Poll List* 1841).

Greatbach, Daniel, Penkhull, 1825–1851: an engraver named Greatbach worked for Spode-Copeland factory.

Green, John, partner in firm of Green, Sergeant & Pepper, Engravers, Brickmakers and Agents until 25th December 1851, (*Staffordshire Advertiser* 24th January 1852) when the business became Green and Pepper. In 1851 his address was Market Street, Hanley.

Green and Pepper, Engravers 1851.

Green, Sergeant & Pepper, engravers, brickmakers, and agents.

Griffiths, George, born 1872, died 1947. Lived in Liverpool Road, Stoke 1908 and later in Newcastle. Worked for Mintons and Doultons.

Grocott, Samuel, Liverpool Road, Stoke, 1851.

Hackwood, Lewis, worked for Wedgwoods, 1799.

Hales, William, worked for Wedgwoods, 1806–1808.

Hall & Brough, High Street, Newcastle-under-Lyme, 1818.

Hall, Charles, Northwood, Hanley, 1834–1851. (*Poll List* 1841.)

Hall, Frank, 5, John Street and 75, Gilman-street, Hanley, 1879–1887.

Hall, Frederick, 79, Gilman Street, Hanley, 1887.

Hall, Robert, Hanley, 1865.

Hall, Thomas, 5, John Street, Hanley, 1887.

Hammersley, G., Edmund Street, Hanley, 1822–23.

Hancock, Aaron, Lower Hadderage, Burslem 1875-1879; Price Street, Burslem, 1887.

Hancock, Henry, Hanley, 1865.

Hancock, James, Tunstall, 1841: born 1821 (*Ms Copy of Census for Tunstall* 1841, Hanley Reference Library).

Hancock, John, Market Street, Tunstall 1834 and 1841 (*Poll List* 1841), 10, Navigation Road, Burslem, 1865.

Hancock, Robert, born 1730 died 1813 (C. Cook, *The Life and Work of Robert Hancock*).

Hancock, William, Piccadilly, Tunstall 1841: born 1821 (*Ms Copy of Census for Tunstall*, 1841.)

Hassall, Joseph, born 1876: Engraver at W.T. Copeland & Sons from 1890.

Hassall, John, Richardo Street, Dresden, 1865.

Hawkins, John, Church Lane, Newcastle-under-Lyme, 1822–23; 3, York Street, Newcastle 1836–1851: married 1824 (*Pottery Mercury*, 7th, July 1824.)

Heath & Baddeley, Burslem, 1865–1889.

Heath, John, Hope Street, Hanley 1834; Slack's Lane, Hanley, 1841 (*Poll List* 1841); Church Street, Hanley 1851: Worked for Wedgwood of Eturia 1840–1877: His wife, Sarah died 22 December 1840 (*Staffordshire Advertiser*, 26th [December, 1840).

Heath, Samuel, Sneyd Green, 1796.

Heath, Simpson & Heath, Slack's Lane, Shelton, 1834.

Heath, Thomas, Vine Street, Hanley 1834.

Heath, William, Sneyd Green, 1851: 81, Hall Street, Burslem. 1889. Worked for Samuel Alcock and Davenports.

Hicks, Richard, Shelton 1796: Old Hall Lane, Hanley, 1802. He later became a master potter: born 1765, died 1844. Served his apprenticeship at the Caughley China Works, Broseley with Thomas Minton, (*Staffordshire Advertiser*, 1801, 1815, 1844; *Register of Deaths and Internments, Bethesda Chapel*, Hanley, 1844; *Poll List*, 1841; L. Jewitt, *Ceramic Art of Great Britain*, 1878).

Hill, William, 12 Boothenwood Terrace, Stoke, 1887.

Higginbottom, Joseph, 25, Gregory Street, Longton, 1865–1879.

Hodgkiss or Hodgkin; Thomas, Stoke-on-Trent, 1818: married at Stoke, 26th February 1806 (*Stoke Parish Register*).

Hodgkiss, R. S., Hanley, 1940–1950.

Holdcroft, E., Market Place, Burslem, 1940.

Hopwood, I., a design has been recorded signed 'I. Hopwood Sculpt. for I. Wyld'.

Hordley, Thomas, born 1795–6, died in 1888 in his 93rd year (*Staffordshire Advertiser* 14th January 1888). Worked for Wedgwoods of Etruria 1842–1847: Address 40, Charles Street, Hanley, 1834–1897. Supplied designs to Ridgway.

Hudson, Alfred, Trentham Road, Longton, 1887.

Hudson, T., King street, Fenton, 1908.

Hughes, J., 147 Brook Street, Hanley 1889–1908.

Hulme, Jesse, portrait artist, designer and engraver. Born 1789 died 1852. Worked for Wedgwoods, 1843–1844.

Hulme, Paul, Engraver, Wedgwoods of Etruria and Barlaston from 1919.

Hulse, James, Engraver, Newcastle-under-Lyme, 1839.

Hulson, John, Seabridge, near Newcastle-under-Lyme, 1834.

Jackson, Charles, Princes Road, Stoke, 1887.

Johnson, John, Sytch, Burslem, 1841, (*Poll List* 1841): Liverpool-road, 1851, Hanley, 1871.

Keay, William, Waterloo Road, Burslem 1834: partner in the firm of Wildblood & Keay, 1822–1834.

Keeling, Daniel, Broad Street, Shelton, 1822–1834: died 16th February, 1844 (*Staffordshire Advertiser* 14th February 1844).

Keeling, Isaac, born 1789 died 1869: Designer and Engraver at Wedgwoods: Wesleyan Minister 1811: author of pamphlets, verses and sermons.

Kelsall, Harry, worked at Minton's.

Kennedy, James, Commercial Street, Burslem 1818–1834. His signature occurs beneath a portrait of William IV on a Coronation Mug (1831) in Hanley Museum, Stoke-on-Trent. He was working for Henry Whitehouse at Little Fenton at 1801.

Kingston, A., 13, Middle Street, Stoke, 1908.

Landon, Archibald, born 1881: Lived in Hanley and Newcastle-under-Lyme: Manager and director of Henry Fennell Ltd., Engravers, Hanley: Specialist in lettering and heraldry.

Latchford, John Henry, head of firm of Latchford Ltd., Honeywall, Stoke-on-Trent, Engravers.

Latham, Joseph, Market Place, Tunstall, born 1821. (*Ms Copy of Census for Tunstall* 1841. Hanley Reference Library).

Lawton, William, Hanley, 1865.

Ledge, Charles, Sleck Lane, Shelton, 1796–1802.

Leigh, John, Engraver and grocer, Whieldon Road, Fenton 1875–1879.

Lewis, Harry, born c 1878 died 1949: worked for Johnson Bros. Ltd.

Lightfoot, Peter, born 1804 died 1885: Lived at Blurton.

Lockett, Stanley, worked for Grimwades Ltd. and Palissy Pottery, Longton.

Longmore, F. W.

Longmore, Thomas, worked for Wedgwoods 1809–1810.

Lucas, Thomas, worked for Turner of Caughley and from c 1783, Josiah Spode at Stoke-on-Trent (S. Shaw, *History of the Staffordshire Potteries*, 1829).

Lucock, John, Stoke-on-Trent, 1796–1802.

Machin, George, born 1821 died 1847 at Burslem. (*Staffordshire Advertiser*, 17th July 1847.)

Maguire, John, Trent Bridge, Stoke, 1834.

Maguire, Joseph, working for the Engraving Establishment of Edward Whitehouse, Little Fenton, 1801 (*Staffordshire Advertiser*, 19th September, 1801): Living at Fenton Vivian 1818.

Malkin, James, 9, Grove Villas, Hanley, 1887.

Martin, Frederick, Shelton: married 1824 to Mary Chatterley (*Pottery Mercury* 26th May 1824).

Martin, George, born 1783 died 1849: Commercial Street, Burslem, 1800–1802. (*Staffordshire Advertiser*, 23rd June 1849.)

Martin, William, Hanley, 1865.

Mason, George, worked at Mintons and Doultons.

Mawdesley, James, born 1818 died 5th January 1852 at Burslem (*Staffordshire Advertiser* 10th January 1852).

Mayer, A., 74, Gilman Street, Hanley, 1889.

Minton, Thomas, born 1766 died 1836, fellow apprentice with Richard Hicks at Caughley. Came to Potteries. Engraved the 'Willow' pattern for Josiah Spode. Founded the firm of Mintons.

Mollart, John, described variously as engraver and china manufacturer (perhaps after leaving Wedgwoods) and went bankrupt in 1813. (*Staffordshire Advertiser* various dates from 1800 to 1813.)

Moreton, George, Cobridge, 1796.

Morris, F., Shelton.

Moss, H. E., Sutherland Chambers, Stoke, 20th Century.

Mullock, James, Tunstall: Died in Cheshire 15th April 1813 (*Staffordshire Advertiser* 17th April 1813, and *Staffordshire Gazette*, 20th April, 1813).

Mullock & James, 2, Lichfield street, Hanley, 1908.

Nagington, W. H., Process photo-engraver, Hope Street, Hanley, founder of firm of W. H. Nagington & Son.

Newark, John, married 7th March 1804 to Sarah Barber.

Norbury, William, Johnson Bros. Ltd., Hanley.

Parker, James, 25, Newcastle Road, Hanley, 1887.

Parker, Martin A., High Street, Hanley, 1851.

Parker, William, High Street, Hanley, 1818–1823.

Parr, James, Elgreave House, Burslem: born 1870, died 1947: Engraver for Meakins; Myott, Son & Co., and Coalport.

Parr, Jesse.

Pedley, James, Charles Street, Hanley, 1834: 103, Normacot Road, Normacot, 1887.

Pepper, Elisha, worked for Wedgwoods 1839–1865: Slack Lane, Hanley 1851–1865: partner in the engraving firms, of Green, Sergeant & Pepper, Green and Pepper; E. Pepper and Son.

Pepper, E. & Son, 40 Vine Street, Hanley, 1865.

Pointon & Sherwin, Vale Place, Hanley 1908: Beck Street, Hanley, 1940.

Poole, John, born 1874 died 1936: address Lord Street, Etruria and Gladstone

Poole, Joseph, Market Place, Hanley, 1822–1823.   [Street, Basford.

Pope, Henry Price, Hanley, 1865.

Pope, John L., William Street, Stoke, 1875–1879.

Pope, William Wilson, started up in business in 1830 in Piccadilly and Pall Mall, Hanley and continued until 1875 or later. Advertised in *Staffordshire Advertiser*, 9th February 1839 and 28th November 1840.

Powell, William, Elgreave Street, Burslem.

Price, Joseph H., Wheatley Place, Hanley 1887.

Price, William, Henry, Copperplate planisher and engraver at various addresses in Hanley from 1865 until 1889.

Price and Son, Moorland Road, Burlsem, 1908.

Procter, George, Audley, 1834: In partnership with Richard Dean until 1841 (*Staffordshire Advertiser*, 4th September, 1841.)

Pye, Frederick.

Radford, Thomas, Shelton 1796–1802. Engraved 'The World in Planisphere' and 'The Prodigal Son' for Greatbach of Fenton. Worked also at Cockpit Hill, Derby.

Reade, Thomas, married 1809 *(Burslem Parish Register)*. Possible the same as Thomas Rhead, Queen's Street, Burslem, 1822–23.

Reynolds, C. H., Victoria House, Ashford Street, Hanley, 1889.

Reynolds, M. J., Stoke Road, Hanley, 1908.

Ridgway, Frederick, J, Penkhull: born 1891, died 1956 served his apprenticeship under his father at Mintons, and succeeded his father as head engraver.

Ridgway, George, Penkhull: born c 1865 died 1946. Worked all his life at Minton's, Stoke-on-Trent, latterly as foreman engraver.

Rigby, Thomas, Newcastle-under-Lyme: born 1802 died 1834 (*Staffordshire Advertiser*, 9th August 1834).

Roberts, W. S., Basford, 1887.

Robinson, Thomas, worked for Wedgwoods 1806–1810.

Robson, Thomas, Bentley Cottage, Cobridge, 1887.

Ross, James, born 1745, died 1821, pupil of Robert Hancock.

Royles, George, Kilncroft, Burslem, 1818.

Ryles, John, engraver and designer: Newcastle-under-Lyme and Hanley, 1839–1864: married at Shelton 18th April 1840 to Anne Turnock.

Ryles, Moses, Lane end and Hanley 1800–1834: described as engraver and 'tomaographer'. Married at Norton-in-the-Moors to Jinny Chetwyn 5th August 1794. (*Norton Parish Register*).

Ryles, Peter, Adventure Place, Shelton: born 1807 died 1841 (*Staffordshire Advertiser*, 16th January, 1841).

Ryles, Robert Daniel, married at Norton-in-the-Moors 9th November 1817 and described as of Lane End (*Staffordshire Advertiser* 22nd November, 1817). Worked for Wedgwoods 1816–1852: Living at Edmund Street, Hanley, 1865.

Ryles & Glassbrook, Gate Street, Hanley, 1834.

Sadler, John, Liverpool: Partner in the firms of Sadler & Green, printers, Liverpool, born 1720 died 1789.

Scarratt, Edwin, Shelton: born 1818 died 1851 (*Staffordshire Advertiser*, 10th [January 1852).

Scott, J. C. W., Hanley, 1889.

Scragg, A. E., Waterloo-road, Burslem, 1940, and Birks Street, Hanley, 1950.

Seabridge, Josiah, Upper Normacot Road, Longton, 1887–1889.

Sergeant, George, Market Street, Hanley, 1851.

Sergeant & Pepper, Slack Lane, Hanley, 1851.

Sheldon & Banks, Cobridge, 1818.

Sheldon, Thomas, Church Street, Burslem, 1822–23.

Shelley, Samuel, Commercial Street, Burslem, 1834. Died 21st March 1844 at Burslem, and described as 'well known among the coursing gents' (*Staffordshire Advertiser*, 23rd March 1844).

Sherratt, R. C., Heron Cross, Fenton, 1865–1889.

Sherrat & Bowden, Fenton, 1879.

Sherwin, Cyril, High Lane, Burslem, 1940.

Sherwin, Henry, flourished 1839–1864: worked for Wedgwoods of Etruria 1860–1864: Exhibited at the 1862 International Exhibition a series of plate designs 'constructed on the parsley leaf &c'. Did a number of local topographical views in 1839.

Sherwin, Hordley and Sherwin, bankrupt 1825. Possibly the same as Sherwin & Company, Miles Bank, 1822–23.

Sherwin, Isaac, partner in the firm of Sherwin, Hordley & Sherwin, engravers and blue manufacturers which became bankrupt in 1825 (*Pottery Mercury* 30th May 1827, *et. seq.*).

Sherwin, Josiah, baptised at Burslem 15th January 1797, Son of Thomas and Sarah Sherwin, and brother of Isaac Sherwin (born 1799). Partner in Sherwin, Hordley [and Sherwin.

Shufflebotham, Henry, Snow Hill, Burslem, 1834.

Shufflebotham, William, married at Stoke 20th August 1794 *(Stoke Parish Registers)* At little Fenton 1800–1802: An engraver of the same name was at Liverpool-road.

Simpson, C., 5, Penkhull Terrace, Stoke, 1889. [Burslem, 1822–23.

Simpson, James, Nunnery Cottage, Shelton 1834: born 1795 died 1838 (*Staffordshire Advertiser*, 21st April 1838).

Simpson, Joseph (or Josiah), Mill-street, Hanley, 1834.

Simpson, William, George-street, Shelton, 1834.

Smith, Frederick John, born 1872 died 1939: worked at Minton's over 40 years but left and went to Doultons. A very meticulous craftsman.

Smith, George, father of F. J. Smith: Engraver at Minton's.

Smith, John, Fenton, 1865; Stoke 1889.

Smith, W., The Grange, Cobridge, 1908.

Smith, William, Slack's Lane, Hanley, 1800–1802. Possible the engraver from Liverpool who is said to have worked for R. Baddeley of Shelton. (S. Shaw, *History of the Staffordshire Potteries*, 1829.)

Sneyd, William, Market Street, Hanley: born 1794, died 13th October 1832 (*Staffordshire Advertiser*, 20th October 1832).

Sparks (or Sparkes), Thomas, born 1773, died 1848 at Hope Street, Shelton (*Staffordshire Advertiser*, 25th March 1848). Address in 1802, Old Hall Street, Hanley; Worked for Wedgwoods 1812–32.

Stanway, Alfred, Hanley, 1887–1889.

Stanway, William, Fountain Buildings, Burslem, 1834–1851.

Steele, Alfred Wright, Engraver and designer, Burslem, 1879–1889.

Steele, Henry, Albion Place, Hanley, 1834.

Steele, Samuel, Hanley, 1865. Chief engraver at Cauldon Works: Later went to [France.

Steele & Simpson, Albion Place, Shelton, 1834.

Stephen, William, Hanley, 1796.

Stoddard, James, Gower Street, Longton, 1875–79.

Thorley, Thomas, 4, Windmill Terrace, Hanley 1865–1879 (*Staffordshire Advertiser* 10th January 1852 announced the death of his only daughter Evelyn aged 9 months).

Toft, Albert, born 1863 died 1943, grandson of Alfonso Toft (information per H. E. Moss).

Toft, Alfonso (or Alphonsus), There may have been two engravers of this name which occurs in directories from 1828 until 1889 at various addresses in Shelton and Hanley including Tinkersclough.

Toft, A. & H., 40, Bryan Street, Hanley, 1864.

Toft, Charles, 72, West Parade, Fenton, 1887.

Toft, H. & Son, Cliff Bank, Stoke, 1889.

Toft, Henry, designer and engraver: partner in the firm of A. & H. Toft: listed at 28 Thomas Street, and Cliff Bank, Stoke 1889–1908.

Toft, Thomas, 78, Bucknall Old Road, Hanley, 1889.

Toft, William, Mill-street, Shelton 1843: His wife died 1st January 1843 aged 30 (*Staffordshire Advertiser*).

Tomkinson, John, Sparrow Street, Smallthorne, 1889.

Tundley, Arthur, Moorland Road, Burslem, 1887–1908.

Turner, Thomas, engraver at Caughley: probably a pupil of Robert Hancock.

Turner, Samuel, working in 1801 for Edward Whitehouse of Little Fenton.

Vernon, Samuel, Shelton 1800–1802: he died in February 1813 at the Half Ways House, near Newcastle-under-Lyme, 'rising from his morning devotions' (*Staffordshire Advertiser*, 13th February, 1813).

Vernon, Wood & Ford, Albion Place, Shelton 1822–23.

Vyse, Charles, 23, Havelock Place, Hanley 1889: head engraver at Doultons of Burslem.

Wall, Michael, Hanley, 1796.

Walsh, engraver at Johnson Bros. Hanley. Went to America where he died.

Walton, John, Burslem, 1796.

Wareham (or Warham) William, Newcastle-under-Lyme, 1865: Worked for Wedgwoods of Etruria, 1860–1874.

Wayle (or Wayte), Henry, 36, High Street and the 'Cock' Inn, Newcastle-under-Lyme, 1836–39.

Wear, William, partner in firms of Bentley, Wear and Bourne; Bentley & Wear; and Bentley, Wear & Wildig, Shelton.

Whalley, John, 86, Stanley Street, Burslem, 1889.

Whitehouse, Edward, Little Fenton, 1796–1802: Employed a number of journeymen and apprentices including Samuel Turner, James Kennedy, Henry Allden
(who had run away) and Joseph Maguire. He issued a warning against employing
these men.

Wildblood, Ambrose Wood, engraver and clothes dealer 24, St John's Square,
Burslem 1851–1865: married at Burslem 27th July 1839 to Elizabeth Seddon
daughter of Joshua Seddon, earthenware manufacturer (*Staffordshire Advertiser*
3 August 1839).

Wildblood, Edmund, King Street, Burslem, 1887.

Wildblood, Henry Edward, grocer and engraver, Smallthorne, 1851.

Wildblood & Keay, Navigation Road, Burslem, 1834.

Wildblood, R., engraver and designer, 33, Hanover Street, Burslem, 1889.

Wildblood, William, Navigation Road, Burslem, 1834–1879: 22, King-street, Burslem, 1889

Wildig & Allen, Hanley.

Wildig, born 1798 died 18th August 1837: partner in firms of Bentley, Wear and
Wildig, and Wildig and Allen.

Williams, A, Dalehall, Burslem, 1908.

Williams, Robert, the Green, Newcaste-under-Lyme, 1818.

Williams, Robert, Newcastle-under-Lyme, 1837 *(Poll List, Newcastle)*.

Williams, Watkin, 45, Hanover Street, Burslem, 1887.

Wilmot (or Willot), John, Milton, 1865–1889, Smallthorne, 1889.

Wood, F. & Son, High Street, Hanley, 1908.

Wood, Hugh, Fords Bank, Tunstall, 1865–1875.

Wood, Job, 9, East View, Hanley, 1875.

Wood, William, George Street, Sandford Hill, Longton, 1879–89.

Woodnoth, B., 34, Grove Road, Fenton, 1889.

Wrench, Thomas, 19, Charles-street, Hanley, 1887.

Wright, Howard H. G., apprenticed at Mintons, worked for Doulton of Burslem
50 years. Born c 1870, died 1939.

Wright, John, Norton-in-the-Moors, 1864.

Wyse, or Wise, William, Worked at Mintons.

Yates, James, Church Street, Hanley, 1834. Among insolvent debtors to be heard
at Stafford, 12th August 1842 was a James Yates, engraver, licensed brewer, and
retailer of beer and tobacco (*Staffordshire Advertiser*, 23rd July 1842:) His address
in 1887 was 90, Church Street, Hanley.

Yates, William, 8, St John's Street, Hanley, 1889.

Sources

NEWSPAPERS
Staffordshire Advertiser
Staffordshire Gazette
Pottery Mercury
Staffordshire Evening Sentinel
North Staffordshire Independent

PARISH REGISTERS
Stoke-upon-Trent
Wolstanton

Burslem
Norton-in-the-Moors
Register of Deaths and Internments,
Bethesda Chapel, Hanley

OTHER RECORDS
Manuscript Copy, Census of Tunstall
1841. (Hanley Reference Library.)
Art Journal
Poll Lists

PRINTED LITERATURE
Simeon Shaw, *History of the Staffordshire Potteries*, 1829.
Llewellyn Jewitt, *Ceramic Art of Great Britain*, 1878.
Cyril Cook, *The Life and Work of Robert Hancock*, 1948.
Geoffrey Bemrose, *19th Century English Pottery and Porcelain*, 1952.
Catalogue, *Exhibition of Printed Pottery*, Hanley Museum, 1937.

DIRECTORIES
The Staffordshire Pottery Directory (Chester and Mort, Hanley and Newcastle, n.d.) c. 1796
John Tregortha, *A view of the Staffordshire Potteries* (Burslem, 1800)
The Staffordshire Directory (T. Allbut, Hanley, 1802)
W. Parsons & T. Bradshaw, *Staffordshire General and Commercial Directory* (Manchester, 1818).
The Staffordshire Pottery Directory, (Allbut, Hanley 1822–23)
Newcastle Pottery Directory, (1822–23)
Pigot & Co., *London and Provincial New Commercial Directory* (1822, 1828, 1830, 1835, 1839, 1841)
W. White, *History Gazetteer and Directory of Staffordshire* (Sheffield 1834 and 1851)
Williams *Commercial Directory* (Manchester, 1846)
Post Office Directory of Staffordshire (1850 and 1860)
Jones's *Mercantile Directory of the Pottery District* (1864)
Keates's *Gazetteer and Directory of the Staffordshire Potteries* (1865, 1867, 1875, 1879, 1882, 1886, 1889)
Frank Porter's *Postal Directory for the Potteries* (1887)
Cotterill's *Police Directory of Newcastle-under-Lyme* (1836 and 1839)

Appendix 3

Books and articles giving lists of names of potters and pottery craftsmen, with sources and other information

Chaffers, William. *Marks and Monograms on European and Oriental Pottery and Porcelain*, 14th edition, 1952.

Lists of manufacturers culled from other published sources, such as John Ward's *History of the Borough of Stoke-upon-Trent*, 1843, Simeon Shaw's *History of the Staffordshire Potteries*, 1829, and local directories].

Gatty, C. T. *Transactions, Historic Society of Lancashire and Cheshire*, 1881.
[Entries concerning Liverpool potters based upon parish registers.]

Haggar, Reginald G. *English Country Pottery*, 1950.
[English toy and figure manufacturers taken from directories, newspaper advertisements, published records and marked pieces.]

Haggar, Reginald G. *Staffordshire Chimney Ornaments*, 1955.
[Lists of Staffordshire manufacturers of earthenware porcelain and parian toys, figures, toby jugs, and ornaments; descriptive list of toby jug types; list of trade modellers.]

Falkner, Frank. *The Wood Family of Burslem*, 1912.
[List of figure models made by the two Ralph Woods of Burslem together with mould numbers and other relevant information.]

Hurst, A. *A Catalogue of the Boynton Collection of Yorkshire Pottery*, 1922.
[List of Yorkshire factories and firms based upon directories and older ceramic authorities such as L. Jewitt's *Ceramic Art of Great Britain*, 1878.]

Jewitt, Llewellyn. *Ceramic Art of Great Britain*, 1878.
[Lists from directories, local records and histories in various parts of England are scattered through this important source-book of English ceramic history.

Chapter xiv, of volume 2, includes a list of patents related to pottery from 1626 until 1877, with names of persons to whom granted, and their object. The entries from 1862 until 1877 were compiled by William Spence.]

John W. D., and Baker, Warren. *Old English Lustre Pottery*, 1951.
[Lists based upon Directories, etc.]

Lancaster, H. Boswell. *Liverpool and her Potters*, 1936.
[Potters and pot-painters of Liverpool from directories, newspaper advertisements, documents and printed records.]

Larsen, Ellouise Baker. *American Historical views on Staffordshire China*, 1939, revised 1950.
[Exhaustive analysis of manufactures, artists, subjects, and sources.]

MacKenna, F. Severne. *Worcester Porcelain*, 1950.
[List of named services.]

Meteyard, Eliza. *Life of Josiah Wedgwood*, 1865–1866.
[Josiah Wedgwood's Ms. list of Potters working in Burslem and the Potteries c 1710–1715.]

Moore, N. Hudson. *The Old China Book*, 1903, reprinted 1936.
[Manufacturers of blue-printed earthenware with American, English and other pictorial views and borders.]

Parker, Alfred. *Transactions of the Thoroton Society of Nottinghamshire*, 1932.
[Nottingham Potters from Burgess roles, Poll books, etc.]

Pountney, J. W. *Old Bristol Potteries* 1920.
[Potters in Bristol apprenticeship list 1671 until 1848.]

Stringer, George Eyre. *New Hall Porcelain*, 1949.
[Patterns produced by New Hall in hard-paste and bone china as then recorded.]

Wedgwood, J. C. *Staffordshire Pottery and its History*, n.d.
[lists compiled from *Tunstall Court-Rolls*, 1671, Josiah Wedgwood's Ms. list of potters at Burslem and other Potteries villages c 1710–15, Whieldon's *Notebook* 1749–1754, Tunnicliff's *Survey* 1787, and Parson & Bradshaw's *Directory* 1818.]

Turner, William. *Ceramics of Swansea and Nantgarw*, 1897.
[Proprietors, artists and craftsmen.]

Williams, Isaac. *Guide to Welsh Porcelain in the National Museum of Wales*, 1931.
[Potters and artists.]

Wright, Reginald W. M. *Catalogue of Bristol and West of England Delft Collection*, Victoria Art Gallery, Bath, 1929.
[Tabulated list of proprietors, apprentices and artists compiled from *Old Bristol Potteries* by W. J. Pountney, 1920.]

Williams, Sydney B. *Antique Blue and White Spode*, 1943.
[Underglaze transfer-printed patterns made by Spode, with their sources.]

Appendix 4

British and American Museums
where pottery and porcelain may be studied

Public Museums: England

Barnard Castle, Co. Durham: Bowes Museum.

Bath, Somerset: Holburne of Menstrie Museum.

Bath, Somerset: Victoria Art Gallery. (Bristol and West of England delftware).

Bedford: Cecil Higgins Museum ((English pottery and porcelain).

Bideford, Devonshire: Museum (North Devon Pottery).

Birmingham, City Art Gallery. (general).

Bootle Museum (Liverpool pottery and porcelain).

Brighton, Sussex: Museum and Art Gallery (The Henry Willett Collection of English Pottery illustrating popular British history: good examples of Astbury-Whieldon and later figures, slipwares, etc.).

Bristol, Gloucestershire: Museum and Art Gallery.

Cambridge; Archaeological Museum.

Cambridge; Fitzwilliam Museum (The J. W. L. Glaisher collection of English pottery, including medieval pottery, slipwares, salt-glazed stonewares including 'Pew' Groups, figures and useful wares, Astbury, Whieldon and Ralph Wood pottery and figures, Wedgwood cream-coloured and industrial earthenware, Leeds and North of England wares, lustre, stoneware, and 19th century figures and chimney ornaments).

Canterbury, Kent: Royal Museum.

Castleford, Yorkshire: Museum (Local pottery).

Cheltenham, Gloucestershire: Museum and Art Gallery.

Derby: Museum and Art Gallery.

Exeter: Royal Albert Memorial Museum (Devonshire slipwares, etc.).

Gloucester: Museum.

Hanley, see Stoke-on-Trent.
Hastings, Sussex: Museum (local Sussex pottery).

Ipswich, Suffolk: Christchurch Museum.

Leeds, Yorkshire: City Art Gallery and Temple Newsam House (Leeds pottery, Staffordshire slipwares, salt-glazed stoneware and figures).
Lewes, Sussex: Sussex Archaeological Society Museum (Sussex pottery).
Lincoln: Usher Art Gallery (Usher Collection of English porcelain).
Liverpool: Museum (Liverpool pottery and porcelain).
London: British Museum (representative Collections of English pottery and porcelain including the Franks Collection, the Harland gift of English salt-glazed stoneware, the Isaac Falcke Collection of Wedgwood pottery, and the Frank Lloyd Collection of early Worcester porcelain. Notable examples of Dwight's factory are included in the collection).
London: The London Museum (English medieval pottery, and Chelsea and Bow porcelain).
London: Victoria and Albert Museum (English pottery and porcelain from medieval to modern times and covering every phase and factory. Notable collections include those of Lady Schreiber and Herbert Allen).

Maidstone, Kent: Museum (Wrotham slipwares).
Manchester: City Art Gallery (the Greg Collection of pottery, including Staffordshire slipwares and salt-glazed stoneware).

Newcastle-on-Tyne: Laing Art Gallery.
Norwich: Castle Museum (Lowestoft porcelain and the Bulwer Collection of teapots).
Northampton Museum and Art-Gallery.
Nottingham: Castle Museum and Art Gallery. (Nottingham stonewares and fine examples of Wedgwood ware.)

Oldham, Lancashire: Museum and Art Gallery (English historical and modern studio pottery).
Oxford: Ashmolean Museum (Medieval pottery).

Plymouth: Museum and Art Gallery.

Port Sunlight: Lady Lever Art Gallery (Wedgwood ware).

Preston: Harris Institute Museum (Cedric Houghton Collection of English pottery and porcelain).

Reading Museum.

Salisbury and South Wiltshire Museum.

Sheffield: Weston Park Museum.

Stoke-on-Trent: Hanley Museum and Art Gallery. (Good general collection of English pottery, particularly strong in slipwares, salt-glazed stonewares, Whieldon wares, Wedgwood and his imitators, Ralph Wood, Staffordshire figures, lustred pottery, mocha, blue-printed, and modern studio pottery: token collections of porcelain).

Sunderland Museum (local manufactures).

Taunton Museum.

York: City Museum and Art Gallery.

York: Yorkshire Museum (Medieval pottery, and Yorkshire pottery and porcelain).

Factory Museums

Barlaston, Stoke-on-Trent: Wedgwood Museum.

Worcester: Porcelain Works Museum.

Public Museums: Scotland

Edinburgh, Royal Scottish Museum.

Glasgow: Art Gallery.

Public Museums: Wales

Cardiff: National Museum of Wales (Welsh pottery and porcelain).

Merthyr Tydfil: Cyfarthfa Castle Museum.

Swansea: Glynn Vivian Museum and Art Gallery (porcelain of Nantgarw and Swansea: Welsh earthenware).

Public Museums: America

Albany: Institute of History and Art.

Baltimore, Maryland: Walters Art Gallery.

Boston, Massachusetts: Museum of Fine Arts (Chelsea, Leeds, Lowestoft, Staffordshire, etc).

Cambridge, Massachusetts: Fogg Museum of Art (the collection includes one of the first Wedgwood copies of the Portland vase).

Chicago, Illinois: Art Institute (Frank W. Gunsaulus collection of Wedgwood pottery and Flaxman drawings and reliefs; early Staffordshire wares including Astbury, Whieldon and Ralph Wood figures and toby jugs) (Lucy Maud Buckingham collection of lustred pottery; English porcelain).

Detroit, Michigan: Institute of Art.

Kansas City, Missouri: William Rockhill Nelson Gallery of Art (notable examples of early Staffordshire pottery including wares by Toft, Astbury and Whieldon).

Lawrence, Kansas: University of Kansas Museum of Art.

Los Angeles, California: Museum of History, Science and Art.

New Haven, Connecticut: Yale University Gallery of Fine Arts (Mabel Brady Garvan collection of blue-printed American-Staffordshire historican and topographical wares).

New York: Metropolitan Museum of Art (pottery and porcelain including important examples of Toft, Wedgwood, Chelsea, etc.).

Philadelphia, Pennsylvania: Museum of Art (English earthenware, stoneware and porcelain).

Princeton, New Yersey: University of Princeton Museum of Historic Art.

Providence, Rhode Island: Rhode Island School of Design.

St. Louis, Missouri: City Art Museum.

Toledo, Ohio: Museum of Art.

Williamstown, Massachusetts: Williams College, Lawrence Art Museum.

Appendix 5

British Potters on foreign soil

The rise to eminence of the Staffordshire cream-coloured earthenware, and its evident popularity in European markets, led (1) to a flow of not-altogether-desirable curious travellers to this country intent on learning more of English manufacturing methods and tools (a feature not of course confined to the pottery industry); (2) to an attempt to lure English craftsmen abroad by the incentive of higher wages, to improve existing production or to re-organise factory administration on English lines; and (3) to the emigration of English potters to establish manufactories on foreign soil, and so reduce production costs.

The correspondence of Josiah Wedgwood reveals his acute awareness of the dangers to his own, and British pottery trade generally arising from the first two considerations, and the lengths to which he was willing to go in order to prevent it.

Some British Potters in Europe

BAGNAL, an unknown potter who established a potworks at Creil (Oise) in 1794 to manufacture faience and other wares of English type, in conjunction with de Saint-Cricq-Cazeaux. This concern was united with that of Montereau early in the 19th century, and continued working until 1895. There is no evidence to link this potter with the Bagnall who was partner in the New Hall concern as suggested by W. B. Honey. Charles Bagnal of the New Hall firm died in 1814 whereas the Bagnal of this factory continued until 1819.

BAYLEY, partner in the firm of Pain, Bayley and Shirley which in 1814 bought the factory founded by de Ferque at Saint-Pierre-les-Calais for the manufacture of *faience fine*.

CLARK, William, of Newcastle. Apparently manufacturing cream-coloured earthenware of English type at Lille, in 1773, and possibly partner in the firm of Clark Shaw et Cie at Montereau.

CLARK, SHAW ET CIE, earthenware manufacturers at Montereau from 1775.

DAVENPORT, James, recorded as a potter at Bornholm Island Factory, Denmark in 1789 making cream-coloured earthenware.

GARDNER, Francis, founder with Franz Xavier Hattenberger of the Verbilki Porcelain Factory at Moscow, c 1765. The factory was controlled by the Gardner family for three generations.

HALFORD (HALFORT), a workman at Leigh's factory at Douai who subsequently worked Martin Dammann's earthenware factory during the final years of its existence from 1804 until 1807.

HALL, workman for, and possibly partner in, the firm of Clark, Shaw et Cie.

LEIGH, Charles and LEIGH, James, brothers who founded a manufactory of *faience fine* at Douai (Nord) in 1781 in conjunction with a French merchant named Bris, trading as Leigh & Cie. In 1784 the firm was styled Houzé de l'Aulnoit & Cie. It declined and finished in 1820.

MEDWAY, Joseph, thrower of 'porcelaine' to a Rotterdam potter in 1649.

MILLY, Charles, started the Popoff Manufactory at Gorbunovo, near Moscow, c 1800–1806.

MORTON, Andrew, a Scotsman, who acted as foreman or manager to a pot factory in Rotterdam in 1629.

PAIN, BAYLEY & SHIRLEY, bought the factory at Saint-Pierre-les-Calais in 1814.

SHAW, George, an English potter who went to France. Probably the George Shaw described by Josiah Wedgwood as a 'deserter' who 'ventured after ten years' exile to set foot again in a country where his life was forfeit, as a decoy-duck for a pottery in France'. Son of Ralph Shaw.

SHAW, Ralph, a Burslem potter who in 1732 took out a patent for what appears to have been an agate ware. He was of a 'litigious and overbearing' type, and when in 1736 a trial for an alleged infringement of his patent by J. Mitchell went against him, was so mortified that he 'went to France, where he carried forward his manufactory; whence some of his family returned to Burslem about 1750; and, in 1783, Mr. Wedgwood wrote a Pamphlet to 'prevent Potters emigrating with his Son to France'.

SHIRLEY, partner in the firm of Pain, Bayley & Shirley.

WARBURTON, Francis, Brother of Peter Warburton with whom he was in partnership until 1802, when he founded an earthenware factory at La-Charité-sur-Loire (Nièvre). In 1803 it was taken over by Le Bault with Michael Willis as manager.

WILLIS, Michael, manager of an earthenware factory at La-Charité-sur-Loire, 1803.

A factory run on English lines was founded by an unnamed Englishman at Choisy-le-Roy (Seine) about 5 miles from Paris 'many years' before 1820 when it was advertised 'To be sold by Private Contract'. It was said to be very extensive, and in full employment.

[*Staffordshire Advertiser* 3 April 1802, 16 September 1820: Simeon Shaw, *History of the Staffordshire Potteries*, 1829: Josiah Wedgwood, *To the Workmen of the Pottery on the Subject of Entering into the Service of Foreign Manufacturers*, 1783: X. de Chavagnac and A. de Grollier, *Histoire des Manufactures Françaises de Porcelaine*, 1906: M. L. Solon, *French Faience*, 1903: J. Houdoy, *Histoire de la Céramique Lilloise*, 1869: K. E. Farrer (Editor), *Correspondence of Josiah Wedgwood, 1781-1794*, 1906: Henri Frantz, *French Pottery and Porcelain*, n.d.: E. Hannover, *Pottery and Porcelain*, tr. by Bernard Rackham 1925: A. Hoynck van Papendrecht, *De Rotterdamsche Plateel- en Tegelbakkers en hun product*, 1920 (Quoted by B. Rackham and H. Read, *English Pottery*, 1924): W. B. Honey, *Dictionary of Europian Ceramic Art* 1952.]

Appendix 6

Classified Bibliography

A.

DOCUMENTARY SOURCES FOR SOME ENGLISH EARTHENWARE AND PORCELAIN FACTORIES AND THEIR PRODUCTS

1. (CHELSEA) Lansdowne Mss. No. 829. *The Case of the Undertaker of the Chelsea Manufactory of Porcelain Ware.* British Museum, London.

2. (DERBY)*William Duesbury's London Account Book. 1751–1753.* British Museum, London. (This has been published.)

3. (BOW) *Memorandum and Account Book of John Bowcocke, 1750–1758.* British Museum, London.

4. (DWIGHT) *Ms. Copy of Notebook.* British Museum, London. (The original notebook has been lost.)

5. (JAMES MORLEY, NOTTINGHAM) *Advertisement Sheet*, with engraved illustrations, n.d. Bodleian Library, Oxford.

6. (WHIELDON) *Hiring Notebook, 1749–1753.* Stoke-on-Trent Museum and Art Gallery.

7. (LEEDS) *Drawing Books*, c 1778–1792). Victoria and Albert Museum, London.

8. (DILLWYN) *Recipe Book*, (in the handwriting of Dillwyn). Victoria and Albert Museum, London.

9. (SADLER AND GREEN) *Recipe Book, 1767.* Reference Library, Liverpool.

10. (STAFFORDSHIRE) Much documentary material for Staffordshire Pottery history exists but is scattered. The richest collection by far is at the Wedgwood Museum, Barlaston, which contains a vast amount of material relative to (1) the Wedgwood family; (2) the relation of the Wedgwood family to other contemporary developments; (3) workmen, and artists, (4) documents throwing light upon the activities of other contemporary firms; (5) pattern books; (6) trials; and (7) documentary pieces.

Other firms possess material of a similar kind although less in quantity, particularly Mintons, Copelands, Doultons and Adams.

The Diaries of Benjamin Plant, John Boyle and J. H. Goddard, all of which have been used in extract, throw light upon nineteenth century developments.

1. General

Jewitt, Llewellyn, *The Ceramic Art of Great Britain*, 1878, 2nd Edition 1883.

Solon, Marc Louis, *The Art of the Old English Potter*, 1883.

Hodgin, John Elliott and Edith, *Examples of Early English Pottery*, 1896.

Luxmoore, C. F. C., *Saltglaze: with the Notes of a Collector*, 1924.

Marryat, Joseph, *A History of Pottery and Porcelain, Mediaeval and Modern*, 3rd edition 1868.

Drinkwater, John, 'Notes on English Salt-glaze brown Stoneware,' *Transactions, English Ceramic Circle*, 1939.

Grant, M. H., *The Makers of Black Basaltes*, 1910.

Hobson, R. L., *Catalogue of the Collection of Pottery in the British Museum*, 1903.

Burton, William, *English Earthenware and Stoneware*, 1904.

Turner, William, *Transfer-printing on Enamels, Porcelain and Pottery*, 1907.

Church, (Sir) Arthur H., *English Earthenware*, 1911.

Burlington Fine Arts Club, *Catalogue of an Exhibition of Early English Earthenware*, 1914.

Rhead, George Wooliscroft, *The Earthenware Collector*, 1920.

Rackham, Bernard, and Read, (Sir) Herbert, *English Pottery*, 1924.

Rackham, Bernard, *Catalogue of the Schreiber Collection*, Victoria and Albert Museum, 1929.

Rackham, Bernard, *Catalogue of the Glaisher Collection*, Fitzwilliam Museum, Cambridge, 1934.

Honey, William Bowyer, *English Pottery and Porcelain*, 1933, 3rd ed., 1947.

Haggar, Reginald George, *English Country Pottery*, 1950.

Bemrose, Geoffrey, *Nineteenth Century English Pottery and Porcelain*, 1952.

Blacker, J. F., *The A.B.C. of English Saltglaze Stoneware*, 1922.

Blacker, J. F., *The A.B.C. of Nineteenth Century Pottery and Porcelain*, n.d.

Charleston, R. J., 'English Pottery and Porcelain', *The Concise Encyclopaedia of Antiques*, Vo. I, 1954.

2. Catalogues

LEEDS. The first pattern book of this factory was issued in 1783 and entitled *Designs of Sundry Articles of Queen's or Cream Colour'd Earthenware manufactured by Hartley, Greens & Co., at Leeds Pottery...* (illustrated with 40 engravings of pottery shapes). This catalogue was reissued in 1785 and 1786. A fresh edition was printed in 1794 with 31 additional plates. This was reprinted c. 1814 and was translated into French and Dutch (copy Leeds Public Library).

DON POTTERY, SWINTON POTTERY and DUNDERDALE OF CASTLEFORD. These factories issued catalogues in emulation of those of Leeds.

WEDGWOOD. Wedgwood's first Catalogue was printed in 1773 as *A Catalogue of the different Articles of Queen's Ware... manufactured by Josiah Wedgwood, Potter to Her Majesty* (1773). Catalogues were issued at regular intervals subsequently. The first French edition was issued in 1775. Later Catalogues were translated into Dutch and German. The editions of 1779 and 1787 are reprinted in Wolf Mankowitz, *Wedgwood* (1953) as are the engravings in the 1774 edition, and those executed by William Blake 1815-1816 for the 1817 edition. This sumptuous monograph is in fact indispensible to a study of Wedgwood wares. A copy of the *Catalogue of cameos, intaglios, medals, etc. formed in porcelain and terra cotta by Josiah Wedgwood* (1817) is in Hanley Reference Library. Later Catalogues were also issued.

3. Recipe books

(These throw light upon obscure processes such as 'mocha' or 'flown' blue, and are therefore useful).

Lakin, Thomas, *Potting, Enamelling and Glass-staining: the valuable Receipts of the late Mr. Thomas Lakin*, 1824.

Shaw, Simeon, *The Chemistry of Pottery*, 1837.

Evans, William, *Art and History of the Potting Business*, 1846.

White, William, *The Complete Practical Potter*. 1847, (recipes of the late John Taylor.)

(Anonymous), *A manual of practical pottery*, n.d.

Bourne, A. W., *A Collection of Ceramic Receipts for many years used by John Bourne of Burslem*. 1884.

Corfield, I. E., *Recipes for making Potters' Colours*. 1884.

4. Medieval

Rackham, Bernard, *Medieval English Pottery*, 1948.
Dunning, G. C., *London Museum, Medieval Catalogue*, 1940.

5. Slipware, Peasant Pottery, Country Pottery

Lomax, C. J., *Quaint Old English Pottery*, 1909.
Bourne, George. *William Smith, Potter and Farmer*, 1919.
Baines, J. Mainwaring, *Sussex Pottery*, (1) *East Sussex*, 1948.
Haggar, Reginald G., *English Country Pottery*, 1950.
Rackham, Bernard, *Early Staffordshire Pottery*, 1951.
Cooper, Ronald, *Pottery of Thomas Toft*, Leeds Art Gallery, 1952.
Roth, H. Ling, *Yorkshire Coriners and Notes on old and Prehistoric Halifax*, 1906.
Haggar, Reginald G., 'Cottage Pottery and Popular Art'. *The Concise Encyclopaedia of Antiques*, Vol. 2, 1955.

6. Delftware

Sweetman, G., *Nathaniel Ireson: A West Country Potter*, 1909.
Downman, E. A., *Blue Dash Chargers*, 1919.
Pountney, W. J., *The Old Bristol Potteries*, 1920.
Howard, G. E., *Early English Drug Jars*, 1931.
Garner, F. H., *English Delftware*, 1948.

7. Lustre Pottery

Thorne, A., *Pink Lustre Pottery*, 1926.
Bosanko, W., *Collecting Old Lustre Ware*, 1916.
John, W. D. and Baker, Warren, *Old English Lustre Pottery*, 1951.

8. North Country

Maling, Christopher T., *The Industrial Resources of the District of the Three Northern Rivers, the Tyne, Wear and Tees*, 2nd ed., 1864.
Crawley, James (Editor), *Potteries of Sunderland and District*, Sunderland Museum, 1951.

9. Dwight, Elers

Plot, Robert, *National History of Oxfordshire*, 1677. second edition, 1706.

Leigh, Charles, *National History of Lancashire, Cheshire, and the Peak of Derbyshire*, 1700.

Honey, W. B., 'Elers Ware', *Transactions, English Ceramic Circle*, 1932–1933.

Cosmo Monkhouse, 'John Dwight'. *Dictionary of National Biography*.

10. Bristol

Owen, Hugh, *Two Centuries of Ceramic Art in Bristol*, 1873.

Pountney, W. J., *The Old Bristol Potteries*, 1920.

11. Leeds and Yorkshire

Kidson, Joseph R. and Frank, *Historical Notices of the Leeds Old Pottery*, 1892.

Oxley, Grabham, *Yorkshire Potteries, Pots and Potters. Yorkshire Philosophical Society Annual Report. 1916.*

Hurst, Arthur, *A Catalogue of the Boynton Collection of Yorkshire Pottery*, 1922.

Towner, Donald, *Handbook of Leeds Pottery*, Leeds City Art Gallery, 1951.

12. Liverpool

Mayer, Joseph, *History of the Art of Pottery in Liverpool*, 1885.

Gatty, Charles T. *The Liverpool Potteries*, 1882.

Entwistle, P., *Catalogue of Liverpool Pottery and Porcelain*, 1907.

Lancaster, H. Boswell, *Liverpool and her Potters*, 1936.

13. Derbyshire, and Nottinghamshire

Bailey, Thomas, *Annals of Nottinghamshire*, 1853.

Williamson, F., *The Derby Pot Manufactory known as Cockpit Hill*, 1931.

Parker, Alfred, 'Nottingham Pottery'. *Transactions, Thoroton Society of Nottinghamshire*, 1932.

14. Studio, Artist, or Individual Potters

Powell, L. B., *Howson Taylor: Master Potter*.

Beard, Charles R., *Catalogue of the Collection of Martinware formed by Mr. Frederick John Nettlefold*, 1936.

Stirling, A. W. M., *William de Morgan and his Wife*, 1922.

Victoria and Albert Museum, *Catalogue of works by William de Morgan*, 1921.

Cooper, Ronald, *The Modern Potter*, 1947.

Digby, George Wingfield, *The Work of the Modern Potter in England*, 1952.

Leach, Bernard, *A Potter's Book*, 1940.

Forsyth, Gordon Mitchell, *Twentieth Century Ceramics*, 1936.

15. Staffordshire
(a) General

Plot, Robert, *The Natural History of Staffordshire*, 1686.

Pitt, William, *Topographical History of Staffordshire*, 1817.

Shaw, Simeon, *History of the Staffordshire Potteries*, 1829.

Ward, John, *History of the Borough of Stoke-upon-Trent*, 1843.

Rhead, G. W. and F. A., *Staffordshire Pots and Potters*, 1906.

Wedgwood, J. C., *Staffordshire Pottery and its History*, 1914.

Haggar, Reginald G., *A Century of Art Education in the Potteries*, 1953.

Earle, Cyril, *The Earle Collection of Early Staffordshire Pottery*, 1915.

Honey, W. B., 'Elers Ware', *Transactions, English Ceramic Circle*, 1932–1933.

(b) Wedgwood

Meteyard, Eliza, *Life of Josiah Wedgwood*, 1865–1866.

Jewitt, Llewellyn, *The Wedgwoods, being a life of Josiah Wedgwood*, 1865.

Meteyard, Eliza, *Handbook of Wedgwood Ware*, 1875.

Rathbone, F., *Old Wedgwood*, 1893.

Smiles, Samuel, *Josiah Wedgwood*, 1894.

Church, (Sir) Arthur H., *Josiah Wedgwood, Master Potter*, 1903.

Farrer, K. E., (Editor) *Wedgwood's letters to Bentley*, 1903.

Rathbone, F., *Catalogue of the Wedgwood Museum*, Etruria, 1909.

Williamson, G. C., *The Imperial Russian Dinner Service*, 1909.

Wedgwood, J. C., *The Wedgwood Family*, 1910.

Wedgwood, Julia, *Personal Life of Josiah Wedgwood*, 1915.

Burton, William, *Josiah Wedgwood and his Pottery*, 1922.

Hobson, R. L., *Chinese Porcelain and Wedgwood Pottery*, Lady Lever Art Gallery, Port Sunlight, 1928.

Barnard, Harry, *Chats on Wedgwood Ware*, 1924.

Gorely, Jean and Wadsworth, Mary, *Catalogue of an Exhibition of Old Wedgwood, Fogg Museum of Art, Harvard University*, 1944.

Honey, William Bowyer, *Wedgwood Ware*, 1948.

Graham, J. M. and Wedgwood, H. C., *Wedgwood*, 1948.

(Josiah Wedgwood & Sons Ltd), *Catalogue, Early Wedgwood Pottery Exhibited at 34 Wigmore Street, London*, 1951.

Mankowitz, Wolf, *The Portland Vase and the Wedgwood Copies*, 1952.

Mankowitz, Wolf, *Wedgwood*, 1953.

Wills, Geoffrey (Editor), *Transactions, The Wedgwood Society*.

(c) Other Factories, Families, Craftsmen

Adams, P. W. L., *The Adams Family*, 1914.

Adams, P. W. L., *Notes on Some North Staffordshire Families*, 1930.

Adams, P. W. L., *John Henry Clive*, 1947.

Turner, William, *William Adams, an Old English Potter*, 1904.

Hayden, Arthur, *Spode and his successors*, 1925.

Williams, Sydney B., *Antique Blue-and-White Spode*, 1943.

Falkner, Frank, *The Wood Family of Burslem*, 1912.

Haggar, Reginald G., *The Masons of Lane Delph*, 1952.

Hollowood, A. Bernard, *The Story of Meakins*, 1951.

Cooper, Ronald, *Pottery of Thomas Toft, Leeds Art Gallery*, 1952.

(d) Staffordshire figures and Toby jugs

Price, R. K., *Astbury, Whieldon and Ralph Wood Figures and Toby Jugs*, 1922.

Partridge, Frank, *Ralph Wood Pottery*, n.d.

Read (Sir) Herbert, *Staffordshire Pottery Figures*, 1929.

Falkner, Frank, *The Wood Family of Burslem*, 1912.

Mackintosh, Sir Harold, *Early English Figure Pottery*, 1938.

Haggar, Reginald, G., *English Pottery Figures, 1660–1860*, 1947.

Rackham, Bernard, *Animals in Staffordshire Pottery*, 1953.

Latham, Bryan, *Victorian Staffordshire Portrait Figures*, 1953.

Haggar, Reginald G., *Staffordshire Chimney Ornaments*, 1955.

Eyles, Desmond, *Good Sir Toby*, 1955.

16. Scotland

Fleming, J. Arnold, *Scottish Pottery*, 1923.

Baird, William, *Annals of Duddington and Portobello*, 1898.

Paul, Iain, *The Scottish Tradition in Pottery*, 1947.

17. Tiles

Furnival, W. J., *Leadless Decorative Tiles, Faience and Mosaic*, 1904.

Haberley, Loyd, *Medieval Paving-tiles*, 1937.

Nichols, J. G., *Specimens of tile pavements*, 1845.

Shurlock, M., *Tiles from Chertsey Abbey*, 1885.

Lane, Arthur, *A Guide to the Collection of Tiles, Victoria and Albert Museum*, 1939.

C.

PRINTED SOURCES: PORCELAIN

1. General

Hughes, Bernard and Therle, *English Porcelain and Bone China, 1743–1850*, 1955.

Hobson, R. L., *Catalogue of the Collection of English Porcelain in the British Museum*, 1905.

Rackham, Bernard, *Catalogue of the Herbert Allen Collection of English Porcelain*, 2nd edition, 1923.

Rackham, Bernard, *Catalogue of the Schreiber Collection, Victoria and Albert Museum*, 2nd edition, 1928.

Honey W. B., *Old English Porcelain* 1928, new edition, 1948.

Dixon, J. L., *English Porcelain of the Eighteenth Century*, 1952.

Savage, George, *Eighteenth Century English Porcelain*, 1952.

Binns, W. Moore, *The first Century of English Porcelain*, 1906.

Burton, William, *A History and Description of English Porcelain*, 1902.

Church, (Sir) Arthur H., *English Porcelain*, 1904.

Eccles, H., and Rackham Bernard, *Analysed Specimens of English Porcelain*, 1922.

Nightingale, J. E., *Contributions towards the History of Early English Porcelain from Contemporary Sources*, 1881.

Solon, M. L., *A Brief Description of Old English Porcelain*, 1903.

Hayden, Arthur, *Old English Porcelain: The Lady Ludlow Collection*, 1932.

Guest, Montague (Ed.), *Lady Schreiber's Journals: Confidences of a Collector of Ceramics*, 2 Vols., 1911.

2. Chelsea

Bemrose, William, *Bow, Chelsea and Derby Porcelain*, 1898.

Blunt, R., (Editor), *The Cheyne Book of Chelsea Porcelain*, 1924.

Bryant, G. F., *Chelsea Porcelain Toys*, 1925.

Hurlbutt, Frank, *Chelsea China*, 1937.

King, William, *Chelsea Porcelain*, 1922.

MacKenna, F. Severne, *Chelsea Porcelain: The Triangle and Raised Anchor Wares*, 1948.

MacKenna, F. Severne, *Chelsea Porcelain: The Red Anchor Wares*, 1951.

MacKenna, F. Severne, *Chelsea Porcelain: The Gold Anchor Wares*, 1952.

Dixon, J. L., *Chelsea Porcelain* (in preparation).

Read, Raphael W., *A Reprint of the Original Catalogue of one Year's curious Production of the Chelsea Porcelain Manufactory*, 1880.

Stoner, Frank, *Chelsea, Bow and Derby Porcelain Figures*, 1955.

Hackenbroch, Yvonne, *Chelsea and other English Porcelain, Pottery and Enamel in the Irwin Untermyer Collection*, 1957.

3. Bow

Bemrose, William, *Bow, Chelsea and Derby Porcelain*, 1898.

Hurlbutt, Frank, *Bow Porcelain*, 1926.

Tiffin, F. W., *A Chronograph of the Bow, Chelsea, and Derby China Factories*, 1875.

Mew, Egan, *Old Bow China*, 1909.

Dixon, J. L., *Bow Porcelain*, (in preparation).

Stoner, Frank, *Chelsea, Bow and Derby Porcelain Figures*, 1955.

Toppin, Aubrey, 'Some recent excavations on the site of the Bow Factory', *Burlington Magazine*, 1922.

4. Derby

Haslem, John, *The Old Derby China Factory*, 1876.

Gillespie, F. Brayshaw, *Derby Porcelain*, 1950.

Hurlbutt, Frank, *Old Derby Porcelain and its Artist-Workmen*, 1925.

Hyam, E. E., *The Early Period of Derby Porcelain*, 1926.

Bemrose, William, *Bow, Chelsea and Derby Porcelain*, 1898.

5. Worcester

Barrett, F. A., *Worcester Porcelain*, 1953.

Hobson, R. L., *Worcester Porcelain*, 1910.

Hobson, R. L., *Catalogue of the Frank Lloyd Collection of Worcester Porcelain in the British Museum*, 1923.

MacKenna, F. Severne, *Worcester Porcelain*, 1950.

Binns, R. W., *A Century of potting in the City of Worcester*, 1865, 2nd ed., 1877.

6. Longton Hall

Bemrose, W., *Longton Hall Porcelain*, 1898.

Watney, Bernard, *Transactions, English Ceramic Circle*.

7. Lowestoft

Murton, A. E., *Lowestoft China*, 1932.

Spelman, W. W. R., *Lowestoft China*, 1905.

Kiddell, A. J. B., *The Connoisseur*, 1937.

Crisp, F. A., *Lowestoft China Factory*, 1907.

8. Caughley and Coalport

Barrett, F. A., *Caughley and Coalport Porcelain*, 1955.

MacKenzie, Compton, *The House of Coalport, 1750–1950*, 1955.

9. Liverpool

Gatty, C. T., *The Liverpool Potteries*, 1882.

Mayer, Joseph, *History of the Art of Pottery in Liverpool*, 1885.

10. Plymouth

MacKenna, F. Severne, *Cookworthy's Plymouth and Bristol Porcelain*, 1946.

Oxford, A. W., *A Catalogue of Bristol and Plymouth Porcelain... Mr. Alfred Trapnell*, 1905.

Worth, R. N., 'William Cookworthy and the Plymouth China Factory', *Transactions Devonshire Association*, 1876.

11. Bristol

Hurlbutt, Frank, *Bristol Porcelain*, 1928.

Oxford, A. W., *A Catalogue of Bristol and Plymouth Porcelain... Mr. Alfred Trapnell*, 1905.

MacKenna, F. Severne, *Champion's Bristol Porcelain*, 1947.

Owen, Hugh, *Two Centuries of Ceramic Art in Bristol*, 1873.

Pountney, W. J., *The Old Bristol Potteries*, 1920.

12. Swansea and Nantgarw

Turner, William, *The Ceramics of Swansea and Nantgarw*, 1897.

Nance, E. Morton, *The Pottery and Porcelain of Swansea and Nantgarw*, 1942.

John, W. D., *Nantgarw Porcelain*, 1948.

Meager, Kildare S., *Swansea and Nantgarw Potteries*, Glynn Vivian Art Gallery, Swansea, 1949.

Williams, I. J., *Guide to the Collection of Welsh Porcelain*, National Museum of Wales, 1931.

Williams, I. J., *The Nantgarw Pottery and its Products*, 1932.

13. New Hall, Staffordshire

Stringer, George Eyre, *New Hall Porcelain*, 1949.

Haggar, Reginald G., 'New Hall: The Last Phase', in *Apollo*, 1951.

14. Spode, Staffordshire

Hayden, Arthur, *Spode and his Successors*, 1924.

Cannon, T. G., *Old Spode*, n.d.

15. Other Staffordshire Factories

Haggar, Reginald G., *The Masons of Lane Delph*, 1952.

16. *Individual Artists and Craftsmen*

Prideaux, John, *Relics of William Cookworthy*, 1853.

Ballantyne, A. Randal, *Robert Hancock and his Works*, 1885.

Cook, Cyril, *The Life and Work of Robert Hancock*, 1948.

Tapp, W. H., *Jeffryes Hamett O'Neale*, 1938.

MacAlister, Mrs. Donald, *William Duesbury's London Account Book, 1751–1753*, 1931.

Tapp, W. H., 'The Gaurons, Father and Son', *Apollo*, 1942.

Honey, W. B., 'English Porcelain: Some independent Decorators', *Apollo*, 1937.

17. *Special Classes of Ware and Special Subjects*

Crisp, F. A., *Armorial China*, 1907.

Tudor-Craig, Sir A., *Armorial Porcelain of the Eighteenth Century*, 1925.

Fisher, Stanley W., *English Blue-and-White Porcelain of the 18th Century*, 1947.

King, W., *English Porcelain Figures of the 18th Century*, 1925.

Ruscoe, W., *English Porcelain Figures, 1744-1848*, 1947.

Stoner, Frank, *Chelsea, Bow and Derby Porcelain Figures*, 1955.

D.

MARK BOOKS

Chaffers, William, *Marks and Monograms on European and Oriental Pottery and Porce-*

Rhead, G. W., *British Pottery Marks*, 1920.   [*lain*. Numerous editions.

Chaffers, William, *The Ceramic Gallery.*

Burton, W., and Hobson, R. L., *Handbook of Marks on Pottery and Porcelain*, 1928.

Cushion, J. P., and Honey, W. B., *Handbook of Pottery and Porcelain Marks*, 1956.

E.

JOURNALS

1. *Learned Societies.*
   Transactions, English Ceramic Circle.
   Transactions, The Wedgwood Society.

2. *Antiques.*
   The Connoisseur.

   The Burlington Magazine.
   Apollo.

3. *Trade Journals.*
   Pottery and Glass.
   Pottery Gazette.
   Pottery Quarterly.

The Authors

WOLF MANKOWITZ was born on November 7, 1924. Educated at Cambridge, where he gained a Tripos in English, he worked afterwards as a lecturer and free-lance journalist. In 1947 he set up as an antique dealer in one small shop, and he now specialises in antique and modern Wedgwood (on which he is an authority) in his retail show-rooms in London's West End; it is above these that most of his writing is done. He has been writing series of articles and short stories for the *Evening Standard* since 1953, and he is also a regular contributor to *Punch*, *The Connoisseur*, *Truth*, and many other national papers and magazines. He is also the author of several books, plays and films, including *The Portland Vase and the Wedgwood Copies*, *A Kid for Two Farthings*, *My Old Man's a Dustman*, and *The Mendelman Fire and other Stories*, and was awarded the 1957 Oscar for the best two-reel short subject film of his play *The Bespoke Overcoat*. In 1956 he was appointed Head of London Story Department for Columbia Pictures. He is married and has three sons.

Born on December 25, 1905, REGINALD G. HAGGAR was formerly Art Director to Mintons Ltd., and for many years was consultant designer to the pottery and tile trade. From 1934 to 1941 he was Head of Stoke School of Art., and from 1941 to 1945 he was Head of Burslem Art School. He has devoted over 25 years to his research into Staffordshire local history, with special reference to the history of English pottery and porcelain, and is therefore an expert on this subject. He is the author of *English Pottery Figures, 1660–1860*, *English Country Pottery*, *The Masons of Lane Delph*, *A Century of Art Education in the Potteries*, and *Staffordshire Chimney Ornaments*, and he also contributes to various art journals. He is a member of the Royal Institute of Painters in Water Colours, President of the Society of Staffordshire Artists, and an exhibitor at the Royal Academy of Arts. He is also married.

KERN COUNTY
LIBRARY SYSTEM